Pascal Plus Data Structures, Algorithms, and Advanced Programming

THIRD EDITION

Nell Dale

The University of Texas at Austin

Susan C. Lilly

IBM

D. C. HEATH AND COMPANY

Lexington, Massachusetts   Toronto

Acquisitions Editor: John Carter Shanklin
Developmental Editor: Katherine Pinard
Production Editor: Ron Hampton
Designer: George McLean
Production Coordinator: Lisa Merrill
Photo Researcher: Billie L. Ingram

Cover Design: Circa 86, Inc.

This material in no way represents the opinion of IBM, nor does it reflect IBM's approval or disapproval.

Trademark Acknowledgments: Turbo Pascal is a trademark of Borland International, Inc.

Published simultaneously in Canada.

Printed in the United States of America.

International Standard Book Number: 0-669-24830-4

Library of Congress Catalog Number: 90-81853

10 9 8 7 6

Pascal Plus Data Structures,
Algorithms, and
Advanced Programming

To my children, David, Joshua, Miriam, and Leah, and to my grandmothers, Mildred Lilly and Ida Schmidt, who remind me daily that no one is too young or too old to enjoy learning.

S.C.L.

To my family.

N.D.

PREFACE

Since the first two editions of this book were published, computer science has seen software engineering techniques put into practice to solve larger and more complex computing problems than ever before. Computer science educators are realizing that we must teach not only the traditional data structures and algorithms with the related concepts of abstract data types, but also a methodology for using them in software solutions to real-world problems.

By merging the study of data structures and algorithms with the related concepts of data abstraction and encapsulation, the first two editions of this textbook were on the leading edge of computer science education and practice. As a result of positive feedback from many of you who have used the earlier editions, we have expanded our treatment of data structures and algorithms and enlarged the discussion of current software engineering methodology.

Emphasis

Because we represent both academia and industry, we know what students need to prepare for real-world experience as computer professionals. In this edition, we offer a balanced presentation of the traditional topics of data structures and algorithms and the concepts derived from both software engineering practices and computer science theory. It doesn't make sense to us to teach students about stacks, for instance, without also teaching them how the stack may be treated as an abstract data type, encapsulated by a set of operations that create and manipulate it. We continue to stress the leading edge of computer science theory and software engineering principles, including modularization, data encapsulation, information hiding, data abstraction, the top-down design of algorithms and data structures in parallel, the analysis of algorithms, and life-cycle software verification methods.

We feel strongly that these principles should be introduced to computer science students early in their education so that they may learn good software practices from the beginning. An understanding of theoretical concepts helps students put new ideas they encounter into place, and practical advice allows them to apply what they have learned. To teach these concepts to students who may not have completed college-level mathematics courses, we have consistently used intuitive explanations, even for topics that have a basis in mathematics, like the analysis of algorithms. In all cases, our highest goal has been to make our explanations as readable and as easily understandable as our programs.

New Material and Organizational Changes

In response to our users' suggestions, we have made several organizational changes and have added new material. We have moved the introduction to the *analysis of algorithms and Big-O* from the end of the text to Chapter 1. These techniques are now used throughout the book to compare alternative implementations of data structures. To make this material accessible to students with any level of math background, the introduction includes both real-life and programming examples.

Dynamic allocation and pointer variables are now introduced in Chapter 3 (Data Design), as part of the coverage of Pascal's built-in data types. This allows us to focus on the concept of dynamic allocation and the syntax used with Pascal pointers, without complicating the discussion with the idea of linked structures. *Linked structures* are now introduced earlier—in Chapter 4 (Stacks), rather than Chapter 6 (Linear Lists)—because of the relative simplicity of the algorithms used to manipulate a stack. To emphasize that there are numerous ways to design a data structure, both sequential and linked representations of stacks, queues, and lists are now completely implemented. We have expanded the analysis of these alternative solutions by comparing them in terms of length of source code, use of storage space, and "efficiency"—in both Big-O notation and actual timed program execution.

We have expanded the coverage of *recursion* by adding new examples of recursive algorithms, as well as a revised explanation of how recursion works. New sections describe techniques for removing recursion and guidelines for when to use recursion effectively.

We have greatly expanded the coverage of *graphs* in Chapter 10, to include the implementation of a simple Graph ADT using an adjacency matrix, as well as procedures for breadth-first and depth-first searches and the solution to the shortest-paths problem.

We have also expanded the coverage of *life-cycle program* verification by adding discussions of testing and debugging techniques to several of the chapters, as well as additional coverage of the use of loop invariants to design correct looping structures.

Because many students are using nonstandard Pascal compilers, we have included some discussion of Turbo Pascal in boxes to enhance their use of the programming language. Turbo Pascal was chosen because it is a popular compiler, but the nonstandard topics discussed are available in many Pascal compilers. Topics include:

- Using **Units** to enforce data encapsulation
- The **Include** compiler directive, used to break a program into multiple files
- Conditional compilation of debugging Writeln's
- Object-oriented programming (OOP) techniques
- How to make calls to New dependent on the amount of space available, to avoid run time errors
- Using Turbo Pascal's file operations (especially the use of the Assign procedure to allow the selection of a file name at run time)

Content and Organization

Chapter 1 reviews the basic goals of high-quality software and the basic principles of software engineering for designing and implementing programs to meet these goals. Because there is more than one way to solve a problem, we discuss how competing solutions can be compared through the analysis of algorithms, using Big-O notation. The techniques for the top-down design of both programs and data structures are reviewed, with an emphasis on modularization, good programming style, and documentation. The separation of the design of a problem solution from its implementation is stressed. The idea of making a schedule for completing a programming assignment is discussed.

ListAndCount, a new sample application program in Chapter 1 that produces a numbered program listing and source-line count (counting comment and "executable" lines separately), shows students that they are already capable of writing useful programs. Most students only run their programs to create a listing and output to turn in for a grade. Here is a program that they can actually *use.* The design of the program is completely explained, and the code is listed both in the text and on the disk that accompanies the book.

Chapter 2 addresses what we see as a critical need in software education: the ability to design and implement correct programs and to verify that they are actually correct. Topics covered in this chapter include the concept of "life-cycle" verification; designing for correctness using preconditions, postconditions, and loop invariants; the use of deskchecking and design/code walkthroughs and inspections to identify errors before testing; debugging techniques, data coverage (black box), and code coverage (clear or white box) approaches; unit testing, test plans, and structured integration testing using stubs and drivers. The application section for this chapter shows how all these concepts can be applied to the development of a binary search procedure.

Chapter 3 presents data abstraction and encapsulation, the software engineering concepts that relate to the design of the data structures used in programs. Data design is considered as a blend of top-down and object-oriented approaches. Treating a data structure as an "object" in a program, we specify an abstract data type (ADT) to represent it; then we proceed top-down, through levels of abstraction, to design and implement the structure and the operations that manipulate it. Three perspectives of data are discussed: abstraction, implementation, and application. These perspectives are illustrated using a real-world example (a library), and then are applied to the built-in data structures that Pascal supports: arrays, records, variant records, and sets. The concept of dynamic allocation is introduced in this chapter, along with the syntax for using Pascal pointer variables. The application section at the end of this chapter reinforces the ideas of data abstraction and encapsulation in creating a user-defined data structure, the string.

Chapter 4 introduces the stack data type. The stack is first considered from its abstract perspective, and the idea of recording the logical abstraction in an ADT specification is stressed. The set of stack operations is then implemented in Pascal using two different representations—an array-based stack and a linked stack. The technique used to link the elements in dynamically allocated storage is described in detail and illustrated with figures. The two stack representations are then analyzed in terms of their number of source lines, their use of storage space, and the efficiency of their operations, using Big-O notation. Finally, the application perspective is illustrated in a "calculator" program that evaluates infix expressions. This three-perspective treatment is used for each of the data structures considered in the book.

Chapter 5 introduces the FIFO queue. In addition to discussing the properties of the queue data structure, this chapter gives a detailed look at the design considerations of selecting among multiple implementation choices. Two array-based implementations are discussed, as well as a linked queue representation. Techniques for testing the queue operations using a batch test driver are examined. The simulation application at the end of the chapter has been completely redesigned to simulate a generic multiple-server/single-queue queuing system. The servers and wait queue are modelled as "objects," and implemented as ADTs. The program also demonstrates an incremental software development technique, using stubs to provide inputs in the initial phase.

Chapter 6 introduces linear lists that are ordered according to key value. The algorithms for the basic list operations are developed using an implementation-independent design notation. The list operations are implemented using both sequential (array-based) and linked (dynamically allocated) representations. These two implementations are compared in detail, in terms of the size of their source code, their storage requirements, Big-O analysis of their operations, and timed test runs.

The completely new *AdManager* program found at the end of Chapter 6 is a relatively large (for CS2) application program that is intended to demonstrate to the students that they have the level of programming skills necessary to write a useful, real-life application program. Because of the length of the program, it is developed incrementally in Chapters 6 and 7. The program uses a number of data structures, which are specified as ADTs and developed independently of their use to stress data encapsulation. The program uses retained data from its previous execution, which is stored in a binary (nontext) file. The use of binary files is explained thoroughly for students that have never used them.

Chapter 7 continues the discussion of linked lists with a number of variations: circular linked lists, linked lists with headers and trailers, and doubly linked lists. The insertion, deletion, and list traversal algorithms are developed and implemented for each variation. An alternative representation of a linked structure, using static allocation (an array of records), is designed. The application section concludes the AdManager program from Chapter 6. This application section demonstrates techniques for enforcing data encapsulation with Turbo Pascal Units. The syntax and effective use of Turbo Units is thoroughly explained with an application example.

In Chapter 8, the discussion of recursion gives the student an intuitive understanding of the concept, and then shows how recursion can be used to solve programming problems. Guidelines for writing recursive procedures and functions are illustrated with many examples. After demonstrating that by-hand simulation of a recursive routine can be very tedious, a simple three-question technique is introduced for verifying the correctness of recursive procedures and functions. Because many students are wary of recursion (after dire warnings to avoid its unintentional use in their first programming course), the introduction to this material is deliberately intuitive and nonmathematical. A more detailed discussion of how recursion works leads to an understanding of how recursion can be replaced with iteration and stacks. The application section at the end of this chapter is a recursive solution of a maze problem. This implementation is compared to a nonrecursive (stack-based) approach to demonstrate how recursion can simplify the solution to some kinds of problems.

Chapter 9 introduces binary search trees as a way to arrange data, giving the flexibility of a linked structure without the liability of slow, sequential access to its elements. The tree operations are developed in detail, then implemented using dynamic allocation with pointer variables. Both recursive and nonrecursive versions of the insertion, deletion, and traversal operations are presented, reinforcing the use of recursion for simplifying programming problems.

The application section at the end of Chapter 9 modifies Program ListAndCount (from Chapter 1) to include a cross reference generator. The application section is intended to give the students the opportunity to see how an existing program can be modified—one of the most common real-world programming assignments. The enhancement of this program to generate a cross reference of the numbered program listing makes the program a useful software development tool that the students should be encouraged to use (and to further enhance).

Chapter 10 presents a collection of other branching structures: heaps, priority queues (implemented with heaps), and graphs. The coverage of graphs is greatly expanded from previous editions, to include the specification of a Graph ADT and the implementation of a set of basic graph operations with an adjacency matrix. Both depth-first and breadth-first search procedures are developed, using the Graph, Stack, and FIFO Queue ADTs. A procedure is developed that prints the shortest paths to all nodes from a single source, using the Graph and Priority Queue ADTs. A single, extended application example (airline connections between cities) is used to illustrate both the basic graph operations and the search techniques. The chapter also describes and illustrates the use of *adjacency list* graph representations.

Chapter 11 presents a number of sorting algorithms and asks the question: Which is best? The sorting algorithms that are illustrated, implemented, and compared include the straight selection sort, two versions of the bubble sort, quick sort, heap sort, and merge sort. The analysis of the sorting algorithms includes a comparison of the size of their source code, their storage requirements, and their efficiency, in terms of both Big-O and timed test runs.

Chapter 12 continues the discussion of algorithm analysis in the context of searching. Various searching algorithms are explained, implemented, and compared, including sequential and binary searches and hashing techniques.

Additional Features

Chapter Goals   A set of goals is presented at the beginning of each chapter to help the students assess what they have learned. These goals are tested in the exercises at the end of each chapter.

Chapter Exercises   Most chapters have more than 35 exercises, many of them new or revised for this edition. The exercises have varying levels of difficulty, including short programming problems, the analysis of algorithms, and problems that test the student's understanding of concepts. For chapters that contain application programs, there are sets of exercises that specifically pertain to the material in the application section of the chapter. These exercises are designed to motivate the students to read the applications carefully. There are also exercises marked for Turbo Pascal programmers. Approximately one-third of the exercises are answered in the back of the text; the answer key for the remaining exercises is in the *Instructor's Guide*. The numbers of those exercises answered in the text are italicized so they can be easily identified.

Application Programs   There are nine completely implemented applications that demonstrate a start-to-finish approach to designing a computer program from program specifications, including:

- the complete program design (specification, discussion, and design of each module)
- the design of each data structure, using ADTs
- the source code for the program (in the text and on disk)
- additional topics (for example, testing approaches, error checking, alternate implementations, suggestions for enhancements)

Program reading is an essential skill for software professionals, but few books include programs of sufficient length for students to get this experience. Eight of the applications are new or reimplemented for this edition. There is a set of exercises and programming assignments based on each application.

Program Disk   The source code for both data structures and application programs is included on a *disk provided with the text*. Having the source code for the ADTs on disk encourages the students to think in terms of reusable code. The source code for the larger application programs is provided to give students practice in modifying programs, without having to spend time rekeying the original program. Throughout the text a computer disk icon (▧) appears alongside a description of a program and its file name.

Programming Assignments   A set of recommended programming assignments for each chapter is included at the end of the book. The assignments represent a range of difficulty levels and were carefully chosen to illustrate the techniques described in the text. These assignments, which include modifications and enhancements to the programs in the application sections of Chapters 1–9, give the students experience in program modification and program "maintenance." A large selection of additional programming assignments is also available in the *Instructor's Guide* (including both hard-copy reproduction masters and ready-to-edit versions on disk).

Instructor's Guide and Disk   An *Instructor's Guide* is available with a complete key to answers to the chapter exercises, transparency masters for classroom teaching, suggestions for how to teach the material covered in each chapter, and a large number of additional programming assignments in a reproducible form. The programming assignments in the text and in the *Instructor's Guide* are included on a disk so that they can be modified by instructors.

Acknowledgments

It is a pleasure to be able to thank the many people who helped us turn this third edition of *Pascal Plus Data Structures, Algorithms, and Advanced Programming* from a list of good ideas into a real book.

It is not always easy to accept criticism of one's "perfect" manuscript. However, we have been extremely lucky to have many technical reviewers whose comments, corrections, and suggestions have enormously enriched this book. The successful completion of this edition is largely due to the scrupulous attention of our eagle-eyed reviewers:

Ken Alford
United States Military Academy

William Brown
Fitchburg State College

Thomas E. Byther
University of Maine at Orono

Cecilia Daly
University of Nebraska at Lincoln

Fadi Deek
New Jersey Institute of Technology

Ernest Ferguson
Southwest Baptist University

Don Girod
Canisius College

John Goodman
Courant Institute

Joseph Lambert
Pennsylvania State University

Forbes Lewis
University of Kentucky

Arthur McCabe
University of New Mexico

James Pleasant
East Tennessee State University

John Sarraille
California State University at Stanislaus

Tim Thurman
University of Kansas

We also thank Susan Regan and Mary Ellen Verona for their suggestions for improving our selection of chapter exercises. Though we cannot list the names of all the students and instructors who helped so much by using and critiquing various editions and manuscripts of this text, we truly appreciate all their comments. Thanks also to Marc Horovitz, publisher of *Garden Railways,* for his technical suggestions for the AdManager program (Chapters 6 and 7).

Anyone who has ever written a textbook knows the amount of time and effort that goes into such a project. Anyone who is related to a textbook author can tell you at whose expense that time is spent writing. Mere thanks to Robert, David, Joshua, Miriam, and Leah seem pretty small compared with the months of tremendous support and indulgence they gave. Thanks also to Diane, Mason, and Mildred Lilly for the many hours they spent covering the home front (that is, babysitting) while manuscript pages were being generated, figures were being corrected, and so on.

Most of all we thank Kitty Pinard, the developmental editor, Carter Shanklin, our acquisitions editor, and our production editor, Ron Hampton, without whose constant help, encouragement, and seemingly endless phone calls, this book would never have made it to press.

B R I E F
C O N T E N T S

CONTENTS

7 Lists Plus   399

8 *Programming with Recursion*   467

Appendixes   *A1*

Glossary   *A16*

Answers to Selected Exercises   *A27*

Programming Assignments   *A78*

Index   *A115*

Programming Tools

CHAPTER 1

GOALS

- To be able to describe the general activities in the software life cycle.
- To be able to describe the goals for "quality" software.
- To be able to explain the following terms: software requirements, software specifications, algorithm, information hiding, abstraction.
- To be able to explain the use of "Big-O" to describe the amount of "work" done by an algorithm.
- To be able to write a top-down design for a given problem, either in English or pseudocode.
- To be able to explain why it is desirable to separate logical properties from implementation in computer programs.
- To be able to list features that make a program readable and modifiable.

Beyond Programming

When we talk about computer programming, we immediately think of writing a program for a computer to execute—the generation of code in some computer language. As a beginning student of computer science, you wrote programs that solved relatively simple problems. Much of your effort at the start went into learning the syntax of a programming language such as Pascal; the language's reserved words, its data types, its constructs for selection (IF-THEN-ELSE, CASE) and looping (WHILE, FOR, or REPEAT), and its input/output mechanisms (Readln, Writeln).

You may have learned a programming methodology that took you from the problem description that your instructor handed out all the way through to the delivery of a good software solution. There are many design techniques, coding standards, and testing methods that programmers before you have come up with to help develop high-quality software. But why bother with all that methodology? Why not just sit down at a computer and write programs? Aren't we wasting a lot of time and effort on technique, when we could just write our programs directly in Pascal, FORTRAN, or COBOL?

If the degree of our programming sophistication never had to rise above the level of trivial programs (like summing a list of prices or averaging grades), we might get away with such a code-first technique (or rather, *lack* of technique). Some new owners of personal computers program this way, hacking away at the code until the program works more or less correctly.

As your programs grow larger and more complex, however, you must pay attention to other software issues in addition to coding. If you become a software professional, you may someday work as part of a team that develops a system containing tens of thousands, or even millions, of lines of code. The activities involved in such a software project's whole "life cycle" clearly go beyond just sitting down at a computer and writing programs. These activities include

- *Problem analysis*   Understanding the nature of the problem to be solved.
- *Requirements definition*   Specifying exactly what the program must do.
- *High- and low-level design*   Recording how the program will meet the requirements, from the "big picture" overview to the detailed design.
- *Implementation of the design*   Coding a program in a computer language.
- *Testing and verification*   Detecting and fixing errors and demonstrating the correctness of the program.
- *Delivery*   Turning over the tested program to the customer or user (or instructor!).
- *Operation*   Actually using the program.
- *Maintenance*   Making changes to fix operational errors and to add or modify functions of the program.

Software development is not simply a matter of going through these steps one after another. Many of these activities take place concurrently. We may be coding one part of the solution while we're designing another part, or defining requirements for a new version of a program while we're still testing the current version. Often a number of people work on different parts of the same program simultaneously. Keeping track of all these activities is not an easy task.

The term *software engineering* is used to refer to a disciplined approach to the development of computer programs, through *all* of these software life-cycle activities. What makes our jobs as programmers or software engineers challenging is the tendency of software to grow in size and complexity and to change at every stage of its development. Part of the discipline in the software-engineering approach is the utilization of tools to manage this size and complexity in order to develop high-quality software.

Software Engineering　A disciplined approach to the design, production, and maintenance of computer programs that are developed on time and within cost estimates, utilizing tools that help to manage the size and complexity of the resulting software products.

A Programmer's Toolbox

What tools does a programmer use? Usually a programmer has several toolboxes, each containing tools that help to build and shape a software product.

Hardware　One toolbox contains the hardware itself: the computers and their peripheral devices (such as monitors, terminals, storage devices, and printers), on which and for which we develop software.

Software　A second toolbox contains various software tools: operating systems to control the computer's resources, text editors to help us input programs, compilers to translate high-level languages like Pascal into something the computer can execute, interactive debugging programs, test data generators, and so on. You've used some of these tools already.

Ideaware　A third toolbox is filled with the shared body of knowledge that programmers have collected over time. This box contains the algorithms that we use to solve common programming problems, as well as data structures for modeling the information processed by our programs. It contains programming methodologies such as top-down design and software concepts including information hiding, data encapsulation, and abstraction. There are also some tools for measuring, evaluating, and proving the correctness of our programs. We will spend most of the rest of this book exploring the contents of this third toolbox.

It might be argued that the use of these tools takes the creativity out of programming, making the design of software a cut-and-dried activity. We don't believe that to be true. Artists and composers are creative, yet their innovations are grounded in the basic principles of their crafts. Similarly, the most creative programmers build high-quality software through the disciplined use of basic programming tools.

The Goal: Quality Software

Writing a program that does something is not enough. A programmer must determine what the software is supposed to do and then write a good program that accomplishes the task. But what constitutes a good program?

Quality software

1. works
2. can be read and understood
3. can be modified, if necessary, without excruciating time and effort
4. is completed on time and within budget

It's not easy to meet these goals, but they are all important. Let's talk a little about each one.

Goal 1: Quality Software Works   The program must do the task it was supposed to do, correctly and completely. The first step in the development process is to determine exactly what the program is required to do. If you don't know that, you cannot write a program that works.

In order to know what the program is supposed to do, we must have some sort of definition of the program's *requirements*. For students, the requirements often come from the instructor's problem description: "Write a program that calculates. . . ." For programmers on a government contract, the requirements document may be hundreds of pages long.

Requirements   A statement of what is to be provided by a computer system or software product.

We develop programs that meet the user's requirements using software specifications. The *specifications* indicate the format of the input and the expected output, details about processing, performance measures (how fast? how big? how accurate?), what to do in case of errors, and so on. The specifications tell exactly *what* the program will do, but not *how* it will be done. Sometimes your instructor will give you detailed specifications; other times you will have to write them yourself, based on the requirements definition, conversations with your instructor, or guesswork. We will discuss this issue in more detail later in this chapter.

Software Specifications   Detailed description of the function, inputs, processing, outputs, and special requirements of a software product, which provides the information needed to design and implement the program.

How do you know when the program is right? The fact that a program should do everything in its requirements correctly suggests that the program should be *complete* (it should "do everything") and *correct* (it should "do it right"). We will spend all of Chapter 2 discussing this subject.

Goal 1 also means that the program should be *usable*. If the program needs data from a person sitting at a terminal, it must issue prompts to tell the user when it expects input. The program's outputs should be readable and understandable; they should make sense to human beings. Creating a good user interface is an important subject in software engineering today.

Finally, Goal 1 means that the program should be *as efficient as it needs to be*. We never go out of our way to write programs that waste time or space in memory, but not all programs demand a certain level of efficiency. When they do, however, we must meet these demands or else the programs will not satisfy the problem's requirements. For instance, a space-launch control program must execute in "real time"; that is, the software must process commands, do calculations, and display results in pace with the activities it is supposed to control. Closer to home, if a desktop publishing program cannot update the screen as fast as the user can type, the program is not as efficient as it needs to be. In such a case, if the software isn't efficient enough, it doesn't meet its requirements, and thus, according to our definition, it doesn't work correctly.

Goal 2: Quality Software Can Be Read and Understood The first goal says that the computer must understand the program; this second goal is more concerned with the human reading it.

You might wonder why anyone would want to read a computer program. Chances are you have already read a number of them in programming textbooks. Reading a well-written program can teach you techniques that will help you to write good programs. In fact, it's hard to imagine how a person could become a good programmer *without* reading good programs.

Think of the last time you had to debug one of your own programs; you probably spent quite a bit of time reading it. A program that has been well designed and clearly written is certainly easier for human readers to understand. Later in this chapter we will describe a software design methodology that produces "structured," well-documented programs that people, as well as computers, can understand.

Although the computer is the ultimate reader of the program, it is unlikely that a program that cannot be understood by its human authors will be correct. In fact, it may not even be possible to determine whether the program *is* correct.

Goal 3: Quality Software Can Be Modified, if Necessary, Without Excruciating Time and Effort When does software need to be modified? Changes occur in every phase of its existence.

Software gets changed in the design phase. When your instructor or employer gives you a programming assignment, you begin to think of how to solve the problem. The next time you meet, however, you may be notified of a small change in the program description.

Software gets changed in the coding phase. You make changes in your program as a result of compilation errors. Sometimes you suddenly see a better solution to a part of the problem after the program has been coded, so you make changes.

Software gets changed in the testing phase. If the program crashes or gives wrong results, you must make corrections.

In an academic environment, the life of the software typically ends when a corrected program gets turned in to be graded. When software is being developed for use, however, most of the changes that are made take place during the "maintenance" phase. Someone may discover an error that wasn't uncovered in testing, someone else may want additional functions, a third party may want to change the input format, and a fourth may want to run the program on another system.

The point is that software changes often and at all phases of its life cycle. Knowing this, software engineers try to develop programs that are easily modifiable. If you think it is easy to change a program, try to make a "small change" in the last program you wrote. It's difficult to remember all the details of a program after some time has passed. Modifications to programs often are not even made by the original authors, but by subsequent maintenance programmers. (Someday you may be the one making the modifications to someone else's program.)

What makes a program easily modifiable? First, it should meet Goal 2; it should be readable and understandable to humans. Second, it should be able to survive little changes without a big mess. The design methodology we will discuss later in this chapter will help you write programs that meet this goal.

Goal 4: *Quality Software Is Completed on Time and Within Budget* You know what happens in school when you turn your program in late. You have probably grieved over an otherwise perfect program that was given only half credit because you turned it in one day late. "But the computer was down five hours last night!" you protest.

Although the consequences of tardiness may seem arbitrary in the academic world, they are significant in the business world. The software for controlling a space launch must be developed and tested before the launch can take place. A patient database system for a new hospital must be installed before the hospital can open. In such cases the program doesn't meet its requirements if it isn't ready when needed.

"Time is money" may sound trite, but failure to meet deadlines is *expensive*. A company generally budgets a certain amount of time and money for the development of a piece of software. As a programmer, you are paid a salary or hourly wage. If your part of the project is only 80% complete when the deadline arrives, the company must pay you—or another programmer—to finish the work. The extra expenditure in salary is not the only cost, however. Other workers may be waiting to integrate your part of the program into the system for testing. If the program is part of a contract with a customer, there may be monetary penalties for missed deadlines. If the program is being developed for commercial sales, your company may lose money if another firm puts a similar product on the market first.

Once you know what your goals are, what do you do to meet them? Where do you start? There are many tools and techniques used by software engineers. In the next few sections of this chapter, we will focus on techniques that will help you understand, design, and code programs.

Getting Started: Understanding the Problem

The First Step

No matter what programming design technique you use, the first steps are the same. Imagine the following all-too-familiar situation. On the third day of class, you are given a 12-page description of Programming Assignment 1, which must be running perfectly and turned in by noon, a week from yesterday. You read the assignment and realize that this program will be three times as large as any program you have ever written. Now, what is your first step?

The responses below are typical of those given by a class of computer science students in such a situation:

1. Panic   39%
2. Pick up a pencil and start writing   26%
3. Drop the course   24%
4. Copy the code from a smart classmate   7%
5. Stop and think   4%

Response 1 is a reasonable reaction from students who have not learned good programming techniques. Students who answer with Response 3 will find their education coming along rather slowly. Response 4 will get you scholastic probation at most universities. Response 2 seems like a good idea, considering the deadline looming ahead. But resist the temptation to grab a pencil; the first step is to *think*. Before you can come up with a program solution, you must understand the problem. Read the assignment, and then read it again. Ask questions of your instructor (or manager, or client).

The problem with writing first is that it tends to lock you into the first solution you think of, which may not be the best approach. There is a natural tendency to believe that once you've put something in writing, you have too much invested in the idea to toss it out and start over.

On the other hand, don't simply think about all the possibilities until the day before your deadline. (Chances are the computer will be down that day!) When you think you understand the problem, only then should you begin writing.

Writing Detailed Specifications

Many writers feel a moment of terror when faced with a blank piece of paper—where to begin? As a programmer, however, you don't have to wonder about where to begin. You can make the first mark and get on with the job by doing an important preliminary task.

Using the assignment description (your "requirements"), write a complete definition of the problem, including the details of the expected inputs and outputs, the necessary processing and error handling, and all the assumptions about the problem. When you finish this task, you will have a *detailed specification*—a formal definition of the problem your program must solve, telling you exactly what the program should do. In addition, the process of writing the specifications will bring to light any holes in the

Cookies for Uncle Sam

What sort of commercially made cookies are suitable for the tastes of American servicemen? Here are excerpts from the *15-page* specification issued by the U.S. military procurement offices:

Type I, oatmeal with chocolate chips. The cookies shall be well-baked. They shall be browned on the bottom surface and outer edges, but not appreciably browned on the top surface. They shall be wholly intact, free of checks or cracks. . . . The cookies shall be tender and crisp with an appetizing flavor, free of a burnt or scorched flavor. . . .

Type II, sandwich. Each cookie shall consist of two round base cakes with a layer of filling between them. The weight of a cookie shall not be less than 21.5 grams with the filling weighing not less than 6.4 grams. The base cakes shall have been uniformly well-baked with a color ranging from not lighter than chip 27885 or darker than chip 11711. . . . The color comparisons shall be made under . . . sky daylight with the objects held in such a way as to avoid specular refractance [glossiness]. . . . The filling shall be centered so that it does not protrude beyond the perimeter of the base edges. . . .

requirements. For instance, are embedded blanks in the input significant or can they be ignored? Do you need to check for errors in the input? On what computer system(s) will your program be run? If you get the answers to these questions at this stage, you can design and code your program correctly from the start.

Sometimes, but not always, your instructor will give you an assignment description that can also function as a detailed specification. Other times you will receive "simple" program specifications, and the pertinent details must be divined by ESP or by hanging around the professor's office. Consider the following directions:

Write a program to count the lines of source code in a Pascal program. The input is a Pascal program. The output shall be a listing of the program, with line numbers preceding each executable line of source code, followed by a report of the line counts.

The programming task described is not complicated, but some important information is missing from these requirements. When you write a detailed specification, you must answer these questions:

Input: Where is the program to be processed? In a single text file? Does the user provide the name of the file?

Output: Where? To a file or to the screen? What goes in the "report of the line counts"?

Processing requirements: Does it matter whether the program to be processed is syntactically correct? What is meant by "line numbers preceding each *executable* line of source code"? Does that mean that blank lines and comment lines should not be counted? Is a declaration "executable"? What comment delimiters are allowed? Will this program be compiled and run on a certain computer system (for example, IBM PC-compatible computers) or on different systems (both personal computers and mainframes)?

You must know some details in order to write and run the program. Other details, if not explicitly stated in the program's requirements, may be handled according to the programmer's preference. Decisions about unstated or ambiguous specifications, called *assumptions,* should always be written explicitly in the program's documentation.

The detailed specification clarifies the problem to be solved. But it does more than that: It also serves as an important piece of written documentation about the program. A detailed specification for the Program ListAndCount is shown in Figure 1-1. There are many ways in which specifications may be expressed and a number of different sections that may be included, depending on the nature of the problem. Our recommended program specification includes the following sections: Inputs, Outputs, Processing Requirements, and Assumptions. If special processing is needed for unusual or error conditions, it too should be specified. Sometimes it is helpful to include a section containing definitions of terms used in the specification. It is also useful to list any testing requirements so that the method for verifying the program is taken into consideration early in the development process.

Figure 1-1
Specification for the Source Lister and Counter

Specifications: Program ListAndCount

Function:

This program shall process the lines of source code in a Pascal program, producing a listing of the program, with line numbers preceding each executable line of source code, followed by a report of the counts of executable and comment source lines of code.

Definitions:

Line of source code: A line of a Pascal program file (all characters up to EOLN), which may contain statements or parts of statements, comments, and/or blanks.
Blank line: A line of source code that does not contain any nonblank characters.
Executable line: A line of source code that contains Pascal statements, declarations, reserved words, etc. (Note: It may contain comments in addition to functional code.)
Comment line: A line of source code that contains *only* Pascal comments. A comment must terminate on the same lines as it begins; it cannot span a line.

Input:

The Pascal program to be processed is contained in a single text file. The user should be prompted to supply the file name.

Figure 1-1 **Output:**

(Continued)

The lines shall be echoprinted to the screen as they are read from the source file. The formatted report output shall be written to a file called *COUNTOUT.* The output shall contain two sections:

1. The *Program Listing* shall consist of all the lines of the Pascal program. Three types of lines are treated as follows:
   (a) Blank line: Print a blank line.
   (b) Executable line: The line shall be printed, preceded by the current line count printed in eight character spaces.
   (c) Comment line: The line shall be printed, preceded by 8 blank spaces (to maintain program formatting and indentation).

2. The *Count Report* shall consist of the following elements, printed with appropriate labels:
   (a) Number of executable lines of code
   (b) Number of comment lines
   (c) Weighted total lines of source code, according to the following formula:

   Weighted lines =
   Executable lines + Minimum (Comment Lines, 10% Executable lines)

Processing Requirements:

1. This program must be able to differentiate between executable and comment lines. Executable and comment lines shall be counted separately; only executable lines shall be preceded by a line number in the program listing.
2. This program must be able to be compiled and run, with minimal changes, on a variety of computer systems.

Assumptions:

1. The Pascal program in the input file is syntactically correct. (For instance, you can assume that all comments terminate.)
2. The program contains only printable characters, including blanks. (It may not contain tabs.)
3. Only (* *) comment delimiters are supported. { } comments are not supported.
4. Nested comments are not supported.
5. A comment must terminate with *) on the same line in which it began; it cannot span across more than one line.
6. An executable line cannot begin with a comment.

The Next Step: Solving the Problem

There is more than one way to solve most problems. If you were asked for directions to Joe's Diner (see Figure 1-2), you could give either of two equally correct answers:

1. "Go east on the big highway to the Y'all Come Inn, and turn left," or
2. "Take the winding country road to Honeysuckle Lodge, and turn right."

The two answers are not the same, but because following either route will get the traveler to Joe's Diner, both answers are *functionally correct.*

If the request for directions contained special requirements, one solution might then be preferable to the other. For instance, "I'm late for dinner. What's the quickest route to Joe's Diner?" calls for the first answer, whereas "Is there a pretty road that I can take to get to Joe's Diner?" suggests the second. If no special requirements are known, the choice is a matter of personal preference—which road do you like better?

In this book we will present numerous *algorithms.* An algorithm is a step-by-step description of the solution to a problem. How we choose between two algorithms that do the same task often depends on the requirements of a particular application. If no relevant requirements exist, the choice may be based on the programmer's own style.

Algorithm   A logical sequence of discrete steps that describe a complete solution to a given problem in a finite amount of time.

Figure 1-2
Map to Joe's Diner

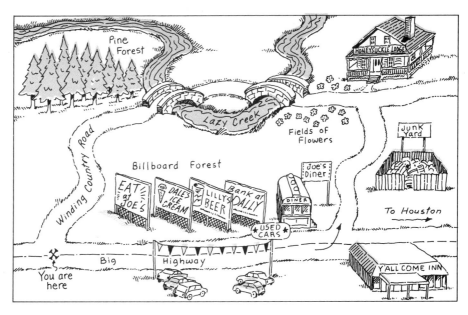

Comparing Algorithms

Often the choice between algorithms comes down to a question of efficiency: Which one takes the least amount of computing time? Which one does the job with the least amount of work? We are talking here of the amount of work that the *computer* does. Later we will also compare algorithms in regard to how much work the *programmer* does. (One is often minimized at the expense of the other.)

To compare the work done by competing algorithms, we must first define a set of objective measures that can be applied to each algorithm. The *analysis of algorithms* is an important area of theoretical computer science; in advanced courses you will undoubtedly see extensive work in this area. In this text you will learn about a small part of this topic, enough to let you determine which of two algorithms requires less work to accomplish a particular task.

How do programmers measure the work that two algorithms perform? The first solution that comes to mind is simply to code the algorithms and then compare the execution times for running the two programs. The one with the shortest execution time will clearly be the better algorithm. Or will it? Using this technique, we can really determine only that Program A is more efficient than Program B *on a particular computer*. Execution times are specific to a particular computer. Of course, we could test the algorithms on all possible computers, but we want a more general measure.

A second possibility is to count the number of instructions or statements executed. This measure, however, varies with the programming language used, as well as with the style of the individual programmer. To standardize this measure somewhat, we could count the number of passes through a critical loop in the algorithm. If each iteration involves a constant amount of work, this measure will give us a meaningful yardstick of efficiency.

These musings lead to the idea of isolating a particular operation fundamental to the algorithm and counting the number of times that this operation is performed. Suppose, for example, that we are summing the elements in an integer array. To measure the amount of work required, we could count the integer addition operations. For an array of 100 elements, there will be 99 addition operations. Note, however, that we do not actually have to count the number of addition operations; it will be some *function* of the number of elements (N) in the array. Therefore we can express the number of addition operations in terms of N: For an array of N elements, there will be $N - 1$ addition operations. Now we can compare the algorithms for the general case, not just for a specific array size.

If we wanted to compare algorithms for multiplying two real matrices together, we could come up with a measure that combines the real multiplication and addition operations required for matrix multiplication. This example brings up an interesting consideration: Sometimes an operation will so dominate the algorithm that the other operations fade into the background "noise." If we want to buy elephants and goldfish, for example, and we are considering two pet suppliers, we really only need to compare the prices of elephants; the cost of the goldfish is trivial in comparison. Similarly, on many computers floating-point multiplication is so much more expensive than addition in terms of computer time that the addition operation is a trivial factor in the efficiency of the whole matrix multiplication algorithm; we might as well count only the multi-

plication operations, ignoring the addition. In analyzing algorithms, we can often find one operation that dominates the algorithm, effectively relegating the others to the "noise" level.

Big-O

We have been talking about work as a function of the size of the input to the operation (for instance, the number of elements in the array to be summed). We can express an approximation of this function using a mathematical notation called **order of magnitude**, or **Big-O**, notation. (This is a letter O, not a zero.) The order of magnitude of a function is identified with the term in the function that increases fastest relative to the size of the problem. For instance, if

$$f(N) = N^4 + 100N^2 + 10N + 50,$$

then f(N) is of order N^4—or, in Big-O notation, $O(N^4)$. That is, for large values of N, N^4 will dominate the function.

How is it that we can just drop the low-order terms? Remember the elephants and goldfish that we talked about earlier? The elephants were so much bigger that we could just ignore the goldfish. Similarly, for large values of N, N^4 is so much larger than 50, 10N, or even $100N^2$ that we can ignore these other terms. This doesn't mean that the other terms do not contribute to the computing time; it only means that they are not significant in our approximation when N is "large."

What is this value *N*? N represents the size of the input to the problem. Most of the problems in this book involve data structures—stacks, queues, lists, trees. Each structure is composed of elements. We might develop algorithms to add an element to the structure, or to modify or delete an element from the structure. We can describe the work done by these operations in terms of N, the number of elements in the structure.

Suppose that we want to write all the elements in a list into a file; how much work is that? The answer depends on how many elements are in the list. Our algorithm is

Open (Rewrite) the file

WHILE more elements in list DO
  Print the next element

If N is the number of elements in the list, the "time" required to do this task is

(N * time-to-print-one-element) + time-to-open-the-file

This algorithm is O(N) because the time required to perform the task is proportional to the number of elements (N)—plus a little to open the file. How can we just ignore the open time in determining the Big-O approximation? Assuming that the time necessary to open (Rewrite) a file is constant, this part of the algorithm is our goldfish. If the list only has a few elements, the time needed to open the file may seem significant, but for large values of N, printing the elements is an elephant in comparison to opening the file.

The order of magnitude of an algorithm does *not* tell you how long in microseconds the solution will take to run on your computer. Sometimes we do need that kind of information. For instance, a word processor's requirements state that the program must be able to spell-check a 50-page document (on a particular computer) in less than 120 seconds. For information like this, we do not use Big-O analysis; we use other measurements. In later chapters we will compare different implementations of a data structure by coding them and then running a test, recording the time on the computer's clock before and after. This kind of "benchmark" test tells us how long the operations take on a particular computer, using a particular compiler. The Big-O analysis, however, allows us to compare algorithms without reference to these factors.

Some Common Orders of Magnitude

A constant computing time is referred to as O(1). *Constant time* means that the time required for the operation is not dependent on the size of the input to the problem. Assigning a value to the I*th* element in an array of N elements is O(1), because an element in an array can be accessed directly through its index.

An O(N) algorithm is said to execute in *linear time*. Printing all the elements in an array of N elements is O(N). Searching for a particular value in an array of unordered elements is also O(N), because you (potentially) must search every element in the whole array to find it.

An $O(\log_2 N)$ algorithm does more work than an O(1) algorithm, but less work than an O(N) algorithm. Finding a value in an array of ordered element using the binary search algorithm is $O(\log_2 N)$. (We will discuss this algorithm in detail in Chapter 2.)

A *quadratic-time*, or $O(N^2)$, algorithm does more work than an O(N) algorithm when N is large. Most simple sorting algorithms (used to put a list of elements in order) are $O(N^2)$ algorithms. A number of "fast" sorting algorithms are $O(N\log_2 N)$. The table that follows illustrates the relative rates of growth of N^2 and $N\log_2 N$. We will discuss this subject at length in Chapter 11.

$O(N^3)$ is called *cubic time*. An example of an $O(N^3)$ algorithm is a routine that increments every element in an $N \times N \times N$ three-dimensional array of integers.

Exponential-time, or $O(2^N)$, algorithms are really costly. As you can see in the table on the following page, exponential times increase very dramatically in relation to the size of N. (It is also interesting to note that the values in the last column grow so quickly that the computation time required for problems of this order may exceed the estimated life span of the universe!)

Note that throughout this discussion, we have been talking about the amount of work the computer must do to execute a program. This determination does not necessarily

Comparison of Rates of Growth

N	$log_2 N$	$N log_2 N$	N^2	N^3	2^N
1	0	1	1	1	2
2	1	2	4	8	4
4	2	8	16	64	16
8	3	24	64	512	256
16	4	64	256	4,096	65,536
32	5	160	1,024	32,768	4,294,967,296
64	6	384	4,096	262,144	About 5 years' worth of instructions on a super computer
128	7	896	16,384	2,097,152	About 600,000 times greater than the age of the universe in nanosecs (for a 6-billion-year estimate)
256	8	2,048	65,536	16,777,216	Don't ask!

relate to the size of the program, say, in lines of code. Consider the following two algorithms to initialize to zero every element in an N-element array.

Algorithm Init1
```
List[1] := 0;
List[2] := 0;
List[3] := 0;
List[4] := 0;
       .
       .
       .
List[N] := 0;
```

Algorithm Init2
```
FOR Index := 1 TO N DO
   List[Index] := 0;
```

Both algorithms are O(N), even though they greatly differ in the number of lines of code.

Now let's look at two different algorithms that calculate the sum of the integers from 1 to N. Algorithm Sum1 is a simple FOR loop that adds successive integers to keep a running total:

Algorithm Sum1
```
Sum := 0;
FOR Count := 1 TO N DO
  Sum := Sum + Count;
```

That seems simple enough. The second algorithm calculates the sum by using a formula. To understand the formula, consider the following calculation when N = 9.

F*amily Laundry*

How long does it take to do a family's weekly laundry? We might describe the answer to this question with the function:

$$f(N) = c * N$$

where N represents the number of family members and c is the average number of minutes that each person's laundry takes. We say that this function is O(N) because the total laundry time depends on the number of people in the family. The "constant," c, may vary a little for different families—depending on the size of their washing machine and how fast they can fold clothes, for instance. That is, the time to do the laundry for two different families might be represented with these functions:

$$f(N) = 100 * N$$
$$g(N) = 90 * N$$

But overall, we describe these functions as O(N).

Now what happens if Grandma and Grandpa come to visit the first family for a week or two? The laundry time function becomes

$$f(N) = 100 * (N + 2)$$

We still say that the function is O(N). How can that be? Doesn't the laundry for two extra people take *any* time to wash, dry, and fold? Of course it does! If N is small (the family consists of Mother, Father, and Baby), the extra laundry for two people is

$$\begin{array}{r} 1 + \ 2 + \ 3 + \ 4 + \ 5 + \ 6 + \ 7 + \ 8 + \ 9 \\ + \ 9 + \ 8 + \ 7 + \ 6 + \ 5 + \ 4 + \ 3 + \ 2 + \ 1 \\ \hline 10 + 10 + 10 + 10 + 10 + 10 + 10 + 10 + 10 \ = \ 10 * 9 = 90 \end{array}$$

We pair up each number from 1 to N with another, such that each pair adds up to N + 1. There are N such pairs, giving us a total of (N + 1) * N. Now, since each number is included twice, we simply divide the product by 2. Using this formula, we can solve the problem: ((9 + 1) * 9)/2 = 45. Now we have a second algorithm:

Algorithm Sum2

```
Sum := ((N + 1) * N) DIV 2;
```

Both of the algorithms code up into short pieces of code. Let's compare them using Big-O notation. The work done by Sum1 is a function of the magnitude of N; as N gets larger, the amount of work grows proportionally. If N is 50, Sum1 will work 10 times as hard as when N is 5. Algorithm Sum1, therefore, is O(N).

significant. But as N grows large (the family consists of Mother, Father, 12 kids, and a live-in baby-sitter), the extra laundry for two people doesn't really make much difference. (The family's laundry is the elephant; the guest's laundry is the goldfish.) When we compare algorithms using Big-O, we are concerned with what happens when N is "large."

If we are asking the question "Can we finish the laundry in time to make the 7:05 train?" we want a precise answer. The Big-O analysis doesn't give us this information. It gives us an approximation. So, if 100 * N, 90 * N, and 100 * (N + 2) are all O(N), how can we say which is "better"? We can't—in Big-O terms, they are all roughly equivalent for large values of N. Can we come up with a better algorithm for getting the laundry done? If the family wins the state lottery, they can drop all their dirty clothes off at a professional laundry 15 minutes' drive from their house (30 minutes roundtrip). Now the function is

$$f(N) = 30$$

This function is O(1). The answer is independent of the number of people in the family. If they switch to a laundry 5 minutes from their house, the function becomes

$$f(N) = 10$$

This function is also O(1). In terms of Big-O, the two professional-laundry solutions are equivalent: No matter how many family members or house guests, it will take a constant amount of the family's time to do the laundry. (We aren't concerned with the professional laundry's time.)

To analyze Sum2, consider the cases when N = 5 and when N = 50. They should take the same amount of time. In fact, whatever value we assign to N, the algorithm will do the same amount of work to solve the problem. Algorithm Sum2, therefore, is O(1).

Does that mean that Sum2 is always faster? Is it always a better choice than Sum1? That depends. Sum2 might seem to do more "work," since the formula involves multiplication and division, while Sum1 is a simple running total. In fact, for very small values of N, Sum2 might actually do more work than Sum1. (Of course, for very large values of N, Sum1 does a proportionally larger amount of work, while Sum2 stays the same.) So the choice between the algorithms depends in part on how they will be used, for small or large values of N.

Another issue is the fact that Sum2 is not as obvious as Sum1; thus it is harder for the programmer (a human) to understand. Sometimes a more efficient solution to a problem is more complicated; we may save computer time at the expense of the programmer's time.

What's the verdict? As usual in the design of computer programs, there are trade-offs. We must look at our program's requirements and then decide which solution is better. Throughout this text we will examine different choices of algorithms and data

*T*op-Down Design for English Majors

The top-down design approach is probably familiar to you from other disciplines—for instance, a term paper for an English composition class. You could read up on a subject, and then just start writing. On the other hand, if you want to write a paper that sticks to the subject and presents an orderly discussion of topics, you had better write an outline first. The highest level of an outline (the Roman numerals) consists of general topics. At each level below (capital letters, numbers, lowercase letters) more detail is recorded. The more detailed information is *hidden* from the higher levels. Once the outline is complete down to the lowest levels, it is a relatively simple task to write the term paper.

The decisions regarding what to write are made before the outline is written and are refined, and perhaps modified, as the outline is developed. By the time you actually begin writing the paper, the decisions about *what* to write have already been made, leaving only the question of *how* to say it.

structures. We will compare them using Big-O, but we will also examine the program's requirements and the "elegance" of the competing solutions. As programmers, we design software solutions with many factors in mind.

Top-Down Design

The detailed specification of the program tells *what* the program must do, but not *how* it will do it. Once you have fully clarified the goals of the program, you can begin to develop and record a strategy for meeting them. One method we will use is called **top-down design**. This method, also called **stepwise refinement**, takes a divide-and-conquer approach. First the problem is broken into several large tasks. Each of these tasks is in turn divided into sections, then the sections are subdivided, and so on. The important feature is that *details are deferred as long as possible* as we go from a general to a specific solution.

The development of a computer program by top-down design begins with a "big picture" solution to the problem defined in the specification. We then devise a general strategy for solving the problem by dividing it into manageable units called **modules**. Next, each of the large modules is subdivided into several tasks. The top level of the top-down design does not need to be written in source code (such as Pascal); it can be written in English or "pseudocode." (Some software development projects even use special design languages that can be compiled.) This divide-and-conquer activity continues until we get down to a level that can be easily translated into lines of code.

Once it has been divided into modules, the problem is simpler to code into a well-structured program. This approach encourages programming in logical units, using procedures and functions. The main module of the top-down design becomes the main program, and subsections develop into procedures. The product of this methodology

Figure 1-3   *Top-Down Problem Solving*

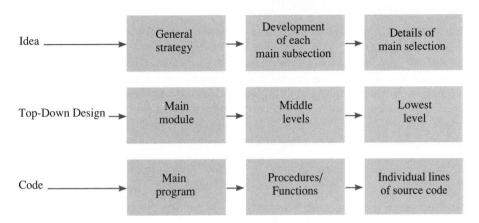

is called a **modular design**. Figure 1-3 shows how the development of the top-down design parallels the thought process for solving the problem.

As an example, let's write part of the top-down design for Program ListAndCount, using the specifications in Figure 1-1.

Main Module

GetFiles
ProcessProgramFile
PrintCountData

The program is now divided into three logical units, each of which will probably be developed into a procedure in the final program. In fact, we can already imagine approximately what the main program will look like:

```
PROGRAM ListAndCount (Input, Output, ProgramFile, ReportFile);
    .
    .
    .
BEGIN (* ListAndCount *)
  GetFiles ( );
  ProcessProgramFile ( );
  PrintCountData ( );

END. (* ListAndCount *)
```

We left out the parameter lists for each of the procedure calls because we haven't yet said anything about the inputs and outputs for these modules. To complete this level of the design, we must specify these inputs and outputs, the *interfaces* to these modules. We may not know at this point how the lower level modules are to be implemented, but we must be able to "call" them.

A Note on the Algorithm "Language"

The algorithms in this book are written in a Pascal-like pseudocode, which is intended to be both easy to read and easy to convert into Pascal code. For the most part, it should be readable without any special instructions by anyone who knows a high-level programming language. The one symbol that may not be intuitively obvious is the backward arrow (←) which means "is assigned the value of." For instance,

Count ← 1

means "Count is assigned the value of 1," and will translate in code to

```
Count := 1;
```

Note, however, that a statement containing ← in our algorithms will not necessarily translate into a single Pascal assignment. For instance,

MinValue ← smallest value in the array

might be coded later as a loop to find the smallest value in the array, inside which MinValue is assigned its value. The statement in the algorithm is much more succinct, and stands in place of the implementation.

    We chose not to use the Pascal assignment symbol (: =) in order to emphasize that the algorithms are not being expressed in code, but rather in a "design" that will later be implemented in some programming language. It is intended that these algorithms should conveniently be coded into any of the large collection of general purpose languages that are similar to Pascal in data and control structures.

■ **GetFiles (ProgramFile, ReportFile)**   /   *Level 1*

Function: Get name of program file from the user. Open the program file for reading and the report file for writing.

Input: From the user: File name of program file

Output: ProgramFile (open for reading)
ReportFile (open for writing)

■ **ProcessProgramFile**
(ProgramFile, ReportFile, ExecCount, CommentCount)   /   *Level 1*

Function: Process every line of program file: Count executable and comment lines; write each line to the report file, with line numbers preceding executable lines.

Input: ProgramFile (contains source lines of Pascal program)
ReportFile (file to contain program listing)

Output: To screen: echoprinted lines of source code
To ReportFile: formatted lines of program listing
Returned to main program: ReportFile, ExecCount, CommentCount

PrintCountData (ReportFile, ExecCount, CommentCount) / *Level 1*

Function: Print report of executable and comment line counts. Calculate and print weighted line count.

Input: ReportFile, ExecCount, CommentCount

Output: ReportFile

We can complete the lower levels of the design by adding a layer of detailed design to their specifications. The first and last of these modules are pretty straightforward. We will look at them in more detail in the application section at the end of this chapter. For now let's look at the second module, ProcessProgramFile, in more detail.

ProcessProgramFile

Initialize counts to zero

WHILE NOT EOF (ProgramFile) DO
    ReadLine from ProgramFile and store in TextLine
    Echoprint TextLine to screen
    CASE LineStatus (TextLine) OF
        BlankLine :
            Print blank line to ReportFile
        CommentLine :
            Increment CommentCount
            Print comment line to ReportFile, preceded by blanks.
        ExecLine :
            Increment ExecCount
            Print line to ReportFile, preceded by ExecCount
END CASE

Note that the design is recorded in a mixture of normal English phrases and Pascal-like structures. While we aren't bound to writing correct Pascal syntax in the design, the use of "pseudocode" gives our design the same kind of structure as the program that will be written.

Much of this design translates fairly directly into Pascal code: assignment statements to initialize and increment counts, Writeln statements to print to the screen and to ReportFile. However, to read the next line from ProgramFile, we must know something about what we mean by *line*. It seems to be a collection of characters, often called a *string*. But how do we store a string? Some versions of Pascal have a built-in data type called **String**, but this is not defined in standard Pascal. Our program requirements tell us that this program may be compiled and run on different computer systems, so we should avoid using a feature that is not standard to all Pascal compilers. Therefore, we decide to create our own string type. At this point in our design (Level 1), however, we don't really need to know how this StringType will be declared. We only need to note that there will need to be an operation to read a "line" from a text file, and to store the characters in a variable of StringType. In fact, we know enough to specify this ReadLine operation.

■ **ReadLine (FileToRead, String)**   /   *Level 2*

Function:	Read all characters until EOLN from FileToRead; store them in String
Input:	FileToRead (a text file)
Output:	FileToRead (updated by read); String (StringType)

Here is the high-level design for the ReadLine operation:

ReadLine

WHILE NOT EOLN (FileToRead) DO
   Read next character from FileToRead
   Store character in String
Readln (FileToRead)

Reading a character from FileToRead will translate directly into a Pascal Read statement:

```
Read (FileToReadFile, Character)
```

Storing the character in String, however, requires us to know how String has been declared. Is StringType an array, a record, or what? Let's put off this decision until we have looked at what else we plan to do with this string.

Looking back at Level 1, we next come to a CASE structure—we will process according to whether TextLine is blank, a comment, or contains executable source code. To determine what kind of line we are processing, we will have to look at the contents of TextLine. Let's specify a function, LineStatus, to do this task.

■ **LineStatus (TextLine)**
returns (BlankLine, CommentLine, or ExecLine)   /   *Level 2*

Function:	Determine whether TextLine is a comment, blank, or executable line of code.
Input:	TextLine (a string)
Output:	LineStatus (BlankLine, CommentLine, or ExecLine)

What needs to be done to determine the type of line? There are three possibilities: The line may be blank, it may contain only comments, or it may contain "executable" code (with or without comments). Figure 1-4 illustrates the various types of lines.

The first case is easy to detect: If the line contains no nonblank characters, it is blank. Since the specifications include assumptions that (1) all comments end on the

Figure 1-4
Types of Lines in a
Pascal Program

```
PROGRAM Example;                                    Executable
                                                    Blank
  (* This program illustrates the various *)        Comment
  (* types of lines in a Pascal program.  *)        Comment
                                                    Blank
VAR                                                 Executable
  Number : Integer; (* a variable *)                Executable
                                                    Blank
BEGIN                                               Executable
  (* Set the variable. *)                           Comment
  Number := 1;                                       Executable
  Writeln (Number); (* print the number *)          Executable
END. (* Example *)                                  Executable
```

same line on which they began, and (2) an executable line cannot begin with a comment, the second case is also simple: If the line begins with a comment delimiter [(∗], then it is a comment line. Otherwise, it is an executable line. Here is the design for function LineStatus:

LineStatus

FindNonBlank (a string operation, returns position of first nonblank character)

IF nonblank not found
   THEN LineStatus ← BlankLine

  ELSE
    IdentifyCommentStart

    IF comment start delimiter identified
       THEN LineStatus ← CommentLine
       ELSE LineStatus ← ExecLine

Most of the algorithm in this Level 2 design will convert directly to Pascal code. However, we will need another level of detail for the FindNonBlank and Identify-CommentStart modules.

How do we know when we are done? The top-down design is complete when all the modules have been broken down, or "decomposed," to a level that is easy to convert to Pascal code. This software design approach is sometimes called **modular decomposition**. The number of levels required is a function of the size and complexity of the problem.

When the design is complete, coding the solution to the problem in Pascal is a straightforward task. We will return to this design later in the chapter and in the Application section at the end of the chapter, which presents the complete design and Pascal solution to the problem.

Information Hiding

One important feature of top-down design is that the details that are specified in lower levels of the program design are hidden from the higher levels. The programmer only sees the details that are relevant at a particular level of the design. This *information hiding* makes certain details inaccessible to the programmer at higher levels. Why is this desirable? Shouldn't the programmer know everything?

No. This is one situation in which a certain amount of ignorance is advantageous. Information hiding prevents the high levels of the design from becoming dependent on low-level design details that are more likely to be changed. Furthermore, you don't want to require a complete understanding of the complicated details of low-level routines for the design of higher level routines. Such a requirement would introduce a greater risk of confusion and errors throughout the whole program.

Information Hiding   The practice of "hiding" the details of a function or structure, making them inaccessible to other parts of the program.

The top-down design technique encourages information hiding within a program by separating the program's function into clear-cut levels of *abstraction*. Once we have stated the function of a low-level procedure and its interface specifications (its calling sequence of inputs and outputs), we can forget *how* the low-level module accomplishes this function. The details are hidden from the higher levels.

Abstraction   The separation of the logical properties of data or function from their implementation in a computer program.

The concepts of information hiding and abstraction are fundamental principles of software engineering. We will come back to them again and again throughout this book.

Designing Data Structures

Programs consist of both algorithms and data. At some point in the design process, we have to come up with appropriate ways of representing the program's data.

Just as we use a top-down approach to develop the algorithms for solving a problem, we can also design the structures to hold the program's data in a top-down manner. In the design of the program's function, we went from a general to a detailed description of the algorithms. In the design of data, we will go from a more abstract view of the data to a more concrete picture, deferring the details as long as possible. In general, it is not necessary or desirable to tie ourselves down early to a particular implementation of a data structure. Just as there are usually multiple functionally correct solutions to programming problems, there are often a number of possibilities for storing the data used in a program.

When Ignorance Is Bliss

To illustrate the value of information hiding, consider the Pascal Read procedure. We use it all the time to input data, but do you know how it works? Its implemention is completely invisible to the user of the procedure. When the program says

```
Read (DataFile, RealNumber);
```

this procedure somehow gets the characters that represent a real number from the appropriate place in DataFile, updates the file cursor to pass the characters that were read, converts these characters into the representation of a real number for this particular computer, and stores that value in an output variable, RealNumber.

Even this simplified explanation of the procedure is inconsequential to the programmer who calls Read. What is important to the user is to have a simple way to call the procedure and to know that Read will assign an appropriate value to the specified variable. The calling program doesn't have to know anything about the internal representation of the file variable or the implementation of real numbers on this machine. It only needs to know the interface to procedure Read. If a change ever is made in the details of how this standard procedure does what it does, the program that calls Read will not have to change.

In designing data structures, we will also use a second design approach: Treating the logical data entity as an "object" in our program, we will determine a set of operations that manipulate it. We can consider this data object and its operations as a single module to design, since all the operations will be dependent on the implementation of the data. This combination of data object and associated operations is called an **abstract data type**. We will talk about this concept in great detail in Chapter 3; for now, let's look at an example.

In designing a solution to Program ListAndCount, we began to discuss the design of TextLine, a variable that held the characters from one line of the program file. We said that an ordered collection of characters can be described as a string. At this point "string" is a *data abstraction*. It has a logical meaning, but not a physical representation. We haven't yet decided how StringType will be represented in terms of Pascal data types. Approaching StringType as an abstract data type, we identify a set of operations that will be performed on strings: reading a line from a file and storing it in a string, printing a string to a file, finding the first/next nonblank character in a string. By defining these operations, we can specify the abstract data type StringType.

Now let's take a top-down approach to the design of the String module, going from our abstraction toward a Pascal implementation. Knowing what operations need to be performed on strings gives us some information we can use in designing StringType. Obviously we will need someplace to store the characters—a "list" of characters. Since we plan to print the characters in the string, we will need to know how long the string is. Now we have decomposed the abstract StringType into a more detailed data description: a list of characters and a length attribute. Let's rewrite the design of ReadLine (Level 2) to include this information.

ReadLine

Set string to empty (length 0)

WHILE NOT EOLN (FileToRead) DO
    Read next character from FileToRead
    Increment string length
    Append character to list of string characters

Readln (FileToRead)

This description of StringType is more detailed than our previous one, but it still contains a level of abstraction; we do not yet know how a "list of characters" will be represented. Of course, eventually we will need to implement the string operations, in terms of Pascal data types. At that point, we might decide to use the following declarations to define StringType:

```
CONST
  MaxString = 80;
TYPE
  StringRangeType = 0 .. MaxString;

  StringType = RECORD
    Length    : StringRangeType;
    Chars     : ARRAY [1 .. MaxString] OF Char
  END; (* StringType *)
```

Given these declarations, we can now code Procedure ReadLine from its design above.

It is important to note that this is not the *only* way we could have represented StringType. Chapters 3 and 6 discuss other string implementations. In terms of the program's correctness, these implementations are equivalent.

This design process suggests a fourth line to be added to Figure 1-3.

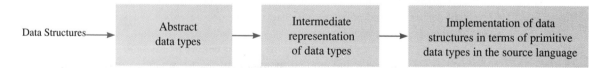

Data Structures → | Abstract data types | → | Intermediate representation of data types | → | Implementation of data structures in terms of primitive data types in the source language |

Throughout this book we will discuss the need for data abstraction. The goal is to be able to manipulate the program's data with regard to its *logical representation,* the abstract data type (ADT), rather than the physical storage of the data structure. To a limited degree, programming languages provide built-in structured data types that hide the physical placement of data in memory; for instance, Pascal provides arrays and records as built-in data structures. We can also build our own programmer-defined structured data types. Several of these (stacks, queues, lists, and trees) are discussed in the chapters that follow. The use of data abstraction to simplify the program design process is discussed in much more detail in Chapter 3.

Implementing the Solution

When you've completed your design, you are ready to code your program. In this section, you will learn how the way you code a program can help you to meet Goals 2 and 3. Let's assume that your good design process has given you a well-structured program. The next key activity in meeting Goals 2 and 3 is to write *well-documented programs*.

Documentation is more than just comments; it includes the written descriptions, specifications, design, and actual source code of a program. Remember that what runs on the computer is in machine language; when you finish a program, the source code will document in human-readable form what that machine code does.

The **external documentation** of a program consists of the written information that is outside the body of the source code. In addition to the detailed specifications, the external documentation may include the history of the program's development and subsequent modifications, the top-down design, "architectural" diagrams of the program's structure, and user's manuals.

The **internal documentation** includes comments, self-documenting code, and program formatting for readability. The goal of all these features is to make the program readable, understandable, and easily modifiable.

Comments

Comments can usually be taken directly from the pseudocode in the top-down design. Effective commentary helps the reader determine what the programmer is trying to do at various points in the program. It is not necessary to comment on every statement, however. In fact, frequent comments like

```
Sum := 0; (* Sum is initialized to zero. *)
```

or

```
Index := Index + 1; (* Increment index value. *)
```

can clutter a program without contributing to its clarity. What constitutes the effective use of comments? In general, it is desirable to comment in the following places.

Declarations   Comment on the intended use of each variable. For example,

```
VAR
    ProgramFile : Text;
    (* input file containing text of Pascal program to process *)
    ReportFile  : Text;
    (* output file containing program listing and count report *)
```

Program Structures   Put a comment before or next to each branch (IF-THEN-ELSE or CASE statement) or loop in the program to explain the function of the whole structure. For example,

```
(* Read "line" from FileToRead, storing characters in String. *)
WHILE NOT EOLN (FileToRead) DO
  BEGIN
    Read (FileToRead, Character);
    String.Length := String.Length + 1;
    String.Characters[String.Length] := Character
  END; (* WHILE *)
```

It is also a good idea to put a comment after each END, especially if it isn't in close proximity to the BEGIN that started the block of statements.

Procedure or Function Calls   Put a comment before or next to each subprogram call to explain its function and effect on the data. It is also useful to put comments on the parameter list of a procedure call, especially if it contains literal values or if there are a lot of parameters. For instance,

```
(* Find position of the first nonblank character in the line. *)
FindNonBlank
    (TextLine,      (* string to search              *)
     1,             (* starting position             *)
     CurPos,        (* position found - returned     *)
     Found);        (* nonblank found? - returned    *)
```

Nonobvious Code   Place a comment on any confusing section of code. Where possible, of course, tricky code should be avoided completely. Comments on complicated or confusing code should be especially clear and precise.

We have seen many instances of programs having as many lines of comments as executable lines of code. Running your program through Program ListAndCount will give you an idea of how many comment lines are in your programs. In general, it's better to err on the side of too many than too few. The important thing is to use the comments in an effective way.

Self-Documenting Code

Self-documenting code uses meaningful identifier names to convey the intended function of variables, constants, and procedure names. For instance,

```
CONST
  T = 0.042;

VAR
  X, Y : Real;

    .

    .

    .

  X := Y * T;
```

doesn't tell us much about the meaning of the constant and variables. On the other hand,

```
CONST
  TaxRate = 0.042;
VAR
  Tax, Price : Real;
  .
  .
  .
  Tax := Price * TaxRate;
```

gives us much more information.

Self-Documenting Code   Source code that uses meaningful names for constant, variable, and subprogram identifiers to clarify their meaning in the program.

Prettyprinting

Program formatting, known as **prettyprinting**, is encouraged by Pascal's relaxed rules about blank spaces and lines. By using blank spaces to indent within control structures such as loops and branches, we can convey the logical structure of a program at a glance. In addition, blank lines can be used to separate the logical units of the program. Program formatting is much more effective when a consistent style is adhered to. Many systems have prettyprinting programs that will do much of the formatting for you, but it's generally not a good idea to rely too heavily on such a tool. We have included some suggestions for program formatting on pages 50–53.

The programs below illustrate how the use of comments, prettyprinting, and self-documenting code can increase the readability of a short program. The first program is functionally correct, but difficult to read and understand.

```
PROGRAM Mystery (Input, Output);
VAR X, Y, Z :REAL;
BEGIN Writeln('Input side lengths:');Readln(X,Y);
IF (X<=0) OR (Y<=0) THEN Writeln('Error')
ELSE BEGIN Z:=SQRT(SQR(X)+SQR(Y)); Writeln(Z) END END.
```

The second program on the following page is functionally identical, but is much easier to read and understand.

```
PROGRAM Hypotenuse (Input, Output);

(* This program reads in two sides of a right triangle,     *)
(* calculates the length of the hypotenuse, and prints      *)
(* the result. The formula used is the Pythagorean Theorem. *)

VAR
  Side1,                  (* first known side        *)
  Side2,                  (* second known side       *)
  Hypot : Real;           (* calculated hypotenuse *)

BEGIN (* Hypotenuse *)

  (* Get the known sides. *)
  Writeln ('Input side lengths:');
  Readln (Side1, Side2);

  (* If no input errors, calculate the hypotenuse *)
  IF (Side1 <= 0) OR (Side2 <= 0)
    THEN Writeln ('Error')
    ELSE
      BEGIN (* no errors in input *)
        Hypot := SQRT (SQR (Side1) + SQR (Side2));
        Writeln (Hypot)
      END (* no errors in input *)

END. (* Hypotenuse *)
```

Using Constants

The use of constants to represent "magic" numbers like pi, nonvariable tax rates, the maximum bounds of an array, and so on makes code more readable and more easily modifiable. The idea here is similar to the concept of data abstraction that we discussed earlier. We use an abstract (a meaningful name) in place of the concrete (a literal value) to increase readability and to facilitate modifiability.

All That . . . and on Schedule

In order to finish programs on time and thus meet Goal 4, software developers must schedule their work. In the best of all programming worlds, creating high-quality software takes time. Unfortunately, few of us work under optimal conditions. Most programmers complain that the hardware is unreliable. This is not true: You can *always* count on the computer to go down for five hours on the last day before your program is due. The problem is to avoid being the victim of this situation. The solution is to make a schedule of milestones to be reached and stick to it. With experience, most programmers can get a feel for the relative amount of time to devote to each part of the development process.

Let's look at an example. On October 5, your professor hands out an assignment that must be completed and turned in three weeks later, on October 26. Since the due date is a Monday and you don't like to spend your weekends in the terminal room, you schedule your completion date as Friday, October 23. Now you make up the following schedule:

Oct. 5   Assignment received. *Think*!
Oct. 7   Requirements completely understood. Any questions about requirements, input, output, assumptions answered. Detailed specifications recorded.
Oct. 9   Top level of design complete.
Oct. 15   All levels of top-down design complete. (Save this design for external program documentation.) All data structures determined.
Oct. 18   Coding complete. (All syntax errors are out.) Begin testing.
Oct. 22   Testing complete.
Oct. 23   Program ready for delivery. (Program meets all standards for delivery, and internal and external documentation are complete.)

Your schedule even has a three-day buffer of safety at the end, just in case the computer goes down or the terminal room is packed. Scheduling your progress will also give you a greater appreciation for the relative time requirements of the various programming activities.

Summary

How are our quality software goals met by the strategy of abstraction and information hiding? When details are hidden at each level, the code becomes simpler and more readable, which in turn makes the program easier to write and modify. The top-down design process produces modular units that are also easier to test, debug, and maintain.

One positive side effect of modular design is that modifications tend to be localized in a small set of modules, and thus the cost of modifications is reduced. Remember that whenever a module is modified it must be retested to make sure that it still works correctly in the program. By localizing the modules affected by changes to the program, we limit the extent of retesting needed. You will find more on this issue in Chapter 2.

Finally, reliability is increased by making the design conform to our logical picture and by delegating confusing details to lower levels of the program. An understanding of the wide range of activities involved in software development—from requirements analysis through the maintenance of the resulting program—leads to an appreciation of a disciplined software-engineering approach. Everyone knows some programming wizard who can sit down and hack out a program in an evening, working alone, coding without a formal design. But we cannot depend on wizardry to control the design, implementation, verification, and maintenance of large, complex software projects that involve the efforts of many programmers. As computers grow larger and more powerful, the problems that people want to solve on them also become larger and more complex. Some people refer to this situation as a software *crisis*. We'd like you to think of it as a software *challenge*.

Application

Software Development Tools 1: List and Count

Abstract Data Type

■ Strings

Software Techniques

■ Top-down design
■ Data design
■ Use of nonstandard Pascal

In this chapter, we began the development of a very useful tool for a programmer to have: a program that will create a numbered listing of a Pascal program and count the "executable" and comment lines in the program.

How is a numbered programming listing more useful than a printout of the Text file that contains the original program? Chapter 2 introduces code walkthroughs and inspections—activities in which the source code of a program is "inspected" by a team of software developers before testing begins. Each member of the team must have a listing of the source code. A numbered listing is very helpful at the meeting, to keep everyone in the same place at the same time.

A numbered listing is also a prerequisite for another tool that we will develop in a later chapter—a cross reference. A cross reference lists all the identifiers (variables, constants, procedures, etc.) used in the program, along with the line numbers of every place where each identifier was used. It is like an index to the program. This tool can be very helpful in debugging a program.

Many computer science students are never given a programming project whose "life cycle" endures beyond delivering it to the customer (turning it in for a grade). They miss seeing the most important part of the software's life: its *use*. That is why we have chosen, for our first application, a programming project that you can actually use as a software development tool. Later we will modify and enhance it—adding the cross reference generator. This modification will have two benefits: (1) You will have experience modifying a program (one of the most common real-world programming assignments), and (2) you will have a more useful tool to add to your collection of software development tools.

Reviewing the Specifications

The specifications for this project are listed in Figure 1-1. Before we go on with the design, let's review and clarify the specifications.

Looking at the Function section, we see that the analysis shall be *line*-based, rather than *statement*-based; a statement may contain many lines of source code. By this measurement, the following program fragment contains 11 lines of source code:

*E*stimating Lines of Code

How long was your last program? How long will this one be? Most programmers don't have a very good idea of how "big" a program to do a particular task must be. Some commercial software companies measure programmer "productivity" in terms of lines of source code designed, coded, and tested in a given time period (a month, for example). While the usefulness of such a measure is debated by software engineers, it is still used in industry. Programmers are sometimes called upon to estimate how many lines of code a program (or section of a program) will be. These estimates, along with some expectation of source-lines-per-programmer-month, are often used on large software projects to schedule the development of various parts of the projects.

While techniques for making such estimations are beyond the scope of this course, you can begin to get a feel for the size of your own programs by using a source line counter like the one we are about to develop. Since lines that contain *only* comments are to be counted separately from lines that contain executable Pascal code, this tool will also give you an idea of how many comments you are using in your programs.

```
IF X < Y (* for X <> Y *)
  THEN
    BEGIN
      Writeln ('X is smaller');
      MinNum := X
    END (* IF *)
  ELSE
    BEGIN
      Writeln ('Y is smaller');
      MinNum := Y
    END; (* ELSE *)
```

This same piece of code could be reformatted in 6 lines of source code:

```
IF X < Y THEN
  BEGIN Writeln ('X is smaller');
        MinNum := X      END (* IF *)
ELSE
  BEGIN Writeln ('Y is smaller');
        MinNum := Y      END; (* ELSE *)
```

A single Pascal program, therefore, could produce many different source line counts, depending on its formatting, though the number of statements would remain the same. It also seems somewhat unfair to count a line that contains only the reserved word BEGIN the same as we count a complex line like

```
Total := ExecCount + Min(ComCount, Round(ExecCount * ComWeight));
```

Is counting source lines, rather than statements, a useful measure? Counting statements isn't completely foolproof, either. The example above consists of a single IF statement, whose IF-part has one compound statement that contains two statements, and whose ELSE-part also has one compound statement that contains two statements. So how many statements are there? (One quick-and-easy method sometimes used to count "statements" is just to count the semicolons that litter a Pascal program.)

Counting lines of source code, rather than statements, makes sense if we understand that the results are more interesting as a *relative* measure than as an absolute measure. That is, the number of source lines in a single program is not meaningful in itself. However, comparing the number of source lines in several programs is much more interesting—assuming the programs are similarly formatted.

For instance, Instructor D requires all her students to conform to a class formatting standard. After the students completed their first programming assignment, they were told to run their programs through ListAndCount and to turn in the numbered listing and count report. The results were very interesting: The solutions ranged from 400 to 700 lines of code, with the average around 580. Some students were writing much more code than others to do the same task. We will also find counting lines of code useful when we start to develop multiple implementations of the same data structure in later chapters. The size of the solution, in lines of code, is one measure that we will use to compare the implementations.

Processing Source Lines

The specifications state that blank lines (lines that contain no nonblank characters before EOLN) should be printed in the listing, but not counted.

How should comments be treated by the source line counter? We could "strip" the comments from the program, and just count the functional Pascal code that is left. However, it might be interesting to look at how many comment lines are in your programs—as a rough measure of the program's documentation. (This is a very rough measure, since we cannot judge the *quality* of the comments from their quantity.) But it provides interesting information, so the specifications have been written to require a count of the comments. In addition, we will calculate a "weighted" total, using the following formula:

Weighted lines =
Executable lines + Minimum (Comment lines, 10% Executable lines).

That is, the number of comment lines will account for no more than 10% of the number of the executable lines in the weighted total. For instance, if a program has 100 executable lines and 20 comment lines, the weighted total is 110—only 10 of the comment lines (10% of the executable lines) contribute to the weighted total. If a program has 100 executable lines and 3 comment lines, the weighted total is 103.

When we speak of "comment lines," we are referring to source lines that contain *only* comments and white space (blanks). The following source lines are comment lines:

```
(* This is a comment. *)
(* This line contains *) (* two comments *)
```

According to the program specifications, the only comment delimiters that we must recognize are (* and *). We are not required to recognize comments in { } delimiters. The assumptions also state that a comment cannot open on one line and close on another—all comments end on the same line in which they begin.

Executable lines consist of source lines that contain functional Pascal text—reserved words, statements, declarations, and so on. The following four source lines are (individual cases of) executable lines:

```
ArrayType = ARRAY [1 .. Max] OF Integer;
Index := Index + 1;
Writeln ('Hello');
THEN
```

We are using "executable" to describe such lines for lack of a better term. While a Writeln statement could be said to execute, it is hard to imagine executing a BEGIN or a type declaration.

Note that a statement that spans two lines is counted as two executable lines, as in the following example:

```
WeightedTotal := ExecCount +
    Min (CommentCount, Round(ExecCount * CommentWeight));
```

since we are counting source lines, not statements.

What about "mixed" lines? For instance, the following source lines:

```
BEGIN (* ListAndCount *)
Index := Index + 1; (* set up to check the next element *)
(* Print answer *) Writeln (Answer);
```

contain comments in addition to "executable" Pascal text. Are these comment lines or executable lines? According to the definition of executable line in the specification, mixed lines are considered to be executable, since they contain functional Pascal text. Comment lines are defined to be lines that contain *only* comment text. However, the assumptions state that no executable line will begin with a comment, so the third example above is not a legal executable line.

Top-Down Design

We began the development of the top-down design earlier in this chapter. Let's review the design of the program. The main program activity is to process the program file, line by line, counting executable and comment lines, and creating a numbered listing. We'll call this activity ProcessProgramFile. Before we can process the file, however, we must ask the user for the file name, and then open (Reset) the file. We must also open (Rewrite) the file that will contain the report. Let's bundle these file-related activities together in a module called GetFiles. Finally, after the program file has been processed and the lines counted, we must write the count report to the output file. We'll call this activity PrintCountData. The main module of our design is

Main Module

GetFiles
ProcessProgramFile
PrintCountData

The main program is now divided into three main sections, or modules. Next the interface (function, inputs, and outputs) to each of these modules must be specified, and its design must be recorded.

The GetFiles Module

The first module, GetFiles, is specified as follows:

GetFiles (ProgramFile, ReportFile) / *Level 1*

> *Function:*   Get name of program file from the user. Open the program file for reading and the report file for writing.
>
> *Input:*   From the user: File name of program file
>
> *Output:*   ProgramFile (open for reading)
> ReportFile (open for writing)

This module seems fairly straightforward. Its design is

GetFiles

Prompt user for ProgramFile name
Read ProgramFile name

Reset the ProgramFile
Rewrite the ReportFile

In the implementation of this module, however, we run into a problem: Once we have read the name of the ProgramFile supplied by the user, what do we do with this information? There is no mechanism in standard Pascal for connecting a file name (such as 'PROGRAM.PAS') with a file variable (such as ProgramFile). However, most Pascal compilers supply an "extension" to the standard language definition to do this function. This leads to a dilemma, for in the Processing Requirements section of the specification, we are told that the program "must be able to be compiled and run, with minimal changes, on a variety of computer systems." If we decide to implement the program for a particular compiler, we will violate this requirement, but if we do not use an extension to standard Pascal, we cannot implement the requirement that the user shall supply the program file name.

Trade-off time: Situations such as this one arise frequently in the real world. What do you do? You must go back to the party that originated the requirements (your instructor, supervisor, or customer) and ask for a clarification. In this case, we (the textbook authors) will supply the answer: The requirement to ask the user for the program file name must be implemented. The requirement to write a program that is "portable" from one machine (and compiler) to another, is mitigated by the phrase "with minimal changes" (see the text of the specification). So you will be allowed to use a nonstandard Pascal extension in this case, as there is no standard way to implement the requirement.

Now, you ask, *which* nonstandard Pascal extension? As this text is being prepared on an IBM PC-compatible system, with programs compiled and tested under Turbo Pascal, that is the extension that will be used in the rest of this discussion. (You should feel free to change the program to fit the compiler you are using for this course. Check your compiler manual for more information.)

To associate the file name with the file variable we will use the Turbo Pascal procedure **Assign**. This procedure takes two parameters: a string containing the file name, and a file variable (type Text). We will declare FileName to be a Turbo Pascal String. This variable will only be used within Procedure GetFiles, so we can contain the nonstandard contamination of our program to this section. According to the specifications, the program output is to be written to a file called COUNTOUT. We will declare a constant for this file name. The declarations and Assign calls can be coded as follows:

```
CONST
  ReportName = 'COUNTOUT';

VAR
  FileName : String[20];   (**** Turbo Pascal Type ****)
    .
    .
    .
(****** Turbo Pascal Code ********)
Assign (ProgramFile, FileName);
Assign (ReportFile, ReportName);
```

NOTE: To make the nonstandard portions stand out from the rest of the program, be sure to identify them explicitly in comments.

Now let's return to the design of module GetFiles. We must first prompt the user for the file name, and read the response. A call to Writeln will suffice for the prompt, but how do we read the file name? Since FileName will be a Turbo String, we can take advantage of the fact that Turbo's Readln procedure can take a String-type parameter.

```
Writeln ('What file would you like to list and count?');
Readln (FileName);
```

We then make the calls to Assign as described above. Finally, we open ProgramFile for reading and ReportFile for writing:

```
Reset (ProgramFile);
Rewrite (ReportFile);
```

The complete code for the GetFiles procedure is in the program listing at the end of this application section.

This procedure works fine, assuming that the user correctly types in the name of a file that contains a Pascal program. In general, this is not a very safe assumption, as human users have a bad habit of making typographical errors. For now, we will leave this procedure as it is. (Modifying this procedure to add *error-proofing* is left as a programming exercise.)

The TerminateProcessing Module

Since we're using a Turbo Pascal extension to implement the GetFiles procedure, we will need to consider Turbo's rules for using files. At the end of the program, we will need to close the files explicitly, using Turbo's **Close** procedure. (This is not required in standard Pascal, but is necessary in Turbo Pascal.) The Close procedure takes one input, the file variable to be closed.

```
Close (ProgramFile);
Close (ReportFile);
```

Rather than placing these calls at the end of the main program, we will add a fourth module to the end of the Level 0 design. The TerminateProcessing procedure will take the two file variables as inputs, and will simply contain the two calls to Close. (If you are using a different compiler, check your manual for information on closing files.)

The ProcessProgramFile Module

The ProcessProgramFile Module has the biggest job: to process the program file, line by line, counting executable and comment lines, and creating a numbered listing. The specification of this module is:

ProcessProgramFile
(ProgramFile, ReportFile, ExecCount, CommentCount) / *Level 1*

> *Function:*   Process every line of program file: Count executable and comment lines; write each line to the report file, with line numbers preceding executable lines.
>
> *Input:*   ProgramFile (contains source lines of Pascal program)
> ReportFile (file to contain program listing)
>
> *Output:*   To screen: echoprinted lines of source code
> To ReportFile: formatted lines of program listing
> Returned to main program: ReportFile, ExecCount, CommentCount

We discussed this module at length in the chapter. Let's review the ProcessProgramFile Level 1 design.

ProcessProgramFile

Initialize ExecCount and CommentCount to 0

WHILE NOT EOF (ProgramFile) DO

ReadLine—Read TextLine from ProgramFile
Echoprint TextLine to screen

```
CASE LineStatus (TextLine) OF
  BlankLine :
    Print blank line to Report File.
  CommentLine :
    Increment CommentCount.
    Print comment line to ReportFile, preceded by blanks.
  ExecLine :
    Increment ExecCount.
    Print line to ReportFile, preceded by ExecCount.
END CASE
```

In this phase of the design process, we see that there are two types of design to consider: the top-down design of the program's function and, at the same time, the design of abstract data types to model data used in the program. At the point in the program where we need to read a line of text and to store it in a variable (TextLine), we must think about what type that variable will be.

The data object that we need to design is logically described as a **string**—a list of characters in a particular order. Since Turbo Pascal has a built-in String type, which we have already used in Procedure GetFiles, can't we just use this type for TextLine? We could, but our requirements tell us to avoid nonstandard Pascal whenever possible, since it will have to be changed to compile under a different system. We know from our discussion of this module in the chapter text that we will need to do many string operations on TextLine. Therefore, we decide to create our own StringType. At this point, we will go on with our top-down design; as we identify string operations that we need, we will add them to a list. When we finish designing ProcessProgramFile, we will come back to the design and implementation of StringType.

The initialization of the line counts will convert directly to code. The next two lines of the design, reading and echo-printing TextLine, suggest two string operations: ReadLine and PrintLine. We add these to our list of string operations.

Next we enter a CASE structure, processing according to whether TextLine is blank, a comment line, or an "executable" line. We'll come back to the LineStatus operation in a moment. We print TextLine to the ReportFile (using the PrintLine operation), preceded by a line number (if it is executable), and increment the line counts as appropriate. The CASE statement can be coded directly from the Level 1 design.

Now let's review the design of the LineStatus operation. There are three possible values for LineStatus: BlankLine, CommentLine, or ExecLine. The first of these is simple to detect. We search TextLine for a nonblank character; if none exists, then the line is blank. That suggests another string operation, FindNonBlank, which takes a string as input, and returns the position of the first nonblank character and a flag to indicate if a nonblank character was found. We add FindNonBlank to the list of string operations.

If the line isn't blank, we have to figure out whether it is a comment or an executable line. To make this determination, we check to see if the first nonblank characters begin a new comment, using a Level 3 module, IdentifyCommentStart. Here is the design for function LineStatus:

LineStatus

FindNonBlank (a string operation, returns position of first nonblank character)

IF nonblank not found
    THEN LineStatus ← BlankLine

ELSE
    IdentifyCommentStart

    IF comment start delimiter identified
        THEN LineStatus ← CommentLine
        ELSE LineStatus ← ExecLine

The assignments to LineStatus can be coded directly, but we will need another level of detail for IdentifyCommentStart, the module that checks for the beginning of a comment. This module inputs TextLine and the current line position (returned from FindNonBlank) and outputs a Boolean flag, InComment. Here is the specification of this module:

IdentifyCommentStart (TextLine, CurPos, InComment)   /   *Level 3*

Function:	If a comment begins at CurPos, InComment is set to True; otherwise InComment is set to False.
Input:	TextLine, CurPos
Output:	InComment (Boolean)

The design for the IdentifyCommentStart module is listed below:

IdentifyCommentStart

InComment ← False

IF character at CurPos = '(' AND length of TextLine > CurPos
    THEN
        IF character at CurPos + 1 = '*'
            THEN InComment ← True

This module is very simple and could be coded directly from the design—almost. How do we access the "character at CurPos" in TextLine, and how do we know TextLine's length? We need string operations to get this information. We will add two functions, CharAt and Length, to our list of string operations.

The StringType Module

By now we have quite a list of string operations. The first thing we need to do is to specify these operations more formally. (We have already informally specified them in passing.) We will use the identifier Strng, instead of the more readable String because Turbo Pascal has a reserved word String, the name of the built-in string type. (Since we already have Turbo-specific code in this program, we had better make it compile under Turbo Pascal!)

ReadLine (FileToRead, Strng)

Function: Read all characters until EOLN from FileToRead; store them in Strng. Assumes file is open.

Input: FileToRead (a text file)

Output: FileToRead (updated by read); Strng

PrintLine (FileToWrite, Strng)

Function: Write string characters to FileToWrite. Assumes file is open.

Input: FileToWrite (a text file), Strng

Output: FileToWrite (updated by write)

FindNonBlank (Strng, Start, Position, Found)

Function: If Found, Position = position of the first nonblank character in Strng following Start position; otherwise, Position = 0

Input: Strng, Start

Output: Position, Found

Length (Strng) returns Integer

Function: Returns the length of Strng. Assumes that Strng is not undefined (it has been read or assigned to).

Input: Strng

Output: Length (Integer)

CharAt (Strng, Position) returns Char

Function: Returns the character in Strng at the specified Position. Assumes that Strng is not undefined, and that Position <= Length(Strng)

Input: Strng, Position

Output: CharAt (Char)

Now that we have the operations specified, we can talk about the implementation of StringType. As we discussed earlier in the chapter, a string is a list of characters. Associated with this list is an attribute called **length**. Our implementation must keep track of both the characters in the string and its length.

The string implementation we have chosen keeps the characters in an array with Length as a separate integer value. The characters and length will be kept together by declaring them as fields in a record:

```
CONST
  MaxString = 80;

TYPE
  StringRangeType = 0 .. MaxString;
```

```
StringType = RECORD
  Length : StringRangeType;
  Chars  : ARRAY [1 .. MaxString] OF Char
END; (* StringType *)
```

Let's look at the two simplest operations, Length and CharAt. The Length operation inputs a string and returns its length. The function contains only a single statement:

```
Length := Strng.Length;
```

The CharAt function inputs a string and a position, and returns the value of the character at the specified position in the string. This function also contains a single statement:

```
CharAt := Strng.Chars[Position];
```

Is it really worthwhile to code functions that contain only a single line? Invoking the function isn't any shorter or simpler than just coding the implementation directly. Perhaps not, but by keeping the implementation hidden from the calling procedure (the string "user"), we are free to change the string implementation without affecting the rest of the program. We will discuss this subject at great length in Chapter 3 and throughout the rest of this book.

The implementations of the string operations are virtually identical to their design. Out of deference to the length of this application, we will not show their designs here, but direct you to look at the code in the program.

The PrintCountData Module

Happily, the final module, PrintCountData, is very short and simple. Here is the interface specification:

▌ **PrintCountData (ReportFile, ExecCount, CommentCount)** / *Level 1*

Function:	Print report of executable and comment line counts. Calculate and print weighted line count.
Input:	ReportFile, ExecCount, CommentCount
Output:	ReportFile (modified)

The design for this module is as follows.

PrintCountData

WeightedTotal = ExecCount + MINIMUM (CommentCount, 10% of ExecCount)

Write ExecCount to ReportFile
Write CommentCount to ReportFile
Write WeightedTotal to ReportFile

We're done! Break out the champagne! What? You say that we're not done; we haven't coded the program yet? That may be true, but we have done the hardest part of the job: We've figured out *what* to write, now we only have to worry about how to write it.

As your programs become larger and more complex, the advantages of recording the top-down design electronically, using an editor or word processor, are obvious. The design is simpler to update. You can print out a listing at any time; that's certainly better than copying over a handwritten document after changes have made it unreadable. But the best part is that, when you are done, you can make a copy of the top-down design file, and then use it as a template for coding the program. That's how we created the program that follows.

The Program

```pascal
PROGRAM ListAndCount (Input, Output, ProgramFile, ReportFile);
  (****************************************************************)
  (* Process the lines of source code in a Pascal program,      *)
  (* producing a listing of the program, with line numbers      *)
  (* preceeding each executable line of source code, followed   *)
  (* by a report of the counts of executable and comment        *)
  (* source lines of code.                                      *)
  (*                                                            *)
  (* NOTE: The GetFiles and TerminateProcessing procedures      *)
  (* contain code that is Turbo Pascal specific.                *)
  (****************************************************************)

CONST
  (* Comment delimiters *)
  LeftPar  = '(';
  Star     = '*';

  (* Maximum characters in StringType variables *)
  MaxString = 80;


TYPE
  LineType   = (BlankLine, CommentLine, ExecLine);

  StringRangeType = 0 .. MaxString;
  StringType      = RECORD
    Length        : StringRangeType;
    Chars         : ARRAY[1 .. MaxString] OF Char
  END; (* StringType *)

VAR
  (* Files *)
  ProgramFile : Text; (* text of Pascal program to process *)
  ReportFile  : Text; (* report output of this program      *)

  (* Count information *)
  CommentCount : Integer; (* count of comment-only lines     *)
  ExecCount    : Integer; (* count of executable lines       *)
```

```
(***************************************************************)
(*                     String Operations                      *)
(***************************************************************)

PROCEDURE ReadLine
  (VAR FileToRead : Text;
   VAR Strng      : StringType);

  (* Read all characters until EOLN from FileToRead; store  *)
  (* them in Strng. Readln is issued. Assumes file is open. *)

BEGIN  (* ReadLine *)

  Strng.Length := 0;

  (* Read characters until the end of the line. *)
  WHILE NOT EOLN (FileToRead) DO
    BEGIN
      Strng.Length := Strng.Length + 1;
      Read (FileToRead, Strng.Chars[Strng.Length])
    END;  (* WHILE *)

  Readln (FileToRead)
END;  (* ReadLine *)

(***************************************************************)

PROCEDURE PrintLine
  (VAR FileToWrite : Text;
   Strng           : StringType);

  (* Write Strng to text file FileToWrite. Assumes that *)
  (* FileToWrite is open for writing.                   *)

VAR
  Position : Integer;

BEGIN  (* PrintLine *)

  (* Write all characters in the string. *)
  FOR Position := 1 TO Strng.Length DO
    Write (FileToWrite, Strng.Chars[Position]);

  Writeln (FileToWrite)
END;  (* PrintLine *)

(***************************************************************)

PROCEDURE FindNonBlank
  (Strng        : StringType;
   Start        : StringRangeType;
   VAR Position : StringRangeType;
   VAR Found    : Boolean);

  (* IF Found, Position = the position of the next nonblank *)
  (* character in Strng, beginning search at Start position; *)
  (* otherwise, Position = 0.                                *)
```

```
VAR
  CurPos : Integer;

BEGIN (* FindNonBlank *)

  Position := Start;
  Found    := False;
  WHILE (Position <= Strng.Length) AND NOT Found DO
    IF Strng.Chars[Position] = ' '
      THEN Position := Position + 1
      ELSE Found := True;

  IF NOT Found
    THEN Position := 0

END; (* FindNonBlank *)
(************************************************************)

FUNCTION Length
  (Strng : StringType) : StringRangeType;

  (* Returns the length of Strng. Assumes that Strng is     *)
  (* not undefined (has a value through read or assignment.) *)

BEGIN (* Length *)
  Length := Strng.Length
END; (* Length *)
(************************************************************)

FUNCTION CharAt
  (Strng    : StringType;
   Position : StringRangeType) : Char;

  (* Returns the character in Strng at Position. Assumes *)
  (* that Strng is not undefined, and that Position <=   *)
  (* Length of Strng.                                    *)

BEGIN (* CharAt *)
  CharAt := Strng.Chars[Position\
END; (* CharAt *)

(************************************************************)
(**                Application Operations                 *)
(************************************************************)

PROCEDURE GetFiles
  (VAR ProgramFile : Text;
   VAR ReportFile  : Text);

  (* Get name of program file from the user. Open the    *)
  (* program file (reset) and the report file (rewrite). *)
  (* NOTE: This procedure contains Turbo Pascal code.    *)
```

```pascal
CONST
  ReportName = 'COUNTOUT';

VAR
  FileName : String[20]; (**** Turbo Pascal Type ****)

BEGIN (* GetFiles *)

  Writeln ('What file would you like to list and count?');
  Readln (FileName);

  (****** Turbo Pascal Code *******)
  Assign (ProgramFile, FileName);
  Assign (ReportFile, ReportName);

  Reset (ProgramFile);
  Rewrite (ReportFile)

END; (* GetFiles *)

(*************************************************************)

FUNCTION Min
  (A, B : Integer) : Integer;

  (* Returns the lesser value of A and B. *)

BEGIN (* Min *)

  IF A < B
    THEN Min := A
    ELSE Min := B

END; (* Min *)

(*************************************************************)

PROCEDURE PrintCountData
  (VAR ReportFile : Text;
   ExecCount      : Integer;
   CommentCount   : Integer);

  (* Print the count information to the report file. *)

CONST
  CommentWeight = 0.10;

VAR
  WeightedTotal : Integer;
```

```
BEGIN (* PrintCountData *)

  WeightedTotal := ExecCount +
    Min (CommentCount, Round (ExecCount * CommentWeight));

  Writeln (ReportFile);
  Writeln (ReportFile);
  Writeln (ReportFile, '----------------------------------');
  Writeln (ReportFile, '        Source Line Counts');
  Writeln (ReportFile);
  Writeln (ReportFile, 'Lines of executable code = ',
           ExecCount : 6);
  Writeln (ReportFile, 'Lines of comments        = ',
           CommentCount : 6);
  Writeln (ReportFile, '----------------------------------');
  Writeln (ReportFile, 'Weighted lines of code   = ',
           WeightedTotal : 6)
END; (* PrintCountData *)

(*************************************************************)

PROCEDURE IdentifyCommentStart
  (TextLine      : StringType;
   CurPos        : StringRangeType;
   VAR InComment : Boolean);

  (* If a comment delimiter is found at CurPos in  *)
  (* TextLine, InComment is set to True; otherwise *)
  (* InComment is set to False.                    *)

BEGIN (* IdentifyCommentStart *)

  InComment := False;

  (* Check first for ( in comment delimiter. *)
  IF (CharAt (TextLine, CurPos) = LeftPar) AND
     (Length (TextLine) > CurPos)
    THEN (* Look for * in comment delimiter. *)
      IF CharAt (TextLine, CurPos + 1) = Star
        THEN InComment := True

END; (* IdentifyCommentStart *)

(*************************************************************)

FUNCTION LineStatus
  (TextLine : StringType) : LineType;

  (* Determine whether text line is blank, a comment, *)
  (* or an executable line of source code.            *)

VAR
  CurPos    : StringRangeType;
  Found     : Boolean; (* nonblank character found? *)
  InComment : Boolean; (* line starts with comment? *)
```

```
BEGIN (* LineStatus *)

  (* Attempt to find the position of the first nonblank *)
  (* character in the line.                             *)
  FindNonBlank
    (TextLine,             (* string to search *)
     1,                    (* start position   *)
     CurPos,               (* position found   *)
     Found);               (* nonblank found?  *)

  IF NOT Found
    THEN
      LineStatus := BlankLine

    ELSE (* line is not blank *)
      BEGIN

        (* Check whether the line starts with a comment *)
        (* start delimiter.                             *)
        IdentifyCommentStart
          (TextLine,     (* line to check     *)
           CurPos,       (* at this position  *)
           InComment);   (* comment started?  *)

        IF InComment
          THEN LineStatus := CommentLine
          ELSE LineStatus := ExecLine

      END (* line is not blank *)
END; (* LineStatus *)

(*****************************************************************)

PROCEDURE ProcessProgramFile
  (VAR ProgramFile  : Text;
   VAR ReportFile   : Text;
   VAR ExecCount    : Integer;
   VAR CommentCount : Integer);

  (* Process the Pascal program in ProgramFile, creating a *)
  (* numbered program listing in ReportFile.               *)

VAR
  TextLine : StringType;   (* line being processed *)

BEGIN (* ProcessProgram File *)

  (* Initialize for processing. *)
  ExecCount    := 0;
  CommentCount := 0;

  WHILE NOT EOF (ProgramFile) DO
    BEGIN

      (* Get the next line from the program file. *)
      ReadLine (ProgramFile, TextLine);
```

```
        (* Echoprint TextLine to the screen. *)
      PrintLine (Output, TextLine);

      (* Process according to whether this line is blank, *)
      (* comment-only, or contains "executable" code.    *)
      CASE LineStatus (TextLine) OF

        BlankLine   :
          BEGIN
            (* Print the line to the report file. *)
            Writeln (ReportFile)
          END; (* BlankLine *)

        CommentLine :
          BEGIN
            CommentCount := CommentCount + 1;

            (* Print the line to the report file. *)
            Write (ReportFile, '        ');
            PrintLine (ReportFile, TextLine)

          END; (* CommentLine *)

        ExecLine    :
          BEGIN
            ExecCount := ExecCount + 1;

            (* Print the line to the report file. *)
            Write (ReportFile, ExecCount:4,'.   ');
            PrintLine (ReportFile, TextLine)

          END (* ExecLine *)

      END (* CASE *)

    END (* WHILE NOT EOF *)

END; (* ProcessProgramFile *)

(***************************************************************)

PROCEDURE TerminateProcessing
  (VAR ProgramFile : Text;
   VAR ReportFile  : Text);

  (* Close ProgramFile and ReportFile.                 *)
  (* NOTE: This procedure contains Turbo Pascal code. *)
BEGIN (* TerminateProcessing *)

  (* Close the files. *)
  Close (ReportFile);
  Close (ProgramFile)

END;  (* TerminateProcessing *)

(***************************************************************)
```

```
BEGIN (* ListAndCount *)

  (* Get Program file name from user; open program (Reset) *)
  (* report (Rewrite) files for processing.                *)
  GetFiles
    (ProgramFile,
     ReportFile);

  (* Process the Pascal program in ProgramFile, creating a *)
  (* numbered program listing in ReportFile.               *)
  ProcessProgramFile
    (ProgramFile,
     ReportFile,
     ExecCount,        (* returned *)
     CommentCount);    (* returned *)

  (* Print the count information to the ReportFile. *)
  PrintCountData
    (ReportFile,
     ExecCount,
     CommentCount);

  (* Close the files. *)
  TerminateProcessing
    (ProgramFile,
     ReportFile);

END.  (* ListAndCount *)
```

The source code for this program is found in file COUNT.PAS on the program disk.

Standards for Program Formatting

Earlier in this application section we mentioned that comparing the relative number of source lines of code is one way to evaluate different solutions to a programming problem. However, the numbers really only make sense if the programs are similarly formatted. Many software companies have program formatting standards that all their programmers must follow. The goal is to make programs easier to read and understand for human readers; the compiler doesn't care, as long as the program is syntactically correct.

If you decide what you want your programs to look like before you start to write them, your programs will have a more consistent style. Some suggestions, based on the style used in this book, are given below.

Capitalization   Few systems require the use of all uppercase letters; most let you mix upper- and lowercase. Here are some ways that mixed case can increase the readability of your program.

We use all capital letters for reserved words to make the program structure stand out:

```
WHILE NOT Found DO
```

We start identifiers with capital letters, and use uppercase letters to break up long names into words:

`DayOfWeek` is more readable than `Dayofweek` or `DAYOFWEEK`

Blank Space   It's free! The compiler doesn't care how many blank spaces you leave between words, or how many blank lines you use. Your resulting "object code" (the machine language that the computer executes) is not increased by adding more blanks in your source code. Blank space can make your program much more readable.

Leave a blank space before and after operators in expressions:

```
Tax := (FullPrice - Discount) * TaxRate:
```

is more readable than

```
Tax:=(FullPrice-Discount)*TaxRate;
```

Use blank lines liberally to break the program into functional units.

Statements

Each statement should be on a separate line.

If a long statement must be broken across lines, try to find a logical place to make the break:

```
FinalGrade := (0.20 * MidTermExam) +
              (0.30 * Homework)    +
              (0.50 * FinalExam);
```

is more readable than

```
FinalGrade := (0.20 * MidTermExam) + (0.30
                    * Homework) + (0.50 * FinalExam);
```

Declarations

In general, declarations should be listed one per line. When there are a lot of variables for a program or subprogram, it's nice to order them according to some scheme. For instance, they can be declared alphabetically. Alternately, the variables of different types can be declared together (i.e., all the Booleans, then all the Integer variables, then the records, arrays, files, and so on).

Variable declarations look nicest if the colons and type names line up vertically:

```
LastName    : String20;
DateOfBirth : DateType;
Salary      : Real;
```

is easier to read than

```
LastName : String20;
DateOfBirth : DateType;
Salary : Real;
```

Indentation   The control structures can be made clear at a glance by the use of proper indentation. Some general rules are listed, following the suggested format for each statement type.

PROGRAM, PROCEDURE, and FUNCTION headings should begin at the left margin. (A nested procedure or function may be indented, however, to make the nesting more clear.)

Each nested or lower level element is indented by (at least) two spaces.

If more than two spaces are used, the number should be consistently applied.

The preferable format for procedure calls is to list the parameters, one per line, indented under the procedure name. Place a comment next to any parameter whose meaning is unclear. For example,

```
DeleteFromString
  (StudentName,   (* string to delete from      *)
   1,             (* position to start deletion  *)
   5,             (* number of chars to delete   *)
   Flag);         (* set if string length error  *)
```

is more clear than

```
DeleteFromString(StudentName, 1, 5, Flag);
```

IF statement:

```
IF Condition
  THEN  (* comment *)
    BEGIN
      (* statements *)
    END  (* IF *)
  ELSE  (* comment *)
    BEGIN
      (* statements *)
    END; (* ELSE *)
```

WITH statement:

```
WITH DataName DO
  BEGIN
    (* statements *)
  END; (* WITH DataName *)
```

CASE statement:

```
CASE Selector OF
  Option1    :
    BEGIN
      (* statements *)
    END; (* Option1 *)

  Option2    :
    BEGIN
      (* statements *)
    END; (* Option2 *)
          .

          .

          .

  OptionN    :
    BEGIN
      (* statements *)
    END (* OptionN   *)
END; (* CASE Selector *)
```

WHILE loop:

```
WHILE Condition DO
  BEGIN
    (* statements *)
  END; (* WHILE loop *)
```

FOR loop:

```
FOR Index := 1 TO Max DO
  BEGIN
    (* statements *)
  END; (* FOR loop *)
```

REPEAT loop:

```
REPEAT
  (* statements *)
UNTIL Condition;
```

▪ *Exercises**

1. Explain what is meant by "software engineering."

2. Which of these statements is always true?
   (a) All of the program requirements must be completely defined before design begins.
   (b) All of the program design must be complete before any coding begins.
   (c) All of the coding must be complete before any testing can begin.
   (d) Different development activities often take place concurrently, overlapping in the software life cycle.

3. Name three computer hardware tools that you have used.

4. Name two software tools that you have used in developing computer programs.

5. Explain what is meant in this chapter by "ideaware."

6. Goal 1, "Quality software works," means that the programs meets its _____ , as documented in the software _____ .

7. Fill in the blanks: Software specifications tell exactly _____ a program will do, but not _____ .

8. Name three program elements that you might see detailed in a software specification.

9. Name two ways in which you can make your programs meet Goal 2: "Quality software can be read and understood."

10. Explain why software might need to be modified
    (a) in the design phase.
    (b) in the coding phase.
    (c) in the testing phase.
    (d) in the maintenance phase.

11. Goal 4 says, "Quality software is completed on time and within budget."
    (a) Explain some of the consequences of not meeting this goal for a student preparing a class programming assignment.
    (b) Explain some of the consequences of not meeting this goal for a team developing a highly competitive new software product.
    (c) Explain some of the consequences of not meeting this goal for a programmer who is developing the user interface (the screen input/output) for a spacecraft launch system.

12. What is the first step in developing any software program?

13. You are working on a class programming assignment, and the details of one of the requirements are ambiguous. What are some ways of dealing with this problem?

14. There is usually one way of solving a problem that is clearly better than any other. (True or False?)

*Questions with italicized numbers are answered in the back of the book.

15. Give an example of an algorithm (other than the examples discussed in the chapter) that is
    (a) O(1).
    (b) O(N).
    (c) O(N²).

16. A routine to calculate the sum of the square roots of some values in array Data contains the following code segment:

```
SumSqrRt := 0.0;
Index := 1;

WHILE Index <= NumElements DO
  BEGIN
    SR := SqrRoot(Data[Index]);
    SumSqrRt := SumSqrRt + SR;
    Index := Index + 1
  END; (* WHILE loop *)
```

    (a) Identify the "goldfish" and the "elephant" operations inside the loop.
    (b) If the function SqrRoot(X) is O(X), what is the order of the sum-of-square-roots algorithm with respect to NumElements?

17. Algorithm 1 does a particular task in a "time" of N³ where N is the number of elements processed. Algorithm 2 does the same task in a "time" of 3N + 1000.
    (a) What are the Big-O requirements of each algorithm?
    (b) Which algorithm is more efficient by Big-O standards?
    (c) Under what conditions, if any, would the "less efficient" algorithm execute more quickly than the "more efficient" algorithm?

18. Three algorithms do the same task. Algorithm 1 is O(√N), Algorithm 2 is O(N), and Algorithm 3 is O(log₂N). Which algorithm should execute the fastest for large values of N? Which one should execute the slowest?

19. A good way to understand the differences in orders of magnitudes for the Big-O notation is to graph functions of the same magnitude. For example, O(1) would be represented by the function f(x) = 1, O(N) would be represented by the function f(x) = x, and O(N²) would be represented by the function f(x) = x². Graph each of these functions on the same coordinate system and compare the rates at which they increase for large values of x.

20. Explain why there might be "trade-offs" between saving computer (execution) time and saving programmer time.

21. Write a top-down design for making a birthday cake.

22. Give an algorithm for calculating your semester grade from the following: five programming assignment grades, each counting 10% of your overall grade; one midterm exam grade, counting 20% of your overall grade; and one final exam grade, counting 30% of your overall grade.

23. What should never be found in the top level of a top-down design?

24. Explain what is meant by "information hiding." Why is the following section of code an example of information hiding?

```
Tax := Rate * TaxableIncome;
Writeln('Your tax liability is', Tax)
```

25. What is meant by "implementation"?

26. What separates the logical properties of a program's data or function from its implementation?

27. Give an example of data abstraction.

28. The documentation of a program should begin as soon as the testing is complete so that the documentation perfectly matches the final correct version of the program. (True or False?)

29. What is meant by "external documentation"? Give two examples.

30. Give three examples of internal documentation from the last program you wrote.

31. Suggest where some comments could be added to the following code segment to make it more understandable:

```
FOR Index := 1 TO MaxIndex DO
  ProcessEntry
    (List,
     Index,
     False,
     100,
     SuccessFlag);
```

32. Use the idea of self-documenting code to make the following code segment more understandable:

```
VAR
  X, Y, Z : Real;
    .
    .
    .
  Z := X * 3.1417 * SQR (Y)
```

33. *True or false?* (Correct any false statements.) Good programming practices dictate that
    (a) a procedure should be written before its specifications.
    (b) when doing top-down design, you should try to avoid changing the main program as you work on lower levels.
    (c) when doing top-down design, you should always first decide on the data structures that will be used.

34. What part of a program's code is analogous to the main module of the top-down design?

35. Dr. Robert gave a test to his class. The best possible score on this test was 19 points. Because he wanted to know the grades as percentages of 100, he wrote a short program to convert the actual grades to percentage grades. A total of 117 students took the test. Each test grade is on a separate line in the input. The program comes up with the correct answer, but, as you can see, it is very poorly written. Can you tell why? Rewrite the program as Program GoodStyle.

```
PROGRAM BADstyle; VAR A, B, C: Integer; BEGIN
FOR C := 0 TO 116 DO begin ReadLN (A); WR1TE (a:5); B := A*100
DIV 19;WRITEln(b) end END.
```

36. Your professor hands out a programming assignment that is supposed to be turned in at a Tuesday morning class two weeks from today. Your sister's wedding is the weekend before your program is due. Make up a schedule that will allow you to get your program done without ruining the wedding weekend.

Problems 37–41 relate to the Application section at the end of this chapter.

37. (Turbo Pascal exercise) Modify the GetFiles procedure in Program ListAndCount to add error-checking. Use the following procedure heading:

```
PROCEDURE GetFiles
  (VAR ProgramFile : Text;
   VAR ReportFile  : Text;
   VAR Successful  : Boolean);

   (* Get name of program file from the user. Open the     *)
   (* program file (Reset) and the report file (Rewrite).  *)
   (* Successful indicates if the file name supplied by     *)
   (* the user is an existing file.                        *)
```

The modified procedure should check the "result" of the call to Reset ProgramFile, and set Successful accordingly. See the description of the Reset procedure in the *Turbo Pascal Reference Guide* for syntactic information.

38. Why did we create functions for the string operations Length and CharAt, when they only contain a single statement each? Name a software engineering principle that relates to this design choice.

39. If the specifications changed to permit both (* *) and {} comment delimiters, how many modules in program ListAndCount would have to be changed? Show how you would modify the program to make this change.

40. If the specifications changed to permit executable statements to begin with a comment, in which module of program ListAndCount would the changes be made? Write the specification of a Level 3 operation called IdentifyCommentClose, which inputs TextLine and CurPos (starting position) and searches for the end of a comment. The operation should update CurPos if the comment terminator is found. Write the procedure. How might you use this operation in implementing the change to allow executable lines to begin with a comment?

41. Describe ProcessProgramFile in terms of Big-O, if N refers to the number of lines in the ProgramFile. Describe LineStatus in terms of Big-O.

Verifying, Debugging, and Testing

GOALS

- To be able to identify several sources of program errors.
- To be able to describe strategies to prevent various categories of software errors.
- To be able to specify the preconditions and postconditions of a program segment or procedure.
- To be able to use loop invariants in order to design error-free loops.
- To be able to show how deskchecking, code walk-throughs, and design and code inspections can improve software quality and reduce software effort.
- To be able to state several testing goals and to indicate when each would be appropriate.
- To be able to describe several integration testing strategies and to indicate when each would be appropriate.
- To be able to explain how program verification techniques can be applied throughout the software development process.

In Chapter 1 we discussed some characteristics of good programs. The first of these was that a good program *works*—it accomplishes its intended function. How do you know when your program meets that goal? The simple answer is, test it.

Let's look at testing in perspective with the rest of the software development process. As programmers, we first make sure that we understand the requirements, and we come up with a general solution. Then we design the solution to the program, using top-down design principles. Next we implement the solution, using good structured coding, with procedures and functions, self-documenting code, and so on.

Once we have the program coded, we compile it repeatedly until there are no more syntax errors. Then we run the program and see what happens. If the program doesn't work, we say that it has a "bug" in it. We try to pinpoint the error and fix it, a process called **debugging**. When all the bugs are out, the program is correct.

Well, maybe. Testing is useful in revealing the presence of bugs in a program, but it doesn't prove their absence. We can only say for sure that the program worked correctly for the cases we tested. This approach seems somewhat haphazard. How do we know which tests or how many of them to run? Debugging a whole program at once isn't easy. And fixing the errors found during such testing can sometimes be a messy task. Too bad we couldn't have detected the errors earlier—while we were designing the program, for instance. They would have been much easier to fix then.

We spent all of Chapter 1 talking about ways to do a good job on the design and implementation part of the programming process. We know how program design can be improved by using a structured design methodology. Is there something similar that we can do to improve our program verification activities?

Yes, there is. Program verification activities don't need to start when the program is completely coded; they can be incorporated into the whole software development process, from the requirements phase on. *Program verification* is more than just testing.

Program Verification   The process of determining the degree to which a software product fulfills its specifications.

Can we really "debug" a program before it has ever been run—or even before it has been written? In this chapter we will discuss a number of topics related to satisfying what Chapter 1 cited as Programming Goal 1: "Quality software works." The topics include

- designing for correctness
- performing code and design walk-throughs and inspections
- using debugging methods
- choosing test goals and data
- writing test plans
- structured integration testing

Where Do Bugs Come From?

When Sherlock Holmes goes off to solve a case, he doesn't start from scratch every time; he knows from experience all kinds of things that help him find solutions. Suppose Sherlock Holmes finds a victim in a muddy field. He immediately looks for footprints in the mud, for he can tell from a footprint what kind of shoe made it. The first print he finds matches the shoes of the victim, so he keeps looking. Now he finds another, and from his vast knowledge of footprints he can tell that it was made by a certain type of boot. He deduces that such a boot would be worn by a particular type of laborer, and from the size and depth of the print he guesses the suspect's height and weight. Now, knowing something about the habits of laborers in this town, he guesses that at 6:30 P.M. the suspect might be found in Clancy's Pub.

In software verification we are often expected to play detective. Given certain clues, we have to find the bugs in programs. If we know what kinds of situations produce program errors, we are more likely to be able to detect and correct problems. We may even be able to step in and *prevent* many errors entirely, just as Sherlock Holmes sometimes intervenes in time to prevent a crime that is about to take place.

Let's look at some types of software errors that show up at various points in program development and testing, and see how they might be avoided.

Errors in the Specifications and Design

What would happen if, shortly before you were supposed to turn in a major class assignment, you discovered that some details in the professor's program description were incorrect? To make matters worse, you found out that the corrections were discussed at the beginning of class on the day you got there late. But somehow you never knew about the problem until your tests of the class data set came up with the wrong answers. What do you do now?

Writing a program to the wrong specifications is probably the worst kind of software error. How bad can it be? Let's look at a true story. Some time ago, a computer company contracted to replace a government agency's obsolete system with new hardware and

software. A large and complicated program was written, based on specifications and algorithms provided by the customer. The new system was checked out at every point in its development to ensure that its functions matched the requirements in the specifications document. When the system was complete and the new software was executed, it was discovered that the results of its calculations did not match those of the old system. A careful comparison of the two systems showed that the specifications of the new software were erroneous because they were based on algorithms taken from the old system's inaccurate documentation. The new program was "correct" in that it accomplished its specified functions, but the program was useless to the customer because it didn't accomplish its intended functions—it didn't work. The cost of correcting the errors measured in the millions of dollars.

How could correcting the error be so expensive? First of all, much of the conceptual and design effort, as well as the coding, was wasted. It took a great deal of time to pinpoint which parts of the specification were in error and then to correct this document before the program could be redesigned. Then much of the software development activity (design, coding, and testing) had to be repeated.

This case is an extreme one, but it illustrates how critical specifications are to the software process. In general, programmers are more expert in software development techniques than in the "application" areas of their programs, such as banking, city planning, satellite control, or medical research. Thus correct program specifications are crucial to the success of program development.

This case also illustrates a basic principle about software costs: The earlier in the development cycle a problem is detected, the cheaper it is to fix. "Cost" may mean dollars to pay programmers, monetary penalties for missed schedules, or points off for turning in a course assignment late. Because the development of the specifications for a software assignment precedes its design and implementation, an undetected error at this point can be very expensive. The longer the problem goes without detection, the higher the cost of fixing it will rise.

Figure 2-1 shows how fast the costs rise in subsequent phases of software development. The vertical axis represents the relative cost of fixing an error; this cost might be in units of hours, or hundreds of dollars, or "programmer months" (the amount of work one programmer can do in a month). The horizontal axis represents the stages in the development of a software product. As you can see, an error that would have taken one unit to fix when you first started designing might take a hundred units to correct when the product is actually in operation!

Many specification errors can be prevented by good communication between the programmers (you) and the party who originated the problem (the professor, manager, or customer). In general, it pays to ask questions when you don't understand something in the program specifications. And the earlier you ask, the better.

A number of questions may come to mind as you first read a programming assignment. What error checking is necessary? What algorithm or data structure is supposed to be used in the solution? What assumptions are reasonable? If you obtain answers to these questions when you first begin working on an assignment, you can incorporate them into your design and implementation of the program. Later in the program's development, unexpected answers to these questions can cost you time and effort. In short, in order to write a program that is correct, you must understand precisely what it is that your program is supposed to do.

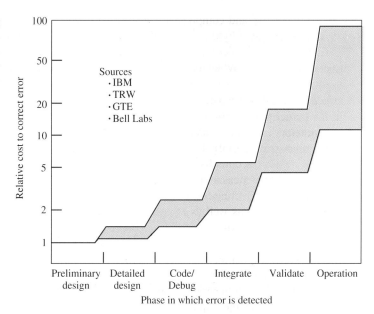

Figure 2-1
This Graph Demon-
strates the Impor-
tance of Early
Detection of Soft-
ware Errors.

Sometimes specifications change during the design or implementation of a program. In this case, a top-down design will help you to pinpoint which sections of the program have to be redone. For instance, to modify Program ListAndCount in Chapter 1 to change the implementation of StringType would not require that the whole program be rewritten. We can see from the top-down design that the offending code is restricted to the String module. The parts of the program that will require changes can usually be located more easily from a design than from the code itself.

Compile-Time Errors

In the process of learning Pascal in your first programming course, you probably made a number of **syntax errors**. These resulted in error messages (for example, "TYPE MISMATCH," "ILLEGAL ASSIGNMENT," " 'END' EXPECTED," and so on) when you tried to compile the program. That's par for the first course.

Now that you are more familiar with the programming language, you can save your debugging skills for tracking down really juicy logical errors. *Try to get the syntax right the first time*. Having your program compile cleanly on the first attempt is not an unreasonable goal. A syntax error wastes computing time and money, as well as programmer time, and it is preventable.

Some programmers argue that looking for syntax errors is a waste of time, that it is faster to let the compiler catch all your typos and syntax errors. Sometimes, however, a coding error will turn out to be a legal statement, syntactically correct but semantically wrong. This situation may cause very obscure, hard-to-locate errors.

Programmers must be familiar with all the idiosyncrasies of the implementation of a programming language at their particular site. For instance, you may be programming in Turbo Pascal on a personal computer at school, whereas in your first job, you may program in VM Pascal on a mainframe computer. More than likely, you will not even

Use of Semicolons in Pascal

Every Pascal programmer at some point gets the infamous compiler error message: "; EXPECTED." There is an issue regarding the use of the semicolon in Pascal. Should it be used at the end of every statement, or should it only be used between statements? In the Pascal programming language, the semicolon is defined as a *separator*, not as a terminator. That is why you do not need to use a semicolon before the keyword END in the following example:

```
(* Initialize Student data.  *)
FOR Index := 1 TO Max DO
  BEGIN
    Student[Index].Name := ' ';
    Student[Index].GPA  := 0.0  (* semicolon not needed here *)
  END (* FOR *)
```

That is also why you *cannot* put a semicolon before the reserved word ELSE:

```
(* Find minimum value. *)
IF X < Y
  THEN Minimum := X;  (* semicolon not allowed here *)
  ELSE Minimum := Y;
```

The semicolon is intended to separate statements, and the **IF-THEN-ELSE** clause is actually one big statement.

be programming in Pascal, for there are literally thousands of computer languages in use. Everyone knows of FORTRAN, COBOL, and BASIC. You may also have heard of LISP, Ada, C, and Modula-2. But you may find yourself programming in SNOBOL, Prolog, JOVIAL, or MUMPS.

Learning the programming language is often the easiest part of a new software assignment. This does not mean, however, that the language is the least important part. In this book we will discuss abstract data types and algorithms that we claim are **language independent**. This means that they can be implemented in almost any general-purpose programming language. The success of the implementation, however, is dependent on a thorough understanding of the features of the programming language. What is considered good programming practice in one language may be poor programming practice in another.

For instance, suppose a program uses a list of data objects, each of which contains several fields. A FORTRAN programmer might implement this abstract data structure as a series of parallel arrays, one array per field. The same implementation would work in Pascal, but it is a poor solution; in Pascal an array of records would be more natural.

Sometimes two programming languages will have rules and features that look similar but work differently. For instance, the language called Modula-2 has rules for naming identifiers (variables, constants, procedures, and so on) that are similar to Pascal's.

Many programmers like to use semicolons at the end of every statement for the sake of maintainability. It is easy to forget to replace the semicolon on the last statement, if you add another statement before the END. For instance, if we add another assignment statement to the first example above,

```
BEGIN
  Student[Index].Name := ' ';
  Student[Index].GPA  := 0.0   (* syntax error here! *)
  Student[Index].ID   := 0
END
```

we will get a compiler error.

It's easier to just use semicolons as statement *terminators* to avoid this problem:

```
BEGIN
  Student[Index].Name := ' ';
  Student[Index].GPA  := 0.0; (* semicolon now required here *)
  Student[Index].ID   := 0;
END
```

We are sympathetic toward this approach. However, the programs in this book use standard Pascal, so we have consistently followed the definition of the semicolon as a separator.

There is an important difference, however; Modula-2 is *case sensitive*. Upper and lowercase letters are considered to be separate characters in Modula-2. This means that DataList, datalist, DATALIST, and Datalist represent four different Modula-2 variables. What seem to be minor details in a programming language manual may turn out to be very important in practice.

Therefore it is worthwhile to develop an expert knowledge of both the control and data structures and the syntax of the language in which you are programming. In general, if you have a good knowledge of your programming language, and are careful, you can avoid syntax errors. The ones you might miss are relatively easy to locate and correct. Most will be flagged by the compiler with an error message. Once you have a "clean" compilation, you can execute your program.

Run-Time Errors

Errors that occur during the execution of a program are usually harder to detect than syntax errors. Some run-time errors stop execution of the program. We say that the program "crashed" or "abnormally terminated."

Run-time errors are often the result of the programmer's making too many assumptions. For instance

```
Result := Dividend / Divisor;
```

is a legitimate assignment statement, *if* we can assume that Divisor will never be zero. If Divisor is zero, however, a run-time error will result.

Sometimes run-time errors occur because the programmer did not fully understand the programming language. For instance, a Turbo Pascal programmer might code the following WHILE loop to search for a value in an array called List (declared as ARRAY [1..MaxIndex] of ValueType):

```
WHILE (Index <= MaxIndex) AND (List[Index] <> Value) DO
   Index := Index + 1;
```

Because Turbo Pascal has "short-circuit" Boolean evaluation, this WHILE condition is legal. The evaluation of the Boolean expression is terminated as soon as the first half of the statement fails. Therefore, when Index > MaxIndex, the loop simply terminates. The Boolean evaluation is "short-circuited."

Standard Pascal, however, may evaluate the entire Boolean expression, even if the outcome is determined after partial evaluation. The WHILE condition above, therefore, could lead to a run-time error when Index > MaxIndex, because List[Index] is not within the legal array bounds. In standard Pascal, the WHILE loop would have to be coded to avoid this error:

```
Found := False;
WHILE (Index <= MaxIndex) AND NOT Found DO
   IF List[Index] = Value
     THEN Found := True
     ELSE Index := Index + 1;
```

Run-time errors also occur because of user errors that have not been anticipated, For instance, if NewValue is declared as an Integer, the statement

```
Read (NewValue)
```

will cause a run-time error (input conversion) if the user inputs a nonnumeric character.

There are many places in a program where potential errors can be predicted. As software designers, we can add checks to a program to handle these errors. In the Chapter 1 application program, for instance, we mentioned that the GetFiles operation, which inputs a file name from the user, is deficient in error checking. If the user mistypes the name of the file, the program crashes trying to reset a nonexistent file.

Pascal automatically makes many checks for run-time errors, so we could just passively let the system take care of them. However, Pascal usually takes care of such errors by terminating the program, and a program that crashes whenever it detects an error condition is not very satisfying to use.

You must not allow conditions that stop your program's execution; your program should stay in control until the user is ready to quit. A program should not crash when it tries to open a file that doesn't exist. (Turbo Pascal, at least, provides a way to detect this situation.) You can include checks for such conditions, followed by appropriate error recovery.

The ability of a program to recover when an error occurs is called *robustness*. If a commercial program is not robust, people will not buy it. Who wants a word processor that crashes if the user says "SAVE" when there is no disk in the drive? We want the program to tell us, "Put your disk in the drive, and hit Enter." For some types of software, robustness is a critical requirement. Programs like an airplane's automatic pilot system or an intensive care unit's patient-monitoring program just can't afford to crash. These are situations in which defensive posture produces good results.

Robustness The ability of a program to recover following an error; the ability of a program to continue to operate within its environment.

In general, you should actively check for error-creating conditions rather than let them abort your program. For instance, it is generally unwise to make too many assumptions about the correctness of input, especially "interactive" input from a keyboard. A better approach is to check explicitly for the correct type and bounds of such input. The programmer can then decide how an error should be handled (request new input, print a message, or go on to the next data) rather than leave the decision to the system. Even the decision to quit should be made by a program that is in control of its own execution. If worse comes to worst, let your program die gracefully.

This does not mean that *everything* that the program inputs must be checked for errors. Sometimes inputs are known to be correct—for instance, input from a file. The decision to include error checking must be based upon the requirements of the program.

Some run-time errors do not stop execution but produce the wrong results. You may have incorrectly implemented an algorithm or used a variable before it was assigned a value. You may have inadvertently swapped two parameters of the same type on a procedure call or forgotten to designate a procedure's output data as a VAR parameter. These "logical" errors are often the hardest to prevent and to locate. Later in this chapter we will talk about debugging techniques to help pinpoint run-time errors. We will also discuss structured testing methods that isolate the part of the program being tested. But knowing that the earlier we find an error the easier it will be to fix, we turn now to ways of catching run-time errors before run time.

Designing for Correctness

It would be nice if there were some tool that would locate the errors in our design or code without our having to even run the program. That sounds unlikely, but consider an analogy from geometry. We wouldn't try to prove the Pythagorean Theorem by proving that it worked on every triangle; that would only demonstrate that the theorem works for every triangle we tried. We prove theorems in geometry mathematically. Why can't we do the same for computer programs?

The verification of program correctness, independent of data testing, is an important area of theoretical computer science research. The goal of this research is to establish a method for proving programs that is analogous to the method for proving theorems in geometry. The necessary techniques exist, but the proofs are often more complicated than the programs themselves. Therefore a major focus of verification research is the attempt to build automated program provers—verifiable programs that will verify other programs.

In the meantime, the formal verification techniques can be carried out by hand, to prove logically that pieces of a program are correct. We will not go into this subject in detail here; for students who are interested in this topic, an explanation of the techniques for verifying assignment statements, branches, and loops is included in Appendix G.

Assertions and Program Design

In this chapter we will consider a couple of ideas upon which verification techniques are based, because these concepts can help us now in our effort to design correctness into our programs. These concepts involve types of assertions that we can make about what our software is trying to do. An *assertion* is a logical proposition that can be true or false. We can make assertions about the state of the program. For instance, following the assignment statement

```
Sum := Part + 1 ;  (* Sum and Part are integers. *)
```

we might assert: "The value of Sum is greater than the value of Part." That assertion might not be very useful or interesting by itself, but let's see what we can do with it. We can demonstrate that the assertion is true by making a logical argument: No matter what value Part has (negative, zero, or positive), when it is increased by 1, the result will be a larger value. Now note what we *didn't* do. We didn't have to run a program containing this assignment statement to verify that the assertion was correct.

The general concept behind formal program verification is that we can make assertions about what the program is intended to do, based on its specifications, and then prove through a logical argument (rather than through execution of the program) that a design or implementation satisfies the assertions. Thus the process can be broken down into two steps: (1) correctly asserting the intended function of the part of the program to be verified and (2) proving that the actual design or implementation does what is asserted. The first step, making assertions, sounds as if it might be useful to us in the process of designing correct programs. After all, we already know that we cannot write correct programs unless we know what they are supposed to do.

Preconditions and Postconditions

Let's take the idea of making assertions down a level in the design process. Suppose we want to design a module (a logical chunk of the program) to perform a specific operation. To ensure that this module fits into the program as a whole, we must clarify what will happen at its *boundaries*—what must be true when we enter the module and what will be true when we come out.

To make the task more concrete, picture the design module as it will eventually be coded, as a procedure that will be called within a program. To be able to call the procedure, we must know its exact interface: the name and the parameter list, which indicates its inputs and outputs. But this isn't enough. We must also know any assumptions that must be true for the operation to function correctly. We call the assertions that must be true on entry into the procedure *preconditions*. The preconditions are like a product disclaimer:

> **WARNING: If you try to execute this operation when the preconditions are not true, the results are not guaranteed.**

For instance, when we said above that following the execution of

```
Sum := Part + 1
```

we can assert that Sum is greater than Part, there was an assumption—a precondition—that Part is not Maxint. If this precondition were violated, our assertion would not be true.

We must also know what conditions will be true when the operation is complete. The *postconditions* are assertions that describe the results of the operation. The postconditions do not tell us how these results are accomplished; they merely tell us what the results should be.

Preconditions Assertions that must be true on entry into an operation or procedure for the postconditions to be guaranteed.

Postconditions Assertions that state what results are to be expected at the exit of an operation or procedure, assuming that the preconditions are true.

Let's take a look at what the preconditions and postconditions might be for a simple operation: a procedure that will delete the last element from a list and return its value as an output. We will add the preconditions and postconditions to the other fields in the procedure's specification (function, inputs, and outputs). Some programmers combine inputs with preconditions and combine outputs with postconditions; we prefer to list them separately for clarity. The specification for GetLast is as follows.

GetLast (List, LastValue)

Function:	Remove the last element from List and return its value in LastValue.
Input:	List
Preconditions:	List is not empty; it contains at least one element.
Output:	List (changed), LastValue
Postconditions:	LastValue = value of last element from List; List = original List minus its last element.

What do these preconditions and postconditions have to do with program verification? By making explicit assertions about what is expected at the interfaces between modules, we can avoid making logical errors based on misunderstandings. For instance, from the precondition we know that we must check outside of this operation for the empty condition; this module *assumes* that there is at least one element. The post-condition tells us that when the value of the last list element is retrieved, that element is deleted from the list. This fact is an important one for the list user to know. If we just want to take a peek at the last value without affecting the list, we cannot use GetLast.

Experienced software developers will tell you that misunderstandings about inter-faces to someone else's modules are one of the main sources of program problems. We will continue to use preconditions and postconditions in specifications at the module or procedure level in this book, because the information they provide helps us to design programs in a truly modular fashion. We can then use the modules we've designed in our programs, confident that we are not introducing errors by making mistakes about assumptions and about what the modules actually do.

Loop Invariants

Taking our design process down a few more levels, we get into the actual control structures of the design: blocks of statements, branches, and loops. Loops are known troublemakers—sometimes they go on forever without ending and sometimes they don't do what we meant them to do. They also have a bad habit of executing one too many times or one too few times.

Using an assertion called a loop invariant can help you design error-free loops. *Loop invariants* are assertions that must be true at the start of every iteration of the loop body and when the loop terminates. (The loop invariant must always be true; that's why it's called an invariant.) The loop invariant is not the same thing as the condition on the WHILE statement, which must also be true at the start of each iteration of the loop body. The loop invariant also says something about the purpose and semantics (meaning) of the loop.

Loop Invariant   Assertion of what conditions must be true on entry into an iteration of the loop body and on exit from the loop.

Let's look at an example. Procedure SumValues has the following specification:

SumValues (List, NumValues, Sum)

Function:	Sum all the elements in List.
Input:	List (an array), NumValues (an integer)
Preconditions:	List contains at least NumValues elements AND NumValues < MaxInt.
Output:	Sum
Postconditions:	Sum = sum of the elements in List[1] .. List[NumElements]

Here's the algorithm used by SumValues:

SumValues

Sum ← 0
Index ← 1

WHILE Index <= NumValues DO
    Add List[Index] to Sum
    Increment Index

What can we assert must be true on entry into the loop in this algorithm? Of course we can say that Index is less than or equal to NumValues; we know that from the condition on the WHILE statement. But we can also assert that, on each entrance into the loop body,

> Sum contains the sum of elements in List[1] .. List[Index − 1].

This assertion is true initially because Sum contains 0, which is the sum of the elements in List[1] .. List[0]. (There are no elements in this range, and we take the sum of "no elements" to be zero.)

When the loop terminates, with Index = NumValues + 1, the invariant asserts that Sum contains the sum of the elements from List[1] to List[Index − 1] (which is now List[(NumValues + 1) − 1], or simply List[NumValues]). Thus we can see that the loop is actually accomplishing what we intended, to sum all the elements in List.

Another check we should always make when dealing with loops is to see whether the loop will ever terminate. Part of the loop invariant will deal with the terminating conditions; this is the part that will usually show up on the WHILE statement. This condition (for example, Index <= NumValues) should be considered together with the initialization (Index ← 1) and its update mechanism within the loop (Increment Index). Because Index starts out at 1 and is unconditionally incremented inside the loop, we know that Index will eventually exceed NumValues. Thus we are certain that the loop will terminate.

A correct loop invariant is very helpful in determining what the loop body is intended to accomplish, therefore it is a good idea to include it as a comment in the code:

```
(* Loop invariant: Index may range from 1 .. NumValues + 1  *)
(* AND Sum = sum of elements in List[1] .. List[Index - 1]. *)
WHILE Index <= NumValues DO
```

Let's take another look at the relationship between the loop invariant and the Boolean expression that controls the loop (that is, Index <= NumValues). On entrance to each iteration of the loop body,

> LoopInvariant AND BooleanExpression

is True, while following the execution of the loop,

> LoopInvariant AND NOT BooleanExpression

is True. Note that the loop invariant is not only true on the entrance into the loop; it is also true on the exit. As we already know, the Boolean expression must be true to enter the loop, and must be false for the loop to terminate.

Now let's write a similar procedure, MultiplyTen, with the following specifications.

▇ MultiplyTen (List, NumValues, Product)

Function:	Calculate the product of the first 10 nonzero elements in List.
Input:	List (an array), NumValues (an integer)
Preconditions:	List contains at least NumValues elements.
Output:	Product
Postconditions:	Product = the product of the first 10 nonzero elements in List[1] .. List[NumElements]. (If there are fewer than 10 non-zero elements in List, Product = Product of all the nonzero elements in List[1] .. List[NumElements].)

This procedure seems almost as easy as SumValues, so we will try to write the algorithm right away.

MultiplyTen

Product ← 1
Index ← 1
NonZeroCount ← 0

WHILE NonZeroCount <= 10 DO
　IF List[Index] <> 0
　　THEN
　　　Multiply List[Index] by Product
　　　Increment NonZeroCount

　Increment Index

First of all let's see whether the loop terminates. The terminating condition says NonZeroCount <= 10 (because we want to calculate the product of the first ten nonzero elements). NonZeroCount starts out at 0 and is incremented whenever the current list element is not 0. But we don't have any guarantees (no preconditions) that the list actually contains ten nonzero elements. If it doesn't, the loop will try to go on looking past the end of the array and the program will crash. (That's one way of terminating a loop!)

Let's try again, this time writing the invariant first. The invariant will consist of all the assertions that must be true on entry into the loop body in order for it to work correctly. For instance, what do we know about Index? Index tells us how far we have processed in the array; therefore its value must be within the range of index values on entrance to the loop. But there's nothing in the loop condition of our algorithm that addresses the issue of range! We have forgotten that we need a condition to stop when Index gets to the end of the array. The loop invariant is a good reminder: We can keep entering the loop while there are still elements to process. Here's the first part of the loop invariant: *Index may range from 1 .. NumValues + 1.*

Why do we say NumValues + 1? Remember that the loop invariant will be true on exit from the loop, as well as on entrance to each iteration. The Boolean expression that will control the loop will say WHILE Index <= NumValues. On entrance to each iteration, the loop invariant AND the Boolean expression will be true. Following the execution of the loop (when Index = NumValues + 1), the Boolean expression will be false, and the loop invariant will still be true.

This part of the loop invariant, as we have phrased it above, is rather wordy. We will express this idea (Index may range from 1 .. NumValues + 1) more concisely as follows:

Loop Invariant Part 1: 1 <= Index <= NumValues + 1

What about NonZeroCount? Before we talk about its range of values, let's ask ourselves what NonZeroCount means in the loop.

Loop Invariant Part 2: NonZeroCount = the number of nonzero elements in List[1] .. List[Index − 1]

When we look at NonZeroCount's meaning in the loop invariant, we see that we've made a mistake in its contribution to the WHILE condition. Coming into each iteration of the loop body, Index tells us which element is *about* to be processed, so Non-ZeroCount is the total number of nonzero elements from List[1] .. List[Index − 1]. NonZeroCount, however, tells us how many nonzero elements have *already* been processed at the top of the loop. So when its value is 10 we want to stop instead of reentering the loop body. There's another part of the loop invariant to indicate that NonZeroCount may range from 0 to 10:

Loop Invariant Part 3: 0 <= NonZeroCount <= 10

This part of the loop invariant will be true on exit from the loop, as well as on entrance to each iteration of the loop body. The associated Boolean expression, NonZeroCount < 10, must be true on entrance to each iteration, and will be false on exit from the loop (assuming that there are ten nonzero elements in the list).

Now that we understand the meanings of Index and NonZeroCount, we can also write the part of the loop invariant that defines Product.

Loop Invariant Part 4: Product = product of the nonzero elements in List[1] .. List[Index − 1]

The resulting condition is

```
WHILE (Index <= NumValues)
 AND (NonZeroCount < 10) DO
```

The revised algorithm is

MultiplyTen (revised)

Product ← 1
Index ← 1
NonZeroCount ← 0

(Loop Invariant: 1 <= Index <= NumValues + 1 AND
0 <= NonZeroCount <= 10 AND NonZeroCount = the number
of nonzero elements in List[1] .. List[Index − 1] AND

Product = product of the nonzero elements in List[1]
.. List[Index − 1].)
WHILE Index <= NumValues
  AND NonZeroCount < 10 DO

  IF List[Index] <> 0
    THEN
      Multiply List[Index] by Product
      Increment NonZeroCount
  Increment Index

This example is simple, but it is typical of the types of problems one gets into with loops. Specifying the initial values, terminating conditions, and the update of the condition inside the loop is not always easy. Should you initialize to 0 and increment before the other processing, or should you initialize to 1 and process and then increment? Should the terminating condition be a less-than comparison or a less-than-or-equal-to comparison? Using invariants to clarify your thinking about what the loop does will help you to write error-free loops.

Deskchecking, Walk-Throughs, and Inspections

When an individual programmer is designing and implementing a program, he or she can find many software errors with pencil and paper. **Deskchecking** the design solution is a very common method of manually verifying a program. The programmer writes down essential data (variables, input values, parameters of subprograms, and so on) and walks through the design, marking changes in the data on the paper. Known trouble spots in the design or code should be double-checked. A checklist of typical errors (such as loops that do not terminate, variables that are used before they are initialized, and incorrect order of parameters on procedure calls) can be used to make the desk-check more effective. A sample checklist for deskchecking a Pascal program appears in Figure 2-2.

Have you ever been really stuck trying to debug a program, and showed it to a classmate or colleague who detected the bug right away? It is generally acknowledged that someone else can detect errors in a program better than the original author can. In an extension of deskchecking, two programmers can trade code listings and check each other's programs. In universities, however, students are often discouraged from examining each other's programs, for it is perceived that this activity leads to cheating. Thus many students gain quite a bit of experience writing programs but don't have much opportunity to practice reading them.

Most sizable computer programs are developed by *teams* of programmers. Two extensions of deskchecking that are effectively used by programming teams are design/code *walk-throughs* and *inspections*. Both walk-throughs and inspections are formal team activities, the intention of which is to move the responsibility for uncovering bugs from the individual programmer to the group. Because testing is time consuming and errors cost more the later they are discovered, the goal of walk-throughs and inspections is to identify errors before testing begins—in fact, as early as possible in the software development process.

Figure 2-2
Checklist for
Deskchecking a
Pascal Program.

1. Does each module in the design have a clear function or purpose?

2. Can large modules be broken down into smaller pieces? (A common rule of thumb is that a program unit—procedure, function, or main program—should fit on one or two pages.)

3. Are all the assumptions valid? Are they well documented?

4. Are the preconditions and postconditions accurate assertions about what should be happening in the module they specify?

5. Is the design correct and complete, as measured against the program specification? Are there any missing cases? Is there faulty logic?

6. Has the design been clearly and correctly implemented in the programming language? Are features of the programming language used appropriately?

7. Is the program designed well for understandability and maintainability?

8. Are all output parameters of procedures assigned values?

9. Are parameters that return values marked VAR? (This is a real error-maker in Pascal!)

10. Are subprograms coded to be consistent with the interfaces (input, output, and intended function) shown in the design?

11. Are the actual parameters of calls to subprograms consistent with the parameters declared in the procedure headings?

12. Is each data object to be initialized set correctly at the proper time? Is each data object set before its value is used?

13. Do all loops terminate?

14. Is the design free of "magic" numbers? (A "magic" number is one whose meaning is not immediately evident to the reader.)

15. Does each constant, type, and variable name have a meaningful name? Are comments included with the declarations to clarify the use of these data objects?

In a **walk-through** the team performs a manual simulation of the program with sample test inputs, keeping track of the program's data by hand on paper or a blackboard. Unlike thorough program testing, the walk-through is not intended to simulate all possible test cases. Instead, its purpose is to stimulate discussion of the way the programmer chose to design or implement the program's requirements.

At an **inspection**, a reader (not necessarily the program's author) goes through the design or code line by line. Inspection participants point out errors, which are recorded on an inspection report. Errors are often uncovered just by the process of reading aloud. Others may have been noted by team members during their preinspection preparation. As with the walk-through, the chief benefit of the team meeting is the discussion that takes place among team members. This interaction among programmers, testers, and other team members can uncover many program errors long before the testing stage begins.

If each participant has a copy of a numbered program listing, it is easier for the group to stay synchronized. In the inspection report, the errors are recorded by line number. Program ListAndCount, which we developed in Chapter 1, is excellent for creating this numbered program listing.

A walk-through or inspection is useful at a number of points in the software development process. At the high-level design stage, the design should be compared to the program requirements, to make sure that all required functions have been included and that this program or module will correctly "interface" with other software in the system. At the low-level design stage, when the design has been filled out with more details, it should be reinspected before it is implemented. When the coding has been completed, a final inspection can be made of the compiled listings. This inspection (or walk-through) ensures that the implementation is consistent with both the requirements and the design. Successful completion of this inspection means that testing of the program can begin.

Program Testing

Eventually, after all the design verification, deskchecking, and inspections have been completed, it is time to execute the code *with the intention of finding any errors that may still remain.* That is, we start testing.

Many programmers are rather lax about program testing. Testing doesn't seem as interesting, challenging, or glamorous as writing the original program. Furthermore, after making a large investment in a particular solution, who wouldn't be reluctant to see it fail? Thorough testing, however, is an integral part of the programming process, and it can be as challenging as the software development.

The challenge is to try to "break" the code in as many different ways as possible. This goal requires you to change roles—to become the adversary, rather than the creator, of the program. For this reason it is often desirable to have someone other than the program's author do the testing. In fact, software companies often have separate staffs for development and testing.

When you first began programming, you probably used the following testing methodology: Compile, then run the whole program over and over again on a set of data inputs provided by the instructor, debugging until your program successfully produced the appropriate outputs. This approach is somewhat effective with the small programs assigned to beginners. Here is an example of the type of program that can be reliably tested on a single test run:

```
PROGRAM EasyTest (Input, Output);

BEGIN
  Writeln ('This is an easily tested program.')
END.
```

Program EasyTest doesn't have any inputs, and there is only one possible output. No matter how many times you test this program, the result should be exactly the same.

Now that your programs are larger and more complex, however, such an approach is not very effective. Why? Simply because the sets of data inputs needed to establish program correctness are correspondingly larger and more complex. Many instructors provide the class with a single large data set to be used for validating a programming assignment. The output produced by running with this data is turned in along with a program listing, as evidence that the program was correctly implemented. Use of a class data set allows instructors to grade programming assignments consistently.

Unfortunately, however, many students take the existence of a class data set as evidence that the single-test-run approach that they used in their first course is sufficient for testing the more complex programs they write in later courses. We strongly suggest that the class data set provided by the instructor be used only as a final test step, to verify a complete program after its various parts have been tested as independent units. What are independently testable units? Single or related groups of subprograms can be tested more reliably than whole programs of any size. For this reason most of the discussion that follows focuses on testing strategies that verify pieces of programs one step at a time.

The testing process is made up of a set of test cases that, taken together, allow us to assert that a program works correctly. We say "assert" rather than "prove" because testing does not generally provide a proof of program correctness.

The goal of each test case is to verify a particular program feature. For instance, we may design several test cases to demonstrate that the program correctly handles various classes of input errors. Other test cases may be designed to check the processing when a data structure (such as an array) is empty, or when it contains the maximum number of elements.

Within each test case, a series of component tasks must be carried out.

- First we determine inputs that will demonstrate the goal of this test case.
- Then we determine the *expected* behavior of the program for the given input. This task is often the most difficult one. For a math function, we might use a chart of values or a calculator to figure out the expected result. For a procedure with complex processing, we might use a deskcheck type of simulation or an alternative solution to the same problem.
- Next we run the program and observe the resulting behavior. This behavior may be observed by looking at either regular program output (something that happens on the terminal or is written on a printer) or output used just for testing.
- Finally we compare the expected behavior and the actual behavior of the program. If they are the same, the test case is successful. If not, an error has been found. In the latter case, we begin the activity known as debugging.

For now we are talking about test cases at a module, or procedure, level. It's much easier to test and debug modules of a program one at a time, rather than trying to get the whole program solution to work all at once. Testing at this level is called **unit testing**.

Let's apply these tasks to a test of a procedure called Divider, with the following specifications:

Divider (Dividend, Divisor, Error, Result)

Function:	Execute the division of Dividend by Divisor.
Input:	Dividend, Divisor (type Real)
Preconditions:	None
Output:	Error (Boolean), Result (Real)
Postconditions:	Error = (Divisor = 0.0)
	Result = Dividend / Divisor (if NOT Error) or
	Result = undefined (if Error)

Here's the procedure we are going to test:

```
PROCEDURE Divider
    (Dividend, Divisor   : Real;
     VAR Error           : Boolean;
     VAR Result          : Real);

    (* Set Error to indicate if Divisor = zero. If no error, *)
    (* set Result = Dividend / Divisor.                      *)

BEGIN (* Divider *)

  (* Check for divisor of 0. *)
  IF Divisor = 0.0

    THEN (* Just set Error; don't do division. *)
      Error := True

    ELSE (* Set Result from calculation. *)
      Result := Dividend / Divisor

END; (* Divider *)
```

For simplicity, let's consider just two test cases: one that calls Procedure Divider with a Divisor value of 0 and one that calls Divider with a nonzero value for Divisor. The procedure will be called from a *test driver*, a program that sets up the parameter values and calls the procedure to be tested. (We'll talk more about test drivers later.) A simple test driver is listed in Figure 2-3 on page 80; it is designed to execute both test cases. That is, it assigns the parameter values for Test 1, calls Divider, and prints the results; then it repeats the process with new test inputs for Test 2. We will run the test, and compare the values output from the test driver with the expected values.

In the first test case, we used values of 8.0 and 0.0 for Dividend and Divisor, respectively. The expected value for Error is True, and the expected value for Result is undefined. The outputs from the test run match, so the test was successful.

In the second test case, we picked values of 8.0 and 2.0 for Dividend and Divisor, respectively. The expected value for Result is 4.0, and the expected value for Error is False. But when we run our test, the actual value of Error is True! Our testing has uncovered an error, so we begin debugging. We quickly see that the value of Error, set to True in Test Case 1, was never reset to False in Test Case 2. Our solution is to add a statement in the ELSE part of the procedure, setting Error to False. The resulting program looks like this:

```
PROCEDURE Divider
    (Dividend, Divisor   : Real;
     VAR Error           : Boolean;
     VAR Result          : Real);

    (* Set Error to indicate if Divisor = zero. If no error, *)
    (* set Result = Dividend / Divisor.                      *)
```

```
BEGIN (* Divider *)

  (* Check for divisor of 0. *)
  IF Divisor = 0.0

    THEN  (* Just set Error; don't do division. *)
      Error := True

    ELSE (* Set Result from calculation; no error. *)
      Result := Dividend / Divisor;
      Error  := False

END;  (* Divider *)
```

Now we run both test cases again. This time Test Case 2 comes out as expected, but Test Case 1 fails to result in Error's being set to True. What happened? Again we go into debug mode, but we just can't see what's wrong. Clearly, when Divisor is 0, as in Test Case 1, we execute the THEN part and Error is set to True. After a while we ask one of our programmer friends to look at it, and he sees the problem right away. Didn't we mean, he asks, to set Error to False as part of the ELSE case? If so, we should have put a BEGIN/END around the two lines under ELSE. Otherwise, Result is calculated in the ELSE case, but Error is set to False in every case. Of course! We should have seen it ourselves, but programmers often can see each other's errors more quickly than their own. We add the BEGIN and END around the two statements in the ELSE part and run the test cases again. This time, both tests are successful. That is, the actual outputs match the predicted values. Here's the final version of the code:

```
PROCEDURE Divider
  (Dividend, Divisor  : Real;
   VAR Error          : Boolean;
   VAR Result         : Real);

  (* Set Error to indicate if Divisor = zero. If no error, *)
  (* set Result = Dividend / Divisor.                      *)
BEGIN (* Divider *)

  (* Check for divisor of 0. *)
  IF Divisor = 0.0

    THEN  (* Just set Error; don't do division. *)
      Error := True

    ELSE  (* Set Result from calculation; no error. *)
      BEGIN
        Result := Dividend / Divisor;
        Error  := False
      END (* divisor not 0 *)
END; (* Divider *)
```

Figure 2-3
Test Driver for Pro-
cedure Divider

```pascal
PROGRAM TestDivider (Input, Output);

VAR
  Dividend, Divisor, Result : Real;
  Error : Boolean;

  (*******************************************)
  (* CODE FOR PROCEDURE DIVIDER GOES HERE *)
  (*******************************************)

  PROCEDURE PrintResults
      (Dividend, Divisor : Real;
       Error             : Boolean;
       Result            : Real);

     (* Print results from one test case. *)
  BEGIN (* PrintResults *)

    Writeln ('Dividend = ', Dividend,
             ' Divisor = ', Divisor);
    Writeln (' Results: Error = ', Error);
    IF NOT Error
      THEN Writeln ('             Result = ', Result)
      ELSE Writeln ('             Result = Undefined')

  END; (* PrintResults *)

(*******************************************)

BEGIN (* TestDivider *)

  (* Test Case 1 *)
  Dividend := 8.0;
  Divisor  := 0.0;
  Divider (Dividend, Divisor, Error, Result);
  Writeln ('TEST 1');
  PrintResults (Dividend, Divisor, Error, Result);

  (* Test Case 2 *)
  Dividend := 8.0;
  Divisor  := 2.0;
  Divider (Dividend, Divisor, Error, Result);
  Writeln ('TEST 2');
  PrintResults (Dividend, Divisor, Error, Result)

END. (* TestDivider *)
```

Debugging with a Plan

We talked in the previous section about checking the output from our test and debugging when errors were detected. We can debug "on the fly" by adding Writeln statements in suspected trouble spots when problems are found. But in an effort to predict and prevent problems as early as possible, can we also *plan* our debugging before we even run the program?

By now you know that the answer is going to be yes. When you write your top-down design, you should identify potential trouble spots. Then temporary "debugging Writeln's" can be inserted into your code in places where errors are likely to occur. For example, to trace the program's execution through a complicated sequence of nested procedures, you might add output statements that indicate when you are entering and leaving each procedure. The debugging output will be even more useful if it also indicates the values of key variables, especially parameters of the procedure or function. The following example shows a series of debugging statements that execute at the beginning and end of procedure Divider:

```
PROCEDURE Divider
   (Dividend, Divisor  : Real;
    VAR Error          : Boolean;
    VAR Result         : Real);

   (* Set Error to indicate if Divisor = zero. If no error, *)
   (* set Result = Dividend / Divisor.                      *)
BEGIN (* Divider *)
   (*** For debugging ***)
   Writeln ('Procedure Divider entered.');
   Writeln ('Dividend = ', Dividend);
   Writeln ('Divisor = ', Divisor);

   (**************************************)
   (* Rest of procedure code goes here.  *)
   (**************************************)

   (*** For debugging: ***)
   Writeln ('Procedure Divider terminated.');
   Writeln ('Error = ', Error);
   Writeln ('Result =', Result)

END; (* Divider * )
```

If hand-testing doesn't reveal all the bugs before you run the program, well-placed debugging lines will at least help you locate the rest of the bugs during execution. Note that this output is only for debugging; these output lines are meant to be seen only by the tester, not by the user of the program. But it's annoying for debugging output to show up mixed with your application's real output, and difficult to debug when the debugging output isn't collected in one place. One way to separate the debugging output from the "real" program output is to declare a separate file to receive these debugging lines, as shown in the following example.

*A*dvanced Debugging Techniques with Turbo Pascal

One way to avoid the wasted space of debugging Writeln's that have been "turned off" is to take advantage of Turbo Pascal's conditional compilation feature. This approach is similar to using the constant DebugFlag to control which debugging Writeln's are executed.

Let's look at an example of this approach. We first declare a "conditional symbol" using the Turbo $DEFINE compiler directive:

```
(*$DEFINE DebugFlag *)
```

We put this statement at the beginning of the program. (Turbo compiler directives are put inside comment delimiters. Turbo will recognize them as comment delimiters because of their special syntax, while other compilers will treat them as comments and ignore them.) Now the symbol DebugFlag can be used as a control for the conditionally compiled debugging Writeln's, using the $IFDEF and $ENDIF compiler directives:

```
(*$IFDEF DebugFlag *)
  Writeln (DebugFile, 'Beginning Test 1');
(*$ENDIF *)
```

```
VAR
   DebugFile : Text; (* file to hold debugging output *)
      .
      .
      .
   Writeln (DebugFile, 'This is the debug output from Test 1.');
```

Usually the debugging Writeln statements are removed from the program, or "commented out," before the program is delivered to the customer or turned in to the professor. (To "comment out" means to turn the statements into comments by surrounding them by comment delimiters.) An advantage of turning the debugging statements into comments is that they can easily and selectively be turned back on for later tests. A disadvantage of this technique is that editing is required throughout the program to change from the testing mode (with debugging) to the operational mode (without debugging).

Another popular technique is to make the debugging Writeln's dependent on a Boolean flag, which can be turned on or off as desired. For instance, a section of code known to be error-prone may be flagged in various spots for trace output by using the Boolean value DebugFlag:

```
CONST
   (*** Set DebugFlag to Control debugging mode: ***)
   DebugFlag = True;
      .
      .
      .
   IF DebugFlag
    THEN Writeln (DebugFile, 'Procedure Divider entered.')
```

These statements mean "If DebugFlag has been defined (using $DEFINE), compile all the statements that follow until $ENDIF is encountered." During the program development stage, therefore, we define DebugFlag, but before we release the tested program to be used, we turn off all the debugging by deleting the $DEFINE directive and recompiling the program. A better alternative is to change $DEFINE to the $UNDEF compiler directive:

```
(*$UNDEF DebugFlag *)
```

In case you want to turn on debugging again at a later time, the $UNDEF directive will act as a placeholder.

How does this approach differ from declaring DebugFlag as a constant and making the execution of the debugging Writeln's dependent on the value of the constant? With a constant to control conditional execution, the IF statements and debugging Writeln's would exist in the compiled code but would not be executed when DebugFlag has been set to False. With conditional compilation, however, the debugging Writeln's would not even be compiled when the flag is off, thus reducing the size of the compiled program. For a large program with a lot of debugging output, space can become an important issue, especially on personal computers.

This flag may be turned on or off by assignment, depending on the programmer's need. Changing to an operational mode (without debugging output) merely involves reassigning DebugFlag to False and then recompiling the program. If a flag is used, the debugging statements can be left in the program; only the IF checks are executed in an operational run of the program. The disadvantage of this technique is that the code for the debugging is always there, making the compiled program larger. If there are a lot of debugging statements, they may waste needed space in a large program. The debugging statements can also clutter up the program, making it harder to read. (This is another example of the trade-offs we face in developing software.)

Some systems have on-line debugging programs which provide trace outputs, making the debugging process much simpler. If the system at your school or workplace has a run-time debugger, use it! Any tool that makes the task easier should be welcome.

A warning about debugging: Beware of the quick fix! Program bugs often travel in swarms, so when you find a bug, don't be too quick to fix it and run your program again. Often as not, fixing one bug generates another. A superficial guess about the cause of a program error usually does not produce a complete solution. In general, the time that it takes to consider all the ramifications of the changes you are making is time well spent.

If you constantly need to debug, there's a deficiency in your design process. The time that it takes to consider all the ramifications of the *design* you are making is time spent best of all.

Developing a Testing Goal

How do we know what kinds of unit test cases are appropriate, and how many are needed? Determining when the set of test cases is sufficient to validate a module of a program is in itself a difficult task. We must first know what the testing requirements are. For instance, should we try to test every possible input?

Data Coverage

In those limited cases where the set of valid inputs, or the **functional domain**, is extremely small, one can verify a subprogram by testing it against every possible input element. This approach, known as "exhaustive" testing, can prove conclusively that the software meets its specifications. For instance, the functional domain of the following procedure consists of the values True and False.

```
PROCEDURE BooleanToInteger
  (Boo     : Boolean;
   VAR Int : Integer);

  (* Input a Boolean value and convert it to an integer *)
  (* value as follows: False = 0, and True = 1.          *)

BEGIN (* BooleanToInteger *)

  (* Set Int according to value of Boo. *)
  IF Boo (* is true *)

    THEN Int := 1
    ELSE Int := 0

END; (* BooleanToInteger *)
```

It is reasonable to apply exhaustive testing to this function, for there are only two possible input values. In most cases the functional domain is very large, however, and thus exhaustive testing is almost always impractical or impossible. What is the functional domain of the following function?

```
PROCEDURE IntegerToBoolean
  (Int       : Integer;
   VAR Boo   : Boolean;
   VAR Error : Boolean);

  (* Input an integer value and convert it to a Boolean *)
  (* value as follows: 0 = False (no error), 1 = True   *)
  (* (no error), any other value sets the Error flag to *)
  (* True and leaves Boo undefined.                     *)
  .
  .
```

It is not practical to test this procedure by running it with every possible data input; the number of elements in the set of Integer values is clearly too large. In such cases we do not attempt exhaustive testing. Instead, we pick some other measurement as a testing goal.

Figure 2-4   *Testing Approaches*

Inputs

- Put in two magic coins.
- Tap with magic wand.

Outputs

- Pull out rabbit.

Black Box Testing
Does the trick work?

Clear Box Testing
How does the trick work?

You can attempt program testing in a haphazard way, entering data randomly until you cause the program to fail. Guessing doesn't hurt (except possibly by wasting your time and the computer's), but it may not help much either. This approach is likely to uncover *some* bugs in a program, but it probably will not find them all. There are, however, strategies for detecting errors in a systematic way.

One goal-oriented approach is to cover general classes of data. You should test at least one example of each category of inputs, as well as boundaries and other special cases. For instance, in Procedure IntegerToBoolean there are three basic classes of data: inputs of 0, 1, and "other." So you should plan three test cases, one for each of these classes. You could try more than three, of course. For example, you might want to try both negative and positive values in the "other" class. Testing, however, is time consuming, and a quick analysis of the program shows that different types of "other" data inputs will all be treated the same way, so the additional test cases don't buy you much.

There are other cases of data coverage. For example, if the input consists of commands, each command must be tested. If the input is a fixed-sized array containing a variable number of records, the maximum number of records should be tested; this is the boundary condition. A way to test for robustness is to try one more than the maximum number of records. It is also a good idea to try an "empty" array or one that contains a single element. Testing based on data coverage is called **black box testing**. The tester must know the external interface to the module—its inputs and expected outputs—but does not need to consider what is being done inside the module (the inside of the black box). (See Figure 2-4.)

Code Coverage

There are also a number of testing strategies based on the concept of code coverage, the execution of statements or groups of statements in the program. This testing approach is called **clear** (or **white**) **box testing**. The tester must look inside the module (through the clear box) to see the code that is being tested.

For instance, one approach requires that every statement in the program be executed at least once. Another approach requires that the test cases cause every **branch**, or code section, in the program to be executed. (A simple IF-THEN-ELSE statement has two branches, one following THEN and the other following ELSE.)

A similar type of code-coverage goal is to test program paths. A **path** is a combination of branches that might be traveled when the program is executed. In **path testing**, we try to execute all the possible program paths in different test cases.

The code-coverage approaches are analogous to the ways forest rangers might check out the trails through the woods before the hiking season opens. If the rangers wanted to test to make sure that all the trails were clearly marked and not blocked by fallen trees, they would check each branch of the trails [see Figure 2-5(a)]. Alternatively, if they wanted to classify each of the various trails (which may be interwoven) according to its length and difficulty from start to finish, they would use path testing [see Figure 2-5(b)].

To create test cases based on code-coverage goals, we select inputs that will drive the execution into the various program paths. How can we tell whether a branch or path is executed? One way to trace execution is to put debugging Writeln's at the beginning of every branch, indicating that this particular branch was entered. Software projects often use tools that help programmers track program execution automatically.

These strategies lend themselves to measurements of the testing process. We can count the number of paths in a program, for example, and keep track of how many have been covered in our test cases. The numbers provide statistics about the current status of testing; for instance, we could say that 75% of the branches of a program had been executed. When a single programmer is writing a single program, such numbers

Figure 2-5(a)
Checking Out All
the Branches

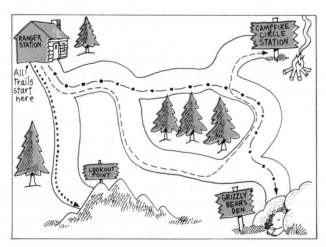

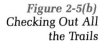

Figure 2-5(b)
Checking Out All
the Trails

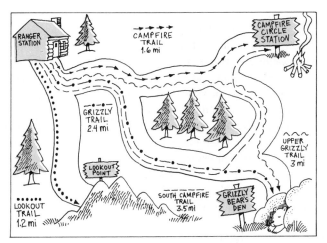

may be superfluous. In a software development environment with many programmers, however, statistics like these are very useful for tracking the progress of testing.

These measurements can also be used to indicate when a certain level of testing has been completed. Achieving 100% path coverage is often not a feasible goal. A software project might have a lower standard (say, 80% branch coverage) that the programmer who wrote the module is required to reach before turning the module over to the project's testing team. Testing in which goals are based on certain measurable factors is called **metric-based testing**.

Test Plans

Deciding on the goal of the test approach—data coverage, code coverage, or (most often) a mixture of the two—precedes the development of a *test plan*. Some test plans are very informal—the goal and a list of test cases, written by hand on a piece of paper. Even this type of test plan may be more than you have ever been required to write for a class programming project. Other test plans (particularly those that are submitted to management or to a customer for approval) are very formal, containing the details of each test case in a standardized format. We'll look at an example of a test plan in the application at the end of this chapter. The main point of this discussion, however, can be summarized in a single word: *plan*.

Test Plan   A document showing the test cases planned for a program or module, their purposes, inputs, expected outputs, and criteria for success.

For program testing to be effective, it must be planned. The required or desired level of testing should be determined and the general strategy and test cases planned before testing begins. In fact, the planning for testing should begin before a single line of code has been written.

Structured Integration Testing

Earlier we looked at a test driver to test Procedure Divider, a program that supplied the test values, made the call, and printed out the results. In this section we will discuss many concepts and tools that will help you put your test cases for individual modules together for structured testing of your whole program. The goal of this type of testing is to integrate the separately tested pieces, so it is called **integration testing**.

A large, complicated program can be tested in a structured way through a method very similar to the structured approach used to design the program. The central idea is to divide and conquer: to test pieces of the program independently and then to use the parts that have been verified as the basis for the next test. The testing can be done using a top-down or a bottom-up approach, or a combination of the two.

Top-Down Testing

In a top-down approach, testing begins at the top levels, to see whether the overall logical design works and whether the interfaces between modules are correct. At each level of testing, this approach works on the assumption that the lower levels will work correctly. We make this assumption by replacing the lower level subprograms with "placeholder" modules called *stubs*. A stub may consist of a single trace Writeln statement, indicating that we have reached the procedure, or a group of debug Writeln's, showing the current values of the parameters. It may also assign values to output parameters if values are needed by the calling procedure (the one being tested).

Stub   A special procedure or function that can be used in top-down testing to stand in for a lower level subprogram.

As an example, consider Program FractionCalc, which reads in operation commands and pairs of values of type FractionType (each fraction value consists of a numerator part and a denominator part), executes the appropriate operation on them, and prints the result. To test the top level of the design, we run the main program.

```
BEGIN (* FractionCalc main program *)
  Finished := False;
  GetCommand (Command);

  (* Process until Finished (on Stop Command). *)
  REPEAT

    GetValues (Fraction1, Fraction2);
    Operate (Command, Fraction1, Fraction2, Result);
    PrintResult (Command, Fraction1, Fraction2, Result);
    GetCommand (Command);
    Finished := (Command = StopCommand)

  UNTIL Finished

END. (* FractionCalc main program *)
```

Stubs are used to stand in for the procedures GetCommand, GetValues, Operate, and PrintResult. A stub for PrintResult, which doesn't have any output parameters, could simply contain a trace Writeln statement:

```
PROCEDURE PrintResult
  (Command               : ComType;
   Value1, Value2, Result : FractionType);

  (* This is a Stub for procedure PrintResult. *)

BEGIN (* PrintResult *)
  Writeln (DebugFile, 'PrintResult entered. ')
END;  (* PrintResult *)
```

A stub for Procedure Operate, which takes the command and two fractions as input and then outputs the result, should also contain a statement to assign a value to Result, because the calling program might try to use the procedure's output. The value assigned to Result in the stub must be legal, but we aren't too concerned with the particular data. To be able to assign a value, we must know something about FractionType. In the main program it is declared as a Pascal record containing integer fields called Numerator and Denominator. The stub for Operate might look as follows:

```
PROCEDURE Operate
  (Command       : ComType;
   Value1, Value2 : FractionType;
   VAR Result    : FractionType);

  (* This is a stub for procedure Operate. *)

BEGIN  (* Operate *)

  Writeln (DebugFile, 'Procedure Operate entered');
  Writeln (DebugFile, 'Command is ', ORD(Command);
  Writeln (DebugFile, 'Value1 is ', Value1.Numerator, '/',
                      Value1.Denominator);
  Writeln (DebugFile, 'Value2 is ', Value2.Numerator, '/',
                      Value2.Denominator);

  (* Set output value for Result, *)
  Result.Numerator   := 1;
  Result.Denominator := 1;

  Writeln (DebugFile, 'Result is ', Result.Numerator, '/',
                      Result.Denominator)

END; (* Operate *)
```

At the next level of testing, the actual procedures are substituted for the stubs, and new stubs are created to stand in for subprograms called from the second-level modules. For instance, the real Procedure Operate contains a CASE statement:

```
(* Process according to command type, *)
CASE Command OF
   AddCommand : Add (Value1, Value2, Result);
   SubCommand : Subtract (Value1, Value2, Result);
   MulCommand : Multiply (Value1, Value2, Result);
   DivCommand : Divide (Value1, Value2, Result)
END; (* CASE *)
```

To support the testing of Procedure Operate, four new stubs are created to stand in for the untested procedures Add, Subtract, Multiply, and Divide. Finally, at the lowest level, these stubs are replaced with real procedures.

It seems like a lot of work to test such a small program, especially when some of the stubs contain so many statements—like Operate, with all of its debug Writeln's. The benefit, however, is that we can now control which module we want to test in any run of the program. In addition, the effort expended to create the stubs is not wasted. When it is time to replace the stub, we can use the stub as a template for editing the real procedure, saving the Writeln statements for use in debugging.

Bottom-Up Testing

An alternative testing approach is to test from the bottom up. With this approach we verify the lowest level subprograms first, using *driver* programs to call them. The test driver sets up data to provide inputs and calls the modules to be tested. (Remember the test driver for Procedure Divider?)

Test Driver   A program that sets up the testing environment by declaring and assigning initial values to variables, then calls the subprogram to be tested.

A bottom-up approach can be useful in testing and debugging a critical module, one in which an error would have significant effects on other modules. "Utility" subprograms, such as mathematical functions, can also be tested with test drivers, independently of the programs that will eventually call them. A bottom-up integration testing approach can also be effective in a group-programming environment, where each programmer writes and tests separate modules. The smaller, tested pieces of the program are later verified together in tests of the whole program.

As an example, let's assume that your assignment is to write program FractionCalc from the previous section with a partner. After working together on the top-down design, the two of you decide to split the effort of coding and testing: Your partner will take care of the **I/O** (input/output) routines (GetCommand, GetValues, and PrintResult) and Procedure Operate, while you write and debug the procedures that calculate the result (Add, Subtract, Multiply, and Divide).

Your assignment is not as trivial a task as it seems. You can't add two values of FractionType with a simple assignment statement such as

```
Sum := Value1 + Value2;
```

You must first calculate the values' lowest common denominator, then adjust and add the numerators, and finally simplify the result.

You are obliged to code and test these low-level procedures bottom up, because your partner won't have the rest of the program finished by the time you are ready to test. You decide to write a simple test driver. The final completed program must provide prompts to ask the user for data and must check the input values for correctness. At this point, however, it is not important how the *real* data is input to the program; you just need to feed your subprograms data of the correct type as conveniently as possible. For instance, your test data might be a line of input containing an operator (such as ' + ' or '*') followed by four integers representing the numerators and denominators of the two operands.

Below is a very simple program that you can use to "drive" your tests. Each time the program is run, a single test case is executed.

```
PROGRAM TestDriver (Input, Output);

(* This driver tests the calculation part of FractionCalc. *)

(* Input: Operator character (+, -, *, or /) in first   *)
(* column, followed by four integers, representing the  *)
(* numerators and denominators of the two fractions.    *)

(***************************************************************)

TYPE
  FractionType = RECORD
    Numerator, Denominator : Integer
  END; (* FractionType *)

VAR
    Operator                : Char;
    Value1, Value2, Result : FractionType;

(***************************************************************)
(*    Procedures Add, Multiply, Subtract, and Divide go here.  *)
(***************************************************************)

BEGIN (* TestDriver *)
  (* Get input values. *)
  Writeln ('Type input values');
  Readln (Operator,
          Value1.Numerator, Value1.Denominator,
          Value2.Numerator, Value2.Denominator);

  (* Echo inputs. *)
  Writeln ('Operator     = ', Operator);
  Writeln ('First value  = ', Value1.Numerator, '/',
           Value1.Denominator);
  Writeln ('Second value = ', Value2.Numerator, '/',
           Value2.Denominator) ;
```

```
(* This section calls the routines to be tested. *)
(* Process according to type of operator.         *)
CASE Operator OF
   '+' : Add      (Value1, Value2, Result);
   '-' : Subtract (Value1, Value2, Result);
   '*' : Multiply (Value1, Value2, Result);
   '/' : Divide   (Value1, Value2, Result)
END; (* CASE *)

(* Print results. *)
Writeln (Value1.Numerator, '/', Value1.Denominator,
         Operator, Value2.Numerator, '/', Value2.Denominator,
         ' = ', Result.Numerator, '/', Result.Denominator)

END. (* TestDriver *)
```

Note that the test driver gets the test data and calls the procedure to be tested. It also provides written output to verify the inputs and outputs. This test driver does not do any error checking to make sure that the inputs are valid, however. For instance, it doesn't verify that the operator (type Char) is really an operator character, as opposed to an 'A' or a '%' character. Remember that the goal of the test driver is to act as a skeleton of the real program, not to *be* the real program. Therefore, the test driver does not need to be as robust as the program it simulates.

You could also have the test driver process multiple test cases by adding a loop around the current processing.

Mixed Testing Approaches

It is often necessary to combine the top-down and bottom-up methods. Critical procedures and utility subprograms (math functions, data input or conversion routines, and so on) can be tested with drivers, and then a top-down approach can be applied to integrate the whole program.

Let's look at how a mixed testing approach could be used to integrate the whole program FractionCalc. While you are testing your part of the program with a test driver, your partner is writing and testing the rest independently, using stubs to stand in for your modules. After your subprograms have been tested, they can be added to your partner's program, which includes the real routines that read the operands and write the results. Now when the program is run, you can verify that the I/O procedures actually input and set up the data correctly for your procedures. This level of testing verifies that the independently tested subprograms work together correctly; that is, it integrates the program pieces.

By now you are probably protesting that these testing approaches are a lot of trouble, and that you barely have time to write your programs, let alone "throwaway code" like stubs and drivers. Structured testing methods *do* require extra work. Test drivers and stubs are software items; they must be written and debugged themselves, even though they probably will not be turned in to a professor or delivered to a customer. These programs are part of a class of *software development tools* that take time to create but are invaluable in simplifying the testing effort.

Programs like these are like the scaffolding that a contractor erects around a building. It takes time and money to build the scaffolding, which will not be part of the final product. But without it, the building could not be constructed. In a large program, where verification plays a major role in the software development process, creating these extra tools may be the only way to test the program.

Practical Considerations

It is obvious from this chapter that program verification techniques are time consuming and, in a job environment, expensive. It would take a long time to do all of the things discussed in this chapter, and a programmer has only so much time to work on any particular program. Certainly not every program is worthy of such cost and effort. How can you tell how much and what kind of verification effort is necessary?

A program's requirements may provide an indication of the level of verification needed. In the classroom your professor may specify the verification requirements as part of a programming assignment. For instance, you may be required to turn in a written test plan and to show what data inputs were used for each test case. Part of your grade may be determined by the completeness of your test data. In the work environment the verification requirements are often specified by a customer in the contract for a particular programming job. For instance, a contract with a military customer may specify that formal reviews or inspections of the software product will be held at various times during the development process.

A higher level of verification effort may be indicated for sections of a program that are particularly complicated or error-prone. In these cases it is wise to start the verification process in the early stages of program development, in order to prevent costly errors in the design.

A program whose correct execution is critical to human life is obviously a candidate for a high level of verification. For instance, a program used for controlling the return of astronauts from a space mission would require a higher level of verification than would a program used for generating a grocery list. As a more down-to-earth example, consider the potential for disaster if a hospital's patient database system had a bug that caused it to lose information about patients' allergies to medications. A similar error in a database program that manages a Christmas card mailing list, however, would have much less severe consequences.

Summary

It should be obvious by now that program verification is not just something you attempt the night before your program is due. Design verification and program testing are activities that go on *throughout* the software life cycle.

Verification activities begin when the software specifications are developed. At this point, the overall testing approach and goals are formulated. Then as program design work begins, these goals are applied: Formal verification techniques may be used for parts of the program, design inspections are held, and thought is given to test cases.

During the implementation phase, the test cases are developed and test data to support them are generated. Code inspections give the programmer extra support in debugging the program before it is ever run. When the code has been compiled and is ready to be run, unit (module-level) testing is done, with stubs and drivers used for support. After these units have been completely tested, they are put together in integration tests. Once errors have been found and corrected, some of the earlier tests are rerun to make sure that the corrections have not introduced any new problems. This is called "regression testing."

Finally, acceptance tests of the whole system are run. When they have been completed, the software is put into use. Is the verification process finished? Hardly! More than half of the total life-cycle costs and effort generally come *after* the program becomes operational, in the maintenance phase. Some changes are made to correct errors in the original program; others are introduced to add new capabilities to the software system. In either case, regression testing must be done after any program modification.

Figure 2-6 shows how the various types of verification activities fit into the software development cycle. Throughout the life cycle one thing remains the same: The earlier in this cycle program errors are detected, the easier (and less costly in time, effort, and money) they are to remove. Program verification is a serious subject; a program that doesn't work isn't worth the disk it's stored on.

Analysis	Make sure that specifications are completely understood. Understand testing requirements.
Design	Design for correctness (using preconditions, postconditions, and loop invariants). Perform design inspections. Formally verify design. Plan testing approach.
Code	Understand programming language well. Perform code inspections. Add debugging Writeln's to program. Write test plan. Construct test drivers and/or stubs. Formally verify code.
Test	Unit test according to test plan. Debug as necessary. Integrate tested modules. Execute regression test after corrections.
Delivery	Execute acceptance tests of complete product.
Maintenance	Execute regression test whenever delivered product is changed to add new function or to correct detected problems.

Figure 2-6
Life-Cycle Verification Activities

Application

The Binary Search and Its Test Driver

Data Structure
- Array

Software Techniques
- Use of a loop invariant
- Analysis of algorithms
- Development of a test driver
- Development of test data

This section illustrates how a combination of techniques can be used to develop and verify a procedure to implement the binary search algorithm. As indicated in this chapter, verification techniques can be applied throughout the software development process. We will use loop invariants to help design the procedure correctly. In order to test the procedure, we will develop a set of test data that will be sufficient to verify the procedure, as well as a test driver that will input this data and call the search procedure.

A search algorithm was chosen for this application section because it will help you in some of your programming assignments. Once this procedure has been designed, implemented, and verified, you can use it in other programs. Reusing pieces of software that have already been developed and tested is a very economical way to build programs. In order to use a procedure like this one in your own programs, however, you must first understand its interface—its inputs, outputs, and any assumptions about them. We will document this interface with the following procedure specification.

BinarySearch (List, NumElements, Value, Location)

Function:	Searches List from index 1 to NumElements for Value; returns Location (an array index) if found, otherwise returns value of 0 in Location.
Input:	List (an array to be searched) NumElements (maximum index used in array) Value (value to search for)
Preconditions:	List's elements can be compared using = and > operators. List contains at least NumElements values. (It is assumed that the calling procedure ensures the validity of the inputs. This routine does not check the array bounds.) The values in List are in sorted order, from smallest to largest.
Output:	Location
Postconditions:	If Value is in List, List[Location] = Value; otherwise, Location = 0.

We now know what the procedure does, which is all that the caller of the procedure needs to know. We do not know *how* the search is done, however. Although this information isn't needed by the caller, it is quite valuable to the programmer, so now let's talk a little about searching.

Searching

Given a sorted array of values and a particular value to search for, the first approach that comes to mind is the simplest: Compare Value to successive array elements, starting with the first element, and searching until (1) Value has been found, (2) we have passed Value's place in the sorted list without finding it, or (3) there are no more elements in the array to examine. The advantage of this algorithm is its simplicity; you have probably written a similar sequential search procedure. The disadvantage is the need to check every element in the array until Value is found. For instance, if Value is the last element in a 1000-element array, this searching algorithm will need to check all 1000 elements before it finds Value.

How can we describe this algorithm in terms of Big-O? In the worst case we will have to check all the values in the list (N), which is O(N). On the average, though, we will have to check half the List (1/2 N). Since we ignore constants in determining the Big-O approximation, 1/2 N comparisons is also O(N). So we can describe a sequential search as an O(N) algorithm.

The Binary Search Algorithm

Can't we do better than that? Think of how you might go about finding a name in a phone book, and you can get an idea of a faster way to search. Let's look for the name "Dale." We open the phone book to the middle and see that the names there begin with M. M is larger than D, so we search the first half of the phone book, the section that contains A to M. We turn to the middle of the first half and see that the names there begin with G. G is larger than D, so we search the first half of this section, from A to G. We turn to the middle page of this section, and find that the names there begin with C. C is smaller than D, so we search the second half of this section—that is, from C to G. And so on, until we are down to the single page that contains the name Dale. This algorithm is illustrated in Figure 2-7.

How do we describe this algorithm using Big-O notation? To figure this out, let's see how many times we can split in half a list of N elements. Assuming that we don't find Value at one of the earlier midpoints, we will have to divide the List $\log_2N$ times at the most, before we run out of elements to split. In case you aren't familiar with logs,

$$2^{\log N} = N$$

That is, if $N = 1024$, $\log_2N = 10$ ($2^{10} = 1024$). How does that apply to our searching algorithms? The sequential search is O(N); in the worst case, we would have to search all 1024 elements of List. The binary search is O($\log_2N$); in the worst case we would have to make $\log_2N + 1$, or 11, search comparisons. A heuristic (a rule of thumb) tells us that a problem that is solved by successively splitting it in half is an O($\log_2N$) algorithm. Figure 2-8 on page 98 illustrates the relative growth of the sequential and binary searches, measured in number of comparisons.

Now that we are convinced of how terrific it is, let's design the BinarySearch procedure.

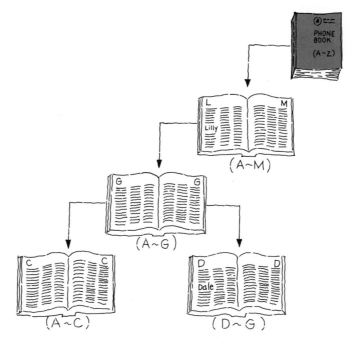

Figure 2-7
A Binary Search of the Phone Book

BinarySearch

Current search area ← List[1] .. List[NumElements]
Found ← False

WHILE more to search in current search area AND NOT Found DO
    Find MidPoint of current search area

    IF Value = List[MidPoint]
        THEN Found ← True
        ELSE
            IF Value < List[MidPoint]
                THEN current search area ← first half of current search area
                ELSE current search area ← second half of current search area

IF Found
    THEN Location ← MidPoint
    ELSE Location ← 0

What do we mean by "current search area"? We begin our search with the whole list to examine; that is, the current search area goes from List[1] to List[NumElements]. In each iteration, we split the current search area in half at MidPoint, and if Value is not found there, we search the appropriate half. The part of the list being searched at any time is the current search area. For instance, in the first iteration of the loop, if Value is less than the element at MidPoint, the new current search area goes from index 1 to the MidPoint. If Value is greater than the element at MidPoint, the new search

Figure 2-8
Comparison of
Sequential and
Binary Searches

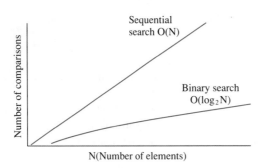

area goes from the MidPoint to index NumElements. Either way, the current search area has been split in half. It looks like we can keep track of the boundaries of the current search area with a pair of indexes, First and Last. In each iteration of the loop, if Value is not found, one of these indexes will be reset to shrink the size of the current search area.

How do we know when to quit searching? There are two possible terminating conditions: (1) Value isn't in the list, and (2) Value has been found.

The first terminating condition, Value isn't in the list, occurs when there's no more to search in the current search area. This condition is a function of the values of First and Last, since these indexes define the current search area. Let's use a loop invariant to describe the situation.

Loop Invariant: Current search area = List[First] .. List[Last].

If First < Last, there are still elements in the array to be examined. What if First = Last? List[First] .. List[Last] would then describe a range of array positions containing one element. As long as there is an element to examine, we continue the search. If First > Last, however, there are no elements in List[First] .. List[Last], so our search is over. Thus we know that the correct condition should be WHILE First <= Last. This takes care of the first terminating condition.

The second terminating condition occurs when Value has been found. This condition is expressed in the WHILE loop as "WHILE NOT Found." That's simple enough. The whole condition is WHILE (First <= Last) AND NOT Found.

Does the loop terminate? Before entering the loop, First will be initialized to 1 and Last to NumElements. In each iteration of the loop either First or Last will be reset to redefine the current search area. Let's look again at this part of the algorithm.

IF Value < List[MidPoint]
   THEN search first half of current search area
   ELSE search second half of current search area

If Value is less than the list element at MidPoint, we want to search the first half of the current search area. We can leave First where it is, and move Last to the MidPoint. Now we've cut the current search area in half. Similarly, if Value is greater than the MidPoint element, we can leave Last where it is and move First to the MidPoint.

IF Value < List[MidPoint]
   THEN Last ← MidPoint
   ELSE First ← MidPoint

First is getting bigger and Last is getting smaller, so we know that they are heading toward each other. But do they ever pass each other? *Uh-oh!* What happens when First = Last? Now MidPoint = First = Last. We keep reassigning First or Last to the same value, and we find ourselves in an infinite loop!

At this point in the design we realize that, since we already know that Value <> List[MidPoint], MidPoint shouldn't be in the new current search area. The correct design for updating the loop control variables is

IF Value < List[MidPoint]
   THEN Last ← MidPoint − 1
   ELSE First ← MidPoint + 1

Now First is always getting larger and Last is always getting smaller, and eventually they must pass each other, so we know that the loop will terminate. The design seems to be in pretty good shape, so we're ready to code the procedure.

The Code—Version 1

```
PROCEDURE BinarySearch
   (List         : ArrayType;
    NumElements  : Integer;
    Value        : ElementType;
    Location     : Integer);

    (* Search List from index 1 to NumElements for Value;   *)
    (* return Location (an array index) if found, otherwise *)
    (* return value of 0 in Location.                       *)

VAR
   Found    : Boolean;   (* has Value been found yet?            *)
   MidPoint : Integer;   (* index of search area's midpoint      *)
   First    : Integer;   (* first index in current search area   *)
   Last     : Integer;   (* last index in current search area    *)

BEGIN  (* BinarySearch *)

  (* Initialize *)
  Found := False;
  First := 1;
  Last  := NumElements;

  (* Search until element found or there are no more.   *)
  (* Current search area = List[First] .. List[Last].   *)
  WHILE (First <= Last) AND NOT Found DO
    BEGIN

       (* Find middle element in the current search area. *)
       MidPoint := First + Last DIV 2;
```

```
                     (* Compare Value to middle element in search area. *)
                  IF List[MidPoint] = Value
                    THEN Found := True
                    ELSE (* Move First or Last to split search area. *)
                      IF List[MidPoint] > Value
                        THEN Last := MidPoint - 1
                        ELSE First := MidPoint + 1
               END;  (* WHILE *)

             (* Set value of Location. *)
             IF Found
               THEN Location := MidPoint
               ELSE Location := 0

       END;  (* BinarySearch *)
```

Developing a Test Driver

The next step is to run the program with the intention of detecting errors—that is, testing. But we cannot run a single procedure. Where is the main program that calls this procedure? Where will the data to test it come from? We decide to write a simple test driver. Each execution of this program will assign values to List, NumElements, and Value and invoke the search routine. The input will come from the standard input file, which in this case is the tester at the keyboard.

Our test driver will be *interactive*; it will ask the tester to indicate the number of elements in the array to be searched. It will then ask for the elements to be input. These values will be stored in the array. Finally, the test driver will ask the tester for values to search for. The test driver will continue processing search values until the tester specifies zero (0) to indicate the test is over. After each call to Procedure Binary Search, the test driver will print out the result of the call. Here is our test driver:

```
PROGRAM TestDriver (Input, Output);

  (* Test driver for setting up array of values and *)
  (* calling a search routine.                      *)

CONST
  MaxElements = 10;
  QuitValue   = 0;

TYPE
  ElementType = Integer;
  ArrayType   = ARRAY[1..MaxElements] OF ElementType;

VAR
  Count       : Integer;      (* number of elements to search *)
  List        : ArrayType;    (* list of elements to search   *)
  SearchValue : ElementType;  (* value to search for in List  *)
  Location    : Integer;      (* index of Value in List       *)
  Finished    : Boolean;      (* tester wants to quit?        *)
```

```
(*****************************************************************)
(*        Code for your search procedure goes here.           *)
(*****************************************************************)

PROCEDURE GetList
  (VAR List  : ArrayType;
   VAR Count : Integer);

  (* Ask tester for list of values to put in search array. *)

VAR
  Index  : Integer;

BEGIN (* GetList *)

  Writeln ('Enter number of test elements (0-10).');
  Readln (Count);

  (* Don't allow more than maximum elements. *)

  IF Count > MaxElements
    THEN Count := MaxElements;

  (* Prompt for test elements. *)

  Writeln ('Enter the test elements, one per line, sorted.');

  (* Read in all the elements. *)

  FOR Index := 1 TO Count DO
    Readln (List[Index])

END;  (* GetList *)

(*****************************************************************)

PROCEDURE PrintList
  (List  : ArrayType;
   Count : Integer);

  (* Print the elements in List. *)

VAR
  Index : Integer;

BEGIN (* PrintList *)

  Writeln;

  (* Print elements of List. *)

  FOR Index := 1 TO Count DO
    Write (List[Index] : 6);

  Writeln;

  (* Print index guide under elements. *)

  Write ('  ');
  FOR Index := 1 TO Count DO
    Write ('  [', Index : 2, ']  ');

  Writeln;
  Writeln

END; (* PrintList *)
```

```
(*************************************************************)
BEGIN  (* Test driver *)

  (* Get list of array elements from tester. *)
  GetList (List, Count);

  Finished := False;

  (* Continue testing until tester wants to quit. *)
  WHILE NOT Finished DO
    BEGIN

      (* Ask user for search value to test for. *)
      Writeln ('Input search value, or 0 to quit:');
      Readln  (SearchValue);

      IF SearchValue <> QuitValue
        THEN
          BEGIN

            (* Call the search procedure to be tested. *)
            BinarySearch (List, Count, SearchValue, Location);

            (* Print the results after the search. *)
            PrintList (List, Count);

            IF Location <> 0
              THEN Writeln (SearchValue,
                   ' found at List[', Location, ']')
              ELSE Writeln (SearchValue, ' not found in List')

          END (* IF not quit value *)

        ELSE (* tester wants to quit *)
          Finished := True

    END (* WHILE *)
END.  (* Test driver *)
```

Now that we have the driver, how do we test it? After all, it is a computer program and may have the same kinds of bugs that our "real" program has. One thing we can do is to write a stub for Procedure BinarySearch, so that we can test the driver separately from the search routine. The stub might look like this:

```
PROCEDURE BinarySearch
   (List        : ArrayType;
    NumElements : Integer;
    Value       : ElementType;
    Location    : Integer);

  (* STUB for Procedure BinarySearch *)

BEGIN (* BinarySearch *)

  Writeln ('**** DEBUG **** Entering BinarySearch ')

END;  (* BinarySearch *)
```

We compile the test driver program with this version of Procedure BinarySearch and do a few test runs. Note that we do not expect the answers to be correct, since we are not running the real search procedure. We just want to make sure that the mechanism for reading in the data, calling the search procedure, and printing the results works.

This test driver seems like a lot of work—its code is longer than the procedure it was designed to test. However, we can get some use out of it later. Note that just by changing the name of the search procedure that is called you can make this driver suitable for testing other search routines. This driver may be helpful to you in testing the procedures developed in Chapter 12.

Developing a Test Plan

When we are satisfied with the test driver, we are ready to test Procedure BinarySearch. First we replace the stub with the real procedure and recompile. Before running the program, however, we need to know what kind of inputs will thoroughly test the procedure. Several types of tests come to mind: List may be empty (any search Value); List may contain only one element (check for Value in list and Value not in list); List may contain a number of elements (check for Value in first list position, Value in middle list position, Value in last list position, Value smaller than any list element, Value greater than any list element).

To make our tests easier to track, we document our planned inputs on a written test plan (see Figure 2-9). As we run the tests, we will record the results.

Figure 2-9
Test Plan for Binary
Search

Test 1

Goal:	Test empty array.
Input:	NumElements = 0, List = (), Value = any
Expected Result:	Location = 0 (Value not found)
Actual Result:	Location = _____

Test 2

Goal:	Testing single element array.
Input:	NumElements = 1, List = (4), Value = 4
Expected Result:	Location = 1 (Value found)
Actual Result:	Location = _____

Test 3

Goal:	Testing single element array.
Input:	NumElements = 1, List = (4), Value = 3
Expected Result:	Location = 0 (Value not found)
Actual Result:	Location = _____

Figure 2-9
(Continued)

Test 4

Goal:	Value in first list position.
Input:	NumElements = 8, Value = 1,
	List = (1, 3, 5, 7, 9, 11, 13, 15)
Expected Result:	Location = 1 (Value found)
Actual Result:	Location = _____

Test 5

Goal:	Value in "middle" list position.
Input:	NumElements = 8, Value = 7,
	List = (1, 3, 5, 7, 9, 11, 13, 15)
Expected Result:	Location = 4 (Value found)
Actual Result:	Location = _____

Test 6

Goal:	Value in last list position.
Input:	NumElements = 8, Value = 15,
	List = (1, 3, 5, 7, 9, 11, 13, 15)
Expected Result:	Location = 8 (Value found)
Actual Result:	Location = _____

Test 7

Goal:	Value less than first list position.
Input:	NumElements = 8, Value = −1,
	List = (1, 3, 5, 7, 9, 11, 13, 15)
Expected Result:	Location = 0 (Value not found)
Actual Result:	Location = _____

Test 8

Goal:	Value greater than last list position.
Input:	NumElements = 8, Value = 100,
	List = (1, 3, 5, 7, 9, 11, 13, 15)
Expected Result:	Location = 0 (Value not found)
Actual Result:	Location = _____

Test 9

Goal:	Value falls between list values.
Input:	NumElements = 8, Value = 10,
	List = (1, 3, 5, 7, 9, 11, 13, 15)
Expected Result:	Location = 0 (Value not found)
Actual Result:	Location = _____

OK, let's run the program! (Each different array size will require a separate execution of the program, but all of the tests on a particular array (such as, Tests 3–9) can be executed in one run of the program.) We execute Test 1 (no elements in list), and run into our first problem. The program tells us that Value is in the list, even though there's nothing in the list! And the Location of Value in the list is not even within the range of possible values. Something is wrong with Location, our output parameter. A glance at the program reveals the first bug: Location isn't declared as an output parameter. We forgot to put VAR in front of its declaration in the parameter list. This is a "really stupid bug"—and one of the most common coding errors in Pascal. Forgetting to designate output parameters as VAR should always be suspected when values output by a procedure contain garbage. We should have used our checklist (see Figure 2-2); we made a number 9 mistake!

When we edit Procedure BinarySearch to make this correction, we decide to add a few debugging Writeln's to the procedure. Just in case there's any problem, we want to have plenty of evidence to look at. (We're wearing our Sherlock Holmes hats now.) We've prefaced all of our debugging output with '**** DEBUG ****', so it will show up clearly. Here is the procedure that we will test:

The Code—Version 2

```
PROCEDURE BinarySearch
    (List         : ArrayType;
     NumElements  : Integer;
     Value        : ElementType;
     VAR Location : Integer);

    (* Search List from index 1 to NumElements for Value;   *)
    (* return Location (an array index) if found, otherwise *)
    (* return value of 0 in Location.                       *)

VAR
    Found    : Boolean;   (* has Value been found yet?           *)
    MidPoint : Integer;   (* index of search area's midpoint     *)
    First    : Integer;   (* first index in current search area  *)
    Last     : Integer;   (* last index in current search area   *)
BEGIN  (* BinarySearch *)

    Writeln ('**** DEBUG **** Entering BinarySearch ');

    (* Initialize *)
    Found := False;
    First := 1;
    Last  := NumElements;

    (* Search until element found or there are no more elements. *)
    (* Current search area = List[First] .. List[Last].          *)
    WHILE (First <= Last) AND NOT Found DO
      BEGIN

        Writeln ('********** ENTERING LOOP **********');
        Writeln ('**** DEBUG **** First       = ', First);
        Writeln ('**** DEBUG **** Last        = ', Last);

        (* Find middle element in the current search area. *)
        MidPoint := First + Last DIV 2;
```

```
               Writeln ('**** DEBUG **** New Midpoint = ', MidPoint);
               (* Compare Value to middle element in the search area. *)
               IF List[MidPoint] = Value
                 THEN Found := True
                 ELSE (* Move First or Last to split search area. *)
                   IF List[MidPoint] > Value
                     THEN Last := MidPoint - 1
                     ELSE First := MidPoint + 1

            END;   (* WHILE *)

         (* Set value of Location. *)
         IF Found
           THEN Location := MidPoint
           ELSE Location := 0;

         Writeln ('**** DEBUG **** Leaving BinarySearch');
         Writeln ('**** DEBUG **** Location = ', Location);
      END;   (* BinarySearch *)
```

We continue testing. Test cases 1–4 come out as expected. But Test 5 goes into an infinite loop. Our debugging Writeln's in the loop produce a repeating series of values:

```
*************** Entering Loop *****************
**** DEBUG **** First       = 4
**** DEBUG **** Last        = 5
**** DEBUG **** New Midpoint = 6
```

Clearly MidPoint is not being correctly calculated. Looking back at the code for Procedure BinarySearch, we see that the calculation of Midpoint indeed is incorrect.

```
MidPoint := First + Last DIV 2;
```

The order of precedence in the expression requires parentheses around the addition operation.

```
MidPoint := (First + Last) DIV 2;
```

We make the correction and run the rest of the tests in our test plan. This time all of our tests succeed.

Programmers are often surprised to find errors in their programs, especially when they have designed them carefully. However, even with a good design, "stupid bugs" often are introduced in the coding phase, as we have seen here.

Here is the final, corrected version of Procedure BinarySearch, which you can use in your programs. The debugging lines have been removed, for we no longer need them. Just in case, however, we have stored in our library a version of the program with the debugging lines in it.

The Code—Final Version

```
PROCEDURE BinarySearch
   (List          : ArrayType;
    NumElements   : Integer;
    Value         : ElementType;
    VAR Location  : Integer);

   (* Search List from index 1 to NumElements for Value;   *)
   (* return Location (an array index) if found, otherwise *)
   (* return value of 0 in Location.                       *)

VAR
   Found     : Boolean;  (* has Value been found yet?         *)
   MidPoint  : Integer;  (* index of search area's midpoint   *)
   First     : Integer;  (* first index in current search area *)
   Last      : Integer;  (* last index in current search area  *)
BEGIN  (* BinarySearch *)

   (* Initialize *)
   Found := False;
   First := 1;
   Last  := NumElements;

   (* Search until element found or there are no more.     *)
   (* Current search area = List[First] .. List[Last].     *)
   WHILE (First <= Last) AND NOT Found DO
     BEGIN

        (* Find middle element in the current search area. *)
        MidPoint := (First + Last) DIV 2;

        (* Compare Value to middle element in the search area. *)
        IF List[MidPoint] = Value
          THEN Found := True
          ELSE (* Move First or Last to split search area. *)
            IF List[MidPoint] > Value
              THEN Last := MidPoint - 1
              ELSE First := MidPoint + 1
     END;  (* WHILE *)

   (* Set value of Location. *)
   IF Found
     THEN Location := MidPoint
     ELSE Location := 0

END;  (* BinarySearch *)
```

This program can be found on the program disk in file BINSRCH.PAS.

■ *Exercises**

1. *True or False?* (Correct any false statements.)
   (a) Software verification begins as soon as the program has been completely coded.
   (b) "Program verification" and "testing" are the same thing.
   (c) Testing is the only way to truly prove that a program is correct.
   (d) Compile-time errors are usually easier to detect and to correct than run-time errors.
   (e) Logical errors can usually be detected by the compiler.

2. Have you ever written a programming assignment with an error in the specifications? If so, at what point did you catch the error? How damaging was the error to your design and code?

3. Explain why the cost of fixing an error is higher the later in the software cycle the error is detected.

4. Differentiate between a syntax error and a logical error in a program. When is each type of error likely to be found?

5. Indicate what kind of error (syntax or logical) is found in each of the following segments of code:
   (a) `(* Set InBounds flag according to value of Number. *)`
   ```
   IF Number <= Max
       THEN InBounds := True;
       ELSE InBounds := False;
   ```
   (b) `(* Set InBounds flag, and reset Number if it is *)`
   `(* out of bounds.                              *)`
   ```
   IF Number <= Max
     THEN
        Inbounds := True
     ELSE
        Inbounds := False;
        Number := Max
   ```
   (c) `TYPE ErrorCode = (OK, OutOfBounds, Undefined, Wrong);`
   ```
      .

      .
   (* If not OK, print warning. *)
   IF ErrorCode <> OK
     THEN Writeln('WARNING! Error = ', ErrorCode)
   ```
   (d) `Error := OK;`
   ```
      (* Process all error codes. *)
   WHILE Error <= Wrong DO
     BEGIN
        ProcessError (Error) ;
        Error := SUCC (Error)
     END
   ```

6. Explain how an expert understanding of your programming language can reduce the amount of time you spend debugging.

7. Give an example of a run-time error that might occur as the result of a programmer's making too many assumptions.

*Questions with italicized numbers are answered in the back of the book.

8. Define "robustness." How can programmers make their programs more robust by taking a defensive approach?

9. What is meant by "designing for correctness"? Name two types of assertions described in this chapter that can contribute to a correct design.

10. Procedure Average takes DataList, an array of reals, and ElementCount, an integer that tells how many elements are stored in the array. It returns the real number DataAvg, which is the average of the data stored in the array. Determine the preconditions and postconditions of this procedure. (You may assume that there is at least one element in the array.)

11. Given the following preconditions and postconditions for Procedure AddElement, determine what would happen if we called AddElement when the list was already full.

    Preconditions: DataList is not full.
    Postconditions: DataList = original DataList plus new element added.

12. (a) Define a "loop invariant."
    (b) Give the loop invariant in the following segment of code:
```
Index := 1;
Found := False;
(* Loop Invariant :                              *)
WHILE (Index <= ElementCount) AND NOT Found DO
  IF DataList[Index] = TargetValue
    THEN Found := True
    ELSE Index := Index + 1;
```

13. Give the loop invariants for the following segments of code:
    (a) `Quot := 0;`
```
(* Loop Invariant :_____ *)
WHILE Number > 5 DO
  BEGIN
    Number := Number - 5;
    Quot   := Quot + 1
  END; (* WHILE *)
```
    (b) `Largest := Data[1];`
        `Index := 2;`
```
(* Loop Invariant :_____ *)
WHILE Index <= 100 DO
  BEGIN
    IF Data[Index] > Largest
      THEN Largest := Data[Index];
    Index := Index + 1
  END; (* WHILE *)
```

14. Explain why the loop invariant contributes more to an understanding of the loop than does the condition on a WHILE statement alone.

15. What should we always be sure to check when trying to verify the correctness of a loop design?

16. Fill in the blanks at the top of page 110 with "True" or "False."

On entrance to an iteration of the loop body, the loop invariant must be _____ and the Boolean expression (in the WHILE or FOR condition) must be _____. To exit from the loop, the loop invariant must be _____ and the Boolean expression (in the WHILE or FOR condition) must be _____.

17. Write the loop that is described by the following loop invariant:

    Loop Invariant: $1 <=$ Index $<=$ MaxList $+ 1$ AND 0 is not found in List[1] .. List[Index $- 1$] AND Sum $=$ Sum of List[1] .. List [Index $- 1$].

18. What is the purpose of conducting design and code inspections?

19. The following program has three separate errors, each of which would cause an infinite loop. As a member of the inspection team, you could save the programmer a lot of testing time by finding the errors during the inspection. Can you help?

```
PROGRAM LoopTime (Input, Output);

VAR
  Count : Integer; (* Loop control variable *)

(***************************************************************

  PROCEDURE Increment (NextNumber : Integer);

    (* Increment the parameter by 1. *)

    BEGIN (* Increment *)
      NextNumber := NextNumber + 1
    END; (* Increment *)

(***************************************************************)

BEGIN (* LoopTime *)

  Count := 1 ;
  WHILE Count < 10 DO
    Write('The number after ', Count); (* Procedure Increment adds
    Increment (Count);                            1 to the value of Count. *)
    Writeln (' is ', Count)

END. (* LoopTime *)
```

Use the following declarations for Problems 20–24:

```
CONST
  MaxList = 100;

TYPE
  ListType = RECORD
    Length : Integer;
    Data   : ARRAY [1..MaxList] OF Integer
  END; (* ListType *)
VAR
  List : ListType;
```

20. The following code fragment is intended to find the first list element with the value 0:

```
Index := 1
WHILE Index < List.Length AND List[Index] <> 0 DO
   Index = Index + 1;
```

   (a) Identify and correct any syntax errors in the code. (Only correct errors that would be flagged at compile time.)
   (b) Using the syntactically correct version from part (a), identify and correct any logical errors in the code.
   (c) Write the loop invariant.

21. The following code fragment is intended to fill List with values from DataFile. The file contains one value per line.

```
WHILE NOT EOF (DataFile) DO
   Readln (DataFile, List.Data[Index]);
   Index := Index + 1;
List.Length := Index;
```

   (a) Identify and correct any syntax errors in the code. (Only correct errors that would be flagged at compile time.)
   (b) Identify two types of logical errors that could occur due to incorrect assumptions about the input file.
   (c) Using the syntactically correct version from part (a), identify and correct any logical errors in the code.
   (d) Write the loop invariant.

22. The following code fragment doesn't work correctly:

```
(* Print all the elements in the list. *)
FOR Index := 1 TO List.Length DO;
   Writeln (List.Data[Index]);
```

   (a) What results would this code produce if it is run as it is now?
   (b) Correct the problem(s).

23. The following code fragment prints out 37 "good" values and then a screen-full of garbage:

```
FOR Index := 1 TO MaxList DO
   Writeln (List.Data[Index]);
```

   What's wrong? Correct the problem.

24. The following function is intended to sum a list of integers:

```
FUNCTION Sum
   (List : ListType);
   (* Sum all the numbers in the list. *)

VAR
   Index : Integer;
BEGIN (* Sum *)
   FOR Index = 1 .. List.Length
      Sum := Sum + List.Data[Count]
END (* Sum *)
```

(a) Identify and correct any syntax errors in the code. (Only correct errors that would be flagged at compile time.)

(b) Using the syntactically correct version from part (a), identify and correct any logical errors in the code.

(c) Write the loop invariant.

25. Is there any way a single programmer (for example, a student working alone on a programming assignment) can benefit from some of the ideas behind the inspection process?

26. When is it appropriate to start planning a program's testing?
    (a) During design or even earlier
    (b) While coding
    (c) As soon as the coding is complete

27. List some of the component activities of running a test case.

28. Differentiate between unit testing and integration testing.

29. Explain the advantages and disadvantages of the following debugging techniques:
    (a) Inserting Writeln's that may be turned off with comment delimiters.
    (b) Using a Boolean flag to turn debugging Writeln's on or off.

30. Add some debugging Writeln statements to the following procedure to make it easier to test and debug. Don't worry about what the procedure does (nothing meaningful); just consider where debugging statements would help.

```
PROCEDURE TestMe
  (FirstNumber,
   SecondNumber    : Integer;
   VAR Answer      : Integer;
   VAR OutOfBounds : Boolean);

VAR
  Temp : Integer;
  Term : Integer;

BEGIN (* TestMe *)

  Temp := FirstNumber * 2;
  Term := Calculate (FirstNumber, SecondNumber);

  Answer := Term - SecondNumber;

  OutOfBounds := (Answer < 0) OR
                 (Answer > Temp)

END; (* TestMe *)
```

31. Differentiate between "data coverage" and "code coverage" in program testing. Which is better?

32. We should try to test every possible input to a program in order to prove that it works correctly. (True or False?)

33. Describe a realistic goal-oriented approach to data-coverage testing of the procedure specified as follows:

FindElement (List, TargetElement, Index, Found)

Function:	Searches List for TargetElement.
Input:	List (an array), TargetElement
Preconditions:	List contains elements of the same type as TargetElement. The elements are in no particular order, and List may be empty.
Output:	Index, Found (Boolean value)
Postconditions:	Found = (TargetElement was found in List) Index = array index of the element if Found.

34. Explain how paths and branches relate to code coverage in testing. Can we attempt 100% path coverage? What is metric-based testing?

35. Differentiate between "top-down" and "bottom-up" integration testing. What software tool is used to support each?

36. You are writing a program that contains a loop controlled by a Boolean function TerminateLoop:

```
REPEAT

  (* Body of loop action goes here. *)

UNTIL TerminateLoop (Factor1, Factor2);
```

You decide to work on testing the loop body, putting off testing the TerminateLoop function until later. Write a stub for Function TerminateLoop.

37. Explain when a test driver is needed. If we advocate a top-down design approach, why would we ever need to test with a test driver?

38. Modify the test driver in this chapter to do multiple tests on the same execution of the program, by prompting the tester to answer the question "Do you want to run another test?" (You will need to add a loop to the test driver program.)

39. Explain the phrase "life-cycle verification."

Data Design

GOALS

- To be able to explain what is meant by "abstract data type" and "data encapsulation."
- To be able to define an abstract data type as an arrangement of data elements and a set of operations on the data.
- To be able to describe a data structure from three perspectives: application, abstraction, and implementation.
- To be able to explain how a specification can be used to record an abstract data type.
- To be able, at the abstract level, to calculate the accessing function, and to describe appropriate applications for the following Pascal built-in data types: one-dimensional arrays, two-dimensional arrays, and records.
- To be able to use the following Pascal built-in data types: variant records, sets, and pointers.
- To be able to differentiate between static and dynamic allocation.
- To be able to define at the abstract level and to implement the user-defined data type StringType.

Data from the Top Down

In Chapter 1 we began to discuss how the top-down design process can be applied to data, as well as to the decomposition of the function of a program. Using this approach, we start out with a logical picture of the data in the program: a list of addresses, a stack of cards, or a set of values. This logical picture, or **data abstraction**, hides the details of how the data will eventually be represented in the basic types that Pascal (or another programming language) supports. As we go through the levels of our design, we refine our view of the data to add the details we need at each level. At the lowest levels we consider how our data abstraction will map onto a physical implementation in terms of the data types provided by programming language. We also mentioned the idea of grouping together a data "object" with a set of operations that manipulate it, treating them as a single module in a program.

This short description of the data design process raises a number of questions: What exactly is data? What do we mean by abstraction, and what's so good about it? What do we mean by implementation, and why do we want to postpone it? And if computer memory is just a long string of bits or bytes, how does Pascal provide us with all the built-in data types we take for granted?

What Do We Mean by Data?

When we talk about the function of a program, we use words like "add," "read," "multiply," "write," "DO," and so on. The function of a program describes what it does in terms of the verbs in the programming language.

The data are the nouns of the programming world: the objects that are manipulated, the information that is processed by a computer program. In a sense, this information is just a bunch of bits that can be turned on or off. The computer itself needs to have data in this form. Human beings, however, tend to think of information in terms of somewhat larger units like numbers and lists; thus we want at least the human-readable portions of our programs to refer to data in a way that makes sense to us. To separate the computer's view of data from our own, we create another view, the *data abstraction*.

Data Abstraction

Lots of people feel more comfortable with things that they perceive as real than with things that they think of as abstract. Thus "data abstraction" may seem more forbidding than a more concrete entity like "integer." Let's take a closer look, however, at that very concrete—and very abstract—integer you've been using since you wrote your earliest programs.

Just what is an integer? Integers are physically represented in different ways on different computers. In the memory of one machine, an integer may be a binary-coded

Figure 3-1
The Decimal Equiv-
alents of an 8-Bit
Binary Number

Binary: | 10011001

Decimal:	153	-25	-102	-103	99
	Unsigned	Sign and magnitude	Ones complement	Twos complement	Binary coded decimal

decimal. In a second it may be a sign-and-magnitude binary. In a third it may be represented in one's complement or two's complement notation. Although chances are you don't know what any of these terms mean, that hasn't stopped you from using integers. (You will learn about these terms in an assembly language course, so we aren't going to explain them here.) Figure 3-1 shows some different representations of an integer number.

The way that integers are physically represented determines how they are manipulated by the computer. As Pascal programmers, however, you don't usually get involved at this level; you simply *use* integers. You only need to know how to declare an Integer type variable and what operations are allowed on integers: assignment, addition, subtraction, multiplication, division, and modulo arithmetic.

Consider the statement

```
Distance := Rate * Time;
```

It's pretty easy to understand the concept behind this statement. The *concept* of multiplication doesn't depend on whether the operands are, say, integers or real numbers, despite the fact that integer multiplication and floating-point multiplication may be implemented in very different ways on the same computer. Computers would not be so popular if, every time we wanted to multiply two numbers, we had to get down to the machine-representation level. But we don't have to: Pascal has surrounded the Integer data type with a nice neat package and has given you just the information you need to create and manipulate data of this type.

Another word for "surround" is "encapsulate." Think of the capsules surrounding the medicine you get from the pharmacist when you're sick. You don't have to know anything about the chemical composition of the medicine inside to recognize the big blue-and-white capsule as your antibiotic or the little yellow capsule as your decongestant. *Data encapsulation* means that the physical representation of a program's data is surrounded. The user of the data doesn't see the implementation, but deals with the data only in terms of its logical picture—its abstraction.

Data Encapsulation   The separation of the representation of data from the applications that use the data at a logical level.

Figure 3-2
A Black Box
Representing an
Integer

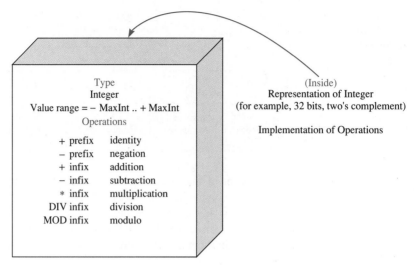

But if the data is encapsulated, how can the user get to it? *Operations* must be provided to allow the user to create, access, and change the data. Let's look at the operations Pascal provides for the encapsulated data type Integer. First of all, you can create ("construct") variables of type Integer, using declarations in the VAR section of your program. Then you can assign values to these integer variables through the use of the : = operator and perform arithmetic operations using $+$, $-$, $*$, DIV, and MOD. Figure 3-2 shows how Pascal has encapsulated the type Integer in a nice neat package.

The point of this discussion is that you have been dealing with a logical data abstraction of "integer" since the very beginning. The advantages of doing so are clear: You can think of the data and the operations in a logical sense and can consider their use without having to worry about implementation details. The lower levels are still there— they're just hidden from you.

Remember that the goal in top-down design is to reduce complexity through abstraction. We extend this goal with another: *to protect our data abstraction through encapsulation*. We refer to an encapsulated data "object," plus the specifications of the operations (procedures and functions) that are provided to create and manipulate the data, as an *abstract data type (ADT)*.

Abstract Data Type   The logical picture of a data type, plus the specifications of the operations required to create and manipulate objects of this data type.

Data Structures

A single integer can be very useful if we need a counter, a sum, or an index in a program, but generally we must also deal with data that has lots of parts, such as a list. When a program's information is made up of component parts, we have to consider an appropriate *data structure*.

Figure 3-3
A Collection of
Books Ordered in
Different Ways

All over the place (unordered)

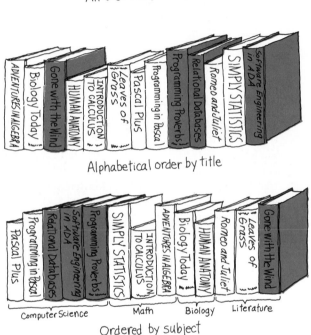

Alphabetical order by title

Ordered by subject

Data structures have a few features worth noting. First, they can be "decomposed" into their component elements. Second, the arrangement of the elements is a feature of the structure that will affect how each element will be accessed. Third, both the arrangement of the elements and the way they are accessed can be encapsulated.

Let's look at a real-life example: a library. A library can be decomposed into its component elements—books. The collection of individual books can be arranged in a number of ways, as shown in Figure 3-3. Obviously the way the books are physically arranged on the shelves determines how one would go about looking for a specific volume. The particular library we're concerned with doesn't let its patrons get their own books, however; if you want a book, you must give your request to the librarian, who gets the book for you.

The library "data structure" is composed of elements (books) in a particular physical arrangement; for instance, it might be ordered on the basis of the Dewey decimal system. Accessing a particular book requires knowledge of the arrangement of the books. The library user doesn't have to know about the structure though, because it

*O*bject-Oriented Programming

Object-oriented programming (OOP) is a programming methodology that has evolved to make computer programs more closely model the real world. New languages (such as SmallTalk) and extensions to existing languages (such as Turbo Pascal, Microsoft QuickPascal) have been created to support the concepts that characterize the OOP methodology. The main properties of an OOP language are

- *Encapsulation:* To create an "object" by combining a data entity with the operations that manipulate it.
- *Inheritance:* To build a hierarchy of objects, with each descendant inheriting access to all its ancestors' operations.
- *Polymorphism:* To be able to define an operation that is shared within an object hierarchy, with an appropriate implementation of the operation that is specific to each object in the hierarchy.

We will discuss the concept of encapsulation in great detail in this text. The other two properties, however, may be less familiar. Let's say that we have two "lists," StudentList (a list of student records) and EmployeeList (a list of employee records). Both lists are implemented as arrays of records, but with different record component types. Since the components are of different types, we need a separate set of procedures and functions for each list to provide the basic list manipulation operations. Although the types of data stored in the lists differ, the operations are nearly identical, because

has been encapsulated: Users access books only through the librarian. The physical structure and abstract picture of the books in the library are not the same. The books might be arranged on the shelves according to the Dewey decimal system. The card catalog provides logical views of the library—ordered by subject, author, or title—that are different than its physical arrangement.

We will use this same approach to data structures in our programs. A data structure will be defined by 1) the logical arrangement of data elements, combined with 2) the set of operations we need to access the elements.

Data Structure   A collection of data elements whose organization is characterized by accessing operations that are used to store and retrieve the individual data elements.

In designing data structures programmers wear many hats. We must determine the logical picture of the data in a particular program, choose the representation of the data, and develop the operations that will encapsulate this arrangement. We will consider data structures from three different perspectives, or levels:

1. *Application (or user) level:* A way of modeling real-life data in a specific context.
2. *Abstract (or logical) level:* An abstract collection of elements and its corresponding set of accessing operations.

the algorithms to manipulate a list (create, search, add and delete elements) are largely independent of the component type. The property of *inheritance* makes it possible to define a parent object (for instance, GenericList), complete with the operations to manipulate a list that contains elements of any data type. Then we can create descendant objects defined for a particular component type, but able to inherit the operations of the parent List object. For instance, descendant objects StudentList and EmployeeList each have their own component types, but both inherit the operations defined for the parent object GenericList.

Certain operations, of course, require implementations specific to the particular list. For instance, to print the list, there must be a PrintList procedure for each type of list, since a knowledge of the component element's contents is needed. *Polymorphism* makes it possible to create different implementations of an operation (like PrintList) for objects in a hierarchy, with the appropriate implementation being chosen by the system, according to the object type. You're already familiar with a type of polymorphism in standard Pascal: the Read(ln) and Write(ln) procedures. They can input parameters of different types, not to mention different numbers of parameters, and still work correctly. The + and * operations are other examples of polymorphism in standard Pascal. The operands might be type Integer or Real; the compiler selects the correct operation according to the operand type.

True OOP methodology is beyond the scope of this text, as well as beyond the limitations of standard Pascal. However, we will use the concept of encapsulation in designing data structures, despite the lack of support for *enforcing* it in standard Pascal.

---

3. *Implementation level:* A specific representation of the structure and its accessing operations in a programming language (such as Pascal).

In our discussion, we refer to the second perspective as the "abstract data type." Since an abstract data type can be a scalar type, as well as a structure that contains component elements, we also use the term "structured data type" to refer to abstract data types that may contain component elements.

Let's see what these different viewpoints mean in terms of our library analogy. At the application level, there are entities like the Library of Congress, the Dimsdale Collection of Rare Books, and the Lubbock City Library.

At the abstract level, we deal with the "what" questions: What is a library? What services (operations) can a library perform? The library may be seen abstractly as "a collection of books," for which these operations are specified:

- Check out a book.
- Check in a book.
- Reserve a book that is currently checked out.
- Pay a fine for an overdue book.
- Pay for a lost book.

How the books are organized on the shelves is not important at the logical level, because the patrons don't actually have access to the books. The abstract viewer of library services is not concerned with how the librarian actually organizes the books in the library. The library user only needs to know what is the correct way to invoke the desired operation. For instance, here is the user's view of the operation to check in a book: Present book at check-in window of library from which book was checked out, and receive fine slip if the book is overdue.

At the implementation level, we deal with the answers to the "how" questions: How are the books cataloged? How are they organized on the shelf? How does the librarian process a book when it is checked in? For instance, the implementation information includes the fact that the books are cataloged according to the Dewey decimal system and arranged in four levels of stacks, with 14 rows of shelves on each level. The librarian needs such knowledge to be able to locate a book. This information also includes the details of what happens when each of the operations takes place. For example, when a book is checked back in, the librarian may use the following algorithm to implement the check-in operation:

CheckInBook

Examine due date to see whether the book is late.

IF book is late
   THEN
      Calculate fines.
      Issue fine slip.

Update library records to show that the book has been returned.
Check reserve list to see if someone is waiting for the book.

IF book is on reserve list
   THEN Put the book on the reserve shelf.
   ELSE Replace the book on the proper shelf, according to
        the library's shelf arrangement scheme.

All this, of course, is invisible to the library user.

The goal of our design approach is to hide the implementation level from the user. Picture a wall separating the application level from the implementation level, as shown in Figure 3-4. Imagine yourself on one side and another programmer on the other. How do the two of you, with your separate views of the data, communicate across this wall? Similarly, how do the library user's view and the librarian's view of the library come together? The library user and the librarian communicate through the data abstraction. The abstract view provides the specification of the accessing operations without telling how the operations work. It tells what but not how. For instance, the abstract view of checking in a book can be summarized in the following specification:

CheckInBook (Library, Book, FineSlip)

Function:	Check in a book.
Input:	Book, Library
Preconditions:	Book was checked out of this Library; Book is presented at the check-in desk.

Figure 3-4
*Communication
between the Appli-
cation Level and
Implementation
Level*

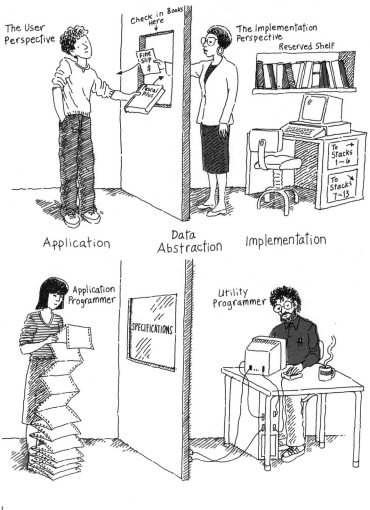

Output:	FineSlip, Library (changed)
Postconditions:	FineSlip is issued if book is overdue.
	Library = original Library + Book

The only communication from the user into the implementation level is in terms of input specifications and allowable assumptions—the preconditions of the accessing routines. The only output from the implementation level back to the user is the transformed data structure described by the output specifications, or postconditions, of the routines. The abstract view encapsulates the data structure, but provides windows through the specified accessing operations.

When you write a program as a class assignment, you often deal with data at all three levels. In a job situation, however, you may not. Sometimes you may program an application that uses a data type that has been implemented by another programmer.

Other times you may develop "utilities" that will be called by other programs. In this book we will ask you to move back and forth between these views.

In later chapters we will use these ideas to build some useful data structures that may be new to you. But first let's explore what built-in structured data types Pascal provides for us.

Built-in Structured Data Types

Programming languages usually provide some structured data types that are built into the language; for instance, Pascal provides records, arrays of various dimensions, and sets. Let's look at each of these from our three perspectives. First we'll examine the abstract view of the structure—how we construct variables of that type and how we access individual elements in our programs. Then from an application perspective we'll discuss what kinds of things can be modeled using each structure. These two points of view are important for you as a Pascal programmer.

Finally, we'll look at how some of the structures may be implemented—how the "logical" accessing mechanism is turned into a location in memory. Understanding the implementation view of a built-in data structure is not critical for you as a programmer. You can just use the structures, as long as you know the syntax. As you read through the implementation sections and see the complex formulas that are needed to access an element of a data structure, you will appreciate why information hiding and data encapsulation are necessary.

One-Dimensional Arrays

Abstract Level   A one-dimensional array is a structured data type made up of a finite, fixed-size collection of ordered homogeneous elements. **Ordered** means that there is a first element, a second element, and so on. (It is the relative position of the elements that is ordered, not necessarily their values.) **Finite** indicates that there is also a last element. **Fixed size** means that the size of the array must be known at compile time; but it doesn't mean that all the slots in the array must contain meaningful elements. Because the elements in an array must all be of the same type, they are physically **homogeneous**. In general, it is desirable for the array elements to be logically homogeneous, as well—that is, for all the elements to have the same purpose. (If we kept a list of numbers in an array of Integers, with the length of the list (an integer) kept in the 0th array slot, the array elements would be physically, but not logically, homogeneous.)

The accessing mechanism of an array is **direct access**, which means we can access any element directly, without first accessing the preceding elements. The desired element is specified using an index, which gives its relative position in the collection. We'll talk later about how Pascal uses the index and some characteristics of the array to figure out exactly where in memory to find the element. That's part of the implementation view, and the array user doesn't need to be concerned with it. (It's encapsulated.)

What operations are defined for arrays? If Pascal didn't have built-in arrays and we were defining arrays ourselves, we would want to specify at least the following two operations:

```
CreateArray (AnArray, IndexRange, ElementType)
  (* procedure to create AnArray with the specified *)
  (* IndexRange to contain data of ElementType      *)

AccessElement (AnArray, Index)
  (* function to return the location of the Index'th *)
  (* element of AnArray                              *)
```

Because arrays are built-in data types, however, the Pascal programming language supplies a special way to perform each of these operations. Pascal's syntax provides a type constructor for creating arrays in memory, as well as a way to directly access an element of an array.

The construct operation is part of the declarations section of a Pascal program. We declare a data type that defines what the array should look like and then create an array variable by declaring it in the VAR section.

For example, a one-dimensional array can be declared with these statements:

```
TYPE
  ListType = ARRAY [1 .. 10] OF Integer;
VAR
  List : ListType;
```

This declaration defines a linearly ordered collection of ten integer elements. Abstractly we can picture List as follows:

Each slot may contain an integer value.

Each element in List can be accessed directly through its relative position in the array. The syntax of the accessing function is described by this syntax diagram:

array-name [indexing-expression]

The indexing expression must have a value in the range declared for the array; in the case of List, the value must be between 1 and 10. The semantics of the accessing function is "Locate the element associated with the indexing expression in the collection of elements identified by array-name."

The accessing function can be used in two ways:

1. to specify a place into which a value is to be copied (such as List[2] : = 5)
2. to specify a place from which a value is to be extracted (such as Number : = List[Index])

Application Level   A one-dimensional array is the natural structure for modeling lists of like data elements. Some examples are a grocery list, a list of prices, a list of phone numbers, a list of student records, and a list of characters (a string). You have probably already used one-dimensional arrays in similar roles in some of your programs.

Implementation Level   Two things must be done to achieve the implementation of any data type: (1) Memory cells must be reserved for the data structure, and (2) the accessing functions must be coded. In the case of a one-dimensional array, the declaration statements tell the compiler how many cells are needed to represent the array. The name of the array is then associated with the characteristics of the array. These characteristics include

1. the upper bound of the index range (Upper)
2. the lower bound of the index range (Lower)
3. the location in memory of the first cell in the array, called the **base address** of the array (Base) (We will designate the base address of a specific array by using the name of the array with no index.)
4. the number of memory locations needed for each element in the array (Size)

During the compilation of the program, the information about the array characteristics is stored in a table called a **dope vector**. When the compiler comes across references to an array element, it uses this information to generate code that will calculate the element's location in memory at runtime.

Before we go on to a concrete example, we will digress for a moment and look at memory. We have used the nonspecific term **cell** instead of *word* or *byte*. By cell we mean the unit of memory that will be assigned to hold a value. This unit is machine-dependent. Figure 3-5 shows several different memory configurations. In practice, how

Figure 3-5   *Memory Configurations*

7	0 7	0 7	0 7	0 7	0 7	0 7	0 7	0
Byte	Byte	Byte	Byte	Byte	Byte	Byte	Byte	
Half word		Half word		Half word		Half word		
Word				Word				
Double word								

IBM 370 Architecture

Word

59   CDC   0

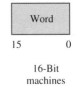

Word

15   0

16-Bit
machines

Word

7   0

8-Bit
machine

memory is configured is a consideration for the compiler writer. In order to be as general as possible, however, we will continue to use the generic term *cell* to represent a location in memory. In the examples that follow, we will assume that an integer or character is stored in one cell and a real number in two cells.

How are the array characteristics used to calculate the number of cells needed and to develop the accessing functions for the following arrays?

```
VAR
   Data        : ARRAY [1 .. 10] OF Integer;
   Values      : ARRAY [-3 .. 2 ] OF Real;
   LetterCount : ARRAY ['A' .. 'Z'] OF Integer;
```

These arrays have the following characteristics:

	Data	*Values*	*LetterCount*
Upper	10	2	'Z'
Lower	1	−3	'A'
Base	unknown	unknown	unknown
Size	1	2	1

We can look at the declaration for Data and immediately see that ten cells will be required. The index type of Values is more complicated, however. To determine the number of cells needed by a particular index type, take the ordinal value (ORD) of the upper bound of the index type, subtract the ordinal value of the lower bound of the index type, then add 1. The result is multiplied by the number of cells per element (Size) to get the number of cells needed for the whole array. The formula is

Number of cells = (ORD(Upper) − ORD(Lower) + 1) * Size

The following table applies this formula to the arrays above:

Index type	*ORD(Upper)*	−	*ORD(Lower)*	+	*1*	=	*Number of elements*	*	*Size*	=	*Number of cells*
[1 .. 10]	10	−	1	+	1	=	10	*	1	=	10
[−3 .. 2]	2	−	(−3)	+	1	=	6	*	2	=	12
['A' .. 'Z']	('Z')	−	('A')	+	1	=	26	*	1	=	26

The compiler assigns memory cells to variables in sequential order. If, when the three declarations above are encountered, the next memory cell available to be assigned is, say, 100, the memory assignments will be as shown on the following page. (We have used 100 to make the arithmetic easier.)

Data	Address		Values	Address		Lettercount	Address
[1]	100		[−3]	110		['A']	122
[2]	101		[−2]	112		['B']	123
.	.		.	.		.	.
.	.		.	.		.	.
.	.		.	.		.	.
[10]	109		[2]	120		['Z']	147

Now we have determined the base address of each array: Data is 100, Values is 110, and LetterCount is 122. The arrangement of these arrays in memory gives us the following relationships:

Given	The program must access
Data[1]	100
Data[9]	108
LetterCount['A']	122
LetterCount['C']	124
Values[-1]	114
Values[0]	116

The accessing function that gives us the position of an element in a one-dimensional array associated with the expression Index is

Address(Index) = Base + Offset of the Index ' th element

How do we calculate the offset? The general formula is

Offset = (ORD(Index) − ORD(Lower)) * Size

The whole accessing function becomes

Address(Index) = Base + ((ORD(Index) − ORD(Lower)) * Size)

Let's apply this formula and see if we do get what we have shown we should.

	Base	+	((ORD(Index)	−	ORD(Lower))	*	Size)	=	Address
Data[1]	100	+	((1	−	1)	*	1)	=	100
Data[9]	100	+	((9	−	1)	*	1)	=	128
LetterCount['A']	122	+	((0	−	0)	*	1)	=	122
LetterCount['C']	122	+	((2	−	0)	*	1)	=	124
Values[−1]	110	+	(((−1)	−	(−3))	*	2)	=	114
Values[0]	110	+	((0	−	(−3))	*	2)	=	116

In Pascal, the upper bound (Upper) for each array is used in error checking. After an indexing expression has been calculated, this value is compared to the Base + Upper. If the calculated expression is greater than or equal to the Base + Upper, the address is not within the array. In that case an error message is printed and execution halts.

Two-Dimensional Arrays

Abstract Level Most of what we have said about the logical view of a one-dimensional array applies as well to a two-dimensional (or multidimensional) array. It is a structured data type made up of a finite, fixed-size collection of ordered homogeneous elements. Its accessing mechanism is direct access: A pair of indexes specifies the desired element by giving its relative position in the collection.

A two-dimensional array is a natural way to represent data that is logically viewed as a table with columns and rows. The following example illustrates the syntax for the type constructor.

```
TYPE
    TableType = ARRAY [1 .. 10, 1 .. 5] OF Integer;

VAR
    Table : TableType;
```

The abstract picture of this structure is a grid with rows and columns:

The accessing function for the two-dimensional array is as follows:

```
                    Table [Row, Col]
                          ↗       ↘
          Specifies which row    Specifies which column
          (First dimension)      (second dimension)
```

Application Level   As mentioned in the previous section, a two-dimensional array is the ideal data structure for modeling data that is logically structured as a table with rows and columns. The first dimension represents rows, and the second dimension represents columns. Each element in the array contains a value, and each dimension represents a relationship.

For example, suppose we wanted to keep track of the progress of six stocks on the New York Stock Exchange over a four-week period. We could use the following data declarations to model this information:

```
CONST
    NumStocks = 6;
    NumWeeks  = 4;

TYPE
    PriceType  = Real;
    StockRange = 1 .. NumStocks;
    WeekRange  = 1 .. NumWeeks;
    TableType  = ARRAY [StockRange, WeekRange] OF PriceType;

VAR
    Stock       : StockRange;
    Week        : WeekRange;
    StockPrices : TableType;
```

The value in StockPrices [Stock, Week] is the average price of a particular stock for a particular week (see Figure 3-6). All the values in a row represent prices for the same stock (one relationship among the data elements); all the values in a column represent average prices for a particular week (a second relationship).

Implementation Level   Let's change hats again and examine how the two-dimensional array is implemented. Remember that in the translation process two things have to be done: Memory space must be reserved for the structure, and the code to be generated for the accessing function must be determined.

In the case of the one-dimensional array, the amount of memory space was calculated by subtracting the ORD of the lower bound of the index range from the ORD of the upper bound of the index range and adding 1. This approach can be extended to the two-dimensional case by applying the same formula to both dimensions and multiplying the two results. To make the formula a little more manageable, let's use UB for upper bound of the index range and LB for lower bound of the index range. The number of elements in a two-dimensional array is calculated by the following formula:

Number of elements =
(ORD(UB first dimension) − ORD(LB first dimension) + 1) *
(ORD(UB second dimension) − ORD(LB second dimension) + 1)

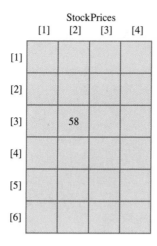

Figure 3-6
A Two-Dimensional
Array Representing
StockPrices

The value in StockPrices[3,2]
represents the average
price of the third stock
for the second week.

Applying this formula to the stock example, we have

$$(ORD(6) - ORD(1) + 1) * (ORD(4) - ORD(1) + 1) = 6 * 4 = 24$$

If you count the number of elements in the table in Figure 3-6, you will find that there are indeed 24. To calculate the number of cells needed to store the array, you simply multiply the number of elements by Size (cells per element). The number of cells needed for StockPrices is 48:

24 elements * 2 cells per real number element = 48

Humans visualize a two-dimensional array as a table with rows and columns; in fact, we will call the first dimension Row and the second dimension Column in the balance of our discussion. Computer memory, however, is one long sequence of cells accessed by addresses beginning at 0. Therefore, a two-dimensional array is usually stored with all the elements of a row (or column) in sequence, followed by all the elements of the next row (or column) in sequence, and so on. If the elements of a row are stored next to one another, the array is said to be stored in **row-major order**. If the elements of a column are stored next to one another, the array is in **column-major order**.

Some languages, such as FORTRAN, store arrays in column-major order. Pascal stores arrays in row-major order. Does the method of storage affect the FORTRAN or Pascal application programmer? Not usually; the accessing mechanism is transparent. We are now looking at two-dimensional arrays from the implementation level, however. At this level it does make a difference, because the accessing function is different for the two methods of storage. We will describe the accessing functions for row-major storage here, leaving the description of the accessing functions for column-major storage as an exercise.

We will develop these functions using integer indexes (omitting the ORDs) because this notation is clearer. [Remember that ORD(l) is 1.] We will then convert to the general case by inserting ORDs in the proper places.

Let's look again at the stock market example. Figure 3-6 shows how we visualize StockPrices. Figure 3-7 shows this table as it looks in memory. Remember, StockPrices

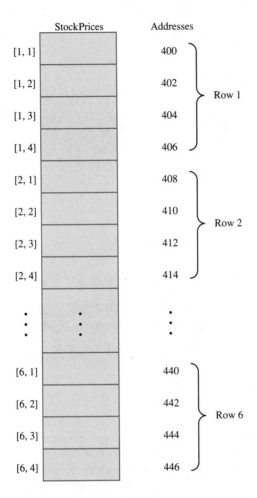

Figure 3-7
StockPrices

is the identifier associated with the first cell in the block of storage set aside for this table. Let's assume that the address is 400.

To access an element in the second row, you must skip over the elements in the first row. To access an element in row I, you must skip over I − 1 rows. How many elements are there in each row? The number of elements in the second dimension tells us. There is one element in a row for each column. Therefore,

UB Column − LB Column + 1

gives us the number of elements in each row. Because there are four columns in StockPrices, there are four elements in a row.

The base address plus the offset (the number of elements in a row times the number of rows to be skipped, multiplied by Size) gives us the first cell in the correct row. Consider this value to be the base address of the correct row. Now the same formula as was used to find the place in the one-dimensional case can be used to find the correct row item: the column index minus the lower bound of the column.

$$\text{Address} = \text{Base} + ((\text{UB Column} - \text{LB Column} + 1) * (\text{Row Index} - 1) * \text{Size}) + ((\text{Column Index} - \text{LB Column}) * \text{Size})$$

Let's apply this formula to several references to StockPrices and see if we do indeed get the right cell. (Look back at Figure 3-6.) Because the number of elements in a row stays constant, we will calculate it only once.

Number of elements in a row of StockPrices = $(4 - 1) + 1 = 4$

	Base address	+	*Elements in row*	*	*(Row index −1)*	*	*Size*	+	*(Col index − LB col)*	*	*Size*	=	*Addr*
StockPrices[1,1]	400	+	(4	*	(1−1)	*	2)	+	(1−1)	*	2	=	400
StockPrices[3,2]	400	+	(4	*	(3−1)	*	2)	+	(2−1)	*	2	=	418
StockPrices[4,1]	400	+	(4	*	(4−1)	*	2)	+	(1−1)	*	2	=	424
StockPrices[6,4]	400	+	(4	*	(6−1)	*	2)	+	(4−1)	*	2	=	446

Following is the complete general formula that is used to access an element in a two-dimensional array stored in row-major order. The index type can be any ordinal type, and the component type of the elements in the array can occupy Size cells.

Address of element at [Row, Col] =

Base +	*Base address plus offset:*
Size *	*cells/element*
[(ORD(UB Col) − ORD(LB Col) + 1)	*elements/row*
* (ORD(Row) − ORD(LB Row))	*rows to skip*
+ (ORD(Col) − ORD(LB Col))]	*row elements to skip*

where

UB Row	=	Upper bound of first dimension.
LB Row	=	Lower bound of first dimension.
UB Col	=	Upper bound of second dimension.
LB Col	=	Lower bound of second dimension.
Row	=	First-dimension index.
Col	=	Second-dimension index.
Base	=	Base address of the array.
Size	=	Number of cells per array element.

Why are we going through all these details to explain something that you as a Pascal programmer don't need to know in order to use arrays in programs? The main reason is to demonstrate how much detail can be hidden from the user. Also, this background will help you later on, when *you* will be implementing the accessing routines for other data structures that are not built into Pascal. Once these accessing routines have been clearly specified, implemented, and thoroughly debugged, you can use them in your programs, just as if these data structures were built into Pascal. You can think of your Pascal compiler as having been enhanced to include these as built-in types. In case you still have any doubts about data encapsulation, just imagine what it would be like if you had to use the long formula we just discussed every time you wanted to access an element of a two-dimensional array!

Last Words on Arrays

The concept of an array can be extended to any number of dimensions. In the exercises we ask you to define a three-dimensional array at the logical level and to give its accessing function.

The discussion of array implementations illustrates the relationship of the physical data structure to the set of accessing operations. The desired direct access by index is facilitated by the organization of the data. Note that the complexity of the accessing function is independent of the size of the array. Thus to access a particular slot in an array is an O(1) operation. Array access must be fast and direct because arrays are used to implement other data structures. It is the need for fast access that has prompted most designers of programming languages to limit indexes to ordinal types. The ORD function is defined on all ordinal types and can be used to directly access the element associated with a particular index.

It is possible, of course, to index an array by any value; however, the complexity of the accessing function depends on the type of index used. If, for example, you wanted to index an array by a set of strings, you could explicitly store the strings in parallel with their corresponding component values. When you wished to retrieve a component value, you would then search the strings to find the corresponding component value. In this case the complexity of the accessing function would be proportional to the size of the array; that is, finding a particular array element would be O(N).

Records

Pascal has another built-in data type called the *record*. This very useful structure is not available in all programming languages. FORTRAN, for instance, does not support records; however, COBOL, a business-oriented language, uses records extensively.

Abstract Level   A record is a structured data type made up of a finite collection of not necessarily homogeneous elements called *fields*. Accessing is done directly through a set of named field selectors.

We'll illustrate the syntax and semantics of the accessing function within the context of the following declarations:

```
TYPE
  CarType = RECORD
    Year  : Integer;
    Maker : ARRAY [1 .. 10] OF Char;
    Price : Real
  END;    (* CarType *)

VAR
  MyCar : CarType;
```

The record variable MyCar is made up of three components. The first, Year, is of type Integer. The second, Maker, is an array data type. The third component, Price, is a real number. The names of the components make up the set of selectors. A picture of MyCar appears in Figure 3-8.

Figure 3-8
MyCar

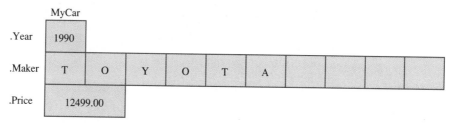

The syntax of the accessing function is the record variable name, followed by a period, followed by the field selector for the component you are interested in.

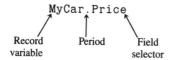

If this expression is on the right-hand side of an assignment statement, a value is being extracted from that place (for example, PricePaid := MyCar.Price). If it is on the left-hand side, a value is being stored in that field of the record (for example, MyCar.Price := 12499.00).

The MyCar.Maker field is an array whose elements are of type Char. In Pascal, you can access that array field as a whole (for example, MyCar.Maker), or you can access individual characters by using the array accessing function on that field.

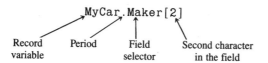

Application Level   Records are very useful for modeling objects that have a number of characteristics. The Record data type allows us to collect various types of data about an object and to refer to the whole object by a single name. We can also refer to the different attributes or fields of the object by name. You have probably seen many examples of records used in this way to represent objects.

Records are also useful for defining other data structures, allowing programmers to combine information describing characteristics of the structure with the storage of the elements. For instance, one way to define a list is to declare the array that will contain its elements and then to declare another variable to indicate how many of the slots in the array are being used.

```
CONST
    MaxList = 1000;    (* maximum elements in List *)
TYPE
    ArrayType = ARRAY [1 .. MaxList] OF Integer;
VAR
    List       : ArrayType;  (* contains the elements *)
    ListCount  : Integer;    (* actual element count  *)
```

If we want to call a procedure to do some processing on this list, we must pass both List and ListCount. (Only the elements in use should be processed, not all the slots in the array.)

Alternatively, we can combine the list elements and the other list information together in a record.

```
CONST
  MaxList = 1000;    (* maximum elements in List *)

TYPE
  ArrayType = ARRAY [1 .. MaxList] OF Integer;

  ListType = RECORD
    Elements  : ArrayType;    (* contains the elements *)
    ListCount : Integer       (* number of slots used  *)
  END;      (* ListType *)

VAR
  List : ListType;    (* contains everything needed *)
                      (* to process the List        *)
```

We will make extensive use of records in this way when we develop representations of our own user-defined data structures.

Implementation Level   A record, like an array, occupies a consecutive block of cells in memory.* The array's accessing function calculates the location of a particular cell from an index; the record's accessing function calculates the location from a named field selector. The basic question, however, is the same: Which cell (or cells) in this consecutive block do you want?

The name of the record variable is associated with a location in memory, the base address of the record. To access each field, we need to know how much of the record to skip to get to the desired field. When a record is declared, the compiler calculates how many cells are needed for each field, and creates a table that relates the field names to their positions within the record. A reference to a record field causes the compiler to examine this table to determine the field's offset from the beginning of the record. The compiler can then generate the field's address by adding the offset to the base. Figure 3-9 shows such a table for CarType. If the base address of MyCar were 1000, the fields of this record would be at the following addresses.

Address of MyCar.Year   =   1000 + 0 = 1000
Address of MyCar.Maker =   1000 + 1 = 1001
Address of MyCar.Price =   1000 + 11 = 1011

Note that MyCar.Maker is the base address of an array. If an element within this array is to be accessed, this base address is used in the array's accessing formula.

---

*In some machines this may not be exactly true, for boundary alignment (full- or half-word) may require that some space in memory be skipped so that the next field starts on a byte that is divisible by 2 or 4. This is true of the IBM 370. See Figure 3.5.

Figure 3-9
CarType

Field	Length	Offset
Year	1	0
Maker	10	1
Price	2	11

Address	
1000	Year field
1001	
1002	
.	Maker field
.	
.	
1010	
1011	Price field
1012	

Other Pascal Built-in Data Types

Arrays are supported by nearly all general-purpose programming languages, and record structures are also commonly provided. Because they are extremely common and will be used extensively in your programs, we have discussed these structures in detail. Pascal also supports a couple of other data structures that are less commonly built in to programming languages. We will discuss variant records, sets, and pointers, to give you the understanding you need to use these data types in your own programs.

Variant Records

Every record variable contains all of the fields defined for its record type, whether or not all of the fields are applicable to the particular instance of the record. For instance, suppose we want to write the procedure described by the following procedure heading:

```
PROCEDURE DrawFigure
  (Figure : FigureType);
  (* Display the figure described by the Figure record. *)
```

Type FigureType is a record that contains all the information necessary to display a circle, ellipse, triangle, or rectangle. Some pieces of information are necessary for *all* shapes: We need to know which shape to display, what color to display it, and whether to fill the figure. Other information, however, varies according to the shape. To display a circular figure, for example, we need to know the center coordinates and the radius, while to display a rectangle we need to know the top-left and bottom-right coordinates. One way to handle this situation is to declare a record that contains all the possible fields that the record might need, as shown below.

```
TYPE
   ShapeType = (Circular, Elliptical, Triangular, Rectangular);
   ColorType = (Red, Blue, Green, Black, Yellow, Magenta);

   CoordType = RECORD
      X : Integer;    (* X-coordinate *)
      Y : Integer     (* Y-coordinate *)
   END; (* CoordType *)

   FigureType = RECORD
      Color    : ColorType;   (* for all shapes            *)
      Fill     : Boolean;     (* for all shapes            *)
      Shape    : ShapeType;   (* for all shapes            *)
      Radius   : Integer;     (* for circles and ellipse   *)
      Center   : CoordType;   (* for circle and ellipse    *)
      RadiusY  : Integer;     (* for ellipse only          *)
      Point1   : CoordType;   (* for triangle and rectangle *)
      Point2   : CoordType;   (* for triangle and rectangle *)
      Point3   : CoordType    (* for triangle only         *)
   END; (* FigureType *)

VAR
   Figure : FigureType;
```

There are two problems with this approach. First, we waste space. For example, if Figure.Shape = Circular, the last four fields are meaningless. The second problem is that the record declaration is confusing; we have to depend on the comments to tell us which fields are logically meaningful for a particular instance of the record.

Pascal provides an alternative: the **variant record**. A variant record has two sections:

1. the *fixed* part, which contains the fields, if any, that must be present in any instance of the record, and
2. the *variant* part, which contains fields that are applicable to a particular instance of the record.

In the example above, the fixed part would contain the Shape, Color, and Fill fields, while the variant part would contain fields appropriate to each type of shape. Let's look at how a variant record version of FigureType might be coded. (ShapeType, ColorType, and CoordType are declared above.)

```
TYPE
   FigureType = RECORD

      (* Fixed Part *)
      Color : ColorType;     (* exists in all variables of *)
      Fill  : Boolean;       (* this record type           *)

      (* Variant Part *)
      CASE Shape : ShapeType OF
         Circular   :  (* fields applicable to circles *)
            (Radius     : Integer;
             CirCenter  : CoordType);
```

```
        Elliptical  :  (* fields applicable to ellipses *)
          (XRadius      : Integer;
           YRadius      : Integer;
           EllCenter    : CoordType);

        Triangular  :  (* fields applicable to triangles *)
          (Point1       : CoordType;
           Point2       : CoordType;
           Point3       : CoordType);

        Rectangular :  (* fields applicable to rectangles *)
          (TopLeft      : CoordType;
           BottomRight  : CoordType)
  END;  (* FigureType *)
```

In the declaration of FigureType above there are "regular" field declarations for the two fixed fields, Color and Fill. But there is a special syntax for the declaration of the Shape field, since its value determines which of the variant parts is applicable. The field that discriminates between the different variants of the record is called the **tag field**. This field's declaration is inserted at the top of the variant part of the record declaration in what resembles a CASE statement. Like a CASE statement, the word CASE precedes the tag field declaration, and the word OF follows it. Unlike a CASE statement, however, the field's type name is included. After all, this is a field declaration, which must include both a field's name and its type.

The lines that follow also resemble a CASE statement. Like a CASE statement, the possible tag field values are listed, each followed by a colon and code that is specific to this value. Unlike a CASE statement, the value-specific code contains field declarations, not statements. These declarations are bracketed by parentheses, much as the value-specific statements in a CASE statement are contained within BEGIN/END. There is no END (* CASE *) following the declarations of the last variant, since the record terminates immediately with an END.

Let's look at how we can use the following variables of this variant record type:

```
VAR
  Circle    : FigureType;
  Ellipse   : FigureType;
  Triangle  : FigureType;
  Rectangle : FigureType;
```

Suppose that we want to display a red circle. We can assign values to the variable Circle, and then call DrawFigure:

```
Circle.Color      := Red;       (* fixed field            *)
Circle.Fill       := True;      (* fixed field            *)
Circle.Shape      := Circular;  (* tag field              *)
Circle.Radius     := 10;        (* circle-specific field  *)
Circle.CirCenter.X := 40;       (* circle-specific field  *)
Circle.CirCenter.Y := 100;      (* circle-specific field  *)

DrawFigure (Circle);
```

Actually, we could have used any of the four variables declared above to contain the circle data, since they all *potentially* contain the fields applicable to circles. It doesn't make much sense to assign Rectangle.Shape := Circular, but it is legitimate syntax. The compiler doesn't care about the semantics of variable names.

However, we must *not* assign values to fields that are inconsistent with the value of the tag field, as shown in the following example:

```
Circle.Shape    := Circular;
Circle.XRadius := 10;                (* No No No! *)
```

Although a radius is relevant to a circle, the XRadius field is only to be used when the Shape field has the value Elliptical. We must only use fields that are declared for the value we assign to the tag field. The programmer is responsible for using the correct fields, since the compiler will not catch this kind of error.

This does not mean, however, that a single variable of type FigureType cannot be used for different variants. We can declare a record of FigureType, use it to contain circle information, and then use it later to contain ellipse information.

```
VAR
  Figure : FigureType;
    .

    .

    .
  Figure.Color := Red;
  Figure.Fill  := True;
  (* Draw a filled red circle. *)
  Figure.Shape        := Circular;
  Figure.Radius       := 10;
  Figure.CirCenter.X := 40;
  Figure.CirCenter.Y := 100;
  DrawFigure (Figure);

  (* Draw a filled red ellipse. *)
  Figure.Shape        := Elliptical;
  Figure.XRadius      := 5;
  Figure.YRadius      := 20;
  Figure.EllCenter.X := 90;
  Figure.EllCenter.Y := 20;
  DrawFigure (Figure);
```

We just can't use Figure to contain the information about a circle and an ellipse *at the same time*.

To understand why it is dangerous to use fields that are inconsistent with the value of the tag field, you need to understand how variant records are generally implemented. Figure 3-10 illustrates the four variant records declared above. Each record contains the Color, Fill, and Shape fields; following these fields space is allotted for the variant parts. Because only one set of variant fields are logically in use at any one time, the various sets of fields can overlay each other in memory. When a variant record dec-

Figure 3-10   *Four Variant Records of FigureType*

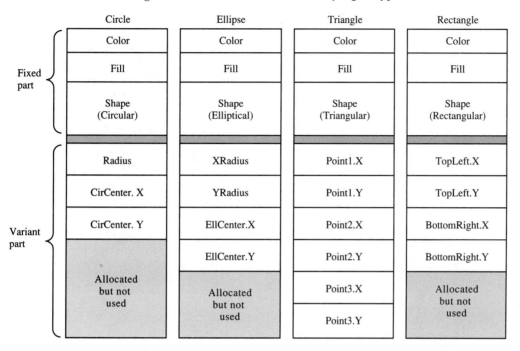

laration is encountered, the compiler only needs to allocate enough space to hold a record variable that uses the largest variant (in this case, a triangle). Any of the other, smaller variants would fit within this space, and whatever space is left over contains logical garbage. If we are careful only to use the correct set of fields, however, this garbage is inaccessible.

The use of a variant record solves both of the problems we discussed above. First, we do not waste as much space, since we do not need to reserve space for every possible field needed in the record, even if they are mutually exclusive. There is some waste, in the case of the smaller variants, since the smallest and largest variants are allocated the same amount of space. There is generally less waste, however, than if a regular record type had been used. Figure 3-11 compares the variant record Triangle (which contains the largest variant) with the nonvariant declaration of Figure at the beginning of this section. The fields in each record that are relevant to a triangle are shaded.

There may be any number of fields (including none) in the fixed part of a variant record. If a record has both a fixed part and a variant part, the fixed part must be defined first. The record definition may contain only one variant part, although field lists in the variant part may themselves contain a variant part (nested variant).

All of the field identifiers within the record definition must be unique. That is, you cannot use the same field name within two of the variants. The fields that specify the "center" of a circle and an ellipse, for instance, have different names. Look back at Figure 3-10 to see how important this is; CirCenter and EllCenter are located at different offsets within the record.

Figure 3-11
Comparing Records and Variant Records (Relevant Fields Are Shaded)

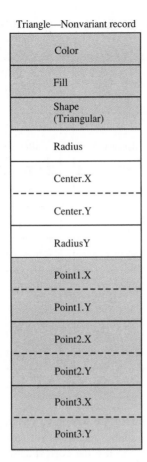

Triangle—Nonvariant record

| Color |
| Fill |
| Shape (Triangular) |
| Radius |
| Center.X |
| Center.Y |
| RadiusY |
| Point1.X |
| Point1.Y |
| Point2.X |
| Point2.Y |
| Point3.X |
| Point3.Y |

Triangle—Variant record

| Color |
| Fill |
| Shape (Triangular) |
| Point1.X |
| Point1.Y |
| Point2.X |
| Point2.Y |
| Point3.X |
| Point3.Y |

The "CASE part" of the variant record declaration is often matched by a CASE statement in the program. For example, the following code might be included in Procedure DrawFigure:

```
CASE Figure.Shape OF
    Circular :
        (* code for displaying a circle goes here *)
    Elliptical :
        (* code for displaying an ellipse goes here *)
    Triangular :
        (* code for displaying a triangle goes here *)
    Rectangular :
        (* code for displaying a rectangle goes here *)
END; (* CASE *)
```

It is possible to declare the tag field using only the type name, rather than the *fieldname : typename* syntax described above. For instance, suppose that the Draw-Figure procedure had the following heading:

```
PROCEDURE DrawFigure
  (Shape   : ShapeType;
   Figure : FigureType);

  (* Display the shape described by the Figure record. *)
```

Since the Shape is input as a parameter to the procedure, this information is redundant in the record. We could change the variant part of the record as follows:

```
    (* Variant Part *)
    CASE ShapeType OF
      Circular    :  (* fields applicable to circles *)
         .
         .
      (* the rest of the variant part as above *)
```

Note that Shape is no longer a record field. However, we no longer need this information in the record, as it is passed to DrawFigure as a parameter.

It is possible to have a variant that does not have any additional fields; that is, a record with a particular tag field value may only need the fixed fields. Suppose that we decide to extend Procedure DrawFigure to draw a colored frame around the entire screen, or to color the whole screen (background) if Fill is True. We modify our type declarations as follows:

```
ShapeType = (Background, Circular, Elliptical,
             Triangular, Rectangular);

  FigureType = RECORD
    (* Fixed Part *)
    Color : ColorType;     (* exists in all variables of *)
    Fill  : Boolean;       (* this record type.          *)

    (* Variant Part *)
    CASE Shape : ShapeType OF
      Background  : ();     (* no add'l fields needed *)
         .
         .
      (* the rest of the variant part as above *)
```

The list of fields for the Background variant is empty; there is nothing between the ( ) delimiters.

Sets

A **set** is a structured data type composed of a finite, *unordered* collection of homogeneous elements called set *members*. To declare a set type, we use the following syntax:

```
TYPE
   typename = SET OF basetype;
```

For instance, to declare the type of a set that can contain members chosen from the subrange 'A' .. 'Z', we use

```
TYPE
   LetterSet = SET OF 'A' .. 'Z';
```

The statements

```
VAR
   Vowels     : LetterSet;
   Consonants : LetterSet;
```

create two set variables of this type. These variables can contain from zero to 26 members (all the possible values defined for this base type).

Just like variables of other types, a set variable must be initialized before it can be manipulated. To put elements into a set, you use an assignment statement. The values to be added to the set are separated by commas and enclosed in square brackets.

```
Vowels := ['A', 'E', 'I', 'O', 'U'];
```

puts the elements 'A', 'E', 'I', 'O', 'U' into the set variable Vowels.

A set-type variable that has been declared but has no value assigned to it is not an empty set; it is a variable that contains logical garbage. If you want a set to be empty, you assign to it the empty set, which is represented by square brackets with no values between them.

```
Letters := [];   (* Letters = empty set. *)
```

Ordering has no meaning in sets, so it doesn't make any difference how you order the values within the set brackets. These two assignment statements produce the same results:

```
Vowels := ['A', 'E', 'I', 'O', 'U'];
Vowels := ['E', 'O', 'A', 'U', 'I'];
```

Subranges can be used to assign values to sets. The statement

```
Letters := ['A' .. 'C'];
```

assigns the letters 'A', 'B', and 'C' to the set variable Letters. Although order is not important in listing set elements, it is relevant in specifying a subrange. For the subrange to contain any values, the second value must be greater than the first. For example,

```
Letters := ['C' .. 'A'];
```

makes Letters the empty set. Because ordering is irrelevant for set elements, we could write

```
Letters := ['P'..'T', 'A'..'C', 'Z', 'K'..'M'];
```

However, it makes better sense to list the values in a more readable order.

To determine if a value is in a set, we use the set operator **IN**. For instance, to test if a character (Ch) is a vowel, we use the following condition:

```
IF Ch IN ['A', 'E', 'I', 'O', 'U']
   THEN ...
```

This IF condition is equivalent to writing

```
IF (Ch = 'A') OR (Ch = 'E' ) OR (Ch = 'I') OR
   (Ch = 'O') OR (Ch = 'U')
   THEN ...
```

Following the assignment statement,

```
Vowels := ['A', 'E', 'I', 'O', 'U'];
```

we could also have used the equivalent statement

```
IF Ch IN Vowels (* contains 'A', 'E', 'I', 'O', 'U' *)
   THEN ...
```

Testing for set membership is easier to read than a long expression in an IF statement. It is usually a much faster operation than evaluating the equivalent IF condition, but this is implementation-dependent.

There are a number of other operations defined for sets, including union, intersection, and difference.

Symbol	Operation	Meaning
+	Union	The union of two set variables is a set made up of those elements that are in *either* or *both* set variables.
*	Intersection	The intersection of two set variables is a set made up of only those elements occurring in *both* set variables.
−	Difference	The difference of two set variables is a set made up of the elements that are in the *first* set variable but *not in the second*.

Four of the relational operators can also be applied to sets, as described in the list that follows.

Expression	Returns True if
Set1 = Set2	Set1 and Set2 are identical.
Set1 <> Set2	there is at least one element in Set1 not in Set2 or there is at least one element in Set2 not in Set1.
Set1 <= Set2	all the elements in Set1 are in Set2.
Set1 >= Set2	all the elements in Set2 are in Set1.

Pointers and Dynamic Memory Allocation

In Chapter 1, we designed and implemented Program ListAndCount to create a listing and source line count of a Pascal program. We plan to modify this program to create a "cross reference" of the identifiers used in the program. A cross reference is like an index; it contains the names of all the identifiers (constants, variables, type names, for instance) as well as a list of line numbers to indicate where each identifier was used. Since generating a cross reference is time-consuming, our modified program should ask the user whether a cross reference is desired. If the user says yes, then a cross reference will be generated in addition to the other program outputs; otherwise, only the source code listing and count report will be created.

If the user desires a cross reference, it will be built as the program is processed line by line. When it is complete, the information in the cross reference will be added to the end of the report file. In the meantime, the information must be kept in some sort of data structure. We'll worry about designing this data structure later; in the meantime let's just call it CrossRefType. In the declarations section of our main program we put the following declarations:

```
TYPE
   CrossRefType = (* the details of this type will go here *)
VAR
   CrossReference : CrossRefType;
```

When we define a type for a data structure and then declare a variable of that type in our global program declarations, that variable is said to be **static**. Its size and existence are determined at compile time, and it will exist for the entire execution of the program.

The variable CrossReference, then, will exist for the whole execution of the program, whether it is used or not. What if the user doesn't want a cross reference to be generated? We don't have to put anything in the data structure, but it will be sitting there anyway, taking up a lot of space in memory.

We know that Pascal can create variables on the fly. The local variables of a procedure, for instance, are created on entrance to the procedure and destroyed on exit, as if they never existed. This is one kind of **dynamic storage allocation**. If Pascal can create dynamic variables, why can't we?

The answer is: *We can*. Pascal allows a program to allocate space for data dynamically, during the course of its execution. That is, we can design a program to do the following:

IF user wants Cross Reference
  THEN
    Allocate CrossRef

The data structure that will hold the cross reference is not declared in the program's VAR section. Unlike a declared variable, its existence will not be determined at compile time; rather it will be created dynamically at run time—if the user wants a cross reference, that is. When the program comes to the part of the code that tells it to "allocate CrossRef," it essentially grabs a chunk of free memory to put the cross reference data structure in. This section of memory does not have a *name*, however; its space is merely reserved.

If it doesn't have a name, how can we assign a value to this space? Although the chunk of memory has no name, it does have an address, and we can declare a variable to contain this address. Then we can assign a value to the chunk by referencing the variable that contains its address. In essence, this variable "points" to the newly allocated, nameless chunk of memory. That's why this variable is called a **pointer**.

Pointer Variables

To allocate space dynamically in Pascal, we declare a **pointer type variable**. Just as Integer-type variables can only contain integer values, and Char-type variables can only contain characters, a Pascal pointer variable can only contain pointer values, which are actual *addresses in memory*.

Since most machines use integers (ranging from 0 to the maximum size of memory) to represent addresses, pointer values look like integers. We must differentiate between Integers as a data type and Pascal pointers. The operations defined for Integers (such as addition and multiplication) and the operations defined for pointers are not the same.

As programmers we are not interested in addresses anyway; we are interested in the data being pointed to. Rather than using actual address values (numbers like 48690), it is convenient to picture the pointers graphically as arrows.

In fact, the Pascal pointer type is denoted by the arrow symbol (↑) followed by the name of the type of data that the pointer will access, or point to. This symbol is called "up-arrow." Since most keyboards do not include this character, the caret character (∧) is usually used as an up-arrow. The following declarations show how a pointer to the cross reference data structure is declared.

```
TYPE
  RefListType   = (* the details of this type will go here *)
  CrossRefType = ∧RefListType;

VAR
  CrossReference : CrossRefType;
```

The up-arrow symbol, ∧, followed by a type name (for example, ∧RefListType), is used to denote the pointer type. A variable of type CrossRefType can point *only* to data of type RefListType. Note that in the TYPE declarations, we have declared RefListType, but we have not declared any variables of this type. We did declare a variable of CrossRefType—a pointer (address). The pointer is small, about the size of an integer, while the structure that will be pointed to will be large.

We could have left out the declaration of CrossRefType and declared CrossReference as follows:

```
VAR
  CrossReference : ^RefListType;
```

Defining the variable CrossReference by the type description ^RefListType is analogous to defining an array variable in the VAR declarations, as in

```
VAR
  Word : ARRAY [1 .. 10] OF Char;
```

The definition of types in the VAR section ("anonymous typing") is legal, but generally not a good practice. In standard Pascal these variables cannot subsequently be used as actual parameters for procedures and functions. That is, we cannot write

```
PROCEDURE ReadWord
  (VAR Word : ARRAY [1 .. 10] OF Char);
```

Similarly, we cannot write

```
PROCEDURE PrintCrossRef
  (CrossRef : ^RefListType);
```

It is a much better practice to declare a type name for the pointer type, and to use the type name in variable declarations.

Using NIL

The pointer variable CrossReference currently does not contain meaningful data. After its declaration, but before any assignments to it, CrossReference contains garbage. Unfortunately, what looks like garbage to us might look like an address to a computer, so we have to be really careful to make sure a pointer has a good value (the address of our data) in it before it is used.

There is, however, a special value that we can assign to a pointer, that says, "This pointer doesn't point to anything." This value is represented by the Pascal reserved word, NIL. For instance, if the user doesn't want a cross reference, we could set CrossReference to NIL using an assignment statement:

```
CrossReference := NIL
```

NIL   A constant in Pascal that can be assigned to a pointer type variable to indicate that the pointer points to nothing.

Usually Pascal implements the NIL value as a zero address; however, the value 0 cannot be substituted for the word NIL in this implementation. The assignment "Cross-Reference : = 0" would cause a compilation error, because the types of CrossRefType (a pointer type) and 0 (an integer) are different.

Now we refer to CrossReference as a **NIL pointer**. Later in our line-by-line processing of the program, we can check the value of CrossReference to decide whether the identifiers in the current line should be added to the cross reference:

```
IF CrossReference <> NIL
   THEN
      (* Add identifiers in the current line to the cross ref. *)
      .
      .
      .
```

Using Procedure New

All right, suppose that the user says "Yes." How do we dynamically allocate the space for the cross reference data? Pascal provides a built-in procedure, **New**, to do this. Procedure New takes one parameter: the name of the pointer variable in which to store the address of the newly allocated space.

```
(* Allocate space for the cross reference data. *)
New (CrossReference);
```

Following the call to New, CrossReference contains the address of the chunk of memory where we will store our cross reference data. How did Procedure New know how much memory to grab? Pascal pointers are *typed pointers*; that is, they are defined to point to data of a specific type. Because of its declaration,

```
TYPE
   CrossRefType = ^RefListType;
```

pointers of CrossRefType (like CrossReference) can *only* point to data of RefListType. The size of RefListType is known at compile time, so Procedure New can figure out how much space to allocate at run time.

NOTE: If the call to New fails because the system has run out of free space, the job will crash at run time. New doesn't return a flag or any kind of warning if we are running low on space; it just causes the program to terminate at run time.

Now we have dynamically allocated space for the cross reference data, and we're almost ready to put some values in it. Before we go any further, however, let's expand our definition of CrossRefType. We know that the cross reference will be a list of identifiers, each of which will contain a list of line references. For now, we'll leave the details of the list entries undefined, and fill in some of the other details.

Crash Protection

Some "extended" versions of Pascal provide tools to help protect against program crashes when a call to New fails. In the following example, we use Turbo Pascal's MaxAvail and SizeOf functions to make the call to New conditional on whether there is enough space to allocate.

```
FreeSpace := MaxAvail;      (* returns the size in bytes of the *)
                            (* largest free block of storage    *)

IF FreeSpace >= SizeOf (RefListType) (* size of list in bytes *)
  THEN New (CrossReference)
  ELSE (* Error processing *)
```

Since we do not make the call to New unless we know that there is enough space, we can avoid an ugly program crash. If space is not available, our program will still be in control.

```
CONST
  MaxEntries = 50; (* we can adjust this as needed *)
TYPE

  EntryType  = RECORD
    ID       : StringType;   (* TO BE DEFINED LATER *)
    LineRefs : LineListType; (* TO BE DEFINED LATER *)
  END; (* EntryType *)

  EntryListType = ARRAY [1 .. MaxEntries] OF EntryType;

  EntryRangeType = 0 .. MaxEntries;

  RefListType = RECORD
    NumEntries : EntryRangeType;
    Entries    : EntryListType;
  END; (* CrossRefType *)

  CrossRefType = ^RefListType;

VAR
  CrossReference : CrossRefType;
```

Accessing Data through Pointers

We cannot access data in dynamically allocated storage by name, because it doesn't have a declared name. Instead, we will reach the data structure through its pointer. The pointer is a *named* variable; the data it points to is sometimes called *referenced* data, since it is referred to through its pointer. The data being pointed to is also called an

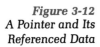

Figure 3-12
A Pointer and Its
Referenced Data

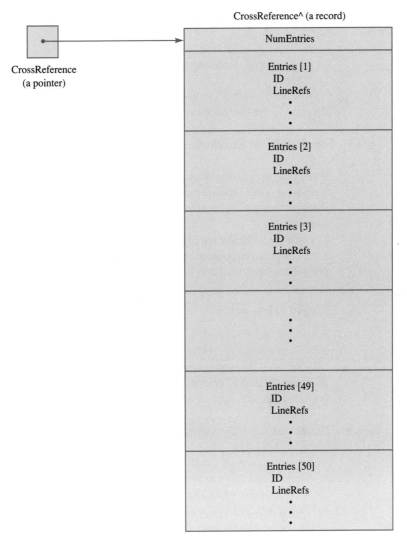

anonymous variable, because it doesn't have a name of its own. We have seen that the symbol ∧, followed by a type identifier, defines a pointer type. The up-arrow symbol, preceded by a variable name, denotes the data object that the pointer variable is pointing to. For instance, CrossReference∧ refers to the data that CrossReference points to. Figure 3-12 illustrates the difference between CrossReference (a pointer) and CrossReference∧ (a record of RefListType).

Now, since CrossReference∧ is a record, we should be able to access its fields in the usual way: We add a dot (period), and then specify the desired field. For instance, to initialize the NumEntries field in the cross reference data we write:

```
CrossReference^.NumEntries := 0;
```

To compare CurrentID (a string) to the ID of the Index'th entry in the entry list, we use the condition

```
IF CurrentID = CrossReference^.Entries[Index].ID
   THEN ...
```

Can you figure out what the following expression references?

```
CrossReference^.Entries[CrossReference^.NumEntries]
```

This example is a little more complicated, so let's take it apart: CrossReference^.Entries is an array, and CrossReference^.NumEntries is the index of the last entry in the array. Putting the index expression inside the [ ] brackets, we can access the last entry in the entry list.

Once we see that CrossReference^ is the referenced "name" of a record, we simply use it in place of a record variable name in the usual ways. Whatever type of data Pointer has been declared to point to, Pointer^ is an object of that type.

Using Dispose

Just as we can allocate data space dynamically, we can also deallocate it. Most Pascal compilers provide a procedure called **Dispose** to free dynamically allocated space. Dispose takes one parameter: a pointer to the memory space that is no longer needed. After we're finished printing out the contents of the cross reference, we no longer need the data structure. The call to

```
Dispose (CrossReference);
```

makes further use of CrossReference illegal until the pointer is redefined by either an assignment statement or another call to New (CrossReference).

What happens when Dispose is called? There is no standard treatment specified in the Pascal language definition; each implementation of Pascal may have its own version of the Dispose procedure. In some implementations the pointer is set to NIL; in others the pointer is left unchanged, with what looks like a valid address stored in it. It is the programmer's responsibility to make sure that undefined pointers are never referenced.

In this particular application, the call to Dispose seems unnecessary, since after the cross reference is written to the output file, the program is about to end anyway. (That will certainly free all the space!) But in general, it's wise to free dynamically allocated space as soon as you are finished with it. A program that makes many calls to New really can use up all the available memory, especially on a PC.

In future chapters you will get a lot more practice using pointers, and you will see what a very powerful tool we have in dynamic storage allocation.

Summary

We have discussed how data can be viewed from multiple perspectives, and we have seen how Pascal encapsulates the implementation of the primitive types and structures built into the language.

As we create user-defined data types, using built-in data types (such as arrays, records, and pointers) to implement them, we will see that there are actually many levels of data abstraction. The abstract view of an array might be seen as the implementation level of the user-defined data structure List, which uses an array to hold its elements. At the abstract level, we do not access the elements of List through their array indexes, but through a set of accessing operations defined especially for objects of ListType. Moving up a level, we might see the abstract view of List as the implementation level of another user-defined data type, ProductInventory. And so on.

PERSPECTIVES ON DATA

Application or user view	Logical or abstract view	Implementation view
Product Inventory	List	Array
List	Array	Row major access function
Array	Row major access function	32-Bit words on IBM 370

What do we gain by separating the views of the data? First, we reduce complexity at the higher levels of the design, making the program easier to understand. Second, we make the program more easily modifiable: The implementation can be completely changed without affecting the program that uses the data structure. We will make use of this advantage in this text, developing various implementations of the same logical data structures in different chapters. Third, we develop software that is *reusable*: The structure and its accessing operations can be used by other programs, for completely different applications, as long as the correct interfaces are maintained. You saw in the first two chapters of this book that the design, implementation, and verification of computer software is a very laborious process. Being able to reuse pieces that are already designed, coded, and tested cuts down on the amount of work we have to do.

In the chapters that follow we will extend these ideas to build other structured data types that Pascal does not provide: stacks, queues, lists, trees and graphs. We will consider these data structures from the abstract view: What is our logical picture of the data, and what accessing operations can we use to create, assign to, and manipulate elements in the data structure? We call the result of this level of design the abstract data type (ADT) and record its description in a data specification.

Next we will change hats and turn to the implementation view of the data structure. We will consider the Pascal type declarations that represent the data structure, as well as the procedures and functions that implement the specifications of the abstract view. Data structures can be implemented in more than one way, so we will look at alternative representations.

Finally, in the applications at the ends of the chapters, we will take the application view of the data, using the data structures we have developed in some real programs.

Application

Strings

Data Types	*Software Techniques*
■ String	■ Design from specifications
■ Array	■ Data encapsulation and information hiding
■ Record	■ Error checking in data structure operations

The user-defined StringType, which was created in the application section of Chapter 1, is such a success that we have been asked to extend it into a whole set of string operations.

The Logical Level: The String ADT

At the logical level, a string is a finite sequence of alphanumeric characters, characterized by a property called **length**. The length refers to the number of characters in the string.

A number of possible operations can be defined for strings. The choice of operations that we implemented in Chapter 1 was driven by the needs of Program ListAndCount. Now we are going to create a set of general operations, independent of any particular application. This module will then be available to use in other programs. The operations that we will implement for the StringType ADT are summarized below:

Operation	*Function*
Length	Determines the number of characters in a string.
CharAt	Returns the character at the specified string position.
EmptyString	Sets a string to empty (length 0).
Append	Appends a character to the end of a string.
ReadLine	Inputs a line of text.
PrintString	Writes the contents of a string.
Substring	Returns a part of a string.
Concat	Returns a new string created by putting two strings end to end.
Compare	Compares two strings to determine their relationship (equal to, less than, or greater than).

A number of other string operations are suggested in the Exercises at the end of this chapter.

The Implementation Level

There are a number of ways that a string can be implemented. One simple string representation is a packed array of characters. For instance, we could use the following declarations to declare a ten-character string called Name:

```
TYPE
  StringType = PACKED ARRAY [1 .. 10] OF Char;
VAR
  Name : StringType;
```

The advantage to using a packed array is the simplicity of writing and comparing string values. For instance, assuming that Name has been assigned a value, we can print it with the statement

```
Write (Name);
```

The disadvantage to this string implementation is that there is no explicit way to determine the *length* of the string. What if the value of string is 'Smith'? This string has five characters, yet the array has space for ten; the last five array positions contain logical garbage [see Figure 3-13(a)]. How do we detect the end of the string?

One solution is to pad all of the character spaces following the string with blanks [see Figure 3-13(b)]. To find the end of the string, we search backward from the end of the array, looking for a nonblank character. The problem with this solution is that it assumes that the blanks are not part of the string. What happens if we want to store the string 'Smith   ' [Figure 3-13(c)]? The trailing blanks are part of the string. Another solution is to put some kind of special end-of-string character into the array position following the last string character [see Figure 3-13(d)]. This approach assumes that the packed array is one array slot larger than the maximum string size, since the end-of-string marker takes a character position.

As long as we are wasting an array slot, however, we might as well use it to *explicitly* store the string's length. We could use the Turbo Pascal approach. Turbo's built-in String type is implemented as an array of characters that is one slot larger than the number of characters the string is declared to hold. For instance, given the following Turbo Pascal declaration:

```
VAR
  Name : String[10];
```

Turbo creates an ARRAY [0 .. 10] OF Char. (All Turbo arrays are "packed.") The last ten array slots contain the string characters; the first slot contains CHR(Length). Thus the length and the characters are kept in a single array structure, as shown in Figure 3-14.

While this is a clever implementation, it violates the idea that the elements in an array should be logically, as well as physically, homogeneous. The first array slot has a purpose that is different than the other array positions.

We decide to use the string representation that we developed in the application section of Chapter 1. A string will be represented by two parts: the collection of characters in

Figure 3-13   Storing a String in a Packed Array

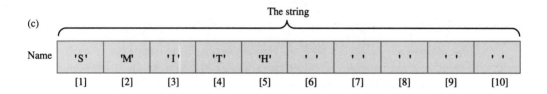

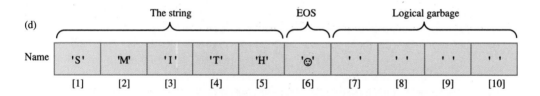

the string itself and an integer value that indicates its length. Because Pascal doesn't allow variable-length arrays, a maximum string length must be chosen. Each string will be stored in an array of the maximum length, but the string characters themselves will constitute only that part of the array from position 1 to the position indicated by the Length field. This string representation is pictured in Figure 3-15.

As we did in Chapter 1, we will implement the string as a record, with an Integer field for Length and an array for the character portion of the string. We will use the following declarations:

```
CONST
    (* Maximum characters in StringType variables *)
    MaxString = 80;

TYPE
    StringRangeType = 0 .. MaxString;
    IndexType       = 1 .. MaxString;
```

Figure 3-14   The Turbo String Implementation

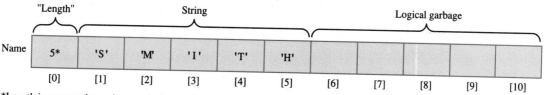

*Length is converted to a character before storing

Figure 3-15   StringType

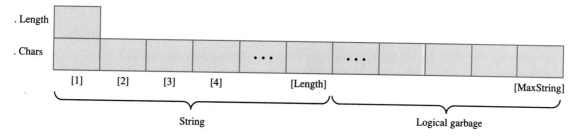

```
StringType      = RECORD
   Length       : StringRangeType;
   Chars        : ARRAY [IndexType] OF Char
END; (* StringType *)

VAR
   String : StringType;
```

Implementing the String Operations

Let's look at the operations one by one, and see how the specifications for each can be implemented as Pascal procedures and functions. We will first show the specification and then develop the algorithm and implement the operation.

 The code for the whole module of string operations is in file STRING.PAS on the program disk.

If your compiler doesn't have strings as a built-in data structure, or you want your program to compile under different compilers, you can use these procedures and functions in your programs.

Length Operation

Length (String) : returns StringRangeType

Function:	Returns the length characteristic of String.
Input:	String (StringType)
Preconditions:	String is not undefined.
Output:	Length (StringRangeType)
Postconditions:	Length = the number of characters in String

Given our representation of a string, writing a function to return its length is very simple. We can get the length directly from the length field in the record.

Length

Length ← String.Length

The code for this function is very short:

```
FUNCTION Length
  (String : StringType) : StringRangeType;
  (* Returns the length characteristic of String. *)
BEGIN (* Length *)
  Length := String.Length
END; (* Length *)
```

Isn't it inefficient to have a one-line function? Wouldn't it be just as easy to use String.Length in the calling program, instead of invoking a function Length (String)?

Remember that the implementation should be invisible to the string user. As the coder of the string operations, you know that this implementation takes only one line of code. The user, however, only sees the operation from the logical level. If you let the user access the length field directly, you violate the concept of an abstract data type. The abstract data structure can be accessed *only* through the set of operations that are defined for it.

CharAt Operation

CharAt (String, Position) : returns Char

Function:	Returns the character in String at the specified Position.
Input:	String (StringType)
	Position (IndexType)
Preconditions:	String is not undefined.
	1 <= Position <= Length (String)
Output:	CharAt (Char)
Postconditions:	CharAt = character in specified Position of String.

If String is encapsulated, how can the string user find out what characters are in the string? A little operation, CharAt, provides this information. The user specifies the string position and CharAt returns the character in this slot. Like Length, this function only contains a single statement:

```
FUNCTION CharAt
  (String   : StringType;
   Position : StringRangeType) : Char;
  (* Returns the character in String at Position. Assumes *)
  (* that String is not undefined, and that 1 <= Position *)
  (* <= Length(String).                                   *)
```

```
BEGIN (* CharAt *)
  CharAt := String.Chars[Position]
END;  (* CharAt *)
```

EmptyString Operation

EmptyString (String)

Function:	Sets String to empty.
Input:	String (StringType)
Preconditions:	None
Output:	String
Postconditions:	Length (String) = 0.

In the postconditions for this operation, we state that "Length (String) = 0," rather than "String.Length = 0." The String ADT user understands the meaning of Length (String)—this operation is already defined. However, String.Length is part of the String ADT's *implementation,* and should not be mentioned in the specification.

This procedure is also trivial to implement—we simply set String.Length to 0. We do not have to set the characters in the Chars field to blanks; if the length of the string is zero, the values in the array are logical garbage.

```
PROCEDURE EmptyString
  (VAR String : StringType);

BEGIN (* EmptyString *)
  String.Length := 0
END; (* EmptyString *)
```

It would have been nice to implement the EmptyString operation as a parameterless function, so that it could be used in comparisons:

```
IF MyString = EmptyString
  THEN ...
```

However, StringType is not a scalar type; it cannot be returned as the value of a function.

Append Operation

Append (String, Character)

Function:	Adds a single character to the end of String.
Input:	String (StringType) Character (Char)
Preconditions:	String is not undefined. Length (String) < MaxString.
Output:	String
Postconditions:	String = original String with Character appended to the end.

Implementing the Append operation is quite simple.

```
PROCEDURE Append
  (VAR String : StringType;
   Character  : Char);
BEGIN (* Append *)

  String.Length := String.Length + 1;
  String.Chars[String.Length] := Character
END; (* Append *)
```

We can create literal strings by initializing a string to the empty string (using the EmptyString operation) and then appending characters one by one. The following code creates the string 'HELLO'.

```
EmptyString (String);
Append (String, 'H');
Append (String, 'E');
Append (String, 'L');
Append (String, 'L');
Append (String, 'O');
```

It would be simpler if we could just use a constant string, such as

```
CONST
  String = 'HELLO';
```

We could, of course, create such a literal string, but we could not then use it with our string operations because it would be of a type other than StringType. Pascal would create a packed array of characters for the constant String declaration. StringType is a record, however, so we have to create strings using Append. We can also create strings from file (or keyboard) input using the ReadLine operation.

ReadLine Operation

▌ **ReadLine (FileToRead, String, Error)**

    Function: Reads a line of characters from FileToRead, and returns it in String. Error flag is set to indicate if the characters will not fit into String.

    Input: FileToRead (Text file)

    Preconditions: FileToRead is open for reading, with file read cursor at first character of current line; EOF will not be encountered.

    Output: FileToRead—file read cursor updated
                        String (StringType)
                        Error (Boolean)

Postconditions: String = up to MaxString characters from the current line of
text in FileToRead.
Error = (number of characters in the current line > MaxString)
File cursor is at first character of next line.

This specification is a modification of the ReadLine operation in the Chapter 1 application section. What happens if we are reading a line that has more characters than String.Chars can hold? We have added a second output, Error, to indicate whether the string is full before the end of the text line in the file.

The main task of ReadLine is to read in and store characters until end-of-line or the string is full. Then we set the string's length field and determine the value of Error. In each iteration of the loop body, we read a character and place it in the next slot in the character array. We can keep track of the current array position using a variable called Pos. Pos will be initialized to 0 (since there may be no characters in the line), and incremented inside the loop body before the call to Read. Here's the algorithm:

ReadLine

Pos ← 0

WHILE more space in string AND more characters to read DO
    Increment Pos
    Read (FileToRead, String.Chars[Pos])

Set String length
Set Error
Move file cursor to next line

Let's use a loop invariant to help us get the looping structure right. To begin we'll look at the first exit condition: running out of space in the string. Pos tells us whether there is "more space in string." Assuming for now that there are more characters to read, we can continue entering the loop body as long as there's room in the string—that is, WHILE Pos < MaxString. This gives us the first part of the loop invariant:

Loop Invariant Part 1: $0 <= Pos <= MaxString$

When Pos = MaxString, we do not reenter the loop body, because Pos would be incremented in the loop body. (Remember, after the execution of the loop, the WHILE condition is False, and the loop invariant is still true.)

What else do we know about Pos? We know that the first Pos slots in the array contain string characters.

Loop Invariant Part 2:   String.Chars[1] .. String.Chars[Pos] contain all the
characters read from the input file.

This information is important when we exit from the loop. To set String.Length, we must know the position of the last character that we put into the character array. Our loop invariant tells us that the last character is in the array slot at position Pos, so String.Length must be set to Pos.

How do we express "more characters to read"? When EOLN (FileToRead) is true, there are no more characters to read. (The EOLN marker, generally one or two characters, will be "flushed" when we move the read cursor to the next line.) The complete WHILE condition is

```
WHILE (Pos < MaxString) AND NOT EOLN (FileToRead) DO
```

How do we set the error flag? If EOLN (FileToRead) is True, we know that all the characters fit into the string, and so Error should be False. Otherwise, an error has occurred; the characters in the line don't all fit in the string. We can set Error with a simple assignment statement:

```
Error := NOT EOLN (FileToRead)
```

We are now ready to code the ReadLine procedure:

```
PROCEDURE ReadLine
   (VAR FileToRead  : Text;
   VAR String       : StringType;
   VAR Error        : Boolean);
   (* Reads a line of characters from FileToRead, and      *)
   (* returns it in String. Error flag is set to indicate *)
   (* if the characters will not fit into String. (If      *)
   (* Error, String contains first MaxString characters.) *)

VAR
   Pos : StringRangeType; (* index into character array *)
BEGIN (* ReadLine *)

   Pos := 0;
   (* Loop Invariant: 0 <= Pos <= MaxString AND        *)
   (* String.Chars[1] .. String.Chars[Pos] contain      *)
   (* all the characters already read from the current *)
   (* line in FileToRead.                               *)
   WHILE NOT EOLN (FileToRead) AND (Pos < MaxString) DO
     BEGIN
       Pos := Pos + 1;
       Read (FileToRead, String.Chars[Pos])
     END; (* WHILE *)
   (* Set Length field = number of characters read. *)
   String.Length := Pos;

   (* Set error to indicate if string too small for line. *)
   Error := NOT EOLN (FileToRead);

   (* Move file read cursor to next line. *)
   Readln (FileToRead)
END; (* ReadLine *)
```

PrintString Operation

▌ **PrintString (String)**

Function:	Prints out the characters in String to FileToWrite.
Input:	FileToWrite (Text)
	String (StringType)
Preconditions:	String is not undefined. File is open for writing.
Output:	FileToWrite
Postconditions:	String is printed to FileToWrite. No end-of-line is printed.

The algorithm for this operation is very simple. The string is printed exactly as it is, character by character, using the standard Pascal procedure Write. No Writeln is issued.

PrintString

FOR Pos := 1 TO String.Length DO
    Write String.Chars[Pos]

The code for this procedure can be implemented directly from the algorithm.

```
PROCEDURE PrintString
  (VAR FileToWrite : Text;
   String          : StringType);

  (* Print String to FileToWrite. Assumes file is open. *)

VAR
  Pos : IndexType; (* loop control variable *)
BEGIN (* PrintString *)

  FOR Pos := 1 TO String.Length DO
    Write (FileToWrite, String.Chars[Pos])

END; (* PrintString *)
```

How would you modify this procedure to create a PrintLine operation?

Substring Operation

▌ **Substring (String, StartPos, Num, Substr, Error)**

Function:	Creates a substring of String that includes Num characters, beginning at position StartPos. Error flag is set to indicate if the substring goes past the end of the original string.
Input:	String (StringType)
	StartPos (IndexType)
	Num (IndexType)—the number of characters to copy into the substring)
Preconditions:	String is not undefined.
	1 <= StartPos <= MaxString
	1 <= Num <= MaxString

Output:	Substr (StringType)
	Error (Boolean)
Postconditions:	Substr contains Num characters from String, beginning at position StartPos. If Error, Substr is undefined.
	Error = (StartPos + Num − 1 > length of String).

This time the postconditions give the user a warning: If Error comes back True, we don't guarantee the contents of Substr. The processing inside the routine in the case of an error is left up to the programmer. The ADT design determines whether, in the case of an error, the output is undefined or has some specified value, as in ReadLine. The main point here is that the specifications should warn the user, in this case: "*Beware!* If there's an error, you don't know what's in Substr."

The preconditions for this operation specify that there are upper and lower bounds on both StartPos and Num. Since both of these parameters are IndexType (the integer range 1 .. MaxString), this precondition is implied by the Input specification. However, we have added these preconditions for clarity. Note that meeting these preconditions does not preclude the possibility of an error; the error condition is a function of both StartPos and Num.

In the algorithm for the Substring operation, we take the characters from String one by one and copy them into Substr. We begin at StartPos and copy Num times, or until we run out of characters in String (the Error condition). Actually, because Substr is undefined when Error occurs, we can check at the start to see whether there will be enough characters in String. If so, we copy; otherwise, we just set Error and quit.

The algorithm is

Substring

Error ← (StartPos + Num − 1 > length of String)

```
IF NOT Error
    THEN
        Copy Num characters from String, beginning with StartPos,
            into Substr
        Substr.Length ← Num
    ELSE we don't do anything (Substr is undefined)
```

The copy task is coded as a FOR loop, as shown in the procedure listing below:

```
PROCEDURE Substring
    (String      : StringType;
     StartPos    : IndexType;
     Num         : IndexType;
     VAR Substr  : StringType;
     VAR Error   : Boolean);

(* Create a substring of String that includes Num      *)
(* characters, beginning at position StartPos. Error   *)
(* flag is set to indicate if the substring goes past  *)
(* the end of the original string.                     *)
```

```
VAR
  Pos : Integer; (* loop control variable *)
BEGIN (* Substring *)

  Error := (StartPos + Num - 1) > String.Length;

  IF NOT Error
    THEN
      BEGIN
        (* Copy Num characters from String to Substr,        *)
        (* beginning at StartPos.                            *)
        (* Loop Invariant: 1 <= Pos <= Num + 1    AND        *)
        (* Substr.Chars[1] .. Substr.Chars[Pos - 1] =        *)
        (* String.Chars[StartPos]..String.Chars[StartPos - 2]. *)
        FOR Pos := 1 TO Num DO
          Substr.Chars[Pos] := String.Chars[StartPos + Pos - 1];

        Substr.Length := Num

      END (* IF not error *)
END; (* Substring *)
```

Concat Operation

Concat (String1, String2, Error)

Function:	Adds the characters in String2 to the end of String1. Error flag is set to indicate if String1's length would exceed the maximum string length.
Input:	String1, String2 (StringType)
Preconditions:	String1 and String2 are not undefined.
Output:	String1 (changed), Error (Boolean)
Postconditions:	String1 = original String1 concatenated with String2. If Error, String1 will be returned unchanged.
	Error = (length of String1 + length of String2 > maximum string length).

The Concat operation "adds" one string to the end of another string. Note that the specification of this concatenation operation has only two strings as parameters, not three. The resulting string is returned in the first string. This time the specification tells us that if an error occurs the first string will be returned unharmed.

To do the concatenation part of the operation, we copy all the characters from the second string into the first string, one at a time, beginning in the first slot after String1's own characters (that is, in position String1.Length + 1). An example of this operation is shown in Figure 3-16.

Figure 3-16   Concat Operation

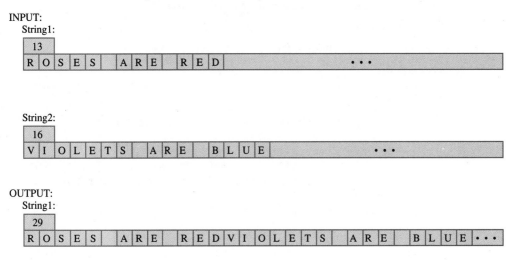

Concat

Error ← (String1.Length + String2.Length) > MaxString

IF NOT Error
    THEN
        Copy all characters in String2 into String1, beginning
           at String1.Length + 1
        Reset String1.Length

    ELSE (Error)
        Do nothing (String1 is returned unchanged)

    This algorithm is fairly straightforward. The copy task is implemented with a FOR
loop, as shown in the procedure below.

```
PROCEDURE Concat
   (VAR String1 : StringType;
    String2     : StringType;
    VAR Error   : Boolean);

   (* Add the characters in String2 to the end of String1.  *)
   (* Error flag is set to indicate if total length exceeds *)
   (* the maximum string length.                            *)

VAR
   LastPos,              (* current last position in String1 *)
   Pos : StringRangeType; (* position in String2             *)

BEGIN (* Concat *)

   (* Error := lengths of two strings exceed MaxString *)
   Error := (String1.Length + String2.Length) > MaxString;
```

```
IF NOT Error
  THEN
    BEGIN

      (* Start String2 immediately after Stringl. *)
      LastPos := Stringl.Length;

      (* Move all the characters from String2. *)
      FOR Pos := 1 TO String2.Length DO
        BEGIN
          LastPos := LastPos + 1;

          (* Copy next character from String2 to  *)
          (* next slot in Stringl.                *)
          Stringl.Chars[LastPos] := String2.Chars[Pos]
        END; (* FOR loop *)

      (* Reset length of resulting string. *)
      Stringl.Length := LastPos

    END (* IF not error *)
END; (* Concat *)
```

The Substring and Concat operations can be used to create two other string operations: Delete and Insert.

The Delete operation is used to remove a number of characters from a string, beginning with the character in a designated position. The Substring operation can be used to break the original string into two parts: the part before the characters to be deleted and the part following them. These two strings can then be concatenated together to produce the string we want. Figure 3-17 illustrates this approach.

The Insert operation is the mirror image of Delete. Insert causes a substring to be inserted into another string at a specified position. We can use the same approach as we did in Delete—use Substring and Concat to take the strings apart and put them back together correctly. Here's the algorithm:

Insert

Get Substring of String, from insertion point to end
    (put the result in EndString)
Get Substring of String, from start to insertion point
    (put the result back in String)
Concatenate String with InString
Concatenate result with EndString

This algorithm is illustrated in Figure 3-18. Implementing the Delete and Insert string operations is left as an exercise.

Compare Operation

▪ **Compare (String1, String2) : returns Relation**

    Function: Makes a lexical comparison between String1 and String2, and returns a value indicating their relation (less than, equal to, or greater than).

Figure 3-17   Delete Operation

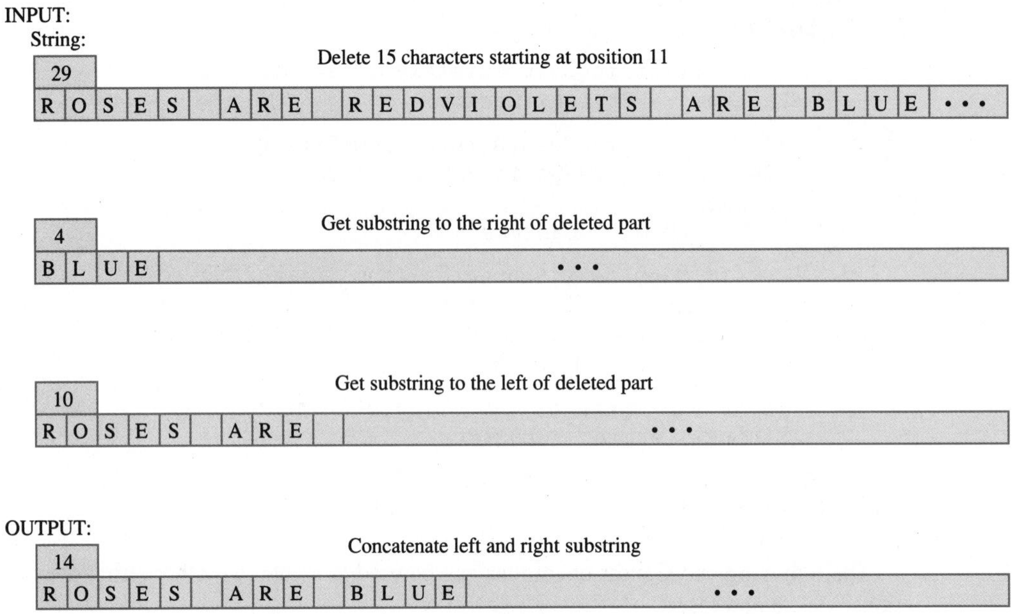

INPUT:
String:

Delete 15 characters starting at position 11

| 29 |
| R | O | S | E | S | | A | R | E | | R | E | D | V | I | O | L | E | T | S | | A | R | E | | B | L | U | E | • • • |

Get substring to the right of deleted part

| 4 |
| B | L | U | E | | • • • |

Get substring to the left of deleted part

| 10 |
| R | O | S | E | S | | A | R | E | | • • • |

OUTPUT:

Concatenate left and right substring

| 14 |
| R | O | S | E | S | | A | R | E | | B | L | U | E | • • • |

Input:	String1, String2 (StringType)
Preconditions:	String1 and String2 are not undefined.
Output:	Compare (Relation)
Postconditions:	Compare = Less, if String1 < String2 (that is, if String1 comes before String2 alphabetically).
	Compare = Equal, if String1 = String2.
	Compare = Greater, if String1 > String2.
	If all the characters match but one string is shorter than the other, the shorter one is assigned the value Less.

Pascal lets us compare packed arrays to each other directly, but an array of characters (such as the Chars part of the StringType record) must be examined character by character. Starting at the beginning of each string, we compare characters in matching positions. As soon as we find two characters that are not the same, their order determines the order of the two strings. We stop comparing in this case, as well as in the case where there are no more characters in the shorter string.

Compare

MinLength ← length of the shorter string
Pos   ← 1
StillMatch ← True

Figure 3-18
Insert Operation

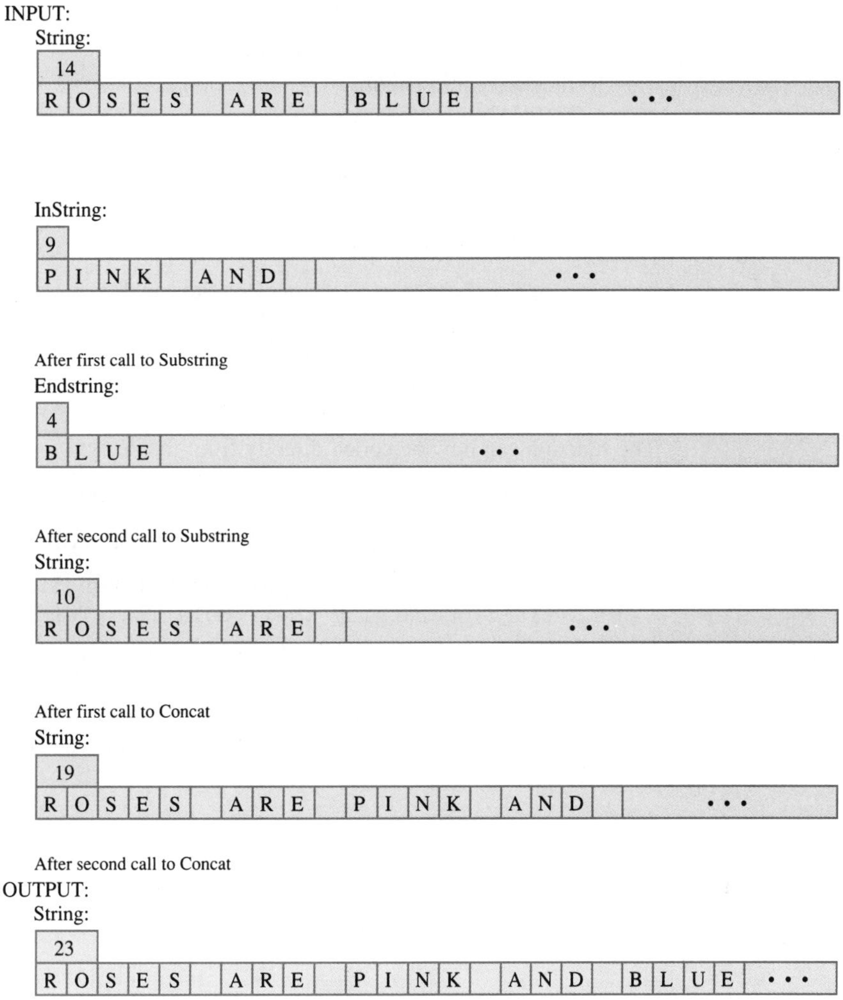

INPUT:
String:

14											
R	O	S	E	S		A	R	E		B	L	U	E	• • •

InString:

9							
P	I	N	K		A	N	D	• • •

After first call to Substring
Endstring:

4			
B	L	U	E	• • •

After second call to Substring
String:

10							
R	O	S	E	S		A	R	E	• • •

After first call to Concat
String:

19												
R	O	S	E	S		A	R	E		P	I	N	K		A	N	D	• • •

After second call to Concat
OUTPUT:
String:

23															
R	O	S	E	S		A	R	E		P	I	N	K		A	N	D		B	L	U	E	• • •

(Loop Invariant: 1 < = Pos < = MinLength + 1 AND
String1.Chars[1] .. String1.Chars [Pos − 1] =
String2.Chars[1] .. String2.Chars [Pos − 1])

WHILE Pos < = MinLength AND StillMatch DO
  IF Pos character in String1 = Pos character in String2
    THEN
      Increment Pos
    ELSE (they don't match)
      StillMatch ← False (so stop checking)
      Compare Pos characters of String1 and String2
        to set Compare output to Less or Greater.

```
IF StillMatch
   THEN (Use lengths to determine order:)
      IF they are equal lengths
         THEN Compare ← Equal
      IF String1 is shorter
         THEN Compare ← Less
      IF String1 is longer
         THEN Compare ← Greater
```

The function's output value is of type Relation, which has the following declaration:

```
TYPE
  Relation = (Less, Greater, Equal);
```

The function can now be coded directly from the design.

```
FUNCTION Compare
    (String1, String2 : StringType) : Relation;

    (* Perform a lexical comparison between String1 and *)
    (* String2, returning their relation (less than,    *)
    (* equal to, or greater than).                      *)
VAR
    Pos        : IndexType;       (* index within strings       *)
    StillMatch : Boolean;         (* True while characters match *)
    MinLength  : StringRangeType; (* length of shorter string    *)
BEGIN (* Compare *)

    (* MinLength := length of the shorter string *)
    IF String1.Length < String2.Length
      THEN MinLength := String1.Length
      ELSE MinLength := String2.Length;

    Pos        := 1;
    StillMatch := True;

    (* Loop Invariant: 1 <= Pos <= MinLength + 1 AND *)
    (* String1.Chars[1] .. String1.Chars[Pos - 1] =  *)
    (* String2.Chars[1] .. String2.Chars[Pos - 1]    *)
    WHILE (Pos <= MinLength) AND StillMatch DO
      BEGIN

        (* Search for characters that do not match. *)
        IF String1.Chars[Pos] = String2.Chars[Pos]
          THEN (* keep comparing *)
            Pos := Pos + 1
```

```
      ELSE (* they don't match *)
        BEGIN
          StillMatch := False;
          IF Stringl.Chars[Pos] < String2.Chars[Pos]
            THEN Compare := Less
            ELSE Compare := Greater
        END (* ELSE they don't match *)
    END; (* WHILE loop *)
  (* If the shorter string ran out of characters, use *)
  (* the lengths to determine ordering.               *)
  IF StillMatch
    THEN
      IF Stringl.Length = String2.Length
        THEN Compare := Equal
        ELSE
          IF Stringl.Length < String2.Length
            THEN Compare := Less
            ELSE Compare := Greater
END; (* Compare *)
```

Error Checking in the String Package

You may have noticed that most of the operations in the string package have limited preconditions. That is, they make few assumptions about the correctness of the input parameters. Instead they make the error checks inside the operations and return an error flag to tell the user when something is wrong.

As discussed in Chapter 2, we could have let Pascal use its error checking on array bounds to see whether we were trying to copy characters past the end of the array that contains the string. If we specified an illegal array position, as in the statement

```
String.Chars [MaxString + 1] := 'A'
```

the message "INDEX OUT OF RANGE" would be printed and the program would crash.

FORTRAN takes another approach to run-time error checking: It leaves the checking to the user. If our program said to set the value of the position MaxString + 1 in the array, FORTRAN would write a value at the calculated address for that element, even though it is not inside the array. In other words, FORTRAN makes the programmer responsible for checking the range.

These two approaches represent different philosophies about error handling. Pascal actively checks for run-time errors and takes control away from the program when it detects an error. FORTRAN does very little run-time checking.

As mentioned in Chapter 2, however, we want to write robust programs that do not lose control. This goal suggests a third approach—checking for errors but leaving the determination of what to do when an error is detected to the programmer. That is, the accessing operations check for errors and set an error flag, but leave the decision of how to handle the error to the programmer. After each call to an accessing routine, the programmer can check the error flag to see whether a problem was detected. If so, the programmer can make a decision about how to handle the situation within the context of the specific program.

The StringType ADT, which we have developed here, uses this third approach. In the planning stage, possible error conditions were identified. Then the specifications were written so as to make clear to the programmer using these operations what the error flag means and what the other ramifications of the situation are (for example, a result is undefined, or the string is returned unchanged). The specifications ensure agreement between the user and the accessing routines about what is being done in the operation.

■ *Exercises**

1. Explain what is meant by "data abstraction."

2. What is data encapsulation? Explain the programming goal "to protect our data abstraction through encapsulation." How can the data user access data that is encapsulated?

3. Describe the Pascal type Real as an abstract data type (ADT). What operations are defined for this data type?

4. Describe the Pascal file type Text as an ADT.
   (a) What operations are defined to create and manipulate this data type?
   (b) Explain how this ADT is an example of data encapsulation that is enforced by Pascal.

5. (a) Describe three properties of an Object-Oriented Programming (OOP) methodology.
   (b) Pascal's + operator can be described as "polymorphic." Name three data types for which it is defined.
   (c) How are the OOP properties enforced in standard Pascal?

6. Name two components of a data structure.

7. Name three different perspectives from which we can view a data structure. Using the logical data structure "a list of student academic records," give examples of what each perspective might tell us about the data.

8. Consider the abstract data type GroceryStore.
   (a) At the application level, describe GroceryStore.
   (b) At the logical level, what operations might be defined for the user (customer) of a GroceryStore?
   (c) Specify (at the logical level) the operation CheckOut.
   (d) Write an algorithm (at the implementation level) for the operation CheckOut.
   (e) Explain how parts (c) and (d) above represent information hiding.

9. What structured data types are built into the Pascal programming language?

10. Based on the following declarations and assuming that DataType has been previously declared, tell whether each statement below is syntactically legal or illegal.

*Questions with italicized numbers are answered in the back of the book.

```
TYPE
   Pointer = ^DataType;
VAR
   P, Q, R : Pointer;
   A, B, C : DataType;
```

(a) New (P)   _____   (f) R := NIL   _____   (k) Dispose (R)   _____
(b) New (Q^)   _____   (g) C := P^   _____   (l) A := New (P)   _____
(c) New (A)   _____   (h) P := ^A   _____   (m) Q^ := NIL   _____
(d) P := R   _____   (i) Dispose (B) _____   (n) P^ := A^   _____
(e) Q := B   _____   (j) Dispose (P^) _____   (o) C := NIL   _____

11. The following code segment has careless errors on two lines. Find and correct the errors and show the output where requested.

```
TYPE
   PtrType = ^Integer;

VAR
   Ptr, Temp: PtrType;
   X : Integer;

BEGIN
   New (Ptr);
   Ptr^ := 4;
   Temp^ := Ptr^;
   Writeln (Ptr, Temp);          Output: _____
   X := 9;
   Temp^ := X;
   Writeln (Ptr^, Temp^);        Output: _____
   New (Ptr);
   Ptr^ := 5;
   Writeln (Ptr^, Temp^)         Output: _____
END;
```

12. Describe the accessing function of a Pascal one-dimensional array at the logical level.

13. What operations does Pascal define for the array data type?

14. (a) Declare a one-dimensional array, Name, that contains 20 characters, indexed by Integer values.
    (b) If each character takes one "cell" in memory, and the base address of Name is 1000, what is the address of the cell referenced in this statement?

    Name[10] := 'A';

15. Describe the accessing function of a two-dimensional array. Give an example of an appropriate use of this data structure.

16. In this chapter we discussed the implementation of a two-dimensional array stored in row-major order. FORTRAN, however, uses column-major rather than row-major storage of arrays. What would be the general formula for accessing an element of a two-dimensional array stored in column-major order?

Use the following declarations for Problems 17 and 18:

```
TYPE
   MonthType = (January, February, March, April, May, June,
      July, August, September, October, November, December);

   WeatherRecType = RECORD
      AvgHiTemp  : Integer;    (* Fahrenheit degrees *)
      AvgLoTemp  : Integer;    (* Fahrenheit degrees *)
      ActualRain : Real;       (* inches            *)
      RecordRain : Real        (* inches            *)
   END; (* WeatherRecType *)
```

Assume that an integer takes one cell in memory, a real number takes two cells, and that the fields are in contiguous memory locations with no gaps.

17. (a) Declare a one-dimensional array type, WeatherListType, of WeatherRecType components, indexed by MonthType. Declare a variable, YearlyWeather, of WeatherListType.
    (b) Assign the value 1.05 to the actual rainfall field of the July record in YearlyWeather.
    (c) If the base address of YearlyWeather is 200, what is the address of the field that you assigned in (b) above?

18. (a) Declare a two-dimensional array, DecadeWeather, of WeatherRecType components, indexed by MonthType in the first dimension and by the Integer subrange 1980 .. 1990 in the second dimension.
    (b) Draw a picture of DecadeWeather.
    (c) Assign the value 26 to the AvgLoTemp field of the March, 1989, record.
    (d) Assuming that the base address of DecadeWeather is 600, what is the address of the field you assigned in (c)?

19. (a) Define a three-dimensional array at the logical level.
    (b) Suggest some applications for three-dimensional arrays.
    (c) Give a general formula for accessing an element in a three-dimensional array. Is there more than one? Explain.

Use the following declarations for Problems 20–23.

```
TYPE
   StringType = ARRAY [1 .. 10] OF Char;

   StudentRecType = RECORD
      FirstName     : StringType;
      LastName      : StringType;
      ID            : Integer;
      GPA           : Real;
      CurrentHours  : Integer;
      TotalHours    : Integer
   END; (* StudentRecType *)
```

Assume that an integer or character takes one cell in memory, a real number or a pointer takes two cells, and that the fields are in contiguous memory locations with no gaps.

20. Construct a field-length-offset table for StudentRecType (as in Figure 3-9).

21. If the base address of Student (a variable of StudentRecType) is 100, what address will the compiler generate as the target of the following assignment statement?

```
Student.GPA := 4.0;
```

22. How much space will the compiler reserve for StudentList, declared below?

```
TYPE
  ListType = ARRAY [1 .. 100] OF StudentRecType;
VAR
  StudentList : ListType;
```

23. Given the following declarations,

```
TYPE
  ListType    = ARRAY [1 .. 100] OF StudentRecType;
  ListPtrType = ^ListType;

VAR
  StudentList : ListPtrType;
```

   (a) How much space will the compiler allocate for the variable StudentList?
   (b) How much space will be allocated at compile time for StudentList^?
   (c) How much space will be allocated at run time by the statement New(StudentList)? (Assume that New allocates exactly the number of "cells" needed by the data type.)
   (d) Write a statement to set the ID of the first student in the list array to 1000.
   (e) Write a loop to print out the ID's of all the students in the list. (Assume that all array positions are in use.)
   (f) Write a loop to add the CurrentHours field of each student in the list to the TotalHours field, and to reset CurrentHours to zero.

24. (a) Define a variant record type to contain a day's weather forecast. Each record of this type must have the following standard information: Date, High and Low temperatures, Humidity. Certain weather conditions (snow, thunderstorm, hurricane, drought, windstorm) may have special fields associated with them.
   (b) Draw a diagram to compare the different variants of this record type (like Figure 3-10).

25. (a) Define a set type to contain the months of the year.
   (b) Declare variables of this set type: WinterMonths, FallMonths, CoolMonths.
   (c) Assign the appropriate set elements to the WinterMonths variable.
   (d) Assign the appropriate set elements to the FallMonths variable.
   (e) Set CoolMonths to the union of FallMonths and WinterMonths.

26. Indicate which of the Pascal built-in data structures would most appropriately be used to model each of the following (more than one may be appropriate for each):
   (a) a chessboard
   (b) a collection of characters used for punctuation (to be used for determining the ends of words)
   (c) information about a single product in an inventory-control program
   (d) a list of famous quotations
   (e) the casualty figures (number of deaths per year) for highway accidents in Texas from 1954 to 1974
   (f) the casualty figures for highway accidents in each of the states from 1954 to 1974

(g) the casualty figures for highway accidents in each of the states from 1954 to 1975, subdivided by month

(h) an electronic address book (name, address, and phone information for all your friends)

(i) a collection of hourly temperatures for a 24-hour period

27. How does Pascal support data abstraction? That is, how does Pascal keep the data structure "user" part of the program from accessing or updating the data in any way other than through the specified operations?

28. (a) Define a subrange type called SmallInt for integers from 1 to 100. Use this type to define SmallSet, a set type which may contain integers from 1 to 100.

(b) Write procedure Multiples, which constructs a set of those multiples of a given number which are less than 100. Use set constructor notation and the built-in union operation.

```
PROCEDURE Multiples
  (Value        : SmallInt;
   VAR MultiSet  : SmallSet);
```

(c) Write a procedure that finds the least common multiple of two numbers by calling Procedure Multiples for each of the two values and then using the built-in intersection operation. Determine the lowest value using the IN operator.

29. Since many Pascal compilers offer a very limited range of values for the set base type, sets are sometimes implemented as arrays of Boolean values, as declared below:

```
CONST
  Min = (* minimum value *)
  Max = (* maximum value *)

TYPE
  Range = Min .. Max;
  SetType = ARRAY [Range] OF Boolean;
```

Each possible set value, from Min to Max, is represented by a Boolean flag in the array. If the flag is True, the value is an element in the set; otherwise the value is not an element in the set. Write an operation to support such a set type for each of the procedure and function headings below:

(a) PROCEDURE EmptySet
```
    (VAR ASet : SetType);

  (* Make ASet the empty set. *)
```
(b) PROCEDURE SetIntersect
```
    (Set1, Set2 : SetType;
     VAR Set3    : SetType);

    (* Set3 = Set1 * Set2. *)
```
(c) PROCEDURE SetUnion
```
    (Set1, Set2 : SetType;
     VAR Set3    : SetType);

    (* Set3 = Set1 + Set2. *)
```
(d) PROCEDURE SetOf
```
    (Value : Range;
     ASet   : SetType);

    (* Put Value in ASet. *)
```

```
(e) FUNCTION InSet
      (ASet : SetType;
       Value : Range) : Boolean;

   (* Determine if Value is an element in ASet. *)
```

30. Rewrite the procedure in Problem 28 using the SetType implementation and operations from Problem 29.

31. (a) Define an object to represent a tic tac toe board.
    (b) Write the operations Initialize, Mark, and Display.

Problems 32–36 relate to the String ADT described in this chapter.

32. Extend the String ADT defined in this chapter to include Procedure ReadFixedString, which will read a specified number of characters (designated by parameter) and assign them to the specified string.
    (a) Write a specification for this operation.
    (b) Write the algorithm for this operation.
    (c) Implement the operation, using the declarations for StringType defined in the package.

33. (a) Write a specification for the string Insert operation.
    (b) Write the string Insert operation, using the algorithm described in the chapter.
    (c) For greater efficiency, reimplement the Insert operation to manipulate the string representation directly, not through Substring and Concat.

34. (a) Write a specification for the string Delete operation.
    (b) Write the string Delete operation, using the algorithm described in the chapter.
    (c) For greater efficiency, reimplement the Delete operation to manipulate the string representation directly, not through Substring and Concat.

35. The string Concat operation must be modified to perform the concatenation, even if Error is true. (If Error occurs, the extra characters should be truncated.)
    (a) Modify the specification of the string Concat operation.
    (b) Modify the Concat procedure.

36. (a) What is the order of the algorithm (Big-O) of the Length operation implemented in the application section?
    (b) A string is implemented as a PACKED ARRAY of Char. The string characters are left-justified in the array, and the rest of the array is padded with blanks. Write a Length function for this string implementation, which will search the string (backward), looking for the first nonblank character. What is the order of this algorithm in Big-O notation?

Stacks

CHAPTER 4

GOALS

- To be able to describe a stack and its operations at a logical level.
- To be able to demonstrate the effect of stack operations on a particular implementation of a stack.
- To be able to implement the stack abstract data type in a static array implementation.
- To be able to implement the stack abstract data type as a linked data structure.
- To be able to explain the difference between static and dynamic allocation of the space in which the stack elements are stored.
- To be able to compare stack implementations in terms of source code length, use of storage space, and Big-O approximations of the stack operations.
- To be able to choose between a static and a dynamic linked stack structure.
- To be able to describe advantages and disadvantages of using dynamically allocated space to contain the stack elements.
- To be able to determine when a stack is an appropriate data structure for a specific problem.
- To be able to design and implement the solution to a problem for which a stack is an appropriate data structure.
- To be able to show how stacks can be used to evaluate infix expressions.
- To be able to evaluate an expression in prefix or postfix notation.
- To be able to discuss issues in designing error checking for a program.

Chapter 3 presented the basic principles of designing structures for data used in computer programs. In this chapter and the ones that follow, we will be using these principles to build a range of new data structures. These structures are not built into most programming languages, as arrays and records are, but have to be created by the programmer in each program before they can be used.

We will discuss each structure at several levels. First we will *define* the abstract data type: What does it "look" like, and what are the logical operations on it? At the next level, we will *build* one or more representations of the data structure, using Pascal declarations, and write subprograms to implement the logical operations. At a third level, we will *use* the structures in various application examples. Let's illustrate these concepts with a simple data structure called a "stack."

The Logical Level

What Is a Stack?

Consider the items pictured in Figure 4-1. Although the objects are all different, each illustrates a common concept—the *stack*.

At the logical level, a stack is an ordered group of homogeneous elements. The removal of existing elements and the addition of new elements can take place only at the *top* of the stack. For instance, if your favorite blue shirt is underneath a faded, old, red one in a stack of shirts, you must first remove the red shirt (the top element) from the stack. Only then can you remove the desired blue shirt, which is now the top element in the stack. The red shirt may then be replaced on the top of the stack or thrown away.

The stack is considered an "ordered" group of items because elements occur in a sequence according to how long they've been in the stack. The items that have been in the stack the longest are at the bottom; the most recent are at the top. At any time, given any two elements in a stack, one is higher than the other. (For instance, the red shirt was higher in the stack than the blue shirt.)

Because items are added and removed only from the top of the stack, the last element to be added is the first to be removed. There is a handy mnemonic to help you remember this rule of stack behavior: A stack is a **"last in, first out" (LIFO)** structure.

Figure 4-1
Real-Life Stacks

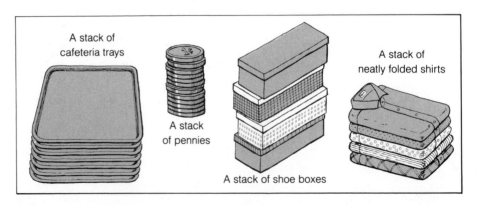

A stack of cafeteria trays

A stack of pennies

A stack of shoe boxes

A stack of neatly folded shirts

Stack   A data structure in which elements are added and removed from only one end; a "last in, first out" (LIFO) structure.

The accessing function of a stack is summarized as follows: Both to retrieve elements and to assign new elements, access only the top of the stack.

Operations on Stacks

The logical picture of the structure is only half the definition of an abstract data type. The other half is a set of operations that allows the user to access and manipulate the elements stored in the structure. Given the logical structure of a stack, what kinds of operations do we need in order to use a stack?

A stack is a dynamic structure; it changes as elements are added to and removed from it. The operation that adds an element to the top of a stack is usually called *Push,* and the operation that takes the top element off the stack is referred to as *Pop*. When we begin using a stack, it should be empty, so another necessary operation is one that creates an empty stack (a stack containing no elements). We'll call this operation *CreateStack*. We must also be able to tell whether a stack contains any elements before we pop it, so we need a Boolean operation *EmptyStack*. As a logical data structure, a stack is never conceptually "full," but for a particular implementation you may need to test whether a stack is full before pushing. We'll call this Boolean operation *FullStack*. We might also want an operation that destroys a stack, getting rid of all the elements left in it and leaving the stack empty. We'll call this operation *DestroyStack*. Figure 4-2 on page 183 shows how a stack, envisioned as a stack of building blocks, is modified by several Push and Pop operations.

We now have a logical picture of a stack and are almost ready to use the stack in a program. The part of the program that uses the stack, of course, won't be concerned with how the stack is actually implemented—we want the implementation level to be hidden, or encapsulated. The accessing operations such as Push and Pop are the windows into the stack encapsulation, through which the stack's data is passed.

We are *almost* ready to use the stack, but to be able to use an abstract data type, the user must have an agreement with the implementation regarding the interfaces to the accessing operations. This agreement, called the abstract data type (**ADT**) **specification**, serves the same purpose as the function specifications discussed in Chapter 1. The following specification describes the stack abstract data type.

Stack ADT Specification

Structure: Elements are added to and removed from the top of the stack.

Operations:

CreateStack (Stack)

Function:	Initializes Stack to an empty state.
Input:	None

Preconditions:	None
Output:	Stack (StackType)
Postconditions:	Stack is empty.

DestroyStack (Stack)

Function:	Removes all elements from Stack, leaving the stack empty.
Input:	Stack (StackType)
Preconditions:	Stack has been created.
Output:	Stack
Postconditions:	Stack is empty.

EmptyStack (Stack) : returns Boolean

Function:	Tests whether Stack is empty.
Input:	Stack (StackType)
Preconditions:	Stack has been created.
Output:	EmptyStack (Boolean)
Postconditions:	EmptyStack = (stack is empty)

FullStack (Stack) : returns Boolean

Function:	Tests whether Stack is full.
Input:	Stack (StackType)
Preconditions:	Stack has been created.
Output:	FullStack (Boolean)
Postconditions:	FullStack = (stack is full)

Push (Stack, NewElement)

Function:	Adds NewElement to the top of Stack.
Input:	Stack, NewElement
Preconditions:	Stack has been created and it is not full.
Output:	Stack
Postconditions:	Stack = original Stack with NewElement added on top

Pop (Stack, PoppedElement)

Function:	Removes top element from Stack and returns it in PoppedElement.
Input:	Stack
Preconditions:	Stack has been created and it is not empty.
Output:	Stack, PoppedElement
Postconditions:	Stack = original Stack with top element removed PoppedElement = top element of original Stack

We have written these specifications informally with a lot of English phrases because this type of specification is easy to read and seems easier to understand. One problem

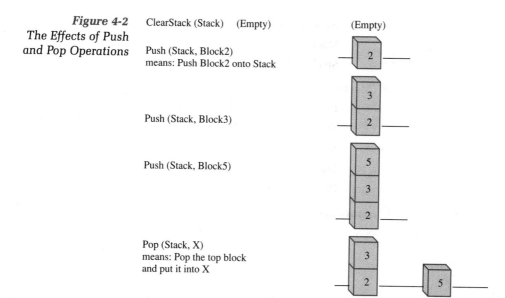

Figure 4-2
The Effects of Push and Pop Operations

with this approach, however, is that English, or "natural-language," descriptions of an operation's function and preconditions and postconditions are often imprecise. There is a whole body of software engineering research concerned with software specification techniques, and many papers and books have been written on the subject. Many people prefer a more mathematical way of expressing what software does, because it is less ambiguous. In this chapter and those that follow, we will stick with natural-language specifications.

The User Level

Now let's look at an example of how the operations in the stack package might be used in a program. Using the Pascal Read procedure to input a real number can be risky, because the program will crash if the input is nonnumeric. To avoid this problem, we can write our own ReadReal procedure, using the following specification:

▪ **ReadReal (Data, RealNumber, Error)**

    Function: Read characters representing a real number from file Data, and convert them to type Real. Number terminates with a blank;

any other nonnumeric (except decimal point) characters generate an error.

Input:	Data (Text)
Preconditions:	Data is open for reading.
Output:	RealNumber (Real), Error (Boolean)
Postconditions:	Error is true if number terminates with nonblank. If Error, RealNumber is undefined; otherwise, RealNumber = Real representation of input characters that terminate with blank. Read cursor is left following terminating character.

This procedure reads in the characters representing a real number and converts them into a value of type Real. Postponing the error processing momentarily, we'll use the following algorithm:

ReadReal

Convert the "whole" part of the number

IF decimal point found
    THEN
        Convert the "decimal" part of the number

Add the whole and decimal parts.

To convert the whole part of the number, we will read and process characters until a nonnumeric character is encountered.

Convert Whole Part

Number ← 0.0

Read Numeral (a character) from Data

WHILE Numeral IN ['0' .. '9'] DO
    Number ← (10 * Number) + numeric equivalent of Numeral
    Read next Numeral from Data

In each iteration, the numeric conversion of the characters that were previously read is multiplied by 10, and the product is added to the numeric equivalent of Numeral. Let's walk through this loop with the input '1234.567':

Before loop (after "priming" read):
        Number = 0.0   Numeral = '1'
After 1st iteration:
        Number = (10 * 0)   + 1 = 1   Numeral = '2'
After 2nd iteration:
        Number = (10 * 1)   + 2 = 12   Numeral = '3'
After 3rd iteration:
        Number = (10 * 12) + 3 = 123   Numeral = '4'
After 4th iteration:
        Number = (10 * 123) + 4 = 1234   Numeral = '.'
Numeral is not IN '0' .. '9'. *Stop!*

When the loop terminates, Number contains the Real number conversion of all the characters we have read, except for the last one. Numeral still contains the last character read. At this point, there are three possible scenarios:

1. Numeral is blank, in which case the real number ended with no decimal part (RealNumber = Number and Error = False).
2. Numeral is a decimal point ('.'), in which case we need to read and convert the decimal part of the number (Error = False so far).
3. Numeral = any other character, in which case Error = True.

Scenarios 1 and 3 terminate the procedure, and need no further decomposition, but scenario 2 needs more work. To convert the characters that follow the decimal point, we need to read characters until a nonnumeric character is encountered. In each iteration of the read loop, the numeric conversion of the characters that were previously read is divided by 10, and the result is added to the numeric equivalent of Numeral.

Convert Decimal Part

Decimal ← 0.0

Read Numeral (a character) from Data

WHILE Numeral IN ['0' .. '9'] DO
    Decimal ← (Decimal / 10) + numeric equivalent of Numeral
    Read next Numeral from Data

Let's walk through this algorithm with the input '567' (the part that follows the decimal point in our original input '1234.567'):

Before loop (after "priming" read):
          Decimal = 0.0   Numeral = '5'
After 1st iteration:
          Decimal = (0 / 10)   + 5 = 5   Numeral = '6'
After 2nd iteration:
          Decimal = (5 / 10)   + 6 = 6.5   Numeral = '7'
After 3rd iteration:
          Decimal = (6.5 / 10) + 7 = 7.65   Numeral = ' '

Whoops—our digits are coming out backward! What we need to do is to start at the *last* digit of the number and move toward the decimal point. That is, we need to process the digits in the reverse order from the order in which they were read.

A stack is a great structure for reversing data, since the last element put into the stack will be the first one out (LIFO). Our Read loop will be modified to read until a nonnumeric character is encountered, pushing each character onto a stack. To simplify the processing, we will assume that the stack is large enough to contain all the characters in the decimal part:

Convert Decimal Part (Read and Push)

CreateStack
Read Numeral from Data

WHILE Numeral IN ['0' .. '9'] DO
   Push Numeral onto stack
   Read next Numeral from Data

Let's trace this loop with the input '567 ' (following a decimal point):

Before loop (after "priming" read):
         Stack = empty   Numeral = '5'
After 1st iteration:
         Stack = '5'   Numeral = '6'
After 2nd iteration:
         Stack = '6' '5'   Numeral = '7'
After 3rd iteration:
         Stack = '7' '6' '5'   Numeral = ' '

After we have read and pushed all the numeric characters, we will enter a second loop. In each iteration of the loop body, we pop the stack, putting the top element in Numeral, and process: The numeric conversion of the characters that were previously popped is divided by 10, and the result is added to the numeric equivalent of Numeral.

Convert Decimal Part (Pop and Calculate)

WHILE stack is not empty DO
   Pop (Stack, Numeral)
   Decimal ← (Decimal / 10) + numeric equivalent of Numeral

Given the stack contents in the example above, let's walk through the rest of the algorithm:

Before loop:
   Stack = '7' '6' '5'   Numeral = ' '   Decimal = 0.0
After 1st iteration:
   Stack = '6' '5'   Numeral = '7'   Decimal = (0 / 10) + 7 = 7
After 2nd iteration:
   Stack = '5'   Numeral = '6'   Decimal = (7 / 10) + 6 = 6.7
After 3rd iteration:
   Stack = empty   Numeral = '5'   Decimal = (6.7/10) + 5 = 5.67

Now the digits are in the correct order, but the result is off by one decimal point. In setting the output parameter, RealNumber, we correct this situation as follows:

Add Whole and Decimal Parts

RealNumber ← Number + (Decimal / 10)

To complete our example, RealNumber := 1234 + (5.67 / 10) = 1234.567.

There is one more possibility to consider. The number might be negative. To determine the sign of the result, we will check the first character; if it is ' − ', we will need to multiply the answer by −1 to get the correct sign.

In coding this procedure we will insert additional error checking to the Convert Decimal Part algorithm to set Error to True if the decimal part terminated in a non-numeric character. If this error occurs, we must destroy the stack, which may still contain elements.

The final procedure follows:

```
PROCEDURE ReadReal
  (VAR Data        : Text;
   VAR RealNumber : Real;
   VAR Error       : Boolean);

  (* Reads a real number from file Data, by reading      *)
  (* characters until blank encountered, and converting  *)
  (* characters to a real number. Error set if nonnumeric *)
  (* character is read before blank is read.             *)

VAR
  Number   : Real;        (* holds whole part of number      *)
  Decimal  : Real;        (* holds decimal part of number    *)
  SignTerm : Real;        (* determines positive or negative *)
  Numeral  : Char;        (* character form of a digit       *)
  Stack    : StackType;   (* stack of characters             *)

  (******************** Nested function ********************)
  FUNCTION Digit
    (Numeral : Char) : Integer;

  BEGIN (* Digit *)
    Digit := ORD(Numeral) - ORD('1') + 1
  END;  (* Digit *)
  (*********************************************************)

BEGIN (* ReadReal *)

  (* Initialize for processing. *)
  Error   := False;
  Number  := 0.0;
  Decimal := 0.0;

  (* Get first character. *)
  Read (Data, Numeral);

  (* Determine if number is positive or negative. *)
  IF Numeral <> '-'
    THEN SignTerm := 1.0
    ELSE (* it is a negative number *)
      BEGIN
        SignTerm := -1.0;
        Read (Data, Numeral)
      END; (* it is a negative number *)

  (* Calculate whole part of real operand. *)
  WHILE Numeral IN ['0' .. '9'] DO
    BEGIN
      Number := (10 * Number) + Digit (Numeral);
      Read (Data, Numeral)
    END; (* WHILE *)
```

```
(* If Numeral is blank then return Number, otherwise check *)
(* for decimal point or nonnumeric character (error).      *)
IF Numeral = ' '
  THEN (* there is no decimal part *)
    RealNumber := Number * SignTerm

  ELSE (* Check for decimal part. *)
    IF Numeral = '.'
      THEN   (* there is a decimal part *)
        BEGIN

          CreateStack (Stack);
          Read (Data, Numeral);

            (* Put all numeric characters on stack. *)
            WHILE Numeral IN ['0' .. '9'] DO
              BEGIN
                Push (Stack, Numeral);
                Read (Data, Numeral)
              END; (* WHILE Numeral IN ['0' .. '9'] *)

          IF Numeral = ' '  (* number ended normally *)
            THEN
              BEGIN (* Convert characters to decimal. *)
                (* Pop stack and perform divisions. *)
                WHILE NOT EmptyStack (Stack) DO
                  BEGIN
                    Pop (Stack, Numeral);
                    Decimal := (Decimal / 10) + Digit(Numeral)
                  END; (* WHILE NOT EmptyStack *)

                (* Set final answer. *)
                RealNumber := (Number + (Decimal / 10))
                  * SignTerm

              END (* IF Numeral = ' ' *)

            ELSE  (* nonnumeric char encountered *)
              BEGIN
                Error := True;
                DestroyStack (Stack)
              END (* nonnumeric char encountered *)
        END (* calculate decimal part *)

      ELSE (* nonnumeric char encountered *)
        Error := True

END; (* ReadReal *)
```

In writing Procedure ReadReal, we have been acting as stack users. We have written an interesting stack application, without even considering how the stack will be implemented. The stack user doesn't need to know the implementation! The details of the implementation are hidden inside the Stack abstract data type.

The Implementation Level

We will now consider the implementation of our abstract stack data structure. After all, unlike Readln and Writeln procedures, Push and Pop are not magically available to the Pascal programmer. You need to write these routines in order to include them in a program.

The Implementation of a Stack as a Static Array

Because all the elements of a stack are of the same type, an array seems like a reasonable structure to contain them. We can put elements in sequential slots in the array, placing the first element pushed in the first array position, the second element pushed in the second array position, and so on. The floating "high-water" mark will be the top element in the stack.

Before we can implement our stack as an array, we need to know how to find the top element when we want to Pop and where to put the new element when we Push. Remember, although we can access any element of an array directly, we have agreed to use the accessing function "last in, first out" for a stack. So we will access the stack elements only through the top, not through the bottom or the middle. Recognizing this distinction from the start is important. Even though the implementation of the stack may be a random-access structure such as an array, the stack itself as a logical entity is not randomly accessed. We can use only its top element.

One way to keep track of the top position in the array containing stack elements is to declare another variable, Top. However, the specifications of the stack operations only show the entity "Stack" passed in and out, not two entities, "Stack" and "Top." We can bundle the array and the top indicator into a single entity, however, by using a Pascal record.

In order to declare the array variable that will contain the stack, we must decide on its maximum size. Let's plan to use a maximum of 100 character elements. We therefore declare

```
CONST
  MaxStack = 100;

TYPE
  StackType  = RECORD
    Elements : ARRAY [1 .. MaxStack] OF Char;
    Top      : 0 .. MaxStack
  END; (* StackType *)

VAR
  Stack : StackType;
```

This data structure is pictured in Figure 4-3. Note that Top can range from 0 through MaxStack, since the stack can be empty. Top is the index of the top element in the stack, not the index of the next free slot in the array.

Figure 4-3
The Array Imple-
mentation of a
Stack

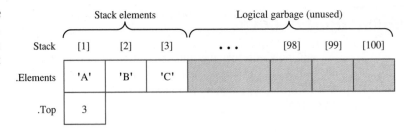

Figure 4-4
An Empty Stack

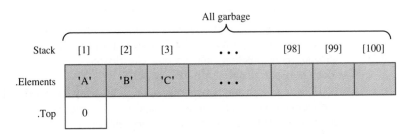

Stack Operations with the Array Implementation

Now we can begin to write functions and procedures to implement the stack operations. Let's first consider how to create an empty stack. It isn't necessary to blank out the whole array; instead, simply set the top indicator to 0, as pictured in Figure 4-4.

It doesn't matter how much garbage is in the array. If the stack's top indicator says that the stack is empty, none of the array slots can be accessed.

The resulting Procedure CreateStack is short and simple.

```
PROCEDURE CreateStack
  (VAR Stack : StackType);

  (* Initializes Stack to empty state. *)

BEGIN (* CreateStack *)
  Stack.Top := 0
END;  (* CreateStack *)
```

In this implementation of a stack, the DestroyStack operation is actually equivalent to Procedure CreateStack. We merely need to set the top indicator to 0 to "destroy" all the values in the stack. Even though they still exist in the array, they no longer exist in the stack.

```
PROCEDURE DestroyStack
  (VAR Stack : StackType);

  (* Destroys all elements in stack, leaving Stack empty. *)

BEGIN (* DestroyStack *)
  Stack.Top := 0
END;  (* DestroyStack *)
```

From this discussion it is obvious that Function EmptyStack will also be very easy to write. Since we set a stack to its empty state by assigning 0 to its top indicator, we can test for EmptyStack by checking to see whether the top indicator is 0.

```
FUNCTION EmptyStack
   (Stack : StackType) : Boolean;

   (* Returns True if Stack is empty; returns False otherwise. *)
BEGIN (* EmptyStack. *)
   EmptyStack := (Stack.Top = 0)
END; (* EmptyStack *)
```

Recall that a stack as an abstract data structure cannot be full; however, a particular implementation may make a test for a full stack necessary. The array implementation of a stack requires the programmer to choose an upper limit for the size of the stack in order to declare the array. Therefore, we must add an extra operation to the stack ADT to check for a full stack. To make this test, we compare the top indicator to the constant MaxStack.

```
FUNCTION FullStack
   (Stack : StackType) : Boolean;

   (* Returns True if Stack is full; returns False otherwise. *)
BEGIN (* FullStack *)
   FullStack := (Stack.Top = MaxStack)
END; (* FullStack *)
```

To add, or Push, an element onto the top of the stack is a two-step task:

Push

Increment the top indicator
Stack array [top indicator] ← new element

Using the declarations above, we can code this operation as follows:

```
PROCEDURE Push
   (VAR Stack  : StackType;
   NewElement : Char);

   (* Adds NewElement to the top of Stack. Assumes that the *)
   (* stack is not full.                                    *)
BEGIN (* Push *)
   Stack.Top := Stack.Top + 1;
   Stack.Elements[Stack.Top] := NewElement
END; (* Push *)
```

Let's take a look at the effect of a Push operation on the stack in Figure 4-5(a). We want to Push (Stack, 'L'). To do so we need to increment the top indicator from 3 to

Figure 4-5
The Effect of a Push
Operation

(a)

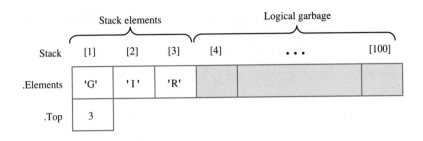

(b)

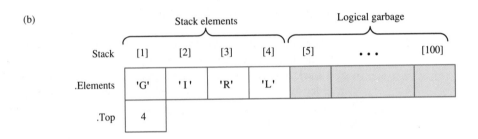

4, and then put our new element, 'L', into the fourth element place. The result is shown in Figure 4-5(b).

Before we call this Push operation in a program, we must make sure that the stack is not already full.

```
IF NOT FullStack (Stack)
  THEN Push (Stack, 'L')
```

If the stack is already full when we try to Push, the resulting condition is called **stack overflow**. Error checking for overflow conditions may be handled in a number of different ways. We could check for overflow inside our Push procedure, instead of making the calling program do the test. In that case we would need to tell the caller whether or not the Push was possible, which we could do by adding a Boolean variable OverFlow to the parameter list. The revised algorithm would be

Push (Checks for overflow)

IF stack is full
    THEN OverFlow ← True
    ELSE (OK to push)
        OverFlow ← False
        Increment top indicator
        Stack array [top indicator] ← new element

Which version of Push we decide to use in a program will *depend on the specifi-cations*. Our Stack ADT specification uses the first version because the precondition for the Push operation states that the stack is not full. If the utility procedures and their calling programs are being written by different programmers, as often happens, it is important to establish whose responsibility it is to check for overflow, for this decision will determine the number of parameters in the interface. (Try writing the second version of Push yourself.)

Stack Overflow   The condition resulting from trying to push an element onto a full stack.

To remove, or Pop, an element from the stack, we do virtually the reverse of the Push operation. The algorithm is

Pop

PoppedElement ← Stack array [top indicator]
Decrement top indicator

The procedure for the Pop operation is as follows:

```
PROCEDURE Pop
  (VAR Stack         : StackType;
   VAR PoppedElement : Char);

  (* Removes the top element from Stack and returns its *)
  (* value in PoppedElement. Assumes that the stack is  *)
  (* not empty.                                         *)
BEGIN (* Pop *)
  PoppedElement := Stack.Elements[Stack.Top];
  Stack.Top := Stack.Top - 1
END; (* Pop *)
```

Figure 4-6 shows how the Pop operation would affect a stack. In Figure 4-6(a), the value in Stack.Top tells us that the top element is stored in Stack.Elements[3]. We

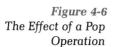

Figure 4-6
The Effect of a Pop
Operation

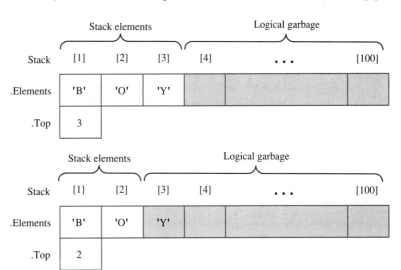

assign the value of the top element, 'Y', to PoppedElement. Then the top indicator is decremented, giving us the stack shown in Figure 4-6(b). Note that after popping, 'Y' is still stored in the third element slot in the array, but we cannot access it through the stack. The 'Y' in the third array position is now logical garbage, since the stack contains only two elements.

To execute the Pop operation illustrated above, we first test for an empty stack and then call our Pop procedure:

```
IF NOT EmptyStack (Stack)
 THEN Pop (Stack, TopElement)
```

If the stack is empty when we try to pop it, the resulting condition is called **stack underflow**. Just as we can test for overflow within the Push operation, we could test for underflow inside the Pop procedure. The algorithm for Pop would have to be modified slightly to return a Boolean value UnderFlow in addition to the popped element.

Pop (Checks for underflow)

IF stack is empty
   THEN UnderFlow ← True
   ELSE (OK to pop)
      UnderFlow ← False
      PoppedElement ← Stack array [top indicator]
      Decrement top indicator

Note that this change would affect the specification for Pop in the stack package, as well as the parameter list of the procedure. Try writing this procedure yourself.

Stack Underflow   The condition resulting from trying to pop an empty stack.

A More General Implementation

Now we have a complete implementation of the Stack of Characters ADT. But what if we want to create a stack of integers? The algorithms of the stack operations themselves are independent of the element type, but there will have to be some coding changes. Obviously we would have to change the Elements field in the record declaration to

```
Elements : ARRAY [1 .. MaxStack] OF Integer;
```

We will also have to change the headings of all the stack operations that specify the element type in the parameter list. For instance,

```
PROCEDURE Push
  (VAR Stack  :  StackType;
   NewElement :  Char);
```

would be changed to

```
PROCEDURE Push
  (VAR Stack  : StackType;
   NewElement : Integer);
```

Pop will have to be modified in the same way.

We can get around having to make all these trivial editing changes throughout our program by adding a type StackElementType to our declarations.

```
TYPE
  StackElementType = Char;  (* or whatever the elements are *)

  StackType = RECORD
    Elements : ARRAY [1 .. MaxStack] OF StackElementType;
    Top      : 0 .. MaxStack
  END; (* StackType *)
```

All of the procedure headings will now use the type StackElementType for the stack elements; for example,

```
PROCEDURE Push
  (VAR Stack  : StackType;
   NewElement : StackElementType);
```

Now a change in element type will result in changes only to the declarations of the program and recompilation. This feature makes the program easier to modify.

The code for the array implementation of the Stack ADT can be found in file STACK1.PAS on the program disk.

The Implementation of a Stack as a Linked Structure

The implementation of a stack in an array is very simple, but it has a serious drawback: The size of a stack must be determined at compile time. When we declare a variable of StackType, memory is allocated to contain the maximum number of stack elements. If we use fewer elements at run time, space is wasted; if we need to push more elements than the array can hold, we cannot. It would be nice if we could just get space for stack elements as we need it.

Chapter 3 introduced the concept of *dynamic storage allocation*, the ability to allocate memory for the program's data at run time. Let's see how we might use this concept to build a stack.

Implementing Procedure Push

We can modify Procedure Push to allocate space for each new element dynamically.

Push

Allocate space for new element
Put new element in the allocated space
Put new element in the stack

Implementing the first part of this operation is simple. As we discussed in Chapter 3, we use the built-in Pascal procedure New to allocate space dynamically:

```
(* Allocate space for new element. *)
New (ElementPtr)
```

This procedure call allocates a piece of memory big enough to hold a stack element and puts its address in the variable ElementPtr. Let's say for the moment that ElementPtr has been declared to be a pointer to StackElementType (the type of data contained in the stack). Now we can put NewElement into the space that was allocated. The situation at this point is pictured in Figure 4-7, with a NewElement of 'E'.

The third part of the Push operation is to "put the new element in the stack." How do we do this? Let's think for a minute what happens after we have pushed a few characters. Space is allocated for each new element, and the characters are put into the space. Figure 4-8 shows the results of calling Push to add the characters 'D', 'A', 'L', and 'E' to the stack.

Whoops—we see our data in the dynamically allocated space, but it's not a stack! There's no order. Even worse, since we haven't returned the pointers to the dynamically allocated space from Procedure Push, we have no way to access any of the elements

Figure 4-7
Putting New Element in the Allocated Space

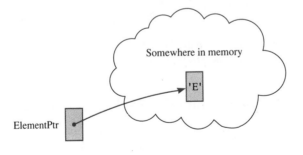

Figure 4-8
After Four Calls to Push

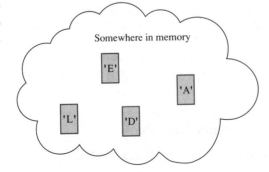

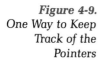
Figure 4-9.
One Way to Keep
Track of the
Pointers

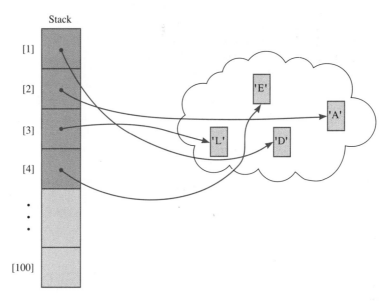

Figure 4-10
Chaining the Stack
Elements Together

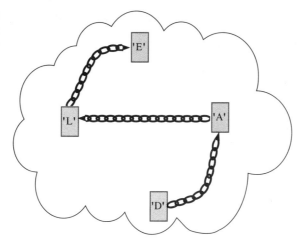

any more. Clearly, the third part of the Push operation will need to do something to fix this situation. Where can we store the pointers to our data?

One possibility that comes to mind is to declare Stack as an array of pointers, and to put the pointer to each new element in this array, as shown in Figure 4-9. This solution would keep track of the pointers to all the elements in the correct order, but it wouldn't solve our original problem: We still need to declare an array of a particular size. Where else could we put the pointers?

It would be nice if we could just chain all the elements together somehow, as shown in Figure 4-10. We'll call each element in this "linked" stack a **node**.

This solution looks promising. Let's see how we might use this idea to implement the stack. First we push the character 'D'. Push calls Procedure New to allocate space for the new node, and puts 'D' into the space. There's now one element in the stack. We don't want to lose the pointer to this element, so we pass it back to the calling program in the Stack parameter. (We will declare StackType to be a pointer to a stack node.) The first Push operation is illustrated in Figure 4-11.

Now we call Push to add the character 'A' to the stack. Push calls New to allocate space for the new element and puts 'A' into the space. Next we want to chain 'A' to 'D', the old stack element. We can establish a link between the two elements by letting one element "point" to the next; that is, we can store the address of the next element in each stack element. To do this, we need to modify the stack node type. Let's make each node in the stack contain two parts: Info and Next. The *Info* field will contain the stack user's data—a character, for instance. The *Next* field will contain the address of the next element in the stack. A single node is pictured in Figure 4-12.

Since we're not ready to start coding yet, let's create a special design terminology to refer to the parts of a node in our algorithms. Let's assume that Ptr points to one of the nodes in a stack, as illustrated in Figure 4-13.

Node(Ptr) refers to the *whole node* pointed to by Ptr.
Info(Ptr)   refers to the *data field* of the node pointed to by Ptr.
Next(Ptr)   refers to the *pointer field* of the node pointed to by Ptr.

As you can see in the figure, the Next field of each node points to the next node in the stack. What about the Next field of the last node? We cannot leave it unassigned. The

Figure 4-11
Pushing the First
Element

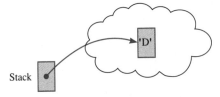

Figure 4-12
A Single Node

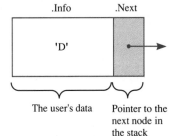

Figure 4-13
Node Terminology

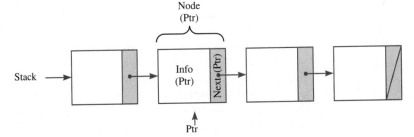

Figure 4-14
The Second Push
Operation

(a)

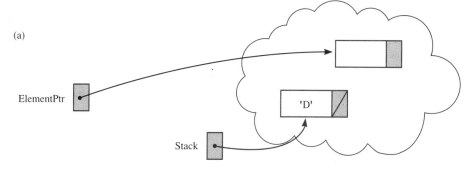

(b)

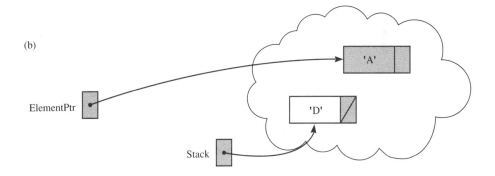

Next field of the last node in the list must contain some special value that is not a valid address. In Chapter 3, we mentioned that there is a special pointer value, NIL, that says, "This pointer doesn't point to anything." We can put NIL in the Next field of the last node, to mark the end of the stack. Graphically, we use a slash across the Next field to represent a NIL pointer.

Now let's return to our Push algorithm. We have allocated a node to contain the new element 'A' using Procedure New [Figure 4-14(a)].

New (ElementPtr)

Then the new value, 'A', is put into the node [Figure 4-14(b)]:

Info(ElementPtr) ← NewElement

Now we are ready to link the new node to the stack. Where should we link it? Should the new node come before or after the node containing 'D'? To answer that question, let's look at how the stack will be accessed: We add elements to the top (push) and remove elements from the top (pop). Last in, first out. Therefore, it would be a good idea to have Stack point to the top element, so that we can access it directly.

Linking the new node to the (previous) top node in the stack is a two-step process:

Figure 4-14
(Continued)

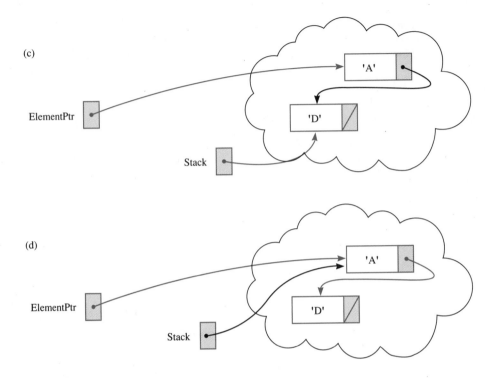

(c)

(d)

Make Next(ElementPtr) point to stack's top node [Figure 4-14(c)]
Make Stack point to the new node [Figure 4-14(d)]

Note that the order of these tasks is critical. If we changed the Stack pointer before making Next(ElementPtr) point to the top of the stack, we would have lost access to the stack nodes! (See Figure 4-15.) This situation is generally true when we are dealing with a linked structure: You must be very careful to change the pointers in the correct order, so that you do not lose access to any of the data.

Before we code the Push algorithm, let's see how the Stack data will be declared. Remember that from the stack user's point of view, nothing will have changed; the heading for Procedure Push will be the same as it was for the static array implementation.

```
PROCEDURE Push
  (VAR Stack   : StackType;
   NewElement : StackElementType);
```

StackElementType will still be declared as the type of data that the user wants to put in the stack. StackType, however, will need new declarations. It is no longer an array; it is a pointer to a single node, the top of the stack. This node has two parts, Info and Next, which suggests a Pascal record implementation. Here are the declarations we will use:

Figure 4-15 Be Careful When You Change Pointers

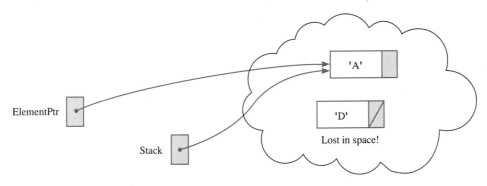

```
TYPE
   StackElementType = Char;                 (* stack user's data type *)

   NodePtrType      = ^StackNodeType;          (* a pointer type *)

   StackNodeType    = RECORD
      Info          : StackElementType;      (* the user's data *)
      Next          : NodePtrType       (* pointer to next node *)
   END; (* StackNodeType *)
```

As mentioned before, StackElementType stays the same. StackNodeType is a record containing the user's data (StackElementType), as well as a pointer to the next node (NodePtrType). Using good Pascal form, NodePtrType has been declared prior to its use in the record declaration:

```
NodePtrType = ^StackNodeType;
```

Remember from Chapter 3 that the ^ character, followed by a type name, is used to denote a pointer to data of that type. That is, a variable of ^StackNodeType can only point to a data of StackNodeType. But StackNodeType is declared *after* the declaration of NodePtrType, which uses it! This situation is an exception to the general rule in Pascal that types must be defined before they can be used. You can see why this situation is allowed: The Next field is declared to be of type NodePtrType. One or the other of the types would have had to be used before its declaration.

Now what is StackType? It is a pointer to the top node in the stack. We already have a type declared to describe a pointer to a stack node, NodePtrType. So we could just declare Stack to be a variable of this type. But we have said that we don't want to change the headings of all the stack procedures; we want to leave the type names alone. We will just define StackType to be equivalent to NodePtrType:

```
TYPE
   StackType = NodePtrType;   (* pointer to stack top *)

VAR
   Stack : StackType;
```

Keep in mind that StackType and NodePtrType are equivalent. That means that variables of StackType (like Stack) can be assigned the value of NodePtrType variables.

Now let's code the Push algorithm. We will use a local variable, ElementPtr, of type NodePtrType. The first two tasks are simple:

```
(* Allocate space for new element. *)
New (ElementPtr);

(* Put new element in the allocated space. *)
ElementPtr^.Info := NewElement;
```

ElementPtr is a pointer to a node. ElementPtr^ is the way that we reference this node; it is a record with two fields. Since ElementPtr^ describes a record, we can access its fields in the usual way—by adding a period, followed by the desired field name. So ElementPtr^.Info refers to the Info field of the record in the dynamically allocated storage pointed to by ElementPtr. (See Figure 4-16.) This field is the same type as the user's data, so we can assign NewElement to it. So far, so good.

Now for the linking task:

Make Next(ElementPtr) point to stack's top node   [Figure 4-14(c)]
Make Stack point to the new node   [Figure 4-14(d)]

Next(ElementPtr) is the Next field of the record in the dynamically allocated storage pointed to by ElementPtr. We can access it just as we accessed the Info field: ElementPtr^.Next. What can we put in this field? It is declared as a pointer, so we can assign it another value of the same pointer type. We want to make this field point to the stack's top node. Since we have a pointer to the stack's top node (Stack), this assignment is simple.

```
ElementPtr^.Next := Stack;
```

Finally, we need to complete the linking by making Stack point to the new node. Stack is declared as a pointer, so we can assign another value of the same pointer type to it.

Figure 4-16
The Fields of the
Node

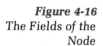

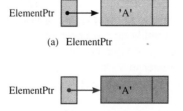

(a) ElementPtr

(b) ElementPtr ↑

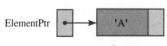

(c) ElementPtr ↑ .Info

Since we have a pointer to the new node (the local variable ElementPtr), this assignment can be made:

```
Stack := ElementPtr;
```

Here is the complete Procedure Push:

```
PROCEDURE Push
  (VAR Stack   : StackType;
   NewElement : StackElementType);

  (* Adds NewElement to the top of Stack. *)
VAR
  ElementPtr  : NodePtrType;
BEGIN (* Push *)

  (* Allocate space for new element. *)
  New (ElementPtr);

  (* Put new element in the allocated space. *)
  ElementPtr^.Info := NewElement;

  (* Link the new node to the top of the stack. *)
  ElementPtr^.Next := Stack;
  Stack := ElementPtr

END;   (* Push *)
```

You have seen how this code will work on a stack that contains at least one value. What happens if this procedure is called when the stack is empty? Space is allocated for the new element and the element is put into the space [Figure 4-17(a)]. Will the procedure correctly link the new node to the top of an empty stack? Let's see. The Next field of the new node is assigned the value of Stack. What is this value when the stack is empty? It is NIL, which is exactly what we want to put in the Next field of the last node of a linked stack [Figure 4-17(b)]. Then Stack is reset to point to the new node [Figure 4-17(c)]. So this procedure works for an empty stack, as well as a stack that contains at least one element.

The coded version of Procedure Push uses pointer-variable terminology where our algorithm used our special node terminology. The following table summarizes the relationship between the design and code terminology.

Comparing Node Design Notation to Pascal Code

Design Notation	Pascal Code
Node(Ptr)	Ptr ↑
Info(Ptr)	Ptr ↑ .Info
Next(Ptr)	Ptr ↑ .Next
Ptr ← Next(Ptr)	Ptr := Ptr ↑ .Next
Info(Ptr) ← Value	Ptr ↑ .Info := Value

Figure 4-17
Pushing into an
Empty Stack

(a)

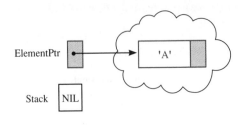

(b)

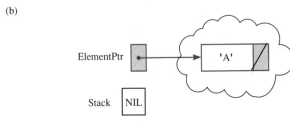

(c)

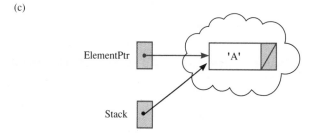

Implementing Procedure Pop

Now let's look at the Pop operation. The algorithm for Pop is

Pop

PoppedElement ← info in top node
Unlink the top node from the stack
Dispose of the old top node

Let's try out this algorithm on the stack in Figure 4-18. We first put the value from the top node into PoppedElement. How do we "unlink" the top node from the stack? If we reset Stack to point to the node *following* the top node, the resulting stack should be correct. Now we can free the space occupied by the old top node by calling the Pascal Dispose procedure.

Whoops! The problem with this algorithm is that it leaves the old top node inaccessible—we no longer have a pointer to this node. Without a pointer, we cannot call Dispose to free the space. When we code the procedure, let's add a local pointer variable to save the address of this space before we reset Stack.

```
PROCEDURE Pop
    (VAR Stack         : StackType;
     VAR PoppedElement : StackElementType);
```

Figure 4-18
Popping the Top
Element

(a)

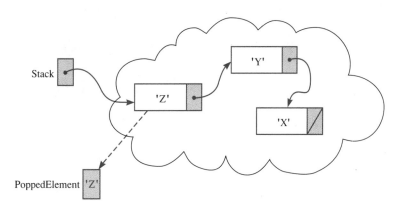

(b)

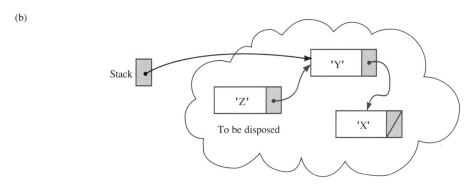

```
(* Removes the top element from Stack and returns its *)
(* value in PoppedElement. Assumes that the stack is  *)
(* not empty.                                         *)

VAR
  TempPtr : NodePtrType;

BEGIN (* Pop *)

  (* PoppedElement := info in top node. *)
  PoppedElement := Stack^.Info;

  (* Unlink the top node from the stack. *)
  TempPtr := Stack;
  Stack := Stack^.Next;

  (* Free the space for the old top node. *)
  Dispose (TempPtr)

END; (* Pop *)
```

Let's walk through this procedure, using the stack in Figure 4-19. PoppedElement is set to the value in the first (top) node, the Info field of the record Stack^ [Figure 4-19(a)]. We save a pointer to the first node, so that we can access it later for the call to

Figure 4-19 Popping the Stack

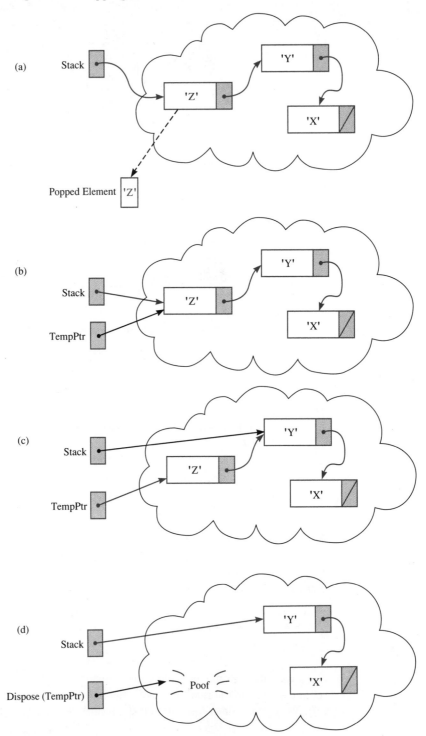

Dispose [Figure 4-19(b)]. Then the external pointer to the stack is advanced to jump over the first node, making the second node the new top element. How do we know the address of the second node? We get it from the Next field of the first node (Stack^.Next). This value is assigned to Stack to complete the unlinking task [Figure 4-19(c)]. Finally, we free the space occupied by the old top node by calling Dispose, giving it the address we saved in TempPtr [Figure 4-19(d)].

Does this procedure work if there is only one node in the stack when Pop is called? Let's see. PoppedElement is assigned the last value in the stack, then we unlink the first/last node from the stack. We save a pointer to the node, as before, and then try to assign Stack^.Next to Stack (Figure 4-20). What is the value of Stack^.Next? Since this is the last node in the list, its Next field should contain NIL. This value is assigned to Stack, which is exactly what we want, since a NIL Stack pointer means that the stack is empty. So the procedure works for a stack of one element.

What happens if the stack is empty when Pop is called? If Stack is NIL, then the assignment statement

```
Stack := Stack^.Next
```

will result in a run-time error. But this is not a problem. The precondition in the specification of this procedure explicitly states that Stack is *not* empty. So this procedure

Figure 4-20
Popping the Last
Element in the
Stack

(a)

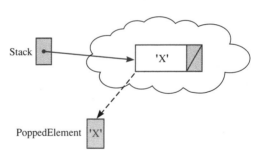

(b)

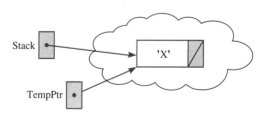

(c)

is not required or expected to protect the caller from this situation. The caller is responsible for checking for an empty stack before the call to Pop.

Implementing the Other Stack Operations

In the explanation of pushing the first element, it was noted that an empty stack is a NIL pointer. This fact has implications for the other stack operations. To create an empty stack, we merely need to set the Stack parameter to NIL:

```
PROCEDURE CreateStack
  (VAR Stack : StackType);

  (* Initializes Stack to empty state. *)

BEGIN (* CreateStack *)
  Stack := NIL
END;  (* CreateStack *)
```

That was simple. Function EmptyStack is correspondingly simple: If we create an empty stack by setting its external pointer to NIL, we can detect an empty stack by looking for a NIL pointer:

```
FUNCTION EmptyStack
  (Stack : StackType) : Boolean;

  (* Returns True if Stack is empty; returns False otherwise. *)

BEGIN (* EmptyStack *)
  EmptyStack := (Stack = NIL)
END; (* EmptyStack *)
```

What about Procedure FullStack? There is no way to detect a full stack; we can continue to Push until the system runs out of memory. Using dynamically allocated space rather than a static (declared variable) array, we no longer have a MaxStack constant to limit stack size. So there really isn't any need to have a full stack function. Of course, if this operation is defined for the Stack ADT, we must supply a function; the caller doesn't need to know how the stack is implemented. So we can just code a stub for FullStack, a dummy function that just sets the return value:

```
FUNCTION FullStack
  (Stack : StackType) : Boolean;

  (* Stub for FullStack operation. *)

BEGIN (* FullStack *)
  FullStack := False
END; (* FullStack *)
```

(Refer back to Chapter 3 for a fuller description of Procedure New. If you are programming in a nonstandard version of Pascal that allows you to check how much free memory you have, like Turbo Pascal, you can write a functional version of FullStack. We leave this as an exercise.)

Finally, we come to Procedure DestroyStack. In the array implementation, this procedure was virtually identical to Procedure CreateStack. We could make the two procedures the same here also—just set Stack to NIL to leave the stack empty—but that leaves all the space occupied by the nodes tied up. It's better to free the node space.

Our DestroyStack operation will loop through all the elements in the stack, removing them one by one, and disposing of the space.

DestroyStack

WHILE more nodes in the stack
    Unlink top node
    Dispose of the node

This process is very much like putting Procedure Pop inside a loop. In fact, we could just write the loop as

```
WHILE NOT EmptyStack (Stack) DO
  Pop (Stack, DummyValue)
```

But for the sake of efficiency (avoiding all the procedure and function calls), not to mention getting some extra practice using pointers, we will write the procedure from scratch.

How do we know when there are "more nodes in the stack"? As long as the Stack pointer is not NIL, the Stack is not empty. So the resulting condition on the loop is WHILE Stack <> NIL. Since the inside of the loop is virtually the same as the unlinking code in Pop, let's just "borrow" it. Here is the resulting procedure.

```
PROCEDURE DestroyStack
  (VAR Stack : StackType);

  (* Destroys all elements in stack, leaving Stack empty. *)

VAR
  TempPtr : NodePtrType;

BEGIN (* DestroyStack *)

  (* Pop all the elements in the stack. *)
  WHILE Stack <> NIL DO
    BEGIN

      (* Unlink the top node from the stack. *)
      TempPtr := Stack;
      Stack := Stack^.Next;

      (* Free the space for the old top node. *)
      Dispose (TempPtr)

    END (* WHILE *)

END;  (* DestroyStack *)
```

The code for the linked implementation of the Stack ADT can be found in file STACK2.PAS on the program disk.

Comparing the Stack Implementations

We have now looked at two very different implementations of the Stack ADT. We can compare these implementations in terms of the length of source code required by running the declarations, procedures, and functions through Program ListAndCount. The results are shown in the following table.

Comparison of Executable Source Lines of Code

	Array Implementation	*Linked Implementation*
Declarations	9	10
CreateStack	5	5
DestroyStack	5	12
FullStack	5	5
EmptyStack	5	5
Push	7	11
Pop	7	11
Total	43	59

As you can see from the table, the array implementation code is shorter than the linked implementation by more than 25 percent. Its logic also seems a little more intuitively obvious than the pointer manipulations, but that is a very subjective measurement.

Now let's compare the storage requirements. An array variable of the maximum stack size will take the same amount of memory, no matter how many array slots are actually used; we need to reserve space for the maximum possible. The linked implementation using dynamically allocated storage space only requires space for the number of elements actually on the stack at run time. Note, however, that the elements are larger, since we must store the link (the Next field) as well as the user's data.

We can also compare the relative "efficiency" of the two implementations in terms of Big-O notation. In both implementations, the CreateStack, FullStack, and EmptyStack operations are clearly $O(1)$. They always take a constant amount of work. What about Push and Pop? Does the number of elements in the stack affect the amount of work done by these operations? No, it does not. In both implementations, we directly access the top of the stack, so these operations also take a constant amount of work. They too are $O(1)$. Only the DestroyStack operation differs from one implementation to the other. The array implementation simply sets the Top field to 0, so it is clearly an $O(1)$ operation. The pointer implementation must process every node in the stack, in order to free the node space. This operation, therefore, is $O(N)$, where N is the number of nodes in the stack. Overall the two stack implementations are roughly equivalent in terms of the amount of work they do, only differing in one of the six operations. Note that if the difference had been in the Push or Pop operation, rather than the less frequently called DestroyStack, it would be more significant. The next table summarizes the Big-O comparison of the stack operations.

Big-O Comparison of Stack Operations

	Array Implementation	*Pointer Implementation*
CreateStack	O(1)	O(1)
DestroyStack	**O(1)**	**O(N)**
FullStack	O(1)	O(1)
EmptyStack	O(1)	O(1)
Push	O(1)	O(1)
Pop	O(1)	O(1)

So which is better? The answer, as usual, is: It depends on the situation. The linked implementation certainly gives more flexibility, and in applications where the number of stack elements can vary greatly, it wastes less space when the stack is small. In situations where the stack size is totally unpredictable, the linked implementation is preferable, since size is largely irrelevant. Why then would we ever want to use the array implementation? Because it is short, simple, and efficient. When MaxStack is small, and we can be sure that we will not need to exceed the declared stack size, the array implementation is a good choice. Also, if you are programming in a language that does not support dynamic storage allocation, an array implementation may be the only good choice.

Debugging Hints for Pascal Pointers

Because the dynamic allocation mechanism presents us with some new syntax, we want to make some suggestions for debugging programs that use Pascal pointers. Let's take a look at several steps you can take to avoid problems with pointer variables.

Avoiding Compile-Time Problems

- Remember that a Pascal pointer variable is a *typed* pointer. That is, it points to data of only one type. In order for pointers to be compared or assigned to each other, they must be of the same (or equivalent) type.
- Don't confuse the pointer with the variable that it points to. If Stack and Ptr are both declared to be of type NodePtrType (a pointer to a node containing fields called Info and Next),

```
Stack := Ptr^.Next;
```

is a legal assignment, because Stack and the Next field of Node(Ptr) are both type NodePtrType. But

```
Stack := Ptr^;
```

is illegal, because Stack is a pointer and Ptr^ is a record.

■ Be careful when using complex pointer expressions. Some compilers limit the complexity of pointer expressions, requiring the programmer to rewrite lengthy expressions using an intermediate variable. For instance, if the compiler will not accept the statement

```
DataVal := Ptr^.Next^.Next^.Next^.Info;
```

the pointer expression can be broken up as follows:

```
TempPtr := Ptr^.Next^.Next;
DataVal := TempPtr^.Next^.Info;
```

In general, if a pointer expression is too complicated for the compiler, it is also too complicated to be easily understood by the programmer.

Avoiding Run-Time Problems

■ The fact that pointer variables contain memory addresses makes programs using pointer variables difficult to debug. For one thing, it is hard to tell whether pointer variables contain valid values. Standard Pascal doesn't allow us to print out the values of pointer variables; even if it did, what would we gain by printing out the value of a pointer? Even if it were syntactically correct (which it isn't) the output from the statement

```
Writeln ('Pointer address = ', Ptr);
```

wouldn't generally tell us much about our data or about its structure. We can, however, print out the values *referenced* by the pointer, by using a debugging Writeln statement such as

```
Writeln ('Data = ', Ptr^.Info);
```

assuming, of course, that Ptr is not a NIL pointer.

■ Be sure that a pointer is not NIL before accessing the data it references. If the pointer Ptr is either NIL or undefined (after a call to Dispose, for instance), accessing Ptr^ will cause a run-time error.

■ Be especially careful with compound expressions in a WHILE loop. The definition of standard Pascal allows the compiler to evaluate both sides of an expression using AND or OR, regardless of the outcome of evaluating the first side. Thus the statement

```
WHILE (Ptr <> NIL) AND (Ptr^.Info <> MyData) DO
```

may cause an error if Ptr is NIL. The expression evaluation does not necessarily stop if the first part fails. (See Chapter 2 for a discussion of short-circuited Boolean evaluation.)

- Remember that Dispose(Ptr) leaves Ptr undefined; trying to use the data referenced by Ptr after a call to Dispose will cause a run-time error.
- Return nodes to available space when you are finished with them. When deleting nodes from a linked structure, use Dispose to return those nodes to available space for later use. Failure to use Dispose may cause your program to run out of memory. If you think you are using Dispose properly and your program still runs out of memory space, check to be sure that it does not have an inadvertent recursive call or an infinite loop. Another possibility is that your implementation of Pascal has a version of Dispose that doesn't return the node to free space, but only sets the pointer to NIL. (Such a procedure is not very useful, but then some implementations of Pascal are not as good as others.) If Dispose does not return the node to free space, the program can run out of memory after many deletions, even if the linked structure is not currently large. Because of its lack of dependability and portability, some programmers don't like to use the Pascal Dispose procedure. They prefer to manage their own free space by saving deleted nodes in a FreeNode (linked) list.
- Keep track of pointers. Changing pointer values prematurely may cause problems when you try to get back to the referenced data. When you are manipulating pointers to add or delete nodes, it is important to assign and reassign the pointers in the correct order so that you don't lose access to the data. (Remember what happened when we changed the pointers incorrectly in Figure 4-15!)

Stack Applications

The example of Procedure ReadReal at the beginning of this chapter hints at the types of applications that use a stack. A stack is the appropriate data structure when information must be saved and then later retrieved in reverse order. A situation requiring you to backtrack to some earlier position may be a good one in which to use a stack. For instance, in trying to find the way out of a maze, you may end up against a wall and need to backtrack to another exit. If you use a stack to save the alternative paths as you pass them, you can retrace your route to an earlier position.

Have you ever wondered how a program determines where to continue executing when it gets to the end of a procedure or function? Many systems use a stack to keep track of the return addresses, parameter values (or their addresses), and other information used by subprograms. For example, when Procedure A is called, its calling information is pushed onto a "run-time stack." Then when Procedure B is called from A, B's calling information is pushed onto the top of the stack. B then calls Procedure C, and C's calling information is pushed onto the stack. When C finishes executing, the stack is popped to retrieve the information needed to return to Procedure B. Then

B finishes executing, and its calling information is popped from the stack. Finally Procedure A completes, and the stack is popped again to get back to the main program. Because it can grow and shrink throughout execution, according to the level of sub-program nesting, a stack is a good structure for storing data on the order of procedure calls within a program. We will return to this topic in Chapter 8 when we discuss recursion.

Stacks are also used extensively in the evaluation of arithmetic expressions. We will consider this use of stacks further in the application program at the end of this chapter.

Summary

We have defined a stack at the logical level as an abstract data type, and we have discussed two implementations of a stack. In the first implementation, an array is used to store the stack elements. In the second implementation, the stack elements are stored in dynamically allocated memory, and linked together using Pascal pointers. By iso-lating the procedures and functions that operate on the actual representation of the stack, we encapsulate the data structure. No matter which implementation we select, we keep the use of the data structure limited to the interfaces recorded in the Stack ADT Specification.

Though our logical picture of a stack is a linear collection of data elements with the newest element (the top) at one end and the oldest element at the other end, the physical representation of the Stack ADT does not have to recreate our mental image. The implementation of the Stack ADT must support the last in, first out (LIFO) property; how this property is supported, however, is another matter. For instance, the Push operation could "time stamp" the stack elements, and put them into an array in any order. To Pop, we would have to search the array, looking for the newest time stamp. This representation is very different from either of the stack implementations we devel-oped in this chapter, but to the user of the Stack ADT they are all functionally equiv-alent. The implementation is transparent to the program that uses the stack because the stack is encapsulated by the operations that surround it.

Can we enforce this encapsulation? That is, can we keep the stack user from access-ing the middle element in the array that houses the stack? Unfortunately standard Pascal does not have a mechanism to enforce data encapsulation. It would be *syntactically correct* to put the following statement in the main program:

```
Stack.Elements[5] := 25;
```

The Pascal compiler does not object to such a statement, though it effectively destroys the logical meaning of the stack's data, which can only be accessed through the top indicator. For now we will have to depend on convention, an agreement that we will manipulate the data in the stack only through the package of stack utility routines. The ability to enforce such data encapsulation is a consideration in the design of new programming languages, as well as extensions to standard Pascal.

Application

Expression Evaluation

Data Structure

- Stacks
- Variant records

Software Techniques

- Approaches for expression evaluation
- Data encapsulation and information hiding
- Need for error checking

In elementary school you learned how to evaluate simple expressions that involve the basic binary operators: addition, subtraction, multiplication, and division. (These are called *binary* operators because they each operate on two operands.) It is easy to see how a child would solve the following problem:

2 + 5 = ?

As expressions become more complicated, the pencil-and-paper solution requires a little more work. A number of tasks must be performed to solve the following problem:

(((13 − 1) / 2) * (3 + 5)) = ?

First we solve for 13 − 1, divide the result by 2, and save this value. Then we evaluate 3 + 5 and save this value. Finally we multiply the first saved value by the second to get the result—48.

Designing a computer program to evaluate the expression is not so simple. Before we can write the program, we must answer the following questions:

How do we know which part of the expression to evaluate first?

Where do we save the intermediate values that contribute to the final result [such as (13 − 1) / 2]?

The first question is easy to answer if the expression to be evaluated is fully parenthesized (that is, if we do not depend on the relative precedence of the operators to tell us which part to evaluate first, but simply rely on the location of the parentheses). The innermost level of parentheses indicates which part of the expression must be evaluated first, and we work outward from there.

The second question, involving the storage of intermediate values, suggests that we must design an appropriate data structure for our solution. If we knew how many intermediate values would be produced, we could declare temporary variables to hold them (Temp1, Temp2, . . . TempN). But obviously the number of intermediate operands produced will vary from expression to expression. Luckily we know of an ideal data structure for saving dynamically changing values for later processing, the stack. Let's consider how we can use a pair of stacks to evaluate the expression

(((13 − 1) / 2) * (3 + 5))

We will use one stack to store the operators and a second to store the operands. Assuming for now that the expression is fully and correctly parenthesized, we will ignore the left parentheses (`'('`). As we pass through the expression from left to right,

Figure 4-21
At the First Right
Parenthesis

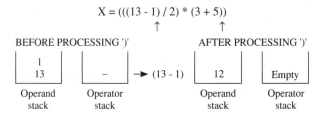

Figure 4-22
At the Second Right
Parenthesis

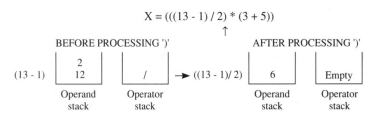

we will push each element onto the appropriate stack, until we come to a right paren-thesis (')'). The left side of Figure 4-21 shows how the two stacks will look when we come to the first right parenthesis. At this point we have reached the innermost level of parentheses (for this term, at least), and we can perform the first operation.

Where are the two operands? They should be the last and next-to-last values pushed onto the operand stack. Where is the operator? It should be the top element on the operator stack. To evaluate the first intermediate operand, we pop the top two elements from the operand stack; these become Operand2 and Operand1, respectively. Then we pop the top element from the operator stack and perform the appropriate operation, 13 − 1, producing the value 12. Note that $13 - 1 = 12$ is an intermediate step in the evaluation of the larger expression. The result of this step, 12, will be one of the operands in the next step, which calculates $(13 - 1) / 2$. Where do we put operands? That's right, on the operand stack, so we push 12 onto the operand stack (see the right side of Figure 4-21).

Now we resume pushing operators and operands onto their respective stacks until we again come to a right parenthesis. Figure 4-22 shows the processing that occurs at this point. We pop Operand2 and Operand1 from the operand stack, pop the top element from the operator stack, and perform the operation, $12/2 = 6$. The result is pushed onto the operand stack, and we resume pushing elements onto the two stacks.

Figure 4-23 shows the processing that occurs when we reach the next right paren-thesis. After popping the operator and two operands, the operation $(3 + 5)$ is per-formed, then the result (8) is pushed onto the operand stack. Note that at this point the operator stack is not empty; there is still an operation left to perform. The '*' operator was encountered before the ' + ' operator, but because of the parentheses, the multi-plication was put on hold (that is, put into the stack) until after the addition could be performed.

Finally we reach the last right parenthesis—and the end of the expression (Figure 4-24). Again we pop the operator and the two operands, perform the operation, and put the result back into the operand stack. At this point the operator stack is empty and the operand stack contains only one value, the evaluated result of the whole expression.

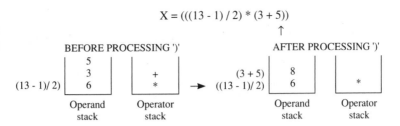

Figure 4-23
At the Third Right
Parenthesis

$X = (((13 - 1) / 2) * (3 + 5))$

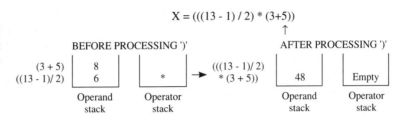

Figure 4-24
At the Fourth (and
Last) Right
Parenthesis

$X = (((13 - 1) / 2) * (3+5))$

Let's use this strategy to write a program for the simple expression calculator specified in Figure 4-25 on page 218.

We have allowed a number of assumptions about the program's input in order to concentrate on the processing of the expression evaluation using stacks. Because we will test and use this expression evaluator as an interactive tool (that is, all the input will come from the keyboard), these are not really legitimate assumptions. We will come back to this point later. For now we will allow these restrictions so that we can develop the algorithms of interest to a stack user.

Data Structures

We have already seen that we will need to use a pair of stacks to hold intermediate values of operands and operators. The specification of the Stack ADT is recorded on pages 181–182. Since we have already developed two complete implementations of the Stack ADT, we do not need to reinvent the wheel; we will use one of the implementations from the chapter.

What is the data type of the stack element? Uh-oh! We have two different types of stack elements: The operators are characters (type Char) and the operands are real numbers (type Real). Since StackElementType must be one type, we cannot use the same set of operations for both stacks. One solution is to make two sets of stack operations, one for stacks of characters and one for stacks of real numbers. We must rename the operations so that the program will be able to invoke the correct operation. For instance, the create operations might be called CreateCharStack and CreateRealStack.

However, it is a shame to have to make two nearly identical sets of stack operations. There is another alternative: We can make StackElementType a *variant record*. (If you are not familiar with variant records in Pascal, you should review the discussion of variant records in Chapter 3 before you continue.)

Figure 4-25
Specifications of
Program Calculator

Specifications: Program Calculator

Function:

This program will evaluate arithmetic expressions containing real numbers and the operators +, −, *, and /.

Input:

The input is a series of arithmetic expressions entered interactively from the keyboard. The user is prompted to enter a fully and correctly parenthesized arithmetic expression made up of operators (the characters '+', '−', '*', and '/'), parentheses, and real numbers. The end of the expression is marked by the expression terminator character, '='. There may be any number (including 0) blanks between the operators, parentheses, real numbers, and expression terminator. The outermost level of the expression does not need parentheses; that is, (3 * (5 + 1)) could also be expressed as 3 * (5 + 1).

Real numbers must be expressed in decimal format: the whole part, followed by a decimal point ('.'), followed by the decimal part. The decimal point and decimal part are optional. Exponential notation (that is, 3.2E3) is not valid. The following are examples of real numbers processed by this program:

   5.0   15.123 0.0   250   27.

Examples of valid expressions (followed by the expression terminator, '=') are:

   (25 + 30.2) =
   100.0 − (5.3 * 12) =
   (2.78 + (53.44 − 3.3)) * 0.5 =
   33 =

Examples of invalid expressions are:

   1 + 2 + 3 =   (Requires parentheses)
   3.2E3 * 5.0 =   (Exponential notation not permitted)
   (1 + 2) + ((3 + 4) =   (Parentheses do not match)
   3.55 * 0.5   (Missing expression terminator)

The user terminates the program by entering the character '#' instead of an assignment statement.

Output:

The user is prompted for each new expression to be evaluated with the following prompt:

   Enter expression to evaluate or # to quit:

After the evaluation of each assignment statement, the results are printed to the screen:

   Result = *value*

where *value* is a real number in decimal format, with a field width of 8 and a decimal field of 4.

Processing Requirements:

1. This program must be able to be compiled and run, with minimal changes, on a variety of computer systems.
2. This program must read real number inputs as characters and make the appropriate conversions.

Assumptions:

1. The expressions will be fully and correctly parenthesized, as described in the Input section.
2. The expressions will be terminated by $' = '$.
3. The operations in expressions will be valid at run time. This means that we will not try to divide by 0.

For instance, we might use the following declarations.

```
TYPE
  ContentsType     =  (Operator, Operand);

  StackElementType = RECORD
    (* no fixed part *)

    (* variant part: *)
    CASE Contents  : ContentsType OF
      Operator     : (Character : Char);
      Operand      : (Value     : Real)
  END; (* StackElementType *)
```

Following this declaration of StackElementType, one set of stack operations will support both the OperandStack and the OperatorStack. Since we know that the element type is irrelevant to the stack operations, the Push and Pop procedures will merely store and retrieve data of the variant record type. The *caller* knows whether the data in the stack is a character operator or a real number operand, and processes the correct record field accordingly.

Top-Down Design

The main module of the Calculator program is a loop that simply reads and evaluates expressions until the user indicates that he or she is finished.

Calculator / *Level 0*
REPEAT
  EvaluateExpression (Finished)
UNTIL Finished

The EvaluateExpression module seems to do all the work. Let's look at its specification:

EvaluateExpression (Finished) / *Level 1*

Function:	Prompt user for arithmetic expression, then read expression and evaluate it. Print results.
Input:	From Input (keyboard): arithmetic expression or end-program character ('#')
Preconditions:	None
Output:	To Output (screen): result of evaluation To main program: Finished (Boolean)
Postconditions:	Evaluation of arithmetic expression is printed to screen. Finished = user entered end-program character instead of expression.

In this module, we will loop through the user's expression, reading it piece by piece, then pushing and popping and performing the operations, as in the example we discussed earlier. Here's the high-level description of this algorithm:

EvaluateExpression

Finished ← False
Prompt user for expression
Get first piece of input

IF first input = EndProgram character
   THEN Finished ← True
   ELSE
      Create operand and operator stacks

      REPEAT
         Process this piece of input
         Get next piece of input
      UNTIL End of expression

      Print result

What exactly is this "piece" of input that gets read before the loop and in each iteration of the loop body? If the piece of input is an operator [' + ', ' − ', '*', '/', '(', or ')'], expression termination character (' = '), or program termination character ('#'), we need only read the next nonblank character from the input stream. On the other hand, if the next piece of the expression input is an operand, we must skip any leading blanks, then read all the characters (digits and decimal point) that constitute the number and convert them into a real number. Let's specify an operation to take care of the input. It will read whatever characters are necessary and return a "token" containing this piece of input. This token may be either a character (if the next piece of input was an operator or termination character) or a real number (if the next piece of input was an operand).

But how can Procedure GetToken return data of two different types? One approach would be to have several output parameters, not all of which are relevant, as illustrated by this procedure heading:

```
PROCEDURE GetToken
   (VAR Token     : ContentsType;   (* Operand or operator *)
    VAR Character : Char;           (* If token = operator *)
    VAR RealNum   : Real);          (* If token = operand  *)
```

However, earlier we discussed the idea of using a single set of stack operations to implement stacks that contain either character or real elements. Our solution was to make the stack element type a variant record that contains one variant for operator type data (Char) and a second variant for operand type data (Real). We can use the same solution here. In fact we can use the same variant record type for both the token and the stack element. Here is the specification for the GetToken operation:

■ **GetToken (Token)** / *Level 2*

    Function: Read "token" from input stream.

    Input: From Input (keyboard): character(s)

    Preconditions: None

    Output: Token (TokenType)

    Postconditions: Token contains one of the following:
                       1. an operand (Real)
                       2. an operator (Char)
                       3. end-expression (Char)
                       4. end-program (Char)

Our algorithm contains processing for each of these cases.

GetToken

Skip leading blank characters.

CASE first nonblank character OF
    '0' .. '9'   : GetOperandToken
    '#'   : Token ← end-program
    '='   : Token ← end-expression
    anything else : Token ← operator character
END CASE

We have used a CASE structure in the design because it is the logical way to describe this operation. This design would be difficult to implement with a standard Pascal CASE statement for two reasons. First, standard Pascal does not support the use of subranges for case label lists; we would have to list each digit separately ('0', '1', '2', etc.). Second, the "anything else" case label is not supported. Therefore, when we code this procedure, the CASE structure will be implemented as a nested IF statement. (Some versions of Pascal, including Turbo Pascal, support both subrange case labels and "ELSE" clauses in CASE statements.)

    The only part of the GetToken algorithm that needs further decomposition is GetOperandToken. This is the module that will read digits (with or without a decimal point) and convert the characters to their Real value. This operation is very similar to the ReadReal procedure developed earlier in this chapter. The main difference is in the terminating conditions. Procedure ReadReal used a blank (' ') as the character that terminated the number, leaving the read cursor ready to read the character that followed the blank. Our specifications, however, do not require any blanks between operands and operators. Therefore, GetOperandToken must consider any nonnumeric digit (except for the decimal point) to be the character that terminates the number.

At first glance this seems to be a minor coding modification, but there are further implications. Consider the following expression:

1234 + 5678

GetOperandToken reads/converts the first four characters before it reads the ' + '. Since ' + ' is neither a digit nor a decimal point, we have finished reading the operand. GetToken returns the Real operand value 1234. On the next call to GetToken, we expect to return the operator ' + ', but instead we read '5'. What happened? The problem is that we read the ' + ' on the first call to GetToken; it was the character that terminated the real number. We had it on the previous call, but it was local data; it is lost to us now.

To solve this problem, we decide that GetToken should return this "preread" character to the caller. On the subsequent call to GetToken, this character is supplied as the next character to look at. That is, in every call to GetToken we read ahead and save the next character to process in a subsequent call. Though we could add NextChar to the parameter list of GetToken, a neater solution is to add a field to the Token record itself. Thus NextChar will be a field in the *fixed part* of the variant record type.

What about the *first* call to GetToken? If the NextChar field has not been initialized, who knows what garbage may be in this field? We will need to create an operation InitToken, which sets the NextChar field of the Token to blank. This procedure must be called before the first call to GetToken in the EvaluateExpression module.

While we are looking at the module, one other problem occurs to us. What if the value in the NextChar field is ' − '? How do we know whether this token is a subtraction operator or a negative operand (for example, − 3.2)? Peeking ahead at the characters that follow doesn't help; we can't differentiate between ' − 3.2' (the ' − ' is an operator) and '5 − 3.2' (the ' − ' is part of the operand) just by looking at the characters that follow the ' − '. What we really need to know is what came *before*. Because the arithmetic operators and operands alternate in expressions, we can keep track of what kind of contents we expect in the next token. We only need to consider operators and operands; we can ignore the parentheses. This suggests one more fixed field, NextToken, in the variant record type. What should InitToken initialize this field to? Since the first (nonparenthesis) token must be an operand, NextToken will be initialized to Operand.

Note that these considerations not only change the algorithm; they also *change the specification* of GetToken:

▌ **GetToken (Token)**—revised version   /   *Level 2*

Function:	Read "token" from input stream.
Input:	From Input (keyboard) : character(s)
	From calling procedure: Token (TokenType)
Preconditions:	Token = Token returned from previous call to GetToken or
	InitToken
Output:	Token (TokenType)
Postconditions:	Token contains one of the following:

                         1. an operand (Real)

                         2. an operator (Char)

                         3. end-expression (Char)

                         4. end-program (Char)

                         Token.NextChar = last character read

Before we revise the algorithm for GetToken, let's redefine the TokenType variant record. When we originally discussed using a variant record for StackElementType, we only considered two variants: one for operators and one for operands. In the specifications for GetToken, we see that the Token can represent two other types of information: end-expression and end-program. Since these are associated with character values, we could put them into the Operator variant, which contains a Char field. Logically, however, they are not arithmetic operators. It would be better to add two new values to ContentsType—EndProgram and EndExpression. Neither of these values require additional fields in the variant part. Here is our "final" version of TokenType:

```
TYPE
  ValueType    = Real;
  ContentsType = (Operator, Operand, EndProgram, EndExpression);

  TokenType    = RECORD   (* variant record! *)
    (* Fixed Part *)
    NextChar   : Char;            (* from last GetToken      *)
    NextToken  : ContentsType;  (* token contents expected *)

    (* Variant Part *)
    CASE Contents : ContentsType   OF
      Operator     : (Character : Char);
      Operand      : (Value     : ValueType);
      EndProgram   : ();  (* no additional fields *)
      EndExpression : ()   (* no additional fields *)
  END; (* TokenType *)
```

As we plan to use the variant record for the stack elements also, we can set Stack-ElementType to the host type, TokenType:

```
StackElementType = TokenType;
```

Now let's look at the revised algorithm for GetToken:

GetToken—revised

Token.NextChar ← first nonblank character

(Process according to character value.)
IF Token.NextToken = Operand AND
   Token.NextChar IN ['0' .. '9', '−']
   THEN GetOperandToken
   ELSE
    IF Token.NextChar = '#'
      THEN Token.Contents ← EndProgram
      ELSE
       IF Token.NextChar = '='
        THEN
         Token.Contents ← EndExpression
         Readln
        ELSE (it is an operator)
         Token.Contents ← Operator
         Token.Character ← Token.NextChar
         Read (Token.NextChar)

Note that we have added a call to Read to the "anything else" case. On entrance to GetToken, the NextChar field contains the last character read but unprocessed. We must "preread" a character to put into NextChar. We have also added a call to Readln in the '=' case. After reading the end-expression character, we must call Readln to get ready for reading the next expression.

   The GetOperandToken module is specified as follows:

■ **GetOperandToken (Token)**   /   *Level 3*

Function:	Read real number "token" from input stream.
Input:	From Input (keyboard) : character(s) From calling procedure: Token (TokenType)
Preconditions:	Token = Token returned from previous call to GetToken or InitToken
Output:	Token (TokenType)
Postconditions:	Token.Contents = Operand Token.Value = Real "value" of character digits Token.NextChar = last character read

Unlike the ReadReal operation in this chapter, GetOperandToken is not required to do any error processing. (We will discuss this issue at the end of this application section.)

   We can "borrow" the general algorithm from Procedure ReadReal. We first calculate the whole part of the number, then (if there is a decimal point) we calculate the decimal part using a stack. We will not repeat the explanation of this algorithm here; you can review the discussion on pages 183–188.

This algorithm uses a stack of characters. To avoid needing to implement another set of stack operations, we can use the character field of TokenType to contain the values we want to push. Now this procedure can use the same stack type as the operand and operator stacks; it will be a stack of TokenType elements.

Many pages and ideas have gone by since we last looked at our Level 1 design for the EvaluateExpression module. Let's review it here, updating it to reflect decisions that have been made since we originally designed it.

EvaluateExpression—revised

Prompt user for expression

Create operand and operator stacks
InitToken (Token)
ExpressionDone ← False

GetToken (Token)

IF Token.Contents = EndProgram
   THEN Finished ← True
   ELSE

     REPEAT
      ProcessToken

      IF Token.Contents = EndExpression
        THEN ExpressionDone ← True
        ELSE GetToken (Token)
     UNTIL ExpressionDone

     Pop operand stack to get final result
     Print result

Let's look now at the ProcessToken module. This operation processes the token that is returned from GetToken according to its contents: If the token contains an operand, it is pushed onto the operand stack and the NextToken field is reset to Operator. If the token contains an arithmetic operator, it is pushed onto the operator stack and NextToken is reset to Operand. Left parentheses are ignored, and right parentheses cause the "top" operation to be performed. Before we record the algorithm, let's take a look at the specification:

■ **ProcessToken (Token, OperatorStack, OperandStack)** / *Level 2*

Function:	Process Token according to contents.
Input:	Token (TokenType)
	OperatorStack (StackType)
	OperandStack (StackType)
Preconditions:	Token = Token returned from call to GetToken
	Stacks have been created.
Output:	Token (NextToken field may be modified)
	OperatorStack, OperandStack (both modified)

Postconditions: IF Token contains operand, THEN OperandStack = previous OperandStack + Token AND OperatorStack is unchanged AND Token.NextToken = Operator.

IF Token contains operator ($+$, $-$, $*$, or $/$), THEN OperatorStack = previous OperatorStack + Token AND OperandStack is unchanged AND Token.NextToken = Operand.

IF Token contains $'('$, THEN both stacks and Token are unchanged.

IF Token contains $')'$, THEN OperatorStack $\leftarrow$ previous OperatorStack minus its top element AND OperandStack $\leftarrow$ previous OperandStack minus its top two elements + result of operation. Token is unchanged.

IF Token contains EndExpression, THEN OperatorStack is empty AND OperandStack contains the result of evaluating the whole expression. Token is unchanged.

The postconditions suggest that the algorithm will be a big nested CASE statement:

ProcessToken

CASE Token.Contents OF
   Operand : Push Token onto OperandStack
             Set Token.NextToken to Operator

   Operator :
    CASE Token.Character OF
     $'+'$, $'-'$, $'*'$, $'/'$: Push Token onto OperatorStack
                    Set Token.NextToken to Operand

     $')'$: Perform operation

     $'('$: Do nothing
    END (CASE Token.Character)

   EndExpression : Perform operation
END (Case Token.Contents)

Why do we need to "perform operation" if the Token contains the end-expression value? Consider the following expression:

$$(4 + 5) - 1 =$$

The Real value 4 is pushed onto OperandStack, the character $'+'$ is pushed onto OperatorStack, and then the 5 is pushed onto OperandStack. The right parenthesis causes the operation to be performed: The operands are popped from OperandStack, the operator is popped from OperatorStack, and the addition is performed: $4 + 5 = 9$. This sum is pushed onto the OperandStack. Then $'-'$ is pushed onto OperatorStack, and 1 joins 9 on the OperandStack. When GetToken returns the token containing EndExpression ($'='$ was read), the expression evaluation is not complete: There is still one operator on the OperatorStack and two operands on the OperandStack. ProcessToken, inputting this token, must perform the final operation, and put the result back on OperandStack.

What would happen if the expression had been completely enclosed in parentheses:

$$((4 + 5) - 1) =$$

This time, the second right parenthesis will cause the final operation to be performed. When GetToken reads the $'='$ and returns the token containing EndExpression, the expression evaluation is already complete: both stacks are empty. We will reflect both of these possible situations in the design of the final module, PerformOperation.

■ **PerformOperation (OperatorStack, OperandStack)** / *Level 3*

Function:	Perform the "top" operation in OperatorStack, using the two top operands in OperandStack, leaving the result at the top of OperandStack.
Input:	OperatorStack, OperandStack
Preconditions:	The stacks have been created.
Output:	OperatorStack, OperandStack
Postconditions:	IF OperatorStack is empty, then both stacks are returned unchanged; otherwise, OperatorStack = previous Operator-Stack − top operator AND OperandStack = previous OperandStack minus its top two elements + result of operation (at top of stack).

The algorithm for this operation is very straightforward:

PerformOperation

IF OperatorStack is not empty
  THEN
    Pop OperatorStack to get Operator
    Pop OperandStack to get Op2
    Pop OperandStack to get Op1

    CASE Operator OF
     $'+'$: NewValue ← Op1 + Op2
     $'-'$: NewValue ← Op1 − Op2
     $'*'$: NewValue ← Op1 * Op2
     $'/'$: NewValue ← Op1 / Op2
    END (CASE)

    Push token containing NewValue onto OperandStack

The top-down design is now complete. Note that, except to define Stack-ElementType, we have not discussed the implementation of StackType. We already have two complete, tested, ready-to-use implementations of the Stack ADT. We can select either one of them to use in our program. We only need to define Stack-ElementType in the declarations and then we can include the other stack declarations, procedures, and functions, without any changes. Actually, since this program does not use all of the stack operations we only need to include the operations that are actually called. Either of the two stack implementations would be appropriate for this application. Because we like the opportunity to get some practice using pointer variables, we have used the linked implementation.

The Program

The source code for Program Calculator follows. To save space, we have abbreviated the program listing by inserting comments in place of the source code for the Stack ADT operations.

The complete source code can be found in file CALC.PAS on the program disk.

```
PROGRAM Calculator (Input, Output);

  (* program specifications repeated here *)

CONST

  (********* Character Constants *********)
  EndExp    = '=';        Escape    = '#';
  Blank     = ' ';        DecPoint  = '.';
  LeftPar   = '(';        RtPar     = ')';
  AddOp     = '+';        MultOp    = '*';
  SubOp     = '-';        DivOp     = '/';
  MinusSign = '-';

TYPE

  ValueType    = Real;
  ContentsType = (Operator, Operand, EndProgram, EndExpression);

  TokenType    = RECORD   (* variant record! *)
    (* Fixed Part *)
    NextChar   : Char;         (* char from last GetToken *)
    NextToken  : ContentsType; (* next token expected    *)

    (* Variant Part *)
    CASE Contents    : ContentsType  OF
      Operator       : (Character : Char);
      Operand        : (Value     : ValueType);
      EndProgram     : ();
      EndExpression  : ()
  END; (* TokenType *)

  (***** Stack Declarations *****)
  StackElementType   = TokenType;
  NodePtrType        = ^StackNodeType;   (* a pointer type *)

  StackNodeType = RECORD
    Info       : StackElementType; (* user's data         *)
    Next       : NodePtrType       (* pointer to next node *)
  END; (* StackNodeType *)
```

```
    StackType = NodePtrType;

VAR
  Finished  : Boolean;        (* Quit processing? *)

(********************************************************************)
(*                     Stack Operations                          *)
(********************************************************************)
(* Include source code for the Stack ADT operations here.       *)
(********************************************************************)
(*                    Evaluate Operations                        *)
(********************************************************************)

PROCEDURE GetToken
  (VAR Token : TokenType);

  (* Get "token" from input stream. On entrance to this      *)
  (* procedure, Token = the token returned from a previous    *)
  (* call to GetToken or InitToken. On exit, Token contains   *)
  (* one of the following types of contents: an Operand, an   *)
  (* Operator, an expression end marker, or a program end     *)
  (* marker; the NextChar field of Token contains the last    *)
  (* character read (the next character to process).          *)

  (***************** Nested Operations *******************)

  FUNCTION Digit
    (Numeral : Char) : Integer;

    (* Convert Numeral to integer value ('1' = 1, '2' = 2, *)
    (* etc.; this is not the ordinal value of the Numeral  *)
    (* character in the character set.)                    *)

  BEGIN (* Digit *)
    Digit := ORD(Numeral) - ORD('1') + 1
  END;  (* Digit *)

  (********************************************************)

  PROCEDURE GetOperandToken
    (VAR Token : TokenType);

    (* Get real number operand token from input string, *)
    (* beginning with previous char, leaving the last   *)
    (* nonnumeric character read in previous char.      *)

  VAR
    Number   : Real;    (* whole part of operand  *)
    SignTerm : Real;    (* term to set pos/neg    *)
    Decimal  : Real;    (* decimal part of operand *)
    DecToken : TokenType; (* stack element        *)
    DecStack : StackType; (* stack of decimal chars *)
```

```
BEGIN (* GetOperandToken *)

  Number  := 0.0;
  Decimal := 0.0;

  (* Check for a minus sign to indicate negative number. *)
  IF Token.NextChar <> MinusSign
    THEN SignTerm := 1.0
    ELSE (* it is a negative number *)
      BEGIN
        SignTerm := -1.0;
        Read (Token.NextChar)
      END; (* it is a negative number *)

  (* Calculate whole part of real operand. *)
  WHILE Token.NextChar IN ['0'..'9'] DO
    BEGIN
      Number := (10 * Number) + Digit(Token.NextChar);
      Read (Token.NextChar)
    END: (* WHILE *)

  (* Calculate decimal part of operand, if any. *)
  IF Token.NextChar = DecPoint
    THEN
      BEGIN

        CreateStack (DecStack);
        Read (Token.NextChar);

        (* Put all decimal characters on stack. *)
        WHILE Token.NextChar IN ['0' .. '9'] DO
          BEGIN
            DecToken.Character := Token.NextChar;
            Push (DecStack, DecToken);
            Read (Token.NextChar)
          END; (* WHILE *)

        (* Pop stack and perform successive divisions. *)
        WHILE NOT EmptyStack (DecStack) DO
          BEGIN
            Pop (DecStack, DecToken);
            Decimal := (Decimal / 10) +
              Digit (DecToken.Character)
          END (* WHILE NOT EmptyStack *)

      END; (* IF char = decimal point *)

  Token.Contents := Operand;
  Token.Value    := (Number + (Decimal / 10)) * SignTerm

END;  (* GetOperandToken *)

(***************************************************************)
```

```
BEGIN (* GetToken *)

  (* Token.NextChar := next nonblank character from Input. *)
  WHILE Token.NextChar = Blank DO
    Read (Token.NextChar);

  (* IF NextChar field is numeric, get operand. *)
  IF (Token.NextToken = Operand) AND
     (Token.NextChar IN ['0' .. '9', '-'])
    THEN    (* Token will be a real number operand. *)
      (* Convert characters to real number. *)
      GetOperandToken (Token)

    ELSE (* previous character is nonnumeric *)
      IF Token.NextChar = Escape
        THEN Token.Contents := EndProgram

      ELSE
        IF Token.NextChar = EndExp
          THEN
            BEGIN
              Token.Contents := EndExpression;
              Readln
            END (* end expression *)

          ELSE (* contains operator *)
            BEGIN
              (* Get operator token *)
              Token.Contents  := Operator;
              Token.Character := Token.NextChar;
              Read (Token.NextChar)
            END (* character is nonnumeric *)

END;  (* GetToken *)

(************************************************************)

PROCEDURE InitToken
  (VAR Token : TokenType);

  (* Initalize Token before call to GetToken. *)

BEGIN (* InitToken *)
  Token.NextChar  := Blank;
  Token.NextToken := Operand
END;  (* InitToken *)

(************************************************************)

PROCEDURE PerformOperation
  (VAR OperatorStack : StackType;
   VAR OperandStack  : StackType);

  (* Performs next operation in the expression evaluation      *)
  (* and leaves result at the top of the OperandStack.         *)
  (* This procedure may be called when OperatorStack is        *)
  (* empty if entire expression was enclosed in parentheses.   *)
```

```
        VAR
          Op1, Op2   : TokenType;
          Operator   : TokenType;
          NewValue   : ValueType;

        BEGIN (* PerformOperation *)

          (* Perform evaluation if there are any operators left in *)
          (* Operators stack.                                      *)
          IF NOT EmptyStack (OperatorStack)
            THEN
              BEGIN
                (* Get operands and operator. *)
                Pop (OperatorStack, Operator);
                Pop (OperandStack, Op2);
                Pop (OperandStack, Op1);

                (* Perform the appropriate operation *)
                CASE Operator.Character OF
                  '+' : NewValue := Op1.Value + Op2.Value;
                  '-' : NewValue := Op1.Value - Op2.Value;
                  '*' : NewValue := Op1.Value * Op2.Value;
                  '/' : NewValue := Op1.Value / Op2.Value
                END;  (* CASE *)

                (* Put the result back on the operands stack. *)
                Op1.Value := NewValue;
                Push (OperandStack, Op1)

              END (* IF operator stack not empty *)
        END; (* PerformOperation *)

        (**************************************************************)

        PROCEDURE ProcessToken
          (VAR Token         : TokenType;
           VAR OperatorStack : StackType;
           VAR OperandStack  : StackType);

          (* Process Token according to contents. On entrance to   *)
          (* this procedure, Token = the token returned from a call *)
          (* to GetToken. On exit the parameters have been modified *)
          (* as listed in the specification postconditions.         *)

        BEGIN (* ProcessToken *)

          (* Process according to token contents. *)
          CASE Token.Contents OF

            Operand : (* Push the token onto the operand stack. *)
              BEGIN
                (* Push the operand on OperandStack. *)
                Push (OperandStack, Token);

                (* Reset NextToken to expect an Operator. *)
                Token.NextToken := Operator
              END; (* Operand *)
```

```
      Operator : (* Process according to character field. *)
        CASE Token.Character OF

          AddOp, SubOp, MultOp, DivOp : (* operator *)
            BEGIN
              (* Push the operator on OperatorStack. *)
              Push (OperatorStack, Token);

              (* Reset NextToken to expect an Operand *)
              Token.NextToken := Operand
            END; (* operator *)

          RtPar : (* end of a suboperation *)
            (* Perform most recent operation; leave *)
            (* result at top of OperandStack.       *)
            PerformOperation (OperatorStack, OperandStack);

          LeftPar : (* do nothing *)

        END; (* CASE Token.Character *)

      EndExpression :
        PerformOperation (OperatorStack, OperandStack)

    END (* CASE Token.Contents *)
END; (* ProcessToken *)

(*************************************************************)

PROCEDURE EvaluateExpression
  (VAR Finished : Boolean);

  (* Prompt user for arithmetic expression, then read    *)
  (* expression. Finished is True if the user enters an   *)
  (* end-program character instead of an expression;      *)
  (* otherwise Finished is False and the expression is    *)
  (* evaluated and the result is printed.                 *)

CONST
  Field     = 8;    (* Field length for printing real number *)
  Precision = 4;  (* Precision for printing real number       *)

VAR
  Token         : TokenType;    (* Stack element       *)
  OperandStack  : StackType;    (* Stack of operands   *)
  OperatorStack : StackType;    (* Stack of operators  *)
  ExpressionDone : Boolean;     (* End of expression   *)

BEGIN (* EvaluateExpression *)

  Writeln ('Enter expression to evaluate (or # to Quit):');

  (* Set up stacks for processing expression. *)
  CreateStack (OperandStack);
  CreateStack (OperatorStack);
  InitToken (Token);
  ExpressionDone := False;
  Finished := False;
```

```
        (* Get first token from input expression. *)
        GetToken (Token);

        (* IF token is end-program, set Finished; otherwise process *)
        (* the expression, token by token.                          *)
        IF Token.Contents = EndProgram
          THEN   (* user wants to quit *)
            BEGIN
              Finished := True;
              Writeln ('Goodbye')
            END (* if user wants to quit *)

          ELSE (* input is expression *)
            BEGIN
              REPEAT

                (* Process the token. *)
                ProcessToken
                  (Token,
                   OperatorStack,
                   OperandStack);

                (* Get the next token from input. *)
                IF Token.Contents = EndExpression
                  THEN ExpressionDone := True
                  ELSE GetToken (Token)

              UNTIL ExpressionDone;

              (* Final result is at top of operands stack. *)
              Pop (OperandStack, Token);
              Writeln ('Result = ', Token.Value:Field:Precision)

            END (* input is an expression *)

  END; (* EvaluateExpression *)

  (*************************************************************)

  BEGIN (* Main program *)

    (* Process all assignment statements until Finished. *)
    REPEAT
      EvaluateExpression (Finished)
    UNTIL Finished

  END. (* Main program *)
```

Error Checking

When we begin testing the calculator program, we begin to doubt the wisdom of making so many assumptions about the requirements for correct input. We cannot expect a person sitting at the keyboard to type every character perfectly. But what does our program do if there is an input error in an expression? Sometimes it gets wrong answers, and sometimes it just crashes.

Pascal will check for many types of run-time errors. It is better, however, to write the error-checking logic into the programs than to rely on the system to catch errors at run time. That way we can choose how to handle the error. Even if we do choose to terminate the program, there is an important difference. If we have our program do the error checking itself, rather than rely on the system to do it, we can *control* the termination of the program. We may, for instance, want the program to print out an error message describing the problem before it stops executing.

In other cases we may not want the program to stop executing. For instance, if the user of our calculator program makes an error in typing the input expression, we would probably want the program to reject that line of input with an error message and then go on to the next expression. If we depend on the system to catch the error, it may terminate the program or generate incorrect results.

How do we decide what action the program should take when an error occurs? As always, we must first consider the requirements of the program. Sometimes the specifications will tell us explicitly what to do in case of each type of error. If not, the best course of action is to try to recover as "gracefully" as possible, with the least damage to the program's execution: clean up the mess, print out a message to warn the user that an error has occurred, then go on to the next processing that is not affected by the error.

Let's look at how we could incorporate error checking into the design of the calculator program. To make this program as robust as possible, we will specify that if there is an input error anywhere within an expression, we will stop processing that expression, print an appropriate error message, and go on to the next expression. What is involved in recovering from an input error? First of all, we want to get rid of the rest of the line. That's easy; a simple Readln will take care of it. What about the stacks? If there are no errors, both stacks end up empty at the end of the expression evaluation. If we stop processing midway through the expression, however, there may be elements left over in the stacks. To get rid of this data, we must destroy the stacks.

One place where input errors might occur is in the GetOperandToken procedure; there may be invalid characters in the operand string (for example, 3.2E2). The ReadReal procedure in this chapter incorporated such checking for input errors. Similar checks could be added to GetOperandToken. This change would require a modification to the specifications of GetOperandToken, as well as GetToken, to add an Error flag to the output.

Other input errors occur if the parentheses are not correct. Let's see what happens, for instance, if the expression is not fully parenthesized. The input lines

3.0 * (1.0 + 6.0 =

will produce a result of 7.0 instead of 21.0; the last operation is never performed. One way to deal with such errors is to replace the call to Pop at the end of EvaluateExpression with a module called GetResult. This module would check the status of the stacks to see if there is a mismatch between the operands and operators. GetResult inputs the two stacks and outputs Result (ValueType) and Error (Boolean), as well as the stacks, which should both be empty at the end of this operation. What conditions would set Error to true? Error is True if

1. OperandStack is empty before popping Result;
2. OperandStack is not empty after popping Result; or
3. OperatorStack is not empty.

If either condition 2 or condition 3 is true, we must destroy the stack, in addition to setting Error. We can't always prevent errors in the input, especially input from a keyboard, but we can try to limit their effect on the continuing execution of the program.

Another source of run-time errors is software limitations. Although there may be nothing wrong with either the input or the logic of the program, execution may be impeded by design decisions like the size of the data structures. For instance, with the static array implementation of StackType, we could run into stack overflow problems if the MaxStack constant was too small. To implement error checking for this condition, we would use the FullStack function to check the status of the stack before Pushing in Procedure ProcessToken. If stack overflow occurs, we would set an Error flag, destroy the stacks, and skip to the next expression.

Another place where a run-time error might occur is in Procedure PerformOperation: If the second operand is 0, a division operation will generate a "division by 0" error. We could remove this assumption from the program specification, and add an explicit check for the error condition in PerformOperation.

We have mentioned several ideas for making Program Calculator a more reliable piece of software. When we add error checking, we decrease the likelihood that the program will fail at run time. By increasing the *robustness* of the program, we also increase the satisfaction of its users.

Other Notations for Expressions

One of the things that makes our calculator clumsy to use is the need for parentheses to indicate the order of evaluation. The way we are used to seeing expressions is called **infix** notation—the operator is *in* between the operands. Infix notation can be fully parenthesized, or it can rely on a scheme of operator precedence, as well as the use of parentheses to override the rules, to express the order of evaluation within an expression. For instance, the multiplication operators $\times$ and / usually have a higher precedence than the addition operators + and $-$. The user of such a precedence scheme reduces the need for parentheses to situations where we want to override the order imposed by the scheme. In the following example, if we want to perform the multiplication operator first,

A + B * C

is sufficient to express the correct order of evaluation of the expression. If we want to do the addition before the multiplication (breaking the rule), however, we must indicate this with parentheses:

(A + B) * C

In one of the programming assignments at the end of the book, you are asked to develop a program that incorporates a precedence scheme into the expression evaluation.

The problem with infix notation is its ambiguity. We must resort to an agreed-upon scheme to determine how to evaluate the expression. There are other ways of writing expressions, however, that do not require parentheses or precedence schemes. We will briefly describe two of them here, and then show how we can convert from infix to another notation with the help of our new friend, the stack.

Prefix Notation

In **prefix notation** the operator *precedes* the operands. For instance, we would write the infix expression "A + B" as " + A B". The infix expression

(A + B) * C

which requires the use of parentheses to designate the order of evaluation, would be written as

* + A B C

Notice two features of the prefix expression:

- The operands maintain the same order as in the equivalent infix expression.
- Parentheses are not needed to designate the expression unambiguously.

We evaluate a prefix expression by scanning from left to right until we find the first operator that is immediately followed by a pair of operands. This binary expression is evaluated, and its result is put back into the expression to replace the operator and operands we used. This process continues until only a single value remains. Let's evaluate the expression

* + 5 2 4

to illustrate the process. The first symbol is an operator, *, so we save it and go on. The second symbol is also an operator, +, so we save it and go on. The third symbol, 5, is an operand, so we save it and look at the next symbol. It is also an operand, 2, so we perform an operation on the two operands. We have saved two operators. Which should we use? We want to use the operator that we saw *most recently*—that is, + .

5 + 2 = 7

so we substitute 7 back into the expression, replacing + 5 2. The next symbol is another operand, 4, so we perform the next operation, using the × that we first saved. Note that our first operand will be the 7 that we already calculated and the second will be 4.

7 * 4 = 28

Now we are at the end of the expression, and we are left with the single value 28 as the result of the expression evaluation.

Use this approach to convince yourself that the prefix expression

* − + 4 3 5 / + 2 4 3

equals 4.

We will leave to the reader the development of this algorithm into a procedure.

HINT: Using the most recent operator implies a "last in, first out" type of solution.

How can we convert an infix expression into a prefix expression? Our solution to this question will make use of the stack routines from this chapter and the string processing routines from Chapter 3.

For simplicity, we will again begin with a fully parenthesized infix expression of the format used in the calculator program. Our output will be a string representing the equivalent prefix expression.

Our general approach will be to loop through the expression, reading a token (in this case, one character) and processing according to its type, until we reach the end of the input expression. (The types are letters, symbols that represent operators, left parentheses, and right parentheses.) If the token is a letter, representing an operand, we will push it onto a stack of operands. If the token represents an operator, we will push it onto a stack of operators. We will ignore left parentheses. So far the processing looks similar to the calculator program's Evaluate module. The processing for a right parenthesis will be different, however. We will pop the last two operands and the most recent operator, convert them to a prefix expression, and push this expression back onto the operand stack. Note that the operand stack no longer contains real numbers; it is now a stack of *strings*.

How do we convert to prefix? If the operators, as well as the operands, are strings, we can use our string routines from Chapter 3 to create an expression that begins with an operator, followed by Operand1 and Operand2, respectively. This can be accomplished by using the Concat procedure. First we concatenate the operator with Operand1; then we concatenate the result with Operand2.

When we reach the end of the input expression, we should find the complete prefix expression string as the top (and only) element in the operand stack.

We can use much of our design from the calculator program. The only changes to the Evaluate module will be to make operands and operators into string type elements before they are pushed onto their respective stacks and to invoke module Convert, rather than module Perform operation, when a right parenthesis is encountered.

Convert

Pop Operand2 from operands stack
Pop Operand1 from operands stack
Pop Operator from operators stack
Concatenate Operator with Operand1
Concatenate result with Operand2
Push the result onto the operands stack

This module directly codes into a Pascal procedure, using Push, Pop, and Concat.

Postfix Notation

In an alternative way of writing expressions, called **postfix notation**, the operator *follows* the operands. For instance, the infix expression A + B would be written as the prefix expression A B +. The infix expression

(A + B) * C

which requires parentheses to indicate the order of evaluation, would be written as the postfix expression

A B + C ∗

Note three features of postfix notation:

- As in prefix notation, the relative order of the operands is maintained.
- Parentheses are not necessary, for postfix expressions are by nature unambiguous.
- A postfix expression is not merely the reverse of the equivalent prefix expression.

The algorithms to convert expressions into postfix notation and to evaluate postfix expressions, like those for prefix notation, make use of the stack data structure.

■ *Exercises**

1. Define the accessing function of a stack at the logical level.

2. Show what is written by the following segments of code, given that Stack is a stack of integer elements and X, Y, and Z are integer variables.

(a)
```
CreateStack (Stack);
  X := 1;
  Y := 0;
  Z := 4;
  Push (Stack, Y);
  Push (Stack, X);
  Push (Stack, X + Z);
  Pop (Stack, Y);
  Push (Stack, SQR(Z));
  Push (Stack, Y);
  Push (Stack, 3);
  Pop (Stack, X);
  Writeln ('X = ', X);
  Writeln ('Y = ', Y);
  Writeln ('Z = ', Z);
  WHILE NOT EmptyStack (Stack) DO
    BEGIN
      Pop(Stack, X);
      Writeln (X)
    END
```

(b)
```
CreateStack (Stack);
  X := 4;
  Z := 0;
  Y := X + 1;
  Push (Stack, Y);
  Push (Stack, Y + 1);
  Push (Stack, X);
  Pop (Stack, Y);
  X := Y + 1;
```

*Questions with italicized numbers are answered in the back of the book.

```
Push (Stack, X);
Push (Stack, Z);
WHILE NOT EmptyStack (Stack) DO
  BEGIN
    Pop (Stack, Z);
    Writeln (Z)
  END;
Writeln ('X = ', X);
Writeln ('Y = ', Y);
Writeln ('Z = ', Z)
```

Use the following information for Exercises 3–6: Stack is implemented as a record containing an array of Elements and a field indicating the index of the Top element, as discussed in this chapter. Letter is a Char variable. In each exercise below, show the result of the operation on the stack. If overflow or underflow occurs, check the appropriate box; otherwise, show the new contents of the array, the Top indicator, and Letter. (*Note:* Some values in the array may not be elements in the stack.)

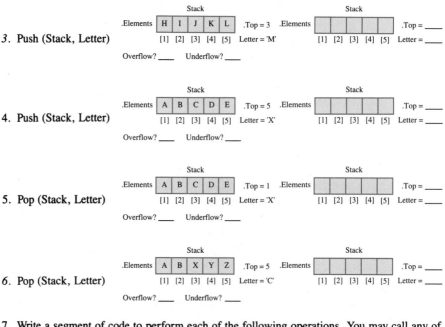

3. Push (Stack, Letter)

4. Push (Stack, Letter)

5. Pop (Stack, Letter)

6. Pop (Stack, Letter)

7. Write a segment of code to perform each of the following operations. You may call any of the procedures or functions specified for the Stack ADT.
   (a) Set SecondElement to the second element in the stack, leaving the stack without its top two elements.
   (b) Set Bottom equal to the bottom element in the stack, leaving the stack empty.
   (c) Set Bottom equal to the bottom element in the stack, leaving the stack unchanged.
   (d) Remove all the zero elements from a stack, leaving all the other elements in the stack.

8. (Multiple choice) If the record implementation of a stack were used, the statement

   ```
   Stack.Elements[1] := Stack.Elements[2]
   ```

   in the main program (setting the top element equal to the second element)
   (a) would cause a syntax error at compile time.

(b) would cause a run-time error.

(c) would not be considered an error by the computer, but would violate the encapsulation of the stack data type.

(d) would be a perfectly legal and appropriate way to accomplish the intended task.

9. (Multiple choice)   The statements

```
Push (Stack, X + 1);
Pop (Stack, X - 1)
```

in the main program

(a) would cause a syntax error at compile time.

(b) would cause a run-time error.

(c) would be legal, but would violate the encapsulation of the stack.

(d) would be perfectly legal and appropriate.

10. Given the following specification of the Push operation:

■ **Push (Stack, NewElement, OverFlow)**

Function:	Add NewElement to the top of the stack, if the stack is not full.
Input:	Stack (StackType) NewElement (StackElementType)
Preconditions:	Stack has been created.
Output:	Stack (changed) OverFlow (Boolean)
Postconditions:	OverFlow = (stack is already full). IF NOT OverFlow, Stack = original Stack with NewElement added on top; otherwise, Stack is unchanged.

(a) Write a procedure to implement this operation, using the array-based stack implementation developed in the chapter.

(b) Write a procedure to implement this operation, using the linked stack implementation developed in the chapter.

11. Given the following specification of the Pop operation:

■ **Pop (Stack, PoppedElement, UnderFlow)**

Function:	Remove top element from Stack and return it in PoppedElement.
Input:	Stack (StackType)
Preconditions:	Stack has been created.
Output:	Stack (changed) PoppedElement (StackElementType) UnderFlow (Boolean)
Postconditions:	UnderFlow = (stack is empty when Pop called). IF NOT UnderFlow, Stack = original Stack with top element deleted, PoppedElement = top element from the stack; otherwise, Stack is unchanged and PoppedElement is undefined.

(a) Write a procedure to implement this operation, using the array-based stack implementation developed in the chapter.

(b) Write a procedure to implement this operation, using the linked stack implementation developed in the chapter.

12. Given the following specification of the StackTop operation:

> **StackTop (Stack): returns StackElementType**
>
> | | |
> |---|---|
> | *Function:* | Returns the value of the top element without changing the stack. |
> | *Input:* | Stack (StackType) |
> | *Preconditions:* | Stack is not empty. |
> | *Output:* | StackTop (StackElementType) |
> | *Postconditions:* | StackTop = value of top element from Stack |
> | | Stack is unchanged |

(a) Write this function as a stack application, using operations from the specifications. (You do not know how the stack is implemented.)

(b) Write this function as a new operation in the stack ADT, using the array-based stack implementation from this chapter.

(c) What change(s), if any, would you have to make to the implementation of this operation if StackElementType was a record type. (Assumes standard Pascal.)

13. A stack is kept in a record (StackDataType) that has two fields: Elements (an array that contains the stack elements) and Top (the index of the current top element). The record variable is not declared, but rather it is allocated dynamically when a stack is needed. The stack is accessed through the following type:

```
TYPE
   StackType = ^StackDataType;
VAR
   Stack : StackType;
```

(a) Is the space for this array-based data structure statically or dynamically allocated?

(b) How much space is reserved for the variable Stack?

(c) Write the CreateStack, DestroyStack, and EmptyStack operations, using the specifications in the Stack ADT.

(d) Is a FullStack operation for this representation meaningful? Write the FullStack operation. (If the operation is not meaningful for this implementation, you should write a stub.)

(e) If you could write the Push and Pop procedures by modifying the source code of one of the stack implementations in the chapter, which one would you choose to modify? Write the Push and Pop operations, using the specifications in the Stack ADT.

14. The CreateStack and DestroyStack operations are virtually identical in some implementations, but they differ in their preconditions. Explain why this difference is important. What would happen if DestroyStack's precondition was not true, when the stack is implemented as a linked structure.

15. Two stacks of positive integers are needed, one containing those elements less than or equal to the value 1000 and the other containing those elements that are larger than 1000. The total number of elements in the small-value stack and the large-value stack combined will not be more than 200 at any time, but we cannot predict how many will be in each stack. (All the elements could be in the small-value stack, they could be evenly divided, both stacks could be empty, etc.) Can you think of a strategy to implement both stacks in one array?

(a) Draw a diagram of how the stack might look.

(b) Write the declarations for such a double-stack structure.

(c) Implement the Push operation; it will assign NewElement to the correct stack according to its value (compared to 1000).

16. A stack of integer elements is implemented as an array with the following declarations:

```
TYPE
   StackType = ARRAY [0 .. MaxStack] OF Integer;
VAR
   Stack : StackType;
```

The index of the top element is kept in Stack[0], and the stack elements are stored in Stack[1] .. Stack[Stack[0]].

(a) How does this implementation fare with the idea of an array as a homogeneous collection of data elements?

(b) How would this implementation change the stack specifications? How would it change the procedures and functions?

17. Each node in a linked stack representation points to its successor. What does the last node point to?

Use the following declarations for Exercises 18 and 19.

```
TYPE
   PtrType  = ^NodeType;
   NodeType = RECORD
     Info   : Integer;
     Next   : PtrType
   END; (* NodeType *)

   StackType = PtrType;

   ListDataType = RECORD
     Length : Integer;
     Info   : ARRAY [1 .. 10] OF Integer
   END; (* ListDataType *)

   ListType = ^ListDataType;

VAR
   Stack : StackType;
   List  : ListType;
   Ptr   : PtrType;
```

18. Mark each statement as syntactically **valid** or **invalid**.

(a) Stack^.Info := '2';

(b) Stack^.Info := List^.Info;

(c) Ptr := Stack^.Next;

(d) Stack^.Info := List^.Info[3];

(e) Ptr^.Next := Stack;

(f) List.Length := List.Length + 1;

(g) Ptr := List;

(h) Ptr := Ptr^.Next;

(i) List^.Info[Ptr^.Info] := Stack^.Info;

19. Describe each of the following as a pointer, array, record, or integer:

(a) `Stack`

(b) `List^`

(c) `List^.Info`

(d) `Stack^.Info`

(e) `Stack^.Next`

(f) `Ptr^.Next^`

(g) `List^.Info[Ptr^.Info]`

20. Write Procedure PrintReverse, given the following specification. Your solution should use a stack. (You may use any of the stack operations defined for the Stack ADT, but you may not assume any knowledge of the implementation of the stack.)

PrintReverse

Function:	Read a string of characters, terminated by a blank, from file Data, and print out the characters in reverse order.
Input:	Data (Text)
Preconditions:	Data is open for reading.
Output:	To screen: characters
Postconditions:	Screen contains characters from file Data, from original read cursor position up to but not including first blank, printed in reverse order. Read cursor is positioned to read character following blank.

21. Write a code segment to read in a string of characters and determine whether they form a palindrome. A palindrome is a sequence of characters that reads the same both forward and backward, for example:

ABLE WAS I ERE I SAW ELBA

The character '.' ends the string. Write a message indicating whether the string is a palindrome. You may assume that the data is correct and that the maximum number of characters is 80.

22. Write a procedure ReplaceElement, with the following specifications:

ReplaceElement (Stack, OldEl, NewEl)

Function:	Replace all occurrences of OldEl in the stack with NewEl.
Input:	Stack (StackType)
	OldEl, NewEl (both StackElementType)
Preconditions:	Stack has been created.
Output:	Stack (changed)
Postconditions:	Stack = original Stack with any occurrence of OldEl changed to NewEl

(You may use any of the operations defined for the Stack ADT, but you may not assume any knowledge of how the stack is implemented.)

23. In each plastic container of Pez candy, the colors are stored in random order. Your little brother only likes the yellow ones, so he painstakingly takes out all the candies, one by one, eats the yellow ones, and keeps the others in order, so that he can return them to the container in exactly the same order as before—minus the yellow candies, of course. Write the algorithm to simulate this process. (You may use any of the stack operations defined in the Stack ADT, but may not assume any knowledge of how the stack is implemented.)

24. True or False?
    (a) Since the two Pop implementations developed in the chapter are both O(1), they take the same amount of time to execute.
    (b) The array-based stack implementation uses more space than the linked implementation, no matter how many elements are actually in the stack.
    (c) If the elements in a stack are stored in an array, then the stack is necessarily a static variable.

25. Assuming that data of StackElementType takes 12 bytes, integers take 2 bytes, and that pointer types take 4 bytes, and MaxStack = 100, compare the space requirements of static array-based versus dynamic linked stack implementations. (In calculating the space requirements of the linked implementation, don't forget to count the external pointer.)

Number of Elements	Static Array-Based	Dynamic Linked Stack
0		
10		
50		
100		

26. Indicate whether a stack would be a logical data structure for each of the following applications.
    (a) A program is to evaluate arithmetic expressions according to the specific order of operators.
    (b) A bank wants to simulate its teller operation to see how waiting times would be affected by adding another teller.
    (c) A program is to receive data that will be saved and processed in the reverse order.
    (d) An address book is to be maintained.
    (e) A word processor is to have a PF key that causes the preceding command to be redisplayed. Every time the PF key is pressed, the program is to show the command that preceded the one currently displayed.
    (f) A dictionary of words used by a spelling checker is to be built and maintained.
    (g) A program is to keep track of patients as they check into a medical clinic, assigning patients to doctors on a first-come, first-served basis.
    (h) A data structure is used to keep track of the return addresses for nested procedures while a program is running.

27. (Turbo Pascal Exercise) Write a functional version of the FullStack operation, using the linked implementation of a stack that was developed in the chapter. This function should use the Turbo Pascal MaxAvail and SizeOf operations to determine whether there is room in memory for another element.

Problems 28–37 refer to the application section at the end of this chapter.

28. If the specifications of Calculator included the assumption that every expression must be fully parenthesized, including parentheses around the outermost operands, how could the program be modified? For instance, 2 + 3 would be expressed as (2 + 3).

29. The call to Pop at the end of EvaluateExpression is to be replaced by a module called GetResult, as discussed in the application text. This module checks the status of the stacks to see if there is a mismatch between the operands and operators. GetResult inputs the two stacks and outputs Result (ValueType) and Error (Boolean), as well as the stacks, which should both be empty at the end of this operation.
    (a) Write the specification of the GetResult operation.
    (b) Write GetResult.
    (c) Show how EvaluateExpression might be changed to use the GetResult operation, including reporting any errors.

30. If the program is modified to let Procedure PerformOperation check for division-by-zero errors, what changes would be required in the specification of this procedure? in the implementation of the procedure?

31. What changes would need to be made to Program Calculator to switch to the array-based stack implementation? What additional error checking, if any, would be required?

32. True or False?
    (a) Parentheses are never needed in prefix or postfix expressions.
    (b) The relative order of the operators in an infix expression is exactly the reverse of the order of the operators in the equivalent postfix expression.
    (c) A postfix expression is merely the reverse of the prefix expression.
    (d) A stack may be used to aid in evaluating a prefix expression.

33. Evaluate the following prefix expressions:
    (a) + * 2 + / 14 2 5 1
    (b) − * 6 3 − 4 1
    (c) + + 2 6 + − 13 2 4

34. Evaluate the following postfix expressions:
    (a) 6 4 + 1 − 3 /
    (b) 1 4 18 6 / 3 + + 5 / +
    (c) 1 16 8 4 2 / / / + 5 *

35. Convert the following infix expressions to prefix notation:
    (a) ((A + 2) * (B + 4)) − 1
    (b) Z − ((((X + 1) * 2) − 5) / Y)
    (c) ((C * 2) + 1) / (A + B)

36. Convert the infix expressions in Exercise 35 to postfix notation.

37. Write an algorithm to convert a nonparenthesized infix expression to the equivalent postfix expression. The order of the evaluating the infix expression is based on the following precedence rules:

    * and / have equal precedence.
    + and − have equal precedence.
    * and / have higher precedence than + and −.

    For instance, the infix expression

    3 − 6 * 7 + 2 / 4 * 5 − 8

    converts to the postfix expression

    3 6 7 * − 2 4 / 5 * + 8 −

    You may use any of the operations specified for the Stack ADT in your algorithm.

FIFO Queues

GOALS

- To be able to describe the structure of a FIFO queue and its operations at a logical level.
- To be able to demonstrate the effect of queue operations on a particular implementation of a FIFO queue.
- To be able to implement the FIFO Queue ADT using a static array-based implementation.
- To be able to implement the FIFO Queue ADT as a linked data structure.
- To be able to compare queue implementations in terms of source code length, use of storage space, and Big-O appoximations of the queue operations.
- To be able to choose between a statically and a dynamically allocated structure.
- To be able to discuss the advantages and disadvantages to using a linked data structure.
- To be able to determine when a FIFO queue is an appropriate data structure for a specific problem.
- To be able to design and implement the solution to a problem for which a queue is an appropriate data structure.
- To be able to design and implement a strategy for testing a queue implementation.

In Chapter 4 we talked about a stack, a data structure with the special property that elements are always added to and removed from the top. We know from experience that many collections of data elements operate in the reverse manner: Elements are added at one end and removed from the other. This structure, called a **FIFO** (First In, First Out) **queue**, has many uses in computer programs. In this chapter we will consider the FIFO queue data structure at three levels: logical, implementation, and application. In the rest of this chapter, "queue" refers to a FIFO queue. (Another queue-type data structure, the priority queue, is discussed in Chapter 10. The accessing function of a priority queue is different from that of a FIFO queue.)

The Logical Level

What Is a Queue?

A **queue** (pronounced like the letter Q) is an ordered, homogeneous group of elements in which new elements are added at one end (the "rear") and elements are removed from the other end (the "front"). As an example of a queue, consider a line of students waiting to pay for their textbooks at a university bookstore (see Figure 5-1). In theory, if not in practice, each new student gets in line at the rear. When the cashier is ready for a new customer, the student at the front of the line is served.

To add elements to a FIFO queue we access the rear of the queue; to remove elements we access the front. The middle elements are logically inaccessible, even if we physically store the queue elements in a random-access structure such as an array. It is convenient to picture the queue as a linear structure with the front at one end and the rear at the other end. However, we must stress that the "ends" of the queue are *abstrac-*

Figure 5-1
A FIFO Queue

Rear of
Queue

Front of
Queue

tions; they may or may not correspond to any physical characteristics of the data structure's implementation. The essential property of the queue is its FIFO access.

FIFO Queue   A data structure in which elements are added to the rear and removed from the front; a "first in, first out" (FIFO) structure.

Like the stack, the queue is a holding structure for data that we will use later. We put a data element onto the queue, and then when we need it we remove it from the queue. If we want to change the value of an element, we must take that element off the queue, change its value, and then return it to the queue. We do not directly manipulate the values of elements that are currently in the queue.

Operations on FIFO Queues

The bookstore example suggests two operations that can be applied to a queue. First, new elements can be added to the rear of the queue, an operation that we will call *Enqueue*. We can also take elements off the front of the queue, an operation that we will call *Dequeue*. Unlike the stack operations Push and Pop, the adding and removing operations on a queue do not have standard names. Enqueue is sometimes called Enq, Add, or Insert; Dequeue is also called Deq, Remove, or Serve.

Another useful queue operation is checking whether the queue is empty. The *EmptyQueue* function returns True if Queue is empty and False otherwise. We can only Dequeue when the queue is not empty. Theoretically we can always Enqueue, for in principle a queue is not limited in size. We know from our experience with stacks, however, that certain implementations (an array representation, for instance) require that we test whether the structure is full before we add another element. This real-world consideration applies to queues as well, so we will define a *FullQueue* operation.

We also need an operation to initialize a queue to an empty state, which we will call *CreateQueue*. As with stacks, we might also want an operation to destroy the whole structure, leaving it empty. We will call this operation *DestroyQueue*.

Figure 5-2 shows how a series of these operations would affect a queue. We have briefly described a set of accessing operations for a FIFO queue. Before we talk about its use and implementation, let's define the specification for the FIFO Queue abstract data type.

FIFO Queue ADT Specification

Structure   Elements are added at the rear and removed from the front of the queue.

Operations:

CreateQueue (Queue)

Function:	Initializes Queue to empty state.
Input:	None
Preconditions:	None

Output:	Queue (QueueType)
Postconditions:	Queue is empty.

DestroyQueue (Queue)

Function:	Removes all elements from Queue, leaving the queue empty.
Input:	Queue (QueueType)
Preconditions:	Queue has been created.
Output:	Queue
Postconditions:	Queue is empty.

EmptyQueue (Queue)   Returns a Boolean value

Function:	Indicates whether Queue is empty.
Input:	Queue to be tested.
Preconditions:	Queue has been created.
Output:	EmptyQueue (Boolean)
Postconditions:	EmptyQueue = (Queue is empty)

FullQueue (Queue)   Returns a Boolean value

Function:	Indicates whether Queue is full.
Input:	Queue to be tested.
Preconditions:	Queue has been created.
Output:	FullQueue (Boolean)
Postconditions:	FullQueue = (Queue is full)

Enqueue (Queue, NewElement)

Function:	Adds NewElement to the rear of Queue.
Input:	Queue, NewElement
Preconditions:	Queue has been created and is not full.
Output:	Queue
Postconditions:	Queue = original Queue with NewElement added to rear.

Dequeue (Queue, DeqElement)

Function:	Removes front element from Queue and returns its value as DeqElement.
Input:	Queue
Preconditions:	Queue has been created and is not empty.
Output:	Queue DeqElement
Postconditions:	Queue = original Queue with front element removed. DeqElement = front element of original Queue.

Figure 5-2
The Effects of
Queue Operations

CreateQueue
(Queue)

EmptyQueue
(Queue)=True

EnQueue
(Queue,A)

EmptyQueue
(Queue)=False

EnQueue
(Queue,B)

DeQueue
(Queue,Customer)

EnQueue
(Queue,C)

DestroyQueue
(Queue)

EmptyQueue
(Queue)=True

Note that in this specification, we made the caller of Enqueue and Dequeue responsible for checking for overflow and underflow conditions. As discussed in Chapter 4, these conditions could be checked inside the routines and a Boolean flag returned. The specifications of the Enqueue and Dequeue routines would have to be changed, of course. One of the exercises at the end of this chapter asks you to design and implement this version of the queue operations. As in Chapter 4, we have used a simple, informal way of specifying the operations.

The User Level

Let's see how the FIFO queue operations might be used in a program. Suppose that we are reading character information in the form

  substring1 .substring2

where *substring1* and *substring2* are the same length (at least one character each) and are separated by a period. We want to write a procedure that reads such a string, and that checks whether its format is correct. Procedure ReadMatchString will output two parameters—String (the string that was read) and StringMatch, a Boolean value that indicates whether the two substrings are actually the same. For instance, if String is 'ABCDEFG.ABCDEFG', StringMatch is true; if String is 'ABCDEFG.ABCDEFQ', StringMatch is false.

The algorithm for this procedure uses a FIFO queue to hold the first substring's characters in the order in which they were read until they are needed for the comparison with the second substring.

StringMatch

Create queue
StringMatch ← True

REPEAT
    Read a character, and put into String.
    IF character <> '.'
        THEN Enqueue the character.
UNTIL character = '.'

WHILE more elements in the queue DO
    Dequeue an element.
    Read the next character and place in string.
    IF Dequeue character <> character read
        THEN StringMatch ← False

This algorithm can be coded into Procedure ReadMatchString, using procedures CreateQueue, Enqueue, and Dequeue and function EmptyQueue, as described in the FIFO queue ADT specifications. We will use the definition of StringType discussed in Chapter 3. (We can assume that the characters read in will not exceed the maximum string length.)

```
PROCEDURE ReadMatchString
   (VAR String     : StringType;
    VAR StringMatch : Boolean);

   (* Reads a String containing two substrings of equal  *)
   (* length, separated by a period. StringMatch is True *)
   (* if the substrings are the same, False otherwise.   *)
```

```
VAR
  StringChar : Char;      (* character read         *)
  QueueChar  : Char;      (* char removed from queue *)
  Queue      : QueueType; (* saves first substring   *)
BEGIN (* ReadMatchString *)

  EmptyString (String);   (* Start with empty string.  *)
  CreateQueue (Queue);    (* Start with an empty queue. *)
  StringMatch := True;    (* Start out optimistic.      *)

  (* Read and Enqueue the characters in the first substring. *)
  REPEAT

    (* Read character and put it into the string. *)
    Read (StringChar);
    Append (String, StringChar);

    (* Put the character in the queue. *)
    IF StringChar <> '.'
      THEN Enqueue (Queue, StringChar)

  UNTIL StringChar = '.';

  (* Read and compare characters in second substring with *)
  (* those in the queue. The FIFO queue preserves the     *)
  (* original order of the first substring's characters.  *)
  WHILE NOT EmptyQueue (Queue) DO
    BEGIN

      Dequeue (Queue, QueueChar);

      (* Read the next character and place in string. *)
      Read (StringChar);
      Append (String, StringChar);
      IF QueueChar <> StringChar
        THEN StringMatch := False

    END (* WHILE *)

END; (* ReadMatchString *)
```

The Implementation Level

Now that we've had the opportunity to be queue users, let's take a look at how a FIFO queue might be implemented in Pascal. As with a stack, the queue can be stored in a static variable, an array, as well as in dynamically allocated memory in a linked structure. We will look at both implementations in this chapter. Note that the queue user should not have to be concerned about which implementation is used, since the interfaces to all the queue operations will be the same.

The Implementation of a Queue as a Static Array

Like a stack, a queue can be stored in a record, with the elements in an array and other information in separate fields.

```
TYPE
  QueueType = RECORD
    Elements : ARRAY [1 .. MaxQueue] OF QueueElementType;

    .
    .  (* other information goes here *)
    .

  END; (* QueueType *)
```

The first question to consider is how we will order the elements in the array. In implementing the stack in Chapter 4, we began by inserting an element in the first array position and then let the top float with subsequent Push and Pop operations. The bottom of the stack, however, was fixed at the first slot in the array. Can we use a similar solution for a queue, keeping the front of the queue fixed in the first array slot and letting the rear move down as we add new elements?

Let's see what happens after a few Enqueue's and Dequeue's if we insert the first element in the first array position, the second element in the second position, and so on. After four calls to Enqueue, the queue would look like this:

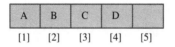

Enqueue (Queue, 'A');
Enqueue (Queue, 'B');
Enqueue (Queue, 'C');
Enqueue (Queue, 'D');

Remember that the front of the queue is fixed at the first slot in the array, whereas the rear of the queue moves down with each Enqueue. Now we Dequeue the front element in the queue:

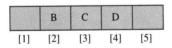

Dequeue (Queue, Element)

This operation deletes the element in the first array slot and leaves a hole. To keep the front of the queue fixed at the top of the array, we need to move every element in the queue up one slot:

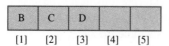

Let's summarize the queue operations corresponding to this queue design. The Enqueue operation would be the same as Push. The Dequeue operation would be more complicated than Pop, because all the remaining elements of the queue would have to be shifted up in the array, to move the new front of the queue up to the first array slot. The CreateQueue, DestroyQueue, EmptyQueue, and FullQueue operations could be the same as the equivalent stack operations.

Before we go any further, we want to stress that this design would work. It may not be the best design for a queue, but it could be successfully implemented. There are multiple *functionally correct* ways to implement the same abstract data structure. One design may not be as good as another (because it uses more space in memory or takes longer to execute) and yet may still be correct. Though we don't advocate the use of poor designs for programs or data structures, the first requirement must always be program correctness.

Now let's evaluate this design. Its strength is its simplicity; it is almost exactly like the package of stack routines that we wrote in Chapter 4. Though the queue is accessed from both ends rather than just one (as in the stack), we only have to keep track of the rear, because the front is fixed. Only the Dequeue operation is more complicated. What is the weakness of the design? The need to move all the elements up every time we remove an element from the queue increases the amount of work needed to Dequeue.

How serious is this weakness? To make this judgment, we have to know something about how the queue will be used. If this queue will be used for storing large numbers of elements at one time, or if the elements in the queue will be large (records with many fields, for instance), the processing required to move up all the elements after the front element has been removed will make this solution a poor one. On the other hand, if the queue generally contains only a few elements and they are small (integers, for instance), all this data movement may not amount to much processing. Further, we need to consider whether performance—how fast the program executes—is of importance in the application that will use the queue. Thus the complete evaluation of the design depends on the requirements of the program.

In the real programming world, however, you don't always know the exact uses or complete requirements of programs. For instance, you may be working on a very large project with a hundred other programmers. Other programmers may be writing the specific application programs for the project while you are producing some utility programs that will be used by all the different applications. If you don't know the requirements of the various users of your package of queue operations, you must design general-purpose utilities. In this situation the design described above is not the best one possible.

Another Queue Design

The need to move the elements in the array was created by our decision to keep the front of the queue fixed in the first array slot. If we keep track of the index of the front as well as the rear, we can let both ends of the queue float in the array.

Figure 5-3 shows how several Enqueue's and Dequeue's would affect the queue. (For simplicity, these figures show only the elements that are in the queue. The other

Figure 5-3
The Effect of
Enqueue and
Dequeue

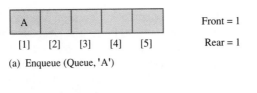

Front = 1
Rear = 1

[1]   [2]   [3]   [4]   [5]

(a) Enqueue (Queue, 'A')

| A | B | | | |

Front = 1
Rear = 2

[1]   [2]   [3]   [4]   [5]

(b) Enqueue (Queue, 'B')

| A | B | C | | |

Front = 1
Rear = 3

[1]   [2]   [3]   [4]   [5]

(c) Enqueue (Queue, 'C')

| | B | C | | |

Front = 2
Rear = 3

[1]   [2]   [3]   [4]   [5]

(d) Dequeue (Queue, Element)   Element = 'A'

slots contain logical garbage, including values that have been Dequeue'ed.) The Enqueue operations have the same effect as before; they add elements to subsequent slots in the array and increment the index of the Rear indicator. The Dequeue operation is simpler, however. Instead of moving elements up to the beginning of the array, it merely increments the Front indicator to the next slot.

Letting the queue elements float in the array creates a new problem when Rear gets to the end of the array. In our first design this situation told us that the queue was full. Now, however, it is possible for the rear of the queue to reach the end of the (physical) array when the (logical) queue is not yet full [Figure 5-4(a)].

Because there may still be space available at the beginning of the array, the obvious solution is to let the queue "wrap around" the end of the array. In other words, the array can be treated as a circular structure, in which the last slot is followed by the first slot [Figure 5-4(b)]. To get the next position for Rear, for instance, we can use an IF statement:

```
IF Rear = MaxQueue
  THEN Rear := 1
  ELSE Rear := Rear + 1;
```

Another way to reset Rear is to use the MOD operator:

```
Rear := (Rear MOD MaxQueue) + 1;
```

This solution leads us to a new problem: How do we know whether a queue is empty or full? In Figure 5-5 we remove the last element, leaving the queue empty. In Figure

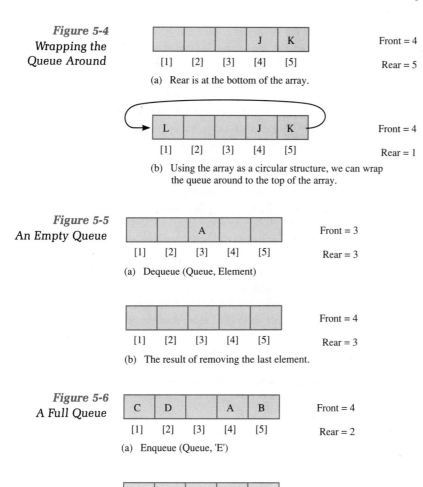

Figure 5-4
Wrapping the
Queue Around

Front = 4

Rear = 5

(a) Rear is at the bottom of the array.

Front = 4

Rear = 1

(b) Using the array as a circular structure, we can wrap
the queue around to the top of the array.

Figure 5-5
An Empty Queue

Front = 3

Rear = 3

(a) Dequeue (Queue, Element)

Front = 4

Rear = 3

(b) The result of removing the last element.

Figure 5-6
A Full Queue

Front = 4

Rear = 2

(a) Enqueue (Queue, 'E')

Front = 4

Rear = 3

(b) The result of adding the last element,
making the queue full.

5-6 we add an element to the last free slot in the queue, leaving the queue full. The values of Front and Rear, however, are identical in the two situations.

The first solution that comes to mind is to add another field to our queue record, in addition to Front and Rear—a count of the elements in the queue. When the count field is 0, the queue is empty; when the count is equal to the maximum number of array slots, the queue is full. Note that keeping this count adds processing to the Enqueue and Dequeue routines. If the queue user frequently needed to know the number of elements in the queue, however, this solution would certainly be a good one. We leave the development of this solution as a homework assignment.

Another common but less intuitive approach is to let Front indicate the index of the array slot *preceding* the front element in the queue, rather than the index of the front element itself. (The reason for this may not be immediately clear, but keep reading.)

If Rear still indicates the index of the rear element in the queue, the queue will be empty when Front = Rear. Before we Dequeue [see Figure 5-7(a)], we first check for the empty condition. Because the queue is not empty, we can Dequeue. Front is incremented to indicate the true location of the front queue element, and the value in that array slot is assigned to DeqElement. (Note that updating the Front index *precedes* assigning the value in this design, for Front does not point to the actual front element at the beginning of Dequeue.) After this Dequeue operation, EmptyQueue will find that Front is now equal to Rear, indicating that the queue is empty [see Figure 5-7(b)].

An additional convention that we must establish to implement this scheme is that the slot indicated by Front (the slot preceding the true front element) will be reserved. It cannot contain a queue element. Thus, if there are 100 array positions, the maximum size of the queue is 99 elements. To test for a full queue, we look to see whether the next space available (after Rear) is the special reserved slot indicated by Front (see Figure 5-8).

To Enqueue, we must first increment Rear so that it contains the index of the next free slot in the array. We can then insert the new element into this space.

Using this scheme, how do we initialize a queue to its empty state? We want Front to indicate the array index that precedes the front of the queue, so that when we first Enqueue the front of the queue will be in the first slot of the array. What is the position that precedes the first array slot? Because the array is circular, the first slot is preceded by the last slot. Thus we initialize Front to MaxQueue. Our test for an empty queue is Front = Rear; therefore, we will initialize Rear to Front, or MaxQueue.

To destroy a whole queue, we merely reinitialize it to its empty state. The data values in the array slots become logical garbage, but they are inaccessible when the queue's front and rear indexes say that the queue is empty. Therefore, as with the array implementation of a stack, the destroy operation will be identical to the create operation.

The declarations and operations for the FIFO Queue ADT follow on page 259.

Figure 5-7
Testing for an
Empty Queue

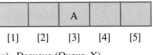

		A		
[1]	[2]	[3]	[4]	[5]

Front = 2

Rear = 3

(a) Dequeue (Queue, X)

[1]	[2]	[3]	[4]	[5]

Front = 3

Rear = 3

(b) Front = Rear

Figure 5-8
Testing for a Full
Queue

C	D	Reserved	A	B
[1]	[2]	[3]	[4]	[5]

Front = 3

Rear = 2

```
(*************************************************************)
(*                      FIFO QUEUE                         *)
(*                Array-Based Implementation               *)
(*************************************************************)
CONST
  MaxQueue = 100;
      (* MaxQueue is the upper array bound; it equals the *)
      (* maximum number of queue elements - 1.           *)
TYPE
  QueueElementType = Char;   (* or whatever is in the queue *)

  IndexType  = 1 .. MaxQueue;

  QueueType  = RECORD
    Elements : ARRAY [IndexType] OF QueueElementType;
    Front    : IndexType; (* index of slot preceding front *)
    Rear     : IndexType  (* index of slot containing rear *)
  END; (* QueueType *)

(*************************************************************)

PROCEDURE CreateQueue
  (VAR Queue : QueueType);

  (* Initialize Queue to empty state. *)

BEGIN (* CreateQueue *)

  Queue.Front := MaxQueue;
  Queue.Rear  := MaxQueue

END; (* CreateQueue *)

(*************************************************************)

PROCEDURE DestroyQueue
  (VAR Queue : QueueType);

  (* Remove all elements from Queue, leaving queue empty. *)

BEGIN (* DestroyQueue *)

  Queue.Front := MaxQueue;
  Queue.Rear  := MaxQueue

END; (* DestroyQueue *)

(*************************************************************)

FUNCTION EmptyQueue
  (Queue : QueueType) : Boolean;

  (* Returns True if Queue is empty; otherwise it is False. *)

BEGIN (* EmptyQueue *)

  (* Queue is empty if Rear indicator = Front indicator. *)
  EmptyQueue := (Queue.Rear = Queue.Front)

END; (* EmptyQueue *)
```

```
(*************************************************************)

FUNCTION FullQueue
  (Queue : QueueType) : Boolean;

  (* Returns True if Queue is full; returns False otherwise. *)

BEGIN (* FullQueue *)

  (* Queue is full if the next available rear position *)
  (* is equal to the front of the queue.               *)
  FullQueue := ((Queue.Rear MOD MaxQueue) + 1 = Queue.Front)

END; (* FullQueue *)

(*************************************************************)

PROCEDURE Enqueue

  (VAR Queue   : QueueType;
   NewElement : QueueElementType);

  (* Add NewElement to the rear of the queue. Assumes *)
  (* that the queue is not full.                      *)

BEGIN (* Enqueue *)

  (* Find the next rear position. Queue.Rear is the    *)
  (* index of the current rear of the queue. The queue *)
  (* may wrap around the end of the array.             *)
  Queue.Rear := (Queue.Rear MOD MaxQueue) + 1;

  (* Add new element to the rear of the queue. *)
  Queue.Elements[Queue.Rear] := NewElement

END; (* Enqueue *)

(*************************************************************)

PROCEDURE Dequeue
  (VAR Queue      : QueueType;
   VAR DeqElement : QueueElementType);

  (* Remove the front element from Queue and return it   *)
  (* in DeqElement. Assumes that the queue is not empty. *)

BEGIN (* Dequeue *)

  (* Update Queue.Front to access the front of the queue. *)
  (* Queue.Front is the index of the array slot preceding *)
  (* the front element in the queue. The queue may wrap   *)
  (* around the end of the array.                         *)
  Queue.Front := (Queue.Front MOD MaxQueue) + 1;

  (* Assign the front element of the queue to DeqElement. *)
  DeqElement := Queue.Elements[Queue.Front]

END; (* Dequeue *)

(*************************************************************)
```

Note that Dequeue, like the stack Pop operation, does not actually remove the value of the element from the array. The value that has just been Dequeue'ed still physically exists in the array. It no longer exists in the queue, however, and cannot be accessed because of the change in Queue.Front.

 The source code for this array-based implementation of a FIFO queue can be found in file QUEUE1.PAS on the program disk.

Comparing Array Implementations

This solution is not nearly so simple or intuitive as our first queue design. What did we gain by adding some amount of complexity to our design? By using a more efficient Dequeue algorithm, we achieved better performance. To find out how much better, let's analyze the first design: Since the amount of work to move all the remaining elements is proportional to the number of elements, this version of Dequeue is an O(N) operation. The second array-based queue design only requires Dequeue to change the values of the Front indicator and to put the value in the new Front slot. The amount of work never exceeds some fixed constant, no matter how many elements are in the queue, so the algorithm is O(1).

All of the other operations, for both array-based designs, are O(1). No matter how many elements are in the queue, they do (essentially) a constant amount of work. That does *not* mean that the two Enqueue operations will be the same in terms of lines of code or time of execution. It only means that the amount of work done by them is roughly equivalent.

The Implementation of a Queue as a Linked Structure

The major weakness of the array-based implementation is the need to declare an array big enough for a structure of the maximum expected size. This size is set at compile time. If a much smaller number of elements is actually needed at run time, we have wasted a lot of space. If a larger number of elements is unexpectedly needed, we are in trouble. We cannot extend the size of the array at run time.

We know, however, from our discussion of stacks in Chapter 4, that we can get around this problem by using dynamic storage allocation to get space for queue elements at run time. This implementation relies on the idea of linking the elements one to the next to form a chain.

In the array-based implementation of a queue, we decided to keep track of two indexes that pointed to the Front and Rear boundaries of the data in the queue. In a linked representation we can use two *pointers,* QFront and QRear, to mark the front and the rear of the queue. (See Figure 5-9. Since by now you realize that dynamically allocated nodes in linked structures exist "somewhere in memory," rather than in adjacent locations like array slots, we are going to show the nodes arranged linearly for clarity.)

The user's data will be stored in dynamically allocated "nodes," along with a pointer to the following node in the queue. Reviewing our design terminology from Chapter 4, let's assume that Ptr points to one of the nodes in a queue.

Figure 5-9
A Linked Queue
Representation

Figure 5-10
The Enqueue
Operation

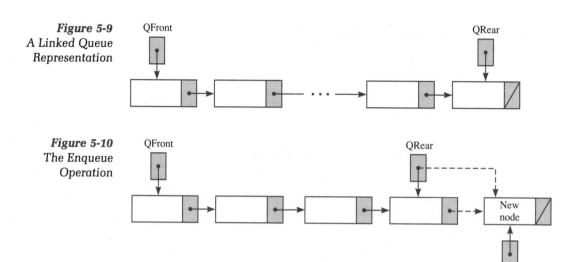

Node(Ptr)	refers to the *whole node* pointed to by Ptr.
Info(Ptr)	refers to the *data field* of the node pointed to by Ptr.
Next(Ptr)	refers to the *pointer field* of the node pointed to by Ptr.

We can Dequeue elements from the queue using an algorithm similar to our stack Pop algorithm, with QFront pointing to the first node in the queue. Because we add new elements to the queue by inserting after the last node, however, we need a new Enqueue algorithm (see Figure 5-10):

Enqueue

Create node for the new element
Insert the new node at the rear of the queue
Update pointer to the rear of the queue

The first of these tasks is familiar from the stack Push operation. We get the space using Pascal's New procedure, and then assign the new element value to the node's Info field. Because the new node will be inserted at the rear end of the queue, however, we will also need to set the node's Next field to NIL.

(Create node for the new element.)
New (NewNode)
Info(NewNode) ← new element
Next(NewNode) ← NIL

The second part of the Enqueue algorithm involves updating the Next field of Node(QRear) to make it point to the new node. This is simple:

(Insert the new node at the rear of the queue.)
Next(QRear) ← NewNode

What happens if the queue is empty, when we Enqueue the first element? In this case, there is no Node(QRear); we must set QFront to point to the new node. We will modify the algorithm to take this condition into account:

(Insert the new node at the rear of the queue.)
IF the queue is empty
    THEN QFront ← NewNode
    ELSE Next(QRear) ← NewNode

The last task in the Enqueue algorithm, updating the QRear pointer, simply involves the assignment QRear ← NewNode. Does this work if this is the first node in the queue? Sure; we always want QRear to be pointing to the rear node following a call to Enqueue, regardless of how many elements are in the queue.

Note the relative positions of QFront and QRear. Had they been reversed (as in Figure 5-11), we could have used our stack Push algorithm for the Enqueue operation. But how could we Dequeue? To delete the last node of the linked queue, we need to be able to reset QFront to point to the node preceding the deleted node. Because our pointers all go forward, we can't get back to the preceding node. To accomplish this task, we would either have to traverse the whole list (an O(N) solution—very inefficient, especially if the queue is long) or else keep a list with pointers in both directions. Use of this kind of a *doubly linked* structure (which we will discuss in Chapter 7) is not necessary if we set up our queue pointers correctly to begin with.

In writing the Enqueue algorithm we noticed that inserting into an empty queue is a special case because we need to make QFront point to the new node also. Similarly, in our Dequeue algorithm we will need to allow for the case of deleting the last node in the queue, leaving the queue empty. If QFront is NIL after we have deleted the front node, we know that the queue is now empty. In this case we will need to set QRear to NIL also. The algorithm for Dequeue'ing the front element from a linked queue is illustrated in Figure 5-12.

Figure 5-11
A Bad Queue Design

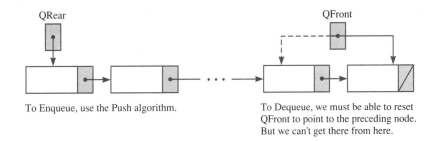

To Enqueue, use the Push algorithm.

To Dequeue, we must be able to reset QFront to point to the preceding node. But we can't get there from here.

Figure 5-12
The Dequeue Operation

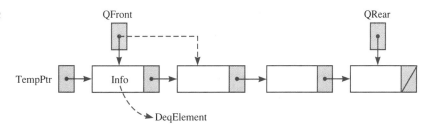

This algorithm assumes that the test for an empty queue was performed before the Dequeue routine was entered, so we know that the queue contains at least one node. (We can make this assumption because this is the precondition for Dequeue in our FIFO Queue ADT specification.) As in Pop, we will need to keep a local pointer to the node being removed, so that we will be able to access it for the call to Dispose after the QFront pointer change.

Dequeue

TempPtr ← QFront (Save it for disposing)
DeqValue ← Info(QFront)
QFront ← Next(QFront)

IF queue is now empty
    THEN QRear ← NIL

Dispose (TempPtr)

How do we know when the queue is empty? Both QFront and QRear should then be NIL pointers. This makes Procedure CreateQueue and Function EmptyQueue extremely simple. What about Function FullQueue? As we said in Chapter 4, there is no way to detect a full structure; we can continue to Enqueue until the system runs out of memory! Using dynamically allocated space rather than a static (declared variable) array, we no longer have a MaxQueue constant to limit our queue size. So there really isn't any need to have a FullQueue function. Since this operation is defined for the FIFO Queue ADT, however, we must supply a function for it. As we did for the linked stack implementation, we will code a stub for FullQueue, a dummy function that just sets the return value. (Of course, if you are programming in a nonstandard version of Pascal that allows you to check how much free memory you have, as Turbo Pascal does, you can write a functional version of FullQueue. We leave this as an exercise.)

In the array-based implementation, operation DestroyQueue merely changed the Front and Rear indexes to make the queue appear to be empty. There was no need to do anything to the data slots in the array; they became logical garbage, inaccessible through the queue operations. In the linked implementation, DestroyQueue must result in an empty queue, but there's more to this operation than just setting QFront and QRear to NIL. We must also free the dynamically allocated space in which the queue elements reside. The algorithm is basically like a loop that performs Dequeue's "unlinking" and "disposing" operations on successive queue elements. At the end of the operation, QFront and QRear are both NIL, so the queue is empty.

DestroyQueue

WHILE more elements
    TempPtr ← QFront (Save it for disposing)
    QFront ← Next(QFront)
    Dispose (TempPtr)

QRear ← NIL

As in the case of changing the stack implementation to a linked structure, we will change only the declarations and the insides of the queue operations. For a queue-using program, the interfaces to the operations will remain the same. Let's look at the declarations first. For simplicity, in our design, we referred to the two queue pointers as QFront and QRear. Our queue operations, however, have only a single Queue reference on the parameter list. In implementing the queue data type, we will combine these two external pointers in a record type, which we will call QueueType. We will access the front of the queue through the pointer Queue.Front and the rear of the queue through the pointer Queue.Rear. Each of these pointers points to a node in the linked queue (or are NIL pointers if the queue is empty). Each queue node has two fields, Info (containing the user's data) and Next (containing the pointer to the next node, or in the case of the last node, NIL). We can implement the FIFO Queue ADT with the following declarations, procedures, and functions:

```
(********************************************************)
(*                    FIFO QUEUE                       *)
(*              Linked Implementation                  *)
(********************************************************)

TYPE

  QueueElementType = Char;   (* or whatever is in the queue *)

  QueuePtrType = ^QueueNodeType;

  QueueNodeType = RECORD
    Info : QueueElementType;   (* the queue user's data      *)
    Next : QueuePtrType        (* pointer to next queue node *)
  END;   (* QueueNodeType *)

  QueueType = RECORD
    Front : QueuePtrType;   (* accesses front of queue *)
    Rear  : QueuePtrType    (* accesses rear of queue  *)
  END; (* QueueType *)

(********************************************************)

PROCEDURE CreateQueue
  (VAR Queue : QueueType);

  (* Initializes Queue to an empty state. *)

BEGIN (* CreateQueue *)

  Queue.Front := NIL;
  Queue.Rear  := NIL
END; (* CreateQueue *)

(********************************************************)

FUNCTION EmptyQueue
  (Queue : QueueType) : Boolean;

  (* Returns True if Queue does not contain any elements; *)
  (* returns False otherwise.                             *)
```

```
BEGIN (* EmptyQueue *)
  EmptyQueue := (Queue.Front = NIL)
END; (* EmptyQueue *)

(****************************************************************)

FUNCTION FullQueue
  (Queue : QueueType) : Boolean;

  (* Returns True if Queue is full; returns False otherwise. *)

BEGIN (* FullQueue *)

  (* This function is not meaningful for this queue *)
  (* implementation, so just return False.          *)
  FullQueue := False

END; (* FullQueue *)

(****************************************************************)

PROCEDURE Enqueue
  (VAR Queue  : QueueType;
   NewElement : QueueElementType);

  (* Adds NewElement to the rear of Queue. Assumes that *)
  (* Queue is not "full."                               *)

VAR
  NewNode : QueuePtrType;

BEGIN (* Enqueue *)

  (* Create a node for the new element. *)
  New (NewNode);
  NewNode^.Info := NewElement;
  NewNode^.Next := NIL;

  (* Insert new node at rear of Queue. *)
  IF Queue.Rear = NIL (* queue is empty *)
    THEN Queue.Front := NewNode
    ELSE Queue.Rear^.Next := NewNode;

  (* Update external pointer to rear of Queue. *)
  Queue.Rear := NewNode

END; (* Enqueue *)

(****************************************************************)

PROCEDURE Dequeue
  (VAR Queue     : QueueType;
   VAR DeqElement : QueueElementType);

  (* Removes front element from Queue and returns its *)
  (* value in DeqElement. Assumes Queue is not empty. *)

VAR
  TempPtr : QueuePtrType;
```

```
BEGIN (* Dequeue *)

  TempPtr := Queue.Front; (* save it for Dispose *)

  (* Take DeqElement from front node of Queue. *)
  DeqElement := Queue.Front^.Info;

  (* Remove front node from Queue. *)
  Queue.Front := Queue.Front^.Next;
  IF Queue.Front = NIL (* queue is now empty *)
    THEN Queue.Rear := NIL;

  Dispose (TempPtr)

END; (* Dequeue *)
(* *********************************************************** *)

PROCEDURE DestroyQueue
  (VAR Queue : QueueType);

VAR
  TempPtr : QueuePtrType;

BEGIN (* DestroyQueue *)

  WHILE Queue.Front <> NIL DO
    BEGIN
      TempPtr := Queue.Front;
      Queue.Front := Queue.Front^.Next;
      Dispose (TempPtr)
    END; (* WHILE *)

  Queue.Rear := NIL

END; (* DestroyQueue *)
```

Source code for this implementation is in file QUEUE2.PAS on the program disk.

A Circular Linked Queue Design

Our QueueType record contains two pointers, one to each end of the queue. This design is based on the linear structure of the linked queue: Given only a pointer to the Front of the queue, we could follow the pointers to get to the Rear, but this makes accessing the Rear (to Enqueue) an O(N) operation. With a pointer to the Rear of the queue, we could not access the Front because the pointers only go from the Front to Rear.

However, we could access both ends of the queue from a single pointer, if we made the queue *circularly linked*. That is, the Next field of the Rear node would point to the Front node of the queue (see Figure 5-13). Now QueueType will simply be a pointer to a single queue node, rather than a record containing two pointers. Queue, the external pointer to the queue, will point to the "rear" node.

One interesting thing about this queue implementation is that it differs from the logical picture of a queue as a linear structure with two ends. This queue is a circular structure with no ends. What makes it a queue is its support of FIFO access.

Figure 5-13
A Circular Linked
Queue

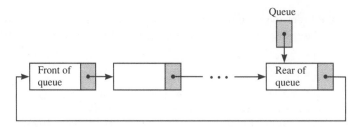

In order to Enqueue, we access the "rear" node directly through the pointer Queue. To Dequeue, we must access the "front" node of the queue. We don't have an external pointer to this node, but we do have a pointer to the node preceding it—Queue. The pointer to the "front" node of the queue is in Next(Queue). An empty queue would be represented by Queue = NIL.

Designing and coding the queue operations using a circular linked implementation is left as an exercise.

Comparing the Queue Implementations

We have now looked at several different implementations of the FIFO Queue ADT. How do they compare? As we compared Stack implementations in Chapter 4, we will look at several different factors: the length of the source code required to implement the solutions, the amount of memory required to store the structure, and the amount of "work" the solution requires, as expressed in Big-O notation. We will compare the two implementations that are completely coded in this chapter.

The size of the source code of the declarations, procedures, and functions for each implementation is summarized in the table that follows. As you can see from the table, the array-based implementation is somewhat smaller (about 30% fewer lines of code) than the linked implementation. This means that there are fewer lines of code to develop and to maintain. However, unlike the array-based stack implementation, the array-based queue implementation is not immediately obvious to the program reader; having

Comparison of Executable Source Lines of Code

	Array Implementation	Linked Implementation
Declarations	10	11
CreateQueue	6	6
DestroyQueue	6	13
FullQueue	5	5
EmptyQueue	5	5
Enqueue	7	14
Dequeue	7	13
Total	46	67

the Front index point to the array slot preceding the actual front element is a little bit tricky. Now that you are more familiar with Pascal pointer syntax and use, you will probably find that the linked implementation of a queue is more intuitive than the array implementation. Deciding which design is easier to understand is very subjective, but it is often a factor in selecting one approach over another.

Now let's compare the storage requirements. An array variable of the maximum queue size will take the same amount of memory, no matter how many array slots are actually used; we need to reserve space for the maximum possible number of elements. The linked implementation using dynamically allocated storage space only requires space for the number of elements actually in the queue at run time, plus space for the external pointer(s). Note, however, that the node elements are larger, since we must store the link (the Next field) as well as the user's data.

Let's see how these implementations would compare if the queue contains strings (each requiring, say, 80 bytes). The maximum number of queue elements is 100 strings (so MaxQueue = 101). On our sample system, an array index (type Integer) takes 2 bytes and a pointer takes 4 bytes. The storage requirements of the array-based implementation are

(80 bytes * 101 array slots) + (2 bytes * 2 indexes) = 8084 bytes

no matter how many elements are in the queue at any time. The linked queue implementation requires

80 bytes (the string) + 4 bytes (the "next" pointer) = 84 bytes

per queue node, plus 8 bytes for the two external Queue pointers. The storage requirements of this queue are graphed in Figure 5-14(a). Note that the linked implementation does not always take less space than the array; when the number of elements in the queue exceeds 96, the linked queue requires more memory, due to the need to store the pointers.

If the queue element type were small, like a character or an integer, the pointer field could be larger than the user's data field. In this case, the space used by the linked representation exceeds that of the array-based representation much faster. Consider a queue that may contain up to 100 integer elements (2 bytes each). The storage requirements for the array-based queue are

(2 bytes (per element) * 101 array slots) + (2 bytes * 2 indexes) = 206 bytes

no matter how many elements are in the queue at any time. The linked queue implementation requires

2 bytes (the Info field) + 4 bytes (the Next field) = 6 bytes

per queue node, plus 8 bytes for the two external Queue pointers. The storage requirements for this queue are graphed in Figure 5-14(b). When the number of elements in this queue exceeds 33, the linked queue requires more memory, due to the need to store pointers that are twice as big as the QueueElementType!

We can also compare the relative "efficiency" of the two implementations, in terms of Big-O. In both implementations, the CreateQueue, FullQueue, and EmptyQueue operations are clearly O(1). They always take a "constant" amount of work. What about

Figure 5-14
Comparison of Stor-
age Requirements

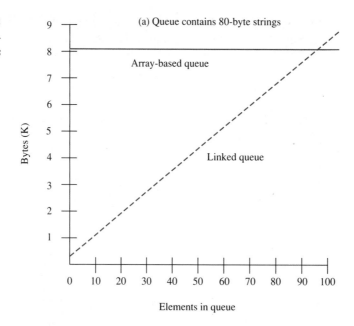

(a) Queue contains 80-byte strings

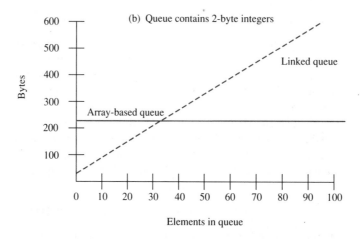

(b) Queue contains 2-byte integers

Enqueue and Dequeue? Does the number of elements in the queue affect the amount of work done by these operations? No, it does not; in both implementations, we can directly access the Front and Rear of the queue. The amount of work done by these operations is independent of the queue size, so these operations are also O(1). Only the DestroyQueue operation differs from one implementation to the other. The array-based implementation merely sets the Front and Rear indexes, so it is clearly an O(1) operation. The linked implementation must process every node in the queue in order to free the node space. This operation, therefore, is O(N), where N is the number of nodes in the queue. As with the array-based and linked implementations of stacks, these two queue implementations are roughly equivalent in terms of the amount of work they do, only differing in one of the six operations. The following table summarizes the Big-O comparison of the queue operations.

Big-O Comparison of the Queue Operations

	Array Implementation	*Linked Implementation*
CreateQueue	O(1)	O(1)
DestroyQueue	**O(1)**	**O(N)**
FullQueue	O(1)	O(1)
EmptyQueue	O(1)	O(1)
Enqueue	O(1)	O(1)
Dequeue	O(1)	O(1)

So which is better? Go back to the comparison of stack implementations in Chapter 4 and read the bottom line there. The answer is the same for the two queue implementations: It depends on the requirements of your application. Some of the kinds of issues to consider when choosing an implementation are listed in the next table.

Considerations for Selecting a Queue Implementation

Situation	*Recommended Implementation*
The number of elements in the queue varies greatly from one program execution to the next.	Linked with pointers
The maximum number of elements cannot be predicted.	Linked with pointers
The maximum number of elements is known, and the usual number is close to the maximum.	Array or linked with pointers
The maximum number of elements is known and is small.	Array or linked with pointers
The maximum number of elements is large and the element size is large.	Linked with pointers
The system or programming language does not support dynamic storage allocation.	Array
The program requirements specify a static implementation.	Array
The program requirements specify the use of dynamic allocation.	Linked with pointers

Testing the Queue Operations

You can test the FIFO Queue ADT independently of the program that will use it with a *test driver*. Although it is possible to write a complicated interactive test driver that allows the tester to specify actions (such as Enqueue and Dequeue), the simplest test driver merely sets up a scenario that will execute the various cases to be tested. To make sure that you have tested all the necessary cases, make a test plan, listing all the queue operations, and what tests are needed for each. (For example, to test Function EmptyQueue, you must call it at least twice, once when the queue is empty and once when it is not.)

We will want to Enqueue elements until the (array-based) queue is full; and then to call functions FullQueue and EmptyQueue to see whether they correctly judge the state of the queue. We can then Dequeue all the elements in the queue, printing them out as we go, to make sure that they are correctly Dequeued. At this point we can call the queue status functions again to see if the empty condition is correctly detected.

We will also want to test out the "tricky" part of the array-based algorithm: Enqueue until the queue is full, Dequeue an element, then Enqueue again, forcing the operation to circle back to the beginning of the array. At each point in the test, you should print out text explaining what the test driver is doing.

We can use the same test driver for testing both queue implementations; we merely replace the declarations and queue operations, leaving the driver's main program alone. Note that we will get different results for the FullQueue function, depending on the implementation.

Since the type of data stored in the queue has no effect on the operations that manipulate the queue, you can change QueueElementType to simplify the test driver. Suppose that the queue in your application program will contain a maximum of 1000 record-type elements, each with many fields (a queue of student information records, for instance). You don't need to Enqueue actual student records, since the queue element type is not relevant to how Enqueue works. For the test driver, you can declare QueueElementType to be Char to simplify setting up the test. You also don't need to test a queue of 1000 elements. Knowing that the code works the same whether MaxQueue is 10 or 1000, you can set MaxQueue to 10 for the test. Of course, when you finish testing, you will need to change MaxQueue and QueueElementType to the correct declarations for your application.

 A sample test driver for testing the FIFO Queue operations can be found in file TESTQ.PAS on the data disk. We suggest that you modify this driver and run it, trying out both implementations of QueueType. (Please let us know if you find any errors.)

*U*sing the Turbo "Include" Feature

One way to simplify your test driver is to put your queue declarations, procedures, and functions in separate file and then to "include" this file in your test driver using the Include compiler directive. The syntax for this compiler directive is

```
(* $I filename *)
```

(As always, the compiler directive is contained within comment delimiters.) This directive simply means "include all the code from the specified text file at this point." For instance, suppose that our test driver is in file TESTQ.PAS and that our queue implementations are in files QUEUE1.PAS (array-based queue) and QUEUE2.PAS (linked queue). File TESTQ.PAS might contain the following code:

```
PROGRAM TestQueue (Input, Output);
  (* Test driver to test the queue routines. *)
  (*$I QUEUE1.PAS *) (* Include the queue types and operations. *)
VAR
  Element : QueueElementType;
  Queue   : QueueType;
BEGIN (* TestQueue *)
  (* Source code of test driver goes here. *)
END.  (* TestQueue *)
```

The Include directive tells the compiler that at this point in the program (before the use of QueueElementType and QueueType in the global declarations), the contents of file QUEUE1.PAS should be included. This directive does not cause the contents of file TESTQ.PAS to be changed; the lines of source code in file QUEUE1.PAS are compiled, but they are not physically added to the test driver's text file.

How does the use of Include files help us? First, the size of each file is smaller and easier to manage. Second, when we are finished testing the first queue implementation, it is easy to switch to the second implementation; we merely change one line in our test driver. We change the $I directive to

```
(*$I QUEUE2.PAS *) (* Include the queue types and operations. *)
```

and we are ready to recompile. This time the compiler will bring in the contents of QUEUE2.PAS instead.

Many compilers have a directive like this one. If you are not programming in Turbo Pascal, check your compiler's manual to see if there is a comparable compiler directive.

Queue Applications

One application area in which queues figure as the prominent data structure is the computer simulation of real-world situations. For instance, consider a bank that is planning to set up drive-in teller windows. There should be enough tellers to service each car within a "reasonable" wait time, but not too many tellers for the number of customers. The bank may want to run a computer simulation of typical customer transactions, using data objects to represent the real-world physical objects like tellers, cars, and the clock.

Queues are also used in many ways by the operating system to schedule the use of the various computer resources. One of these resources is the central processing unit (CPU) itself. When you tell the computer to run a particular program on a multiuser system, the operating system adds your request to its "job queue." When your request gets to the front of the queue, the program you requested is executed. Similarly, queues are used to allocate time to the various users of the input/output (I/O) devices—printers, disks, tapes, and so forth. The operating system maintains queues of requests to print, read, or write to each of these devices.

Summary

In this chapter we have examined the definition and operations of a FIFO queue. We have also discussed some of the design considerations encountered when an array is used to contain the elements of a queue. Though the array itself is a random-access structure, our logical view of the queue as a FIFO structure limits us to accessing only the elements in the front and rear positions of the queue stored in the array. As with stacks, the problem with a static array-based implementation is the need to determine the queue size before compilation. The queue is logically a dynamic structure, but the array is physically a static structure.

The linked implementation of a FIFO queue allows us to allocate space for queue elements as needed. Now that you are getting used to Pascal pointers, this implementation will become more intuitive—perhaps more intuitive, even, than the array implementation that we developed.

There is virtually always more than one functionally correct design for the same data structure. When multiple correct solutions exist, the requirements and specifications of the problem may determine which is the best design.

In the design of data structures and algorithms, you will find that there are often trade-offs. A more complex algorithm may result in more efficient execution; a solution that takes longer to execute may save much memory space. As always, we must base our design decisions on what we know of the problem's requirements.

Application

Simulation

Data Structure

- FIFO Queue

Software Techniques

- Time-driven simulation
- Top-down design
- Data encapsulation
- Incremental program development
- Testing and evaluation

Before astronauts go up into space, they spend many hours in a spaceship simulator, a physical model of a space vehicle in which they can experience all the things that will happen to them in space. The spaceship simulator is a *physical model* of another object. The technique that is used to make the model behave as the real object is called **simulation**. We can use similar techniques to build *computer models* of objects and events rather than physical models.

A model can be thought of as a series of rules that describe the behavior of a real-world system. We change the rules and watch the effects of these changes on the behavior we are observing.

Let's look at a very useful type of simulation that uses queues as the basic data structure. In fact, the real-world system is called a *queueing system*. A queueing system is made up of servers and queues of objects to be served. We deal with queueing systems all the time in our daily lives. When you stand in line to check out at the grocery store or to cash a check at the bank, you are dealing with a queueing system. When you submit a batch "job" (such as a compilation) on a mainframe computer, your job must wait in line until the CPU finishes the jobs scheduled ahead of it. The operating system is a queueing system. When you make a phone call to reserve an airline ticket and get a recording that says, "Thank you for calling Air Busters. Your call will be answered by the next available operator. Please wait:"—you are dealing with a queueing system.

Please wait. Waiting is the critical element. The objective of a queueing system is to utilize the servers (the tellers, checkers, CPU, operators, and so on) as fully as possible, while keeping the wait time within a reasonable limit. These goals usually require a compromise between cost and customer satisfaction.

To put this on a personal level, no one likes to stand in line. If there were one checkout counter for each customer in a supermarket, the customers would be delighted. The supermarket, however, would not be in business very long. So a compromise is made: The number of cashiers is kept within the limits set by the store's budget, and the average customer is not kept waiting *too* long.

How does a company figure out the optimal compromise between the number of servers and the wait time? One way is by experience; the company tries out different numbers of servers and sees how things work out. There are two problems with this approach: It takes too long and it is too expensive. Another way of examining this problem is by using a computer simulation. To simulate a queueing system, we must know four things:

1. the number of events and how they affect the system,
2. the number of servers,
3. the distribution of arrival times, and
4. the expected service time.

The simulation program uses these parameters to predict the average wait time. The interactions of these parameters are the rules of the model. By changing these parameters, we change the rules. The average wait times are then examined to determine what a reasonable compromise would be.

Before we start designing a simulation program, let's walk through a simple simulation of a real-life example. Consider the case of a drive-in bank with one teller. How long does the average car have to wait? If business gets better and cars start to arrive more frequently, what would be the effect on the average wait time? When would the bank need to open a second drive-in window?

This problem is clearly a queueing problem. We have a *server* (the teller) and *objects being served* (customers in cars), and the *average wait time* is what we are interested in observing.

The events in this system are the arrivals and the departures of customers. Suppose that the number of servers is 1, the average transaction takes 5 minutes, and a new customer arrives about every 3 minutes. Let's look at how we can solve this problem as a time-driven simulation. A *time-driven simulation* is one in which the program has a counter that represents a clock. To simulate the passing of a unit of time (a minute, for example), we increment the clock. We will run the simulation for a predetermined amount of time, say, 100 minutes. (Of course, simulated time passes much more quickly than real time; 100 simulated minutes will pass in a flash on the computer.)

From a software point of view, the simulation is a big loop that executes a set of rules for each value of the clock—from 1 to 100, in our example. Here are the rules that are processed in the loop body:

Rule 1. If a customer arrives, he or she gets in line.
Rule 2. If the teller is free and if there is anyone waiting, the first customer in line leaves the line and advances to the teller's window. The service time is set to five minutes.
Rule 3. If a customer is at the teller's window, the time remaining for that customer to be serviced is decremented.
Rule 4. If there are customers in line, the additional minute that they have remained in the queue is recorded.

The output from the simulation is the average wait time. We calculate this value using the following formula:

Average wait time = total wait time for all customers / number of customers

Given this output, the bank can see whether their customers have an unreasonable wait in a one-teller system. If so, the bank can repeat the simulation with two tellers.

We have described this example in terms of a single teller and a specific arrival rate and transaction time. In fact, these simulation parameters should be varied to see what effect the changes have on the average wait time. Therefore these values will be read as inputs to the program.

Since there are so many different applications that might use this program—modeling bank queues, phone call waiting systems, CPU "job queues," doctor's office waiting room, and so on—we will write our program as a *generic* time-driven queueing system simulator. That is, the same program can be used to simulate many different real-world systems. We will refer to the bank tellers, phone operators, etc., as *servers*, and the objects to be serviced (customers, patients, etc.) as *jobs*. This program will simulate a *multiple*-server/*single*-queue system. That is, the jobs waiting to be served are stored in a single queue. (In contrast, grocery stores are usually multiple-server/multiple-queue systems.) The specifications of this program are listed in Figure 5-15.

Figure 5-15
Specifications for
Program Simulation

Specification: Program Simulation

Function:

The program will simulate a queueing system, using the following variable simulation parameters: length of simulation, average time between arrivals, number of servers, and average transaction time.

Input:

The simulation parameters are entered interactively, and include:

1. The length of the simulation,
2. The average transaction time,
3. The number of servers, and
4. The average time between job arrivals.

The program must prompt the user for each input, and each input (a positive integer) is entered on a separate line.

At the end of each simulation, the program will prompt the user to ask if another simulation is desired. If the user responds positively, the program will prompt the user to input a new set of simulation parameters.

Output:

The outputs are printed both to the screen and to a report file. The screen output will be the resulting average wait time for the current simulation, labeled. Following the execution of the last simulation, the following message will be printed to the screen:

"Simulation is complete. Summary in file REPORT.SIM."

The output in file REPORT.SIM will consist of the set of simulation parameters, the resulting average wait time, and the number of jobs that are still waiting when the simulation time runs out. The output for each set of parameters should be printed on a single line, resulting in a tabular listing. A header line should be written to the file at the beginning of the program to label the columns, and a trailer section should be written to the end of the file, describing the meaning of the columns in the table.

Figure 5-15
(Continued)

Processing Requirements:

1. The program must include processing to guard against range errors in the user's inputs. The maximum values allowed for each parameter must be described as constants, so that they can be "tuned" if necessary. Use the following initial values:

Maximum Servers	10
Maximum Simulation Length	10000
Maximum Transaction Time	1000
Maximum Time between Arrivals	1000

2. Real number output should be specified to two decimal places.
3. The number of elements in the wait queue at any given time cannot be predicted.

Assumptions:

1. No more than one job arrives per time unit.
2. User inputs can be assumed to be numeric (that is, you can use Read(ln) to input an integer value).

Data Design

In a computer simulation, each physical object in the real-world system can be represented as a data object. Actions in the real world are represented as operations that manipulate these data objects. From a software standpoint, the combination of a data object and a set of operations equals an abstract data type.

Before we begin the top-down design, let's give some thought to what kind of data objects our simulation must model. There are two main objects in the simulation: the servers and the jobs waiting. How can each of these be described as an ADT?

The Server ADT

From the abstract perspective, this data object is a *list of servers*. Each server has a "timer" to indicate how many clock units are left on the job that the server is currently processing. What operations must be defined for this ADT? Before the server list can be used, it must be initialized to set all of the servers to "free." We'll call this operation InitServers. Looking back at the rules to be processed in the loop body, we see that we need an operation to engage a free server (Rule 2). We'll call this operation EngageServer. How do we know which, if any, server is free? We need another operation GetFreeServerID to tell us which server is available or to indicate that no server is free. Finally, we need an operation to decrement the timers of all the active servers to indicate that a clock unit has passed (Rule 3). We'll call this operation UpdateServers. The ADT can be described with the following specification:

Server ADT Specification

Structure   List of server elements, each of which has a Server ID and Timer associated with it.

Operations:

InitServers (Servers, NumServers)

Function:	Initializes NumServers elements to "free" status.
Input:	NumServers (Integer)
Preconditions:	$1 <=$ NumServers $<=$ maximum number of servers allowed.
Output:	Servers (ServerType)
Postconditions:	Servers contains NumServers free servers.

GetFreeServerID (Servers, ServerID, Found)

Function:	Searches Servers for a free server; if Found, returns ServerID.
Input:	Servers (ServerType)
Preconditions:	Servers has been initialized.
Output:	ServerID (ServerIDType) Found (Boolean)
Postconditions:	Found = free server found. IF Found, ServerID = ID of free server. (*Note:* This operation does *not* engage the server; it just identifies it.)

EngageServer (Servers, ServerID, TransactTime)

Function:	Engages the designated server for TransactTime.
Input:	Servers (ServerType) ServerID (ServerIDType) TransactTime (Integer)
Preconditions:	Servers has been initialized AND the server with ServerID is free.
Output:	Servers
Postconditions:	Timer of server with ServerID = TransactTime.

UpdateServers (Servers)

Function:	Increments the timer of each server that is currently engaged.
Input:	Servers (ServerType)
Preconditions:	Servers has been initialized.
Output:	Servers
Postconditions:	Timer of each engaged server = previous timer value $-$ 1.

The WaitQueue ADT

At the abstract level, the jobs waiting in line to be processed can be described as a queue of "wait timers." Let's see if we can use the FIFO Queue ADT that we discussed in this chapter. Rule 1 tells us that if a job arrives, it should be put in line; this is the Enqueue operation. Rule 2 suggests two queue operations: We need to know if there is anyone waiting in line (the EmptyQueue operation), and we need to be able to remove the first job from the WaitQueue (the Dequeue operation). Finally, Rule 4 says that the wait timers of all the jobs still in line must be incremented to show the passing of a clock unit. This is an operation that is not supported by the FIFO Queue ADT that we developed in the chapter. Let's add its specification to the ADT:

UpdateQueue (Queue)

Function:	Increment the time of every job waiting.
Input:	Queue (QueueType)
Preconditions:	Queue has been created.
Output:	Servers
Postconditions:	Timer of each job waiting = previous timer value + 1.

With the addition of UpdateQueue, we can use the FIFO Queue ADT that we discussed in this chapter.

Just to prove how committed we are to the idea of data encapsulation, we are not going to discuss the implementation of the Server and WaitQueue ADTs until we finish designing the program. We believe that the information in the specifications tells us enough that we can use these data types without knowing anything more. In fact, we will give these modules to another programmer to implement however she wishes, and we'll write the rest of our program without knowing the representation of these data types. When we finish our design, we'll get the implementation of these data structures from our friend.

Top-Down Design

Now we're ready to design the program. The specification tells us that the program must continue to run simulations and printing results with different sets of parameters until the user is ready to quit. This suggests a loop, each iteration of which will invoke the ExecuteSimulation module. Before we can process the first simulation we must do some "initialization"—opening the report file and writing the report header, for instance. After we finish the last simulation, we must do some "termination" processing—writing the report trailer, for example. There might be other initialization and termination activities; for now we will just specify a module for each of these. The top level of the design is

Simulation   /   *Level 0*

Initialize

REPEAT
    ExecuteSimulation
    Finished ← ReadyToStop
UNTIL Finished

Terminate

The main work of the program is in the ExecuteSimulation module. It must get the simulation parameters, run the simulation, and print out the result to the screen and the report file. Let's look at its specification:

■ **ExecuteSimulation (ReportFile)** / *Level 1*

Function:	Run one simulation with user-supplied parameters and print results to screen and ReportFile.
Input:	ReportFile (Text) From user (keyboard): simulation parameters
Preconditions:	ReportFile is open for writing.
Output:	ReportFile (updated)
Postconditions:	Calculated average wait time is printed to screen; parameters and average wait time are printed to ReportFile on one line (in format of output table).

Here is the design for this important module:

ExecuteSimulation

GetParameters (parameters include time limit, number of servers, transaction time, and minutes between arrivals)

Initialize simulation variables

WHILE more time on the clock DO
    Update the clock, server timers, and wait queue timers.
    ReceiveJob if one arrives.
    StartJob if server free and job waiting.

Clean up leftover jobs in wait queue.
Calculate average wait time.

PrintResults

This design gives an overall view of a simulation but leaves many questions unanswered. Clearly more levels of the top-down design are needed.

The GetParameters module gets all the parameters for this execution of the simulation. Since it returns so many different values, we decide to make its output a single parameter, a record that contains a field for each simulation parameter:

```
TYPE
  ParametersType = RECORD
    TimeLimit    : Integer; (* length of simulation  *)
    NumServers   : Integer; (* number of servers     *)
    TransactTime : Integer; (* avg transaction time  *)
    TimeBtwnJobs : Integer  (* avg time btwn arrivals *)
  END; (* ParametersType *)
```

The module specification is

> **GetParameters (Parameters)**   /   *Level 2*
>
> | | |
> |---|---|
> | *Function:* | Get valid parameters for the current simulation. |
> | *Input:* | From keyboard: TimeLimit, NumServers, TransactTime, TimeBtwnJobs |
> | *Preconditions:* | User inputs are integers. |
> | *Output:* | Parameters (ParametersType) |
> | *Postconditions:* | All field values in Parameters record are valid according to specifications. |

The GetParameters module must prompt the user for each parameter value, read the response, check the response to make sure that it falls within the bounds listed in the program specifications, and—if the response is not valid—ask for another value. Clearly this is going to be a lot of work. However, we do not want to get distracted with this right now. We really want to get on to the main processing of this program, the execution of the simulation using these parameters. We decide to *postpone the design and coding of this module* until we have had a chance to test the simulation processing. But this module outputs the simulation parameters. How can we postpone coding it? We will code a **stub** to stand in its place. The stub will simply assign sample simulation parameters to the record:

```
PROCEDURE GetParameters
  (VAR Parameters : ParametersType);

BEGIN (* GetParameters *)

  (*** STUB ***)
  Parameters.TimeLength    := 100;
  Parameters.TransactTime  := 5;
  Parameters.NumServers    := 2;
  Parameters.TimeBtwnJobs  := 3

END;  (* GetParameters *)
```

We'll use this stub until we're convinced that our main simulation processing works; then we will come back and code this module to get real values from the user. This means that we will be coding and testing our program *incrementally*.

Now let's get back to the Level 1 design. Our next job is to initialize the simulation variables. What are these variables? First of all, there are the servers and wait queue. We have specified operations to initialize each of these. As we saw in reference to the bank teller example, we must keep track of two values, (1) the total wait time for all jobs and (2) the number of jobs that are served. These are the values that are used to calculate the average wait time. The last variable to initialize is the clock.

InitSim

InitServers (Servers, Parameters.NumServers)
CreateQueue (WaitQueue)
TotalWait ← 0
NumJobs ← 0
Clock ← 0

Now we come to the WHILE loop in the ExecuteSimulation (Level 1) design. Our first job is to update the clock and timers. Here is the specification of this module:

▎ **UpdateClock (Clock, Servers, WaitQueue)** / *Level 2*

Function:	Increment the Clock and the wait timers for each job in the WaitQueue; decrement the timer for each active server.
Input:	Clock (Integer) Servers (ServerType) WaitQueue (QueueType)
Preconditions:	All inputs have been initialized; clock and timer values < MaxInt
Output:	Clock, Servers, WaitQueue
Postconditions:	Clock = previous clock value + 1. Timer of each active server = its previous value − 1. Timer of each job in WaitQueue = its previous value + 1.

Since we have specified operations to update the Servers and WaitQueue, this module will be very simple to design and code:

Update Clock

Clock ← Clock + 1
UpdateServers (Servers)
UpdateQueue (WaitQueue)

Our next activity inside the loop body of ExecuteSimulation is to receive a new job—if one arrives. How do we know whether or not a job has arrived in this particular clock unit? The answer is a function of two factors: the simulation parameter Time-BtwnJobs (the average time between job arrivals) and luck.

Luck? We're writing a computer program that bases calculations on sheer luck? Well, not exactly. Let's express TimeBtwnJobs another way—as the *probability* that a job will arrive in any given clock unit. Probabilities range from 0.0 (no chance) to 1.0 (a sure thing). If on the average a new job arrives every five minutes, then the chance of a customer arriving in any given minute is 0.2 (1 chance in 5). Therefore, the probability of a new job arriving in this iteration of the loop body is 1.0 / TimeBtwnJobs. Let's call this value ArrivalProb.

Now what about *luck*? In computer terms, luck can be represented by the use of a **random-number generator**. Many Pascal compilers have a built-in function that returns a random number. We simulate the arrival of a customer by generating a random number between 0.0 and 1.0 and apply the following rules:

1. If the random number is between 0.0 and ArrivalProb, a job has arrived; and
2. If the random number is greater than ArrivalProb and less than 1.0, no job arrived in this clock unit.

If a job was received, the ReceiveJob module will put it into the WaitQueue. Therefore, this module needs two inputs: WaitQueue and TimeBtwnJobs, and outputs a possibly changed WaitQueue.

ReceiveJob (WaitQueue, TimeBtwnJobs)   /   *Level 2*

Function:	If a job arrives, put it on the WaitQueue.
Input:	WaitQueue (QueueType)
	TimeBtwnJobs (Integer)
Preconditions:	WaitQueue has been created.
	1 <= TimeBtwnJobs <= maximum value specified.
Output:	WaitQueue (may be changed)
Postconditions:	IF job arrived, WaitQueue = previous WaitQueue + new job with wait timer value of 0.

To design this module, we need to consider what is being stored in the wait queue. As queue users, we do *not* need to know how the queue structure will be implemented, but we do need to know about QueueElementType. Each element in the queue is a "job." Each job has a "wait timer." Does each job have any other information associated with it? In the real-life application, there *will* be other information: all the information needed for the system to process the job (fill an order, start a compilation, cash a check, and so on). But in the simulation world, we are not actually going to process the job; we are only going to see how long jobs have to wait. Therefore, the WaitQueue can be a *queue of wait timers*. A timer can be represented as a simple integer value; it starts out at 0 and is incremented in each clock cycle. Now we know enough to record the design for ReceiveJob:

ReceiveJob

ArrivalProb ← 1.0 / TimeBtwnJobs
JobArrives ← (Random <= ArrivalProb)
IF JobArrives
  THEN Enqueue a 0 timer value in WaitQueue

NOTE: Because not all Pascal systems provide a random-number generator, we have included the code for a version of this operation in the program listed below. In keeping with tradition, we have coded the random-number generator as a function. This approach goes against current thinking about good style, however, because the function must access (and change) a global variable called a **seed**. This variable is set to any real value to initialize the function and is changed each time the function is called.

Finally we come to the last activity in the ExecuteSimulation loop body: If a server is free and a job is waiting, start a job. Clearly the module must input and output Servers and WaitQueue. What other parameters does it need? To be able to set up the job to be served for the correct amount of time, we must input the transaction time (from the Parameters record). If a job starts, two other variables are changed: the number of jobs served (NumJobs) and the total wait time of jobs served (TotalWait). The StartJob module has the following specification:

StartJob (TransactTime, Servers, WaitQueue, NumJobs, TotalWait) / *Level 2*

Function:	If a server is free and a job is waiting, start a new job to be served for TransactTime and update NumJobs and TotalWait.
Input:	TransactTime (Integer)
	Servers (ServerType)
	WaitQueue (QueueType)
	NumJobs (Integer)
	TotalWait (Real)
Preconditions:	All parameters have been initialized.
Output:	Servers, WaitQueue, NumJobs, TotalWait.
Postconditions:	If a server is free and WaitQueue is not empty:
	WaitQueue is dequeue'ed.
	NumJobs = previous value of NumJobs + 1.
	TotalWait = previous value of TotalWait + wait timer dequeue'ed from WaitQueue.
	Free server is engaged for TransactTime.

Using our Server and FIFO Queue operations, this module is easy to design:

StartJob

```
GetFreeServerID (Servers, ServerId, Found)
IF Found AND NOT EmptyQueue (WaitQueue)
    THEN
        Dequeue (WaitQueue, Job)
        Increment NumJobs
        TotalWait ← TotalWait + Job
        EngageServer (Servers, ServerID, TransactTime)
```

This module ends the work that must be done by the ExecuteSimulation loop. When the loop terminates (after the clock hits the TimeLimit), this version of the simulation is finished. Now we need to clean up the wait queue, calculate the average wait time, and print out the results.

The CleanupWaitQueue module will return the WaitQueue empty, as well as a count of the number of jobs that were never serviced.

▶ **CleanupWaitQueue (WaitQueue, JobsWaiting)**   /   *Level 2*

Function:	Remove all jobs from WaitQueue, and return count of the jobs removed.
Input:	WaitQueue (QueueType).
Preconditions:	WaitQueue has been initialized (it does not necessarily contain any elements).
Output:	WaitQueue, JobsWaiting (Integer)
Postconditions:	WaitQueue is empty. JobsWaiting = number of elements removed from WaitQueue.

The algorithm is simple:

JobsWaiting ← 0
WHILE NOT EmptyQueue (WaitQueue) DO
    Dequeue WaitQueue (ignore value removed from queue)
    Increment JobsWaiting

Finally we are ready to calculate the average wait time—the information that we have been waiting for:

AverageWait ← TotalWait / NumJobs

What happens if no jobs were ever received? If the simulation was run for a short TimeLimit, with a relatively large TimeBtwnJobs parameter, it is possible that NumJobs is = 0. Division by zero will cause the program to crash at run time, so it is better to check for this condition explicitly:

IF NumJobs > 0
    THEN AverageWait ← TotalWait / NumJobs
    ELSE AverageWait ← 0

All that is left in the ExecuteSimulation (Level 1) design is to print the results.

▶ **PrintResults (ReportFile, Parameters, AverageWait, JobsWaiting)**   /   *Level 2*

Function:	Print results of this simulation to the screen and ReportFile.
Input:	ReportFile (Text) Parameters (ParametersType) AverageWait (Real) JobsWaiting (Integer)
Preconditions:	All input variables have values.
Output:	To ReportFile: a single line containing parameter and result data for this simulation, formatted for tabular output. To Screen: Average wait time.
Postconditions:	Data has been printed to ReportFile and screen.

The output that is specified to be printed to the screen can be generated with a simple Writeln statement:

```
Writeln ('Average wait time = ',
         AverageWait: FieldWidth: DecimalWidth);
```

Printing the ReportFile output, however, requires us to know how the columns in the table were set up. This reminds us that there are two other file output operations—one to print the report "header" (the title and column headings) and one to print the report "trailer" (text regarding the meaning of the columns). These procedures will be called by the Initialize and Terminate modules, respectively, of the main program. Let's specify these two operations:

▌ **PrintReportHeader (ReportFile)** / *Level 2—under Initialize*

Function:	Open ReportFile for writing; print title and table headings.
Input:	ReportFile (Text)
Preconditions:	ReportFile either does not exist, or exists and previous contents will be destroyed by Rewrite.
Output:	ReportFile
Postconditions:	ReportFile is open and contains title and table headings.

▌ **PrintReportTrailer (ReportFile)** / *Level 2—under Terminate*

Function:	Print trailing messages; close ReportFile.
Input:	ReportFile (Text)
Preconditions:	ReportFile has been opened for writing.
Output:	ReportFile
Postconditions:	ReportFile is complete and closed.

(References above to "closing" ReportFile do not reflect standard Pascal, but do reflect requirements by most Pascal compilers to explicitly close files before the program terminates.)

The work required to get the output printed with title centered and the columns straight is not important to developing and testing the simulator. Like GetParameters, these print operations can be coded in the second development iteration. Our final program needs these operations, of course, but we just don't need them *now*. Straight tabular output is irrelevant to testing whether the simulation works. So we will put the coding of these three operations on hold, and replace them for now with stubs:

```
PROCEDURE PrintResults
  (VAR ReportFile : Text;
   Parameters     : ParametersType;
   AverageWait    : Real;
   JobsWaiting    : Integer);

  (* Print results to screen and report file. *)
```

```
BEGIN (* PrintResults *)

   (*** STUB ***)
   Writeln ('Average wait time = ', AverageWait:8:2)

END;  (* PrintResults *)
(***************************************************************)

PROCEDURE PrintReportHeader
   (VAR ReportFile : Text);

BEGIN (* PrintReportHeader *)

   (*** STUB ***)
   Assign  (ReportFile, 'REPORT.SIM');  (*** Turbo Pascal ***)
   Rewrite (ReportFile);
   Writeln (ReportFile, 'Starting Simulation')

END;  (* PrintReportHeader *)
(***************************************************************)

PROCEDURE PrintReportTrailer
   (VAR ReportFile : Text);

BEGIN (* PrintReportTrailer *)

   (*** STUB ***)
   Writeln (ReportFile, 'Ending Simulation');
   Close (ReportFile)   (*** Turbo Pascal ***)

END; (* PrintReportHeader *)
```

Let's return to the Level 0 design and complete our top-down design. The Initialize module will call PrintReportHeader, so it will need to input ReportFile. It will do one other job, initializing the Seed for the random-number generator. Seed is customarily a global variable. The Terminate module will call PrintReportTrailer, and then print out the terminating screen message: "Simulation is complete. Summary in file REPORT.SIM." These two modules need no further explanation or decomposition. The ExecuteSimulation module has already been discussed in great detail.

All that is left to discuss in the Level 0 design is how we know whether the user is ReadyToStop.

ReadyToStop returns Boolean / *Level 1*

Function:	Ask if user is ready to stop and return answer.
Input:	None
Preconditions:	User is alive.
Output:	ReadyToStop (Boolean)
Postconditions:	ReadyToStop = True if user answered 'Y' or 'y' and False if user answered 'N' or 'n'.

This kind of Boolean function is very common: We ask the user a question, and then read the answer. If the answer is 'Y' or 'y', the function returns True. If the answer is 'N' or 'n', the function returns False. The only problem is if the answer is '4' or 'U' or '%' or any other invalid character. Therefore, the algorithm for this operation must loop until the user gives a valid answer:

ReadyToStop

Print question
AnswerValid ← False
REPEAT
  Read Answer
  IF Answer IN ['Y', 'y', 'N', 'n']
    THEN AnswerValid ← True
UNTIL AnswerValid

Set ReadyToStop based on Answer

This completes the top-down design of Program Simulation (except for the input/output procedures that we are postponing to the second development iteration).

Data Design (Part II)

As we promised earlier, we developed the top-down design of this program without ever knowing how the Servers and WaitQueue were implemented. Meanwhile, our friend has been busy developing these data structures for us. Let's see what she came up with.

The Server ADT

The list of servers is represented as a record with two fields: the number of servers that are active (NumServers) and an array of server "timers." The timers are simple integer values that indicate how much time is left on the current job. A timer value of 0 means that the server is free. The GetFreeServerID and EngageServer operations require a ServerID to be passed. This Server representation simply uses the array index as the ServerID. Here are the declarations that support this ADT:

```
CONST
  MaxServers = 10;

TYPE
  ServerIDType = 1 .. MaxServers;

  ServerType = RECORD
    NumServers : 0 .. MaxServers;
    ServerList : ARRAY [ServerIdType] OF Integer
  END; (* ServerType *)

VAR
  Server : ServerType;
```

We will look briefly at the design of the Server operations. You may want to review the specifications on pages 278–279. The InitServer operation sets the NumServers field of the Server record to the input parameter value. The first NumServer positions in the array are then set to 0, indicating that all the servers are free.

The GetFreeServerID operations searches the first NumServers positions of the array for a zero (free) timer value, using a loop. If a nonzero value is found, Found is set to True and Server ID is set to the index of its array slot; otherwise Found is False.

The EngageServer is the simplest of all: It merely sets the ServerID'th array slot to TransactTime.

Finally the UpdateServers operation loops through the active servers (in array slots 1 through NumServers), decrementing nonzero values by 1. The code that supports the Server operations is found in the program listing.

The WaitQueue ADT

Since we already have two perfectly good FIFO queue implementations to choose from, the implementation of this ADT is easy. But which to pick? The program specifications indicate that the number of queue elements cannot be predicted, so the linked implementation with dynamically allocated nodes is a better choice. To the operations already coded for this implementation, our programmer friend has added the implementation of UpdateQueue. The linked queue is traversed, from Front to Rear, and each node value is incremented. The code for the queue operations is found in the program listing.

Coding the Simulation Program

Using the top-down design and the two data structures provided by our programmer friend, we can now code the program. After we complete the coding, we run the program, letting the program execute four simulations. The average wait times printed to the screen are 3.21, 0.88, 7.03, and 0.52. How can that be? The program inputs are now coming from the GetParameters stub, not from the tester. Each time ExecuteSimulation calls GetParameters, the same parameters are returned. So how can the simulation come up with different results for each simulation?

It is the random-number generator supplying a little "luck," just as in real life, a bank teller might be really busy one Thursday morning and bored the next. Let's try using a bigger time limit. We change the TimeLimit field in the GetParameters stub to 1000 clock units, recompile, and run the program again. This time the four executions of the simulation are much more alike: 2.01, 2.92, 2.27, and 4.40.

We start the program again, and let it run four more executions of the simulation with the same time limit. This time we get exactly the same results as the previous run! How can that be? Aren't the random numbers random? Much theoretical work has gone into the development of algorithm to produce random numbers. Given a particular function to produce random numbers and the current output from the function (Seed), however, the next value is completely predictable—not random at all! Since our program initially resets Seed to the same value, each run of the program produces the same sequence of "random" numbers. Therefore the numbers from such a function are called **pseudo-random**. For simulation purposes, however, pseudorandom numbers are sufficient. If a simulation is run for a long enough period of time, the theory of random numbers says that the wait time will converge no matter what kind of random number generator you use. As we saw, with a larger TimeLimit value, the results were more alike.

How do we know whether the program is working? The results seem more or less "reasonable," but how do we know they are *correct*? A good way to see what the program is doing is to trace its execution using debugging Writeln's. We add Writeln's throughout the program—when we Enqueue and Dequeue, when we Engage a server, and so on. Then we walk through the debug output, comparing what the program is doing to what we expect it to do.

Another way to test out this program is to run it with different values of input parameters, and to see if the results change in predictable ways. To make this test, however, we will need to code the real GetParameters routine.

The Program

We add the functional version of GetParameters, as well as the three print report operations, to complete the program. The final version of the Simulation program is listed below. To save space, we have abbreviated the program listing by inserting a comment in place of the source code for the FIFO Queue ADT operations.

The complete source code is in file SIM.PAS on the program disk.

We think that you will enjoy running the program on the disk. If you are not using Turbo Pascal, be sure to replace any Turbo code with code appropriate to your compiler!

```
PROGRAM Simulation (Input, Output, ReportFile);

  (* Repeat Program Specifications *)
CONST
  MaxServers    = 10;     (* maximum number of servers     *)
  MaxTimeLimit  = 10000;  (* maximum simulation length     *)
  MaxTransact   = 1000;   (* maximum length of transaction *)
  MaxArrivalGap = 1000;   (* maximum gap between arrivals   *)
TYPE

  (************* Simulation Parameters Type *************)
  ParametersType = RECORD
    TimeLimit    : Integer;  (* length of simulation      *)
    NumServers   : Integer;  (* number of servers         *)
    TransactTime : Integer;  (* average transaction time  *)
    TimeBtwnJobs : Integer   (* average time between job  *)
                             (* arrivals, in clock units  *)

  END; (* ParametersType *)

  (*************** Queue Type Declarations ***************)
  QueueElementType = Integer;

  QueuePtrType = ^QueueNodeType;

  QueueNodeType = RECORD
    Info : QueueElementType;  (* the queue user's data     *)
    Next : QueuePtrType       (* pointer to next queue node *)
  END; (* QueueNodeType *)
```

```
QueueType = RECORD
  Front : QueuePtrType; (* accesses front of queue *)
  Rear  : QueuePtrType; (* accesses rear of queue  *)
END;  (* QueueType *)

(*************** Server Type Declarations **************)

ServerIdType = 1 .. MaxServers;

ServerType = RECORD
  NumServers : 0 .. MaxServers;
  ServerList : ARRAY [ServerIDType] OF Integer
    (* the value in each slot represents job time   *)
    (* remaining, zero represents that server is free. *)
END; (* ServerType *)

VAR
  Finished   : Boolean;   (* User wants to quit program? *)
  ReportFile : Text;      (* output file                 *)
  Seed       : Real;      (* global Random function seed *)

(*********************************************************)
(*                  Queue ADT Operations               *)
(*********************************************************)
(* Include source code for the CreateQueue, EmptyQueue, *)
(* Enqueue, and Dequeue operations here.                *)
(*********************************************************)

PROCEDURE UpdateQueue
  (VAR Queue : QueueType);

  (* Increment all queue elements by 1. *)

VAR
  TempPtr : QueuePtrType;

BEGIN (* UpdateQueue *)

  TempPtr := Queue.Front;
  WHILE TempPtr <> NIL DO
    BEGIN
      TempPtr^.Info := TempPtr^.Info + 1;
      TempPtr := TempPtr^.Next
    END (* WHILE *)

END;  (* UpdateQueue *)

(*********************************************************)
(*                  Server ADT Operations              *)
(*********************************************************)

PROCEDURE InitServers
  (VAR Servers : ServerType;
   NumServers  : Integer);

  (* Initialize the requested number of servers to "free." *)
```

```
VAR
  Index : Integer;
BEGIN (* InitServers *)

  Servers.NumServers := NumServers;

  (* Mark the servers as free (0 clock units left on job). *)
  FOR Index := 1 TO NumServers DO
    Servers.ServerList[Index] := 0
END;  (* InitServers *)

(***********************************************************)

PROCEDURE GetFreeServerID
  (Servers    : ServerType;
   VAR ServerID : ServerIDType;
   VAR Found    : Boolean);
  (* IF a free server is found, Found = True and ServerID = *)
  (* the ID of a free server; otherwise Found = False.      *)

VAR
  Index : Integer;
BEGIN (* GetFreeServerID *)

  Found := False;
  Index := 1;

  WITH Servers DO
    BEGIN

      (* Loop Invariant: 1 <= Index <= NumServers + 1     *)
      (* AND ServerList[1] .. ServerList[Index - 1] does *)
      (* not contain a zero value.                        *)
      WHILE (Index <= NumServers) AND NOT Found DO
        IF ServerList[Index] = 0
          THEN Found := True
          ELSE Index := Index + 1
    END; (* WITH Servers *)

  IF Found
    THEN ServerID := Index
END;  (* GetFreeServerID *)

(***********************************************************)

PROCEDURE EngageServer
  (VAR Servers : ServerType;
   ServerID    : ServerIdType;
   TransactTime : Integer);

  (* Mark the designated server as busy for TransactTime. *)
```

```
BEGIN  (* EngageServer *)

  Servers.ServerList [ServerID] := TransactTime

END;   (* EngageServer *)

(***********************************************************)

PROCEDURE UpdateServers
  (VAR Servers : ServerType);

  (* Decrement all servers that are in use. *)

VAR
  Index : Integer;

BEGIN  (* UpdateServers *)

  WITH Servers DO
    FOR Index := 1 TO NumServers DO
      IF ServerList[Index] <> 0
        THEN ServerList[Index] := ServerList[Index] - 1

END;   (* UpdateServers *)

(***************************************************************)
(*                 User Input/Output Operations              *)
(***************************************************************)

PROCEDURE GetParameters
  (VAR Parameters : ParametersType);

  (*************** Nested Procedure ********************)
  PROCEDURE GetValue
    (LowBound   : Integer;
     UpBound    : Integer;
     VAR Value  : Integer);

      (* Get value from user in range LowBound .. Upbound. *)

  VAR
    ValueValid : Boolean;

  BEGIN  (* GetValue *)

    ValueValid := False;   (* Be pessimistic. *)

    (* Read answer and check for the specified bounds. *)
    REPEAT
      Readln (Value);
      Writeln;
      IF (Value < LowBound) OR (Value > UpBound)
        THEN Write ('Value must in the range from ',
               LowBound, ' to ', UpBound, '. Please reenter:  ')
        ELSE ValueValid := True
    UNTIL ValueValid

  END;   (* GetValue *)
  (***************************************************************)
```

```
BEGIN (* GetParameters *)

  WITH Parameters DO
    BEGIN

      Writeln ('Please enter all times in clock units.');
      Writeln;
      Write (' Length of simulation:  ');
      GetValue (1, MaxTimeLimit, TimeLimit);

      Write (' Average transaction time:  ');
      GetValue (1, MaxTransact, TransactTime);

      Write (' Number of servers:  ');
      GetValue (1, MaxServers, NumServers);

      Write (' Average clock units between arrivals:  ');
      GetValue (1, MaxArrivalGap, TimeBtwnJobs);
      Writeln

    END (* WITH Parameters *)

END; (* GetParameters *)

(***********************************************************)

FUNCTION ReadyToStop :  Boolean;

  (* Ask user if ready to stop and return answer. *)

VAR
  Answer      : Char;
  AnswerValid : Boolean;

BEGIN (* ReadyToStop *)

  Writeln;
  Writeln ('Do you want to run another simulation? (Y/N)');

  (* Continue until user gives valid answer. *)
  AnswerValid := False;

  REPEAT
    Readln (Answer);

    IF Answer IN ['Y', 'y', 'N', 'n']
      THEN AnswerValid := True
      ELSE Writeln ('Please answer with "Y" or "N".')

  UNTIL AnswerValid;

  ReadyToStop := (Answer = 'N') OR (Answer = 'n')

END; (* ReadyToStop *)

(***********************************************************)

PROCEDURE PrintReportHeader
  (VAR ReportFile : Text);

  (* Open ReportFile for writing, and print title and *)
  (* table headings to ReportFile.                    *)
```

```
BEGIN (* PrintReportHeader *)

  (**** Turbo Pascal Code ****)
  Assign (ReportFile, 'REPORT.SIM');

  (* Open the ReportFile for writing. *)
  Rewrite (ReportFile);

  (* Print Report header info. *)
  Writeln (ReportFile,
    '                   S I M U L A T I O N');
  Writeln (ReportFile);
  Writeln (ReportFile,
    'Simulation Number of  Average   Time Betwn  Average  Jobs');
  Writeln (ReportFile,
    ' Length    Servers  Transactn  Arrivals      Wait    Left');
  Writeln (ReportFile,

    '_____')

END;  (* PrintReportHeader *)

(***********************************************************)

PROCEDURE PrintResults
  (VAR ReportFile : Text;
   Parameters     : ParametersType;
   AverageWait    : Real;
   JobsWaiting    : Integer);

  (* Print results to screen and report file. *)

BEGIN (* PrintResults *)

  (* Print result of this simulation to screen. *)
  Writeln ('Average wait time = ', AverageWait:8:2);

  (* Print result of this set of parameters to ReportFile. *)
  Writeln (ReportFile);

  WITH Parameters DO
    Writeln (ReportFile,
             TimeLimit    : 6,     (* length of simulation *)
             NumServers   : 11,    (* number of servers    *)
             TransactTime : 11,    (* avg transaction time *)
             TimeBtwnJobs : 11,    (* time between jobs     *)
             AverageWait  : 12 : 2,  (* average wait time *)
             JobsWaiting  : 8)     (* jobs left in queue   *)

END;  (* PrintResults *)

(***********************************************************)

PROCEDURE PrintReportTrailer
  (VAR ReportFile : Text);

  (* Print terminating messages to ReportFile; close file. *)
```

```
BEGIN (* PrintReportTrailer *)

  (* Print trailer message to report file. *)
  Writeln (ReportFile);
  Writeln (ReportFile,

 '_____');
  Writeln (ReportFile,
    'All times are expressed in clock units. Average wait    ');
  Writeln (ReportFile,
    'time reflects the wait time of jobs served; it does not ');
  Writeln (ReportFile,
    'reflect the wait time of jobs that were not yet served. ');
  Writeln (ReportFile,
    'Jobs Left reflects the number of jobs that were waiting ');
  Writeln (ReportFile,
    'to be served when the Simulation time limit was reached.');

  (* Close the report file -- Turbo Pascal Code. *)
  Close (ReportFile)

END;  (* PrintReportTrailer *)

(**************************************************************)
(*              Other Application Operations                *)
(**************************************************************)

PROCEDURE Initialize
  (VAR ReportFile : Text);

BEGIN (* Initialize *)

  (* Initialize Seed for random number generator. *)
  Seed := 4.0;

  (* Open report file and print starting messages to *)
  (* report file and screen.                         *)
  PrintReportHeader (ReportFile)

END;  (* Initialize *)

(**************************************************************)

FUNCTION Random : Real;

  (* Returns a pseudo-random number between 0.0 and 1.0.  *)
  (* Assumes that Seed, a global variable, was previously *)
  (* initialized.                                         *)

CONST
  Pi = 3.14159;

VAR
  Temp : Real; (* temporary variable *)
```

```
BEGIN (* Random *)

   Temp     := Seed + Pi;
   Temp     := Exp (5.0 * Ln(Temp));
   Seed     := Temp - Trunc(Temp);
   Random   := Seed

END; (* Random *)

(************************************************************)

PROCEDURE ReceiveJob
   (VAR WaitQueue : QueueType;
    TimeBtwnJobs  : Integer);

   (* If job arrives, put it on the wait queue. *)

VAR
   ArrivalProb : Real; (* probability of arrival this time *)

BEGIN (* ReceiveJob *)

   ArrivalProb := 1.0 / TimeBtwnJobs;

   (* If a job arrives, add a zero value to the queue  *)
   (* to indicate a job with a current wait time of 0. *)
   IF Random <= ArrivalProb
      THEN Enqueue (WaitQueue, 0)

END;  (* ReceiveJob *)

(************************************************************)

PROCEDURE StartJob
   (TransactTime   : Integer;
    VAR Servers    : ServerType;
    VAR WaitQueue  : QueueType;
    VAR NumJobs    : Integer;
    VAR TotalWait  : Real);

   (* If server free and job waiting, start next job. *)

VAR
   ServerID : ServerIDType;      (* ID of free server       *)
   Job      : QueueElementType;  (* time waiting in queue    *)
   Found    : Boolean;           (* free server found?       *)

BEGIN (* StartJob *)

   (* Get ID of a free server. *)
   GetFreeServerID (Servers, ServerID, Found);
```

```
    (* If a server is free AND a job is waiting, start a job. *)
    IF Found AND (NOT EmptyQueue (WaitQueue))
      THEN
        BEGIN
          (* Remove first job from the wait queue. The value *)
          (* of Job represents time spent waiting in queue.   *)
          Dequeue (WaitQueue, Job);

          (* Increment NumJobs and TotalWait. *)
          NumJobs := NumJobs + 1;
          TotalWait := TotalWait + Job;

          (* Engage the free server for TransactTime. *)
          EngageServer (Servers, ServerID, TransactTime)

        END (* IF server free and job waiting *)
END;   (* StartJob *)

(************************************************************)

PROCEDURE CleanupWaitQueue
  (VAR WaitQueue   : QueueType;
   VAR JobsWaiting : Integer);

  (* Remove all remaining jobs from queue, counting jobs. *)

VAR
  Job : QueueElementType;

BEGIN (* CleanupWaitQueue *)

  JobsWaiting := 0;

  (* WHILE more elements in the queue, Dequeue and count. *)
  WHILE NOT EmptyQueue (WaitQueue) DO
    BEGIN
      Dequeue (WaitQueue, Job);
      JobsWaiting := JobsWaiting + 1
    END (* WHILE *)

END;   (* CleanupWaitQueue *)

(************************************************************)

PROCEDURE UpdateClock
  (VAR Clock     : Integer;
   VAR Servers   : ServerType;
   VAR WaitQueue : QueueType);

  (* Update data for clock tick: Increment clock and all *)
  (* the times of jobs waiting in queue; decrement times  *)
  (* in Servers list.                                     *)
```

```
BEGIN (* UpdateClock *)

  Clock := Clock + 1;

  (* Decrement all the nonzero times in Servers list. *)
  UpdateServers (Servers);

  (* Increment all the values in the WaitQueue. *)
  UpdateQueue (WaitQueue)

END;  (* UpdateClock *)
(*************************************************************)

PROCEDURE ExecuteSimulation
  (VAR ReportFile : Text);

  (* Get parameters and run one simulation; print results. *)

VAR
  Parameters   : ParametersType;  (* parameters from user    *)
  Servers      : ServerType;      (* list of servers         *)
  Clock        : Integer;         (* simulated clock minutes *)
  WaitQueue    : QueueType;       (* jobs waiting for service *)
  TotalWait    : Real;            (* wait time for all jobs   *)
  NumJobs      : Integer;         (* total jobs started       *)
  AverageWait  : Real;            (* average time waiting     *)
  JobsWaiting  : Integer;         (* jobs never served        *)

  (******************** Nested Procedure ********************)

PROCEDURE InitSim;
  (* Initialize local variables before simulation. *)
BEGIN (* InitSim *)

  (* Initialize all servers to "free." *)
  InitServers (Servers, Parameters.NumServers);

  (* Create queue to hold jobs waiting for service. *)
  CreateQueue (WaitQueue);

  (* Initialize scalar variables. *)
  TotalWait := 0.0;
  NumJobs   := 0;
  Clock     := 0

END;  (* InitSim *)
(*************************************************************)

BEGIN (* ExecuteSimulation *)

  (* Get simulation parameters from user. *)
  GetParameters (Parameters);

  (* Initialize local variables for this simulation. *)
  InitSim;
```

```
(* Run simulation for specified time limit. *)
WHILE Clock <= Parameters.TimeLimit DO
  BEGIN

    (* Update data for clock tick. *)
    UpdateClock (Clock, Servers, WaitQueue);

    (* If job arrives, put it on the wait queue. *)
    ReceiveJob (WaitQueue, Parameters.TimeBtwnJobs);

    (* If server free and job waiting, start next job. *)
    StartJob (Parameters.TransactTime, Servers,
              WaitQueue, NumJobs, TotalWait)

  END; (* WHILE Clock <= TimeLimit *)

(* Clean up data from this simulation. *)
CleanupWaitQueue (WaitQueue, JobsWaiting);

(* Calculate results and print. *)
IF NumJobs > 0
  THEN AverageWait := TotalWait / NumJobs
  ELSE AverageWait := 0.0;

PrintResults (ReportFile, Parameters, AverageWait, JobsWaiting)

END;  (* ExecuteSimulation *)
(*************************************************************)

PROCEDURE Terminate
  (VAR ReportFile : Text);

BEGIN (* Terminate *)

  (* Print terminating messages to report file and screen. *)
  PrintReportTrailer (ReportFile);

  (* Print trailer message to screen. *)
  Writeln ('Simulation is complete. Summary in file REPORT.SIM.')

END;  (* Terminate *)
(*************************************************************)

BEGIN (* Simulation *)

  (* Initialize for processing. *)
  Initialize (ReportFile);

  (* Continue processing until user wants to quit. *)
  REPEAT

    (* Run simulation of one parameter set and print results. *)
    ExecuteSimulation (ReportFile);

    (* Ask user if another simulation desired and set Finished. *)
    Finished := ReadyToStop

  UNTIL Finished;
```

```
(* Terminate processing. *)
Terminate (ReportFile)

END.  (* Simulation *)
```

Running the Final Program

The output from file REPORT.SIM for a sample test of the program is shown in the following table. (Blank lines have been deleted between some output lines to enhance readability.) We want to answer our original question about the drive-in bank. Is one teller enough? The test demonstrates cases where the transaction time is five minutes, new jobs arrive every three minutes, and the number of servers varies from one to four. We have run each set of parameters for 100, 500, 1000, and 5000 clock units (minutes in this case) respectively.

Output from One Run of Program Simulation

SIMULATION

Simulation Length	Number of Servers	Average Transactn	Time Betwn Arrivals	Average Wait	Jobs Left
100	1	5	3	18.00	14
500	1	5	3	106.65	58
1000	1	5	3	202.55	132
5000	1	5	3	1042.11	686
100	2	5	3	2.19	3
500	2	5	3	1.41	1
1000	2	5	3	3.89	0
5000	2	5	3	2.99	2
100	3	5	3	0.09	0
500	3	5	3	0.13	0
1000	3	5	3	0.28	1
5000	3	5	3	0.22	0
100	4	5	3	0.00	0
500	4	5	3	0.03	0
1000	4	5	3	0.01	0
5000	4	5	3	0.01	0

```
All times are expressed in clock units. Average wait
time reflects the wait time of jobs served; it does not
reflect the wait time of jobs that were not yet served.
Jobs Left reflects the number of jobs that were waiting
to be served when the simulation time limit was reached.
```

The results of this very simple simulation illustrate two important facts about simulations. Notice that some of the wait times just keep getting bigger and bigger, the longer that the simulation is run, whereas others stay approximately the same.

The numbers that keep increasing represent cases where the queue is unstable. A queue is unstable when the objects to be served are arriving faster than they can possibly be served. Clearly, when there is only one server, and the transaction time exceeds the time between arrivals, the line can only get longer and longer! This drive-in bank will have very unhappy customers—or more likely, no customers at all. It is possible to identify unstable queues: If the probability multiplied by the service time, divided by the number of servers, is greater than 1.0, the queue will be unstable.

With more servers, the queue is stable, and the average wait times stay about the same, no matter how long we run the simulation. Now the management of the bank needs to decide: How long is a reasonable wait? With three or four tellers, the customers barely have to wait at all. But more tellers are expensive for the bank. However, with two tellers the average wait time hovers between 1 and 4 minutes; this seems reasonable.

This program is not only fun to run; it is also fun to modify. There are many interesting ways to vary this program. For instance, the transaction times might vary as follows: 20% of the jobs take two clock units, 50% of the jobs take four clock units, and 30% of the clock take seven clock units. (This might be typical of a pediatric clinic where there are three typical types of patients: 20% come in for inoculations, 50% come in sick, and 30% come in for annual checkups.) How do you determine how long a particular job will take? You guessed it: Use a random-number generator.

■ *Exercises**

1. Define the accessing function of a FIFO queue at the logical level.

2. Show what is written by the following segments of code, given that Queue is a FIFO queue of integers; Stack is a stack of integers; and X, Y, and Z are integer variables.

(a)
```
CreateQueue (Queue);
X := 0;
Y := 1;
Enqueue (Queue, X);
Enqueue (Queue, Y);
Dequeue (Queue, Y);
Z := Y + 5;
Enqueue (Queue, Z);
Enqueue (Queue, 7);
Dequeue (Queue, X);
Enqueue (Queue, Y);
WHILE NOT EmptyQueue (Queue) DO
  BEGIN
    Dequeue (Queue, Z);
    Writeln (Z)
  END; (* WHILE *)
```
(b)
```
CreateStack (Stack);
CreateQueue (Queue);
```

*Questions with italicized numbers are answered in the back of the book.

```
X := 0;
Y := 1;
Z := X + Y;
WHILE Z < 10 DO
    BEGIN
      IF Z MOD 2 = 0
          THEN Push (Stack, Z)
          ELSE Enqueue (Queue, Z);
        X := Y;
        Y := Z;
        Z := X + Y
    END; (* WHILE Z *)

Write ('Stack contains ');
WHILE NOT EmptyStack (Stack) DO
    BEGIN
        Pop (Stack, Z);
        Write (Z)
    END; (* WHILE *)

Writeln;
Write ('Queue contains ');
WHILE NOT EmptyQueue (Queue) DO
    BEGIN
        Dequeue (Queue, Z);
        Write (Z)
    END; (* WHILE *)
```

3. True or False?
    (a) The comparison of the implementations of a FIFO queue in this chapter proves that there is always one implementation of a data structure that is clearly the best.
    (b) The statement Dequeue(Queue, Q + 5) would cause a run-time error.
    (c) All data structures that are called "queues" have the first in, first out accessing function.

In Exercises 4–9, show the result of the given operations on the queues, using the final array-based implementation discussed in this chapter. If overflow or underflow occurs, mark the appropriate spot; otherwise, show any changes to the queue. (Note that some of the values shown in the array may not be elements of the queue.)

4. Enqueue (Queue, 'J');

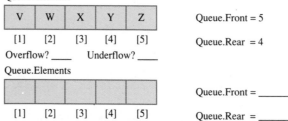

Queue.Elements

V	W	X	Y	Z
[1]	[2]	[3]	[4]	[5]

Queue.Front = 5

Queue.Rear = 4

Overflow? _____   Underflow? _____

Queue.Elements

[1]	[2]	[3]	[4]	[5]

Queue.Front = _____

Queue.Rear = _____

5. Enqueue (Queue, 'K');

Queue.Elements

V	W	X	Y	Z
[1]	[2]	[3]	[4]	[5]

Queue.Front = 4

Queue.Rear = 5

Overflow? _____   Underflow? _____

Queue.Elements

[1]	[2]	[3]	[4]	[5]

Queue.Front = _____

Queue.Rear = _____

6. Enqueue (Queue, 'L');

Queue.Elements

V	W	X	Y	Z
[1]	[2]	[3]	[4]	[5]

Queue.Front = 1

Queue.Rear = 4

Overflow? _____   Underflow? _____

Queue.Elements

[1]	[2]	[3]	[4]	[5]

Queue.Front = _____

Queue.Rear = _____

7. Dequeue (Queue, QueueValue);

Queue.Elements

V	W	X	Y	Z
[1]	[2]	[3]	[4]	[5]

Queue.Front = 3

Queue.Rear = 3

Overflow? _____   Underflow? _____

Queue.Elements

[1]	[2]	[3]	[4]	[5]

Queue.Front = _____

Queue.Rear = _____

QueueValue = _____

8. Dequeue (Queue, QueueValue);

Queue.Elements

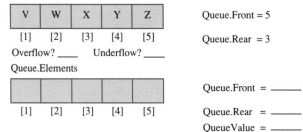

V	W	X	Y	Z
[1]	[2]	[3]	[4]	[5]

Queue.Front = 5

Queue.Rear = 3

Overflow? _____ Underflow? _____

Queue.Elements

[1]	[2]	[3]	[4]	[5]

Queue.Front = _____

Queue.Rear = _____

QueueValue = _____

9. Dequeue (Queue, QueueValue);

Queue.Elements

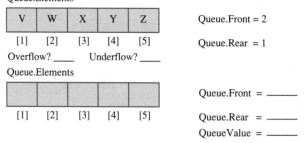

V	W	X	Y	Z
[1]	[2]	[3]	[4]	[5]

Queue.Front = 2

Queue.Rear = 1

Overflow? _____ Underflow? _____

Queue.Elements

[1]	[2]	[3]	[4]	[5]

Queue.Front = _____

Queue.Rear = _____

QueueValue = _____

10. Indicate whether each of the following applications would be suitable for a FIFO queue.
    (a) An ailing company wants to evaluate employee records in order to lay off some workers on the basis of service time (the most recently hired employees will be laid off first).
    (b) A program is to keep track of patients as they check into a clinic, assigning them to doctors on a first-come, first-served basis.
    (c) A program to solve a maze is to backtrack to an earlier position (the last place where a choice was made) when a dead-end position is reached.
    (d) An inventory of parts is to be processed by part number.
    (e) An operating system is to process requests for computer resources by allocating the resources in the order in which they are requested.
    (f) A grocery chain wants to run a simulation to see how average customer wait time would be affected by changing the number of checkout lines in the stores.
    (g) A dictionary of words used by a spelling checker is to be created.
    (h) Customers are to take numbers at a bakery and be served in order when their numbers come up.
    (i) Gamblers are to take numbers in the lottery and win if their numbers are picked.

11. Given the following specification:

Enqueue (Queue, NewElement, OverFlow)

Function:	Adds NewElement to the rear of the Queue.
Input:	Queue (QueueType) NewElement (QueueElementType)
Preconditions:	Queue has been created.
Output:	Queue (changed) OverFlow (Boolean)
Postconditions:	OverFlow = (queue is already full) IF NOT OverFlow, Queue = original Queue with NewElement added at the rear.

(a) Write Procedure Enqueue using the array-based implementation discussed in the chapter.

(b) Write Procedure Enqueue using the linked implementation discussed in the chapter.

12. Given the following specification:

Dequeue (Queue, DeqElement, UnderFlow)

Function:	Remove the front element from Queue and return its value in DeqElement.
Input:	Queue (QueueType)
Preconditions:	Queue has been created.
Output:	Queue (changed) DeqElement (QueueElementType) UnderFlow (Boolean)
Postconditions:	UnderFlow = (queue is already empty) IF NOT UnderFlow, Queue = original Queue with front element removed AND DeqElement = front element from original queue.

(a) Write Procedure Dequeue using the array-based implementation discussed in the chapter.

(b) Write Procedure Dequeue using the linked implementation discussed in the chapter.

Use the following information for Exercises 13–16: The user of the queue operations needs to know how many elements are in the queue, so we must add another function, QueueCount, to the ADT. To simplify the processing, we decide to modify our *array-based* queue implementation to add a field, Count, to the record that contains the queue.

```
TYPE
  QueueType = RECORD
    Elements : ARRAY [IndexType] OF QueueElementType;
      (* holds the queue elements *)
    Front : IndexType;
      (* index of array slot containing front element *)
    Rear  : IndexType;
      (* index of array slot containing rear element *)
    Count : Integer
      (* number of elements in the queue *)
  END; (* QueueType *)
```

Note that you no longer need to reserve an unused slot in the array to differentiate between an empty and full queue.

13. Write Function QueueCount, using the queue declarations above and the following specifications:

▎ **QueueCount (Queue) returns Integer**

> *Function:*   Returns the number of elements in Queue.
>
> *Input:*   Queue (QueueType)
>
> *Preconditions:*   Queue has been created.
>
> *Output:*   QueueCount (Integer)
>
> *Postconditions:*   QueueCount = number of elements in Queue.

14. Write the CreateQueue and DestroyQueue procedures that would go with the declarations above, using the FIFO Queue ADT specification in this chapter. How does this implementation compare to the equivalent array-based queue operations in the chapter, using Big-O notation?

15. Write the FullQueue and EmptyQueue that would go with the declarations above, using the FIFO Queue ADT specification in this chapter.

16. Write the Enqueue and Dequeue procedures that would go with the declarations above, using the FIFO Queue ADT specification in this chapter.

Use the following information for Exercises 17–19: The user of the queue operations needs to know how many elements are in the queue, so we must add another function, QueueCount, to the package. To simplify the processing, we decide to modify our *linked* queue implementation to add a field Count to the record that contains the queue.

```
TYPE
   QueueType = RECORD
      Count : Integer;       (* number of queue elements *)
      Front : QueuePtrType;  (* accesses front of queue  *)
      Rear  : QueuePtrType;  (* accesses rear of queue   *)
   END; (* QueueType *)
```

17. (a) Write Function QueueCount, using the queue declarations above and the following specifications:

▎ **QueueCount (Queue) returns Integer**

> *Function:*   Returns the number of elements in Queue.
>
> *Input:*   Queue (QueueType)
>
> *Preconditions:*   Queue has been created.
>
> *Output:*   QueueCount (Integer)
>
> *Postconditions:*   QueueCount = number of elements in Queue

(b) Write Function QueueCount using the linked queue declarations in the chapter (does not contain Count field in the record).

(c) Compare the implementation of QueueCount in (a) and (b) above, using Big-O notation.

18. Write the CreateQueue and DestroyQueue procedures that would go with the declarations for a linked queue above, using the FIFO Queue ADT specification in this chapter. How does this implementation compare to the equivalent linked queue operations in the chapter, using Big-O notation?

19. Write the FullQueue and EmptyQueue functions that would go with the declarations for a linked queue above, using the FIFO Queue ADT specification in this chapter.

20. A *deque* (pronounced "deck") is what you get when you cross a stack with a schizophrenic queue. You can add to and delete from either end of a deque. Maybe it should be called a *FOLIFOLO* (First Or Last In, First Or Last Out) structure. Using an array to contain the elements in the deque, write
    (a) the declarations that you would use to implement DequeType.
    (b) the specifications and implementation of Procedure CreateDeque (initialize to empty).
    (c) the specifications and implementation of Procedure InDequeFront (add element to front).
    (d) the specifications and implementation of Procedure InDequeRear (add element to rear).
    (e) the specifications and implementation of Procedure OutDequeFront (remove element from front).
    (f) the specifications and implementation of Procedure OutDequeRear (remove element from rear).

21. Repeat Exercise 20, using a *linked* deque representation.

22. A queue is kept in a record (QueueDataType) that has three fields: Elements (an array that contains the queue elements); Front (the index of the array slot preceding the front element); and Rear (the index of the array slot containing the rear element). The record variable is not declared, but rather it is allocated dynamically when a queue is needed. The queue is accessed through the following type:

```
TYPE
  QueueType = ^QueueDataType;

VAR
  Queue : QueueType;
```

(a) Is the space for this array-based data structure statically or dynamically allocated?
(b) How much space is reserved for the variable Queue at the beginning of the program's execution?
(c) Write the CreateQueue, DestroyQueue, and EmptyQueue operations, using the specifications in the FIFO Queue ADT.
(d) Is a FullQueue operation for this representation meaningful? Write a FullQueue operation. (If the operation is not meaningful for this implementation, you should write a stub.)
(e) If you could write the Enqueue and Dequeue procedures by modifying the source code of one of the queue implementations in the chapter, which one would you choose to modify?

23. Using the following specifications:

> **PrintQueue (Queue)**
>
> | | |
> |---|---|
> | *Function:* | Print the elements in Queue |
> | *Input:* | Queue (QueueType) |
> | *Preconditions:* | Queue has been created. |
> | *Output:* | To screen: the elements in queue, printed one per line. |
> | *Postconditions:* | The elements are printed; the Queue is unchanged. |

(a) Write Procedure PrintQueue as an operation provided as part of the FIFO Queue ADT, using the array-based queue implementation from the chapter.

(b) Write Procedure PrintQueue as an operation provided as part of the FIFO Queue ADT, using the linked queue implementation from the chapter.

(c) Write Procedure PrintQueue, using only the operations provided in the FIFO Queue ADT Specification, without any knowledge of how the queue is implemented.

(d) Do the procedures in (a), (b), and (c) differ in efficiency in terms of execution speed? In terms of Big-O notation?

24. A queue is implemented as a circular linked structure, as described in the chapter, with the external pointer accessing the "rear" element.

(a) Draw a sketch of a queue with one node.

(b) Implement the CreateQueue, DestroyQueue, and EmptyQueue operations.

(c) Implement the Enqueue and Dequeue operations.

(d) Does this implementation change the storage requirements of the queue, as compared with the linear linked queue? Does it change the Big-O approximations of the work required to do each operation?

25. A queue contains 12-byte elements. Assuming that a pointer takes 4 bytes and an integer takes 2 bytes, and that the maximum queue size is 80 elements:

(a) Fill in the chart showing the storage requirements, using the implementations developed in the chapter:

Number of Elements	Array-Based Implementation	Linked Implementation
0		
10		
30		
50		
80		

(b) At what point does the linked implementation take more space than the array-based implementation?

Use the following declarations for Exercises 26 and 27.

```
TYPE
  PtrType  = ^NodeType;
  NodeType = RECORD
    Info  : Integer;
    Next  : PtrType
  END; (* NodeType *)


  StackType = PtrType;

  QueueType = RECORD
    Front  : PtrType;
    Rear   : PtrType
  END; (* QueueType *)

VAR
  Stack : StackType;
  Queue : QueueType;
  Ptr   : PtrType;
```

26. Mark each statement as syntactically **valid** or **invalid**.
    (a) Stack^.Info := Queue^.Front.Info;
    (b) Stack^.Info := Ptr^.Next^.Info;
    (c) Ptr := Queue.Front;
    (d) Queue.Rear.Info := Ptr.Info;
    (e) Queue.Front := Queue.Rear;
    (f) Queue.Front^ := 2;
    (g) Queue.Front^.Next := Ptr;

27. Describe each of the following as a pointer, array, record, or integer:
    (a) Queue
    (b) Queue.Rear
    (c) Queue.Rear^
    (d) Queue.Front^.Info
    (e) Queue.Front^.Next^
    (f) Queue.Front^.Next

Use the following information for Exercises 28–30: A particular operating system queues the user jobs that are waiting to be executed according to the following scheme.

■ System users have relative priorities based on their user ID numbers:

Users 0–99	Highest (for example, company executives)
Users 100–199	Next to highest (for example, executive secretaries)
Users 200–299	Next highest (for example, technical leaders)
.	
.	
.	
Users 800–899	Next to lowest (for example, regular programmers)
Users 900–999	Lowest (those whose jobs only run at 3 A.M. on weekends)

- Within each priority group the jobs execute in the order in which they arrive in the system.
- If there is a highest priority job queued, it will execute before any other job; if not, if there is a next to highest priority job queued, it will run before any lower priority jobs; and so on. That is, a lower priority job will run only when there are no higher priority jobs waiting.
- The system has an array of FIFO queues to hold the queues for the various priority levels:

```
Jobs : ARRAY [0 .. 9] OF QueueType;
      (* queues of job "tokens" for each priority level *)
```

In completing the following exercises, you may call any of the queue operations specified in the FIFO queue package.

28. Write Procedure AddJob, which receives a user ID and a token (representing the job to be executed) and adds the token to the appropriate queue for that user's priority level.

29. Write Procedure GetNextJob, which returns the token for the highest priority job that is queued for execution. (The token should be removed from the queue.)

30. The system is going down for maintenance. All jobs that are waiting to be executed will have to be purged from the job queues. Fortunately this system is very friendly; it notifies users when their jobs are being canceled so that the users will know to resubmit the jobs later. Procedure Notify, with Token and Messages, as input, will take care of this notification. Write a procedure CleanUpJobs that sends Message 7 to all the users with queued jobs (call Procedure Notify to do this). The highest priority users should be notified first, of course.

31. (Turbo Pascal Exercise) Write a functional version of the FullQueue operation, using the linked implementation of a queue that was developed in the chapter. This function should use the Turbo Pascal MaxAvail and SizeOf operations to determine whether there is room in memory for another element.

Exercises 32–39 refer to the simulation application in this chapter.

32. In a simulation program, 10% of the jobs take 10 minutes, 35% of the jobs take 15 minutes, and the rest of the jobs take 30 minutes. Write the algorithm for determining TransactionTime for any given clock cycle.

33. (a) The program developed in this chapter simulates a multiple-server/single-queue system. Name two real-life examples of such a queueing system. Identify the servers and the objects being served.
    (b) Name two real-life examples of a multiple-server/multiple-queue system. Identify the servers and the objects being served.

34. The program developed in this chapter is a time-driven simulation. The length of the wait time for each job could also be established by "time-stamping" each job as it arrives, and calculating the elapsed time when the job is served. How would the program be modified to use this approach? (Describe the modifications; you do not have to write the code.)

35. The WaitQueue ADT is to be implemented using the array-based queue representation developed in this chapter.
    (a) What modifications must be made to the program to support this change?
    (b) Write the UpdateQueue operation, using this implementation.
    (c) What additional error-checking, if any, should be done?

36. Write a version of UpdateQueue that does not know how the queue is implemented. Your procedure must use the FIFO Queue ADT operations to access the elements in the queue:

WHILE more elements to process DO
    Dequeue element
    Increment element
    Enqueue element

Be careful. If you Enqueue each element after it is incremented, the queue will never be empty. You must find some way to mark the "end" of the queue.

37. Does your Pascal compiler have a random number function? If so, how is it invoked? How is the seed initialized?

38. (a) Why were the GetParameters and the report output procedures implemented as stubs in the first version of this program?
    (b) If we had postponed implementing ReadyToStop, a stub would have been necessary for this function. Write a stub for the ReadyToStop function.

39. Suggest ways to error-proof the GetParameters procedure.

Linear Lists

CHAPTER 6

GOALS

- To be able to describe a list at a logical level.
- To be able to describe how an ordered list may be implemented as a sequential or a linked structure.
- To be able to implement the following list operations for both sequential and linked implementations:
    Create and destroy a list
    Determine whether the list is empty or full
    Insert an element
    Retrieve an element
    Modify an element
    Delete an element
    Print the list elements in order
- To be able to contrast the sequential and linked implementations of a list in terms of the Big-O approximations of their operations.

The Logical Level

We all know intuitively what a "list" is; in our everyday lives we use lists all the time—grocery lists, lists of things to do, lists of addresses, lists of party guests.

In computer programs, lists are very useful and common data structures. From a programming point of view, a list is a *homogeneous* collection of elements, with a linear relationship between the elements. This means that, at the logical level, each element in the list except the first one has a unique predecessor and each element except the last one has a unique successor. (At the implementation level, there is also a relationship between the elements, but the physical relationship may not be the same as the logical one.) Lists can be unordered—their elements may be placed into the list in no particular order. Lists can also be ordered in different ways. For instance, stacks and queues are lists that are ordered according to the time when their elements were added.

Lists can also be ordered *by value*; for instance, a list of strings can be ordered alphabetically, or a list of grades can be ordered numerically. Often a value-ordered list is called a **sorted list**. When the elements in a value-ordered list are records, rather than scalar data, their logical (and often physical) order is determined by one of the fields in the record, the record *key*. For example, a list of students on the Honor Roll can be ordered alphabetically by name, or numerically by student ID. In the first case, the Name field of the record is the key; in the second case, the ID field is the key. Such value-ordered lists are also called **key-ordered lists**.

If a list cannot contain records with duplicate keys, it is considered to have *unique keys*. (To generalize our list nomenclature, we can consider a list of scalar values to be a list whose elements are keys.) This chapter deals with lists of elements with unique keys, ordered from smallest to largest key value.

Key   Field in a record whose value is used to determine the logical (and/or physical) order of the records in a list.

There are many different operations that programmers can provide for lists. For different applications we can imagine all kinds of things users might need to do to a list of elements. The List abstract data type (ADT) specification given here contains a small collection of basic operations to create and destroy a list, to determine whether a list is empty or full, to retrieve an element given its key, to add a new element, to delete or modify an existing element, and to print all the elements in the list.

List ADT Specification

Structure   The list elements are of ListElementType, and contain a key field called Key, of KeyType. The list is logically ordered from smallest unique element key value to largest; that is, the key value of the predecessor of an element is less than the key value of the element, which is less than the key value of the successor of the element.

Operations:

CreateList (List)

Function:	Initializes List to empty state.
Input:	None
Preconditions:	None
Output:	List (ListType)
Postconditions:	List exists and is empty.

DestroyList (List)

Function:	Destroys all elements, leaving List in empty state.
Input:	List (ListType)
Preconditions:	List has been created.
Output:	List
Postconditions:	List is empty.

EmptyList (List)   Returns Boolean value

Function:	Determines whether List is empty.
Input:	List (ListType)
Preconditions:	List has been created.
Output:	EmptyList (Boolean)
Postconditions:	EmptyList = (List is empty).

FullList (List)   Returns Boolean value

Function:	Determines whether List is full.
Input:	List (ListType)
Preconditions:	List has been created.
Output:	FullList (Boolean)
Postconditions:	FullList = (List is full).

RetrieveElement (List, KeyValue, Element, Found)

Function:	If Found, a copy of the element that contains the key KeyValue is returned.
Input:	List (ListType) KeyValue (KeyType)
Preconditions:	List has been created.
Output:	Element (ListElementType) Found (Boolean)

Postconditions:	Found = (element with key of KeyValue exists in List). IF Found, Element = *copy* of element from list with Key of KeyValue; otherwise, Element is undefined. List is unchanged.

InsertElement (List, NewElement)

Function:	Adds NewElement to List.
Input:	List (ListType) NewElement (ListElementType)
Preconditions:	List is not full; NewElement is not in List.
Output:	List
Postconditions:	List = original list + NewElement.

ModifyElement (List, ModElement)

Function:	Replace existing list element with same key as ModElement.
Input:	List (ListType) ModElement (ListElementType)
Preconditions:	Element with same key as ModElement exists in List.
Output:	List
Postconditions:	List = original list with value of ModElement replacing like-keyed original element.

DeleteElement (List, DeleteVal)

Function:	Deletes the element containing the key DeleteVal from List.
Input:	List (ListType) DeleteVal (KeyType)
Preconditions:	Element with key of DeleteVal is in the list and only appears once.
Output:	List
Postconditions:	List = original list with DeleteVal removed.

PrintList (List)

Function:	Prints all the elements in List in order from smallest to largest key value.
Input:	List (ListType)
Preconditions:	List has been created.
Output:	List elements (to standard output)
Postconditions:	List elements have been printed in order from smallest to largest key value. List is unchanged.

This is a basic set of the operations that might be needed to create and maintain an ordered list of elements. The specifications of the operations are somewhat arbitrary. For instance, we specified in the preconditions of the DeleteElement operation that the element to delete must exist in the list. It would be just as legitimate to specify a DeleteElement operation that does not require the element to be in the list and that returns a Boolean value Found, as well as the element data, if it exists. This is a design choice. For your own programs, you may want to modify or enhance this set of operations. The specifications for some other list operations that you can implement are given in the exercises at the end of this chapter.

The User Level

The set of "primitive" operations that we are providing for the List ADT is rather small. One way to be able to do more operations on the list is to add operations to the ADT. Another way is to create special-purpose routines that *use* the primitive list operations. For instance, the ModifyElement operation specified above cannot be used to change the value of an element's key field, since it replaces the list element with the same key. We could add a ChangeKey operation to the List ADT. Alternatively, we could write a procedure to modify the key of an element in the list, using the List ADT operations.

```
PROCEDURE ChangeKey
    (VAR List : ListType;
    OldKey    : KeyType;
    NewKey    : KeyType);

    (* Change the key of the element containing OldKey to *)
    (* NewKey. Preconditions: List has been created, and  *)
    (* contains an element with the key OldKey.            *)

VAR
    Found   : Boolean;
    Element : ListElementType;
BEGIN (* ChangeKey *)

    (* Get a copy of the element containing OldKey. *)
    RetrieveElement (List, OldKey, Element, Found);

    (* Delete the element from the list. *)
    DeleteElement (List, OldKey);

    (* Modify key and reinsert element into list. *)
    Element.Key := NewKey;
    InsertElement (List, Element)
END;  (* ChangeKey *)
```

In this procedure, we first called RetrieveElement to get the element whose key is to be changed. Unlike Pop or Dequeue, RetrieveElement does not remove the element from the List; it merely returns a copy of its data. We call DeleteElement to delete the element from the list. Since the Element that is returned from RetrieveElement is a *copy* of the list element, we cannot merely assign values to the fields of this variable to effect a change to the list. We must also call InsertElement to replace this element in the list.

Another operation that our List ADT does not perform is one to read records (of ListElementType) from a file and to create a list containing those elements. Without knowing how the list is implemented, we can write procedure CreateListFromFile, using the operations specified in the List ADT. (FileType is declared as a FILE OF ListElementType. Each call to Read inputs the next sequential record from the file.)

```
PROCEDURE CreateListFromFile
  (VAR DataFile : FileType;
   VAR List     : ListType);

  (* Reads all the records from DataFile and creates List     *)
  (* that contains the same records. Preconditions: DataFile *)
  (* exists and is closed; List has not been created yet.     *)

VAR
  Element : ListElementType;
BEGIN (* CreateListFromFile *)
  (* Open DataFile for reading. *)
  Reset (DataFile);

  (* Create empty List. *)
  CreateList (List);

  (* Read all records from file and insert them into List. *)
  WHILE NOT EOF (DataFile) DO
    BEGIN
      Read (DataFile, Element);
      InsertElement (List, Element)
    END   (* WHILE *)

END;  (* CreateListFromFile *)
```

We have made calls to the list operations specified for the List ADT, creating and modifying lists *without even knowing how the list is implemented*. At a user level, these are logical operations on a list. At a lower level, these operations will be implemented as Pascal procedures or functions that manipulate an array or other data-storing medium holding the list's elements. As we have seen with stacks and queues, there are multiple functionally correct ways to implement an abstract data type. Between the user picture and the eventual representation in the computer's memory, there are intermediate levels of abstractions and design decisions. For instance, how will the logical order of the list elements be reflected in their physical ordering? Will the list be represented as a sequential or a linked structure? If a linked structure is chosen, will its elements be stored in statically or dynamically allocated memory?

The Implementation Level

We said earlier that the logical order of the list elements may or may not be mirrored in the way that they are physically stored in a data structure. The way that the list elements are physically arranged affects the way that we access the elements of the list. This arrangement may have implications for how efficient the list operations are. For instance, there is nothing in the specification of the List ADT that *requires* us to implement the list with the elements stored in order. If we stored the elements in an array, completely unordered, we could still implement all the List operations. With this list representation, the InsertElement algorithm could be an O(1) operation, since we do not care about the order of the elements. (If the elements were ordered, the InsertElement operation would be O(N), as we shall discuss later.) However, the PrintList operation, which requires that the elements be printed *in order*, would be $O(N^2)$ (or at best, $O(N\log_2 N)$, as we will see in Chapter 11). For a list whose elements are physically sorted, this operation is O(N). We leave further exploration of the implementation of the List ADT in an unordered structure as an exercise.

In this chapter we will develop two list representations that preserve the order of the list elements. That is, the elements are physically stored in such a way that, from one list element, we can access its logical successor directly. We will first look at a *sequential list* representation. The distinguishing feature of this implementation is that the elements are stored sequentially, in adjacent slots in an array. The order of the elements is implicit in their placement in the array.

Array-based list implementations are so common that many people refer to an "array" of data when they really mean a "list," as if the two were interchangeable. Of course, we know this to be a misnomer; an array is one place to store list elements, but it is not the only implementation choice.

The second approach that we will discuss is a *linked list* representation. In a linked implementation, the data elements are not constrained to be stored in physically contiguous, sequential order; rather the individual elements are stored "somewhere in memory," and their order is maintained by explicit links between them.

We want to emphasize that the choice between sequential and linked list representations is not the same as the choice between static and dynamic storage allocation. These are separate issues. We typically store arrays in variables that have been declared, as illustrated in Figure 6-1(a), but an array-based implementation does not necessarily use static storage. The whole array could exist in a dynamically allocated area of memory; that is, we could get space for the whole structure at once using Procedure New, as illustrated in Figure 6-1(b).

We tend to think of linked structures as being in dynamically allocated storage, as illustrated in Figure 6-2(a), but this is not a requirement. A linked list could be implemented in an array; the elements might be stored in the array in any order, and "linked" by their indexes [Figure 6-2(b)], as we shall discuss in Chapter 7.

We will develop both sequential and linked implementations of a list of record elements (of type ListElementType) that are ordered according to a unique key field. The key is assumed to be a field called Key in the record. If the list element type in

Figure 6-1
Sequential Lists in Static and Dynamic Storage

(a) A sequential list in static storage

```
TYPE
   ListType = ARRAY[1 .. 5] OF Char;

VAR
   List : ListType;  (* an array *)
```

(b) A sequential list in dynamic storage

```
TYPE
   ArrayType = ARRAY[1 .. 5] OF Char;
   ListType  = ^ArrayType;

VAR
   List : ListType; (* pointer to array *)
   .
   .
   .
   New (List); (* allocate array space *)
```

Figure 6-2
Linked Lists in Static and Dynamic Storage

(a) A linked list in dynamic storage

```
TYPE
   PtrType  = ^NodeType;
   ListType = PtrType;

   NodeType = RECORD
     Info : Char;
     Next : PtrType
   END; (* NodeType *)

VAR
   List : ListType; (* a node pointer *)
   .
   .
   .
   New (List); (* allocate first node *)
```

(b) A linked list in static storage

```
TYPE
   PointerType = 0 .. 5;

   NodeType = RECORD
     Info : Char;
     Next : PointerType
   END; (* NodeType *)

   ListType = RECORD
     Nodes : ARRAY[1 .. 5] OF NodeType;
     Start : PointerType; (* index of first list node *)
     Free  : PointerType  (* index of first free node *)
   END; (* ListType *)

VAR
   List  : ListType;
```

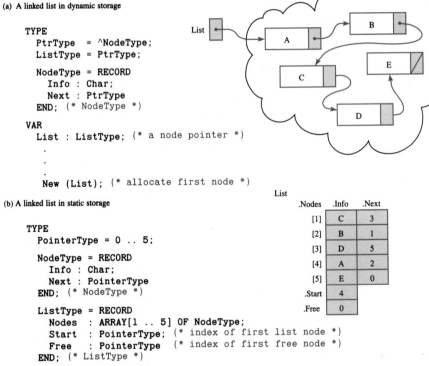

your application program uses a different name for the key field, you will need to modify all the references to the key in the list operations to use the correct field name.

The following declarations describe the data type of the elements to be stored in the list:

```
TYPE

  KeyType = Integer;        (* or any type that can be compared  *)
                            (* using <, >, <=, >=, <>, and =     *)
  ListElementType = RECORD  (* the user's data type              *)
    Key : KeyType;          (* field on which list is ordered *)
      .
      .                     (* other fields in user's data       *)
      .
  END;  (* ListElementType *)
```

List Design Terminology

Before we go on, let's establish a design terminology that we can use in our algorithms, independent of the eventual list implementation. Assuming that Location "accesses" a particular list element,

Node(Location)   refers to all the data at Location.
Info(Location)   refers to the user's data at Location.
Key(Location)   refers to the key of the user's data at Location.
Next(Location)   accesses the node following Node(Location).

What then is *Location*? For an array-based implementation, Location is an index, since we access array slots through their indexes. For example, the design statement

Print element Info(Location)

means "Print the user's data at the array slot at index Location"; eventually it might be coded as

```
PrintElement (List.Info[Location])
```

For a linked implementation whose elements are in dynamically allocated storage, Location is a pointer, since we access dynamic storage through pointer values (addresses in memory). The design statement above might be coded as

```
PrintElement (Location^.Info);
```

What about Next(Location)? We have used this notation before with pointers to refer to the "next" field of Node(Location). For example, the design statement

Location ← Next(Location)

would eventually be coded as

```
Location := Location^.Next;    (* Location is a pointer *)
```

But what does Next(Location) mean in an array-based sequential implementation? To answer this question, consider how we access the next list element stored in an array: We increment the Location, that is, the index. The design statement above, therefore, might be coded as

```
Location := Location + 1;   (* Location is an array index *)
```

We have not introduced this list design terminology just to force you into learning the syntax of another computer "language." We simply want to encourage you to think of the list, and the parts of the list elements, as *abstractions*. We have intentionally made the design notation similar to the syntax of function calls to emphasize that, at the design stage, the implementation details can be hidden. There is a lower level of detail that will be encapsulated in the "functions" Node, Key, Info, and Next. For instance, you can think of Key(Location) as a function call that returns the value of the Key at Location. How that key is accessed is not important at this level.

In fact, if the key field is a scalar type, you could actually implement the function Key. (This function would be internal to the List ADT; it is for the use of the list operations, not for the list user.) Function Key inputs a Location and returns the Key of the element at that location. For instance, for a linked list implementation, we might implement the following function Key:

```
FUNCTION Key
  (Location : LocationType) : KeyType;
  (* Returns the key of Node(Location). *)
BEGIN (* Key *)
  Key := Location^.Info.Key (* whatever the key field name is *)

END;  (* Key *)
```

In our designs, however, we often use these "functions" on the left side of assignment statements. For example, in inserting a new element into a list, we might use the design statement:

Info(Location) ← NewElement

Though the intent is clear, this use of a function would be illegal in Pascal. So we will use this "pseudofunction" notation in our algorithms to stress that *information hiding is taking place,* but we will not attempt to extend it into our code. Using this design terminology, we hope to record algorithms that can be coded for both sequential and linked list implementations.

Sequential List Implementations

The elements in the sequential list implementation will be stored in an array of records:

```
Info : ARRAY [1 .. MaxElements] OF ListElementType;
```

What makes this a sequential representation is not the array itself, but the *arrangement* of the elements within the array. The first (smallest key value) element will be stored in the first array slot, the second (next smallest key value) element in the second slot, and so on. Now we know where the list begins—in the first array slot. Where does the list end? The *array* ends at the slot with index MaxElements, but the *list* may not fill the whole array. Therefore, we will keep track of the number of list elements; we'll call this value *Length*. Now we know that the last (largest key value) element in the list is in the array slot with index Length. As we did for strings, stacks, and queues, we will bundle together the array and its supporting data in a record type:

```
CONST
  MaxElements = 100;   (* maximum number of elements in list *)
TYPE
  KeyType = Integer;   (* or any type that can be compared *)
                       (* using <, >, <=, >=, <>, and =    *)

  ListElementType = RECORD          (* the user's data type *)
    Key     : KeyType;     (* field on which list is ordered *)
    .
    .                      (* other fields in user's data as needed *)
    .
  END; (* ListElementType *)

  IndexType = 0 .. MaxElements;

  ListType = RECORD
    Length : IndexType;
    Info   : ARRAY [1 .. MaxElements] OF ListElementType;
  END; (* ListType *)
VAR
  List : ListType;
```

Figure 6-3 depicts a sequential list of the students on the Honor Roll. The elements are ordered according to their key fields, which are strings. (For simplicity, only the key fields are shown.) The element whose key comes first alphabetically is in List.Info[1], the next element is in List.Info[2], and so on. The element whose key comes last alphabetically is in List.Info[List.Length].

Now let's look at the operations we have specified for the List ADT. Because of the structural resemblance of this implementation to the array-based stack, several of the operations will seem familiar to you. An empty list is one whose Length field is zero.

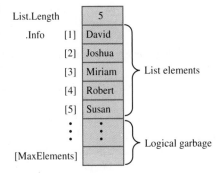

Figure 6-3
A Sequential List

List.Length

.Info

[1] David

[2] Joshua

[3] Miriam   } List elements

[4] Robert

[5] Susan

[MaxElements]   } Logical garbage

Thus the CreateList, DestroyList, and EmptyList operations merely set or check the value of the Length field. They can be coded without additional decomposition.

```
PROCEDURE CreateList
  (VAR List : ListType);

  (* Creates list in empty state. *)

BEGIN (* CreateList *)
  List.Length := 0
END;   (* CreateList *)

(*************************************************************)

PROCEDURE DestroyList
  (VAR List : ListType);

  (* "Destroys" all list elements, leaving List empty. *)

BEGIN (* DestroyList *)
  List.Length := 0  (* all elements become logical garbage *)
END;   (* DestroyList *)

(*************************************************************)

FUNCTION EmptyList
  (List : ListType) : Boolean;

  (* Returns True if List is empty; returns False otherwise. *)

BEGIN (* EmptyList *)
  EmptyList := (List.Length = 0)
END;   (* EmptyList *)
```

Like the array-based implementations of stacks and queues, this list implementation requires a FullList operation, to make sure that we do not try to insert another element when all the array slots are full. Since the array has MaxElements slots, the FullList operation simply compares the list's Length to MaxElements.

```
FUNCTION FullList
  (List : ListType) : Boolean;
```

```
     (* Returns True if List is full; returns False otherwise. *)

BEGIN  (* FullList *)
  FullList := (List.Length = MaxElements)
END;   (* FullList *)
```

The PrintList Operation

The PrintList operation processes all the elements in the list (not the array). We begin with the first element in the list, and continue until all the elements have been printed.

PrintList

Location ← start of list

WHILE more elements in list DO
    Print element Info(Location)
    Location ← Next(Location)

Now let's look at this algorithm in detail.

Location ← start of list

Location, remember, is an array index. The first element of the list is stored in the first array slot, so this will be coded as

```
Location := 1;
```

Now let's look at the loop. On entrance to each iteration of the loop body, all the list elements up to, but not including, List.Info[Location] have been printed.

    Loop Invariant Part 1:   List.Info[1] .. List.Info[Location − 1] have been printed.

How do we know if there are "more elements in the list"? To make sure that the loop terminates, we must put some upper bounds on the value of Location. We want to stop looping when the whole list has been printed; this will occur when Location − 1 equals List.Length.

    Loop Invariant Part 2:   1 <= Location <= List.Length + 1.

The resulting condition is

```
WHILE Location <= List.Length DO
```

Meanwhile, inside the loop, we print the element Info(Location)—that is, the element in the array slot with index Location. This will be coded as

```
PrintElement (List.Info[Location]);
```

Nested Procedure PrintElement, of course, will be application-specific; its implementation will depend on what data is being stored in the list. Right now we only know the name of one field—Key.

Finally, does the loop terminate? The second part of the loop invariant limits the execution of the loop, but the loop terminates only if Location is incremented inside the loop. The last line of the algorithm

Location ← Next(Location)

provides this function. What is Next(Location)? Since Location is an array index, Next(Location) is the index of the next list element, that is, Location + 1. This becomes

```
Location := Location + 1;
```

The resulting Procedure PrintList is

```
PROCEDURE PrintList
  (List : ListType);
  (* Print all the elements in List in order. *)
VAR
  Location : 1 .. MaxElements + 1;
  (***************** Nested Procedure *****************)
  PROCEDURE PrintElement
    (Element : ListElementType);
    (* Print fields of single element. *)
  BEGIN (* PrintElement *)
    Writeln ('Key = ', Element.Key)
    (* other statements as needed *)
  END; (* PrintElement *)
  (****************************************************)
BEGIN (* PrintList *)
  Location := 1;   (* Start at beginning. *)
  (* Loop Invariant: List.Info[1] .. List.Info[Location - 1]  *)
  (* has been printed AND 1 <= Location <= List.Length + 1.   *)
  WHILE Location <= List.Length DO
    BEGIN
      PrintElement (List.Info[Location]);
      Location := Location + 1
    END (* WHILE *)
END;   (* PrintList *)
```

You may have noticed that this algorithm could have been described (and coded) more succinctly as a FOR loop:

FOR Location := 1 (start of list) TO List.Length (end of list) DO
    Print element Info(Location)

However, this limits the algorithm's use to the array-based implementation. As you will see later, we can reuse the more general PrintList algorithm when we develop the linked list implementation.

Finding a List Element

All of the remaining list operations—to retrieve, modify, insert, and delete an element—require searching the list either to find the element to process or to find the appropriate place to insert. To support these operations, let's write a little procedure, FindElement. This procedure takes the list and a key value as inputs and searches the list for the element with this key. If the element is found, FindElement returns the index of the desired element's location (a value between 1 and MaxElements). What if the element with the specified key is not found, as in the case when we are inserting a new element? If the element is not found, the procedure will return a value of 0 for the location. However, as long as we're searching the list, it would be useful to know where an element with this key would belong if it *were* in the list. Therefore, Find-Element will also return the index of the element's *logical predecessor* in the list.

Here is the specification of procedure FindElement:

FindElement (List, KeyValue, Location, PredLoc)

Function:	Searches the list for the element whose key is KeyValue.
Input:	List (ListType) KeyValue (KeyType)
Preconditions:	List has been created.
Output:	Location (IndexType) PredLoc (IndexType)
Postconditions:	IF KeyValue is found in a list element, then Location = index of the element with key KeyValue and PredLoc = index of the preceding list element. If KeyValue is found in the first element, PredLoc = 0. IF KeyValue is not found in a list element, then Location = 0 and PredLoc = index of the list element that is the logical predecessor of an element containing KeyValue.

For simplicity we will use a **sequential search**. We will start at the beginning of the list and loop until (1) we have passed all the elements in the list whose keys are smaller than KeyValue, or (2) we have reached the end of the list. Then we will set the output parameters based on the loop terminating conditions. Here's the general approach:

FindElement

Index ← start of list

WHILE more to search DO
    Index ← Next(Index)

Set Location and PredLoc based on loop terminating condition.

Let's look at details. To develop our loop condition "more to search," we'll use a loop invariant. There are two conditions mentioned above that cause the search to stop. The first condition that stops the search is that we have passed the point in the list where KeyValue might be found. Since the list is ordered by key value, it is not necessary to search the entire list; we only need to search until we find a key that is larger than the one we are looking for. This tells us that on entrance to the loop, all the key values that have already been examined are less than KeyValue.

Loop Invariant Part 1: All values in Key(1) .. Key(Index − 1) are less than KeyValue.

The second condition that stops the search is that there are no more elements left to examine; that is, we have gotten to the end of the list. (This condition occurs when KeyValue is larger than any key in the list.) We now know the range of values that Index might have.

Loop Invariant Part 2: 1 <= Index <= List.Length + 1.

Let's review what the loop invariant tells us: Part 1 says not to search after passing the place in the list where KeyValue might be; Part 2 says not to search after the last list element has been examined. (Note in Part 2 that the search stops when List.Length is reached, not MaxElements, because we are searching a list, not an array.) Each part of the loop invariant contributes to the loop condition. The resulting WHILE condition is

```
WHILE  Key(Index)   <   KeyValue          (Part 1)
       AND Index  <=  List.Length DO      (Part 2)
```

When the loop terminates, the loop invariant will still be true, and the loop condition will be false. Are we sure that the loop will terminate? Looking at the inside of the loop, we see that on every iteration, Index is incremented. Eventually, if we don't pass the location of the correct element, Location will be incremented past List.Length. So we know that the loop will terminate eventually.

The only problem with coding this WHILE condition is the Boolean evaluation issue we discussed in Chapter 2. If KeyValue is larger than any of the keys in the list, we may have a run-time failure when Index > List.Length. We must not evaluate the expression Key(Index) <= KeyValue when Index is not a legitimate index in the list. To get around this problem, we will replace Part 1 of the compound condition with a Boolean flag, MoreToSearch, and move the Part 1 test inside the loop. This correction is reflected in the coded version of Procedure FindElement below.

When the loop terminates, we set the output parameters, Location and PredLoc. There are three possible situations:

1. *Index > List.Length.* If we reach the end of the list without finding an element whose key is as large as KeyValue, then the element is not in the list, so we set Location to 0. We also know that the last element examined was at the end of the list, so PredLoc is set to Index − 1, or List.Length. [See Figure 6-4(a).]
2. *Index <= List.Length AND Key(Index) = KeyValue.* In this case, we have found the element within the list. Location is set to Index and PredLoc is set to Index − 1. [See Figure 6-4(b).]
3. *Index <= List.Length AND Key(Index) <> KeyValue.* In this case, we have passed the location where the element belongs, but it isn't in the list. Location is set to 0

Figure 6-4
Finding an Element
in a Sequential List

(a) Index > List.Length. (Find Susan)

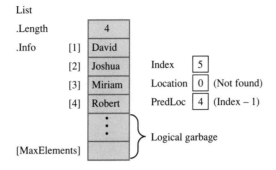

(b) Index <= List.Length AND Key(Index) = KeyValue. (Find Miriam)

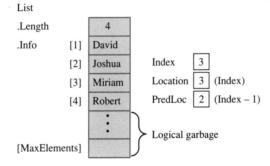

(c) Index <= List.Length AND Key(Index) <> KeyValue. (Find Leah)

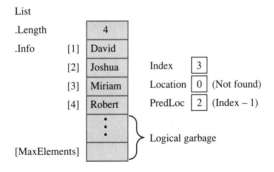

*Figure 6-4
Finding an Element
in a Sequential List*

to indicate that the element wasn't found, and PredLoc is set to Index − 1. [See Figure 6-4(c).] Note that if we wanted to insert an element with KeyValue, it would belong in the slot following PredLoc.

The assignment of the output parameters is coded as a nested IF-THEN-ELSE structure. In all three cases we set PredLoc to Index − 1, so this assignment is made before the IF. The code is shown below:

```
PROCEDURE FindElement
  (List          : ListType;
   KeyValue      : KeyType;
   VAR Location  : IndexType;
   VAR PredLoc   : IndexType);

  (* Search List for element with KeyValue. If KeyValue is   *)
  (* found in a list element, then Location = index of the   *)
  (* element with key KeyValue and PredLoc = index of the    *)
  (* preceding list element. If KeyValue is found in the     *)
  (* first element, PredLoc = 0. If KeyValue is not found    *)
  (* in the list, then Location = 0 and PredLoc = index of   *)
  (* logical predecessor of an element containing KeyValue.  *)

VAR
  Index        : Integer;
  MoreToSearch : Boolean;

BEGIN (* FindElement *)

  (* Set up to search. *)
  Index := 1;  (* start of list *)
  MoreToSearch := True; (* not done yet *)

  (* Loop Invariant: Values in Key(1) .. Key(Index - 1) are *)
  (* less than KeyValue AND 1 <= Index <= List.Length + 1. *)
  WHILE MoreToSearch AND (Index <= List.Length) DO
    IF List.Info[Index].Key < KeyValue
      THEN Index := Index + 1
      ELSE MoreToSearch := False;

  (* Set output parameters *)
  PredLoc := Index - 1;
  IF Index > List.Length
    THEN  (* KeyValue not found before end of list. *)
      Location := 0
    ELSE  (* Index is within List length *)
      IF List.Info[Index].Key = KeyValue
        THEN Location := Index (* KeyValue found *)
        ELSE Location := 0 (* KeyValue's place passed. *)

END; (* FindElement *)
```

Note that Procedure FindElement is not included in our List ADT Specification. Should we add it? *No*—this procedure is provided for the use of the List operations, not for the List user. It is logically *internal* to the List ADT. If we do not want the list user to know anything about how the list is stored, there is no reason to provide information about the inner workings (array indexes, pointers, or whatever) of the list implementation. Our goal is information hiding; therefore, this procedure is off-limits to the list user.

In standard Pascal, however, there is no mechanism for making this procedure inaccessible to the program that uses the List operations. Nesting can be used to make a procedure or function internal to a single other subprogram, but there is no way to make it internal to a group of subprograms. Languages such as Ada and Modula2, as well as "extended" versions of Pascal, such as Turbo Pascal, do provide this mechanism. If we are limited to standard Pascal, however, we must simply *agree* to use Procedure FindElement only from within the list operations.

The RetrieveElement Operation

The RetrieveElement operation allows the list user to access the list element with a specified key, if that element exists in the list. The List and the value to search for (KeyValue) are inputs to this operation, and a copy of the Element (if found) and a flag (Found) are returned. The basic algorithm is

RetrieveElement

Find Location of KeyValue in List

Found ← (KeyValue was found in list)

IF Found
   THEN Element ← Info(Location)

This procedure is very easy to code, since the hardest part (finding KeyValue in the List) has already been implemented—we can call Procedure FindElement:

```
FindElement (List, KeyValue, Location, Ignore);
```

If KeyValue is found, Location will be the index of its position; otherwise Location will be zero. (We ignore the PredLoc output parameter, because it is irrelevant to this operation.) Procedure RetrieveElement is listed below:

```
PROCEDURE RetrieveElement
   (List        : ListType;
    KeyValue    : KeyType;
    VAR Element : ListElementType;
    VAR Found   : Boolean);
   (* IF Found the Element with key KeyValue is returned;   *)
   (* otherwise, Element is undefined. List is not changed. *)
VAR
   Location : IndexType; (* location of element in array *)
   Ignore   : IndexType; (* n/a to this operation        *)
BEGIN (* RetrieveElement *)
   (* Find Location of KeyValue. Returns 0 if not found. *)
   FindElement (List, KeyValue, Location, Ignore);
   Found := (Location <> 0);
   IF Found
     THEN Element := List.Info[Location]
END; (* RetrieveElement *)
```

The RetrieveElement operation is illustrated in Figure 6-5. Note that a *copy* of the list element is returned. The caller does not access data that is in the list.

The ModifyElement Operation

The ModifyElement operation has two inputs: the List and an element that is to be put into the list (ModElement), replacing the existing element with the same key. To modify a list element that is known to be in the list, we use the following algorithm:

Find Location of element with ModElement.Key
Info(Location) ← ModElement

Since we have a procedure (FindElement) to do the first task, this procedure is really easy. The preconditions of ModifyElement state that there *must* be an element in the list with this key, so we do not need to check the value of Location to see whether the element was found.

```
PROCEDURE ModifyElement
  (VAR List    : ListType;
   ModElement : ListElementType);

  (* Replace the list element with ModElement.Key with the *)
  (* new value of ModElement. Assumes that this element    *)
  (* exists in List.                                       *)

VAR
  Location : IndexType; (* index of element to modify *)
  Ignore   : IndexType; (* n/a to this operation      *)
BEGIN (* ModifyElement *)

  (* Find Location of KeyValue in List. *)
  FindElement (List, ModElement.Key, Location, Ignore);

  (* Modify the element values. *)
  List.Info[Location] := ModElement

END;  (* ModifyElement *)
```

Figure 6-5
The Retrieve-
Element Operation

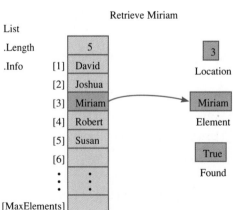

As we discussed earlier, this operation cannot be used to change the key of an element. To do this, you must delete the element with the original key and insert an element with the new key.

The InsertElement Operation

To add an element to a value-ordered list, we must first find the place where the new element belongs. Unlike a stack (where we always add to the top) or a queue (where we always add to the rear), the list's insertion location is not fixed. Where the element belongs depends on the value of its key field.

We'll use an example to illustrate the insertion operation. Let's say that Leah has made the Honor Roll. To add the element Leah to the sequential list pictured in Figure 6-6(a), maintaining the alphabetic ordering, we use the following algorithm:

InsertElement

Find the place where the new element belongs.
Create space for the new element.
Put new element in the list.

Figure 6-6
Inserting into a
Sequential List

(a) Before inserting Leah

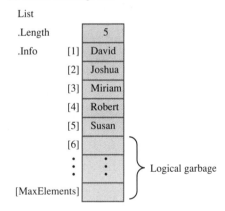

(b) After inserting Leah

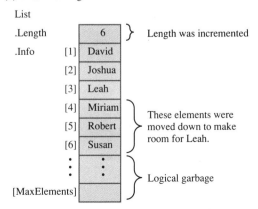

The first task involves traversing the list until we find the first element that is greater than the one we want to add (in this case, Miriam). FindElement will do this task for us; the loop terminates when the insertion point is reached.

```
FindElement (List, NewElement.Key, Location, PredLoc);
```

Since the key value of the element to be inserted is not found, Location is 0; PredLoc, however, gives us the index of the element that will precede the new element in the list.

Now that we know where the element belongs, we need to create space for it. Since the list is sequential, the element Leah must be put into the slot between its alphabetic predecessor (at index PredLoc) and successor (at index PredLoc + 1). But this slot is occupied. To "create space for the new element," we must move down all the list elements that follow it, from PredLoc + 1 to List.Length.

Create Space for New Element

FOR Index := List.Length DOWNTO PredLoc − 1 DO
   Info(Index + 1) ← Info(Index)

Now the array slot at index PredLoc + 1 is free; we put the new element in the list in this position and increment the Length field of the list. Figure 6-6(b) shows the resulting list.

Put New Element in List

Info(PredLoc + 1) ← new element
Increment List.Length

The complete InsertElement procedure is

```
PROCEDURE InsertElement
   (VAR List    : ListType;
    NewElement : ListElementType);

   (* Add NewElement to List, leaving ordered structure of *)
   (* List intact. Assumes List is not full.               *)

VAR
   Location : IndexType;   (* used for FindElement interface *)
   PredLoc  : IndexType;   (* index of preceding element     *)
   Index    : IndexType;   (* used for moving data           *)

BEGIN (* InsertElement *)

   (* Find the insertion place. Since this key is not in *)
   (* the list, Location will be 0. PredLoc is the index *)
   (* of the element that precedes the insertion place,  *)
   (* or zero if inserting before first list element.    *)
   FindElement (List, NewElement.Key, Location, PredLoc);

   (* Create space for new element. *)
   FOR Index := List.Length DOWNTO PredLoc + 1 DO
     List.Info[Index + 1] := List.Info[Index];
```

```
(* Put new element in list. *)
List.Info[PredLoc + 1] := NewElement;
List.Length := List.Length + 1
END;  (* InsertElement *)
```

Does this procedure work if the new element belongs at the beginning or end of the list? Draw yourself a picture to see how the procedure works in each of these cases.

The DeleteElement Operation

The DeleteElement operation takes two inputs: the List and the key of the element that is to be deleted (DeleteVal). We will use the following algorithm:

DeleteElement

Find the element in the list
Remove the element from the list

The first part of the algorithm is easy; we can call Procedure FindElement.

```
FindElement (List, DeleteVal, Location, Ignore);
```

On return from FindElement, Location contains the index of the element with the key DeleteVal. (We can ignore the last parameter, since the index of the predecessor node is irrelevant to this operation.) Since the preconditions of DeleteElement state that there *must* be an element in the list with this key, we do not need to check the value of Location to see whether the element was found.

How do we "remove the element from the list"? Let's look at our Honor Roll example [Figure 6-7(a)]. Removing Susan from the Honor Roll is easy, for hers is the last element in the list [see Figure 6-7(b)]. If David drops off the Honor Roll, however, we need to move up all the elements that follow to fill in the space [see Figure 6-7(c)]. In the sequential implementation, we do not actually remove the element; instead we cover it up with the element that previously followed it. Each successive element must be moved up to cover up its predecessor. Finally, we decrement the Length of the List.

Remove the Element

FOR Index := Location + 1 TO List.Length DO
    Info(Index − 1) ← Info(Index)

Decrement List.Length

What happens when we are trying to remove the last element in the list, that is, the element at List.Info[List.Length]? There are no elements following it in the list, so the value in this slot doesn't get "covered up." The loop is never entered, since there aren't any values in the range Location + 1 .. List.Length, when List.Length = Location. Decrementing List.Length, in effect, implements the deletion of the element from the list. The deleted element's value is still in the *array,* but it is no longer in the *list*. For instance, Susan is still in array slot 6 in Figure 6-7(b), but there are only five elements in the list. This element is logically (though not physically) inaccessible.

Figure 6-7
Deleting from a
Sequential List

(a) The original list

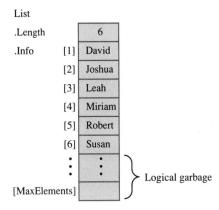

(b) Delete Susan

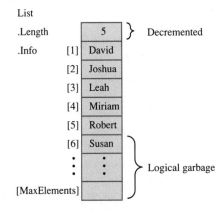

(c) Delete David

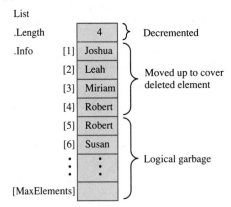

Here is the completed Procedure DeleteElement:

```
PROCEDURE DeleteElement
  (VAR List    : ListType;
   DeleteVal : KeyType);

  (* Delete the element containing the key DeleteVal from  *)
  (* List. Assumes this element exists in the list.        *)

VAR
  Location : IndexType;    (* index of element to delete    *)
  Ignore   : IndexType;    (* n/a for this operation        *)
  Index    : Integer;      (* used for loop moving elements *)
BEGIN (* DeleteElement *)

  (* Find the position of element with key of DeleteVal.  *)
  FindElement (List, DeleteVal, Location, Ignore);

  (* "Remove" the element from the list by moving up its *)
  (* successors to cover it.                             *)
  FOR Index := Location + 1 TO List.Length DO
    List.Info[Index - 1] := List.Info[Index];

  List.Length := List.Length - 1

END;  (* DeleteElement *)
```

Notes on the Sequential List Implementation

In many of the list operations, we have declared a local variable Location, which contains the array index of the list element being processed. The values of array indexes never get outside of the set of list operations; this information is *internal* to the implementation of the List ADT. If the list user wants a record in the list, the RetrieveElement operation does not give the user the index of the record; instead it returns a copy of the record itself. If the user changes values in this record, those changes are not reflected in the list unless the user calls ModifyElement. The list user is never allowed to see or manipulate the physical structure in which the list is stored. These details of the list implementation are hidden; the list has been encapsulated by the ADT.

In the RetrieveElement and PrintList procedures, which use the list but do not change it, we have made List a value parameter. While this is logically the correct choice, it may not be very practical when the List is very large. Pascal causes a copy to be made of each parameter that is passed by value; therefore, it is usually a better idea to pass large structures by reference (VAR), even when they are input-only parameters. When you pass an input parameter by reference, you should document this information in a comment, as shown below:

```
PROCEDURE PrintList
  (VAR List : ListType);

  (* Print all the List elements. NOTE: List is an input  *)
  (* parameter passed by reference to conserve space.     *)
```

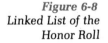   The code for the sequential implementation of the List ADT can be found in file LIST1.PAS on the program disk.

Linked List Implementations

In a **linked list** representation, the data elements are not constrained to be stored in sequential order; rather, the individual elements are stored "somewhere" in memory. The order of the elements is maintained by *explicit* links between them. Figure 6-8 shows pictorially how our Honor Roll data would be represented as a linked list.

We will construct the linked list structure much like the linked versions of the Stack and FIFO Queue ADTs. Each node contains both data and an explicit link to the next node in the list. Since the list is linear, the link field of the last node contains NIL, a special pointer value that says, "This pointer doesn't point to anything." An external pointer (e.g., List) tells us where the list starts. You cannot access nodes in a linked list directly or randomly; that is, you cannot get directly to the twenty-fifth element in the list, as you can with a sequential representation. Rather, you access the first node through the external pointer, the second node through the first node's "next" pointer, the third node through the second node's "next" pointer, and so on, to the end of the list.

In discussing the advantages of the linked stack and queue representations, we focused on the issue of dynamic storage allocation. Since the nodes were created dynamically, we did not have to declare an array variable large enough to store the maximum number of elements, thus saving space when the list was smaller. There are, however, other advantages to a linked implementation, unrelated to the issue of storage allocation. In fact, as you will see in Chapter 7, a linked list does not have to be stored in dynamically allocated space; we can store the elements in an array and link them explicitly using array indexes instead of pointers. So what's so great about linking?

Using a linked structure streamlines the algorithms that manipulate the elements. For instance, we can avoid all of the data movement that was necessary to insert and delete into a sequential list. With a linked representation, the existing elements stay where they are as others are added and deleted. What changes are the links that establish the order of the elements.

Implementing a Linked List

Each node in a linked list must contain at least two fields. The first is the *Info* field, which contains the list user's data. As we said above, we will assume that the Info field is a record, which contains a field called Key, on whose value the list is ordered. The second field, the *Next* field, contains the pointer, or link, to the next node in the list.

Figure 6-8
Linked List of the
Honor Roll

In this chapter we will implement a linked list whose nodes are dynamically allocated, using Procedure New. The following declarations are used for this list representation:

```
TYPE
   KeyType = Integer;      (* or any type that can be compared  *)
                           (* using <, >, <=, >=, <>, and =     *)

   ListElementType = RECORD (* the user's data type             *)
     Key : KeyType;         (* field on which list is ordered *)
       .                  ⎤
       .                  ⎬ (* other fields in user's data      *)
       .                  ⎦
   END; (* ListElementType *)

   PointerType = ^NodeType;

   NodeType = RECORD
     Info   : ListElementType;      (* list user's data      *)
     Next   : PointerType           (* pointer to next node *)
   END; (* NodeType *)

   ListType = PointerType;

VAR
   List : ListType;                 (* pointer to start of List *)
```

Note that the list *user's* data types (ListElementType and KeyType) are unchanged from the sequential implementation. From the user's perspective, nothing has changed.

In fact, from the List ADT programmer's perspective, something else hasn't changed much: The algorithms for the list operations will be very similar to the ones we developed for the sequential implementation.

Using the declarations above, to create an empty list we merely set List (the external pointer to the linked list) to NIL. Here is the procedure to implement this operation:

```
PROCEDURE CreateList
   (VAR List : ListType);

   (* Creates list in empty state. *)
BEGIN (* CreateList *)
   List := NIL
END; (* CreateList *)
```

We can use the knowledge that an empty list is one whose pointer is NIL to write a short EmptyList function:

```
FUNCTION EmptyList
   (List : ListType) : Boolean;

   (* Returns True if List is empty; returns False otherwise. *)
```

```
BEGIN (* EmptyList *)
  EmptyList := (List = NIL)
END;  (* EmptyList *)
```

What about the FullList operation we specified in our list package? Unfortunately, when the list is "full" (all the space available for new nodes has been used), the program will crash with a run-time error if we try to get more space. So a FullList operation is not very useful with this implementation. As we did for linked stacks and queues, we will merely create a stub for the FullList operation.

```
FUNCTION FullList
  (List : ListType) : Boolean;

  (* Stub for FullList operation, which is meaningless in *)
  (* this implementation.                                 *)

BEGIN (* FullList *)
  FullList := False
END;  (* FullList *)
```

(Of course, if your Pascal compiler provides a nonstandard extension to check the amount of free memory, you can write a functional version of this operation.)

The DestroyList operation for a linked list is more complicated than its sequential list counterpart, since the dynamically allocated space used by the elements must be freed. The easiest approach is just to unlink each successive node in the list and free it. Since this is exactly like our DestroyStack operation in Chapter 4, we'll just "borrow" the code, changing "Stack" references to "List."

```
PROCEDURE DestroyList
  (VAR List : ListType);

  (* Destroys all list elements, leaving List empty. *)

VAR
  TempPtr : PointerType;

BEGIN (* DestroyList *)

  (* Remove all elements from the list, freeing the space. *)
  WHILE List <> NIL DO
    BEGIN

      (* Unlink the first node from the list. *)
      TempPtr := List;
      List := List^.Next;

      (* Free the space from the node. *)
      Dispose (TempPtr)

    END (* WHILE *)

END; (* DestroyList *)
```

Printing the List

The PrintList operation specified in our list package prints out all the elements (the Info part of each node) of the linked list. Let's review the algorithm for PrintList that we developed for the sequential implementation of the list.

PrintList

Location ← start of list

WHILE more elements in list DO
    Print element Info(Location)
    Location ← Next(Location)

As noted before, we can reuse this algorithm for the linked list implementation, even though the way that we access list elements has changed. In the sequential list, we accessed list elements using Location—an array index. What does Location mean in the linked implementation? It is a pointer variable, the address in memory of a list node. With this in mind, let's examine this algorithm.

To access the beginning of the list, we initialize Location by setting it equal to the external pointer, List. Next we see the loop control "WHILE more elements in list DO." How do we know if there are more elements? When Location is equal to the special value in the Next field of the last node (NIL), we know that we have reached the end of the list. If the list is empty, we stop; otherwise we perform the processing inside the loop. First we print the data in the Info field of the node currently pointed to by Location. Then we advance Location by setting it to the value of the Next field of the current node. This loop causes Location to move through, or "traverse," all the elements in the list, until it finally becomes NIL.

The implementation of PrintList, using pointer types, is shown below.

```
PROCEDURE PrintList
  (List: ListType);

  (* Prints out the value of the Info field of each *)
  (* node in the linked list pointed to by List.    *)
VAR
  Location : PointerType; (* traversing pointer *)

  (**************** Nested Procedure ****************)

  PROCEDURE PrintElement
    (Element : ListElementType);

    (* Print fields of single element. *)

  BEGIN (* PrintElement *)

    Writeln ('Key = ', Element.Key);

    (* other statements as needed *)

  END; (* PrintElement *)

  (***********************************************************)
```

```
BEGIN (* PrintList *)
  Location := List;  (* Start at beginning of list. *)
  (* Print all elements until the end of the list. *)
  WHILE Location <> NIL DO
    BEGIN
      (* Print data and advance the pointer. *)
      PrintElement (Location^.Info);
      Location := Location^.Next
    END (* WHILE *)
END; (* PrintList *)
```

The implementation changed, but the basic algorithm to print the list stayed the same. The table that follows compares the array and pointer syntax that describes our list design notation.

From the Design Notation to Pascal Syntax

Design Notation	Sequential (array-based)	Linked (pointer-based)
Location	an array index	a pointer variable
Node(Location)	List.Info[Location]	Location^
Info(Location)	List.Info[Location]	Location^. Info
Key(Location)	List.Info[Location].Key	Location^. Info.Key
Next(Location)	Location + 1	Location^. Next

Finding a List Element

The rest of the List ADT operations (retrieve, modify, insert, and delete), require searching the list to find the element to process. As we did for the sequential list implementation, we will write a procedure, FindElement, to simplify these other operations. This procedure takes a pointer to the list and a key value as inputs, and searches the list for the element with the specified key. If the element is found, the output parameter Location returns a pointer to the node with the desired key; otherwise, Location is NIL. As before, the procedure also returns PredLoc, the location (a pointer) of the element that logically precedes the element we are searching for. In the linked list implementation, the pointer to the preceding node is useful both in inserting and in deleting elements.

Here is the specification of procedure FindElement for the linked implementation:

FindElement (List, KeyValue, Location, PredLoc)

Function:	Searches the list for the element whose key is KeyValue.
Input:	List (ListType)
	KeyValue (KeyType)

Preconditions:	List has been created.	
Output:	Location (PointerType)	
	PredLoc (PointerType)	
Postconditions:	IF KeyValue is found in the list, then Location = pointer to the node with key KeyValue and PredLoc = pointer to the preceding list node. If KeyValue is found in the first node, PredLoc = NIL.	
	IF KeyValue is not found in a list node, then Location = NIL and PredLoc = pointer to the list node that is the logical predecessor of a node with the key KeyValue.	

The algorithm is similar to the sequential list version of this procedure: Starting at the beginning of the list, we loop until (1) we have passed all the elements in the list whose keys are smaller than KeyValue, or (2) we have reached the end of the list. Then we set the output parameters based on the loop terminating conditions.

FindElement

Location ← start of list

WHILE Key(Location) < KeyValue AND more nodes in list DO
   Location ← Next(Location)

Set Location and PredLoc based on loop terminating conditions.

Location starts out accessing the first node and is advanced in each iteration to access the next node. Since the end of the list is marked by a NIL "Next" pointer, "more nodes in list" becomes "Location <> NIL." As in the sequential list version of this procedure, we again run into the Boolean evaluation issue:

```
WHILE (Location^.Info.Key < KeyValue) AND (Location <> NIL) DO
```

may cause a run-time error when we reach the end of the list. Therefore, the coding of this procedure uses a Boolean flag in place of the first half of the WHILE condition and moves the test inside the loop. This change is reflected in the code, listed below.

The last task is to "set Location and PredLoc based on the loop terminating conditions." As before, there are three conditions:

1. *Location = NIL.* If we reach the end of the list without finding an element whose key is as large as KeyValue, then the element is not in the list. Location correctly has the value of NIL. We also know that, if we want to insert an element with the key KeyValue, it belongs at the end of the list, so PredLoc is set to point to the last node. [See Figure 6-9(a).]
2. *Location <> NIL AND Key(Location) = KeyValue.* In this case, we have found the element within the list. Location correctly points to the node with the specified key, and PredLoc is set to point to the preceding node. [See Figure 6-9(b).]
3. *Location <> NIL AND Key(Location) <> KeyValue.* In this case, we have passed the location where the element belongs, but it isn't in the list. Location is reset to

Figure 6-9
Finding an Element
in a Linked List

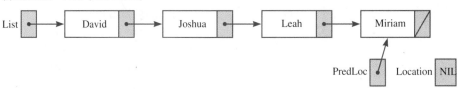

(a) Location = NIL. (Find Robert)

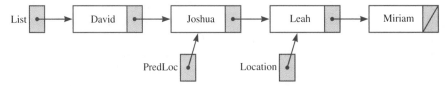

(b) Location <> NIL AND Key(Location) = KeyValue. (Find Leah)

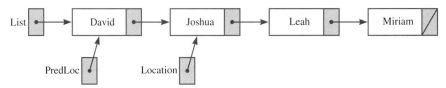

(c) Location <> NIL AND Key(Location) <> KeyValue. (Find Diane)

NIL to indicate that the element wasn't found, and PredLoc is set to point to the last node whose key was less than KeyValue. [See Figure 6-9(c).]

Setting Location is easy, but setting PredLoc is a problem. In the sequential list implementation, this is a simple task. Given the location (index) of an array slot, it is easy to figure out its predecessor—we merely set PredLoc to Index − 1. Given the pointer to a node in a linked list, however, we cannot figure out the address of its predecessor in the list. The links go in only one direction.

One way to solve this problem is to modify our algorithm slightly to "peek ahead" one node:

Location ← start of List

WHILE Key(*Next*(Location)) < KeyValue AND more nodes in list DO
    Location ← Next(Location)

Trying this out on the examples in Figure 6-9, we quickly notice that the first node (the one containing David) gets skipped in the comparison. We have to make a special check, before we enter the loop, for the case that there is no key in the list smaller than KeyValue.

The "peek ahead" approach requires us to worry about different cases, based on the position of the key in the list. Another approach is to use a *pair* of pointers to traverse the list. As Location moves along the list, searching for a node that contains a key larger than KeyValue, PredLoc trails behind by one node. Using a second pointer will complicate our search loop slightly. We initialize Location to List and PredLoc to

Figure 6-10
The Inchworm
Effect

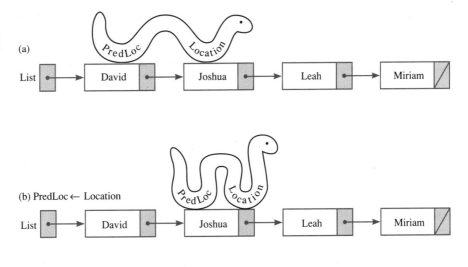

(a)

(b) PredLoc ← Location

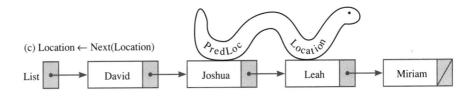

(c) Location ← Next(Location)

NIL. Then, inside the loop, we advance both pointers. As Figure 6-10 shows, the process resembles the movement of an inchworm. PredLoc (the tail of the inchworm) catches up with Location (the head), and then Location advances.

Now, when the loop terminates, it is easy to set the output parameters. In the first case (Location = NIL), PredLoc is already set to the correct value. If the list is empty, PredLoc is still NIL; otherwise, PredLoc points to the last node in the list [Figure 6-9(a)].

In the second case (Location <> NIL AND Key(Location) = KeyValue), the node with KeyValue was found. Both Location and PredLoc are already correct: Location points to the node with the key KeyValue, and PredLoc points to the node that precedes it [Figure 6-9(b)], or is NIL if Node(Location) is the first one in the list.

In the third case (Location <> NIL AND Key(Location) <> KeyValue), KeyValue does not appear in the list. When the loop terminates, PredLoc points to the node that would logically precede a node with the key KeyValue. Location points to the node that would logically follow a node with the key KeyValue [Figure 6-9(c)]. Thus PredLoc is already correct, but we must reset Location to NIL to indicate that KeyValue does not appear in the list.

Letting PredLoc trail Location in searching the list makes setting the output parameters easy; in most cases, they are already correct on exit from the loop. The code for the complete Procedure FindElement is shown on the following pages.

```
PROCEDURE FindElement
  (List          : ListType:
   KeyValue      : KeyType;
   VAR Location  : PointerType;
   VAR PredLoc   : PointerType);

  (* IF KeyValue is found in list, then Location = pointer  *)
  (* to the node with key KeyValue and PredLoc = pointer to *)
  (* the preceding list node. If KeyValue is found in the   *)
  (* first node, PredLoc = NIL. IF KeyValue is not found in *)
  (* a list node, then Location = NIL and PredLoc = pointer *)
  (* to the list node that is the logical predecessor of a  *)
  (* node with the key KeyValue.                            *)
VAR
  MoreToSearch : Boolean;

BEGIN (* FindElement *)

  (* Set up to search. *)
  Location := List;           (* start of list *)
  PredLoc  := NIL;
  MoreToSearch := True;

  (* Search for node containing KeyValue until:       *)
  (*    (1) we reach KeyValue's place in the list, or *)
  (*    (2) we reach the end of the list.             *)
  WHILE MoreToSearch AND (Location <> NIL) DO
    IF Location^.Info.Key < KeyValue
      THEN (* keep looking — advance both pointers *)
        BEGIN
          PredLoc  := Location;
          Location := Location^.Next
        END (* Key(Location) < KeyValue *)

      ELSE MoreToSearch := False;

  (* If Location does not point to a node containing  *)
  (* KeyValue, reset Location to NIL.                 *)
  IF Location <> NIL
    THEN
      IF Location^.Info.Key <> KeyValue
        THEN Location := NIL

END; (* FindElement *)
```

As in the sequential list implementation, Procedure FindElement is internal to the List ADT; it is to be used only by the list operations. The list *user* should never be able to access list data through the pointers; rather, the access mechanism is encapsulated by the List ADT operations. With the help of Procedure FindElement, the rest of the list operations will be very simple to write.

The RetrieveElement Operation

The RetrieveElement operation allows the list user to retrieve a copy of the list element with a specified key value, if it exists in the list. The List and the value to search for (KeyValue) are inputs to this operation, and the Element (if found) and a flag (Found) are returned. The basic algorithm is identical to the sequential list version of the operation:

RetrieveElement

Find Location of KeyValue in List
Found ← (KeyValue was found in list)

IF Found
   THEN Element ← Info(Location)

Procedure FindElement will give us the location of KeyValue in the list:

```
FindElement (List, KeyValue, Location, Ignore);
```

If KeyValue is found, Location will point to its node, and we can assign its Info field to Element; otherwise Location will be NIL. (We ignore the value of the PredLoc parameter, since it is irrelevant to this operation.) Procedure RetrieveElement is listed below:

```
PROCEDURE RetrieveElement
   (List        : ListType;
    KeyValue    : KeyType;
    VAR Element : ListElementType;
    VAR Found   : Boolean);

   (* IF Found the Element with key KeyValue is returned;  *)
   (* otherwise, Element is undefined.                     *)
VAR
  Location : PointerType; (* points to node with KeyValue *)
  Ignore   : PointerType; (* n/a to this operation        *)
BEGIN (* RetrieveElement *)

  (* Find Location of KeyValue in List. Returns NIL value for *)
  (* Location if the key was not found in the list.           *)
  FindElement (List, KeyValue, Location, Ignore);

  Found := (Location <> NIL);

  IF Found
    THEN Element := Location^.Info
END;  (* RetrieveElement *)
```

The ModifyElement Operation

The linked list version of Procedure ModifyElement is almost identical to the sequential list code. We need to make only minor editing changes, as the algorithms are exactly the same.

```
PROCEDURE ModifyElement
  (VAR List    : ListType;
   ModElement : ListElementType);

  (* Replace the list element with ModElement.Key with the *)
  (* new value of ModElement. Assumes that this element    *)
  (* exists in List.                                       *)
VAR
  Location : PointerType; (* points to node to modify *)
  Ignore   : PointerType; (* n/a to this operation    *)
BEGIN (* ModifyElement *)

  (* Find Location of ModElement's key in List. *)
  FindElement (List, ModElement.Key, Location, Ignore);

  (* Modify the element values. *)
  Location^.Info := ModElement

END;  (* ModifyElement *)
```

It is not necessary to check the value of Location to see if the search was successful; the preconditions guarantee that the element with the desired key is in the list.

The InsertElement Operation

To insert a new element into the linked list, we will use the general algorithm developed for the sequential list implementation:

InsertElement

Find the place where the new element belongs.
Create space for the new element.
Put new element in the list.

   This algorithm is illustrated in Figure 6-11. The first task is simple: we just call FindElement:

```
FindElement (List, NewElement.Key, Ignore, PredLoc);
```

Of course, we do not expect to find NewElement's key in the list. In fact, the preconditions guarantee that it will not be in the list yet. So we can ignore the value returned for FindElement's formal parameter Location (it will be NIL). PredLoc, however, is very interesting to us since it points to the node that should precede the new node in the list.

Figure 6-11
Inserting into a
Linked List

(a) Find the place where the new node belongs (Insert Leah)

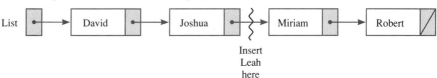

Insert
Leah
here

(b) Create space for the new element

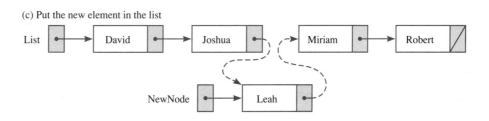

(c) Put the new element in the list

The second task is to create space for the new element. In the sequential version of InsertElement, we had to move all the data elements down one slot, from the insertion location to the end of the list, to make room for the new element. One of the advantages to a linked list implementation is that all this data movement can be avoided, because the space for the new element does not come out of the existing structure. Instead we create space dynamically at run time by asking the system to allocate some free memory space, using Procedure New. We can then put the value of NewElement into the Info part of the new node.

Create Space for the New Element

New (NewNode)
Info(NewNode) ← NewElement

The last task of the insert algorithm is to put the new element in the list. To complete the insertion, we must manipulate the pointers to link the new node into its appropriate position in the list. There are four cases to consider: (1) inserting into an empty list; (2) inserting before the first node in the list; (3) inserting into the "middle" of the list; and (4) inserting after the last node in the list.

In the first case, we merely need to set Next(NewNode) to NIL and to set List (the external pointer to the list) to point to the new node [Figure 6-12(a)].

Figure 6-12
Four Insert Cases

(a) Insert into empty list (Insert Leah)

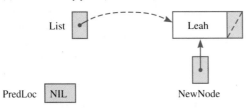

(b) Insert at beginning of list (Insert David)

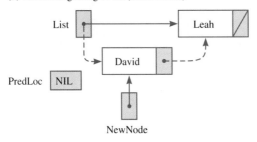

(c) Insert in middle of list (Insert Joshua)

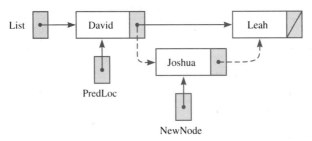

(d) Insert at end of list (Insert Miriam)

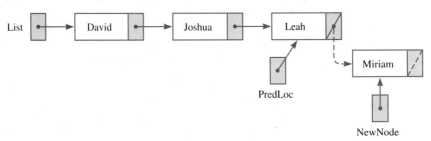

Inserting into an Empty List

Next(NewNode) ← NIL
List ← NewNode

The second case is similar: We set Next(NewNode) to point to the first list node and then set List to point to the new node [Figure 6-12(b)].

Inserting at the Front of the List

Next(NewNode) ← List
List ← NewNode

Actually, since List = NIL when the list is empty, the first case is the same as the second, so we will combine them.

In the third case (inserting into the "middle" of the list), we link the new node into place after its predecessor (Node(PredLoc)), as shown in Figure 6-12(c).

Next(NewNode) ← Next(PredLoc)
Next(PredLoc) ← NewNode

In the fourth case (inserting at the end of the list), we link the new node after Node(PredLoc) and set its Next field to NIL, as illustrated in Figure 6-12(d).

Next(NewNode) ← NIL
Next(PredLoc) ← NewNode

Since Next(PredLoc) = NIL when we are inserting at the end of the list, the third and fourth cases can also be combined. The whole algorithm for the InsertElement operation is shown below:

InsertElement

(Find the insert location.)
FindElement (List, NewElement.Key, Ignore, PredLoc)

(Create node for new element.)
New (NewNode)
Info(NewNode) ← NewElement

(Insert the element.)
IF list is empty OR inserting at beginning of list
  THEN
      Next(NewNode) ← List
      List ← NewNode

  ELSE (inserting in the middle or at the end)
      Next(NewNode) ← Next(PredLoc)
      Next(PredLoc) ← NewNode

How do we know if the list is empty or if we are inserting at the beginning of the list? In either of these cases, the value of PredLoc returned from FindElement will be NIL.

The code to implement this insert algorithm as a Pascal procedure is given below.

```
PROCEDURE InsertElement
  (VAR List   : ListType;
   NewElement : ListElementType);

  (* Add NewElement to List, leaving key value-ordered *)
  (* structure of List intact. Assumes that an element *)
  (* with same key is not already in the list.         *)
```

```
VAR
  NewNode  : PointerType;    (* pointer to the new node    *)
  PredLoc  : PointerType;    (* pointer to preceding node *)
  Ignore   : PointerType;    (* not used                   *)
BEGIN  (* InsertElement *)

  (* Find the insert location. *)
  FindElement (List, NewElement.Key, Ignore, PredLoc);

  (* Allocate a new node, and put NewElement into it. *)
  New(NewNode);
  NewNode^.Info := NewElement;

  (* Insert the new node into the list. *)
  IF PredLoc = NIL
    THEN (* list is empty OR inserting at beginning of list *)
      BEGIN
        NewNode^.Next := List;
        List := NewNode
      END (* inserting first element *)

    ELSE (* inserting in the middle or at the end *)
      BEGIN
        NewNode^.Next := PredLoc^.Next;
        PredLoc^.Next := NewNode
      END (* inserting in middle or at end *)
END;  (* InsertElement *)
```

The DeleteElement Operation

The last operation specified for our List ADT is the deletion of nodes that are no longer needed. The basic tasks for the delete algorithm are

DeleteElement

Find the element in the list.
Remove the element from the list.

Procedure FindElement will give us a pointer to the node we wish to delete, as well as a pointer to its predecessor in the list, if there is one:

```
FindElement (List, DeleteVal, Location, PredLoc)
```

The second task, to remove the element from the list, has two parts. First we must "unlink" the deleted element from the list; then we dispose of its node space. When unlinking the deleted element, we must pay attention to the node's position in the list. We will consider four cases: (1) deleting the only list element, leaving the list empty; (2) deleting the first node; (3) deleting a "middle" node; and (4) deleting the last node.

In the first case, we merely set List to NIL, as pictured in Figure 6-13(a). In the second case (deleting the first node in the list), we set List to Next(Location), as shown in Figure 6-13(b). Since Next(Location) = NIL when the delete node is the only node

Figure 6-13   *Deleting from a Linked List*

(a) Delete only list node (Delete David)

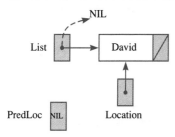

(b) Delete first list node (Delete David)

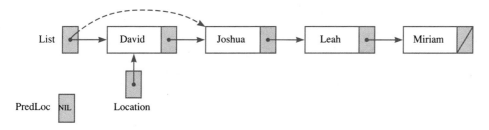

(c) Delete "middle" node (Delete Leah)

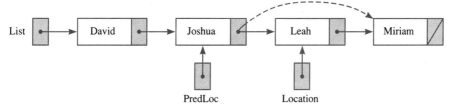

(d) Delete last node (Delete Miriam)

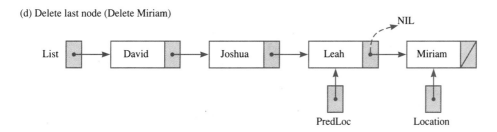

in the list, these two cases can be combined in the code. We can detect both these cases by checking for a NIL pointer in PredLoc.

In the third case (deleting a middle node), we must make the link from the preceding node "jump over" the deleted node [Figure 6-13(c)]:

Next(PredLoc) ← Next(Location)

In the fourth case (deleting the last node), we merely set Next(PredLoc) to NIL, as pictured in Figure 6-13(d). Since Next(Location) = NIL when the delete node is at the end of the list, the third and fourth cases can be combined.

After unlinking Node(Location), we dispose of its space with a call to Dispose(Location). The code for Procedure DeleteElement is shown below:

```
PROCEDURE DeleteElement
   (VAR List   : ListType;
    DeleteVal : KeyType);

   (* Removes the node containing the key DeleteVal from   *)
   (* the linked list pointed to by List. Assumes that this *)
   (* key is present in the list.                           *)

VAR
   Location : PointerType;   (* points to delete node    *)
   PredLoc  : PointerType;   (* points to preceding node *)
BEGIN (* DeleteElement *)

   (* Find the element to delete. On return from this  *)
   (* procedure, Location points to the node to delete *)
   (* and PredLoc points to the node preceding it, or  *)
   (* is NIL if we're deleting the first node in list. *)
   FindElement (List, DeleteVal, Location, PredLoc);

   (* Unlink the delete node from the list. *)
   IF PredLoc = NIL (* deleting first node in list *)
      THEN List := Location^.Next
      ELSE PredLoc^.Next := Location^.Next;

   (* Free the node space to be reused. *)
   Dispose (Location)
END; (* DeleteElement *)
```

We've now designed and implemented the operations that were specified for the List ADT. You can probably think of a number of other useful operations that you could perform on a list: finding the previous or succeeding element, merging two lists, counting the list elements, and so on. Some other list operations are specified in the homework exercises.

The code for the linked implementation of the List ADT can be found in file LIST2.PAS on the program disk.

Analyzing the List Implementations

Now let's compare the sequential and linked implementations of the List ADT. Just as we compared Stack and Queue implementations, we will look at several different factors: the length of the source code required to implement the solutions, the amount of memory required to store the structure, and the amount of "work" the solution does.

The size of the source code of the declarations, procedures, and functions for each implementation is summarized in the table that follows. As you can see from the chart, the linked implementation takes about 15% more lines of code than the sequential implementation. Most of the operations (marked in the table with asterisks) take the same number of lines in both implementations; these are the operations that are almost identical, developed from the same design-language algorithms. Deciding which design is easier to understand is very subjective. Which implementation seems simpler to you?

Comparison of Executable Source Lines of Code

	Sequential Implementation	Linked Implementation
Declarations	6	7
CreateList (*)	5	5
DestroyList	5	12
FullList (*)	5	5
EmptyList (*)	5	5
PrintList (*)	17	17
FindElement	24	24
RetrieveElement (*)	14	14
ModifyElement (*)	10	10
InsertElement	14	23
DeleteElement	13	13
Total	118	135

Now let's compare the storage requirements. An array variable of the maximum list size will take the same amount of memory, no matter how many array slots are actually used, because we need to reserve space for the maximum possible. The linked implementation using dynamically allocated storage space requires only enough space for the number of elements actually in the list at run time. However, as we discussed in detail in Chapter 5, each node element is larger, since we must store the link (the Next field) as well as the user's data.

We can also compare the relative "efficiency" of the two implementations. As mentioned before, most of the operations are nearly identical in the two implementations. The CreateList, FullList, and EmptyList operations in both implementations are clearly O(1). As in the stack and queue operations, DestroyList is a O(1) operation for a sequential list but becomes a O(N) operation for a linked list. The sequential implementation merely marks the list as empty, while the linked implementation must actually access each list element to free its dynamically allocated space.

The two PrintList operations traverse a list element by element. As each element in the list is processed once, PrintList is O(N) for both list representations.

Both implementations of the FindElement procedure use sequential searches. Beginning at the first element, they examine one element after another until the correct element (or place) is found. Since they must potentially search through all the elements in a list, the loops in both procedures are O(N). The code to set the output parameters is O(1). Thus both versions of FindElement are O(N). This does not mean that they take the same amount of time to execute. The linked list version reassigns two pointers in each iteration of the loop body (the search pointer Location and the trailing pointer PredLoc), while the sequential list version only increments an index. Thus we might expect the sequential version to be a little quicker, but by less than one order of magnitude. (The linked version might take 50% longer, but not 10 times longer to execute.)

The RetrieveElement and ModifyElement operations are virtually identical for the two implementations. They first call FindElement [O(N)] and then assign the output parameters [O(1)]. Since O(N) + O(1) = O(N), these operations are O(N) in both implementations.

In both list implementations, the InsertElement operations call FindElement to find the insertion position; therefore, the search parts of these algorithms are O(N). The sequential list must also move down all the elements that follow the insertion position to make room for the new element. The number of elements to be moved ranges from 0, when we insert to the end of the list, to List.Length, when we insert to the beginning of the list. So the insertion part of the algorithm is also O(N) for the sequential list. Since O(N) + O(N) = O(N), the sequential list's InsertElement operation is O(N).

The insertion part of the algorithm for the linked list representation simply requires the reassignment of a couple of pointers. This makes the insertion task O(1) for a linked list, which is one of the main advantages of linking. However, adding the insertion task to the search task gives us O(N) + O(1) = O(N)— the same Big-O approximation as for the sequential list! Doesn't the linking offer any advantage in efficiency? Remember that the Big-O evaluations are only rough approximations of the amount of work that an operation does. The next section presents a timed test to see whether the linked list's insertion operation really is faster.

The DeleteElement operation is similar to InsertElement. In both implementations, the search task is performed by FindElement, an O(N) operation. Then the sequential list's insert operation "deletes" the element by moving up all the subsequent elements in the list, which adds O(N). The whole procedure is O(N) + O(N), or O(N). The linked list deletes the element by unlinking it from the list and calling Dispose, which adds O(1) to the search task. The whole procedure is O(N) + O(1), or O(N). Thus both DeleteElement operations are O(N); for large values of N, they are roughly equivalent.

This does not mean that they will take the same amount of time to execute, however. The sequential implementation requires a great deal of data movement for both InsertElement and DeleteElement. Does all this data movement really make any difference? It doesn't matter too much in our Honor Roll example; the list is very small. If there are 1000 students on the Honor Roll, however, the data movement starts to add up.

The table that follows summarizes the Big-O comparison of the list operations for sequential and linked implementations.

Big-O Comparison of List Operations

	Sequential Implementation	Linked Implementation
CreateList (*)	O(1)	O(1)
DestroyList	**O(1)**	**O(N)**
FullList (*)	O(1)	O(1)
EmptyList (*)	O(1)	O(1)
PrintList (*)	O(N)	O(N)
FindElement	O(N)	O(N)
InsertElement		
FindElement O(N) +	**O(N)**	**O(1)**
Total	O(N)	O(N)
RetrieveElement (*)		
FindElement O(N) +	O(1)	O(1)
Total	O(N)	O(N)
ModifyElement (*)		
FindElement O(N) +	O(1)	O(1)
Total	O(N)	O(N)
DeleteElement		
FindElement O(N) +	**O(N)**	**O(1)**
Total	O(N)	O(N)

Starred operations are nearly identical in the two implementations, developed from the same algorithm. The areas where the implementations differ are marked in boldface.

Let's look at an actual timed test case, with real numbers. The table on the following page shows how long it takes on one computer to insert and then delete 1000 elements (key values 1 through 1000) in various orders. The test program ran three cases:

1. *Mixed inserts/deletes*. The test program inserted the elements "random" order; then deleted them in the same mixed order.
2. *End of list inserts/deletes*. The test program inserted elements with keys from 1 through 1000, in order; then deleted the elements in reverse order (1000 through 1), so that insertions and deletions always took place at the end of the list.
3. *Front of list inserts/deletes*. The test program inserted elements in reverse order, from key 1000 through 1; and then deleted the elements in order (1 through 1000), so that insertions and deletions always took place at the beginning of the list.

As you can see from the information in the next table, the linked implementation is faster for random additions and deletions to the list (Case 1). This result is as we expected, due to the data movement required in the sequential list implementation.

Results of the Timed Implementation Comparisons*

	Sequential Implementation	Linked Implementation
Case 1: Random		
Insert 1–1000 (Random order)	3.79	1.48
Delete 1–1000 (Random order)	3.79	1.43
Case 2: List End		
Insert 1–1000 (In order)	1.98	2.86
Delete 1000–1 (Reverse order)	1.98	2.86
Case 3: List Start		
Insert 1000–1 (Reverse order)	5.61	0.05
Delete 1–1000 (In order)	5.65	0.06

*Time (in seconds) to insert and delete 1000 list elements. Tests were run on IBM-compatible computer (Intel 386 25 MHz) using test driver and List ADT implementation code compiled with Turbo Pascal 5.5.

In Case 2, we minimize the data movement by inserting and deleting only at the end of the list. The search task requires N comparisons, which means we have to search the whole list. However, the create/delete space task is O(1) for both implementations, since no elements must be moved. This is the *best* case for the sequential list, and in fact, the sequential list operations were a little faster than the linked list's. This result can be attributed to the quicker sequential list version of FindElement, as we discussed earlier.

If we maximize the data movement by inserting and deleting only at the front of the list (Case 3), the search task becomes O(1); we always find the place with one comparison. The linked version's create/delete space task is O(1) as always, resulting in O(1) InsertElement and DeleteElement operations. However, this is the *worst* case for the sequential list; all the elements in the list must be moved down for each insertion, and they must all be moved up for each deletion. The results of the timed test reflect this disparity: The sequential list took *100 times as long* as the linked list to perform the same operations.

Though we cannot avoid the data movement in the sequential implementation, we can improve the searching task by replacing the sequential search with the binary search we developed in Chapter 2. This modification will improve the "search" part of the algorithm from $O(N)$ to $O(\log_2 N)$. We cannot make a similar improvement, however, for searching the linked list, since we cannot access the elements randomly; we can only access an element through its predecessor in the list. Chapter 9 discusses the binary search tree, a linked structure that supports $O(\log_2 N)$ searches.

Testing the List Operations

By means of a test driver, we can test the List ADT independently of the program that will use it. The simplest kind of test driver sets up a scenario that will execute the various cases to be tested. To make sure that you have tested all the necessary cases, you should make a test plan, listing all the list operations and the tests needed for each.

The same test driver can be used to test both the sequential and linked list implementations; we merely replace the declarations and list operations, leaving the driver's main program alone. Except for Function FullList, you should get the same test results for both implementations.

Since the only field in the user's data type that is relevant to your test is Key, you can simplify ListElementType for your tests. You can also set MaxElements to a relatively small number for your tests. Knowing that the code works the same whether MaxElements is 5 or 1000, you can set MaxElements to 5 for the test. Of course, when you finish testing, you will need to change MaxElement and ListElementType to the correct declarations for your application.

 The code for a sample list test driver can be found in file TESTLIST.PAS on the program disk.

The Application Level

Ordered lists are used in all kinds of computer applications. It would be an unusual program that didn't use an ordered list of data of some kind. You have probably written programs that used a value-ordered list, implemented sequentially in an array. In general, the programs you have written using sequential lists could have been written with a linked implementation.

Choosing to use a sequential or linked implementation for a particular application depends greatly on what you want to do with the data stored in the list. We have already compared the operations that were specified in the List ADT. There are other operations that might be specified for an ordered list, some of which are better for one implementation than another. For instance, if the dominant activity in your application is to access the Nth element in the list, or if you need to print out the elements in reverse order, a sequential list would be preferable to a linked list. On the other hand, if the maximum number of elements in the list cannot be predicted, a linked list would be preferable, especially if the list elements for the application are large.

Summary

We have seen how lists may be represented in a sequential or linked representation and how they may be implemented with static (an array) or dynamic variables. The List ADT specification at the beginning of this chapter didn't mention any of these design issues, so we were free to implement the abstract data structure list in many ways.

There was nothing in the specification of this ADT to say that the list was sequential or linked, or that its elements were stored in statically or dynamically allocated storage.

We could specify a number of other operations for the list package. Some operations, such as one to find the preceding node in a list, are easy to implement for a sequential list but would be difficult to implement using a list that is linked in one direction (like the lists in this chapter). This operation would be simpler if the list had links going both forward and backward. We can think of many variations for representing a linked list in order to simplify the kinds of operations that are specified for the list: doubly linked lists, circular lists, lists that are accessed from both the beginning and the end. We will continue this discussion in Chapter 7.

The idea of linking the elements in a data structure is not specific to the type of list we have been discussing in this chapter. In Chapters 4 and 5 we implemented stacks and queues as linked structures; we will use this powerful tool to implement many other data structures in this book.

We will also return in Chapter 7 to an alternative implementation of a linked list. Sometimes it is better, or necessary, to use a static implementation instead of dynamic allocation. The change of implementation, however, will not change the specification of our list operations, and for the most part, will not even change their general algorithms.

Application

Advertising Manager

Data Structures
- List with sequential retrieval
- FIFO queue
- Strings
- Binary file

Software Techniques
- Top-down design
- Data encapsulation
- Writing software specifications
- User interface issues
- Program with retained data
- Incremental software development

Your brother-in-law Marc started a hobby magazine, a small business that is finally becoming successful. He uses his personal computer for desktop publishing, but he does all of his bookkeeping by hand. Now that he has quite a few advertisers, writing up the bills has become a real chore for him. So he has called you with a proposition: Could you write a program to automate this part of his business?

The Specification

Obviously, your "customer" isn't able to give you a formal specification. Your brother-in-law has a pretty good idea of what he wants, however, and you know what kind of information goes into a specification. So the two of you go out for a pizza, and together you come up with a software specification for Program AdManager.

Marc tells you that he currently does his billing as follows: Every time an advertiser places an ad for the current issue of the magazine, Marc writes down a description of the ad on a slip of paper. "What kind of information goes in this description?" you ask. He tells you that he writes down the name of the advertiser, and the billing address (if it is a new advertiser), as well as the size and color of the ad. His magazine has four ad sizes: full-, half-, quarter-, and eighth-page, each with a set price. If an advertiser wants a color—red, blue, green, or yellow—in addition to black, there is a fee. The fee is higher, of course, for ads with full–color photographs.

All of these slips of paper are kept in a folder. When he is ready to "dummy" the magazine (position all the ads on magazine pages), he goes through the file and writes down a list of the ads by size—all the full-page ads, then all the half-page ads, and so on. After the ads are in place, he positions his magazine articles, photos, and stories on the pages. When they are complete, he sends the pages to a commercial printer.

Finally, while the magazine is at the printer, Marc gets around to the billing. He collects all the slips of paper, and types up the bills, using a calculator to add the charges for the ads in the current issue to the advertiser's previous balance. (He requires first-time advertisers to pay at the time of their order, but good customers get credit.) This is the part of his business that Marc hates. It's so *uncreative*. Since he uses a computer in his business, he'd like to automate this billing.

Now that you have an idea of the general problem, you start a draft of the specifications. You know some of the inputs: all of the information that Marc writes down on slips of paper—advertiser names, addresses, ad sizes and colors. You know the main output: the bills. The two of you decide that the bills should be written to a text file called BILLS, not to the printer; Marc will print them out later using the operating system's PRINT command.

Since ads for each issue are collected over a period of several weeks, some data must be retained from one execution of the program to the next. This *retained data* will also be saved in a file. You note the existence of this file under Inputs and Outputs in the specifications. Marc doesn't plan to use or modify this information directly, so the file format is not important to him. Therefore, you do not need to mention the *format* of this file in the program specifications—its implementation is part of the program's data design.

Marc is getting impatient: "Okay, you've written down all these inputs and outputs—but what do I *do?*" Marc is the program's *user*; he is interested in the *user interface*. He wants to know how he, the human being, will interact with your program. He starts to tell you about a great program that he has used before: "It has choice bars and pulldown windows and color and graphics and a mouse and . . ."

"*Wait a minute!*" you yell, "I don't know *how* to program all that stuff!"

"Can't you learn?" Marc asks.

"I'm sure that I could figure it out *someday*," you answer, "but I thought that you want this program really soon."

The two of you come to a compromise: You will write the initial program with a simple textual command interface, with prompts to tell Marc what to enter. This way, he can start using the program right away. Later, you will try to modify it to have a choice bar and pulldown windows and whatever "bells and whistles" he wants. You note in the Programming Requirements part of your specification that the part of the program that handles the user interface should be very modular, so that it will be easy to replace later.

You finish up with a discussion of exactly what commands the program will process: commands to add a new advertiser, to place an ad in the current issue, to generate all the bills, to record an advertiser's payment when the check arrives, and to quit. You go home to draft the program specifications and by midnight, you have written the specification that is listed in Figure 6-14.

The next day you show the program specification to Marc. "This looks great!" he says, then adds hopefully, "How about a command to generate a list of ads from largest to smallest, to use for dummying?" You promise to add this operation in a future "delivery" of this software.

The Design

As always, you start with a design phase. You can see from the inputs and outputs that data design is going to be central to this program. The main data object is some kind of *list of advertisers*. Let's call this object AdList. Each advertiser has associated with it several pieces of information:

1. A name
2. A billing address
3. A list of advertisements for the current issue
4. The previous balance (money owed from ads in previous issues)

This description of an advertiser suggests a record, with a field declared for each piece of information. Since the billing statements in the BILLS file will be ordered alphabetically by advertiser name, this seems to be the key field. You tentatively use the following pseudo-declaration for the list element type:

```
AdRecType = RECORD  (* all data for one advertiser *)
  Key      : (* advertiser name - a string                *)
  Address  : (* billing address - type to be determined   *)
  Ads      : (* list of current ads - type to be determined *)
  Balance  : Integer
END; (* AdRecType *)
```

You don't really need to decide at this point how the list of advertiser records will be implemented. Assuming that it is a list, however, you know of a set of basic operations that are available to manipulate AdList—the ones that are specified in the List ADT.

How does AdList relate to the program's *retained data*, which is saved in a file between executions of the program? The retained data is the same information in some kind of file format. Figure 6-15 illustrates the relationship between the retained data and AdList. You can put off deciding how both the file and AdList are implemented until later. For now you can start the top-down design.

AdManager / *Level 0*

Initialize
Finished ← False
REPEAT
  GetCommand

Figure 6-14
The Specifications
of Program
AdManager

Specification: Program AdManager

Function

This program will support the organization and billing of the ads in a small magazine.

Input

1. File ADS.DAT contains the data created in previous executions of the program, if it has been run before.
2. The user enters data interactively from the keyboard, as described under Processing Requirements below.

Output

1. File ADS.DAT is used to save the state of the advertising data between executions of the program. This data includes the descriptions of the current issue's ads (size and color) and each advertiser's address and previous balance.
2. File BILLS is a text file that contains the bills for the current issue. Each bill must contain the advertiser's name and address, an itemized list of the current issue's advertisements, the previous balance, and the total amount due.
3. Input prompts and messages to the user are written to the screen, as described under Processing Requirements below.

Processing Requirements

1. The program must process the following commands:

   Bill Advertisers: Create text file BILLS to contain the advertisers' statements. The statements will be ordered alphabetically by advertiser name.

   New Advertiser: Add a new advertiser to the ad data; prompt user for name and address.

   Accept Ad: Add an advertisement to the ad data; prompt user for advertiser name, size, and color.

   Receive Payment: Update ad data to reflect a payment from an advertiser. Prompt user for advertiser name and amount of new payment. Advise user of current balance before and after payment.

   Quit: Save state of ad data and terminate program.

2. The program should keep track of the "current advertiser" being processed, so that this name can be used as a default in commands to accept ads or receive payments. The user can press Enter to accept the current advertiser, or can type a new name.

3. The program is to be used interactively; it must supply helpful prompts and messages to the user. The user-input part of the program should be implemented modularly to allow it to be replaced at a later date with a different user interface.

Assumptions

1. The program will be used on the magazine's IBM PC-compatible computer.
2. The ad data will fit in memory.

Figure 6-15
The Program Data
(AdList) and
Retained Data
(AdFile)

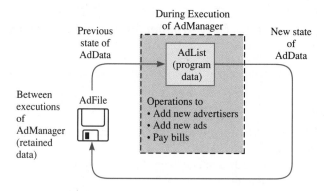

CASE Command OF
    BillAdvertisers   : GenerateBills
    NewAdvertiser   : AddNewAdvertiser
    AcceptAd   : ProcessAd
    ReceivePayment : ProcessPayment
    Quit   : Finished ← True
END CASE

UNTIL Finished

Terminate

Initialization Processing

The main job of the Initialize (Level 1) module is to get the information from the previous execution of the program—the program's retained data—from the file, and to use this data to rebuild the AdList. Creating a list from data in a file is not one of the basic operations specified in the List ADT, so you specify a level 2 operation ReadListFromFile:

ReadListFromFile (AdFile, AdList) / *Level 2*

Function:	Read advertiser data from the AdFile, and store in AdList.
Input:	AdFile (AdFileType)
Preconditions:	AdFile is closed; AdList has not been created.
Output:	AdList (ListType)
Postconditions:	AdList contains all of the information stored in AdFile. AdFile is unchanged.

The algorithm for this operation is:

CreateList (AdList)

Open the AdFile for reading.

WHILE more data in AdFile DO
    Read all the data for one advertiser into AdRec.
    InsertElement (AdList, AdRec)

How do you "read all the data for one advertiser into AdRec"? The answer depends on how the data is stored in the file. We said earlier that Marc doesn't care how the data is stored between executions of the program, so it is up to you to determine the format of AdFile. One approach is to keep the data in a text file, reading and writing all the record fields one at a time. Using a text file requires you to convert back and forth between the way the data is formatted in the text file and the way the data is stored in a record.

A simpler alternative is to use a *binary* (nontext) file. In case you have not used such files before, we will quickly review how text files and binary files are used in Pascal.

As you already know, a *Text file* is a file whose component type is a character. You can read from a text file, one character component at a time using the Read procedure:

```
Read (TextFile, Character);
```

Read takes a single file component (a *character*) from TextFile, stores it in Character, and moves the file read cursor to the next component.

The component type of a *binary (or nontext) file* does not have to be a character; Pascal allows you to declare files of other component types. For instance, AdFile can have a component type of AdRecType:

```
TYPE
  AdFileType = FILE OF AdRecType;

VAR
  AdFile : AdFileType;
  AdRec  : AdRecType;
```

To read a component from AdFile, you use the Pascal Read procedure:

```
Read (AdFile, AdRec);
```

Read takes a single file component (a *record* of AdRecType) from AdFile, stores it in AdRec, and moves the file read cursor to the next component—the next record in the file. As usual, before reading from the file, it must be opened with the Reset procedure. If the file has been opened with Rewrite, the Pascal Write procedure is used to write a single record of the component type to the file. Because you can read or write a whole record at a time, you can avoid the conversion process that the use of a Text file would necessitate.

Using a binary file to contain records of AdRecType, you can "read all the data for one advertiser" with a single call to Read. Opening the file for reading is accomplished with a call to Reset. We can tell if there is "more data in AdFile" (the loop condition) by checking whether EOF (AdFile) is true.

There is only one other issue to consider—what happens the *first* time that the program is run? Since there is no retained data from a previous execution, the call to Reset (AdFile) would cause the program to crash. To get around this problem you decide to create an empty AdFile, using a separate little program that simply Rewrites and then Closes AdFile. The first time that Program AdManager is run, ReadList-FromFile will Reset the empty file and encounter EOF immediately; AdList will be returned empty.

For now, this is the only task that we have identified to be performed by Procedure Initialize, so let's go on with the Level 0 design. Following initialization, a big loop is entered: *REPEAT ... UNTIL Finished*. In each iteration of the loop body, a command is input from the user and processed.

Getting a Command

You told Marc that you'd work on a fancy user interface later. Meanwhile, you decide to create a set of *operations* for getting user inputs, rather than putting scattered calls to Read throughout the program. The operation to input a command is called GetCommand:

■ **GetCommand (Command)**   /   *Level 1*

Function:	Read a command from user.
Input:	From keyboard: command input
Preconditions:	User is awake.
Output:	To Screen: prompt to user
	To calling program: Command (CommandType)
Postconditions:	Command = valid command value

Before we can design this operation, we need to know more about the output value. A value of CommandType indicates which command the user has specified. (The commands that must be supported are listed in the Processing Requirements section of the specification.) In Pascal, the natural way to represent such values is to use an enumerated type:

```
CommandType =
  (BillAdvertisers, (* generate billing statements  *)
   NewAdvertiser,   (* add a new customer to list   *)
   AcceptAd,        (* add an ad to the ad list     *)
   ReceivePayment,  (* subtract payment from balance *)
   Quit);           (* quit program                 *)
```

Of course the user cannot type such a value directly into the computer. Instead, you must prompt the user to type in a value that your program will convert to CommandType. For instance, the user can type the words "BILL", "QUIT", etc. To make it easy for the user, you decide to prompt him enter a single letter command—"B" for Bill-Advertisers, "Q" for Quit, and so on.

To input the command, you read the character and then convert it to the appropriate CommandType value. You could perform this conversion with a big CASE statement. Another way to convert the value is to use a *command table*. A simple command table can be declared as follows:

```
TYPE
   CommandTableType = ARRAY['A' .. 'Z'] OF CommandType;
VAR
   CommandTable : CommandTableType;
```

As part of the program's initialization processing, the CommandTable is initialized to contain the appropriate CommandType values at the indexes that correspond with the single letter inputs. For instance, Procedure InitCommandTable will include the statements

```
CommandTable['A'] := AcceptAd;
CommandTable['B'] := BillAdvertisers;
```

and so on.

In the GetCommand operation, the single-character command is read from the keyboard; then its corresponding CommandType value is retrieved from the table:

```
Read (ComLetter);
Command := CommandTable[ComLetter];
```

Of course, not all the array slots from 'A' to 'Z' are in use— they do not all correspond to valid commands. We do not want to take a chance on picking up "garbage" out of an uninitialized array slot if the user makes a typing error. Therefore, we will add an extra value to CommandType: Unknown. This value will be put into all the unused array slots, as illustrated in Figure 6-16. This design solution makes two changes to your program: (1) You must add a call to Procedure InitCommandTable to the Level 1 Initialize module; and (2) There is a second input to GetCommand—the CommandTable.

Figure 6-16
The CommandTable

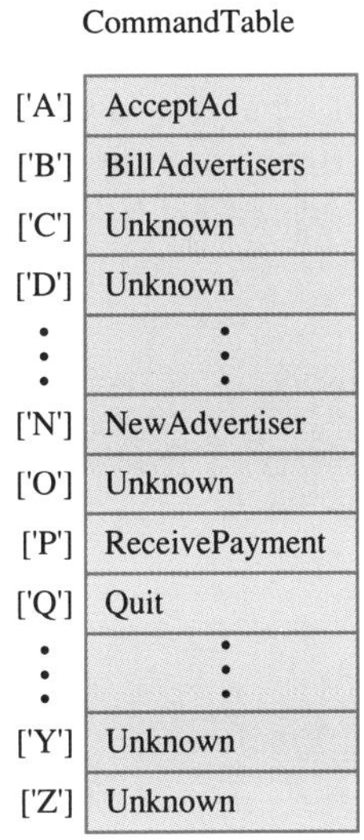

CommandTable

['A']	AcceptAd
['B']	BillAdvertisers
['C']	Unknown
['D']	Unknown
⋮	⋮
['N']	NewAdvertiser
['O']	Unknown
['P']	ReceivePayment
['Q']	Quit
⋮	⋮
['Y']	Unknown
['Z']	Unknown

Before you record the GetCommand design, you give some thought to other possible errors. What if the user types a lowercase letter? What if the user types a nonalphabetic character? There are no array slots corresponding to these characters, but you do not want the program to crash. Therefore, you add error checking to the design for GetCommand, and keep reading command characters until the user inputs a valid command.

GetCommand (CommandTable, Command)

Command ← Unknown

Print instruction prompt

REPEAT
   Readln (ComLetter)
   Convert ComLetter to upper-case if necessary.
   IF ComLetter IN ['A' .. 'Z']
      THEN Command ← CommandTable [ComLetter]
      ELSE Print error message.

UNTIL Command <> Unknown

Processing the Command

Now that the command is known, the program must process it. The Level 0 design contains a big CASE statement to select the appropriate operation for each command. We will go through the design for the NewAdvertiser, AcceptAd, and Quit commands here, paying close attention to the issues of data representation. We will leave stubs in place of the modules that support the ReceivePayment and BillAdvertisers commands, and develop them in the application section at the end of Chapter 7.

The NewAdvertiser Command

The NewAdvertiser command requires you to add a new advertiser to AdList. In addition to updating AdList, the AddNewAdvertiser operation also returns the name of the new advertiser. Why? It is likely that the *next operation* that the user will want to perform is to enter an ad for this advertiser; thus this advertiser's name will act as the "default" unless the user says otherwise. Here is the specification for AddNewAdvertiser:

■ AddNewAdvertiser (AdList, Advertiser) / *Level 1*

Function:	Adds new advertiser to AdList. Returns the Advertiser name for use in next operation.
Input:	AdList (ListType)
Preconditions:	AdList has been created.
Output:	AdList (ListType) Advertiser (StringType)
Postconditions:	Record for Advertiser exists in AdList.

The algorithm follows. Note that the user inputs are encapsulated by operations—GetAdvertiserName and GetAddress—to make it simpler to modify the user interface later.

AddNewAdvertiser

GetAdvertiserName (Advertiser)

Call RetrieveElement to look for this Advertiser (key)

IF Advertiser NOT found in AdList
   THEN (add this advertiser)
      AdRec.Key ← Advertiser
      GetAddress (AdRec.Address)

      AdRec.Ads ← empty state

      AdRec.Balance ← 0

      InsertElement (AdList, AdRec)

      Print success message to user.

   ELSE Print error message (advertiser already in list)

Assuming that the user-input operations take care of their tasks, most of this algorithm can be coded directly. One data issue stands out, however—how do you set "AdRec.Ads ← empty state"? You have not yet determined what the Ads field will be. Let's think in terms of data abstraction: Ads is some sort of collection of advertisement information. As ads are accepted from a particular advertiser, they are added to this collection; later when we generate the bills, the ads are removed from the collection and their costs are calculated. Although the FIFO property is not absolutely *required* by this description, the collection of ads can easily be considered a *queue of ads*. We will declare the Ads field of AdRecType to be of QueueType, with a QueueElementType of AdInfoType:

```
TYPE
  AdInfoType = RECORD
    AdSize   : AdSizeType; (* size of this advertisement  *)
    AdColor  : AdColorType (* color of this advertisement *)
  END; (* AdInfoType *)

  QueueElementType = AdInfoType;
```

Now, back in AddNewAdvertiser, setting AdRec.Ads to an "empty state" merely involves a call to CreateQueue (AdRec.Ads).

The AcceptAd Command

The AcceptAd command results in the execution of the ProcessAd operation. This operation inputs the Advertiser name from the previous operation, in case the user wishes to continue processing the same advertiser without retyping the name.

▶ **ProcessAd (AdList, Advertiser)** / *Level 1*

Function:	Add a new advertisement to the ad queue of the specified Advertiser.
Input:	AdList (ListType)
	Advertiser (value from previous operation)
Preconditions:	AdList has been created.
Output:	AdList
	Advertiser (may be reset to new name)
Postconditions:	If Advertiser specified by user is in AdList, a new ad is added to the ad queue for this Advertiser.

This operation also processes data entered by the user—the advertiser name, the ad size and color. Inputting this information is encapsulated in the user-input operations, GetAdvertiserName and GetAdInfo.

ProcessAd

GetAdvertiserName (Advertiser)—from the user

Call RetrieveElement to get AdRec for this Advertiser (key)

IF Advertiser found in AdList
   THEN
     GetAdInfo (AdInfo)—from the user

     IF NOT FullQueue (AdRec.Ads)
       THEN
         Enqueue (AdRec.Ads, AdInfo)
         ModifyElement (AdList, AdRec)
         Print success message to user.
       ELSE Print error message (ad queue full)

   ELSE Print error message (advertiser not in list)

The BillAdvertisers and ReceivePayment Commands

Because this program is longer than anything you have written before, you decide to postpone developing these two important modules until the rest of this program is running correctly. In the meantime, you code stubs to stand in for the GenerateBills and ProcessPayment procedures. These stubs will merely print messages to the screen. We will resume the development of these modules in the application section at the end of Chapter 7.

The Quit Command

This command is the easiest one of all: we merely set Finished to True. This will cause us to exit the loop and to enter the termination processing.

Termination Processing

Before we end the program, we have one more task: to save the data from AdList to use again next time the program is run. This operation is the reverse of Procedure ReadListFromFile: You must write all the data in AdList back into AdFile.

▌ **WriteListToFile (AdFile, AdList)**

Function:	Rewrite the AdFile to contain the current contents of AdList.
Input:	AdList (ListType)
Preconditions:	AdList has been created.
Output:	AdFile (AdFileType)
Postconditions:	AdFile contains all the records that are in AdList; the file is closed. AdList is not changed.

This procedure will go through the AdList, retrieving one record after another and writing them to AdFile:

WriteListToFile

Open AdFile for writing (Rewrite).

WHILE more elements in AdList DO
  Get the next element from AdList.
  Write the element to AdFile.

When you get to the first task in the loop body you run into trouble. How do you "get the *next* advertiser record from AdList"? There is a RetrieveElement operation in the List ADT that retrieves elements according to a specified key. But you do not know the key of the "next" advertiser in the list. There is no operation in the List ADT to perform "get next" types of retrievals.

You decide to add this capability to the List ADT by creating a GetElement operation. The specification of this operation is listed here; we will discuss the changes to the list implementation later.

▌ **GetElement (List, GetPosition, Element, Found)**

Function:	If Found, return a copy of the requested element from List.
Input:	List (ListType) GetPosition (GetFirst or GetNext)
Preconditions:	List has been created. If GetPosition = GetNext, a call was previously made with GetPosition = GetFirst.
Output:	Element (ListElementType) Found (Boolean) List ("current" position updated)
Postconditions:	Found = (element found in list) IF Found, Element = copy of requested element from list; otherwise, Element is undefined. If GetPosition = GetFirst, the returned element has the smallest key in the list; if Get-Position = GetNext, the returned element has the next larger key than the element returned from the last call to GetElement.

Using this list operation, you can implement the WHILE loop in WriteListToFile. You must make a minor change, to read the first element before the loop:

WriteListToFile (revised)

Open AdFile for writing (Rewrite).
GetElement (AdList, GetFirst, Element, Found)

WHILE Found DO
    Write Element to AdFile.
    GetElement (AdList, GetNext, Element, Found)

Should you also destroy the AdList? Although AdList may be implemented as a linked structure in dynamically allocated memory, you do not really have to call DestroyList to free its space. The space is automatically "freed" by the program's termination.

The User Input Operations

To simplify changing the user interface at a later time, you have decided that all user inputs will be processed by a set of special input operations. In developing the top-down design, you have identified a number of these operations: GetCommand, GetAdvertiserName, GetAddress, GetAdInfo. All of these operations are similar: They print a prompt to tell the user what kind of information to enter; then they read the user's answer(s). We will not go through the user input operation designs here; the designs and code are so similar that we direct you to look at the program listing at the end of this application. The operations are grouped together under a "banner" comment, User Input Operations.

Implementing the Data Structures

In our top-down design of Program AdManager, we've managed to use all kinds of data structures without determining exactly how they would be implemented. We've said that AdList is a "list"— therefore, we can use the operations specified for the List ADT. We referred to the collection of ads for an advertiser as an "ad queue," and subsequently used the operations that were specified for the FIFO Queue ADT. We have created another ADT on the fly—the CommandTable, with operations Init-CommandTable and GetCommand. In *using* the operations provided for these structures independently of their implementations, we see the enormous power of information hiding. We are freed from the implementation-level details, and are able to develop programs that focus on the data abstraction: What does this data *mean* to us?

Before we can run the program, of course, we need to provide the underlying implementations of the structures: the type declarations, procedures, and functions.

Implementing AdList

The AdList is a list of records of AdRecType, each of which represents all the data about a particular advertiser:

```
TYPE
  AdRecType = RECORD
    Key      : KeyType;          (* Record key: Company name *)
    Address  : AddressType;      (* Billing address          *)
    Ads      : QueueType;        (* Current issue's ads       *)
    Balance  : Integer           (* Outstanding balance ($)   *)
  END;  (* AdRecType *)
```

```
        ListElementType = AdRecType;
```

In this chapter, we have developed two complete implementations of the List ADT. Which of them should you use to represent AdList? Although either implementation would be functionally correct, the linked list is a better choice. Why? When Marc first starts using this program, the list will be empty. Over time, as he adds more and more advertisers, the list will grow. There is no reason that we should put a limit on the number of advertisers, other than that imposed by the amount of memory in the computer. Therefore, the linked implementation with dynamically allocated nodes is preferred.

However, you cannot use the version of the linked list from the chapter without making any changes; you must implement the GetElement operation. Here's the basic algorithm:

GetElement

IF GetPosition = GetFirst
    THEN Location ← pointer to first element in list
    ELSE Location ← pointer to the "next" element in list

Found ← (Location <> NIL)

IF Found
    THEN Element ← Info(Location)

The option to GetFirst is simple to implement; we merely set Location to point to Node(List). The option to GetNext, however, does not fit into our picture of a linked list. As it is implemented, the list does not have any notion of a *current position*, so how do we know which element comes *next*?

To support retrieval by position, we change the declarations of ListType. ListType will no longer be a simple pointer; instead it will be a record that contains two pointers:

```
TYPE
  ListType  = RECORD
    Start   : PointerType;  (* access first node in list  *)
    Current : PointerType   (* accesses "current" node    *)
  END; (* ListType *)
```

This data type is illustrated in Figure 6-17(a). The first pointer, Start, is the external pointer to the list elements. The second pointer, Current, points to the "current" element to retrieve from the list. (This pointer is somewhat analogous to the read cursor for a file, which always points to the next data to be read from a file.)

To retrieve the next element from the list, we simply set Location to List.Current. GetElement must also do one more task: After retrieving an element (setting Element to Info(Location)), Current must be updated to point to the element that follows the one that was retrieved, as illustrated in Figure 6-17(b). If we have just retrieved the last element in the list, Current is reset to NIL, as pictured in Figure 6-17(c). A subsequent call to GetElement to retrieve the next element would return a value of False for Found. If the Current pointer is NIL, there is no "next" element.

This implementation change requires minor editing changes to the other list operations to replace references to "List" (the external pointer to the list) with "List.Start."

Figure 6-17   ListType That Supports Retrieval by Position

(a) List

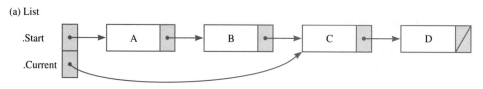

(b) Following call to GetElement (List, GetNext, Element, Found)

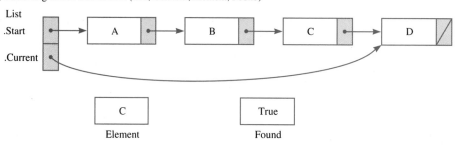

(c) Following call to GetElement (List, GetNext, Element, Found)

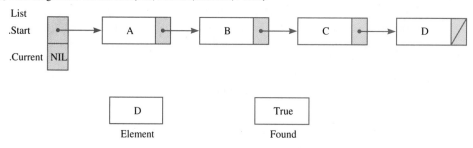

Implementing the Ad Queues

The Ads field of AdRecType is declared to be a queue whose component elements are of AdInfoType. We have two completely implemented versions of a FIFO Queue, developed in Chapter 5. Which queue implementation should we use? In this case, there is not much choice. Given the decision to represent AdFile as a binary file, you *cannot* use the linked queue implementation here. The storage for the queue must exist entirely within the record if we plan to save the record in the binary file. Figure 6-18 illustrates the problem: If we use a linked queue, whose elements are stored in dynamically allocated memory, only the pointers to the Front and Rear nodes of the queue actually exist in the advertiser record. The value of these pointers can be saved in the AdFile, but these addresses are meaningless next time we execute the program—we have lost the data that they point to.

Using an array-based queue implementation means that you must pick a value for MaxQueue. You ask Marc for an expert opinion, and he tells you that the most ads that

Figure 6-18   Storing the Ad Queue to AdFile

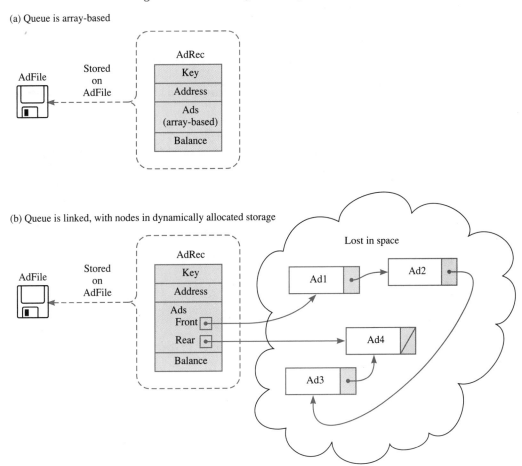

(a) Queue is array-based

(b) Queue is linked, with nodes in dynamically allocated storage

any one advertiser has ever placed in a single issue is 3. To be on the safe side, you decide to set MaxQueue to 6. You record this limitation in the Assumptions section of the Program Specification.

Implementing Strings

A number of places in the data design we have referred to "strings." While you could use the StringType from Chapter 3, the requirements for string operations are really very modest: You need to be able to read, write, and compare strings and to convert them to upper-case. The StringType from Chapter 3 is overkill for your needs. In addition, to be able to use the List ADT operations without further modification, you must be able to compare values of the key type using the < and = operators. The key field of AdList is the advertiser name, a string. Because packed arrays can be directly compared and written (using Write and Writeln), StringType is represented as a fixed-length string stored in a packed array of characters.

```
CONST
  MaxString = 40; (* maximum characters in a string *)
  BlankString = '                                        ';
TYPE
  StringType = PACKED ARRAY [1 .. MaxString] OF Char;
```

The string characters are left justified in the string, with blanks filling the unused slots.

The Program

The code for Program AdManager is shown below. The algorithms have been coded in standard Pascal, except for file operations that are not supported in standard Pascal (Assign and Close), which have been coded in Turbo Pascal. All Turbo code has been marked as such with comments. If you are using a different compiler, the Turbo code should be replaced with statements appropriate to your compiler.

To save space, the source code for the FIFO Queue and List ADT operations (except for GetElement) has not been reprinted here. This code is included in the chapter text.

File ADMGR.PAS on the program disk contains the code for the complete program.

```
PROGRAM AdManager (Input, Output, AdFile, Bills);

  (* Insert program specification here. *)

CONST
  MaxQueue  = 6;  (* max ads for one advertiser per issue *)
  MaxString = 40; (* max characters in a string           *)
  BlankString = '                                        ';

TYPE
  (******************* String Data Type *******************)
  StringType = PACKED ARRAY [1 .. MaxString] OF Char;

  (*************** Advertising Data Types ****************)
  AdSizeType  = (FullPage, HalfPage, QuarterPage, EighthPage);
  AdColorType = (NoColor, Red, Blue, Yellow, Green, FullColor);

  (*********** Advertisement Queue Data Types ************)
  AdInfoType = RECORD
    AdSize   : AdSizeType;
    AdColor  : AdColorType
  END; (* AdInfoType *)

  QueueElementType = AdInfoType;

  IndexType = 1 .. MaxQueue;

  QueueType  = RECORD  (* FIFO Queue Implementation *)
    Elements : ARRAY [IndexType] OF QueueElementType;
    Front    : IndexType; (* index of slot preceding front *)
    Rear     : IndexType  (* index of slot containing rear *)
  END; (* QueueType *)
```

```
(****************** Ad Record Data Type ***************)
KeyType = StringType;  (* advertiser name *)

AddressType    = RECORD
  StreetAddr   : StringType;
  CityStateZip : StringType
END; (* AddressType *)

AdRecType = RECORD
  Key     : KeyType;        (* Record key: Company name *)
  Address : AddressType;    (* Billing address          *)
  Ads     : QueueType;      (* Current issue's ads      *)
  Balance : Integer         (* Outstanding balance ($)  *)
END; (* AdRecType *)

AdFileType = FILE OF AdRecType;

(****************** List Implementation ***************)
ListElementType = AdRecType;
PointerType     = ^NodeType;

NodeType = RECORD
  Info  : ListElementType;      (* list user's data     *)
  Next  : PointerType           (* pointer to next node *)
END; (* NodeType *)

ListType  = RECORD
  Start   : PointerType;        (* pointer to first node   *)
  Current : PointerType         (* pointer to current node *)
END; (* ListType *)

GetPositionType = (GetFirst, GetNext);

(****************** User Command Data Types ***********)
CommandType =
  (BillAdvertisers, (* generate billing statements   *)
   NewAdvertiser,   (* add a new advertiser to list  *)
   AcceptAd,        (* add an ad to the ad list      *)
   ReceivePayment,  (* subtract payment from balance *)
   Quit,            (* quit program (saves data)     *)
   Unknown);        (* command undetermined          *)

CommandTableType = ARRAY ['A' .. 'Z'] OF CommandType;
  (* relates single letter commands to CommandType *)

(********************************************************)
(*                  Global Data                        *)
(********************************************************)

VAR
  AdList          : ListType;         (* contains ad information    *)
  AdFile          : AdFileType;       (* saves ad information       *)
  CommandTable    : CommandTableType; (* letter to command          *)
  Finished        : Boolean;          (* finished running program?  *)
  Command         : CommandType;      (* user's command request     *)
  CurrentAdvertiser : StringType;     (* last advertiser processed  *)
```

```
(**************************************************************)
(*                      String Operations                    *)
(**************************************************************)
PROCEDURE ReadString
  (VAR ReadFile : Text;
   VAR Str      : StringType);

  (* Read characters from ReadFile until MaxString characters *)
  (* have been read from input or EOLN. (No call to Readln.)  *)

VAR
  Index : Integer;

BEGIN (* ReadString *)

  Str := BlankString;
  Index := 1;

  (* Loop Invariant: 1 <= Index <= MaxString + 1 AND        *)
  (* Str[1] .. Str[Index - 1] contain characters read AND *)
  (* Str[Index] .. Str[MaxString] contain blanks.          *)
  WHILE (Index <= MaxString) AND NOT EOLN (ReadFile) DO
    BEGIN
      Read (ReadFile, Str[Index]);
      Index := Index + 1
    END (* WHILE *)

END;  (* ReadString *)

(**************************************************************)

PROCEDURE ReadLine
  (VAR ReadFile : Text;
   VAR Str      : StringType);

  (* Read characters from ReadFile until MaxString characters *)
  (* have been read from input or EOLN; store in Str; Readln. *)

BEGIN (* ReadLine *)
  ReadString (ReadFile, Str);
  Readln (ReadFile)
END;  (* ReadLine *)

(**************************************************************)

FUNCTION Cap
  (Character : Char) : Char;

  (* Returns the upper-case equivalent if Character is *)
  (* between 'a' and 'z'; otherwise returns Character  *)
  (* unchanged.                                        *)

BEGIN (* Cap *)
  IF Character IN ['a' .. 'z']
    THEN Cap := CHR(ORD(Character) - (ORD('a') - ORD('A')))
    ELSE Cap := Character
END; (* Cap *)
```

```
(**********************************************************)

PROCEDURE UpCase
  (VAR Str : StringType);

  (* Convert Str to all upper-case equivalent. *)

VAR
  Index : Integer;

BEGIN (* UpCase *)
  FOR Index := 1 TO MaxString DO
    Str[Index] := Cap(Str[Index])
END; (* UpCase *)
```

```
(***********************************************************)
(*                 FIFO Queue Operations                 *)
(***********************************************************)
(* Insert the source code for the CreateQueue, EmptyQueue, *)
(* FullQueue, Enqueue, and Dequeue operations (array-based *)
(* implementation) from Chapter 5.                         *)
```

```
(***********************************************************)
(*                  List ADT Operations                  *)
(***********************************************************)
(* Insert the source code for the CreateList, FindElement, *)
(* RetrieveElement, InsertElement, and ModifyElement       *)
(* operations (linked implementation) from Chapter 6.      *)
(* References to List (external pointer) must be changed    *)
(* to List.Start.                                          *)
(***********************************************************)
```

```
PROCEDURE GetElement
  (VAR List     : ListType;
   GetPosition : GetPositionType;
   VAR Element : ListElementType;
   VAR Found   : Boolean);

  (* IF Found, Element = copy of requested list element;  *)
  (* otherwise, Element is undefined. If GetPosition is    *)
  (* GetFirst, the returned element has the smallest key   *)
  (* in the list; if GetPosition is GetNext, the returned *)
  (* element has the next larger key than the element      *)
  (* returned from the last call to GetElement.            *)

VAR
  Location : PointerType;

BEGIN (* GetElement *)

  IF GetPosition = GetFirst
    THEN Location := List.Start
    ELSE Location := List.Current;
```

```
      IF Location <> NIL
        THEN
          BEGIN
            Found := True;
            Element := Location^.Info;
            List.Current := Location^.Next
          END (* IF element found *)
        ELSE Found := False

  END;  (* GetElement *)

  (**************************************************************)
  (*                USER INPUT OPERATIONS                     *)
  (**************************************************************)

  PROCEDURE GetAdvertiserName
    (VAR Advertiser : StringType);

    (* Prompt user and get new advertiser name. The value *)
    (* input for Advertiser is returned unchanged if user *)
    (* types Enter without giving a new name.             *)

  VAR
    AdName : StringType;

  BEGIN (* GetAdvertiserName *)

    (* Get name of advertiser. *)
    IF Advertiser = BlankString
      THEN Write ('>>> Enter advertiser name: ')
      ELSE (* may use previous Advertiser name *)
        Write ('>>> Enter advertiser name, or press Enter to use ',
          Advertiser);

    ReadLine (Input, AdName);
    IF AdName <> BlankString
      THEN (* reassign Advertiser *)
        BEGIN
          UpCase (AdName);
          Advertiser := AdName
        END (* IF *)

  END; (* GetAdvertiserName *)

  (**********************************************************)

  PROCEDURE GetAddress
    (VAR Address : AddressType);

    (* Prompt user for address; store response in Address. *)
```

```
BEGIN (* GetAddress *)

  Write ('>>> Enter street address:        ');
  ReadLine (Input, Address.StreetAddr);

  Write ('>>> Enter City, State, Zip code: ');
  ReadLine (Input, Address.CityStateZip)

END;  (* GetAddress *)

(***********************************************************)

PROCEDURE GetAnswer
  (MaxAnswer   : Integer;
   VAR  Answer : Integer);

    (* Returns integer answer between 1 and MaxAnswer. *)

VAR
  UserPicked : Boolean;  (* user picked legal answer? *)
  Character  : Char;     (* user's answer character   *)

BEGIN (* GetAnswer *)

  UserPicked := False;

  REPEAT

    (* Read user's answer in character form. *)
    Readln (Character);

    (* Convert the key choice to a number. *)
    IF Character IN ['1' .. '9']
      THEN
        BEGIN
          (* Convert character to integer. *)
          Answer := ORD(Character) - ORD('1') + 1;
          IF (Answer >= 1) AND (Answer <= MaxAnswer)
            THEN UserPicked := True
        END; (* IF *)

    IF NOT UserPicked
      THEN Write ('>>> Please reenter value between 1 and ',
          MaxAnswer,': ')

  UNTIL UserPicked

END; (* GetAnswer *)

(***********************************************************)
```

```
PROCEDURE GetAdInfo
  (VAR AdInfo : AdInfoType);

  (* Get ad size and color information. *)

VAR
  AdSize     : AdSizeType;      (* size of new ad           *)
  AdColor    : AdColorType;     (* color of new ad          *)
  SizeNum    : Integer;         (* user's answer: ad size *)
  ColorNum   : Integer;         (* user's answer: color   *)
BEGIN (* GetAdInfo *)

  (* Get ad size information. *)
  Writeln;
  Writeln ('1 - Full  2 - Half  3 - Quarter  4 - Eighth');
  Write ('>>> Select size by number: ');
  GetAnswer (4, SizeNum);
  Writeln;
  FOR AdSize := FullPage TO EighthPage DO
    IF ORD(AdSize) = SizeNum - 1
      THEN AdInfo.AdSize := AdSize;

  (* Get ad color information. *)
  Writeln;
  Write ('1 - Black only  2 - Red  3 - Blue  ');
  Writeln ('4 - Yellow   5 - Green  6 - Full color');
  Write ('>>> Select color by number: ');
  GetAnswer (6, ColorNum);
  Writeln;
  FOR AdColor := NoColor TO FullColor DO
    IF ORD(AdColor) = ColorNum - 1
      THEN AdInfo.AdColor := AdColor

END;  (* GetAdInfo *)

(****************************************************************)
(*                  Command Table Operations                  *)
(****************************************************************)

PROCEDURE InitCommandTable
  (VAR CommandTable : CommandTableType);

  (* Initialize CommandTable to correct values to convert   *)
  (* user's single letter commands to command type.         *)

VAR
  Index : Char;
```

```
BEGIN (* InitCommandTable *)

  (* Initialize all fields to Unknown. *)
  FOR Index := 'A' TO 'Z' DO
    CommandTable [Index] := Unknown;

  (* Assign all the letters that are in use. *)
  CommandTable ['A'] := AcceptAd;
  CommandTable ['B'] := BillAdvertisers;
  CommandTable ['N'] := NewAdvertiser;
  CommandTable ['P'] := ReceivePayment;
  CommandTable ['Q'] := Quit

END;   (* InitCommandTable *)

(*************************************************************)

PROCEDURE GetCommand
  (CommandTable : CommandTableType;
   VAR Command  : CommandType);

VAR
  ComLetter : Char;

  (****************** Nested Procedure ******************)
  PROCEDURE PrintCommands;

  BEGIN (* PrintCommands *)
    Writeln (' ------------------------------------------------');
    Writeln (' A - Accept New Ad        N - Add New Advertiser');
    Writeln (' P - Process Payment      B - Bill Advertisers  ');
    Writeln (' Q - Quit');
    Writeln;
    Write ('>>> Enter single letter for command: ')
  END;   (* PrintCommands *)
  (*************************************************************)

BEGIN (* GetCommand *)

  Command := Unknown;

  PrintCommands;

  REPEAT

    Readln (ComLetter);
    Writeln;
    ComLetter := Cap(ComLetter);

    IF ComLetter IN ['A' .. 'Z']
      THEN Command := CommandTable [ComLetter]
      ELSE Write ('>>> Please choose from commands above: ')

  UNTIL Command <> Unknown

END;   (* GetCommand *)
```

```
(****************************************************************)
(*                    Application Operations                  *)
(****************************************************************)

PROCEDURE ReadListFromFile
  (VAR AdFile : AdFileType;
   VAR AdList : ListType);

  (* Copy all records from AdFile into the AdList. AdFile *)
  (* is not open when this procedure is called, and is    *)
  (* left closed at the end of the procedure.             *)
  (* NOTE: This procedure contains Turbo Pascal code.     *)


VAR
  AdRec      : AdRecType;

BEGIN (* ReadListFromFile *)

  (* Create empty AdList. *)
  CreateList (AdList);

  Assign (AdFile, 'ADS.DAT'); (* Turbo Pascal code *)
  Reset  (AdFile);

  (* Read all records; insert in list. *)
  WHILE NOT EOF (AdFile) DO
    BEGIN
      Read (AdFile, AdRec);
      InsertElement (AdList, AdRec)
    END; (* WHILE *)

  (* Close the file. *)
  Close (AdFile)            (* Turbo Pascal code *)

END; (* ReadListFromFile *)

(****************************************************************)

PROCEDURE WriteListToFile
  (VAR AdFile : AdFileType;
   VAR AdList : ListType);

  (* Rewrite the AdFile to contain the current contents *)
  (* of AdList. AdList is not changed.                  *)
  (* NOTE: This procedure contains Turbo Pascal code.   *)

VAR
  AdRec : ListElementType;      (* element from the list *)
  Found : Boolean;              (* record found in list? *)

BEGIN (* WriteListToFile *)

  (* Open file for processing. *)
  Assign (AdFile, 'ADS.DAT');        (* Turbo Pascal code *)
  Rewrite (AdFile);
```

```
    (* Get the first element from the list. *)
    GetElement (AdList, GetFirst, AdRec, Found);

  WHILE Found DO
    BEGIN

      (* Print the element to the file. *)
      Write (AdFile, AdRec);

      (* Get the next element from the list. *)
      GetElement (AdList, GetNext, AdRec, Found)

    END; (* WHILE *)

  (* Close the file. *)
  Close (AdFile)        (* Turbo Pascal code *)

END;  (* WriteListToFile *)

(*************************************************************)

PROCEDURE Initialize
  (VAR AdFile       : AdFileType;
   VAR AdList       : ListType;
   VAR CommandTable : CommandTableType);

  (* Set up the AdList and CommandTable for processing. *)

BEGIN (* Initialize *)

  Writeln
   ('*****************************************************');
  Writeln
   ('****************** AD MANAGER ********************');
  Writeln;

  (* Read advertising data from AdFile; store in list. *)
  ReadListFromFile (AdFile, AdList);

  (* Initialize CommandTable for converting user's commands. *)
  InitCommandTable (CommandTable)

END;  (* Initialize *)

(*************************************************************)

PROCEDURE AddNewAdvertiser
  (VAR AdList     : ListType;
   VAR Advertiser : StringType);

  (* Add new advertiser to the AdList. Returns Advertiser *)
  (* name, in case user wants to continue processing.     *)

VAR
  AdRec   : AdRecType;
  Found   : Boolean;
```

```
BEGIN (* AddNewAdvertiser *)

  (* Get info for new advertiser. *)
  Advertiser := BlankString;
  GetAdvertiserName (Advertiser);

  (* Made sure this advertiser is not in AdList.*)
  RetrieveElement (AdList, Advertiser, AdRec, Found);

  IF NOT Found
    THEN
      BEGIN

        AdRec.Key := Advertiser;

        (* Get new advertiser's address from user. *)
        GetAddress (AdRec.Address);

        (* Set ad queue to empty. *)
        CreateQueue (AdRec.Ads);

        (* Set account balance to $0. *)
        AdRec.Balance := 0;

        (* Insert record for new advertiser into AdList. *)
        InsertElement (AdList, AdRec);

        Writeln ('New advertiser added: ', Advertiser)

      END (* IF not in list *)
    ELSE Writeln ('This advertiser is already in the Ad List.')

END;  (* AddNewAdvertiser *)

(*****************************************************************)

PROCEDURE ProcessAd
  (VAR AdList    : ListType;
   VAR Advertiser : KeyType);

  (* Add a new advertising order to the AdList. This      *)
  (* procedure can use the previous value of Advertiser,  *)
  (* or can reset the Advertiser name.                    *)

VAR
  AdRec     : AdRecType;   (* one advertiser's data  *)
  Found     : Boolean;     (* Advertiser in AdList?  *)
  AdInfo    : AdInfoType;  (* info for the new ad    *)

BEGIN (* ProcessAd *)

  GetAdvertiserName (Advertiser);

  (* Get the ad record for this advertiser. *)
  RetrieveElement (AdList, Advertiser, AdRec, Found);
```

```
                   (* Make sure this Advertiser already in AdList. *)
                   IF Found
                     THEN
                       BEGIN

                         (* Get ad size and color information. *)
                         GetAdInfo (AdInfo);

                         (* Insert the new ad into the ad queue. *)
                         IF NOT FullQueue (AdRec.Ads)
                           THEN
                             BEGIN
                               (* Add this ad to the ad queue. *)
                               Enqueue (AdRec.Ads, AdInfo);

                               (* Make the change in the AdList. *)
                               ModifyElement (AdList, AdRec);

                               (* Tell user what's been done. *)
                               Writeln ('Accepted new ad for ', Advertiser)

                             END (* IF NOT FullQueue *)
                           ELSE Writeln ('Ad Queue Full - Call your programmer!')
                       END (* IF Found *)
                     ELSE Writeln ('This advertiser is not in the list!')

END;  (* ProcessAd *)

(**************************************************************)

PROCEDURE GenerateBills
  (VAR AdList : ListType);

  (* Generate bills for all the advertisers. *)

BEGIN (* GenerateBills *)
  (**************** STUB ****************)
  Writeln ('BILLS PROCESSING TO BE ADDED.')
  (**************** STUB ****************)
END;  (* GenerateBills *)

(**************************************************************)

PROCEDURE ProcessPayment
  (VAR AdList     : ListType;
   VAR Advertiser : KeyType);

BEGIN (* ProcessPayment *)
  (***************** STUB ****************)
  Writeln ('PAYMENT PROCESSING TO BE ADDED.')
  (**************** STUB ****************)
END;  (* ProcessPayment *)
```

```
(***************************************************************)
(*                       Main Program                        *)
(***************************************************************)
BEGIN (* AdManager *)

  Initialize (AdFile, AdList, CommandTable);

  Finished := False;
  CurrentAdvertiser := BlankString;

  (* Process until the user is ready to quit. *)

  REPEAT

    (* Get user's command. *)
    GetCommand (CommandTable, Command);

    (* Process according to user's request. *)
    CASE Command OF

      BillAdvertisers : (* generate advertiser's statements *)
        GenerateBills (AdList);

      NewAdvertiser   : (* add a new advertiser to list   *)
        AddNewAdvertiser (AdList, CurrentAdvertiser);

      AcceptAd        : (* add an ad to the ad list       *)
        ProcessAd (AdList, CurrentAdvertiser);

      ReceivePayment  : (* subtract payment from balance *)
        ProcessPayment (AdList, CurrentAdvertiser);

      Quit            : (* quit program *)
        Finished := True

    END (* CASE *)
  UNTIL Finished;

  (* Save AdList for next execution of the program. *)
  WriteListToFile (AdFile, AdList)

END.  (* AdManager *)
```

We will return to this application program at the end of Chapter 7, to complete the billing and payment processing, and to see how the ADTs can be packaged in a way that will make their data encapsulation enforceable.

▪ *Exercises**

1. (a) Explain the difference between a sequential and a linked representation of a list.

(b) Give an example of a problem for which a sequential list would be the better solution.

(c) Give an example of a problem for which a linked list would be the better solution.

2. True or False. If you answer False, correct the statement.

(a) An array is a random-access structure.

(b) A sequential list is a random-access structure.

*Questions with italicized numbers are answered in the back of the book.

(c) A linked list is a random-access structure.

(d) A sequential list is always stored in a static variable.

(e) The elements in a linked list can be stored in an array.

3. In relation to compile/execution time, what is meant by
   (a) a static variable?
   (b) a dynamic variable?

Use the linked list pictured below in Exercises 4–7. The number listed on each node is the value of a field called Key in the Info part of the node.

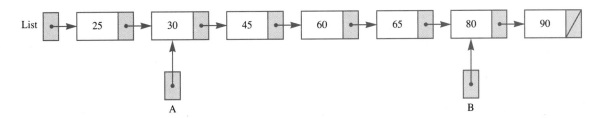

4. Give the values of the following expressions:
   (a) A∧.Info.Key
   (b) B∧.Next∧.Info.Key
   (c) List∧.Next∧.Next∧.Info.Key

5. Are the following statements True or False?
   (a) List∧.Next = A
   (b) A∧.Next∧.Info.Key = 60
   (c) B∧.Next = NIL
   (d) List∧.Info = 25

6. Decide whether the *syntax* in the following statements is valid or invalid. If it is valid, mark it OK; if it is invalid, explain what is wrong.
   (a) List∧.Next := A∧.Next;
   (b) List∧.Next := B∧.Next∧;
   (c) List∧ := B;
   (d) B := A∧.Next∧.Info;
   (e) A∧.Info.Key := B∧.Info.Key;
   (f) List := B∧.Next∧.Next;
   (g) B := B∧.Next∧.Next∧.Next;

7. Write a statement to do each of the following:
   (a) Make List point to the node containing 45.
   (b) Make B point to the last node in the list.
   (c) Make List point to an empty list.
   (d) Set the key value of the node containing 45 to 46.

8. Show what is written by the following segment of code:

```
New (List);
New (Ptr);
List∧.Info.Key := 2;
Ptr∧.Info.Key := 5;
```

```
List := Ptr;
Ptr^.Info := 7;
Writeln(Ptr^.Info.Key, List^.Info.Key);
```

9. Show what is written by the following segment of code:

```
New (List);
List^.Info.Key := 10;
New (Ptr);
Ptr^.Info.Key := 18;
Ptr^.Next := NIL;
List^.Next := Ptr;
New (Ptr);
Ptr^.Info.Key := 20;
Ptr^.Next := List;
List := Ptr;
WHILE Ptr <> NIL DO
  BEGIN
    Writeln (Ptr^.Info.Key);
    Ptr := Ptr^.Next
  END;  (* WHILE *)
```

In Exercises 10–13, choose the phrase that most accurately describes each code segment:

   (a) syntactically correct
   (b) syntactically correct, but poor style because an anonymous type is used
   (c) syntactically incorrect because of a forward reference
   (d) syntactically incorrect because an anonymous type is used

10. TYPE
```
    PtrType  = ^DataNode;
    DataType = Integer;

    DataNode = RECORD
      Data   : DataType;
      Next   : PtrType
    END; (* DataNode *)
```

11. TYPE
```
    DataNode = RECORD
      Data   : DataType;
      Next   : PtrType
    END; (* DataNode *)

    DataType = Integer;
    PtrType  = ^DataNode;
```

12. TYPE
```
    DataNode = RECORD
      Data   : DataType;
      Next    : ^DataNode
    END; (* DataNode *)
```

13. FUNCTION ValueEven (Ptr : ^DataNode) : Boolean;

    (* Indicates whether the data in this node is even. *)
    (* DataType is type Integer.   *)
BEGIN (* ValueEven *)
  ValueEven := (Ptr^.Data MOD 2 = 0)
END; (* ValueEven *)

14. Answer True or False, using the declarations below. If the answer is False, explain why. (The following declarations are global to the program.)

TYPE
  PtrType = ^ListNodeType;

  ListNodeType = RECORD
    Info : ListElementType;
    Next : PtrType
  END; (* ListNodeType *)

VAR
  Ptr   : PtrType;
  OneNode : ListNodeType;

(a) The space for the variable Ptr is dynamically allocated at run time.
(b) The space for Ptr^ is dynamically allocated at run time.
(c) Ptr^ is undefined until a call is made to New.
(d) After the declarations, Ptr = NIL.
(e) After the statement New(Ptr), Ptr^.Next is NIL.
(f) Since Ptr accesses a record of ListNodeType, Ptr and OneNode take the same amount of space in memory.
(g) The declaration of OneNode is syntactically incorrect, because NodeType records can only be allocated dynamically.

15. Discuss changes, if any, that would have to be made to the list operations if nonunique (duplicate) keys are allowed in the list.

16. (Turbo Pascal) Write a functional version of the FullList operation for the linked list implementation in this chapter.

17. The List ADT is to be extended with a Boolean function, ValueInList, which inputs a list and a KeyType value and determines whether there is an element with this key in the list.
(a) Write the specifications for this function.
(b) Write the function, using the sequential list implementation from the chapter.
(c) Write the function, using the linked list implementation from the chapter.
(d) Describe ValueInList in terms of Big-O.

18. The InsertElement in the List ADT is to be modified to perform a *conditional insertion*. The insertion is only to be made if an element with the same key is not already in the list. A Boolean output parameter, ElementExists, is set to indicate if the element is already in the list on entrance to this procedure.
(a) Modify the specifications of InsertElement.
(b) Modify the InsertElement procedure for the sequential list implementation.
(c) Modify the InsertElement procedure for the linked list implementation.

19. The DeleteElement in the List ADT is to be modified to perform a *conditional deletion*. The deletion is only to be made if an element with the specified key is in the list. A Boolean output parameter, NotInList, is set to indicate if the element is not in the list on entrance to this procedure.
    (a) Modify the specifications of DeleteElement.
    (b) Modify the DeleteElement procedure for the sequential list implementation.
    (c) Modify the DeleteElement procedure for the linked list implementation.

20. The List ADT is to be extended with Procedure MergeLists, with the following specification:

▌ **MergeLists (List1, List2, NewList)**

Function:	Merges the elements in List1 and List2 into a single list, NewList.
Input:	List1, List2 (ListType)
Preconditions:	List1 and List2 are ordered lists (or empty lists). NewList is empty. The lists are ordered from smallest to largest element.
Output:	List1, List2, NewList (ListType)
Postconditions:	List1 and List2 are empty. NewList is an ordered list containing all the elements in List1 and List2.

   (a) Write MergeLists, using the sequential list implementation described in the chapter.
   (b) Write MergeLists, using the linked list implementation described in the chapter.
   (c) Describe the algorithm you used for MergeLists in terms of Big-O.
   (d) Compare the implementation of MergeLists using seqential and linked implementations, in terms of space requirements.

21. The List ADT is to be extended by the addition of Procedure SplitList, which has the following specifications:

▌ **SplitList (MainList, SplitValue, List1, List2)**

Function:	Splits the elements in MainList into two lists, List1 and List2, according to the key value of each element. All elements with keys less than SplitValue will be put into List1; all elements with keys greater than or equal to SplitValue will be put into List2.
Input:	MainList (ListType) SplitValue (KeyType)
Preconditions:	MainList is an ordered linked list (or an empty list). SplitValue is a valid key value.
Output:	MainList (changed) List1, List2 (ListType)
Postconditions:	List1 is an ordered list containing all the elements from the original MainList that are less than SplitValue. List2 is an ordered list containing all the other elements from MainList. MainList is empty.

   (a) Write SplitList, using the sequential list implementation described in the chapter.
   (b) Write SplitList, using the linked list implementation described in the chapter.

(c) Describe the algorithm you used for SplitList in terms of Big-O.

(d) Compare the implementation of SplitList using seqential and linked implementations, in terms of space requirements.

22. The list data is to be retained between executions of the program. Therefore, the List ADT must be extended with two procedures, CreateListFromFile and CreateFileFromList, with the following specifications:

▪ **CreateListFromFile (DataFile, List)**

Function:	Creates a list containing all the records in DataFile.
Input:	DataFile (FileType)
Preconditions:	DataFile exists and is not open. List has not been created.
Output:	List (ListType)
Postconditions:	List contains all the records that are in DataFile. DataFile is unchanged.

▪ **CreateFileFromList (DataFile, List)**

Function:	Creates a file containing all the records in List.
Input:	List (ListType)
Preconditions:	DataFile is not open. List has been created.
Output:	DataFile (FileType)
Postconditions:	DataFile contains all the records that are in List. List is unchanged.

FileType is declared as a File OF ListElementType. (If you are not familiar with binary (nontext) files, read the description in the application section, page 367.)

(a) Write the two procedures, using the sequential list implementation from the chapter.

(b) Write the two procedures, using the linked list implementation in the chapter.

23. The List ADT is to be extended by the addition of Procedure GetElement, which inputs List and an integer, Position, and outputs a copy of the element in the specified list position and a Boolean value, Found. For instance, if Position is 1, a copy of the first list element is returned; if Position is 12, a copy of the twelfth list element is returned (if it exists).

(a) Write the specifications for GetElement.

(b) Write GetElement, using the sequential list implementation described in the chapter.

(c) Write GetElement, using the linked list implementation described in the chapter.

(d) Compare the sequential and linked versions of GetElement, in terms of Big-O.

24. The List ADT is to be extended by the addition of Procedure ReversePrint, which inputs List, and prints out the elements in reverse key order (from largest to smallest key).

(a) Write the specifications for ReversePrint.

(b) Write ReversePrint, using the sequential list implementation described in the chapter.

(c) What supporting data structure could be used to write ReversePrint, using the linked list implementation described in the chapter? Write the procedure. (You may call the operations of a supporting ADT without providing their implementations.)

(d) Compare the sequential and linked versions of ReversePrint, in terms of code length, space requirements, and Big-O.

Use the following declarations for Exercises 25–27. Assume that the list of students will be ordered from smallest to largest by identification number (IdNum).

```
TYPE
   StringType = PACKED ARRAY [1 .. 20] OF Char;

   StudentDataType = RECORD
      IdNum      : Integer;      (* key field *)
      FirstName  : StringType;
      LastName   : StringType;
      GPA        : Real
   END;  (* StudentDataType *)

   PointerType = ^ListNodeType;

   ListNodeType = RECORD
      Info : StudentDataType;
      Next : PointerType
   END;  (* ListNodeType *)

   ListType = PointerType;

VAR
   StudentList : ListType;
```

25. StudentList is ordered by the key field, IdNum. Procedure ReorderList is used to reorder the nodes in the list by grade point average (GPA), from smallest to largest value. (This procedure is an extension of the List ADT and can use details about the list's implementation.)
    (a) Write the specification of ReorderList.
    (b) Write Procedure ReorderList.
    (c) Describe your procedure in terms of Big-O.

26. Procedure MakeSublist is used to create a list that contains a subset of the elements in the original list. The inputs are a list and a StringType value. The procedure creates a new list that contains all the elements with the same LastName field as the input string. (This procedure is an extension of the List ADT, and can use details about the list's implementation.)
    (a) Write the specification of MakeSublist.
    (b) Write Procedure MakeSublist.
    (c) Describe your procedure in terms of Big-O.

27. StudentList is to be reimplemented as a sequential list. Write the declarations for ListType, assuming a maximum list size of 100.

Use the following declarations in Exercises 28–33.

```
TYPE
   CreditRatingType = (Poor, Fair, Good, Excellent);

   ListElementType = RECORD
      AccountNumber : Integer;
      CompanyName   : StringType;
      BalanceDue    : Real;
      CreditRating  : CreditRatingType
   END;  (* ListElementType *)
```

```
PointerType = ^ListNodeType;

ListNodeType = RECORD
  Info : ListElementType;
  Next : PointerType
END; (* ListNodeType *)

ListType = RECORD
  Count      : Integer;      (* number of elements in list *)
  ListPtr    : PointerType;  (* pointer to first node       *)
  CurrentPtr : PointerType   (* pointer to "current" node   *)
END; (* ListType *)
VAR
  List : ListType;
```

These list declarations support a list that is used for many tasks that require sequential processing; that is, the first element is processed, then the second, then the third, and so on. List.ListPtr always points to the first element in the list, whereas List.CurrentPtr is used mark the "current" position in traversing the list.

28. Draw a sketch of List when there are four nodes, and the third node is the current list position.

29. Procedure ResetList inputs List and resets the CurrentPtr field to the beginning of the list of elements.
    (a) Write the specification of Procedure ResetList.
    (b) Write Procedure ResetList, using the declarations above.

30. Procedure GetCurrentElement inputs List and returns the Info part of the "current" element in the list, as well as a Boolean flag indicating whether there are any more elements. The CurrentPtr field of List should be advanced to point to the succeeding element. If there are no more elements, NoMore should be set to True and CurrentElement should be reset to the beginning of the list.
    (a) Write the specifications of Procedure GetCurrentElement.
    (b) Write Procedure GetCurrentElement, using the declarations above.

31. Show how the declarations above would be modified to implement the list as an array-based sequential list.

32. Write a procedure that moves all the companies with a CreditRating of Poor and a Balance greater than $1000 to another list (of ListType), deleting them from the original List. This procedure is *not* part of the List ADT, and does not know anything of the implementation of the list. Your procedure may call Procedures ResetList and GetCurrentElement (described in the previous exercises).

33. Write a procedure that prints the names of all the companies with an Excellent credit rating. This procedure is *not* part of the List ADT, and does not know anything of the implementation of the list. Your procedure may call Procedures ResetList and GetCurrentElement (described in the previous exercises), and Procedure PrintLine, which prints a StringType value.

34. Some computers have fairly small ranges of allowable integers. One way to store a really large integer is to put each digit in a node of a linked list. The following list represents the integer 92578:

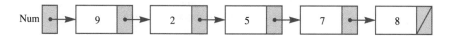

Real numbers, of course, are allowed a much greater range than are integers, so the large integer can be converted into a variable of type Real. Write a function called MakeReal that inputs a pointer to a linked list of digits that represent a large integer, and returns the real-number equivalent of the number.

Questions 35–40 refer to subjects discussed in the application section of the chapter.

35. DataFile is declared as a File OF StringType, and String is declared as StringType. Answer True or False to each statement; if you answer False, explain your answer.
    (a) The component type of DataFile is a character.
    (b) The component type of a binary file must be declared as a record type.
    (c) Writeln (DataFile, String) causes one string to be written to DataFile.
    (d) Read (DataFile, String) causes the next character in DataFile to be added to the end of String.
    (e) Read (DataFile, String) changes the variable DataFile.
    (f) Reset (DataFile) causes a run-time error (in standard Pascal) if DataFile does not exist.

36. The GetCommand operation in Program AdManager is reimplemented to require the user to type the commands as single words: BILL, PAY, QUIT.
    (a) Describe a command table data structure to support the GetCommand operation. What is needed to initialize this data structure before a call to GetCommand?
    (b) Give the algorithm for GetCommand, using the data structure you have described in part (a) as the command table.
    (c) Describe the GetCommand operation in the chapter in terms of Big-O. Describe the GetCommand operation in (b) above in terms of Big-O.

37. Describe the situation that required the modification of the declarations of ListType.

38. The ads for each advertiser were kept in an array-based queue.
    (a) Explain why an array-based queue implementation was chosen to represent the ad queue, rather than a linked implementation that would have allowed "unlimited" numbers of ads for each advertiser.
    (b) Suppose the specifications state that a maximum number of ads per advertiser can *not* be set. Design a way that the retained data could be stored to support this requirement. (You do not need to code the solution.)

39. What changes must be made to the program to add commands to ListAdvertisers ('L') and Save ('S')?

Lists Plus

CHAPTER 7

GOALS

- To be able to implement a circular linked list.
- To be able to implement a linked list with a header node or a trailer node or both.
- To be able to implement a doubly linked list.
- To be able to discuss design issues for implementing lists with nonunique keys.
- To be able to implement a linked list in an array of records.
- To be able to explain the trade-offs between static and dynamic storage allocation.

In Chapter 6 you saw how a useful data structure, the value-ordered list, can be represented as either a sequential or a linked structure. There are many variations of list structures, lists with restricted access (such as the stack and the queue) and lists with special requirements whose operations can be simplified by using different implementations of the linked list. There are also times when dynamic allocation isn't possible or feasible, and when a linked list must be kept in a static structure.

As we consider many different possible implementations, note that the specifications of the structure do not change. From the user's perspective, the list (or stack or queue) is a logical structure that can be manipulated through a set of operations. It shouldn't matter to the list-using part of the program if we change the implementation. This point is repeated over and over because it is probably the most important concept you will learn from this book.

Circular Linked Lists

The linked list that we implemented in Chapter 6 is characterized by a *linear* (linelike) relationship between the elements: Each element (except the first one) has a unique predecessor, and each element (except the last one) has a unique successor. There is a problem with using linear linked lists: Given a pointer to a node anywhere in the list, we can access all of the nodes that follow, but none of the nodes that precede it. With a singly linked linear list structure (a list with all its pointers in one direction), we must always have a pointer to the beginning of the list to be able to access all the nodes in the list.

We can, however, change the linear list slightly, making the pointer in the Next field of the last node point back to the first node instead of containing NIL (Figure 7-1). Now our list is a *circular linked list* rather than a linear linked list. We can start at any node in the list and traverse the whole list. Thus we can make our external pointer to the list point to any node and still be able to access every node in the list. In fact, a truly circular list may not have a first or a last node—just a ring of elements linked to each other.

Circular Linked List   A list in which every node has a successor; the "last" element is succeeded by the "first" element.

The advantage of using a circular list with data that is linear in nature (for instance, nodes whose values are ordered smallest to largest) is that we can reach both ends of

Figure 7-1
A Circular Linked
List

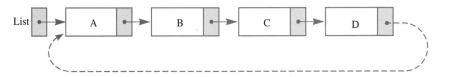

the list using a single external pointer. It is convenient, but not necessary, to let the external pointer point to the (logical) last node in the list. Then we can easily access both ends of the list: List points to the last node, and List^.Next points to the first node in the list [Figure 7-2(a)]. The Next field of the node in a list with only one element points to the element itself [Figure 7-2(b)]. An empty circular list is represented by a NIL value for the external pointer to the list [Figure 7-2(c)].

We mentioned this type of list structure in Chapter 5, when we discussed circular linked queues. We let the external pointer (Queue) point to the Rear node; Queue^.Next then points to the Front node. In this chapter we will look at how the List ADT (as specified in Chapter 6) would be implemented as a circular linked list. We will develop some of the operations in detail; the rest will be left as an exercise.

There is no need to change the declarations of the list structure to make the list circular, rather than linear. After all, the fields in the nodes are the same; only the *value* of the next field of the last node has changed. How does the circular nature of the list change the implementation of the list operations? Since an empty circular list is one with a NIL pointer, the CreateList and EmptyList operations will not change at all. However, using a circular list requires an obvious change in algorithms that *traverse* the list (destroying, printing, or searching the list, for instance). We no longer stop when the traversing pointer becomes NIL. Unless the list is empty, the pointer will never become NIL. Instead we must look for the external pointer itself as a stop sign.

Printing a Circular List

As a simple example of how to traverse a circular list, let's write the PrintList procedure that was specified in Chapter 6. We initialize a temporary pointer (Ptr) to List, the external pointer. List points to the last element in the list. Since we want to start printing at the beginning of the list, we can print one node ahead of the pointer; that is, we print Info(Next(Ptr)). We continue until Ptr comes full circle—when Ptr = List. Note that this algorithm works even when there is only one node in the list—when Ptr, List, and Next(Ptr) are all equal [as in Figure 7-2(b)].

Figure 7-2
Circular Linked Lists with the External Pointer Pointing to the List Rear Element

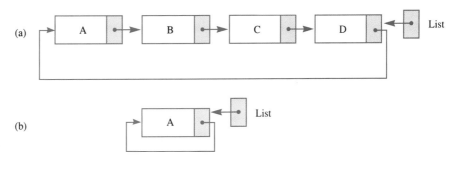

PrintList (List is circular)

Ptr ← List

REPEAT
  Print element Info(Next(Ptr))
  Ptr ← Next(Ptr)
UNTIL Ptr = List

We have used a REPEAT-UNTIL looping structure to delay checking if Ptr = List until after we have printed. If we had used a WHILE looping structure

WHILE Ptr <> List DO
  Print "next" element and advance Ptr

we run into a problem—when we start out Ptr = List. Even if we modify the condition to peek ahead

WHILE Next(Ptr) <> List DO
  Print "next" element and advance Ptr

we have a problem when there is only one element in the list, since Next(Ptr) = Ptr = List. We will not enter the loop to print the single element. Therefore we have used a REPEAT-UNTIL looping structure; now the check is made after the loop has been entered.

    We do run into a problem, however, when the list is empty [Figure 7-2(c)]. References to Next(Ptr) are illegal when Ptr is NIL. We can resolve this problem by checking for this possibility ahead of time and avoiding the loop if the list is empty. The complete PrintList procedure is shown below.

```
PROCEDURE PrintList
  (List : ListType);

  (* Print all the elements in the list in order.  *)
  (* NOTE: The list is circular; List points to the *)
  (* last node in the list.                         *)

VAR
  Ptr: PointerType; (* traversing pointer *)

  (**************** Nested Procedure ****************)

  PROCEDURE PrintElement
    (Element : ListElementType);

    (* Print fields of single element. *)

  BEGIN (* PrintElement *)
    Writeln ('Key = ', Element.Key);
    (* other statements as needed *)
  END; (* PrintElement *)

  (***************************************************)
```

```
BEGIN (* PrintList *)
  Ptr := List;
  (* Make sure that the list isn't empty. *)
  IF Ptr <> NIL
    THEN    (* Print all the elements. *)
      REPEAT
        PrintElement (Ptr^.Next^.Info);
        Ptr := Ptr^.Next
      UNTIL Ptr = List
END; (* PrintList *)
```

Finding a List Element

Many of the List ADT operations require us to search the list to find the element to process. As we did for the list implementations in Chapter 6, we will write a procedure, FindElement, to simplify these other operations. This procedure inputs a pointer to the list and a key value to search for. If the element is found, the output parameter Location will return a pointer to the node with the desired key; otherwise, Location will be NIL. To simplify the insertion and deletion operations, FindElement also returns PredLoc, a pointer to the element that logically precedes the element we are searching for. We will make one change to the specification for FindElement in Chapter 6—if the search key is found in the "first" (smallest keyed) list element, PredLoc will be a pointer to its list predecessor (a pointer to the "last" list element), instead of NIL.

In the linear list implementation, we searched the list looking for the delete key using a pair of pointers, Location and PredLoc. (Remember the inchworm?) We will modify this approach slightly for the circular list. In the linear list version, we initialized Location to point to the first node in the list, and set PredLoc to NIL [Figure 7-3(a)].

Figure 7-3
Initializing for the Search

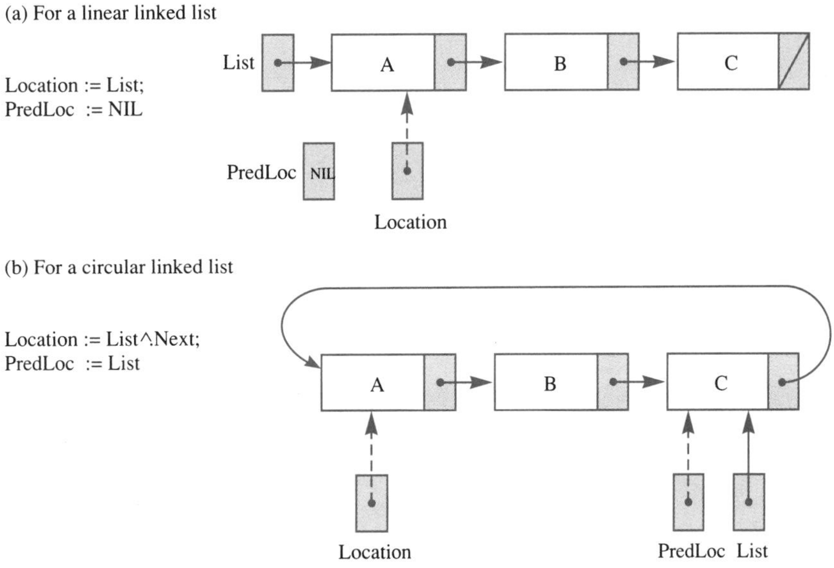

(a) For a linear linked list

Location := List;
PredLoc := NIL

(b) For a circular linked list

Location := List^Next;
PredLoc := List

For the circular list search, we will initialize Location to point to the first node, and PredLoc to point to its "predecessor"—the last node in the list [Figure 7-3(b)].

Initialize for Search

Location ← Next(List)
PredLoc ← List

The search loop executes until (1) a key greater than or equal to KeyValue is encountered, or (2) we reach the "end" of the list. The second condition occurs not when Location = NIL, but when Location = List:

WHILE Key(Location) < KeyValue AND Location <> List DO
    Advance the pointers (inchworm-style)

Following the execution of the loop, if KeyValue is found, Location points to the list node that contains KeyValue and PredLoc points to its predecessor in the list [Figure 7-4(a)]. Note that if KeyValue is the smallest key in the list, PredLoc will be pointing to its predecessor—the last node in the circular list [Figure 7- 4(b)]. If KeyValue was not in the list, PredLoc points to its logical predecessor in the list, and Location should be set to NIL [Figure 7-4(c)]. There is one special case, however; if KeyValue is greater than any element in the list, PredLoc needs to be reset to point to the last list element [Figure 7-4(d)]. This leaves PredLoc set correctly for inserting an element whose key is larger than any currently in the list.

The only other special case occurs when the list is empty: In this case, both Location and PredLoc should be assigned the value NIL. The procedure has been coded to assign the output parameters to the correct values for the special cases, and then to reassign them if it is necessary to search (the general case). Here is the resulting procedure:

```
PROCEDURE FindElement
    (List         : ListType;
     KeyValue     : KeyType;
     VAR Location : PointerType;
     VAR PredLoc  : PointerType);

    (* List is a pointer to the last node in a circular list.  *)
    (* IF KeyValue is found in list, then Location = pointer    *)
    (* to the node with key KeyValue and PredLoc = pointer to   *)
    (* the preceding list node. IF KeyValue is not found in a   *)
    (* list node, then Location = NIL and PredLoc = pointer to  *)
    (* the list node that is the logical predecessor of a node  *)
    (* with the key KeyValue.                                   *)

BEGIN (* FindElement *)

    (* Set to defaults for KeyValue > all keys OR empty list. *)
    Location := NIL;
    PredLoc  := List; (* = NIL if List is empty *)

    (* IF not special case (empty list or KeyValue > all keys *)
    (* in list, THEN search for KeyValue.                     *)
```

```
IF List <> NIL
  THEN    (* List is not empty *)
    IF KeyValue <= List^.Info.Key
      THEN
        BEGIN (* search for the key *)
          (* Set up to search. *)
          Location := List^.Next;    (* "start" of list *)
          (* Loop Invariant: The keys of all the elements *)
          (* "preceding" Node(Location) are smaller than  *)
          (* KeyValue AND Next(PredLoc) = Location.        *)
          WHILE (Location^.Info.Key < KeyValue) AND
                (Location <> List) DO
            BEGIN
              PredLoc  := Location;
              Location := Location^.Next
            END; (* WHILE *)
          (* If Location does not point to the node that *)
          (* contains KeyValue, reset Location to NIL.    *)
          IF Location^.Info.Key <> KeyValue
            THEN Location := NIL
        END (* IF KeyValue <= Key(List) *)
END; (* FindElement *)
```

Note that we did not need to use a Boolean variable in the WHILE loop condition. Can you explain why it was needed for the linear list search but not needed for the circular list search?

Inserting into a Circular List

The algorithm to insert an element into a circular linked list is similar to that for the linear list insertion:

InsertElement

Find the place where the new element belongs
Create space for the new element
Put new element in the list

The first task is simple: we just call FindElement:

FindElement (List, NewElement.Key, Ignore, PredLoc)

Of course, we will not find the element; it is the PredLoc pointer that interests us. The new element will be linked into the list immediately after Node(PredLoc).

The second task, creating space for the new element, is the same: We allocate space for the node using Procedure New, and then assign the NewElement to Info(NewNode).

Figure 7-4
*The FindElement
Operation for a Cir-
cular List*

(a) The general case (Find B)

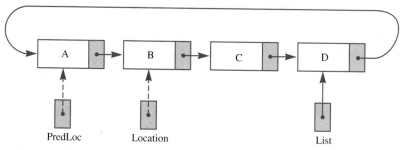

(b) Searching for the smallest list element (Find A)

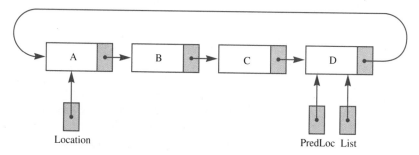

(c) Searching for element that isn't there (Find C)

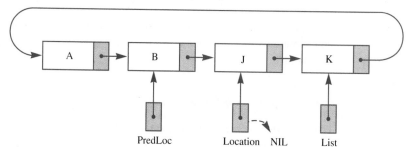

(d) Searching for element bigger than any in the list (Find E)

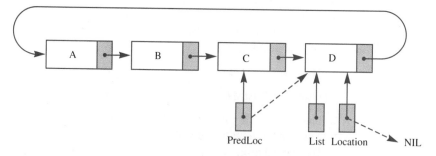

Now we are ready to link the new element into the list. In the general case (inserting into the "middle" of the list), we link Node(NewNode) after Node(PredLoc):

Put New Element in List (General Case)

Next(NewNode) ← Next(PredLoc)
Next(PredLoc) ← NewNode

This case is illustrated in Figure 7-5(a). What are the special cases? First, we have the case of inserting the first element into an empty List. In this case, we want to make List point to the new node, and to make the new node point to itself [Figure 7-5(b)].

Put New Element into Empty List (Special Case)

List ← NewNode
Next(NewNode) ← NewNode

In the insertion algorithm for the linear linked list we also had a special case when the new element key was smaller than any other key in the list. Since Node(NewNode) became the first node in the list, we had to change List (the external pointer) to point to the new node. The external pointer to a circular list, however, doesn't point to the first node in the list—it points to the last node. Therefore, inserting the "smallest" list element is not a special case for a circular linked list [Figure 7-5(c)].

Inserting the "largest" list element at the end of the list *is* a special case, however. In addition to linking the node to its predecessor (the previous last list node) and its successor (the first list node), we must modify List to point to Node(NewNode)—the new last node in the circular list [Figure 7-5(d)].

Put New Node at End of List (Special Case)

Next(NewNode) ← Next(PredLoc)
Next(PredLoc) ← NewNode

List ← NewNode

The statements to link the new node to the end of the list are the same as the general case, plus the assignment of the external pointer, List. Rather than checking for this special case before the search, we can treat it together with the general case: search for the insertion place and link in the new node. Then, if we detect that we have added the new node to the end of the list, we will reassign List to point to the new node. To detect this condition, we compare NewElement.Key to Key(List).

IF NewElement.Key > Key(List)
  THEN List ← NewNode

The resulting implementation of Procedure InsertElement is shown below.

```
PROCEDURE InsertElement
  (VAR List    : ListType;
   NewElement : ListElementType);

  (* Add NewElement to List, leaving key value-ordered *)
  (* structure of List intact. List points to the last *)
  (* node in a circular linked list.                   *)
```

```
VAR
  NewNode    : PointerType; (* pointer to the new node *)
  PredLoc    : PointerType; (* pointer to predecessor  *)
  Ignore     : PointerType; (* n/a to insertions       *)
BEGIN (* InsertElement *)

  (* Look for the insertion place: Next(PredLoc). *)
  FindElement (List, NewElement.Key, Ignore, PredLoc);

  (* Allocate a new node, and put NewElement into it. *)
  New(NewNode);
  NewNode^.Info := NewElement;

  (* Insert the new node into the list. *)
  IF List = NIL
    THEN (* We are inserting into an empty list. *)
      BEGIN
        List := NewNode;
        NewNode^.Next := NewNode
      END (* IF List = NIL *)

    ELSE (* inserting into an existing list *)
      BEGIN
        (* Connect the pointers to complete insert. *)
        NewNode^.Next := PredLoc^.Next;
        PredLoc^.Next := NewNode;

        (* IF this is last node in list, reassign List. *)
        IF NewElement.Key > List^.Info.Key
          THEN List := NewNode
      END (* inserting into existing list *)
END; (* InsertElement *)
```

Deleting from a Circular List

To delete an element from the circular linked list, we use the same general algorithm we developed for the linear list:

DeleteElement

Find the element in the list
Remove the element from the list
Free the node

For the first task, we use our trusty helper, FindElement:

FindElement (List, DeleteVal, Location, PredLoc)

On return from FindElement, Location will be pointing to the node we wish to delete, and PredLoc will be pointing to its predecessor in the list. To remove Node(Location) from the list, we simply reset Next(PredLoc) to jump over the node we are deleting:

Next(PredLoc) ← Next(Location)

Figure 7-5

Inserting into a Circular Linked List

(a) The general case (Insert C)

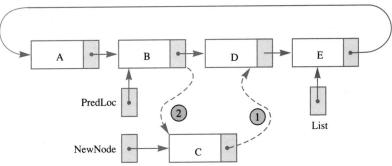

(b) Special case: The empty list (Insert A)

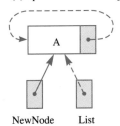

(c) Special case (?): Inserting to front of list (Insert A)

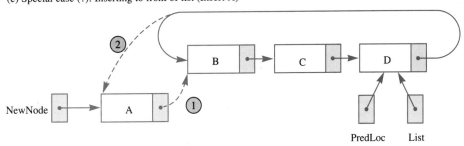

(d) Special case: Inserting to end of list (Insert E)

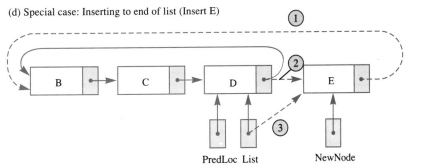

That works for the general case, at least [see Figure 7-6(a)]. What kind of special cases do we have to consider? In the linear list version, we had to check for deleting the first (or first-and-only) element. From our experience with the insertion operation, we might surmise that deleting the smallest element (the first node) of the circular list is *not* a special case; Figure 7-6(b) shows that guess to be correct. However, deleting the *only* node in a circular list is a special case, as we see in Figure 7-6(c). The external pointer List must be set to NIL to indicate that the list is now empty. We can detect this situation by checking to see if PredLoc = Location after FindElement; if so, the node we are deleting is the only one in the list.

We might also guess that deleting the largest list element (the last node) from a circular list is a special case. As Figure 7-6(d) illustrates, when we delete the last node, we first do the general-case processing to unlink Node(Location) from the list, then we reset the external pointer to point to its predecessor, Node(PredLoc). We can detect this situation by checking whether Location = List after the search.

The complete Procedure DeleteElement is shown below:

```
PROCEDURE DeleteElement
  (VAR List   : ListType;
   DeleteVal : KeyType);

  (* Removes the node containing the key DeleteVal from   *)
  (* the linked list pointed to by List. Assumes that this *)
  (* key is present in the list. NOTE: List is the pointer *)
  (* to the last node in a circular linked list.           *)

VAR
  Location : PointerType;
  PredLoc  : PointerType;
BEGIN (* DeleteElement *)

  (* Find location of DeleteVal in List. *)
  FindElement (List, DeleteVal, Location, PredLoc);

  (* Check if this is the only node in the list. *)
  IF PredLoc = Location
    THEN List := NIL
    ELSE (* not the only node in the list *)
      BEGIN
        PredLoc^.Next := Location^.Next;

        IF Location = List (* deleting largest list node *)
          THEN List := PredLoc
      END; (* not the only node *)

  (* Free the node space to be reused. *)
  Dispose (Location)
END; (* DeleteElement *)
```

Having worked through a number of the list operations in detail, we will leave the implementation of the other operations specified for the List ADT as an exercise. None

Figure 7-6
Deleting from a Circular Linked List

(a) The general case (Delete B)

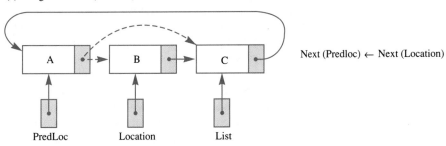

Next (Predloc) ← Next (Location)

(b) Special case (?): Deleting the smallest element (Delete A)

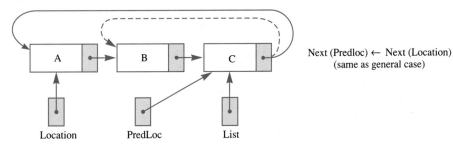

Next (Predloc) ← Next (Location)
(same as general case)

(c) Special case: Deleting the only element (Delete A)

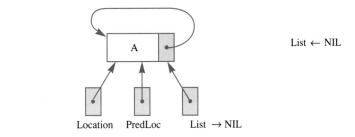

List ← NIL

(d) Special case: Deleting the largest element (Delete C)

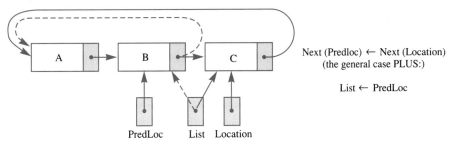

Next (Predloc) ← Next (Location)
(the general case PLUS:)

List ← PredLoc

of the operations we have looked at so far have become shorter or much simpler by changing the implementation to a circular list. Why then might we want to use a circular, rather than linear, linked list? Circular lists are good for applications that require access to both ends of the list. (The circular linked version of the FIFO queue in Chapter 5 is a good example of this.)

For instance, suppose an application requires a value-ordered list to be built by inserting elements that are already sorted. Each call to InsertElement would perform a lengthy search process O(N) for each insertion, since we would always be adding the last element in the list. Look at how the FindElement operation treats a KeyValue that is larger than any in the list: Since it can access the last element of a circular linked list directly, the search operation is O(1).

   The code for the circular list operations we have developed here is in file CIRCL-IST.PAS on the program disk.

Linked Lists with Headers and Trailers

In writing the insert and delete algorithms for linked lists, we saw that special cases arise when we are dealing with the first and the last nodes. One way to simplify these algorithms is to make sure that we *never* insert or delete at the ends of the list.

How can this be accomplished? Let's suppose that the elements in a linked list are arranged according to the value in some key field—for example, numerically by identification number or alphabetically by last name. If the range of possible values for this field can be determined, it is often a simple matter to set up dummy nodes with values outside of this range. A *header node*, containing a value smaller than any possible list element, can be placed at the beginning of the list. A *trailer node*, containing a value larger than any legitimate element, can be placed at the end of the list. The header and the trailer are regular nodes of the same type as the real data nodes in the list. They have a different purpose, however; instead of storing list data, they act as placeholders.

Header Node   Placeholder node at the beginning of a list; used to simplify list processing, or to contain information about the list, or both.

Trailer Node   Placeholder node at the end of a list; used to simplify list processing.

If a list of students is ordered by last name, for example, we might assume that there will be no students named '   ' (all blanks) or 'ZZZZZZZZZZ'. We can therefore initialize our linked list to contain header and trailer nodes with these values in the key field. A version of Procedure CreateList that initializes the header and trailer nodes of such a list is given below. MinValue and MaxValue are constants representing the minimum and maximum possible values for the Name field. The list that is created by this procedure is pictured in Figure 7-7.

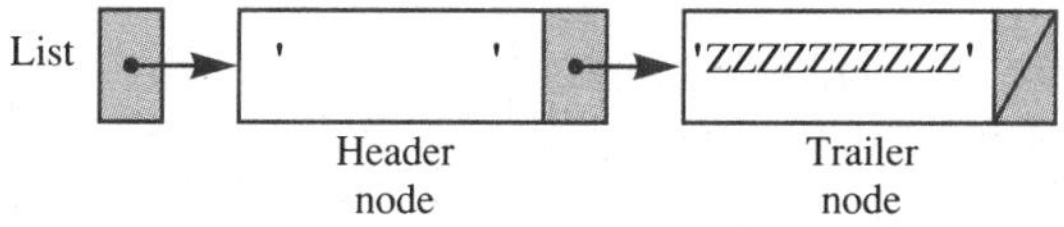

Figure 7-7
*An "Empty" List
with a Header and
a Trailer*

```
(* Add to declarations of ListElementType: *)
CONST
  MinValue = '          ';
  MaxValue = 'ZZZZZZZZZZ';
    .
    .
    .
PROCEDURE CreateList
  (VAR List : ListType);

  (* Initializes a header and a trailer node for the list.  *)
  (* The list will be ordered alphabetically with respect    *)
  (* to the Key field. Assumes that the list is empty.       *)
BEGIN (* CreateList *)

  (* Set up the header. *)
  New (List);
  List^.Info.Key := MinValue;

  (* Set up the trailer node. *)
  New (List^.Next);   (* hooks trailer to header *)
  List^.Next^.Info.Key := MaxValue;
  List^.Next^.Next     := NIL

END;   (* CreateList *)
```

How do we know whether the list is empty? Our old standby EmptyList operation

```
EmptyList := (List = NIL)
```

won't work when an "empty" list contains two nodes! Look again at Figure 7-7: We know that Node(List) contains the key MinValue, and that its successor Node(Next(List)) contains the key MaxValue. The first node in the list, empty or not, will always contain MinValue. Our EmptyList operation, therefore, only needs to check whether the second node in the list is the one with the key MaxValue.

EmptyList ← (Key(Next(List)) = MaxValue)

The complete Function EmptyList is shown here:

```
FUNCTION EmptyList
  (List : ListType) : Boolean;

  (* Returns True if List is empty; returns False otherwise. *)
  (* An empty list contains only a header and trailer node.  *)
```

```
BEGIN  (* EmptyList *)
  EmptyList := (List^.Next^.Info.Key = MaxValue)
END;  (* EmptyList *)
```

Finding an Element in a List with a Header and Trailer

The FindElement procedure can be slimmed down when there is a header and a trailer node: We never have to deal with finding KeyValue in the first node, or with a KeyValue that is larger than any key in the list. The search becomes trivial; we loop until we come across a key that is greater than or equal to KeyValue. The code for this procedure is shown below:

```
PROCEDURE FindElement
    (List          : ListType;
     KeyValue      : KeyType;
     VAR Location  : PointerType;
     VAR PredLoc   : PointerType);

    (* IF KeyValue is found in list, then Location = pointer  *)
    (* to the node with key KeyValue and PredLoc = pointer to *)
    (* the preceding list node. IF KeyValue is not found in   *)
    (* a list node, then Location = NIL and PredLoc = pointer *)
    (* to the list node that is the logical predecessor of a  *)
    (* node with the key KeyValue. The list has a header and  *)
    (* a trailer node.                                        *)

BEGIN  (* FindElement *)

  (* Set up to search. *)
  Location := List;    (* start of list *)

  (* Search for node containing KeyValue until:        *)
  (*    (1) we reach KeyValue's place in the list, or *)
  (*    (2) we reach the trailer node.                 *)
  WHILE Location^.Info.Key < KeyValue DO
    BEGIN
      PredLoc   := Location;
      Location := Location^.Next
    END;  (* Key(Location) < KeyValue *)

  (* If Location does not point to a node that contains *)
  (* KeyValue, reset Location to NIL.                   *)
  IF Location^.Info.Key <> KeyValue
    THEN Location := NIL

END;  (* FindElement *)
```

Inserting and Deleting from a List with a Header and Trailer

When we insert into or delete from a list that has a header and a trailer node, there will be only one case to consider: the case of inserting or deleting in the middle of the list.

Figure 7-8   *A Linked List with Header and Trailer*

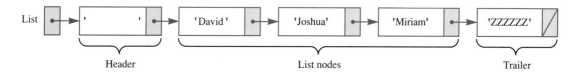

No value for the key field will be smaller than that in the header node or larger than that in the trailer node. (See Figure 7-8.)

How much shorter are the insertion and deletion operations? The code for inserting and deleting into the list we created above is shown here.

```
PROCEDURE InsertElement
   (VAR List    : ListType;
    NewElement : ListElementType);

   (* Add NewElement to List, leaving key value-ordered *)
   (* structure of List intact. The list is linear and  *)
   (* contains a header and trailer node.                *)

VAR
   NewNode : PointerType; (* pointer to the new node *)
   PredLoc : PointerType; (* pointer to predecessor  *)
   Ignore  : PointerType; (* n/a to insertion        *)

BEGIN (* InsertElement *)

   (* Find the insertion place. *)
   FindElement (List, NewElement.Key, Ignore, PredLoc);

   (* Allocate a new node, and put NewElement into it. *)
   New (NewNode);
   NewNode^.Info := NewElement;

   (* Connect the pointers to complete insertion. *)
   NewNode^.Next := PredLoc^.Next;
   PredLoc^.Next := NewNode

END; (* InsertElement *)

(***********************************************************)

PROCEDURE DeleteElement
   (VAR List   : ListType;
    DeleteVal : KeyType);

   (* Removes the node containing the key DeleteVal from *)
   (* the linked list pointed to by List. Assumes that   *)
   (* this key is present in the list. The linear linked *)
   (* list contains header and trailer nodes, so all     *)
   (* deletions will be "middle" nodes.                  *)
```

```
VAR
  Location : PointerType;
  PredLoc  : PointerType;

BEGIN  (* DeleteElement *)

  (* Find element to delete. *)
  FindElement (List, DeleteVal, Location, PredLoc);

  (* Remove the node from the list. *)
  PredLoc^.Next := Location^.Next;

  (* Free the node space to be reused. *)
  Dispose (Location)

END;  (* DeleteElement *)
```

As you can see in the following table, by adding a header and trailer to the list, the FindElement, InsertElement, and DeleteElement operations are pared down significantly. CreateList, however, is increased in size, due to the need to create and link the header and trailer nodes.

Code Length Comparison of Selected List Operations

	Linked List (Ch. 6)	Circular Linked List	Linked with Header and Trailer	Doubly Linked with Header and Trailer
CreateList	5	5	9	11
FindElement	24	24	15	11
InsertElement	23	25	14	16
DeleteElement	13	18	11	12

Is the efficiency of the insertion and deletion operations (in terms of Big-O) altered by the reduction in code size? Looking at the header-and-trailer version of Procedure InsertElement, we see that the search for the insertion place is O(N) and connecting the pointers is O(1)—just as it was before. Similarly, in Procedure DeleteElement, the search for the element to delete is O(N) and resetting the pointers to remove the node is O(1)—as it was before. Although the old versions of the insert and delete operations had more "cases" (first, middle, or last element), in any given invocation, only one case would apply. The old versions of these procedures had more lines of code, but they didn't do more work in terms of Big-O.

Printing a List with a Header and Trailer

Printing all the elements in a list that has a header and trailer is not much different from printing any other linear linked list, except for the fact that not all the nodes contain list elements. Assuming that the user does not want the values of the header and trailer to be printed (they are *internal* to the list's implementation), we must set up our print loop to avoid these nodes. We will use the algorithm we developed for printing a linear list, but there will be minor changes in the implementation.

PrintList

Location ← start of list

WHILE more elements in list DO
    Print element Info(Location)
    Location ← Next(Location)

Two things must change to implement this algorithm for a list that has a header and trailer node: the initialization of the loop control variable (Location) and the terminating condition. Where is the "start of list" when the list has a header node? The first node in the list that contains user data is Node(Next(List)), so we will initialize Location to point to this node. Where is the end of the list? The last node in the list that contains user data is the node before the trailer node. So our terminating condition must look for the special trailer value, MaxValue. What if the list is "empty"? The first node examined will contain the key MaxValue, and we terminate without entering the loop. The resulting Procedure PrintList is shown below:

```
PROCEDURE PrintList
  (List: ListType);

  (* Prints out the value of the Info field of each *)
  (* node in the linked list pointed to by List.    *)

VAR
  Location : PointerType;  (* traversing pointer *)

  (******************************************************)
  (* Code for nested procedure PrintElement goes here. *)
  (******************************************************)

BEGIN  (* PrintList *)
  Location := List^.Next;   (* node following header *)

  (* Print all elements until trailer node found. *)
  WHILE Location^.Info.Key <> MaxValue DO
    BEGIN
      (* Print data and advance the pointer. *)
      PrintElement (Location^.Info);
      Location := Location^.Next
    END  (* WHILE *)
END;  (* PrintList *)
```

Other Uses of Header Nodes

A header node may also be used for a totally different purpose. There may be times when you wish to carry some special information about the list, data that you will need often. For instance, suppose a list package has an operation ListCount specified. You could traverse the list and count the nodes, or you could keep a count of the number of elements in the list in a separate variable, ListCount. Another solution, one that binds the information to the list itself, is to store the count in the Info part of a header node, incrementing and decrementing the count as you insert into and delete from the list. (This approach assumes that the Info part of the node is either an integer, a record that contains an integer field, or a variant record with fields defined for both header and regular nodes.)

Depending on the particular application, you may want to use a header, a trailer, both, or neither. While header and trailer nodes are nice because of the simpler search, insertion, and deletion algorithms, they do have a drawback: We must be very careful to document the range of legal key values, to make sure that the key of the header is truly "smaller" than any valid key and that the key of the trailer is truly "larger" than any valid key. (Maybe there is a student named 'ZZZZZZZZZZ'!)

Doubly Linked Lists

We have discussed using circular linked lists to enable us to reach any node in the list from any starting point. Although this structure has advantages over a simple linear linked list, it is still too limited for certain types of applications. Suppose we want to be able to delete a particular node in a list, given only a pointer to that node (Location). This task involves changing the Next field of the node preceding Node(Location). As we saw in the previous chapter, however, given a pointer to Node(Location), we cannot access its predecessor in the list.

Another task that is difficult to perform on a linear linked list is traversing the list in reverse. For instance, suppose we have a list of student records, ordered by grade point average (GPA) from lowest to highest. The Dean of Students might want a printout of the students' records, ordered from highest to lowest, to use in preparing the Dean's List.

In cases like these, where we need to be able to access the node that *precedes* a given node, a doubly linked list is useful. In a *doubly linked list*, the nodes are linked in both directions. Each node of a doubly linked list contains three parts:

Info: the data stored in the node
Next: the pointer to the following node
Back: the pointer to the preceding node

We will extend our list design notation to include *Back(Location)*, to indicate the contents of the Back pointer field of the node pointed to by Location.

Figure 7-9
A Linear Doubly
Linked List

Doubly Linked List   A linked list in which each node is linked to both its successor and its predecessor.

A linear doubly linked list is pictured in Figure 7-9. Note that the Back field of the first node, as well as the Next field of the last node, contains a NIL pointer. The following declarations might be used to declare such a list:

```
TYPE
  PointerType = ^NodeType;

  NodeType = RECORD
    Info  : ListElementType;    (* the user's data       *)
    Next  : PointerType;        (* accesses next node    *)
    Back  : PointerType;        (* accesses preceding node *)
  END;      (* NodeType *)

  ListType = PointerType;
```

Using the declarations above, let's write Procedure CreateList for a list that is doubly linked with both a header and a trailer node.

```
PROCEDURE CreateList
  (VAR List : ListType);

  (* Initializes a header and a trailer node for the list.  *)
  (* The list will be doubly linked.                        *)

BEGIN (* CreateList *)

  (* Set up the header node. *)
  New (List);
  List^.Info.Key := MinValue;
  List^.Back := NIL;

  (* Set up the trailer node. *)
  New (List^.Next); (* Create trailer linked to header. *)
  List^.Next^.Info.Key := MaxValue;
  List^.Next^.Back := List;
  List^.Next^.Next := NIL

END;    (* CreateList *)
```

Finding an Element in a Doubly Linked List

In the FindElement procedure, we no longer need to use the inchworm search; instead we can get the predecessor to any node through its Back pointer. We will change the

FindElement interface slightly; since we no longer need PredLoc, we will return one pointer, Location. If KeyValue is found in the list, Key(Location) = KeyValue; otherwise, Location points to the node that is the logical *successor* in the list. (We can easily get to the preceding node through the Back pointer.) So that the caller can tell the difference, FindElement will also return a Boolean parameter, Found. The procedure shown below searches a doubly linked list with both a header and a trailer node.

```
PROCEDURE FindElement
  (List          : ListType;
   KeyValue      : KeyType;
   VAR Location  : PointerType;
   VAR Found     : Boolean);

  (* IF KeyValue is found in the list, Found is True and *)
  (* Location points to the node containing KeyValue.    *)
  (* IF KeyValue is not found in a list node, then Found *)
  (* is False and Location points to the list node that  *)
  (* is the logical successor of a node with KeyValue.   *)
  (* List is doubly linked with a header and trailer.    *)
BEGIN (* FindElement *)

  Location := List;  (* start of list *)

  (* Loop Invariant: The keys of all nodes "preceding" *)
  (* Node(Location) are less than KeyValue.            *)

  WHILE Location^.Info.Key < KeyValue DO
    Location := Location^.Next;

  Found := (Location^.Info.Key = KeyValue)

END; (* FindElement *)
```

Operations on a Doubly Linked List

The algorithms for the insertion and deletion operations on a doubly linked list are somewhat more complicated than those for operations on a singly linked list. The reason is clear: There are more pointers to keep track of in a doubly linked list.

For example, consider the InsertElement operation. To link the new node, Node(NewNode), after a given node, Node(Location), in a singly linked list, we need to change two pointers: NewNode^.Next and Location^.Next [see Figure 7-10(a)]. The same operation on a doubly linked list requires four pointer changes [see Figure 7-10(b)].

To find the insertion place we call FindElement:

FindElement (List, NewElement.Key, Location, Found)

On return from FindElement, Location is pointing to the node that should *follow* the new node. As usual, we allocate space for the new element using Procedure New, and put NewElement into the space. Now we are ready to link Node(NewNode) into the list.

Figure 7-10

*Insertions into
Singly and Doubly
Linked Lists*

(a) Inserting into a singly linked list (Insert Leah)

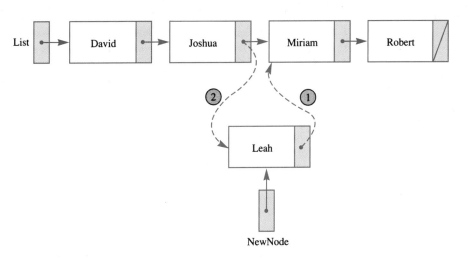

(b) Inserting into a doubly linked list

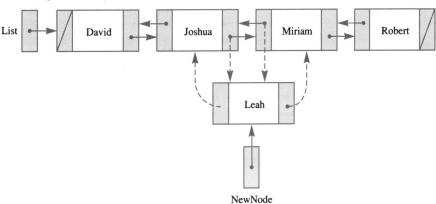

Because of the complexity of the operation, it is important to be careful about the order in which you change the pointers. For instance, when inserting Node(NewNode) before Node(Location), if we change the pointer in Back(Location) first, we lose our pointer to Node(Location)'s predecessor. The correct order for the pointer changes are illustrated in Figure 7-11.

Back(NewNode)   ← Back(Location)
Next(NewNode)   ← Location
Next(Back(Location)) ← NewNode
Back(Location)   ← NewNode

The complete Procedure InsertElement is shown below.

```
PROCEDURE InsertElement
  (VAR List    : ListType;
   NewElement : ListElementType);
```

Figure 7-11
Linking the New
Node into the List

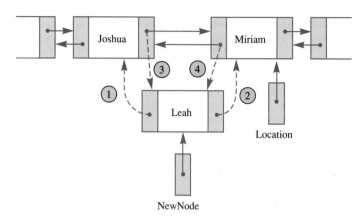

```
(* Add NewElement to List, leaving key value-ordered     *)
(* structure of List intact. The list is linear and      *)
(* doubly linked, and contains a header and trailer node. *)
VAR
  NewNode  : PointerType; (* pointer to the new node   *)
  Location : PointerType; (* points to following node  *)
  Found    : Boolean;     (* returned from FindElement *)
BEGIN (* InsertElement *)

  (* Find the insertion place. Location points to the *)
  (* node that will follow the new node in the list.  *)
  FindElement (List, NewElement.Key, Location, Found);

  (* Allocate a new node, and put NewElement into it. *)
  New (NewNode);
  NewNode^.Info := NewElement;

  (* Connect the pointers to complete insertion. *)
  NewNode^.Back := Location^.Back;
  NewNode^.Next := Location;
  Location^.Back^.Next := NewNode;
  Location^.Back := NewNode
END; (* InsertElement *)
```

One of the useful features of a doubly linked list is that we don't need a pointer to a node's predecessor in order to delete the node. Through the Back pointer field, we can alter the Next field of the preceding node to make it jump over the unwanted node:

Next(Back(Location)) ← Next(Location)

Then we make the Back pointer of the succeeding node point to the preceding node:

Back(Next(Location)) ← Back(Location)

Below is the version of DeleteElement for a doubly linked list that has a header and a trailer node. This operation is pictured in Figure 7-12.

Figure 7-12
Deleting from a
Doubly Linked List

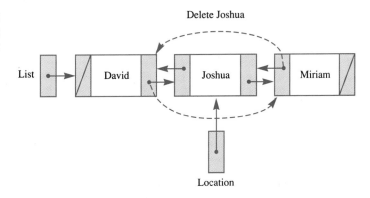

```
PROCEDURE DeleteElement
   (VAR List  : ListType;
   DeleteVal : KeyType);

(* Removes the node containing the key DeleteVal from *)
(* the linked list pointed to by List. Assumes that   *)
(* this key is present in the list. The doubly linked *)
(* list contains header and trailer nodes; so all     *)
(* deletions will be "middle" nodes.                  *)

VAR
   Location : PointerType; (* pointer to node to delete *)
   Found    : Boolean;     (* DeleteVal found in List?  *)

BEGIN (* DeleteElement *)

   (* Find the node to delete. *)
   FindElement (List, DeleteVal, Location, Found);

   (* Unlink the node from the list. *)
   Location^.Back^.Next := Location^.Next;
   Location^.Next^.Back := Location^.Back;

   (* Free the node space to be reused. *)
   Dispose (Location)

END; (* DeleteElement *)
```

The number of lines of executable code required to support these operations on a doubly linked list with a header and trailer are summarized in the table found on page 416.

Variations on a Doubly Linked List

As we saw above, doubly linked lists can have headers and trailers. With or without headers and trailers, a doubly linked list may be circular (rather than linear), as pictured in Figure 7-13.

One advantage of a doubly linked list is the ability to traverse the list backward. When a list is linked only in one direction, it is not simple to traverse it in the other

Figure 7-13   *A Circular Doubly Linked List*

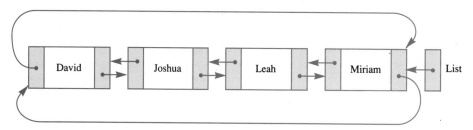

direction. Since a doubly linked list is linked in both directions, traversing the list forward or backward is equally simple. Let's add an operation to our List ADT to print all the elements in the list in reverse order. Procedure PrintReverse, shown below, prints the elements of a *circular doubly linked list*.

```
PROCEDURE PrintReverse
  (List : ListType);

  (* Prints the elements in the list in reverse order. *)
  (* List is a pointer to the last node in the list    *)

VAR
  Ptr : PointerType; (* traversing pointer *)

  (*****************************************************)
  (* Code for nested procedure PrintElement goes here. *)
  (*****************************************************)

BEGIN (* PrintReverse *)

  Ptr := List;    (* Start at the end of the list. *)
  (* Make sure that the list isn't empty. *)
  IF Ptr <> NIL
    THEN (* Print the list backward. *)
      REPEAT
        PrintElement (Ptr^.Info);
        Ptr := Ptr^.Back
      UNTIL Ptr = List

END; (* PrintReverse *)
```

This task, which is trivial with a doubly linked list, would be much more complicated if the list were singly linked. We could traverse the whole list, pushing the pointers to the nodes onto a stack of pointers, and then process those pointers in reverse order by popping and printing. Another approach would be to write a recursive procedure, as we shall do in Chapter 8.

Lists with Duplicate Elements

The lists we have discussed so far in this chapter and Chapter 6 were all composed of elements with unique keys; that is, there were no duplicate keys in the list. For instance, a list of university students might be made up of elements of the following type:

```
ListElementType = RECORD
    StudentID : Integer;
    LastName  : StringType;
    FirstName : StringType;
    GPA       : Real
END; (* ListElementType *)
```

The list might be ordered according to Student ID. In this case, there would be no duplicate keys in the list, as each student has a unique ID number [Figure 7-14(a)]. However, if the list was created for assigning class rank, and GPA was the key on which the elements were ordered, there would almost certainly be some duplicate keys [Figure 7-14(b)]. If the list was to be ordered alphabetically by the students' names, we would have to insert the elements using the values of two fields, rather than a single field, as the key. We would then need to use a special comparison algorithm in place of simple Boolean expressions like

```
WHILE NewElement.Key > Location^.Info.Key DO
```

Figure 7-14   *Duplicate Keys in a List*

(a) Ordered by ID (unique key)

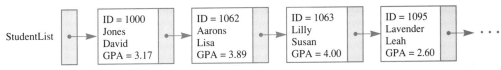

(b) Ordered by GPA (duplicate keys possible)

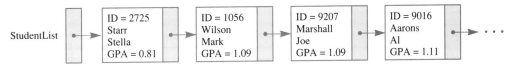

(c) Ordered by LastName/FirstName (duplicate keys possible)

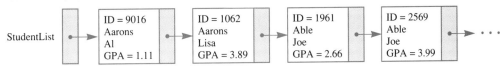

Instead we would first search the list for an element with the same LastName, and then search within the subsequent elements with that LastName for the insertion position, comparing the new element's FirstName to the FirstName field of the element in the list [Figure 7-14(c)].

When lists are not ordered according to a unique key, the operations specified for the list must be changed to reflect this situation. Some of the changes would be internal to the operation; for instance, in the InsertElement operation, the search for the insertion place might be changed to continue looping

```
WHILE NewElement.GPA >= Location^.Info.GPA DO
```

if the list were ordered by GPA.

Other changes, however, must be reflected in the specifications of the operations themselves. For instance, what is returned by GetElement, which searches a list for an element with a specific key, when the keys are not unique? Does it return the first element with the specified key, or a list of the elements that have this key? What is done by DeleteElement, which takes a list and the key of the element to delete, if there are multiple elements with that key? Should they all be deleted? Should the procedure specification be changed to take a list and copy of the element (rather than a key value), to make sure that the procedure deletes only a particular element? Similar questions can be raised for the ModifyElement operation. These are no longer a purely *internal* issues, since the list user must understand the interfaces and the functions of the operations.

We will not tell you a single algorithmic answer to the problem of elements with duplicate keys, for the solution depends on how the list will be used. These are design choices that you, as the programmer, will have to make and to record in the specification of the data structure. In the programs that you are writing now, you are probably wearing two hats: one as the list user and one as the list implementer. In many real-world programming situations, you will be using data structures that another programmer has implemented. Good communications skills (and well-documented specifications) are essential for the programmers who write "utilities" that other programmers use.

Implementation of a Linked List as an Array of Records

We mentioned briefly in Chapter 6 that the values in a linked list are not necessarily stored in dynamically allocated memory. They can also be stored in a *static* structure, the array. Let's see how this implementation might work. The elements in the list can be stored in an array of records, with each node in the list consisting of a record with (at least) two fields, Info and Next. Unlike the sequential list implementation, these records can be stored *in any physical order* in the array. Their logical order will be specified explicitly through the value in their Next fields. The Next field should point out which node (array slot) comes next in the list. We don't need to use a Pascal pointer (address in memory) for this; we only need to know the index ("address" in the array) of the succeeding list element.

Why Use an Array?

We have seen that dynamic allocation has many advantages, so why would we even discuss using a static implementation instead? The main reason is that there are a number of programming languages that do not have dynamic allocation or pointer types. You can still use linked lists if you are programming in one of these languages (in FORTRAN, for instance), but you would have to represent pointers as array indexes. We have discussed that dynamic allocation is only one issue in choosing a linked implementation; another advantage is the efficiency of the insert and delete algorithms. Most of the algorithms that we have discussed for operations on a linked list can be used for either a static or a dynamic implementation. The main difference is the requirement that we manage our own free space in an array-based implementation.

Using pointer variables also presents a problem when we need to save the information in a data structure between runs of a program. Suppose we want to write all the nodes in a list to a file and then use this file as input the next time we run the program. If the links are pointer-type values—actual addresses—they will be meaningless on the next run of the program. We must save the user data part of each node in the file, and then rebuild the linked structure the next time we run the program. An array index, however, will still be valid on the next run of the program. We can store the whole array, including the Next fields (indexes), and then read it back in the next time we run the program.

How Is an Array Used?

Let's get back to our discussion of how a linked list can be implemented in an array. As we have said, the Next field of each node tells us the array index of the succeeding node. The beginning of the list is accessed through a "pointer" that contains the array index of the first element in the list. Figure 7-15 shows how an ordered list containing the elements David, Joshua, Leah, Miriam, and Robert might be stored in an array of records called Nodes. Do you see how the order of the elements in the list is explicitly indicated by the chain of Next indexes?

What goes in the Next field of the last list element? Its "NIL" value must be an invalid address for a real list element. Because the Nodes array indexes begin at 1, the value 0 is not a valid index into the array; that is, there is no Nodes[0]. Therefore 0 makes an ideal value to use as a "NIL" address. We could use the literal value 0 in our programs:

```
WHILE Location <> 0 DO
```

but it is better programming style to declare a constant. We can't use the identifier NIL, however, since this is a Pascal reserved word. We'll use the identifier Null instead:

```
CONSTANT
  Null = 0;
```

When an array of records implementation is used to represent a linked list, the programmer must write routines to manage the free space available for new list elements. Where is this free space? Look again at Figure 7-15. All of the array elements

Figure 7-15
*An Ordered List
Stored in an Array*

Nodes	.Info	.Next	Start	1
[1]	David	5		
[2]				
[3]	Miriam	7		
[4]				
[5]	Joshua	8		
[6]				
[7]	Robert	0		
[8]	Leah	3		
[9]				
[10]				

that do not contain values in the list constitute free space. Instead of the built-in procedure New, which allocates memory dynamically, we must write our own procedure to allocate nodes from the free space. We will call this procedure GetNode. When elements are deleted from the list, we need to free the node space. We can't use the Pascal procedure Dispose, since it only works for dynamically allocated space. We will write our own procedure, FreeNode, to put a node back in the pool of free space.

In fact, this collection of unused array elements can be linked together into a second list, a linked list of free nodes. Figure 7-16 shows the array Nodes with both the list of values and the list of free space linked through their Next fields. The list of values begins at Start, at index 1 (containing the value David). Following the links in the Next field, we see that the list continues with the array slots at index 5 (Joshua), 8 (Leah), 3 (Miriam), and 7 (Robert), in that order. The free list begins at Free, at index 2. Following the links in the Next field, we see that the free list also includes the array slots at index 6, 4, 9, and 10. You see two Null values in the Next field column because there are two linked lists contained in the Nodes array.

Now let's look at how the list will be declared. As we have done before, we can bundle the array of records with its supporting data (Start and Free) using a record type:

```
CONST
  Null        = 0;      (* "NIL" array index      *)
  MaxElements = 100;    (* maximum nodes in List *)
```

Figure 7-16
*An Array with
Linked Lists of
Values and Free
Space*

Nodes	.Info	.Next
[1]	David	5
[2]	Garbage	6
[3]	Miriam	7
[4]	Garbage	9
[5]	Joshua	8
[6]	Garbage	4
[7]	Robert	0
[8]	Leah	3
[9]	Garbage	10
[10]	Garbage	0

Start   1

Free   2

```
TYPE
   KeyType = Integer;   (* or any type that can be compared *)
                        (* using <, >, <=, >=, <>, and =     *)

   ListElementType = RECORD   (* the user's data type        *)
      Key : KeyType;    (* field on which list is ordered    *)
      (* other fields in user's data as needed *)
   END; (* ListElementType *)

   PointerType = 0..MaxElements;

   NodeType = RECORD
      Info   : ListElementType;  (* the user's data        *)
      Next   : PointerType       (* pointer to next node *)
   END; (* NodeType *)

   NodeSpaceType = ARRAY[1 .. MaxElements] OF NodeType;

   ListType = RECORD
      Nodes : NodeSpaceType; (* array of all nodes          *)
      Start : PointerType;   (* index of 1st list element *)
      Free  : PointerType    (* index of 1st free node     *)
   END; (* ListType *)

VAR
   List : ListType;
```

We will always access a field of a given node by its array index (a "pointer" in this implementation) and its field specification. For instance, we can set the key field of the first node in the list with the statement

```
List.Nodes[List.Start].Info.Key := NewKey
```

The pointer field of this node (the index of the next element in the list) can be set to Null with the statement

```
List.Nodes[List.Start].Next := Null
```

Because these variable expressions are so long, we will use the Pascal WITH statement in our procedures. For instance, the preceding two statements can be written within a WITH statement to remove the explicit references to List; we can refer directly to the fields in the record List.

```
WITH List DO
  BEGIN
    Nodes[Start].Info.Key := NewKey;
    Nodes[Start].Next := Null
  END (* WITH List *)
```

Creating an Empty List

We can mark the list as empty by setting its Start field to Null.

```
WITH List DO
  Start := Null
```

But we're not finished. Before we can add any nodes to this list, we must consider how the free list is to be managed. Note that all the space for the *maximum possible* number of list elements has been declared in the array Nodes. All of these nodes should start out linked together in the list of free-space nodes, which is accessed through the pointer field, Free. Building the Free list must be done before any lists are used, so we include it in our CreateList operation. The free nodes can be linked together in any order, of course, but it is simplest to string them together sequentially, as illustrated in Figure 7-17.

```
PROCEDURE CreateList
  (VAR List : ListType);

  (* Initializes List to empty state. Chains all nodes *)
  (* together into free-node list.                     *)
VAR
  Ptr : PointerType;
```

Figure 7-17
Initializing the Free
List to Contain All
the Nodes in the
Array

Nodes	.Info	.Next
[1]	Garbage	2
[2]	Garbage	3
[3]	Garbage	4
[4]	Garbage	5
[5]	Garbage	6
[6]	Garbage	7
[7]	Garbage	8
[8]	Garbage	9
[9]	Garbage	10
[10]	Garbage	0

Start 0

Free 1

```
BEGIN (* CreateList *)
  WITH List DO
    BEGIN
      (* Mark beginning of list as Null. *)
      Start := Null

      (* Make Free list point to the first node. *)
      Free := 1;

      (* Chain each node to the free-space list. *)
      FOR Ptr := 1 TO (MaxElements - 1) DO
        Nodes[Ptr].Next := Ptr + 1;

      (* Mark the end of the free-space list with Null. *)
      Nodes[MaxElements].Next := Null

    END (* WITH List *)
END; (* CreateList *)
```

GetNode and FreeNode

We said earlier that we will need to do our own memory management by writing procedures GetNode and FreeNode. GetNode inputs a List and returns a node "pointer" (the index of an entry in the array Nodes). Using our box-and-arrow pictures, let's see how these operations will work. Figure 7-18 shows the two linked lists, one containing

Figure 7-18   *The Two Lists*

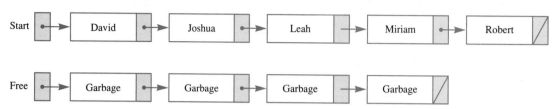

the user's data (accessed through List.Start) and the other containing nodes that are not in use (accessed through List.Free). As calls are made to GetNode, nodes are moved from the list of free nodes to the list of elements. Because the free list doesn't contain "real" data and isn't ordered in any way, we can take any node from it. The simplest approach is just to take the first element from the free list. This is very similar to the linked version of the stack operation, Pop. Figure 7-19 illustrates how the GetNode operation affects the free list.

GetNode (List, NewNode)

IF free list is not empty
   THEN
        NewNode ← Free   [see Figure 7-19 (a)]
        Free ← Next (Free)   [see Figure 7-19 (b)]

What should we do if the free list *is* empty? Somehow we need to tell the calling program that GetNode failed. One way would be to add a success flag to the parameter list. Another simple solution is simply to set the output parameter NewNode to Null. We won't have Procedure GetNode print out an error message, or cause the program to crash—as Pascal's Procedure New does when there's no more space! The *caller* should check the returned parameter and decide how to deal with such an error; a low-level utility program such as GetNode should not make the decision. Here is Procedure GetNode:

```
PROCEDURE GetNode
   (VAR List    : ListType;
    VAR NewNode : PointerType);

   (* Returns a pointer to a free node; returns Null if no *)
   (* more nodes are available in free space.             *)
BEGIN  (* GetNode *)

   WITH List DO
     BEGIN

        (* Try to get space from the free list. *)
        NewNode := Free;

        IF Free <> Null
           THEN Free := Nodes[Free].Next

     END (* WITH List *)
END;  (* GetNode *)
```

Figure 7-19
The GetNode
Operation

(a) NewNode ← Free

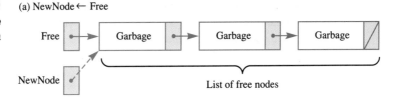

(b) Free ← Next (Free)

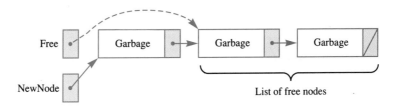

Figure 7-20
The FreeNode
Operation

(a) Next (OldNode) ← Free

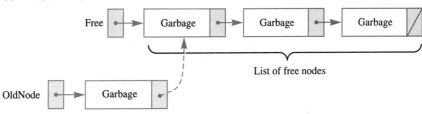

(b) Free ← OldNode

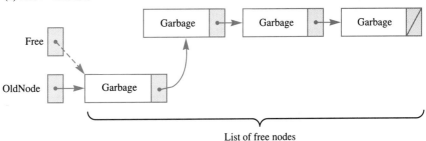

Calls to FreeNode move nodes back into the list of available nodes. We could add them anywhere in the free list, but the simplest approach is just to insert them at the beginning of the list. Figure 7-20 illustrates how the FreeNode operation affects the free list.

FreeNode (List, OldNode)

Next(OldNode) ← Free   [see Figure 7-20(a)]
Free ← OldNode   [see Figure 7-20(b)]

This operation is just like the linked version of Procedure Push, with OldNode as the pointer to the node being returned to the free list. (In fact, we could just consider the free "list" to be a linked *free-space stack*.)

```
PROCEDURE FreeNode
   (VAR List : ListType;
    OldNode  : PointerType);

   (* Puts the node pointed to by OldNode into the list *)
   (* of free nodes.                                     *)

BEGIN (* FreeNode *)

   WITH List DO
     BEGIN
       Nodes[OldNode].Next := Free;
       Free := OldNode
     END (* WITH List *)

END; (* FreeNode *)
```

The GetNode and FreeNode operations are not visible in the specification for the list package. Can you see why? These are *internal* routines that are called from inside the other list processing. They are not supposed to be visible to the list user, just as New and Dispose should be internal to the list operations when the list is implemented with dynamic allocation.

Implementing the Other List Operations

The list operations discussed in Chapter 6 can all be converted easily from the pointer variable representation to this array implementation. Figure 7-21 shows how the two implementations correspond. To show you how easy it is to change the implementation, we will code the PrintList operation. First let's review the algorithm.

PrintList

Location ← start of list

WHILE more elements in list DO
    Print element Info(Location)
    Location ← Next(Location)

    Here is the coded procedure:

```
PROCEDURE PrintList
   (List : ListType);

   (* Prints all the elements in the list. *)
```

Figure 7-21
Two Implementa-
tions of Linked Lists

Algorithm	Array of Records	Dynamic Storage
Allocate a node	GetNode (List, Ptr)	New (Ptr)
Free a node	FreeNode (List, Ptr)	Dispose (Ptr)
Info (Ptr)	List.Nodes[Ptr].Info	Ptr ∧.Info
Key (Ptr)	List.Nodes[Ptr].Info.Key	Ptr ∧.Info.Key
Next (Ptr)	List.Nodes[Ptr].Next	Ptr ∧.Next
Ptr ← Start of list	Ptr := List.Start	Ptr := List
WHILE more elements in list	WHILE Ptr < > Null DO	WHILE Ptr < > NIL DO

```
VAR
  Location : PointerType; (* traversing pointer *)

  (*******************************************************)
  (* Code for nested procedure PrintElement goes here. *)
  (*******************************************************)

BEGIN (* PrintList *)

  WITH List DO
    BEGIN
      Location : = Start;

      WHILE Location <> Null DO
        BEGIN
          PrintElement ([Nodes[Location].Info]);
          Location : = Nodes[Location].Next
        END (* WHILE *)

    END (* WITH List *)
END;      (* PrintList *)
```

Using the data from Figure 7-16, let's see what is written by this segment of code. Location is originally set to 1 (the value of the external pointer Start), and the value of Nodes[1].Info ('David') is printed. Then Location is advanced to Nodes[1].Next, or 5. Because 5 is not equal to our Null value (0), the loop is repeated. Nodes[5].Info ('Joshua') is printed, and Location is advanced to Nodes[5].Next, or 8. Again Location is not Null, so the loop is repeated.

This cycle continues until Location = 7. Then Nodes[7].Info ('Robert') is printed, and Location is advanced to Nodes[7].Next, or 0. This is our Null value, which signifies the end of the list, and we exit the loop.

Inserting and Deleting from the List

Now let's look at how insertions and deletions affect the list. We want to insert an element with the key Karen into the list pictured in Figure 7-22(a). We will use the usual InsertElement algorithm:

Figure 7-22
Inserting and Deleting from an Array-Based Linked List

(a) Original list

Nodes	.Info	.Next
[1]	David	5
[2]	Garbage	6
[3]	Miriam	7
[4]	Garbage	9
[5]	Joshua	8
[6]	Garbage	4
[7]	Robert	0
[8]	Leah	3
[9]	Garbage	10
[10]	Garbage	0

Start [1]
Free [2]

List contains
David
Joshua
Leah
Miriam
Robert

(b) After inserting Karen

Nodes	.Info	.Next
[1]	David	5
[2]	**Karen**	**8**
[3]	Miriam	7
[4]	Garbage	9
[5]	**Joshua**	**2**
[6]	Garbage	4
[7]	Robert	0
[8]	Leah	3
[9]	Garbage	10
[10]	Garbage	0

Start [1]
Free [6]

List contains
David
Joshua
Karen
Leah
Miriam
Robert

(c) After deleting Leah

Nodes	.Info	.Next
[1]	David	5
[2]	**Karen**	**3**
[3]	Miriam	7
[4]	Garbage	9
[5]	Joshua	2
[6]	Garbage	4
[7]	Robert	0
[8]	**Garbage**	**6**
[9]	Garbage	10
[10]	Garbage	0

Start [1]
Free [8]

List contains
David
Joshua
Karen
Miriam
Robert

InsertElement

Find the place where the new element belongs
Create space for the new element
Put new element in the list

To find the place, we search for a node whose key is larger than Karen; Karen belongs in the list just before this node. Tracing through the links, from Start (1) to 5 to 8, we find an element whose key (Leah) is greater than Karen, at array index 8. Let's assume that the search was implemented with a trailing pointer, so we have access to this node's predecessor—Joshua, at array index 5. Now we know the insertion place.

Next we need to create space for the new element, so we call GetNode. GetNode returns the index of the first free slot (2), and updates the free list to start at index 6 (Next(slot 2)). The new element with the key Karen is stored in the new node, at index 2.

Finally, we link the new node in place between its predecessor (at index 5) and its successor (at index 8). The results of the insertion are illustrated in Figure 7-22(b). Trace the nodes in the list, using the Next indexes to see that the insertion was done correctly.

Now let's delete the node containing the key Leah. We will use the usual Delete-Element algorithm:

DeleteElement

Find the element in the list
Remove the element from the list

To find the element in the list, we search: Beginning at the Start index, we follow the trail of Next indexes until we find Leah's node at index 8. As usual, the search was implemented with a trailing pointer, so we know that the predecessor to the node to delete is at index 2 (containing Karen).

To remove Leah, we reset the Next field of its predecessor to jump over Leah's node. This leaves the list of values correct, but we still must return the node at index 8 to the free list. The FreeNode operation takes care of this task, "pushing" Leah's old node onto the free list. The result of the deletion is illustrated in Figure 7-22(c).

Changing the linked list operations that we coded in Chapter 6 to this implementation is so simple that we leave the coding as an exercise. The table in Figure 7-21 can be used as a guide. You can also implement linked lists with headers, trailers, double links, and circular lists with an array-based storage of the nodes.

More Applications of Linked Lists

While a linked list can be used to implement virtually any list application, its real strength is in applications that largely process the list elements in order. In the application section of Chapter 6, we maintained a linked list of customer accounts, used for generating bills. This application, in which the list elements are largely processed in order, is a good use of a linked list.

This is not to say that we cannot do "random access" operations on a linked list. Our List ADT specifications include operations that are access elements in random order—for instance, procedures GetElement, ModifyElement, and DeleteElement manipulate a particular element in the list. However, the only way to find an element is to search the list, beginning at the first element, and continuing sequentially to examine element after element. This search is O(N), since the amount of work required is directly proportional to the number of elements in the list. A particular element in a sequentially ordered list in an array, in contrast, can be found with a binary search, decreasing the search algorithm to $O(\log_2 N)$. For a large list, the O(N) sequential search can be quite time-consuming. There is a linked structure that supports $O(\log_2 N)$ searches: the binary search tree. We will discuss this data structure in detail in Chapter 9.

Although often either a linked or a sequential representation of a list can be used with good results, there are times when a linked representation is a much better choice. For instance, linked lists are often used to implement sparse tables. A *sparse table* is a table with relatively few nonzero elements. Consider a table of company sales figures in which the rows represent the different salespeople and the columns represent the various products sold by the company. Each element in the table contains the total quantity of a particular product that has been sold by one of the salespeople. If the various salespeople specialize, each selling only a small range of different products, it is likely that many or most of the numbers in the table will be zero (see Figure 7-23). This is an example of a sparse table.

Though it is natural to think of implementing a table as a two-dimensional array, a sparse table may be more efficiently implemented (with regard to space) as a linked list structure. One way to represent a sparse table with linked lists is pictured in Figure 7-24. The rows represent the different salespeople and the columns represent the different product numbers. Each row and column has a header node.

Linked lists are also used to implement other list-type data structures that are *not* ordered by key value. One use of linked lists is in a line editor, with each line node

Figure 7-23 A Sparse Table

Product number (columns)

	003	004	026	056	072	124	155	237	274	287	...	822	853	933	945	949
Addams	0	36	91	0	0	0	0	0	0	28	...	0	0	0	0	0
Baker	93	0	0	33	59	0	0	0	0	0	...	0	0	56	0	0
Cole	39	0	0	26	55	0	0	0	0	33	...	0	0	39	0	5
Dale	0	0	0	0	0	0	0	0	0	0	...	0	76	47	98	45
•																
•																
•																
Xavier	0	20	23	33	64	0	0	0	0	0	...	36	0	0	0	0
Young	0	0	0	0	0	54	46	78	36	0	...	71	0	0	0	0
Zorro	48	0	0	0	0	0	0	0	0	69	...	0	87	0	67	0

Salesperson name (rows)

Figure 7-24 *A Sparse Table Represented as Linked Lists with Header Notes*

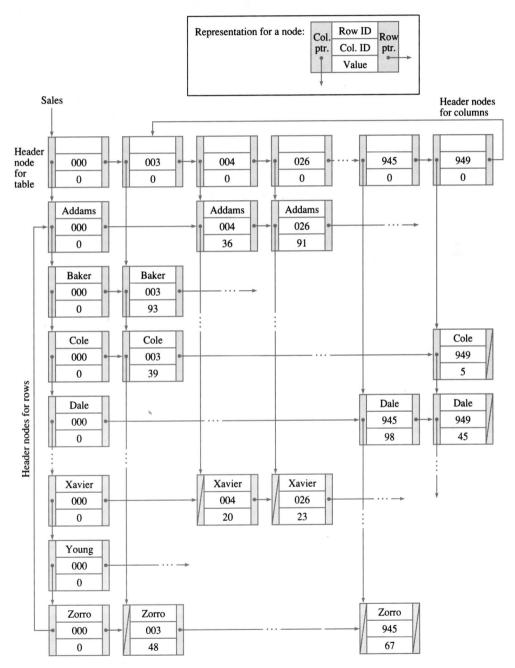

containing a line of text and a pointer to the next line. Because you cannot predict how many lines will be needed, this application would appropriately be implemented with dynamically allocated nodes.

In Chapter 3 you saw how strings can be implemented with arrays. Variable-length strings can also be represented as linked lists. A string may be declared as a record that contains a string count and a pointer to the linked list of characters. In one simple representation, each node contains a single character and a pointer to the next node [see Figure 7-25(a)]. Character manipulation is straightforward with this string implementation, but unfortunately more space is used for the pointers than for the characters. If space is limited, each node can contain several characters, as well as a pointer to the next node [Figure 7-25(b)]. This representation saves space, at the cost of increasing the complexity of the algorithms that manipulate the characters in the strings.

Another use of linked lists for storing data that is not ordered by key is the representation of integers larger than MaxInt. For instance, if an integer variable is stored in 16 bits, integer values can only range from -32768 to $+32767$. If you wanted to perform Integer operations on values larger (or smaller) than this range, you could implement your own LargeInteger type using linked lists. In the simplest case, each node in the list represents one digit in the number [Figure 7-26(a) on page 441]. This solution uses more space for the pointers than for the characters. To save space, each node can contain several digits, as illustrated in Figure 7-26(b). Another consideration involves the manipulation of the integers—in what order should the digits be stored? Adding two integers stored as shown in Figure 7-26(c) is a little bit messy: We need to start adding with the digits at the ends of each list $(6 + 1)$. To simplify arithmetic

Figure 7-25   Linked String Representations

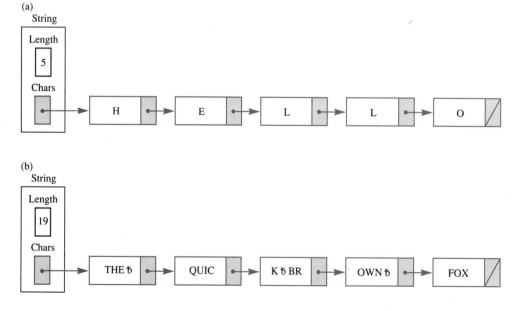

Figure 7-26   Representing Large Integers with Linked Lists

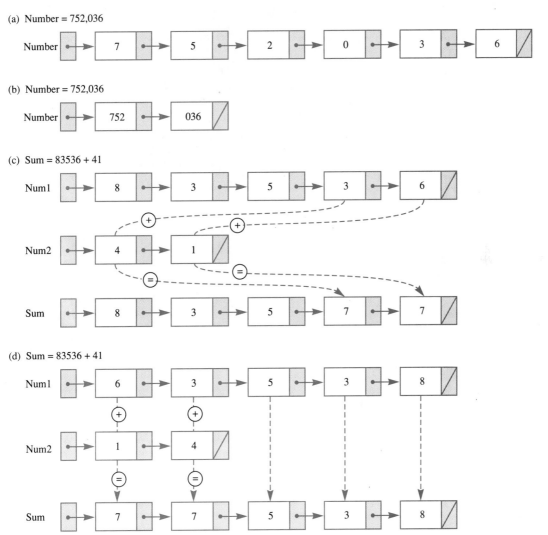

(a) Number = 752,036

(b) Number = 752,036

(c) Sum = 83536 + 41

(d) Sum = 83536 + 41

operations, it would be more convenient to store the digits in reverse order, as shown in Figure 7-26(d).

An operating system is a program that manages and allocates the resources of a computer system. Operating systems use linked lists in many ways. The allocation of memory space (one of the system resources) may be managed using a doubly linked list of variably sized blocks of memory. Doubly linking the lists facilitates the removal of blocks from the middle of the list. In a multiuser system, the operating system may keep track of user jobs waiting to be executed through linked queues of "control blocks" (records that contain information about the user's ID, the program to be run, the files associated with the program, and so forth).

Summary

In this chapter we have looked at a number of variations on the linked list theme. Obviously, given the wide variety of applications that use lists, there are many interesting ways that a programmer can implement this abstract data structure. All of the implementations are supported by a common method of development: As programmers, we determine the needs of the application and then decide on a physical representation for the data. Along with the declarations of the data type, we must provide a set of basic operations so that the user of the data type can create and access elements in the structure. For lists, these operations generally include procedures and functions to create a list, add, delete, and modify elements, traverse a list, and determine whether the list is empty. We don't expect—or allow—the user to manipulate the data structure directly. As discussed in previous chapters, this set of operations encapsulates the list's ADT.

The idea of linking the elements in a list has been extended in this chapter to include circular lists, doubly linked lists, and lists with header and trailer nodes. In fact, the idea of linking the elements is a possibility to consider in the design of many types of data structures.

The dynamic allocation of the space for nodes in a linked structure allows the program to get just what it needs during execution. In a program where the amount of data to be stored is very unpredictable or may vary widely, the dynamic allocation of space has major advantages. A pointer variable provides efficient access to a node, for it contains the node's actual address in memory. (Remember from Chapter 3 that the address of data stored in an array must be computed from the base address and the array index.)

We will continue to use linked representations of data structures in the chapters that follow and will typically implement them with dynamic storage allocation. A static implementation of these linked structures is also possible, however, and in some cases desirable or necessary (especially in languages that do not support dynamic allocation).

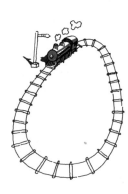

Application

Advertising Manager—Part 2

Data Structure	*Software Techniques*
■ AdRateTable	■ Data encapsulation using Turbo Pascal Units
	■ Incremental program development

In the application section at the end of Chapter 6, we discussed a program to handle the billing for a small magazine's advertisers. We now continue the development of this application with two goals: (1) to complete the GenerateBills and ProcessPayment modules; and (2) to implement an abstract data type in a way that will enforce the concept of data encapsulation. To accomplish the second goal, we will need to use tools that are not included in standard Pascal—we will use the *Unit* feature of Turbo Pascal (versions 4.0 and later).*

*If you are programming in a different nonstandard version of Pascal, your instructor and your user's manual can help you convert this program to work with your compiler.

The ReceivePayment Command

The ReceivePayment command is handled by the ProcessPayment module:

■ **ProcessPayment (AdList, Advertiser)** / *Level 1*

Function:	Credit the advertiser record of the specified Advertiser with a payment input by the user.
Input:	AdList (ListType) Advertiser (from previous operation) From keyboard: Advertiser, amount of payment
Preconditions:	AdList has been created.
Output:	AdList (updated) Advertiser (may be reset by user) To screen: previous balance, new balance info
Postconditions:	If Advertiser is in AdList, the balance of this advertiser's ad record is reduced by the payment amount input by user.

The design for this module is very straightforward:

ProcessPayment

GetAdvertiserName (Advertiser)

RetrieveElement with key = Advertiser
IF Found

   THEN
      Print current balance to screen.
      GetPayment (Payment)—a user input operation
      Calculate new balance.
      ModifyElement to record new balance.
      Print new balance to screen.

   ELSE Print error message (advertiser not in list)

Except for GetPayment, which we will discuss in a moment, there is nothing in this module that needs further decomposition. The procedure listed below replaces the ProcessPayment stub in the program listing in Chapter 6:

```
PROCEDURE ProcessPayment
  (VAR AdList     : ListType;
   VAR Advertiser : KeyType);

  (* Subtract payment from an advertiser's balance due. *)
  (* This procedure can use the current Advertiser or   *)
  (* can reset Advertiser name.                         *)
```

```
VAR
  AdRec   : AdRecType;   (* one advertiser's data *)
  Found   : Boolean;
  Payment : Integer;

BEGIN (* ProcessPayment *)

  GetAdvertiserName (Advertiser);

  (* Get the ad record for this advertiser. *)
  RetrieveElement
    (AdList,         (* list to retrieve element from  *)
     Advertiser,     (* key value to retrieve          *)
     AdRec,          (* list element returned          *)
     Found);         (* list element found in list?    *)

  IF Found
    THEN
      BEGIN
        Writeln ('Current balance is $', AdRec.Balance);

        (* Get amount of payment. *)
        GetPayment (Payment);

        (* Subtract the payment from the balance. *)
        AdRec.Balance := AdRec.Balance - Payment;

        (* Update the record in the AdList. *)
        ModifyElement (AdList, AdRec);

        Writeln ('New balance = ', AdRec.Balance)

      END (* IF Found *)
    ELSE Writeln ('This advertiser is not in the list!')

END;  (* ProcessPayment *)
```

The GetPayment procedure should be added to the group of user-input operations in Program AdManager.

```
PROCEDURE GetPayment
  (VAR Payment : Integer);

  (* Prompt user for amount of payment and read answer. *)

BEGIN (* GetPayment *)

  (* Get amount of payment. *)
  Write ('Enter amount of payment (whole $): ');
  Readln  (Payment)

END;  (* GetPayment *)
```

The BillAdvertisers Command

We come at last to the original *raison d'etre* for this program: the operation to generate the advertisers' bills. As specified in Figure 6-14 on page 365, the bills will be written to a Text file, which Marc will print out later using the operating system's PRINT command. To calculate an advertiser's bill, you need to know the rates for ads of different sizes and colors. That's simple, Marc tells you—he has a printed "rate sheet" that he sends out to advertisers. Here is the specification for this module:

▶ **GenerateBills (AdList)** / *Level 1*

Function:	Generate bills for all the advertisers. Each bill must contain the advertiser's name and address, and show the itemized prices of all current issue ads, the previous balance, and the total amount due.
Input:	AdList (ListType)
Preconditions:	AdList has been created.
Output:	AdList (ad queues emptied) To BILLS file: text of all advertisers' bills.
Postconditions:	File BILLS contains the text of all of the advertisers' bills. The ad queues in AdList are left empty, ready for next issue's ads. The outstanding balance field of each advertiser record = its previous value + the cost of all the ads removed from the ad queue.

Here's the design for this module:

GenerateBills

Open the BILLS file for writing.

GetElement (AdList, GetFirst, AdRec, Found)

WHILE AdRec was Found DO
    ProcessAccount—process ad record for this advertiser.
    ModifyElement (AdList, AdRec)
    GetElement (AdList, GetNext, AdRec, Found)

Print message to user (bills are in file BILLS)

After opening the Bills file, you loop through all of the advertiser records in AdList, processing each one. Each record contains all the information for a single advertiser; thus each record will result in one bill being added to the Bills file. The ProcessAccount (Level 2) module does all the work for one advertiser's account.

▶ **ProcessAccount (Bills, AdRec)** / *Level 2*

Function:	Write the bill for one advertiser. Calculate the cost of the current ads and add to the balance; the ad queue is left empty, ready for next issue's ads.

Input:	Bills (Text)
	AdRec (AdRecType)
Preconditions:	The Bills file is open. AdRec contains all the information about one advertiser's account.
Output:	To Bills (file): text of one advertiser's bill.
	To caller: AdRec (changed)
Postconditions:	AdRec.Ads (the ad queue) is empty.
	AdRec.Balance has been increased by the amount of the current ads. Billing statement for this account has been written to Bills file.

Here is the algorithm for this module:

ProcessAccount

PrintBillHeader—prints title, advertiser name, address

CurrentBill ← 0

WHILE NOT EmptyQueue (AdRec.Ads) DO

Dequeue (AdRec.Ads, Ad)

(Calculate charges for this ad.)
SizeCharge ← cost of ad of Ad.AdSize
ColorCharge ← cost of color of Ad.AdColor
AdCost ← SizeCharge + ColorCharge
CurrentBill ← CurrentBill + AdCost

(Write the charges for this ad to the Bill file.)
Write ad size description and SizeCharge.
Write ad color description and ColorCharge.
Write "TOTAL = " AdCost.
(END WHILE)

(Write totals to the Bill file.)
Write CurrentBill and AdRec.Balance (previous balance)
AdRec.Balance ← AdRec.Balance + CurrentBill
Write AdRec.Balance (new balance)

The ad data Dequeue'd from the current advertiser's ad queue is a record that contains two fields, AdSize and AdColor. The size and color data and the information in Marc's rate sheet determines the price of each ad. There is only one thing in this design that needs further discussion. What is the computer data equivalent of this rate sheet? Rather than dealing with the advertising rates in this module, you decide to treat AdRates as a little ADT, with operations to extract size and color rates and string-type descriptions:

▸ GetSizeRate (AdSize, SizeRate)

Function:	Retrieve the rate for an ad of AdSize.
Input:	AdSize (AdSizeType)
Preconditions:	none
Output:	SizeRate (Integer)
Postconditions:	SizeRate = price for ad of AdSize.

▸ GetColorRate (AdColor, ColorRate)

Function:	Retrieve the rate for an ad of AdColor.
Input:	AdColor (AdColorType)
Preconditions:	none
Output:	ColorRate (Integer)
Postconditions:	ColorRate = price for ad of AdColor.

▸ GetSizeName (AdSize, SizeName)

Function:	Retrieve the string description of AdSize.
Input:	AdSize (AdSizeType)
Preconditions:	none
Output:	SizeName (DescripType)
Postconditions:	SizeName = string describing AdSize.

▸ GetColorName (AdColor, ColorName)

Function:	Retrieve the string description of AdColor.
Input:	AdColor (AdColorType)
Preconditions:	none
Output:	ColorName (DescripType)
Postconditions:	ColorName = string describing AdColor.

Using these AdRates operations, the GenerateBills module can be implemented as shown below. These procedures replace the GenerateBills stub that we used in the AdManager program in Chapter 6.

```
PROCEDURE GenerateBills
  (VAR AdList : ListType);

  (* Generate bills for all the advertisers, using rate  *)
  (* data from AdRates ADT. Show the itemized prices      *)
  (* of all current issue ads, the previous balance, and *)
  (* the total amount due. The ad queue is left empty,    *)
  (* ready for the next issue's ads.                      *)
  (* NOTE: This procedure contains Turbo Pascal code.     *)
```

```
VAR
  AdRec    : AdRecType;  (* ad list element (1 advertiser) *)
  Found    : Boolean;    (* element was found in list?      *)
  Bills    : Text;       (* file to contain statements      *)

(****************** Nested Procedure *********************)
PROCEDURE ProcessAccount
  (VAR Bills : Text;
   VAR AdRec : AdRecType);

  (* Write the bill for one advertiser. Calculate cost  *)
  (* of the current ads, and add to the balance; the ad *)
  (* queue is left empty, ready for next issue's ads.    *)

VAR
  Ad          : AdInfoType;  (* current ad being priced *)
  AdNum       : Integer;     (* current ad number       *)
  AdCost      : Integer;     (* current ad total price  *)
  SizeCharge  : Integer;     (* current ad size cost    *)
  SizeName    : DescripType; (* size description        *)
  ColorCharge : Integer;     (* current ad color cost   *)
  ColorName   : DescripType; (* color description       *)
  CurrentBill : Integer;     (* all ads total cost      *)

  (******************** Nested Procedure **************)
  PROCEDURE PrintBillHeader;

  BEGIN (* PrintBillHeader *)

    Writeln (Bills,
      '*********************************************************');
    Writeln (Bills,
      '***            Garden Railways Magazine            ***');
    Writeln (Bills,
      '*********************************************************');
    Writeln (Bills);
    Writeln (Bills, 'TO: ', AdRec.Key);
    Writeln (Bills, '    ', AdRec.Address.StreetAddr);
    Writeln (Bills, '    ', AdRec.Address.CityStateZip);
    Writeln (Bills);
    Writeln (Bills, 'CURRENT ADS:')

  END;  (* PrintBillHeader *)
  (*********************************************************)

BEGIN (* ProcessAccount *)

  PrintBillHeader;

  CurrentBill := 0;
  AdNum := 0;
```

```
    WHILE NOT EmptyQueue (AdRec.Ads) DO
      BEGIN
        (* Get next ad off the queue. *)
        Dequeue (AdRec.Ads, Ad);

        (* Calculate charges for this ad. *)
        AdNum   := AdNum + 1;
        GetSizeRate  (Ad.AdSize, SizeCharge);
        GetColorRate (Ad.AdColor, ColorCharge);    '
        AdCost := SizeCharge + ColorCharge;
        CurrentBill := CurrentBill + AdCost;

        (* Print the charges for this ad to the bill. *)
        GetSizeName  (Ad.AdSize, SizeName);
        GetColorName (Ad.AdColor, ColorName);
        Writeln (Bills, '  Ad #',Adnum:1, '   ',
                 SizeName,'  ', SizeCharge);
        Writeln (Bills, '            ',ColorName, '   ',ColorCharge);
        Writeln (Bills, '            TOTAL = ', AdCost)

      END; (* WHILE *)

    Writeln (Bills);
    Writeln (Bills, 'Total for current ads  = $', CurrentBill);
    Writeln (Bills, 'Previous balance       = $', AdRec.Balance);
    AdRec.Balance := AdRec.Balance + CurrentBill;
    Writeln (Bills, '---------------------------------------------');
    Writeln (Bills, 'PLEASE PAY NEW BALANCE = $', AdRec.Balance);
    Writeln (Bills);
    Writeln (Bills)

END;  (* ProcessAccount *)

(*****************************************************************)

BEGIN (* GenerateBills *)

  Assign (Bills, 'BILLS');      (*** Turbo Pascal code ****)
  Rewrite (Bills);

  (* Retrieve the first advertiser's record from AdList. *)
  GetElement
    (AdList,             (* retrieve from AdList   *)
     GetFirst,           (* get the first element  *)
     AdRec,              (* element returned       *)
     Found);             (* element was found?     *)

  (* Process all advertisers in AdList. *)
  WHILE Found DO
    BEGIN

      (* Process ad record for one advertiser. Calculate *)
      (* current bill; add to balance; print. Leave ad   *)
      (* queue empty, ready for next issue's ads.        *)
      ProcessAccount (Bills, AdRec);
```

```
                    (* Replace the updated record in the list. *)
                    ModifyElement (AdList, AdRec);

                    (* Retrieve the next advertiser's record from AdList. *)
                    GetElement
                      (AdList,              (* retrieve from AdList   *)
                       GetNext,             (* get the next element   *)
                       AdRec,               (* element returned       *)
                       Found)               (* element was found?     *)

              END;  (* WHILE Found *)

        Writeln ('The statements for this issue are in file BILLS.');

        Close (Bills)              (**** Turbo Pascal code ****)
  END;  (* GenerateBills *)
```

A listing of a bill created with this module is shown in Figure 7-27.

The AdRates ADT

Standard Pascal does not provide a mechanism to enforce the separation of the user and implementation views of a data type. In order to do so, you decide to implement the AdRates ADT using a nonstandard feature of Turbo Pascal—the **unit,** a collection of constants, types, variables, procedures, and functions that are compiled separately from the main program. The unit has two sections:

1. The **Interface** section contains all of the declarations (constants, types, and variables) and subprogram *interfaces* that are exported from the unit.
2. The **Implementation** section contains all of the declarations and subprogram *implementations* that are entirely encapsulated by the unit.

Here is a simplified outline of a Turbo Pascal unit:

```
UNIT UnitName;

INTERFACE

    (* "Public" declarations of constants, types and variables *)

    (* Exported procedure and function "specifications"        *)


IMPLEMENTATION

    (* "Private" constant, type, and variable declarations  *)

    (* Internal procedures and functions                    *)

    (* Implementations of exported procedures and functions *)


BEGIN (* Unit *)

    (* Unit "initialization", if any. *)

END. (* Unit *)
```

The "specifications" of exported procedures and functions are simply the subprogram headings—*without* the procedure and function bodies. Then where are the bodies? They are in the Implementation section, along with "private" declarations, hidden from the program that uses the unit.

Let's look at how the AdRates ADT can be implemented as a Turbo Pascal unit. What does the *user* of the AdRates unit (Procedure ProcessAccount) need to know? The user must know the interfaces of the AdRates operations—how to call the operations, as well as the types of all the parameters. For instance, to use Procedure GetAdRate to determine the price of an ad of AdSize, we must know the legal values of AdSizeType. Similarly, to call GetColorRate, we must know the definition of AdColorType. Therefore, the declarations of these types must be "exported" from the unit; they belong in the unit's Interface section. What about AdRatesType—the type of the AdRates data structure? We want to encapsulate this type, so it will be declared inside the Implementation section of the unit.

To summarize, the Interface section will contain the headings of the procedures that are exported from the unit—GetSizeRate, GetSizeName, GetColorRate, and GetColorName. It is good style to include information from the procedure's specification in a comment under each heading. The Interface section also contains the data types that are used in the procedure interfaces—AdSizeType, AdColorType, and DescripType (the string that describes a size or color).

Figure 7-27
One Advertiser's
Bill

```
*************************************************************
*                  Garden Railways Magazine                *
*************************************************************
TO: CHOOCHOOS INC.
    PO Box 100
    Austin, Texas 78757

CURRENT ADS:
    Ad #1    Full Page                              400
             Four Color Processing                  325
             TOTAL = 725
    Ad #2    Quarter Page                           140
             1 Extra Color Blue                     100
             TOTAL = 240
    Ad #3    Half Page                              250
             Black (no color)                         0
             TOTAL = 250

Total for current ads   = $1215
Previous balance        = $350
------------------------------------------------
PLEASE PAY NEW BALANCE = $1565
```

Implementing the AdRates ADT

Now let's look at the contents of the AdRates unit's Implementation section. The AdRates structure contains two types of data: information about ad sizes and information about ad colors. For each size and each color, there are two types of data: the price and the name—a string description of the size or color. This suggests the following declarations:

```
TYPE
  RateInfoType  = RECORD
    Price        : Integer;
    Name         : DescripType
  END; (* RateInfoType *)

  AdRatesType  = RECORD
    SizeRates  : ARRAY [AdSizeType]  OF RateInfoType;
    ColorRates : ARRAY [AdColorType] OF RateInfoType
  END; (* AdRatesType *)
VAR
  AdRateTable : AdRatesType;
```

The variable AdRates is declared in the VAR part of the Implementation section; it exists completely *inside* the unit, invisible to Procedure ProcessAccount, which uses the AdRates operations. The declarations inside the Implementation section of a unit are essentially "global" unit declarations—the types can be used anywhere within the unit, and the variables declared there (like AdRateTable) exist for the entire execution of the program that uses the unit.

The procedure bodies for the four AdRates operations are also inside the Implementation section. Using the declarations above, each of the four procedures contains only a single statement. For instance, the procedure to get the price of an ad of AdSize is implemented as follows:

```
PROCEDURE GetSizeRate
  (AdSize        : AdSizeType;
   VAR SizeRate : Integer);

BEGIN (* GetSizeRate *)
  SizeRate := AdRateTable.SizeRates[AdSize].Price
END;  (* GetSizeRate *)
```

The other three procedures are similar. It is not necessary syntactically to repeat the entire procedure heading in the Implementation section—you can leave out the parameter list:

```
PROCEDURE GetSizeRate;

BEGIN (* GetSizeRate *)
  SizeRate := AdRateTable.SizeRates[AdSize].Price
END;  (* GetSizeRate *)
```

However, we recommend the practice of repeating the entire heading as good documentation style.

We haven't yet established how the price and description information got into the AdRateTable. One approach is to add an initialization step that fills in the table with"hardcoded"values:

```
AdRateTable.SizeRates[FullPage] := 400;
AdRateTable.SizeRates[HalfPage] := 250;
```

and so on. However, Marc warns you that he will probably raise his rates later this year. The two of you decide to put the current rates in a text file, ADPRICES, so that Marc can edit the prices whenever he needs to. You decide to create another operation, GetAdRates, to read this text file and store the rate information into the AdRateTable.

■ GetAdRates

Function:	Read the ad rates from the ADPRICES text file, and store in AdRateTable.
Input:	From ADPRICES (File): rate names and prices
Preconditions:	ADPRICES exists and is not open.
Output:	AdRateTable (used globally from unit)
Postconditions:	AdRateTable contains the rate names and prices from the ADPRICES file. The file is left closed and unchanged.

Before reading the file, of course, you must define the format of File ADPRICES. This description is added to the Inputs section of the specification:

File **ADPRICES** is a text file that contains ad rate information. Each line contains a Name-Price pair, in the following format:

Col 1-40: Name (String)   Col 41-43: Price (Integer)

The lines are ordered as follows: 1. full page, 2. half-page, 3. quarter page, 4. eighth page, 5. no extra color, 6. extra color: red, 7. extra color: blue, 8. extra color: green, 9. extra color: yellow, 10. full-color.

Sample text of file ADPRICES is listed in Figure 7-28. Marc is happy with this file format, since the Name fields"document" the file. It will be easy for him to edit this file to change ad rates. You are also happy with this format, since the resulting GetAdRates module is very simple:

GetAdRates

Open file ADPRICES for reading (Reset).

```
FOR AdSize := FullPage TO EighthPage DO
    Read Name; store in AdRates.SizeRates[AdSize].Name
    Read Price; store in AdRates.SizeRates[AdSize].Price
```

```
Full Page                           400
Half Page                           250
Quarter Page                        140
Eighth Page                         75
Black (no color)                    0
1 Extra Color Red                   100
1 Extra Color Blue                  100
1 Extra Color Yellow                100
1 Extra Color Green                 100
Four Color Processing               325
```

```
         1         2         3         4
123456789012345678901234567890123456789012345
              (Column number)
```

```
FOR AdColor := NoColor TO FullColor DO
    Read Name; store in AdRates.ColorRates[AdColor].Name
    Read Price; store in AdRates.ColorRates[AdColor].Price
```

Figure 7-29 shows the contents of AdRates, after GetAdPrices initializes it with the values from file ADPRICES.

How does Procedure GetAdPrices fit into the unit we have been describing? The source code of the procedure itself is included in the unit's Implementation section. Because it isn't specified in the Interface section, the user cannot call it. However, it needs to be called once from *somewhere* before any of the other AdRates operations are invoked. We can put the call to GetAdPrices in the unit's *Initialization* section—between the BEGIN and END at the very end of the unit. The unit's initialization section is executed before the beginning of the main program's execution.

Now let's look at the source code for the whole AdRates unit:

```
UNIT AdRates;
  (* Unit that encapsulates the advertising rate information. *)
  (****************************************************************)

INTERFACE
  (****************************************************************)
(** "Public" declarations of constants, types, and variables **)
CONST
  MaxDescription = 40;

TYPE
  AdSizeType  = (FullPage, HalfPage, QuarterPage, EighthPage);
  AdColorType = (NoColor, Red, Blue, Yellow, Green, FullColor);
  DescripType = PACKED ARRAY [1 .. MaxDescription] OF Char;
(**** Exported procedure and function "specifications" *******)
```

Figure 7-29
AdRateTable after
Initialization

AdRateTable			.Price	.Name
.SizeRates	[FullPage]		400	Full Page
	[HalfPage]		250	Half Page
	[QuarterPage]		140	Quarter Page
	[EighthPage]		75	Eighth Page
.ColorRates	[NoColor]		0	No Color
	[Red]		100	1 Extra Color Red
	[Blue]		100	1 Extra Color Blue
	[Yellow]		100	1 Extra Color Yellow
	[Green]		100	1 Extra Color Green
	[FullColor]		325	Four Color Processing

```
PROCEDURE GetSizeRate
  (AdSize        : AdSizeType;
   VAR SizeRate : Integer);

  (* Function:      Retrieve the rate for an ad of AdSize. *)
  (* Preconditions: None.                                  *)
  (* Postconditions: SizeRate = price for ad of AdSize.    *)

PROCEDURE GetColorRate
  (AdColor        : AdColorType;
   VAR ColorRate : Integer);

  (* Function:      Retrieve the rate for an ad of AdColor.*)
  (* Preconditions: None.                                  *)
  (* Postconditions: ColorRate = price for an ad of AdColor.*)

PROCEDURE GetSizeName
  (AdSize        : AdSizeType;
   VAR SizeName : DescripType);

  (* Function:      Retrieve the string describing AdSize. *)
  (* Preconditions: None.                                  *)
  (* Postconditions: SizeName = string describing AdSize.  *)

PROCEDURE GetColorName
  (AdColor        : AdColorType;
   VAR ColorName : DescripType);

  (* Function:      Retrieve the string describing AdColor.*)
  (* Preconditions: None.                                  *)
  (* Postconditions: ColorName = string describing AdColor. *)
```

```pascal
(*************************************************************)
IMPLEMENTATION
(*************************************************************)
(* "Private" declarations of constants, types, variables *)
TYPE
  RateInfoType = RECORD
    Price      : Integer;
    Name       : DescripType
  END; (* RateInfoType *)

  AdRatesType  = RECORD
    SizeRates  : ARRAY [AdSizeType]  OF RateInfoType;
    ColorRates : ARRAY [AdColorType] OF RateInfoType
  END; (* AdRatesType *)

VAR
  AdRateTable : AdRatesType;

(*********** Internal Procedures and Functions  ***********)
PROCEDURE GetAdRates;

  (* Read the ad rates from the ADPRICES text file, and *)
  (* store in AdRateTable.                              *)

VAR
  RatesFile : Text;          (* file that contains rate info *)
  AdSize    : AdSizeType;    (* loop control variable        *)
  AdColor   : AdColorType;   (* loop control variable        *)
  Index     : Integer;       (* index into string            *)

BEGIN (* GetAdRates *)

  Assign (RatesFile, 'ADPRICES');   (**** Turbo Pascal code ****)
  Reset  (RatesFile);

  (* Read ad rates from RatesFile. File format: *)
  (*   Col  1 - 40: Name (e.g., 'Full Page')    *)
  (*   Col 41 - 43: Rate (Integer).             *)
  WITH AdRateTable DO
    BEGIN

      (* Read all the size names/prices from the file. *)
      FOR AdSize := FullPage TO EighthPage DO
        BEGIN
          FOR Index := 1 TO MaxDescription DO
            Read (RatesFile, SizeRates[AdSize].Name[Index]);
          Readln (RatesFile, SizeRates[AdSize].Price)
        END; (* FOR AdSize *)
```

```
            (* Read the color names/prices from the file. *)
          FOR AdColor := NoColor TO FullColor DO
            BEGIN
              FOR Index := 1 TO MaxDescription DO
                Read (RatesFile, ColorRates[AdColor].Name[Index]);
                Readln (RatesFile, ColorRates[AdColor].Price)
            END (* FOR AdColor *)
      END; (* WITH *)
    (* Close the RatesFile. *)
    Close (RatesFile)          (**** Turbo Pascal code ****)
  END;  (* GetAdRates *)
(*************************************************************)
(*    Implementations of Exported Procedures and Functions    *)
(*************************************************************)
PROCEDURE GetSizeRate
  (AdSize        : AdSizeType;
   VAR SizeRate : Integer);

BEGIN (* GetSizeRate *)
  SizeRate := AdRateTable.SizeRates[AdSize].Price
END;  (* GetSizeRate *)
(*************************************************************)

PROCEDURE GetSizeName
  (AdSize        : AdSizeType;
   VAR SizeName : DescripType);

BEGIN (* GetSizeName *)
  SizeName := AdRateTable.SizeRates[AdSize].Name
END;  (* GetSizeName *)
(*************************************************************)

PROCEDURE GetColorRate
  (AdColor        : AdColorType;
   VAR ColorRate : Integer);

BEGIN (* GetColorRate *)
  ColorRate := AdRateTable.ColorRates[AdColor].Price
END;  (* GetColorRate *)
(*************************************************************)

PROCEDURE GetColorName
  (AdColor        : AdColorType;
   VAR ColorName : DescripType);

BEGIN (* GetColorName *)
  ColorName := AdRateTable.ColorRates[AdColor].Name
END;  (* GetColorName *)
```

```
(****************** Initialization Section ******************)

BEGIN (* Unit AdRates *)

  (* Initialize AdRateTable with values from file. *)
  GetAdRates

END. (* Unit AdRates *)
```

The source code for this unit is listed in file ADRATES.PAS.

Using the Unit

How does Program AdManager use this unit? It does not include its source code with the Include compiler directive that we discussed in Chapter 5. The source code for a unit is kept in its own text file. Before it is used, the unit must first be compiled to disk. The compiler generates the unit's object code into a special file called a **.TPU** (**T**urbo **P**ascal **U**nit) file. For instance, for the AdRates unit, the compiler would generate a file called ADRATES.TPU. Now we merely have to put a USES statement at the beginning of Program AdManager, immediately after the PROGRAM statement:

```
PROGRAM AdManager (Input, Output, AdFile, Bills);
  USES ADRATES;
```

Following the USES statement, Program AdManager can use any constant, type, or procedure declared in the Interface section of Unit AdRates. When Program AdManager is compiled, the ADRATES.TPU provides all the information exported from the AdRates ADT. If this program tries to use any declarations from the Implementation section of the AdRates unit, however, a compilation error occurs. To Program AdManager, it is as if the declarations in the Implementation section of the unit do not even exist.

At run-time, when Program AdManager is loaded into memory, the unit's initialization section (the call to GetAdRates) is executed before the first statement of the main program.

Other ADTs from this program (e.g., the AdList and CommandTable ADTs) can be reimplemented as Turbo Pascal units, using the approach illustrated here. We leave this modification as a programming assignment.

■ *Exercises**

1. Complete the List ADT operations for the circular link list in this chapter: CreateList, EmptyList, FullList, DestroyList, RetrieveElement, ModifyElement.

2. Implement the FIFO Queue ADT as a circular linked list, with the external pointer accessing the "rear" node of the queue.

3. Write a procedure PrintReverse that takes a pointer to the first element in a circular singly linked list and prints out the elements in reverse order. For instance, for the following list, PrintReverse(List) would output 'ZYX'. (Hint: Use a stack of pointers. You may assume that all of the specified stack operations have already been written.)

*Question with italicized numbers are answered in the back of the book.

4. Choose appropriate minimum and maximum values for a header and trailer node in a list of employee records. The list is ordered with respect to a 4-digit unique employee ID number.

5. Write a procedure to merge two lists of school club members. Since many students may belong to both clubs, duplicate names need to be eliminated in the merge process. The lists are represented as linear linked lists with headers and trailers; the Key field in the Info part of each node is the student name, declared as a PACKED ARRAY[1.20] OF Char. Use the following specification:

MergeLists

Function:	Merge List1 and List2 to produce NewList.
Input:	List1, List2 (ListType)
Preconditions:	List1 and List2 point to ordered linked lists with header and trailer nodes containing MinKey and MaxKey respectively. NewList is undefined.
Output:	List1, List2, NewList (ListType)
Postconditions:	NewList points to a list containing all the elements of List1 and List2, with no duplicate keys. (If there were elements with the same key in List1 and List2, the element from List1 should be used.) List1 and List2 are empty.

6. (a) Write a procedure, PrintReverse, which inputs the external pointer to a singly linked list and prints the elements in reverse order, using the following approach: Traverse the list from first to last node, reversing the direction of each Next pointer, as illustrated below:

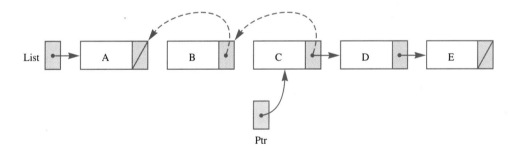

When you reach the end of the list, you have a linked list whose elements are in the reverse order from the original list. Now traverse this list, processing each element by printing the element and re-inverting its Next pointer, as illustrated below:

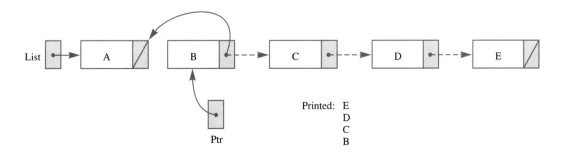

When you reach the (original) beginning of the list, the whole list is printed in reverse order, and the links are back to their original values.

(b) Describe the order of this algorithm. How many times is each node accessed?

7. A list is implemented as a circular singly linked list, with a header node containing an impossibly small value. The node accessed by the external pointer List is considered the "current" node in the list.

(a) Write Procedure ResetList, which takes the List pointer and advances it to access the first node in the list (the one following the header node).

(b) Write Procedure GetCurrentElement, which takes the List pointer and returns both the node's Info part and a Boolean flag indicating whether the end of the list was reached (i.e., if the current node is the header). This procedure should also advance the List pointer to access the node that succeeds the current node, leaving the list ready for another call to GetCurrentElement to retrieve the next element.

(c) Write Procedure PrintListElements, which uses ResetList and GetCurrentElement to access the list data. Procedure PrintInfo is available to print out the Info part of one node; it takes one parameter of type ListElementType.

8. Using the circular doubly linked list below, give the expression corresponding to each of the following descriptions.

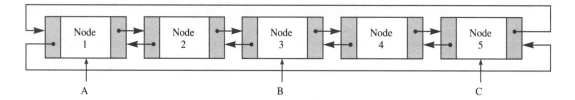

(For example, the expression for the Info field of Node 1, referenced from pointer A, would be A^.Info.)

(a) The Info field of Node 1, referenced from pointer C
(b) The Info field of Node 2, referenced from pointer B
(c) The Next field of Node 2, referenced from pointer A
(d) The Next field of Node 4, referenced from pointer C
(e) Node 1, referenced from pointer B
(f) The Back field of Node 4, referenced from pointer C
(g) The Back field of Node 1, referenced from pointer A

Use the declarations of a doubly linked list below to answer Exercises 9 to 13:

```
TYPE
   StringType = PACKED ARRAY[1 .. 20] OF Char;

   ListElementType = RECORD
     Name : StringType;
      ID   : Integer
   END;  (* ListElementType *)

   DblPtrType = ^NodeType;
```

```
NodeType = RECORD
  Info   : ListElementType; (* the user's data          *)
  Next   : PointerType;      (* accesses next node       *)
  Back   : PointerType       (* accesses preceding node *)
END;   (* NodeType *)
DblListType = DblPtrType;
```

```
VAR
  List : DblListType;
```

9. Identify the type of each of the following expressions as a pointer, a record, a character, a character string, or an integer.
   (a) `List^.Next`
   (b) `List^.Next^`
   (c) `List^.Info.Name`
   (d) `Ptr^.Back^.Info.ID`
   (e) `Ptr^.Back`
   (f) `Ptr^.Info.Name[1]`

10. Write Procedure InsertElement, using the declarations above and the List ADT specifications in Chapter 6, assuming that the doubly linked list does not contain a header or trailer node.

11. Write Procedure DeleteElement, using the declarations above and the List ADT specification in Chapter 6, assuming that the doubly linked list does not contain a header or trailer node.

12. Write Procedure DoubleLink, which takes a singly linked list and creates a linear doubly linked list containing the same elements. You should dispose the nodes of the singly linked list. (Use the declarations above for the doubly linked list, and the declarations of ListType in Chapter 6 to represent the singly linked list.)

13. Under what circumstances will the following code segments have the same effect and under what circumstances will they have different effects? What preconditions, if any, are needed for each?

```
(* Print the list backwards. Ptr accesses the last *)
(* element in the list.                            *)

Segment 1:
WHILE Ptr <> NIL DO
  BEGIN
    Writeln (Ptr^.Info);
    Ptr := Ptr^.Back
  END; (* WHILE *)

Segment 2:
REPEAT
  Writeln(Ptr^.Info);
  Ptr := Ptr^.Back
UNTIL Ptr = NIL;
```

14. A text file contains integer elements, one per line, ordered from smallest to largest. You must read the elements from the file and create an ordered linked list containing the values:

```
WHILE NOT EOF (DataFile) DO
  BEGIN
    (* Get a number from the file *)
    Readln (DataFile, Val);

    (* Add the number to the list *)
    InsertElement (List, Val)
  END; (* WHILE *)
```

You can use the regular InsertElement procedure from Chapter 6, but it seems like a waste of time to traverse the whole list looking for the insertion point, because you know that you'll always be inserting at the end of the list. You decide to use a circular (singly) linked list, with the external pointer List accessing the last element. Write a procedure InsertLast that takes the List pointer and a value and adds the value to the end of the list.

15. The InsertElement in the List ADT is to be modified to perform a *conditional insertion*. The insertion is only to be made if an element with the same key is not already in the list. A Boolean output parameter, ElementExists, is set to indicate if the element is already in the list on entrance to this procedure.
    (a) Modify the specifications of InsertElement.
    (b) Modify the InsertElement procedure for a circular linked list whose external pointer accesses the element with the largest key.
    (c) Modify the InsertElement procedure for a doubly linked list with a header and trailer node.

16. The DeleteElement in the List ADT is to be modified to perform a *conditional deletion*. The deletion is only to be made if an element with the specified key is in the list. A Boolean output parameter, NotInList, is set to indicate if the element is not in the list on entrance to this procedure.
    (a) Modify the specifications of DeleteElement.
    (b) Modify the DeleteElement procedure for a circular linked list whose external pointer accesses the element with the largest key.
    (c) Modify the DeleteElement procedure for a doubly linked list with a header and trailer node.

List

Nodes	.Info	.Next
[1]	12	0
[2]	19	5
[3]	8	2
[4]	6	10
[5]	14	1
[6]	32	7
[7]	67	9
[8]	95	0
[9]	68	8
[10]	11	6

Start 4

Free 3

17. Use the linked list contained in the array pictured below to answer the following questions.
  (a) What elements are in the list?
  (b) What array positions are part of the free-space list?
  (c) What would the array look like after deletion of 68?
  (d) What would the array look like after insertion of 17?

18. An array of records is used to contain a doubly linked list, with the Next and Back fields indicating the index of the linked nodes in each direction.
  (a) Show how the array would look after it was initialized to an empty state, with all the nodes linked into the free-space list. (Note that the free nodes only have to be linked in one direction.)

List

Nodes	.Info	.Next	.Back
[1]			
[2]			
[3]			
[4]			
[5]			
[6]			
[7]			
[8]			
[9]			
[10]			

Start ☐
Free ☐

  (b) Fill in the contents of the array after the following numbers have been inserted into their proper places in the doubly linked list: 17, 4, 25.

List

Nodes	.Info	.Next	.Back
[1]			
[2]			
[3]			
[4]			
[5]			
[6]			
[7]			
[8]			
[9]			
[10]			

Start ☐
Free ☐

(c) Show how the array in part (b) would look after 17 was deleted.

List

Nodes   .Info .Next .Back

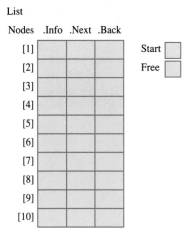

19. Complete the implementation of the linked list stored in an array of records by coding FindElement, InsertElement, DeleteElement, ModifyElement, and RetrieveElement operations.

20. (a) Using a linked list implemented in an array of records to contain the queue elements, rewrite the FIFO queue declarations and the operations specified in Chapter 5.
    (b) Should and/or can you implement a FullQueue operation using this linked implementation?

21. Type BigInteger is implemented with the following declarations:

```
TYPE
    PointerType = ^NodeType;
    NodeType    = RECORD
        Digit   : 0 .. 9;
        Next    : PointerType
    END; (* NodeType *)

BigInteger = PointerType;
    (* digits are stored in reverse order *)
```

The digits are stored in a BigInteger linked list in reverse order; for example: the number 567890 is represented by the following list:

(a) Write a procedure that "adds" two inputs of BigInteger type, and returns a third BigInteger list.
(b) Write a procedure that inputs two BigInteger lists and "subtracts" the second from the first, returning a third BigInteger list.
(c) Write a procedure that prints the digits of a BigInteger input parameter in the correct order.

22. A line editor is represented by a doubly linked list of nodes, each of which contain an 80-column line of text (LineType). There is one external pointer (LinePtrType) to this list, which points to the "current" line position in the text being edited. The list has a header node, which contains the string:

    '----Top of File----'

    and a trailer node, which contains the string:

    '----Bottom of File----'.

    (a) Draw a sketch of this data structure.
    (b) Write the TYPE declarations to support this data structure. (Be sure to include constants for the header and trailer node values.)
    (c) Code the CreateList operation, which sets up the header and trailer nodes.
    (d) Code the following operations on this structure:

```
PROCEDURE GoToTop
   (VAR LinePtr : LinePtrType);
   (* LinePtr is set to access "first" line. *)
PROCEDURE GoToBottom
   (VAR LinePtr : LinePtrType);
   (* LinePtr is set to access "last" line. *)
```

    (e) Describe GoToTop and GoToBottom in terms of Big-O. How could the list be changed to make these operations O(1)?
    (f) Code the InsertLine operation, using the following heading:

```
PROCEDURE InsertLine
   (LinePtr : LinePtrType;
   NewLine : LineType);
   (* Insert NewLine after the "current" line. *)
```

    (g) Why is it not necessary to make LinePtr a VAR parameter? Will this procedure work when inserting the first text line?
    (h) Code the PrintText operation, using the following procedure heading:

```
PROCEDURE PrintText
   (LinePtr : LinePtrType);
   (* Print all the lines from "first" to "last." *)
```

    (i) After the call, *PrintText (TextLine),* which node does TextLine access?

Exercises 23 to 28 refer to the application section at the end of this chapter.

23. List the components of the Interface section of a Turbo Pascal unit. List the components of the Implementation section.

24. What is the purpose of the initialization section of a Turbo Pascal unit?

25. True or False? If False, correct the statement.
    (a) The following statement, if placed in Procedure ProcessAccount, would cause a run-time error:

```
Writeln ('Price=', AdRateTable.SizeRates[AdSize].Price);
```

    (b) The following statement, if placed in Procedure ProcessAccount, would cause a compile-time error:

```
Writeln (MaxDescription);
```

(c) The unit must be in a separate file from the program that uses it.

(d) The main advantage to implementing the AdRates ADT as a unit, instead of including the declarations and procedures in Program AdManager, is the efficiency of execution.

(e) To use the exported types and interfaces from the AdRates unit, you must "include" the source code for the unit into the main program with the Include ($I) compiler directive.

(f) You can put variables that are "global" to the unit in the unit's Interface section.

26. Since Marc only uses the BillAdvertisers command once a month, the AdRateTable only needs to be initialized when billing is about to take place. You decide to put the call to GetAdRates at the beginning of the GenerateBills procedure. How must the unit be modified to support this change?

27. There is an input operation in Program AdManager which has the potential for a run-time error if the user makes a typographical error. Identify the operation. Describe how this operation could be modified to make it error-proof.

28. (Turbo Pascal) The CommandTable ADT is to be reimplemented as a Turbo Pascal unit. The CommandTable should be "global" data to the unit; that is, it should be a variable declared in the unit's Implementation section.

(a) Implement the unit. (CommandTable should not be seen on the parameter lists of the operations in this unit.)

(b) What changes must be made to the AdManager program to replace the CommandTable declarations and operations with the use of the unit?

(c) Describe how the use of this unit could enforce data encapsulation of the CommandTable data structure.

Programming with Recursion

GOALS

- To be able to do the following, given a recursive routine:
    determine whether the routine will halt,
    determine the base case(s),
    determine the general case(s),
    determine what the routine does,
    determine whether the routine is correct and, if it is not, correct it.

- To be able to do the following, given a simple recursive problem:
    determine the base case(s),
    determine the general case(s),
    design and code the solution as a recursive procedure or function.

- To be able to verify a recursive routine, according to the Three-Question Method.

- To be able to decide whether a recursive solution is appropriate for a problem.

- To be able to compare and contrast dynamic storage allocation and static storage allocation in relation to using recursion.

- To be able to explain how recursion works internally by showing the contents of the run-time stack.

- To be able to replace a recursive solution with iteration and/or the use of a stack.

- To be able to explain why recursion may or may not be a good choice to implement the solution of a problem.

"Don't Ever Do This!"

As a beginning programmer, you may have been told never to use a function name within the function on the right-hand side of an assignment statement, as in the following code segment:

```
FUNCTION Sum : Integer;

  (* Sums five integers from the input stream. *)

VAR
  Count  : Integer;   (* loop control variable  *)
  Number : Integer;   (* number read from input *)
BEGIN  (* Sum *)

  Sum := 0;
  FOR Count := 1 TO 5 DO
    BEGIN
      Read (Number);
      Sum := Sum + Number
    END  (* FOR *)
END;  (* Sum *)
```

You were probably told that using a function name as in the statement, Sum := Sum + Number, would cause something mysterious and undesirable to occur—the function would call itself *recursively.* If we tried to execute

```
Sum := Sum + Number;
```

the Sum on the *right*-hand side of the assignment would cause Function Sum to start again through a recursive call. In this case the recursive call is inadvertent; we should have calculated the sum with a local variable, which would be assigned to Sum at the end of the function. But there are many situations in which recursion is used on purpose, as a programming tool.

Recursion is a very powerful programming technique that can be used in place of iteration (loops). It involves a different way of looking at repetitive actions, by allowing a subprogram to call itself to solve a "smaller" version of its original problem. In this chapter we will explore how to understand and write recursive functions and procedures. We will also look at how recursion works in a high-level language such as Pascal, as well as the factors to consider in choosing an iterative or a recursive solution to a problem.

The Classic Example of Recursion

Mathematicians often define concepts in terms of the process used to generate them. For instance, *n*! (read "n factorial") is used to calculate the number of permutations of *n* elements. One mathematical description of *n*! is

$$n! = \begin{cases} 1, & \text{if } n = 0 \\ n * (n - 1) * (n - 2) * \cdots * 1, & \text{if } n > 0 \end{cases}$$

Consider the case of 4!. Because *n* > 0, we use the second part of the definition:

4! = 4 * 3 * 2 * 1 = 24

This description of N! provides a different definition for each value of *n,* for the three dots stand in for the intermediate factors. That is, the definition of 2! is 2 * 1, the definition of 3! is 3 * 2 * 1, and so forth.

We can also express *n*! with a single definition for any nonnegative value of *n*:

$$n! = \begin{cases} 1, & \text{if } n = 0 \\ n * (n - 1)!, & \text{if } n > 0 \end{cases}$$

This definition is *recursive,* because we express the factorial function in terms of itself.

Let's consider the recursive calculation of 4! intuitively. Because 4 is not equal to 0, we use the second half of the definition:

4! = 4 * (4 − 1)! = 4 * 3!

Of course, we can't do the multiplication yet, because we don't know the value of 3!. So we call up our good friend Sue Ann, who has a Ph.D. in math, to find the value of 3!.

Sue Ann has the same formula we have for calculating the factorial function, so she knows that

3! = 3 * (3 − 1)! = 3 * 2!

She doesn't know the value of 2!, however, so she puts you on hold and calls up her friend Max, who has an M.S. in math.

Max has the same formula Sue Ann has, so he quickly calculates that

$$2! = 2 * (2 - 1)! = 2 * 1!$$

But Max can't complete the multiplication because he doesn't know the value of 1! He puts Sue Ann on hold and calls up his mother, who has a B.A. in math education.

Max's mother has the same formula Max has, so she quickly figures out that

$$1! = 1 * (1 - 1)! = 1 * 0!$$

Of course, she can't perform the multiplication, because she doesn't have the value of 0!. So Mom puts Max on hold and calls up her colleague Bernie, who has a B.A. in English literature.

Bernie doesn't need to know any math to figure out that $0! = 1$ because he can read that information in the first clause of the formula ($n! = 1$, if $n = 0$). He reports the answer immediately to Max's mother. She can now complete her calculations:

$$1! = 1 * 0! = 1 * 1 = 1.$$

She reports back to Max, who now performs the multiplication in his formula and learns that

$$2! = 2 * 1! = 2 * 1 = 2.$$

He reports back to Sue Ann, who can now finish her calculation:

$$3! = 3 * 2! = 3 * 2 = 6.$$

Sue Ann calls you with this exciting bit of information. You can now complete your calculation:

$$4! = 4 * 3! = 4 * 6 = 24.$$

Programming Recursively

Of course, the use of recursion is not limited to mathematicians with telephones. Computer languages such as Pascal that support recursion give the programmer a powerful tool for solving certain kinds of problems by reducing the complexity or hiding the details of the problem.

We will consider recursive solutions to several simple problems. In our initial discussion, you may wonder why a recursive solution would ever be preferred to an iterative, or nonrecursive one, for the iterative solution may seem simpler and more efficient. Don't worry. There are, as you will see later, situations in which the use of recursion produces a much simpler—and more elegant—program.

Coding the Factorial Function

A recursive function or procedure is one that calls itself. In the previous section Sue Ann, Max, Max's mom, and Bernie all had the same formula for solving the factorial function. When we construct a recursive Pascal function NFact for solving $n!$, we know where we can get the value of $(n - 1)!$ that we need in the formula. We already have a function for doing this calculation: NFact. Of course, the actual parameter $(N - 1)$ in the recursive call will be different from the parameter in the original call (N). (The recursive call is the one within the function.) As we will see, this is an important and necessary consideration.

A Pascal function for calculating $n!$ for a nonnegative integer N may be coded as follows. NonNegative is a subrange (TYPE NonNegative = 0 .. MaxInt) because the factorial function is only defined for values greater than or equal to zero.

Walkthrough of NFact (4)

Line	Action
1	$4 <> 0$, so skip to ELSE clause.
3	NFact := 4 * NFact $(4 - 1)$
	First recursive call returns us to the beginning of the function, with $N = 3$.
1	$3 <> 0$, so skip to ELSE clause.
3	NFact := 3 * NFact $(3 - 1)$
	Second recursive call returns us to the beginning of the function, with $N = 2$.
1	$2 <> 0$, so skip to ELSE clause.
3	NFact := 2 * NFact $(2 - 1)$
	Third recursive call returns us to the beginning of the function, with $N = 1$.
1	$1 <> 0$, so skip to ELSE clause.
3	NFact := 1 * NFact $(1 - 1)$
	Fourth recursive call returns us to the beginning of the function, with $N = 0$.
1	$0 = 0$, so go to line 2.
2	NFact := 1
	The value of NFact (0) is returned to the calling statement, the fourth recursive call.
3	NFact := 1 * NFact $(0) = 1 * 1 = 1$
	The value of NFact (1) is returned to the calling statement, the third recursive call.
3	NFact := 2 * NFact $(1) = 2 * 1 = 2$
	The value of NFact (2) is returned to the calling statement, the second recursive call.
3	NFact := 3 * NFact $(2) = 3 * 2 = 6$
	The value of NFact (3) is returned to the calling statement, the first recursive call.
3	NFact := 4 * NFact $(3) = 4 * 6 = 24$
	The function now returns a value of 24 to the original calling statement—for example, Writeln (NFact (4)).

```
FUNCTION NFact
  (N : NonNegative) : NonNegative;

  (* Calculates the value of N! recursively. *)
BEGIN   (* NFact *)
  IF N = 0                              (* line 1 *)
    THEN NFact := 1                     (* line 2 *)
    ELSE NFact := N * NFact (N - 1)     (* line 3 *)
END;  (* NFact *)
```

Notice the two uses of NFact in line 3. On the left side of the assignment statement, NFact is the function name receiving a value. This use is the one that you are accustomed to seeing. On the right side of the assignment statement, NFact is a recursive call to the function, with the parameter N − 1.

Let's walk through the calculation of 4! using function NFact. The original value of N is 4. The steps in the calculation are shown in the preceding table.

For purposes of comparison, let's look at the recursive and iterative solutions to this problem side by side:

```
FUNCTION NFact
  (N : NonNegative) : NonNegative;

  (* Calculates the value of N! *)

(* iterative *)                    (* recursive *)

VAR                                (* no local variables *)
  Fact    : NonNegative;
  Count   : NonNegative;

BEGIN (* NFact - iterative *)  BEGIN (* NFact - recursive *)
  Fact := 1;                     IF N = 0
  FOR Count := 2 TO N DO           THEN NFact := 1
    Fact := Fact * Count;          ELSE (* N > 0 *)
  NFact := Fact                      NFact := N * NFact (N - 1)
END;    (* NFact *)            END;    (* NFact *)
```

These two versions of NFact illustrate a couple of differences between recursive and iterative functions. First, an iterative algorithm uses a *looping construct* such as the FOR loop (or WHILE or REPEAT .. UNTIL) to control the execution. The recursive solution uses a *branching structure* (IF-THEN-ELSE). The iterative version needs a couple of local variables, whereas the recursive version uses the parameters of the function to provide all its information. Sometimes, as we will see later, the recursive solution needs more parameters than the equivalent iterative one. Data values used in the iterative solution are usually initialized inside the routine, above the loop. Similar data values used in a recursive solution are usually initialized by the choice of parameter values in the initial call to the routine.

Verifying Recursive Procedures and Functions

The kind of walkthrough we did above, to check the validity of a recursive function or procedure, is time consuming, tedious, and often confusing. Furthermore, simulating the execution of NFact (4) tells us that the function works when N = 4, but it doesn't tell us whether the function is valid for *all* nonnegative values of N. It would be useful to have a technique that would help us determine inductively whether a recursive algorithm will work.

The Three-Question Method

We will use the Three-Question Method of verifying recursive procedures and functions. To verify that a recursive solution works, you must be able to answer yes to all three of these questions.

1. *The Base-Case Question:* Is there a nonrecursive way out of the procedure or function, and does the routine work correctly for this "base" case?
2. *The Smaller-Caller Question:* Does each recursive call to the procedure or function involve a smaller case of the original problem, leading inescapably to the base case?
3. *The General-Case Question:* Assuming that the recursive call(s) works correctly, does the whole procedure or function work correctly?

Let's apply these three questions to Function NFact.

1. *The Base-Case Question:* The base case occurs when N = 0. NFact is then assigned a value of 1, which is the correct value of 0!, and no further (recursive) calls to NFact are made. The answer is yes.
2. *The Smaller-Caller Question:* To answer this question we must look at the parameters passed in the recursive call. In Function NFact, the recursive call passes N − 1. Each subsequent recursive call sends a decremented value of the parameter, until the value sent is finally 0. At this point, as we verified with the base-case question above, we have reached the smallest case, and no further recursive calls are made. The answer is yes.
3. *The General-Case Question:* In the case of a function like NFact, we need to verify that the formula we are using will actually result in the correct solution. Assuming that the recursive call NFact (N − 1) will give us the correct value of $(n − 1)!$, we get the assignment of N * (N − 1)! to NFact. This is the definition of a factorial, so we know that the function works for all positive integers. In answering the first question, we have already ascertained that the function works for N = 0. (The function is defined only for nonnegative integers.) So the answer is yes.

Those of you who are familiar with *inductive proofs* will recognize what we have done. Having made the assumption that the function will work for some base case $(n - 1)$, we can now show that applying the function to the next value, $(n - 1) + 1$, or n, results in the correct formula for calculating $n!$.

Writing Recursive Procedures and Functions

The questions used for verifying recursive procedures and functions can also be used as a guide for *writing* recursive subprograms. You can use the following approach to write any recursive routine:

- First, get an exact definition of the problem to be solved. (This, of course, is the first step in solving any programming problem.)
- Next, determine the *size* of the problem to be solved on this call to the subprogram. On the initial call to the procedure or function, the size of the whole problem will be expressed in the value(s) of the parameter(s).
- Third, identify and solve the *base case(s)* in which the problem can be expressed nonrecursively. This will assure a yes answer to the base-case question.
- Last, identify and solve the *general case(s)* correctly in terms of a smaller case of the same problem—a recursive call. This will assure yes answers to the smaller-caller and general-case questions.

In the case of NFact, the definition of the problem is summarized in the definition of the factorial function. The size of the problem is the number of values to be multiplied: N. The base case occurs when N = 0, in which case we take the nonrecursive path. Finally, the general case occurs when N > 0, resulting in a recursive call to NFact for a smaller case: NFact (N − 1).

Writing a Boolean Function

Let's apply this approach to writing a function, ValueInList, that searches for a value in a list and returns a Boolean flag indicating whether the value was found. List is declared as an ARRAY [1..MaxList] OF ValueType. The recursive solution to this problem is as follows:

ValueInList ← (Value is in the first position?) OR
           (Value is in the rest of the array?)

We can answer the first question just by comparing Value to List[1]. But how do we know whether Value is in the rest of the array? If only we had a function that would search the rest of the array. *But we do have one!* Function ValueInList searches for a value in an array. We simply need to start searching List at the second position, instead of the first (a smaller case). To do this, we need to pass the search starting place to ValueInList as a parameter. We also need to know where the end of the list is so that we can stop searching if the value isn't there. Thus we will use the following procedure specification:

ValueInList (List, Value, StartIndex, EndIndex) Returns Boolean

Function:	Searches List for Value between StartIndex and EndIndex.
Input:	List (ListType) Value (ValueType) StartIndex, EndIndex (Integer)
Preconditions:	List[StartIndex] .. List[EndIndex] contains values.
Output:	ValueInList (Boolean)
Postconditions:	ValueInList = (Value exists in List[StartIndex] .. List[EndIndex])

To search the whole list, we would invoke the function with the statement

```
IF ValueInList (List, Value, 1, MaxList)
   THEN . . .
```

The general case of this algorithm is the part that searches the rest of the list. This case will involve a recursive call to ValueInList, specifying a smaller part of the array to be searched:

```
ValueInList := ValueInList (List, Value, StartIndex + 1,
   EndIndex);
```

By incrementing StartIndex, we have effectively diminished the size of the problem to be solved by the recursive call. That is, searching the array from StartIndex + 1 to EndIndex is a smaller task than searching from StartIndex to EndIndex. Figure 8-1 shows Function ValueInList frozen in midexecution.

Finally, we need to know when to stop searching. In this problem we have two base cases: (1) when the value is found (return True), and (2) when we have reached the end of the list without finding the value (return False). In either case we can stop making recursive invocations to ValueInList.

Let's summarize what we have discussed and then write Function ValueInList.

Figure 8-1
Function ValueIn-
List in
Midexecution

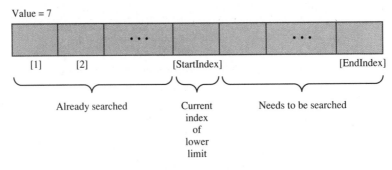

Function ValueInList

Definition:	Search List for Value. Return True if Value is found; return False otherwise.
Size:	The number of slots to search in List[StartIndex] .. List[EndIndex].
Base Cases:	(1) If List[StartIndex] = Value, ValueInList ← True.
	(2) If StartIndex = EndIndex (whole list has been searched) and List[StartIndex] <> Value, ValueInList ← False.
General Case:	Search the rest of the list for Value. This is a recursive invocation of ValueInList with StartIndex incremented (smaller caller).

The code for Function ValueInList is given below.

```
FUNCTION ValueInList
  (List       : ListType;
   Value      : ValueType;
   StartIndex : Integer;
   EndIndex   : Integer)  : Boolean;

  (* ValueInList is True if Value is found within the index *)
  (* range StartIndex to EndIndex; otherwise it is False.   *)
BEGIN (* ValueInList *)

  IF List[StartIndex] = Value
    THEN (* Base Case 1: Value found *)
      ValueInList := True
    ELSE
      IF StartIndex = EndIndex
        THEN (* Base Case 2: Value not in list *)
          ValueInList := False
        ELSE (* General Case: search the rest of List *)
          ValueInList := (* this is the recursive call: *)
            ValueInList (List, Value, StartIndex + 1, EndIndex)
END; (* ValueInList *)
```

Note that it is the parameter StartIndex that acts as a counter index through the array; it is initialized in the original invocation of ValueInList and incremented on each recursive call. The equivalent iterative solution would use a local counter, initialized inside the function above the loop and incremented by an assignment statement inside the loop.

Use the Three-Question Method to verify this function yourself.

Using Recursion to Simplify Solutions

So far the examples we have looked at could just as easily (or more easily) have been written as iterative routines. At the end of the chapter, we will talk more about choosing between iterative and recursive solutions. There are many problems, however, in which using recursion simplifies the solution.

The first problem we will look at is a function, Combinations, that tells us how many combinations of a certain size can be made out of a total group of elements. For instance, if we have twenty different books to pass out to four students, we can easily see that—to be equitable—we should give each student five books. But how many combinations of five books can be made out of a group of twenty books?

There is a mathematical formula that can be used for solving this problem. Given that C is the total number of combinations, Group is the total size of the group to pick from, Members is the size of each subgroup, and Group $>=$ Members,

$$C\ (Group,\ Members)\ =$$

$$\begin{cases} Group, & \text{if Members} = 1 \\ 1, & \text{if Members} = Group \\ C\ (Group\ -\ 1,\ Members\ -\ 1)\ +\ C(Group\ -\ 1,\ Members), & \text{if Group} > Members > 1 \end{cases}$$

Because this definition of Combinations is recursive, it is easy to see how a recursive function could be used to solve the problem.

Let's summarize our problem.

■ Function Combinations

Definition: Calculate how many combinations of Members size can be made from the total Group size.

Size: Size of Group, Members.

Base Cases: (1) If Members = 1, Combinations ← Group
(2) If Members = Group, Combinations ← 1

General Case: If Group > Members > 1, Combinations ←
Combinations (Group − 1, Members − 1) +
Combinations (Group − 1, Members).

The resulting recursive function, Combinations, is listed below. (PosInteger is declared as a subrange type that includes the integers from 1 .. MaxInt).

```
FUNCTION Combinations
  (Group, Members : PosInteger) : PosInteger;

  (* Returns the number of combinations of Members size *)
  (* that can be constructed from the total Group size. *)
```

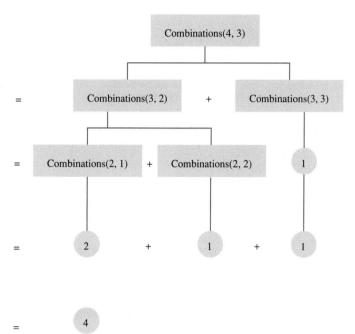

Figure 8-2
Calculating
Combinations (4, 3)

```
BEGIN (* Combinations *)

  IF Members = 1
    THEN (* Base Case 1 *)
      Combinations := Group
    ELSE
      IF Members = Group
        THEN (* Base Case 2 *)
          Combinations := 1
        ELSE (* General Case *)
          Combinations := Combinations (Group - 1, Members - 1)
                        + Combinations (Group - 1, Members)
END;  (* Combinations *)
```

The processing of this function to calculate the number of combinations of three elements that can be made from a set of four is shown in Figure 8-2.

Returning to our original problem, we can now find out how many combinations of five books can be made from the original set of twenty books with the statement

```
Writeln ('Number of combinations = ', Combinations (20, 5));
```

Writing a recursive solution to a problem that is characterized by a recursive definition, like Combinations or NFact above, is fairly straightforward.

Recursive List Processing

Let's look next at a different kind of problem, a procedure that prints out the elements in a linked list. The list has been implemented using the following declarations:

```
TYPE
  PointerType = ^NodeType;

  NodeType = RECORD
    Info : Integer;
    Next : PointerType
  END;         (* NodeType *)

  ListType = PointerType;
```

By now you are probably protesting that this task is so simple to accomplish iteratively (WHILE Ptr <> NIL DO) that it does not make any sense to write it recursively. So let's make the task more fun: Print out the elements in the list in *reverse* order. This problem is much more easily and "elegantly" solved recursively.

What is the task to be performed? The algorithm is given below and illustrated in Figure 8-3.

RevPrint

Print out the second through last elements in the list in reverse order.

Then print the first element in the list.

The second part of the task is simple. If List points to the first node in the list, we can print out its contents with the statement Write (List^.Info). The first part of the task— printing out all the other nodes in the list in reverse order—is also simple, because we have a routine that prints out lists in reverse order: We just call Procedure RevPrint recursively. Of course, we have to adjust the parameter somewhat, to RevPrint (List^.Next). This call says "Print, in reverse order, the linked list pointed to by List^.Next." This task in turn is accomplished recursively in two steps:

Figure 8-3   *Recursive RevPrint*

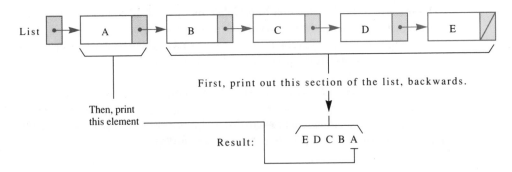

RevPrint the rest of the list (third through last elements).
Then Write the second element in the list.

And of course the first part of this task is accomplished recursively. Where does it all end? We need a base case. We can stop calling RevPrint when we have completed its smallest case: RevPrint-ing a list of one element. Then the value of List^.Next will be NIL, and we can stop making recursive calls. Let's summarize the problem.

Procedure RevPrint

Definition:	Print out the list in reverse order.
Size:	Number of elements in the list pointed to by List
Base Case:	If the list is empty, do nothing.
General Case:	RevPrint the list pointed to by List^.Next, then print List^.Info.

The other recursive routines that we have written have been functions; the RevPrint operation is a procedure.

```
PROCEDURE RevPrint
  (List : ListType);
  (* Prints out the elements in the list in reverse order. *)
  (* This is a recursive solution.                         *)
BEGIN (* RevPrint *)

  IF List <> NIL
    THEN (* General Case *)
      BEGIN
        RevPrint (List^.Next);
        Write (List^.Info)
      END (* General Case *)

    (* ELSE (Base Case) list is empty -- do nothing  *)
END; (* Revprint *)
```

To print out the whole linked list pointed to by DataList, we would use the following procedure call: RevPrint (DataList).
    Let's verify this procedure using the Three-Question Method.

1. *The Base-Case Question:* The base case is implied. When List = NIL, we return to the statement following the last recursive call to RevPrint, and no further recursive calls are made. The answer is yes.
2. *The Smaller-Caller Question:* The recursive call passes the list pointed to by List^.Next, which is one node smaller than the list pointed to by List. The answer is yes.
3. *The General-Case Question:* We assume that RevPrint (List^.Next) correctly prints out the rest of the list in reverse order; this call, followed by the statement printing the value of the first element, gives us the whole list, printed in reverse order. So the answer is yes.

How would you change Procedure RevPrint (in addition to changing its name) to make it print out the list in order?

A Recursive Version of Binary Search

In the application section of Chapter 2, we developed the binary search procedure. Let's review the algorithm:

BinarySearch

Examine the middle element in the list
IF the middle element contains the desired key
    THEN stop searching
    ELSE
        IF the middle element is larger than the desired key
            THEN
                BinarySearch the first half of the list
            ELSE (middle element is smaller than the key)
                BinarySearch the second half of the list

Though the procedure that we wrote in Chapter 2 was iterative, this really is a *recursive algorithm*. The solution is expressed in smaller versions of the original problem: If the answer isn't found in the middle position, BinarySearch (a recursive call) the appropriate half of the list (a smaller problem). Let's summarize the problem:

Procedure BinarySearch

Definition:	Search the list for position of Value.
Size:	The number of elements in List[FromLocation] .. List[ToLocation]
Base Cases:	(1) IF FromLocation > ToLocation, Location ← 0. (2) IF List[MidPoint] = Value, Location ← MidPoint.
General Cases:	(1) IF List[MidPoint] > Value, BinarySearch the first half of list. (2) IF List[MidPoint] < Value, BinarySearch the second half of list.

Here is the recursive version of the procedure:

```
PROCEDURE BinarySearch
   (List         : ArrayType;
    FromLocation : Integer;
    ToLocation   : Integer;
    Value        : ElementType;
    VAR Location : Integer);
```

```
    (* Search List from FromLocation to ToLocation for Value; *)
    (* return Location (an array index) if found, otherwise   *)
    (* return value of 0 in Location.                         *)
VAR
  MidPoint : Integer;  (* index of search area's midpoint   *)
BEGIN (* BinarySearch *)

  IF FromLocation > ToLocation   (* Base Case 1 *)
    THEN Location := 0

    ELSE (* there's more to search *)
      BEGIN

        (* Find middle element in the current search area. *)
        MidPoint := (FromLocation + ToLocation) DIV 2;

        IF List [MidPoint] = Value (* Base Case 2 *)
          THEN Location := MidPoint

        ELSE
          IF List[MidPoint] > Value
            THEN (* General Case 1 *)

              (* BinarySearch first half of the list. *)
              BinarySearch (List, FromLocation,
                MidPoint - 1, Value, Location)

            ELSE (* General Case 2 *)

              (* BinarySearch second half of the list. *)
              BinarySearch (List, MidPoint + 1,
                ToLocation, Value, Location)

      END (* more to search *)
END;  (* BinarySearch *)
```

How does this version of the code compare with the iterative version in Chapter 2? We'll look at the objective measures first: In terms of lines of code, the two procedures are neck-and-neck; the recursive version is only a few lines shorter. The recursive version has one more parameter than the iterative version, since we must input the FromLocation to define the lower bounds of the current search area. The iterative version assumed that the lower bounds was 1. Finally, the iterative version used four local variables, while the recursive version uses only one.

The subjective measure asks: Which procedure is easier to write and to understand? We think that the recursive procedure wins this round—it works the way that we naturally think of the problem: divide and conquer.

The issue of the change in the number of parameters is problematical if we want to replace one version of BinarySearch with another. We would not want to have to change the interface on all the calls to an existing iterative version of the search procedure. How then do we pass the lower bounds to successive calls to the search procedure? It would be better if we kept the interface to BinarySearch as it was specified in Chapter

2, and rename the recursive version shown above to BinSearch. Then we could simply code the BinarySearch procedure to make a call to the recursive BinSearch procedure.

A final issue in the implementation of this procedure involves the List parameter. List is not changed by the BinarySearch procedure, as it is logically an input parameter. However, passing a *copy* of a large structure to a procedure is a poor idea, so we will make List a VAR parameter. As usual, decisions like this one should be documented with a comment. As explained in the following sections, passing large structures as VAR parameters is an especially important consideration when dealing with a recursive implementation, where the initial call to a procedure may hide many levels of recursive calls.

```
PROCEDURE BinarySearch
   (VAR List       : ArrayType;
    NumElements    : Integer;
    Value          : ElementType;
    VAR Location : Integer);
   (* Search List for Value; return its Location, if found, or *)
   (* Location of 0, if not found. NOTE: List is passed as a   *)
   (* VAR parameter because of its size and is not modified by *)
   (* this procedure.                                          *)
BEGIN (* BinarySearch *)
   (* Call recursive binary search procedure. *)
   BinSearch
     (List,          (* list to search *)
      1,             (* FromLocation   *)
      NumElements,   (* ToLocation     *)
      Value,         (* search value   *)
      Location)      (* location found *)
END; (* BinarySearch *)
```

Using this procedure, the interface to calls to BinarySearch does not have to be changed.

How Recursion Works

In order to understand how recursion works and why some programming languages allow it and some do not, we will have to take a detour and look at how languages associate places in memory with variable names. The association of a memory address with a variable name is called **binding**. The point in the compile/execute cycle when binding occurs is called the **binding time**. We want to stress that binding time refers to a point of time in a process, not the amount of clock time that it takes to bind a variable.

Programming languages are usually classified as having either static storage allocation or dynamic storage allocation. Static storage allocation associates variables with memory locations at compile time; dynamic storage allocation associates variables with memory locations at execution time. We know from our discussion of pointer variables that Pascal is a language that supports dynamic storage allocation. As we look at how static and dynamic storage allocation work, consider the following question: *When are the parameters of a procedure bound to a particular address in memory?* The answer to this question tells something about whether recursion can be supported.

Static Storage Allocation

As a program is being translated, the compiler creates a table called a **symbol table**. When a variable is declared, it is entered into the symbol table, and a memory location—an address—is assigned to it. For example, let's see how the compiler would translate the following Pascal declarations:

```
VAR
    GirlCount, BoyCount, TotalKids : Integer;
```

To simplify this discussion, we'll assume that integers take only one memory location. The VAR statement causes three entries to be made in the symbol table:

Symbol	Address
GirlCount	0000
BoyCount	0001
TotalKids	0002

That is, *at compile time,*

GirlCount is *bound* to Address 0000.
BoyCount is *bound* to Address 0001.
TotalKids is *bound* to Address 0002.

Whenever a variable is used later in the program, the compiler searches the symbol table for its actual address, and substitutes that address for the variable name. After all, meaningful variable names are for the convenience of the human reader; addresses, however, are meaningful to computers. For example, the assignment statement, "TotalKids := GirlCount + BoyCount;" is translated into machine instructions that execute the following actions:

- Get the contents of Address 0000.
- Add it to the contents of Address 0001.
- Put the result into Address 0002.

The object code itself is then stored in a different part of memory. Let's say that the translated instructions begin at Address 1000. At the beginning of the program, control is transferred to Address 1000. The instruction stored there is executed; then the instruction in 1001 is executed; and so on.

Where are the parameters of subprograms stored? With static storage allocation, the formal parameters of a subprogram are assumed to be in a particular place; for instance, the compiler might set aside space for the parameter values immediately preceding the code for each subprogram. Consider a procedure with two Integer-type parameters,

GirlCount and BoyCount, as well as a local variable TotalKids. Let's assume that the procedure's code begins at an address we'll call CountKids. The compiler leaves room for the two formal parameters and the local variable at addresses CountKids − 1, CountKids − 2, and CountKids − 3, respectively. Given the procedure heading and declaration below:

```
PROCEDURE CountKids
   (GirlCount, BoyCount : Integer);

VAR
   TotalKids : Integer;
```

the statement "TotalKids := GirlCount + BoyCount;" in the body of the procedure would generate the following actions:

- Get the contents of Address CountKids − 1.
- Add it to the contents of Address CountKids − 2.
- Store the result in Address CountKids − 3.

Figure 8-4 shows how a program with two subprograms might be arranged in memory.

This discussion has been simplified somewhat, since the compiler sets aside space not only for the parameters and local variables, but also for the return address (the location in memory of the next instruction to process, following the completion of the procedure) and the computer's current register values. However, we have illustrated

Figure 8-4
Static Allocation of Space for a Program with Two Subprograms

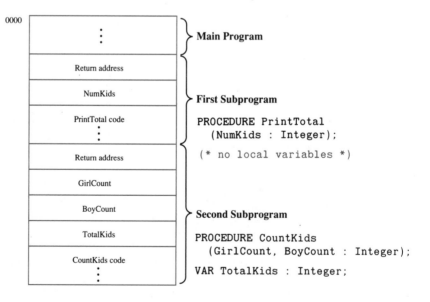

```
PROCEDURE PrintTotal
   (NumKids : Integer);

(* no local variables *)
```

```
PROCEDURE CountKids
   (GirlCount, BoyCount : Integer);

VAR TotalKids : Integer;
```

the main point: The procedure's formal parameters and local variables are bound to actual addresses in memory at *compile time*.

We can compare the static allocation scheme to one way of allocating seats in an auditorium where a lecture is to be held. A finite number of invitations are issued for the event, and the exact number of chairs needed are set up before the lecture. Each invited guest has a reserved seat. If anyone brings friends, however, there will be nowhere for them to sit.

What is the implication of binding variables to memory locations before the program executes? Each parameter and local variable has but a single location assigned to it at compile time. (They are like invited guests with reserved seats.) If each call to a procedure is an independent event, there is no problem. But in the case of recursion, each recursive call is dependent on the state of the values in the previous call. Where is the storage for the multiple versions of the parameters and local variables generated by recursive calls? Because the intermediate values of the parameters and local variables must be retained, the recursive call cannot store its arguments in the fixed number of locations that were set up at compile time. The values from the previous recursive call would be overwritten and lost. Thus a language that uses only static storage allocation *cannot* support recursion.

Dynamic Storage Allocation

The situation described above is like a class of students that must share one copy of a workbook. Joe writes his exercise answers in the space provided in the workbook, then Mary erases his answers, and writes hers in the same space. This process continues until each student in the class writes his or her answers into the workbook, obliterating all the answers that came before. Obviously this situation is not practical. Clearly what is needed is for each student to read from the single copy of the workbook, then to write his or her answers on a separate piece of paper. In computer terms, what each invocation of a procedure needs is its own work space. Dynamic storage allocation provides this solution.

With dynamic storage allocation, variables are not bound to actual addresses in memory until *run time*. The compiler references variables not by their actual addresses, but by relative addresses. Of particular interest to us, the compiler references the parameters and local variables of a procedure or function relative to some address known at run time, not relative to the location of the subprogram's code.

Let's look at a simplified version of how this might work in Pascal. (The actual implementation depends on the particular machine and compiler.) When a subprogram is invoked, it needs space to keep its formal parameters, its local variables, and the return address (the address in the calling program to which the computer returns when the subprogram completes its execution). Just like students sharing one copy of a workbook, each invocation of a procedure or function needs its own work space. This work space is called an **activation record**. A simplified version of an activation record for Function NFact might have the following "declarations":

```
TYPE
  ActivationRecordType = RECORD
    Return    : AddressType;   (* return address   *)
    NFact     : NonNegative;   (* returned value   *)
    N         : NonNegative;   (* formal parameter *)
  END; (* ActivationRecordType *)
```

Each call to a procedure or function, including recursive calls, generates a new activation record. Within the subprogram, references to the parameters and local variables use the values in the activation record. When the subprogram ends, the activation record is released. How does this happen? Your source code doesn't need to allocate and free activation records; the compiler adds a "prologue" to the beginning of each procedure and an "epilogue" to the end of each procedure. The next table compares the source code for Function NFact with a simplified version of the "code" executed at run time. (Of course the code executed at run time is object code, but we are listing the source code "equivalent" so that it makes sense to the reader.)

Run-time Version of NFact (Simplified)

What Your Source Code Says	*What the Run-time System Does*

FUNCTION NFact
  (N : NonNegative) : NonNegative;
 	
BEGIN (* NFact *)
 	
  IF N = 0
    THEN NFact := 1
    ELSE NFact := N * NFact (N − 1)
 	
END;   (* NFact *)
	(* Procedure Prologue: *)
	New (ActRec);
	ActRec^.Return := RetAddr;
	ActRec^.N := N;
	(* ActRec^.NFact = undefined *)
	IF ActRec^.N = 0
	  THEN ActRec^.NFact := 1
	  ELSE ActRec^.NFact :=
	    ActRec^.N *
	    NFact (ActRec^.N − 1);
	
	(* Procedure Epilogue *)
	NFact^ := ActRec^.NFact;
	RetAddr := ActRec^.Return;
	Dispose (ActRec);
	Jump (goto) to RetAddr.

What happens to the activation record of one subprogram when a second subprogram is invoked? Consider a program whose main program calls Proc1, which then calls Proc2. When the program begins executing, the "main" activation record is generated. (Since the main program's activation record exists for the entire execution of the program, the program's global data can be considered "static.") At the first procedure call an activation record is generated for Proc1:

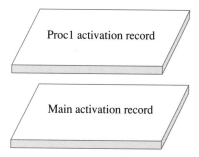

When Proc2 is called from within Proc1, its activation record is generated. Since Proc1 has not finished executing, its activation record is still around; just like the mathematicians with telephones, one waits "on hold" until the next call is finished:

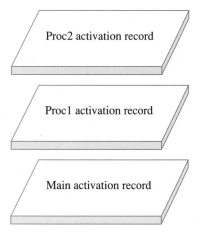

When Proc2 finishes executing, its activation record is released. But which of the other two activation records becomes the active one: Proc1's or Main's? Proc1's activation record is now active, of course. The order of activation follows the Last-In-First-Out rule. We know of a structure that supports LIFO access—the stack—so it should come as no surprise that the structure that keeps track of the activation records at run time is called the **run-time stack**.

When a procedure or function is invoked, its activation record is pushed onto the run-time stack. Each nested level of procedure calls adds another activation record to the stack. As each subprogram completes its execution, its activation record is popped from the stack. Recursive procedure or function calls, like calls to any other subprograms, cause a new activation record to be generated. The level of recursive calls in a program determines how many activation records for this subprogram are pushed onto the run-time stack at any one time.

Using dynamic allocation might be compared to another way of allocating seats in an auditorium where a lecture has been scheduled. A finite number of invitations is issued, but each guest is asked to bring his or her own chair. In addition, each guest

Figure 8-5
The Sample Pro-
gram Loaded in
Memory

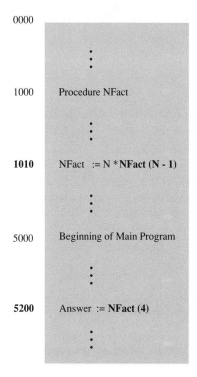

can invite an unlimited number of friends, as long as they all bring their own chairs. Of course, if the number of extra guests gets out of hand, the space in the auditorium will run out, and there will not be enough room for any more friends or chairs. Similarly, the level of recursion in a program must eventually be limited by the amount of memory available in the run-time stack.

Let's walk through Function NFact again, to see how its execution affects the run-time stack. Here is the function:

```
FUNCTION NFact
  (N : NonNegative) : NonNegative;
BEGIN (* NFact *)
  IF N = 0
    THEN NFact := 1
    ELSE NFact := N * NFact (N — 1)
END; (* NFact *)
```

Let's say that the main program is loaded in memory beginning at location 5000, and that the initial call to NFact is made in a statement at memory location 5200. The NFact procedure is loaded in memory at location 1000, with the recursive call made in the statement at location 1010. Figure 8-5 shows a simplified version of how this example program is loaded in memory. (These numbers have been picked arbitrarily, so that we will have actual numbers to show in the Return address field of the activation record.)

When NFact is called the first time from the statement in the main program at address 5200:

```
Answer := NFact (4);
```

an activation record is pushed onto the run-time stack to hold three pieces of data: the return address (5200), the formal parameter N (4), and the value returned from the function (NFact), which has not yet been evaluated. This activation record is now on the top of the run-time stack:

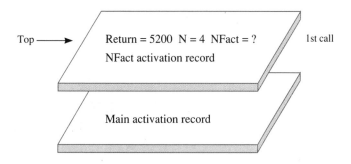

The code is now executed. Is N (the N value in the top activation record) equal to 0? No, it is 4, so the ELSE branch is taken:

```
NFact := N * NFact(N - 1);
```

This time the function NFact is called from a different place. It is called recursively from within the function, from the statement at location 1010. After the value of NFact (N − 1) is calculated, we will return to this location to calculate the value returned from the function. A new activation record is pushed onto the run-time stack:

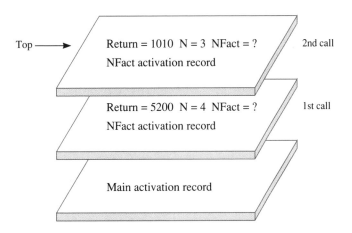

Figure 8-6

The Run-time Stack
During the Execu-
tion of NFact

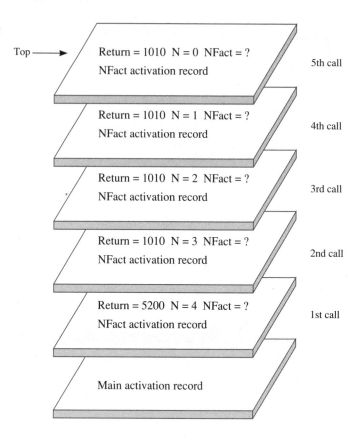

Again the code is executed. Is N (the value in the top activation record) equal to 0? No, N = 3, so the ELSE branch is taken:

```
NFact := N * NFact(N - 1);
```

So the function NFact is again called recursively from the instruction at location 1010. This process continues until the situation looks as shown in Figure 8-6. Now, as the code is being executed, we again ask the question: Is N (the value of N in the top activation record) equal to 0? *Yes*. This time we take the THEN branch, storing the value 1 in NFact (the NFact in the top activation record, that is). The fifth invocation of the function has executed to completion, and the value of NFact in the top activation record is returned from the function. The run-time stack is popped to release the top activation record, leaving the activation record of the fourth call to NFact at the top of the run-time stack. We don't restart the function from the top, however. As with any procedure or function call, we return to execute the instruction following the call to NFact. This was the return address (location 1010) stored in the activation record.

The next instruction is where the returned value (1) is multiplied by the value of N in the top activation record (1) and the result (1) is stored in NFact (the instance of NFact in the top activation record, that is). Now the fourth invocation of the function is complete, and the value of NFact in the top activation record is returned from the function. Again the run-time stack is popped to release the top activation record, leaving the activation record of the third call to NFact at the top of the run-time stack. We return to execute the instruction following the recursive call to NFact.

This process continues until we are back to the first call:

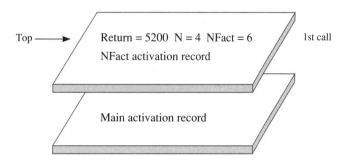

and 6 has just been returned as the value of NFact (N − 1). This value is multiplied by the value of N in the top activation record (that is, 4) and the result, 24, is stored in the NFact field of the top activation record. This assignment completes the execution of the initial call to Function NFact. The value of NFact in the top activation record (24) is returned to the place of the original call, and the activation record is popped. This leaves the main activation record at the top of the run-time stack. The final value of Nfact is stored in the variable Answer, and the statement following the original call is executed.

The fact that the parameters for the recursive calls have to be passed in their activation records makes it clear why we must pass large structures as VAR parameters, even if they are not changed by the procedure. For instance, in the BinarySearch procedure, if we do not make List a VAR parameter, each recursive call will put a *copy* of the whole list into the activation record! Passing List as a VAR parameter, however, only puts the *address* of the List array into the activation record.

Debugging Recursive Routines

Because of their nested calls to themselves, recursive routines can be confusing to debug. The most serious problem is the possibility that the routine will recurse forever. A typical symptom of this problem is an error message such as "STACK OVERFLOW," telling us that the system has run out of space in the run-time stack, due to the level of recursive calls. Using the Three-Question Method to verify recursive procedures and functions should help us avoid the problem of never finishing. If we can answer yes to the base-case and smaller-caller questions, we should be able to guarantee that the routine will eventually end—theoretically, at least.

That does not guarantee, however, that the program will not fail due to lack of space. We saw in the previous section that a procedure call requires a certain amount of overhead to save the parameters, the return address, and the local data. A call to a recursive procedure may generate many, many levels of procedure calls to itself—more than the system can handle.

One error that programmers often make when they first start writing recursive routines is to use a looping structure instead of a branching one. Because they tend to think of the problem in terms of a repetitive action, they inadvertently use a WHILE rather than an IF statement. The main body of the recursive routine should always be a breakdown into base and recursive cases. Hence, we use a branching statement, not a looping statement. It's a good idea to double check your recursive subprograms to make sure that you used an IF or CASE statement to get a branching effect.

Recursive routines are good places to put debug Writeln's during testing. Print out the parameters and local variables, if any, at the beginning and end of the subprogram. Be sure to print the values of the parameters on the recursive call(s) to make sure that each call is trying to solve a problem smaller than the previous one.

Removing Recursion

In cases where a recursive solution is not desired, either because the language doesn't support recursion or because the recursive solution is deemed too costly in terms of space or time, a recursive algorithm can be implemented as a nonrecursive procedure or function. There are two general techniques that are often substituted for recursion: iteration and stacking.

Iteration

When the recursive call is the last action executed in a recursive procedure, an interesting situation occurs. The recursive call causes an activation record to be put on the run-time stack to contain the procedure's parameters and local variables. When this recursive call finishes executing, the run-time stack is popped and the previous values of the variables are restored. But since the recursive call is the last statement in the procedure, the procedure terminates without using these values. The pushing and popping of activation records is superfluous. All we really need to do is to change the "smaller-caller" variable(s) on the recursive call's parameter list, and "jump" back to the beginning of the procedure. That is, what we really need is a *loop*.

For instance, as noted later in this chapter, Function ValueInList is a poor use of recursion. However, it is simple to remove the recursion from this function. The last statement executed in the general case is the recursive call to itself. Let's see how to replace the recursion with a loop.

The recursive solution has two base cases: One occurs if we find the value and the other occurs if we reach the end of the list without finding the value. The base cases solve the problem without further executions of the function. In the iterative solution, the base cases become the terminating conditions of the loop:

WHILE NOT Found AND more elements to examine DO

When the terminating conditions are met, the problem is solved without further executions of the loop body.

In the general case of the recursive solution, ValueInList is called to search the remaining, unsearched part of the list. Each recursive execution of the function processes a smaller version of the problem. The smaller-caller question is answered affirmatively because StartIndex is incremented, shrinking the unsearched part of the list on every recursive call. Similarly, in an iterative solution, each subsequent execution of the loop body processes a smaller version of the problem. The unsearched part of the list is shrunk on each execution of the loop body by incrementing StartIndex.

IF Value is in List[StartIndex]
   THEN Found ← True
   ELSE Increment StartIndex

Here is the iterative version of the function:

```
FUNCTION ValueInList
   (VAR List    : ListType;
    Value       : ValueType;
    StartIndex  : Integer;
    EndIndex    : Integer)  : Boolean;

   (* ValueInList is True if Value is found within the index *)
   (* range StartIndex to EndIndex; otherwise it is False.   *)
   (* NOTE: List is passed as a VAR parameter because of its  *)
   (* size; it is not modified by this function.              *)
VAR
   Found : Boolean;
BEGIN (* ValueInList *)

   Found := False;

   (* While "base cases" have not occurred, do "general case." *)
   WHILE NOT Found AND (StartIndex <= EndIndex) DO
     IF Value = List[StartIndex]
       THEN Found := True
       ELSE StartIndex := StartIndex + 1;

   ValueInList := Found

END; (* ValueInList *)
```

Cases where the recursive call is the last statement executed are called **tail recursion**. Note that the recursive call is not necessarily the last statement in the procedure. For instance, the recursive call in the following version of ValueInList is still tail recursion, even though it is *not* the last statement in the procedure:

```
BEGIN (* ValueInList *)

  IF List[StartIndex] = Val
    THEN (* Base Case 1: Value found, *)
      ValueInList := True
    ELSE
      IF StartIndex <> EndIndex
        THEN (* General Case: Search the rest of List. *)
          ValueInList := (* this is the recursive call: *)
            ValueInList (List, Val, StartIndex + 1, EndIndex)
        ELSE (* Base Case 2: Value not in list. *)
          ValueInList := False

END; (* ValueInList *)
```

The recursive call is the last statement *executed* in the general case—thus it is tail recursion. Tail recursion is usually replaced by iteration to remove recursion from the solution.

Stacking

When the recursive call is *not* the last action executed in a recursive procedure, we cannot simply substitute a loop for the recursion. For instance, in Procedure RevPrint we make the recursive call and then print the value in the current node. In cases like this, we must replace the stacking that was done by the *system* with stacking that is done by the *programmer.*

How would we write Procedure RevPrint nonrecursively? As we traverse the list, we must keep track of the pointer to each node, until we reach the end of the list (when our traversing pointer equals NIL). When we reach the end of the list, we print the Info field of the last node. Then we back up and print again, back up and print, and so on, until we have printed the first list element.

We know of a data structure in which we can store pointers and retrieve them in reverse order: the stack. The general task for RevPrint is

RevPrint (iterative)

Create an empty stack of pointers.
Ptr ← pointer to first node in list

WHILE the list is not empty DO
    Push Ptr onto the stack
    Advance Ptr

WHILE the stack is not empty
    Pop the stack to get Ptr (to previous node)
    Print Info(Ptr)

A nonrecursive RevPrint procedure may be coded as follows:

```
PROCEDURE RevPrint
  (List : ListType);
```

```
(* Prints out the elements in the list in reverse *)
(* order. This is a nonrecursive procedure.       *)
VAR
  Stack : StackType;
  Ptr   : PointerType;
BEGIN (* RevPrint *)

  (* Push pointers to all nodes onto stack. *)
  CreateStack (Stack);
  Ptr := List;
  WHILE Ptr <> NIL DO
    BEGIN
      Push (Stack, Ptr);
      Ptr := Ptr^.Next
    END; (* WHILE Ptr <> NIL *)
  (* Retrieve pointers in reverse order and print elements. *)
  WHILE NOT EmptyStack (Stack) DO
    BEGIN
      Pop (Stack, Ptr);          (* Get the next pointer. *)
      Writeln (Ptr^.Info)        (* Print the data.       *)
    END (* WHILE not empty *)
END; (* RevPrint *)
```

Notice that the nonrecursive version of RevPrint is quite a bit longer than its recursive counterpart, especially if we add in the code for the stack routines Push, Pop, CreateStack, and EmptyStack. This verbosity is caused by our need to stack and unstack the pointers explicitly. In the recursive version, we just called RevPrint recursively, and let the run-time stack keep track of the pointers.

Deciding Whether to Use a Recursive Solution

There are several factors to consider in deciding whether or not to use a recursive solution to a problem. The main issues are the clarity and the efficiency of the solution. Let's talk about efficiency first. In general, a recursive solution is more costly in terms of both computer time and space. (This is not an absolute decree; it really depends on the computer and the compiler.) A recursive solution usually requires more "overhead" because of the nested recursive procedure or function calls, in terms of both time (the procedure prologues and epilogues must be run for each recursive call) and space (an activation record must be created). A call to a recursive routine may hide many layers of internal recursive calls. For instance, the call to an iterative solution to NFact involves a single function invocation, causing one activation record to be put on the run-time stack. Invoking the recursive version of NFact, however, requires $N + 1$ function calls and $N + 1$ activation records to be pushed onto the run-time stack. That is, the depth of recursion is O(N). For some problems, the system just may not have enough space in the run-time stack to run a recursive solution.

As an extreme example, consider the original version of the recursive function ValueInList. Every time it is invoked, it saves copies of the parameters, including the whole array, List, which is passed as a value parameter. As we search farther and farther in the list, nesting more and more levels of recursive calls, the amount of memory needed for the run-time stack becomes considerable. If the list contains 100 elements and the one we are looking for is not in the list, we will end up saving 100 copies of the 100-element array. Eventually we will be using up so much memory that we may run out of space altogether! This is an extreme example of one of the "overhead" problems of recursive calls. In this particular case we might make List a VAR parameter (something generally not done in functions) so that new copies of the array would not be generated on every invocation of ValueInList. (The address of the one and only copy of List would be passed instead.) Still, the level of recursion is O(N) and the iterative solution is about the same length and just as clear. Thus ValueInList is a poor use of recursion.

Another problem to look for is the possibility that a particular recursive solution might just be *inherently* inefficient. Such inefficiency is not a reflection of how we choose to implement the algorithm; rather, it is an indictment of the algorithm itself. For instance, look back at Function Combinations, which we discussed earlier in this chapter. The example of this function illustrated in Figure 8-2 [Combinations (4, 3)] seems straightforward enough. But consider the execution of Combinations (6, 4), as illustrated in Figure 8-7. The inherent problem with this function is that the same values are calculated over and over. Combinations (4, 3) is calculated in two different places, and Combinations (3, 2) is calculated in three places, as are Combinations (2, 1) and Combinations (2, 2). It is unlikely that we could solve a combinatorial problem of any large size using this procedure. The problem is that the program will run "forever"— or until it exhausts the capacity of the computer; it is an exponential-time [$O(2^N)$] solution to a linear time [O(N)] problem. Although our recursive function is very easy to understand, it was not a practical solution. In such cases an iterative solution must be sought.

The issue of the clarity of the solution is still an important factor, however. For many problems a recursive solution is simpler and more natural for the programmer to write. The total amount of work required to solve a problem can be envisioned as an iceberg. By using recursive programming, the applications programmer may limit his or her view to the tip of the iceberg. The system will take care of the great bulk of the work below the surface. Compare, for example, the recursive and nonrecursive versions of Procedure RevPrint. In the recursive version we let the system take care of the stacking that we had to do explicitly in the nonrecursive procedure. Thus recursion is a tool that can help reduce the complexity of a program by hiding some of the implementation details. With the cost of computer time and memory decreasing and the cost of a programmer's time rising, it is worthwhile to use recursive solutions to such problems.

To summarize, it is good to use recursion when:

- *The depth of recursive calls is relatively "shallow,"* some fraction of the size of the problem. For instance, the level of recursive calls in the BinarySearch procedure is $O(\log_2 N)$; this is a good candidate for recursion. The depth of recursive calls in the NFact and ValueInList routines, however, is O(N).

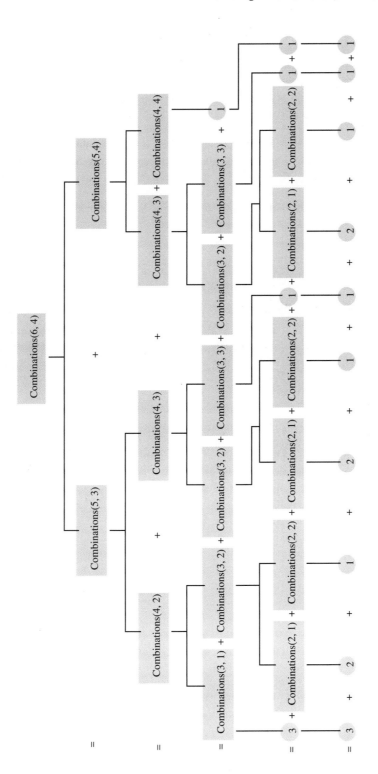

Figure 8-7   *Calculating Combinations (6, 4)*

■ *The recursive version does about the same amount of work as the nonrecursive version*. You can compare the Big-O approximations to determine this. For instance, we have determined that the $O(2^N)$ recursive version of Combinations is a poor use of recursion, compared to an $O(N)$ iterative version. Both the recursive and iterative versions of BinarySearch, however, are $O(\log_2 N)$. BinarySearch is a good example of a recursive procedure.

■ *The recursive version is shorter and simpler than the nonrecursive solution*. By this rule, NFact and ValueInList are not good uses of recursive programming. They illustrate how to understand and write recursive procedures and functions, but they could more efficiently be written iteratively—without any loss of clarity in the solution. RevPrint is a better use of recursion. Its recursive solution is very simple to understand, and the nonrecursive equivalent is much less elegant.

Summary

Recursion is a very powerful computing tool. Used appropriately, recursion can simplify the solution of a problem, often resulting in shorter, more easily understood source code. As usual in computing, there are trade-offs: Recursive procedures are often less efficient, in terms of both time and space, due to the overhead of many levels of procedure calls. How expensive this cost is depends on the computer system and compiler.

A recursive solution to a problem must have at least one base case—that is, a case where the solution is derived nonrecursively. Without a base case, the procedure or function will recurse forever (or at least until the computer runs out of memory). The recursive solution also has one or more general cases that include recursive calls to the procedure or function. The recursive calls must involve a "smaller caller." One (or more) of the actual parameter values must change in each recursive call to redefine the problem to be smaller than it was on the previous call. Thus each recursive call leads the solution of the problem toward the base case(s).

A typical implementation of recursion involves the use of a stack. Each call to a subprogram generates an activation record to contain its return address, parameters, and local variables. The activation records are accessed in a Last-In-First-Out manner. Thus a stack is the choice of data structure. Recursion can be supported by systems and languages that use dynamic storage allocation. The procedure parameters and local variables are not bound to addresses until an activation record is created at run time. Thus multiple copies of the intermediate values of recursive calls to the program can be supported, as new activation records are created for them.

With static storage allocation, in contrast, a single location is reserved at compile time for each parameter and local variable of a procedure. There is no place to store intermediate values calculated by repeated nested calls to the same procedure. Therefore, systems and languages with only static storage allocation cannot support recursion.

When recursion is not possible or appropriate, a recursive algorithm can be implemented nonrecursively by using a looping structure and, in some cases, by pushing and popping relevant values onto a stack. This programmer-controlled stack explicitly replaces the system's run-time stack. While such nonrecursive solutions are often more efficient in terms of time and space, there is usually a trade-off in terms of the elegance of the solution.

In the application program at the end of this chapter, we will develop a recursive solution to the problem of finding the way out of a maze. This problem was included in the first edition of this book as a stack application. We said earlier that any recursive solution can be implemented using iteration or a stack. Our application problem illustrates another way of looking at this idea: Any stack problem may be a good place to use recursion.

Application

Escape from a Maze

Data Structure

■ Two-dimensional array

Software Technique

■ Recursive algorithm

As a child, did you ever dream of playing in a maze? How fun and scary it would have been to get lost and then, just at sundown, find your way out. If you had thought about it, you might have come up with the idea of marking your path as you went along. If you were trapped, you could then go back to the last crossing and take the other path.

This technique of going back to the last decision point and trying another way is called **backtracking**. We will illustrate this very useful problem-solving technique in the context of trying to get out of a maze.

Given a maze and a starting point within it, you are to determine whether there is a way out. There is only one exit from the maze. You may move horizontally or vertically (but not diagonally) in any direction in which there is an open path, but you may not move in a direction that is blocked. If you move into a position where you are blocked on three sides, you must go back the way you came (backtrack) and try another path.

We will write a program that uses this technique to escape from a maze, according to the specifications in Figure 8-8 on page 502.

The Design

Before we consider how to represent the maze, let's look at an overview of the processing of this problem with a Level 0 design:

MazeExit / *Level 0*

GetMazeFromFile

WHILE more starting points in the file DO
    GetStartPoint
    PrintMaze
    TryToEscape
    PrintResults

From the logical perspective, the maze itself can be thought of as a two-dimensional grid of "positions" in the maze. Each position can be identified by its Row and Column

Figure 8-8
Specifications of
Program MazeExit

Specifications: Program MazeExit

Function:

This program uses a backtracking technique to escape from a maze.

Input:

The input comes from a text file, MazeFile. It contains the original maze, represented as a square matrix of symbols, with one row of the matrix per line. Each symbol is a character that indicates whether the corresponding maze position is an open path ('O'), a trap (' + '), or the exit ('E'). The size of the maze is 10 × 10 positions.

Following the original maze in the file, there will be a series of starting position coordinates. Each line will contain a pair of values, representing the row and column of the starting position in the maze. You are to process each of these starting points until EOF is encountered.

Output:

For each starting position, print the following:

1. The maze, with the starting point represented by a '*' symbol
2. A message that indicates the result of the escape attempt:
   "HOORAY! I am free!" *or* "HELP! I am trapped!"
3. The number of positions tried before a solution was found

Processing Requirements:

Begin processing each starting position at the specified coordinates, and continue moving until you find the way out or have no more moves to try. You may move horizontally or vertically into any position that is an open path ('O'), but not into a position that is blocked (' + '). If you move into the exit position ('E'), you have exited the maze.

(Don't worry if the number of positions tried is greater than the number of positions in the maze; there may be positions that were duplicated during backtracking.)

Assumptions:

MazeFile exists; all input from MazeFile is correct.

---

numbers—values between 1 and 10, according to the specifications. Each position contains a Symbol that represents its contents: Open (an open path), Trap (a dead end), Exit (exit from the maze), or Start (the starting point for the escape attempt). The specifications tell us that the file input designates an open path by 'O', a trap by ' + ', and the exit by 'E'. The starting point is to be marked with the character '*'. For convenience, in our illustrations, we will use these characters to represent the contents of the maze positions. Figure 8-9 shows the logical picture of a maze.

From the high-level design we can determine that we will need maze operations to (1) mark a position on the maze and (2) return the "symbol" value of a maze position— open, trap, or exit. These operations can be specified as follows:

Figure 8-9   *Picture of a Maze*

Maze	[1]	[2]	[3]	[4]	[5]	[6]	[7]	[8]	[9]	[10]
[1]	O	O	+	E	+	O	O	+	+	+
[2]	O	+	+	O	+	O·	+	O	O	O
[3]	O	O	O	O	O	O	+	O	+	O
[4]	+	+	+	+	+	O	+	+	O	O
[5]	O	O	O	+	O	O	O	+	O	+
[6]	O	+	O	+	O	+	+	+	O	+
[7]	O	+	O	+	O	O	O	+	O	O
[8]	+	+	O	+	+	+	O	+	+	O
[9]	O	+	O	O	O	O	O	+	+	O
[10]	O	+	O	+	+	O	+	O	O	O

Exit

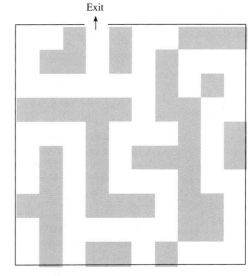

Key to symbols:

+   Trap (hedge)
O   Open path
E   Exit from maze

Key to Maze

☐   Open path
▨   Trap (hedge)

■ **MarkMaze (Maze, Row, Column, Symbol)**

Function:	Set the maze position at the specified Row and Column to the value of Symbol.
Input:	Maze (MazeType) Row, Column (Integer) Symbol (SymbolType)
Preconditions:	Row and Column are within maze bounds (1–10).
Output:	Maze (MazeType)
Postconditions:	Maze is updated to include modified Symbol value at the position specified by Row and Column.

■ **MazePosition (Maze, Row, Column) returns SymbolType**

Function:	Returns the Symbol value of the maze position at the specified Row and Column.
Input:	Maze (MazeType) Row, Column (Integer)
Preconditions:	Row and Column are within maze bounds (1–10).
Output:	MazePosition (SymbolType)
Postconditions:	MazePosition = symbol value of the maze position at the specified Row and Column.

Using these Maze ADT operations, we can describe much of the program's processing. In the GetMazeFromFile module, we will input the original Maze from MazeFile by reading the values, row by row, and calling MarkMaze to put the appropriate symbols (Open, Trap, or Exit) into the specified positions in the maze. In the GetStartPoint module, we mark a starting point by calling MarkMaze to set the designated maze position to the Start symbol. The PrintMaze module prints out the maze row by row, using the MazePosition function to retrieve the symbol value of each maze position. Printing the results of the escape attempt merely involves a call or two to Writeln. The Level 1 designs for the GetMazeFromFile, GetStartPoint, PrintMaze, and PrintResult modules are straightforward, so let's go on to the interesting part of the problem: *How do we get out of the maze?*

Escape Processing

Let's look more closely at the TryToEscape module. It needs to know the position (Row and Column) of the starting point. It does some processing and then returns the results—whether the escape was successful and a count of how many moves we had to make in the escape attempt. Here is the module's specification:

TryToEscape (Maze, Row, Column, Free, NumTries)   /   *Level 1*

Function:	Given a Maze and starting position, determine if there is an escape path and determine how many positions have to be tried during the escape.
Input:	Maze (MazeType) Row, Column (Integer)
Preconditions:	Maze has been initialized with values from MazeFile.
Output:	Free (Boolean) NumTries (Integer)
Postconditions:	Free indicates whether an escape path was found; NumTries = number of positions tried during the escape. (A position may be tried more than once because of backtracking.)

What is this escape processing? Beginning at the starting point, we can move in any direction—up, down, right, or left—that is, either an Open path ('O') or the Exit ('E'). Given the part of the maze shown in Figure 8-10, this means that we could move up

Figure 8-10
The Starting
Position

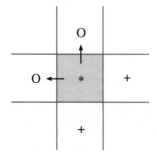

Figure 8-11
After the First Move

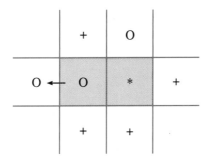

Figure 8-12
After the Second
Move

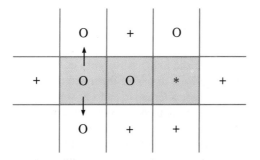

or left, into an Open path. However, we cannot move down or right, where there are Traps (' + ').

Let's say that we move to the left. Now we are facing the same kind of situation (see Figure 8-11). We can move in any direction where we are not trapped. Because the positions above and below the current position are blocked, we do not try these. To the right is the Start position ('*'). There's no use going back there, so we move again to the left.

Again we are in the same kind of situation (see Figure 8-12): We can move in any direction that is not blocked. There is a Trap to the left, so we don't move there. There are Open positions above and below and to the right. We just came from the position to the right, so it's not worth going back there. In fact, this is the same situation we faced in Figure 8-11, when we decided not to go back into the Start position. That time, because we saw the Start symbol in the maze position, we knew not to move into the spot. This time, however, it is just another Open position. How do we know not to go back?

If you were hiking in an uncharted area, you might mark your trail by breaking twigs or leaving stones in the path you had traveled. We can use that same idea here: We'll mark the trail of positions that we've already tried by replacing the Open symbol with a special symbol, Tried. (We will use a little stone ('.') to depict the Tried symbol.)

We have two choices in Figure 8-12: up and down. We decide to go up (see Figure 8-13). Now we face the usual choice with a modified restriction: We can go in any direction that is not blocked or *already tried*. Uh-oh! Our new position is blocked in all the untried directions. We are trapped.

But we don't know for sure that there is no way to get out of the maze. We only know that the path we tried doesn't get us there. We passed up a couple of Open

· *Figure 8-13*

After the Third Move, Marking Our Trail

positions (see Figures 8-10 and 8-13) as we were going along the path that led us into the deadend. We could go back to one of them and try another path from there. Even better, we can collect *all* these alternative paths as we pass them; then if we get trapped we can go back to the path most recently passed and resume the escape attempt.

This line of thinking leads us to the idea of using a data structure that we are already familiar with—the stack—to collect the alternative moves. Every time we enter a position, we put all the possible alternatives (Open positions adjacent to the current position) onto a stack. Then to move, we pop the top alternative off the stack. This move takes us to a new position, from which we will push all of the alternative moves onto the stack, and so on. The following algorithm describes this solution:

TryToEscape—Stack Version

Create empty stack.
Free ← False
HopelesslyTrapped ← False
NumTries ← 0

WHILE NOT Free AND NOT HopelesslyTrapped DO
    Mark current position as Tried.
    Increment NumTries

    Push the positions (Row and Column) of all of possible moves (up, down, right, or
        left positions that are marked as Open or Exit) onto stack.
    IF stack is empty
      THEN
        HopelesslyTrapped ← True
      ELSE
        Pop new current position off the stack
        Free ← (current maze position = Exit)

A Recursive Solution

This solution sounds as if it would work, but before we actually try it we notice something else in the discussion. Every time we made a move, we said, "Now we are facing the same situation. . . ." Every time we moved into a new position, we faced a version of the same problem that led us to call TryToEscape in the first place. This suggests a recursive solution to the problem; perhaps we can use recursion to let the system take care of the backtracking, instead of using a stack.

Let's look at the *general case* of a recursive version of the TryToEscape procedure. The general case is when the current position, on entering the procedure, is Open. Our current position is described by Row and Column numbers. What are the recursive calls that would solve the problem of escaping from the maze? We could TryToEscape up or down or right or left. Actually, we could TryToEscape in *all* of these directions. Here's a first pass at a recursive algorithm for TryToEscape:

TryToEscape—Recursive Version 1

Increment NumTries
IF base case
   THEN
     Do something nonrecursive
   ELSE (general case)
     Mark current position as Tried.
     TryToEscape (Maze, Row + 1, Column, Free, NumTries)
     TryToEscape (Maze, Row − 1, Column, Free, NumTries)
     TryToEscape (Maze, Row, Column + 1, Free, NumTries)
     TryToEscape (Maze, Row, Column − 1, Free, NumTries)

What is the base case? This is the case that can be solved nonrecursively, ensuring that the procedure will eventually end. The situations we might face when we enter procedure TryToEscape are summarized in the next table.

TryToEscape Processing

If the Content of Current Position Is	Then TryToEscape Should
Tried	Do nothing. (Exit from procedure.)
Trap	Do nothing. (Exit from procedure.)
Exit	Set Free to True.
Open	Execute general case.

In addition, since a call to TryToEscape may cause Free to be set to True, a subsequent call may be made with Free already True. In this case we don't want to do anything except exit the procedure. Let's summarize these conditions in a second draft of the TryToEscape algorithm.

TryToEscape—Recursive Version 2

Increment NumTries
CurrentPosition ← MazePosition (Maze, Row, Column)

IF CurrentPosition <> Tried AND
  CurrentPosition <> Trap AND
  NOT Free
  THEN
    IF CurrentPosition = Exit
      THEN Free ← True (another base case)
      ELSE (General Case: Current Position = Open)

      (Mark this position so we don't try it again.)
      MarkMaze (Maze, Row, Column, Tried)

      (Try all the adjacent positions.)
      TryToEscape (Maze, Row + 1, Column, Free, NumTries)
      TryToEscape (Maze, Row − 1, Column, Free, NumTries)
      TryToEscape (Maze, Row, Column + 1, Free, NumTries)
      TryToEscape (Maze, Row, Column − 1, Free, NumTries)

Verifying the Design

Let's use our three questions to verify that this recursive procedure will work.

1. *The Base-Case Question:* The base cases occur when the current position is not an Open path, in which case we should stop searching this path (do nothing), and when Free is already True on entrance to the procedure, in which case we already know the answer to the problem and can quit.

2. *The Smaller-Caller Question:* We need to show here that the portion of the maze left to be processed is smaller on each recursive call. Maze is passed as a VAR parameter; as we process each Open position, we set the value of this position to the Tried symbol. As Open positions are found, therefore, the size of the maze that is left to process becomes "smaller." We usually look at the parameters of the recursive calls to see how the size of the problem is changing. In this case we can see that the Row and Column parameters are adjusted to guide the search for the exit into new paths adjacent to the current position. This observation, however, leads us to note a shortcoming of our design: As we increment and decrement the Row and Column parameters, what will keep us from going right off the edge of the maze? The design will need to be modified to account for the edges of the maze. We'll finish our proof and then come back to this problem.

3. *The General-Case Question:* Let's assume that a call to TryToEscape will correctly tell us whether an escape can be made from a given position. If we can escape from some known position in the maze, then we can also escape from an Open position adjacent to that position. So if we check all the positions adjacent to the starting point (the four calls to TryToEscape) and find that any of them leads to an escape, then we know that we can escape from the starting point. The converse is also true: If none of the adjacent positions leads to the exit, then the starting point cannot lead

to an exit. So the general case should solve the problem, assuming that the recursive calls do what they're supposed to do.

The Boundary Problem

We noticed during our verification of the smaller-caller question that there isn't anything to keep us from going over the edges of the maze as Row and Column are incremented and decremented in the recursive calls. We can add explicit checks for the lower and upper bounds of the array index:

IF (Row < 1) OR (Row > 10) OR (Column < 1) OR (Column > 10)
    THEN (another base case)
        Do nothing, just exit

Another way to handle this condition is to modify the data structure that supports the maze so that the existing conditions will take care of the problem. We can add a "hedge" that borders the whole maze (another row on the top and bottom of the maze, and another column on the left side and right side of the maze), setting all of these border positions to the Trap symbol. Then if the current position is in the border, it will be processed the same way as any other Trap position; that is, we will just exit the recursive call to the procedure.

We don't need any special processing in TryToEscape to handle the array borders. We will need to add an initialization step at the beginning of the program to set these rows and columns to the Trap value.

Finishing the Design

Let's review and refine the top level of our program and then complete the design. There are only a couple of changes to be made in the top level. Because TryToEscape is a recursive procedure, Free and NumTries must be initialized before the initial call. Also, because we decided to mark our trail through the maze by changing some of its positions from Open to Tried symbols, we had better use a fresh copy of the original maze each time we process a new starting point. We'll keep the original maze that we read from the file in a variable called OriginalMaze, and copy it into Maze before we do any other processing inside the main loop.

MazeExit / *Level 0*

GetMazeFromFile (MazeFile, OriginalMaze)

WHILE more starting points in the file DO

  CopyMaze (OriginalMaze, Maze)

  GetStartPoint (MazeFile, Maze, Row, Column)

  PrintMaze (Maze)

  (Set initial values for call to TryToEscape.)
  Free ← False
  NumTries ← 0

  TryToEscape (Maze, Row, Column, Free, NumTries)

  PrintResults (Free, NumTries)

Now let's look at some of the lower levels of the design. We first have to read the maze position values from the text file. This module has the following specification:

▶ **GetMazeFromFile (MazeFile, Maze)**

Function:	Get the original maze from the file for processing.
Input:	From MazeFile (Text)—maze position values, one row of maze values per text line.
Preconditions:	MazeFile exists, and contains valid data. It is not open on entrance to this procedure.
Output:	Maze (MazeType)
Postconditions:	Maze is initialized to original values from file, with borders set to Trap symbols. MazeFile is left open for later reads.

We said in the previous section that we would need to add an initialization step at the beginning of the program, to set up the borders of the maze as Trap positions. This step can be included inside the GetMazeFromFile processing:

GetMazeFromFile

Initialize—set border positions to Trap symbols

Open MazeFile for reading.

(Read the maze from the file row by row.)
FOR Row := first row of maze TO last row of maze DO
   FOR Column := first column of maze TO last column DO
     Read (MazeFile, Symbol)
     MarkMaze (Maze, Row, Column, Symbol)
   Readln (MazeFile)

The GetStartPoint module reads a pair of maze position coordinates—Row and Column—from the MazeFile, and marks the starting point in the maze.

▶ **GetStartPoint (MazeFile, Maze, Row, Column)** / *Level 1*

Function:	Gets next starting point coordinates from the file, and marks starting point in the maze.
Input:	From MazeFile: Row, Column (Integer) Maze (MazeType)
Preconditions:	MazeFile is open for reading; Row and Column indicate an "open" path position in the maze.
Output:	Maze (changed) Row, Column (Integer)
Postconditions:	The maze position with the specified Row and Column is marked with the Start symbol. MazeFile is left open for next call to Read.

The algorithm for this module is very simple:

GetStartPoint

Readln (MazeFile, Row, Column)

MarkMaze (Maze, Row, Column, Start)

The design of TryToEscape was discussed previously. The last modules, PrintMaze and PrintResult, are also trivial and can be coded without further design, with the program specification used as a guide.

Representing the Maze

We've managed to get all the way through the design without tying ourselves down to a representation of the maze. While we could probably think up more interesting structures to implement the maze, the most natural is a two-dimensional array of symbols, with the symbol in each position (Open, Trap, Exit, or Tried) represented by its single-character equivalent.

Using this representation, each maze operation contains only a single statement:

```
(* in MarkMaze: *)
Maze[Row, Column] := Symbol;

(* in MazePosition: *)
MazePosition := Maze[Row, Column];

(* in CopyMaze: *)
ToMaze := FromMaze;
```

Is it worth implementing these little one-liners, instead of just referencing the array in the calling program? These tiny operations have allowed us to encapsulate the maze implementation. We could change the implementation with no change to the many references to these operations throughout the program.

The Program

The code for this program is listed below, and is contained in the file MAZE.PAS on the program disk.

```
PROGRAM MazeExit (Input, Output, MazeFile);

  (* repeat program specification here *)
CONST
  (* Maze character symbols *)
  Start   =  '*';        (* starting point for escape    *)
  Exit    =  'E';        (* exit position from the maze   *)
  Trap    =  '+';        (* dead-end trap position        *)
  Open    =  'O';        (* open path in the maze         *)
  Tried   =  '.';        (* maze position already tried   *)

  (* Maze dimensions *)
  MinMaze = 1;
  MaxMaze = 10;
```

```
TYPE
  SymbolType = Char;
    (* legal symbols limited to symbols listed above *)

  MazeRange = 0 .. 11;    (* includes border positions *)

  MazeType  = ARRAY [MazeRange, MazeRange] OF SymbolType;
    (* legal component values limited to symbols above *)
VAR
  OriginalMaze : MazeType;   (* original maze read from file  *)
  Maze         : MazeType;   (* "working" copy of Maze        *)
  Row          : MazeRange;  (* starting row position         *)
  Column       : MazeRange;  (* starting column position      *)
  Free         : Boolean;    (* freed from the maze?          *)
  NumTries     : Integer;    (* number of squares visited     *)
  MazeFile     : Text;       (* text file containing Maze and *)
                             (* sets of starting coordinates  *)

(*************************************************************)
(*                   Maze Operations                       *)
(*************************************************************)
PROCEDURE MarkMaze
  (VAR Maze : MazeType;
   Row      : MazeRange;
   Column   : MazeRange;
   Symbol   : SymbolType);

  (* Set the designated position of Maze to Symbol. *)

BEGIN (* MazePosition *)
  Maze[Row, Column] := Symbol
END;  (* MazePosition *)

(*************************************************************)

FUNCTION MazePosition
  (VAR Maze : MazeType;
   Row      : MazeRange;
   Column   : MazeRange) : SymbolType;

  (* Return symbol value of Maze at Row/Column position. *)
  (* NOTE: Maze is passed as a VAR parameter because of  *)
  (* its size; it is not modified by this function.      *)

BEGIN (* MazePosition *)
  MazePosition := Maze[Row, Column]
END;  (* MazePosition *)

(*************************************************************)

PROCEDURE CopyMaze
  (VAR FromMaze : MazeType;
   VAR ToMaze   : MazeType);

  (* Copy FromMaze to ToMaze. *)
```

```
    BEGIN (* CopyMaze *)
      ToMaze := FromMaze
    END;  (* CopyMaze *)

    (***********************************************************)
    (*                  Input Operations                     *)
    (***********************************************************)
    PROCEDURE GetMazeFromFile
      (VAR MazeFile : Text;
       VAR Maze     : MazeType);

      (* Reads values for maze positions into the Maze from    *)
      (* MazeFile. Each data line contains one row of the maze *)
      (* with Open, Trap, or Exit characters representing the  *)
      (* status of each maze position.                         *)

    VAR
      Row     : MazeRange;   (* row index      *)
      Column  : MazeRange;   (* column index   *)
      Symbol  : SymbolType;  (* position value *)

    BEGIN (* GetMazeFromFile *)

      (* Set right and left border columns to Trap symbol. *)
      FOR Row := (MinMaze - 1) TO (MaxMaze + 1) DO
        BEGIN
          MarkMaze (Maze, Row, MinMaze - 1, Trap);
          MarkMaze (Maze, Row, MaxMaze + 1, Trap)
        END; (* FOR Row *)

      (* Set top and bottom border rows to Trap symbol. *)
      FOR Column := MinMaze TO MaxMaze DO
        BEGIN
          MarkMaze (Maze, MinMaze - 1, Column, Trap);
          MarkMaze (Maze, MaxMaze + 1, Column, Trap)
        END; (* FOR Column *)

      (* Open the maze text file for reading. *)
      Assign (MazeFile, 'MAZEFILE');   (**** Turbo Pascal ****)
      Reset  (MazeFile);

      (* Read all rows. *)
      FOR Row := MinMaze TO MaxMaze DO
        BEGIN
          (* Read one row. *)
          FOR Column := MinMaze TO MaxMaze DO
            BEGIN
              Read (MazeFile, Symbol);
              MarkMaze (Maze, Row, Column, Symbol)
            END; (* FOR Column *)

          (* Go to the next line in the file. *)
          Readln (MazeFile)

        END (* FOR Row *)
    END; (* GetMazeFromFile *)
```

```
(* *********************************************************** )

PROCEDURE GetStartPoint
  (VAR MazeFile : Text;
   VAR Maze     : MazeType;
   VAR Row      : MazeRange;
   VAR Column   : MazeRange);

  (* Get the next starting position from MazeFile, and   *)
  (* mark it on the maze. Return Row and Column numbers. *)

BEGIN (* GetStartPoint *)

  (* Read the starting coordinates from the maze file. *)
  Readln (MazeFile, Row, Column);

  (* Mark the starting position on the maze. *)
  MarkMaze (Maze, Row, Column, Start)

END;   (* GetStartPoint *)
(* *********************************************************** )
(*                    Output Operations                      *)
(* *********************************************************** )

PROCEDURE PrintMaze
  (VAR Maze : MazeType);

  (* Prints out the maze, with surrounding Trap characters. *)
  (* NOTE: Maze is a VAR parameter because of its size; it  *)
  (* is not modified by this procedure.                     *)

VAR
  Row, Column : MazeRange;

BEGIN (* PrintMaze *)

  Writeln;
  Writeln ('------------------------------------------------');
  Writeln;

  (* Print out all the rows *)
  FOR Row := (MinMaze - 1) TO (MaxMaze + 1) DO
    BEGIN

      (* Print out one row *)
      FOR Column := (MinMaze - 1) TO (MaxMaze + 1) DO
        Write (MazePosition(Maze, Row, Column));

      (* Skip to the next line. *)
      Writeln

    END  (* FOR Row *)
END;   (* PrintMaze *)

(* *********************************************************** )
```

```
      PROCEDURE PrintResult
        (Free     : Boolean;
         NumTries : Integer);

         (* Print out the result of the escape attempt. *)

      BEGIN (* PrintResult *)

        IF Free
          THEN Writeln (' HOORAY! I am free! ')
          ELSE Writeln (' HELP! I am trapped! ');

        Writeln (' Number of moves to try to escape = ', NumTries)

       END;    (* PrintResult *)

      (****************************************************************)
      (*                    Application Operation                    *)
      (****************************************************************)

      PROCEDURE TryToEscape
        (VAR Maze      : MazeType;
         Row           : MazeRange;
         Column        : MazeRange;
         VAR Free      : Boolean;
         VAR NumTries  : Integer);

         (* Tries all open avenues of escape from the maze, *)
         (* beginning at the specified row and column. This *)
         (* is a recursive solution.                        *)

      BEGIN (* TryToEscape *)

        NumTries := NumTries + 1;

        (* Rule out the base cases: current position already *)
        (* tried or a trap, or already free from maze.       *)
        IF (MazePosition (Maze, Row, Column) <> Tried) AND
           (MazePosition (Maze, Row, Column] <> Trap) AND NOT Free
          THEN    (* see if we're free. *)
            IF MazePosition (Maze, Row, Column) = Exit
              THEN Free := True
              ELSE (* This position Open; keep looking. *)
                BEGIN

                    (* Mark this position so we don't try it again. *)
                    MarkMaze (Maze, Row, Column, Tried);

                    (* Try all the surrounding positions. *)
                    TryToEscape (Maze, Row + 1, Column, Free, NumTries);
                    TryToEscape (Maze, Row - 1, Column, Free, NumTries);
                    TryToEscape (Maze, Row, Column + 1, Free, NumTries);
                    TryToEscape (Maze, Row, Column - 1, Free, NumTries)

                END (* Position open; keep trying. *)

      END;   (* TryToEscape *)
```

```
(***************************************************************)
(*                        Main Program                       *)
(***************************************************************)
BEGIN (* MazeExit *)

  (* Get the original maze from the file. *)
  GetMazeFromFile (MazeFile, OriginalMaze);

  (* Process all of the starting points in the maze file. *)
  WHILE NOT EOF(MazeFile) DO
    BEGIN

      (* Start again with a clean copy of the maze. *)
      CopyMaze (OriginalMaze, Maze);

      (* Get the next starting point; mark it in Maze. *)
      GetStartPoint (MazeFile, Maze, Row, Column);

      (* Print the maze, with the starting point marked. *)
      PrintMaze (Maze);

      (* Initialize for an escape attempt. *)
      Free    := False;
      NumTries := 0;

      (* Make an escape attempt. Return Free and number *)
      (* of moves made in the attempt to get free.      *)
      TryToEscape (Maze, Row, Column, Free, NumTries);

      (* Print out the results of this escape attempt. *)
      PrintResult (Free, NumTries)

    END (* WHILE *)
END. (* MazeExit *)
```

Testing the Program

In our first attempt at testing this program, we try out the input and output routines (GetMazeFromFile, GetStartPoint, PrintMaze) with a sample file of data, commenting out the call to TryToEscape in the main program. When we see that those procedures work correctly, we get up our nerve to try running the program with the recursive procedure TryToEscape restored. To make sure that we can trace its execution through all the recursive calls, we put in a debug Writeln at the start of TryToEscape, before any other statements:

```
Writeln(' TryToEscape entered with Row = ', Row,
        ' and Column = ', Column, ' and Free = ', Free);
```

Then we run the program using a variety of starting positions. The debugging output helps us to check whether the procedure is really solving the problem as we had expected. It does seem to work, but we are really surprised at how many recursive calls have to be made. Sometimes NumTries is larger than the total number of positions in the maze! We realize that we shouldn't be surprised, for we can come back to a position more than once, only to find that we have already been there (in these cases we exit immediately).

Looking through the debugging output, we realize that some of the calls are being made to TryToEscape even after we have determined that we are Free. For instance, if Free is set to True on the first of the four recursive calls in the general case, we still make the other three recursive calls, exiting immediately because Free is True (one of the base cases). We can avoid these extra calls by putting a condition *before* the recursive calls in the general case, only making the call IF NOT Free:

```
(* in the general case *)
    .
    .
    .

TryToEscape (to the position above)

IF NOT Free
   THEN TryToEscape (to the position below)
IF NOT Free
   THEN TryToEscape (to the position on the right)
IF NOT Free
   THEN TryToEscape (to the position on the left)
```

We make this change to the TryToEscape procedure and run the program again on the same input file. This time some (but not all) of the values of NumTries are smaller. A comparison of the output values for the two versions of TryToEscape is shown in the next table. Note that if there is no escape, it doesn't help to make the calls to TryToEscape conditional—Free will never be True. If we do escape, however, there is a noticeable difference between the two versions.

A Comparison of Output of the Two Versions of Procedure TryToEscape

Starting Coordinates		Result	Number of Moves to Determine Result	
Row	Column		Version 1	Version 2
1	2	Freed	33	20
10	1	Trapped	9	9
10	8	Trapped	65	65
7	6	Freed	121	108
1	7	Freed	125	115
8	7	Freed	121	106
7	9	Trapped	65	65
9	3	Freed	121	100
7	1	Freed	121	82
2	8	Trapped	65	65

The Recursive Solution vs. a Nonrecursive Solution

One of the techniques we mentioned for deciding whether to use a recursive solution to a problem was to ask if the recursive solution produced a shorter and simpler program. It just so happens that there's a nonrecursive solution to this same program; it uses the stacking algorithm discussed earlier to handle the backtracking.

Well . . . was it worth recursing?

The recursive version of this program, as shown in the preceding listing, contains 140 executable source lines of code. The "equivalent" nonrecursive program has 170 source lines of code. It is longer because of the additional code needed to declare the stack type and to define the stack procedures. The nonrecursive version is also less clear; it takes some time to become convinced that all the pushing and popping really solves the problem of getting out of the maze. In this case the recursive solution is a good choice.

▪ *Exercises**

---

1. Explain what is meant by
   (a) base case
   (b) general (or recursive) case
   (c) run-time stack
   (d) binding time
   (e) tail recursion

2. True or False? If false, correct the statement. *Recursive procedures and functions . . .*
   (a) usually have fewer parameters than the equivalent nonrecursive routines.
   (b) often have fewer local variables than the equivalent nonrecursive routines.
   (c) generally use WHILE or FOR statements as their main control structure.
   (d) are possible only in languages with static storage allocation.
   (e) should be used whenever execution speed is critical.
   (f) are always shorter and clearer than the equivalent nonrecursive routines.
   (g) must always contain a path that does not contain a recursive call.
   (h) are always less "efficient," in terms of Big-O.

3. Use the Three-Question Method to verify the ValueInList function in this chapter.

4. Describe the Three-Question Method of verifying recursive routines in relation to an inductive proof.

5. What data structure would you most likely see in a nonrecursive implementation of a recursive algorithm?

6. Change Procedure RevPrint to Procedure PrintList, which prints out the elements in the list in order. Does one of these routines constitute a better use of recursion? If so, which one?

Use the following function in answering Exercises 7 and 8:

```
FUNCTION Puzzle (Base, Limit : NonNegative) : Integer;
```

*Questions with italicized numbers are answered in the back of the book.

```
BEGIN (* Puzzle *)

  IF Base > Limit
    THEN Puzzle := -1
    ELSE
      IF Base = Limit
        THEN Puzzle := 1
        ELSE Puzzle := Base * Puzzle (Base + 1, Limit)

END; (* Puzzle *)
```

7. Identify
   (a) the base case(s) of Function Puzzle.
   (b) the general case(s) of Function Puzzle.

8. Show what would be written by the following calls to the recursive function Puzzle.
   (a) `Writeln (Puzzle (14, 10));`
   (b) `Writeln (Puzzle (4, 7));`
   (c) `Writeln (Puzzle (0, 0));`

9. Given the following function:

```
FUNCTION Func
   (Num : NumType) : NumType;

BEGIN (* Func *)
  IF Num = 0
    THEN Func := 0
    ELSE Func := Num + Func (Num + 1)
END; (* Func *)
```

   (a) Write a type declaration of NumType that will allow this function to pass the smaller-caller test.
   (b) Is Func (7) a legal call, given your declaration of NumType? If so, what is returned from the function?
   (c) Is Func (0) a legal call, given your declaration of NumType? If so, what is returned from the function?
   (d) Is Func (−5) a legal call, given your declaration of NumType? If so, what is returned from the function?
   (e) Is Func (−5.2) a legal call, given your declaration of NumType? If so, what is returned from the function?

10. Put comments on the following routines to identify the base and general cases and explain what each routine does.
    (a) `FUNCTION Power`
        `(Base, Exponent : Integer) : Integer;`

```
( * _____ * )

BEGIN (* Power *)
  IF Exponent = 0
    THEN Power := 1
    ELSE Power := Base * Power (Base, Exponent - 1)
END; (* Power *)
```

(b) FUNCTION Factorial
       (Num : Integer) : Integer;

    (* _____ *)

    BEGIN (* Factorial *)
      IF Num > 0
        THEN Factorial := Num * Factorial (Num - 1)
        ELSE
          IF Num = 0
            THEN Factorial := 1
            ELSE Writeln ('**** ERROR ****')
    END; (* Factorial *)

(c) PROCEDURE Sort
       (VAR Data   : ArrayType;
        FromIndex : IndexType;
        ToIndex   : IndexType);

    (* _____ *)

    VAR
      Maxi : IndexType; .

    BEGIN (* Sort *)
      IF FromIndex <> ToIndex
        THEN
          BEGIN

            (* Find index of the largest element in *)
            (* array between FromIndex and ToIndex. *)
            Maxi := MaxPosition (Data, FromIndex, ToIndex);

            Swap (Data[Maxi], Data[ToIndex]);

            Sort(Data, FromIndex, ToIndex - 1)

          END (* IF *)
    END; (* Sort *)

11. (a) Fill in the blanks to complete the function:

    FUNCTION Sum
       (List   : ArrayType;
        FromIndex : IndexType;
        ToIndex   : IndexType) : Integer;

       (* Computes the sum of the array elements *)
       (* between FromIndex and ToIndex.   *)

    BEGIN (* Sum *)

      IF FromIndex _____ ToIndex

        THEN (* _____ case *)

          Sum := _____

        ELSE (* _____ case *)

```
        Sum : = _____
    END; (* Sum *)
```

(b) Show how you would call this function to sum all the elements in an array called Numbers, which contains MaxArray elements.

(c) What run-time problem might you have with this function as it is coded?

12. You must assign the grades for a programming class. Right now the class is studying recursion, and they have been given this simple assignment: Write a recursive procedure SumSquares that takes a pointer to a linked list of integer elements and returns the sum of the squares of the elements.

Example:

SumSquares(List) = (5 * 5) + (2 * 2) + (3 * 3) + (1 * 1) = 39

Assume that the list is not empty.

You have received quite a variety of solutions. Grade the procedures below, marking errors where you see them.

```
(a) FUNCTION SumSquares
        (List : ListType) : Integer;

    BEGIN (* SumSquares *)
      SumSquares : = 0;

      IF List <> NIL
          THEN SumSquares : = SQR (List^.Info) +
                                  SumSquares(List^.Next)

    END; (* SumSquares *)

(b) FUNCTION SumSquares
        (List : ListType) : Integer;

    VAR
      Sum : Integer;

    BEGIN (* SumSquares *)

      Sum : = 0;

      WHILE List <> NIL DO
        BEGIN
          Sum : =List^.Info + Sum;
          List : = List^.Next
        END; (* WHILE *)

      SumSquares : = Sum

    END; (* SumSquares *)

(c) FUNCTION SumSquares
        (List : ListType) : Integer;
```

```
    BEGIN  (* SumSquares *)

      IF List = NIL
        THEN SumSquares := 0
        ELSE SumSquares := SQR(List^.Info) +
                            SumSquares(List^.Next)

    END;  (* SumSquares *)
```

(d) FUNCTION SumSquares
```
      (List : ListType) : Integer;

    BEGIN  (* SumSquares *)

      IF List^.Next = NIL
        THEN SumSquares := SQR(List^.Info)
        ELSE SumSquares := SQR(List^.Info) +
                            SumSquares(List^.Next)

    END;  (* SumSquares *)
```

(e) FUNCTION SumSquares
```
      (List : ListType) : Integer;

    BEGIN  (* SumSquares *)

      IF List = NIL
        THEN SumSquares := 0
        ELSE SumSquares := SumSquares(List^.Next) *
                            SumSquares(List^.Next)

    END;  (* SumSquares *)
```

13. The Fibonacci sequence is the series of integers

0, 1, 1, 2, 3, 5, 8, 13, 21, 34, 55, 89 . . .

Do you see the pattern? Each element in the series is the sum of the preceding two elements. There is a recursive formula for calculating the Nth number of the sequence (the 0th number is Fib(0) = 0):

$$\text{Fib}(N) = \begin{cases} N, & \text{if } N = 0 \text{ or } 1 \\ \text{Fib}(N-2) + \text{Fib}(N-1), & \text{if } N > 1 \end{cases}$$

That seems pretty intuitive. It just says that for N greater than 1, the Nth Fibonacci number is the sum of the $(N-2)th$ and $(N-1)th$ Fibonacci numbers.

(a) Write Fib as a recursive function.

(b) Calculate the value of Fib(6) by hand. What does this exercise tell you about the efficiency of the recursive solution? Would you call this a good use of recursion?

(c) Write a nonrecursive version of Function Fib.

14. A function SqrRoot (Num, Ans, Tol) calculates an approximation of the square root of Num, starting with an approximate answer (Ans), within the specified tolerance (Tol). The function uses Newton's method, as defined below:

$$\text{SqrRoot (Num, Ans, Tol)} = \begin{cases} \text{Ans}, & \text{if } |\text{Ans}^2 - \text{Num}| <= \text{Tol} \\ \text{SqrRoot (Num, (Ans}^2 + \text{Num)} / (2 * \text{Ans), Tol),} & \text{if } |\text{Ans}^2 - \text{Num}| > \text{Tol} \end{cases}$$

(a) What limitations must be made on the values of the parameters, if this method is to work correctly? Write type declarations to support the parameter types.

(b) Write a recursive version of Function SqrRoot, using the type declarations from part (a) to define the parameters.

(c) Write a nonrecursive version of Function SqrRoot.

15. A sequential search procedure has the following heading:

```
PROCEDURE Search
  (List        : ListType;    (* list to search      *)
   Value       : KeyType;     (* value to search for *)
   VAR Location : LocType;    (* location of value   *)
   VAR Found    : Boolean);   (* search successful?  *)
```

(a) Complete the procedure as a recursive search, assuming that List is the external pointer to a linked list of elements ordered by their key field, from smallest to largest (use the linked list declarations from Chapter 6). LocType is a pointer to a list node. If not Found, Location is undefined.

(b) Complete the procedure as a recursive search, assuming that the list values are stored sequentially in an array. The list elements are ordered by their key field, from smallest to largest (use the sequential list declarations from Chapter 6). LocType is an array index. If Value is not Found in the list, Location is undefined. (Note that the recursive routine will have to be a nested procedure, because the parameter list of this procedure does not include enough information to support a recursive solution. You cannot change the parameter list of Search.)

16. We want to count the number of paths possible to move in a two-dimensional grid from row 1, column 1 to row N, column N. Steps are restricted to going up or to the right, but not diagonally. The illustration below shows 3 of many paths, if N = 10:

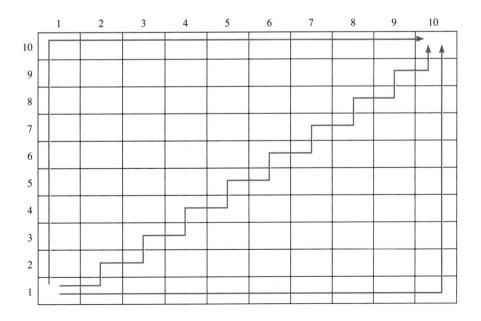

(a) The following function, NumPaths, is supposed to count the number of paths, but it has some problems. Debug the function.

```
FUNCTION NumPaths
   (Row, Col, N : Integer) : Integer;

BEGIN (* NumPaths *)
   IF Row = N
      THEN NumPaths := 1
      ELSE
         IF Col = N
            THEN NumPaths := NumPaths + 1
            ELSE NumPaths := NumPaths (Row + 1, Col) *
                             NumPaths (Row, Col + 1)

END; (* NumPaths *)
```

(b) After you have corrected the function, trace the execution of NumPaths (4) by hand. Why is this algorithm inefficient?

(c) The efficiency of this operation can be improved by keeping intermediate values of NumPaths in a two-dimensional array of Integer values. This keeps the function from having to recalculate values that it has already done. Design and code a version of NumPaths that uses this approach.

(d) Show an invocation of the version of NumPaths in part (c), including any array initialization necessary.

(e) How do the two versions of NumPaths compare in terms of time efficiency? Space efficiency?

17. Given the following function:

```
FUNCTION Ulam
   (Num : Integer) : Integer;

BEGIN (* Ulam *)

   IF Num < 2
      THEN Ulam := 1
      ELSE
         IF Num MOD 2 = 0
            THEN Ulam := Ulam (Num DIV 2)
            ELSE Ulam := Ulam (3 * Num + 1)

END; (* Ulam *)
```

(a) What problems come up in verifying this function?

(b) How many recursive calls are made by the following initial calls:

```
Writeln (Ulam (7));
Writeln (Ulam (8));
Writeln (Ulam (15));
```

18. Explain the relationship between dynamic storage allocation and recursion.

19. What do we mean by binding time, and what does it have to do with recursion?

20. Given the following values in List:

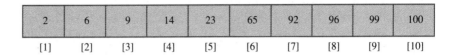

2	6	9	14	23	65	92	96	99	100
[1]	[2]	[3]	[4]	[5]	[6]	[7]	[8]	[9]	[10]

show the contents of the run-time stack during the execution of this call to BinarySearch:

```
BinarySearch
   (List,       (* list to search *)
   1,           (* from location  *)
   10,          (* to location    *)
   99,          (* search value   *)
   Location);   (* returned       *)
```

21. The input to the following two recursive routines is a pointer to a singly linked list of numbers, whose elements are unique (no duplicates) and unordered. Each node in the list contains two fields, Info (a number) and Next (a pointer to the next node).
   (a) Write a recursive function, MinLoc, that inputs a pointer to a list of unordered numbers and returns a pointer to the node that contains the minimum value in the list.
   (b) Write a recursive procedure, Sort, that inputs a pointer to an unordered list of numbers and reorders the values in the list from smallest to largest. This procedure may call the recursive MinLoc function that you wrote in part (a). (*Hint:* It is easier to swap the values in the Info part of the nodes than to try to reorder the nodes in the list.)

22. True or False? If false, correct the statement. *A recursive solution should be used when . . .*
   (a) computing time is critical.
   (b) the nonrecursive solution would be longer and more difficult to write.
   (c) computing space is critical.
   (d) your instructor says to use recursion.

Exercises 23–25 refer to the Maze application at the end of the chapter.

23. What are the base case(s) and general case(s) of the TryToEscape procedure?

24. Describe a scheme to improve the efficiency of the escape attempt by marking the OriginalMaze with the results of previous attempts.

25. A very large maze (MaxMaze = 100) contains very few open paths relative to the number of trap positions. To save space, you decide to represent the Maze ADT as an array of MaxMaze pointers, where each pointer accesses a list of Open, Tried, or Exit path positions in one row, as illustrated below:

Maze

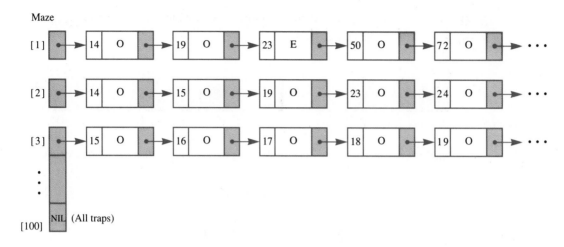

(a) Write type declarations to support MazeType.
(b) Describe algorithms for the revised MarkMaze and MazePosition operations.
(c) Because the maze is large, we do not want to keep two copies. Instead we will reset the maze to its original state after each escape attempt. Write procedure CleanupMaze, using the type declarations from part (a).
(d) Describe how this change of data representation affects the rest of Program MazeExit.

Binary Search Trees

GOALS

- To be able to define and use the following terminology:
  - binary tree
  - binary search tree
  - root
  - parent
  - child
  - ancestor
  - descendant
  - level
  - height
  - subtree
- To be able to define a binary search tree at the logical level.
- To be able to show what a binary search tree would look like after a series of insertions and deletions.
- To be able to implement the following binary search tree algorithms in Pascal:
  - creating an empty tree,
  - inserting an element,
  - deleting an element,
  - retrieving an element,
  - modifying an element,
  - traversing a tree in preorder, inorder, and postorder.

We have discussed some of the advantages of using a linear linked list to store value-ordered information. One of the drawbacks of using a linear linked list is the time it takes to search a long list. A sequential search of (possibly) all the nodes in the whole list is an O(N) operation. In Chapter 2 we saw how a binary search could find an element in an ordered list stored sequentially in an array. The binary search is an O(log₂N) operation. It would be nice if we could binary search a linked list, but there is no practical way to find the midpoint of a linked list of nodes. We can, however, reorganize the list's elements into a linked structure that is just perfect for binary searching: the *binary search tree*. The binary search tree provides us with a structure that retains the flexibility of a linked list while allowing quicker O(log₂N) access to any node in the list.

This chapter introduces some basic tree vocabulary and then develops the algorithms and implementations of the operations needed to use a binary search tree. We will assume that each element stored in the binary search tree is a record that contains a number of fields, including a field that is designated as a unique key. (In the figures that illustrate trees, we will only show the key values for simplicity.)

The Logical Level

Each node in a singly linked list may point to one other node: the one whose value follows it. Thus a singly linked list is a *linear* structure; each node in the list has a unique successor. A *binary tree* is a structure in which each node is capable of having *two* successor nodes, called *children*. Each of the children, being nodes in the binary tree, can also have up to two child nodes, and these children can also have up to two children, and so on, giving the tree its branching structure. The "beginning" of the tree is a unique starting node called the **root**.

Binary Tree   A structure with a unique starting node (the root), in which each node is capable of having two child nodes, and in which a unique path exists from the root to every other node.

Root   The top, or base, node of a tree structure.

Figure 9-1 depicts a binary tree. The root node of this binary tree contains the value A. Each node in the tree may have 0, 1, or 2 children. The node to the left of a node, if it exists, is called its **left child**. For instance, the left child of the root node contains the value B. The node to the right of a node, if it exists, is its **right child**. The right child of the root node contains the value C. The root node is the *parent* of the nodes containing B and C. (Some people use the terms *left son, right son,* and *father* to describe these relationships.) If a node in the tree has no children, it is called a *leaf*. For instance, the nodes containing G, H, E, I, and J are leaf nodes.

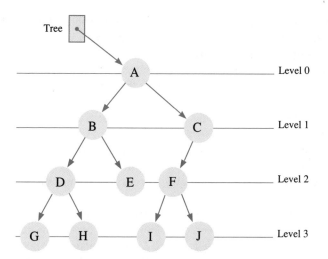

Figure 9-1
A Binary Tree

Leaf Node   Tree node that has no children.

In addition to specifying that a node may have up to two children, the definition of a binary tree states that a unique path exists from the root to every other node. This means that every node (except the root) has a unique parent. In the structure pictured below, the nodes have the correct number of children, but the unique path rule is violated: There are two paths from the root to the node containing D. Therefore this structure is not a binary tree:

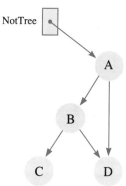

Note, in Figure 9-1, that each of the root node's children is itself the root of a smaller binary tree, or **subtree**. The root node's left child, containing B, is the root of its **left subtree**, while the right child, containing C, is the root of its **right subtree**. In fact, any node in the tree can be considered the root node of a subtree. The subtree whose root node has the value B also includes the nodes with values D, G, H, and E. These nodes are the **descendants** of the node containing B. The descendants of the node containing C are the nodes with the values F, I, and J. A node is the **ancestor** of another node if it is the parent of the node, or the parent of some other ancestor of that node. (Yes, this is a recursive definition.) The ancestors of the node with the value G are the nodes containing D, B, and A. Obviously, the root of the tree is the ancestor of every other node in the tree.

The **level** of a node refers to its distance from the root. If we designate the level of the root as 0 (zero), the nodes containing B and C are Level 1 nodes, the nodes containing D, E, and F are Level 2 nodes, and the nodes containing G, H, I, and J are Level 3 nodes.

The maximum level in a tree determines its **height**. The maximum number of nodes at any level is 2^N. However, often levels do not contain the maximum number of nodes. For instance, in Figure 9-1, Level 2 could contain four nodes, but because the node containing C in Level 1 only has one child, Level 2 contains three nodes. Level 3, which could contain eight nodes, only has four. We could make many differently shaped binary trees out of the 10 nodes in this tree. A few variations are illustrated in Figure 9-2. It is easy to see that the maximum number of levels in a binary tree with N nodes is N. What is the minimum number of levels? If we fill the tree by giving every node in each level two children until we run out of nodes, the tree will have $\log_2 N + 1$ levels [Figure 9-2(a)]. Demonstrate this to yourself by drawing "full" trees with 8 [$\log_2(8) = 3$] and 16 [$\log_2(16) = 4$] nodes. What if there are 7, 12, or 18 nodes?

The height of a tree is the critical factor in determining how efficiently we can search for elements. Consider the maximum-height tree in Figure 9-2(c). If we begin searching at the root node and follow the pointers from one node to the next, accessing the node with the value J (the farthest from the root) is an O(N) operation—no better than searching a linear list! On the other hand, given the minimum-height tree depicted in Figure 9-2(a), to access the node containing J, we only have to look at 3 other nodes— the ones containing E, A, and G—before we find J. Thus, if the tree is of minimum height, its *structure* supports $O(\log_2 N)$ access to any element.

However, the *arrangement* of the values in the tree pictured in Figure 9-2(a) does not lend itself to quick searching. Let's say that we want to find the value G. We begin searching at the root of the tree. This node contains E, not G, so we need to keep searching. But which of its children should we look at next, the right or the left? There is no special order to the nodes, so we will have to check *both* subtrees. We could search the tree, level by level, until we come across the value we are searching for. But that is an O(N) search operation, which is no better than searching a linked list!

To support $O(\log_2 N)$ searching, we will add a special property to the binary tree structure. We will put all the nodes with values *smaller* than the value in the root into its left subtree, and all the nodes with values *larger* than the value in the root into its right subtree. Figure 9-3 on page 532 shows the nodes from Figure 9-2(a) rearranged to satisfy this property. The root node, which contains E, accesses two subtrees. The left subtree contains all the values smaller than E and the right subtree contains all the values larger than E.

Figure 9-2 *Binary Trees with Ten Nodes*

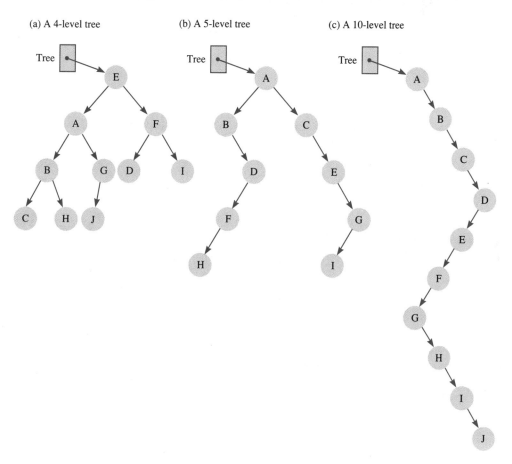

(a) A 4-level tree (b) A 5-level tree (c) A 10-level tree

Searching for the value G, we look first in the root node. G is larger than E, so we know that G must be in the root node's right subtree. The right child of the root node contains H. Now what? Do we go to the right or to the left? This subtree is also arranged according to the binary search property: The nodes with smaller values are to the left and the nodes with larger values are to the right. The value of this node, H, is greater than G, so we search to its left. The left child of this node contains the value F, which is smaller than G, so we reapply the rule and move to the right. The node to the right contains G; we have found the node we were searching for.

A binary tree with this special property is called a **binary search tree**. Like any binary tree, it gets its branching structure by allowing each node to have up to two child nodes. It gets its easy-to-search structure by maintaining the binary search property: The left child of any node (if there is one) is the root of the subtree that contains all of the values smaller than the node. The right child of any node (if there is one) is the root of the subtree that contains all of the values that are larger than the node.

Figure 9-3
A Binary Search
Tree

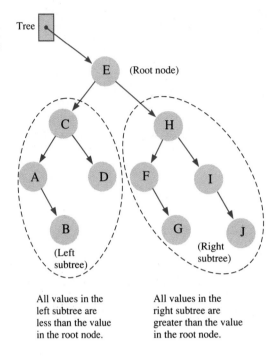

All values in the
left subtree are
less than the value
in the root node.

All values in the
right subtree are
greater than the value
in the root node.

Binary Search Tree   A binary tree in which the key value in any node is greater than the key value in its left child and any of its children (the nodes in the left subtree) and less than the key value in its right child and any of its children (the nodes in the right subtree).

Four comparisons instead of up to 10 doesn't sound like such a big deal, but as the number of elements in the structure increases, the difference becomes impressive. In the worst case—searching for the last node in a linear linked list—you must look at every node in the list; on the average you must search half the list. If the list contains 1000 nodes, you must make 1000 comparisons to find the last node! If the 1000 nodes were arranged in a binary search tree of minimum height, you would never make more than 10 ($\log_2 (1000) < 10$) comparisons, no matter which node you were seeking!

The Binary Search Tree ADT

Now let's specify the logical structure and the operations defined for a Binary Search Tree ADT. There are many operations that one might want to define to manipulate a binary search tree. We have included a "basic" set of operations in this specification; some other operations are specified in the exercises at the end of the chapter. In specifying these operations we will assume that the tree is accessed through the root (a pointer of type TreeType), that the elements are of type TreeElementType, and that the key field of each element is type KeyType.

Binary Search Tree ADT Specification

Structure   The placement of each element in the binary tree must satisfy the binary search property: The value of the key of an element is larger than the value of the key of any element in its left subtree, and smaller than the value of the key of any element in its right subtree.

Operations:

CreateTree (Tree)

Function:	Initializes Tree to empty state.
Input:	None
Preconditions:	None
Output:	Tree (TreeType)
Postconditions:	Tree accesses an empty tree.

DestroyTree (Tree)

Function:	Destroys all tree elements, leaving Tree empty.
Input:	Tree (TreeType)
Preconditions:	Tree has been created.
Output:	Tree (empty)
Postconditions:	Tree accesses an empty tree.

RetrieveElement (Tree, KeyValue, Element, ValueInTree)

Function:	Searches the binary search tree for the element whose key is KeyValue, and returns a copy of the element.
Input:	Tree (TreeType) KeyValue (KeyType)
Preconditions:	Tree accesses the root of a binary search tree.
Output:	Element (TreeElementType) ValueInTree (Boolean)
Postconditions:	ValueInTree = (Tree contains element whose key = KeyValue). IF ValueInTree, Element = a copy of the element containing KeyValue; otherwise Element is unchanged.

InsertElement (Tree, Element)

Function:	Adds Element to the binary search tree.
Input:	Tree (TreeType) Element (TreeElementType)

Preconditions:	Tree accesses the root of a binary search tree. The tree may be empty; it does not contain a node with the same key value as Element.
Output:	Tree
Postconditions:	Element exists in the binary search tree, leaving the tree in accordance with the description of its structure above.

ModifyElement (Tree, ModElement)

Function:	ModElement replaces existing tree element with same key.
Input:	Tree (TreeType) ModElement (TreeElementType)
Preconditions:	Element with same key as ModElement exists in Tree.
Output:	Tree
Postconditions:	Tree = original tree with value of ModElement replacing like-keyed original element

DeleteElement (Tree, KeyValue)

Function:	Deletes Element containing KeyValue from the binary search tree.
Input:	Tree (TreeType) KeyValue (KeyType)
Preconditions:	Tree accesses the root of a binary search tree; an element with the key KeyValue is known to exist in the tree.
Output:	Tree
Postconditions:	Element containing KeyValue is not in the tree; tree is in accordance with the description of its structure above.

PrintTree (Tree, TraversalOrder)

Function:	Prints all the elements in the binary search tree in the order indicated by TraversalOrder.
Input:	Tree (TreeType) TraversalOrder (TraversalType) is one of the following options: Inorder, Preorder, or Postorder. (These will be explained later in the chapter.)
Preconditions:	Tree accesses the root of a binary search tree; the tree may be empty.
Output:	List all of the elements in the tree (to standard output)
Postconditions:	Tree is not changed. Elements are printed to standard output.

These operations are similar to those provided to the user of the List ADT. From the user's point of view, the important thing is to be able to access and manipulate the data stored in the tree. Of course, the algorithms we'll develop to implement the operations will be different from those for the list operations.

The Implementation Level

We will develop the algorithms for the operations specified above and implement them as a linked structure whose nodes are allocated dynamically.

Tree Data Design

The nodes in a tree, like those in a linked list, consist of several parts. Because we are implementing the tree as a linked structure, we will access the nodes through their pointers. Before we go on, let's modify our node design terminology to describe tree nodes. Assuming that Ptr points to a particular node in the tree,

Node(Ptr)   refers to all the data at Ptr.
Info(Ptr)   refers to the tree user's data in Node(Ptr).
Key(Ptr)   refers to the key of the tree user's data in Node(Ptr).
Left(Ptr)   points to the left child of Node(Ptr).
Right(Ptr)   points to the right child of Node(Ptr).

The Left and Right fields, which contain pointers, will be used in the tree algorithms to link together the data stored in the tree. These fields are not accessed by the tree user.

Developing algorithms using this node terminology gives us the flexibility to choose different physical representations of the data structure. When we code examples of each operation, we will represent the binary search tree with dynamic allocation and pointer variables, using the following declarations:

```
TYPE
  KeyType = Integer;             (* the type of key in Info part *)

  TreeElementType = RECORD   (* the type of the user's data   *)
    Key : KeyType;

    .
    .      (* Declare other fields as needed. *)
    .
  END;    (* TreeElementType *)

  TreePtrType = ^TreeNodeType;

  TreeNodeType = RECORD
    Info  : TreeElementType;   (* the user's data         *)
    Left  : TreePtrType;       (* pointer to left child   *)
    Right : TreePtrType        (* pointer to right child *)
  END; (* TreeNodeType *)

  TreeType = TreePtrType;

VAR
  Tree : TreeType;
```

The Info field of the tree node, which contains the data that the user is interested in, may be of any data type. If it is of a simple type, such as Integer or Char, this whole field determines the order of the data; that is, Info is the Key. In applications that use binary search trees, however, the Info portion of the node typically contains a whole record of data.

We assume that the key is a field called Key in the Info record. If the element type in your application program uses a different name for the key field, you will need to modify all the references to the key in the tree operations to use the correct field name.

Another alternative is to make your code more design-like. If the keys are scalar types, you can leave the references to *Key(Ptr)* in your programs by implementing a function, Key. (We mentioned this idea in Chapter 6.) This function is internal to the Binary Search Tree ADT—it is for the use of the tree operations, not for the tree user.* Function Key inputs a pointer and returns the value of the key of the node pointed to by Ptr, as shown in the following example:

```
FUNCTION Key
  (Ptr : TreePtrType) : KeyType;
  (* Returns the key of Node(Ptr). *)

BEGIN (* Key *)

  Key := Ptr^.Info.Key   (* or whatever the key field name is *)

END;  (* Key *)
```

Now design-like expressions like "IF Key(Ptr) = KeyValue" are syntactically legal. Using this scheme, the code stays easy to read—"Key(Ptr)" is more readable than "Ptr^.Info.Key"—and the only editing change to correct the name of the key field would be within Function Key.

In most figures, we will depict tree nodes simply as circles labeled with the key value and linked with arrows. In figures that illustrate the details of the pointer manipulations, we will use a three-part node diagram, as shown below:

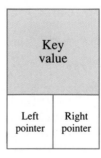

---

*If this ADT were implemented as a Turbo Pascal unit, Key would be in the Implementation Section; its heading would not be put into the Interface Section.

Creating a Binary Search Tree

Creating an empty binary search tree, using the declarations above, is easy: We simply set Tree, the external pointer, to NIL.

```
PROCEDURE CreateTree
  (VAR Tree : TreeType);

  (* Initializes Tree to empty state. *)
BEGIN (* CreateTree *)
  Tree := NIL
END;  (* CreateTree *)
```

This procedure has no preconditions; it will work fine whether or not Tree has previously been used to access a binary search tree. If the tree is not empty when CreateTree is called, however, all access to the node(s) in the tree will be lost. Thus CreateTree should not be used to reset a tree to the empty state; any nodes in the tree will be left stranded, unable to be Disposed of. If you want to get rid of an existing tree, you should call DestroyTree. (We will discuss the DestroyTree procedure later.)

Searching a Binary Search Tree

From the lessons we learned in developing the operations for linked lists, we know that an "all-purpose" search operation is a useful tool. Rather than coding separate searches for the retrieve, insert, delete, and modify operations, we will implement one search routine, FindNode. Then the other tree operations can call FindNode to perform a search. This procedure will not be one of the operations provided to the tree ADT user; it is an "internal" procedure that is only visible to the set of tree operations.*

Procedure FindNode inputs a pointer to a binary search tree (Tree) and the key of the element to find (KeyValue). It outputs a pointer to the desired node (NodePtr), if the key value is found. For the retrieve and modify operations, NodePtr is all we need to complete the operations. However, in deleting elements from linked lists, we saw that we must be able to access the *preceding* node, in order to reset the Next field to jump over the deleted node. A similar situation exists for the tree delete operation: We need to access the *parent* node, in order to reset the Left or Right pointer to jump over the deleted node. Therefore, Procedure FindNode will also return a pointer to the parent node, ParentPtr.

*If this ADT were implemented as a Turbo Pascal unit, FindNode would be in the Implementation Section, its heading would not be put into the Interface Section.

What do we do if KeyValue is not in the tree, as is the case when we are inserting a new element? In this case, we will return a NIL pointer for NodePtr. In inserting an element into a linked list, we searched for the node that logically precedes the new node, and reset its Next field to point to the new node. Similarly, when we insert into a binary search tree, we will set the Right or Left pointer of the parent node (the node that should "precede" the new node in the tree) to point to the new node. So ParentPtr will be useful in inserting, as well as deleting, elements. (We'll come back to this point in the development of the insert operation.)

What is the value of ParentPtr if KeyValue is found in the root node of the tree? In this case, there is no parent node, so we set ParentPtr to NIL.

Here is the specification of the *internal* tree procedure, FindNode:

■ FindNode (Tree, KeyValue, NodePtr, ParentPtr)

Function:	Searches the binary search tree for the node whose key is KeyValue.
Input:	Tree (TreeType)
	KeyValue (KeyType)
Preconditions:	Tree accesses the root of a binary search tree.
Output:	NodePtr (TreePtrType)
	ParentPtr (TreePtrType)
Postconditions:	IF KeyValue is found in a tree node, then NodePtr = pointer to the node that contains KeyValue and ParentPtr = pointer to Node(NodePtr)'s parent node. If KeyValue is found in the root node, ParentPtr = NIL. IF KeyValue is not found in a tree node, then NodePtr = NIL and ParentPtr = pointer to the node in the tree that is the logical parent of a node containing KeyValue.

Let's look at the search algorithm in detail. We will use NodePtr and ParentPtr (the output parameters) to search the tree. Because we access the tree through its root, we initialize NodePtr to the external pointer, Tree. The initial value of ParentPtr is NIL; in case we find KeyValue in the root node, ParentPtr will have the appropriate value. Found, a local variable, is initially False. Now we begin to search:

FindNode

WHILE more elements to search AND NOT Found DO
  IF Key(NodePtr) = KeyValue
    THEN Found ← True
    ELSE Advance pointers.

What do we mean by "advance pointers"? First ParentPtr catches up to NodePtr. (Remember the inchworm?) Then we advance NodePtr to point to the appropriate one of Node(NodePtr)'s children. But which child: *Right* or *Left?* This depends on the value in the node. If Key(NodePtr) is greater than KeyValue, we set NodePtr to point to the node's left child; otherwise we set NodePtr to point to the node's right child.

Advance Pointers

ParentPtr ← NodePtr

IF Key(NodePtr) > KeyValue
   THEN NodePtr ← Left(NodePtr)
   ELSE NodePtr ← Right(NodePtr)

When does the loop terminate? There are two terminating conditions: First, we stop searching if the correct node is found. In this case, NodePtr points to the node containing KeyValue, and ParentPtr points to this node's parent. Second, if KeyValue does not exist in the tree, we search until we fall out of the tree. At this point, NodePtr = NIL, and ParentPtr points to the node that *would be* the parent of a node containing KeyValue—if it did exist in the tree. (We will use this value of ParentPtr when we insert into a tree.) The resulting loop condition is

```
WHILE (NodePtr <> NIL) AND NOT Found
```

The algorithm illustrates that the maximum number of comparisons in a binary search tree equals the height of the tree. As we discussed earlier, this may range from $\log_2 N$ to N (where N is the number of tree elements), depending on the shape of the tree.

The complete procedure, using the declarations above, is

```
PROCEDURE FindNode
  (Tree          : TreeType;
   KeyValue      : KeyType;
   VAR NodePtr   : TreePtrType;
   VAR ParentPtr : TreePtrType);

  (* Find the node that contains KeyValue; set NodePtr to   *)
  (* point to the node and ParentPtr to point to its parent *)

VAR
  Found : Boolean;  (* KeyValue found in tree? *)

BEGIN (* FindNode *)

  (* Set up to search. *)
  NodePtr   := Tree;
  ParentPtr := NIL;
  Found     := False;

  (* Search until no more nodes to search or until found.  *)
  (* Loop Invariant: Node containing key does not exist in *)
  (* an ancestor of Node(NodePtr).                         *)
  WHILE (NodePtr <> NIL) AND NOT Found DO
    IF NodePtr^.Info.Key = KeyValue
      THEN Found := True
```

```
                    ELSE (* Advance pointers. *)
                     BEGIN

                       ParentPtr := NodePtr;

                       IF NodePtr^.Info.Key > KeyValue
                         THEN NodePtr := NodePtr^.Left
                         ELSE NodePtr := NodePtr^.Right

                     END (* advance pointers *)
            END; (* FindNode *)
```

Let's trace this operation, using the tree in Figure 9-4. We want to find the element with the key 18. NodePtr is initially set to Tree, the external pointer. NodePtr^.Info.Key < 18 (KeyValue), so we advance the pointers. ParentPtr now points to the root node and we move NodePtr to the right; it now points to the node with the key 20. This key is greater than KeyValue, so we advance the pointers. Now ParentPtr points to the node with the key 20, and we move NodePtr to the left; NodePtr now points to the node with the key 18. Now NodePtr^.Info.Key = KeyValue. Found is true, so we stop looping. We exit the procedure with NodePtr pointing to the node with the desired key, and with ParentPtr pointing to this node's parent.

Next, let's look at an example where the key is not found in the tree. We want to find the element with the key 7. NodePtr is initially set to Tree. The key of the root node is greater than 7, so we move to the left. Now NodePtr points to the node containing 9 and ParentPtr points to the root node. KeyValue (7) is less than 9, so we move again to the left. Now NodePtr = NIL; it has fallen out of the tree. Since there's no more to search in this subtree, we stop looping. We exit the procedure with NodePtr = NIL and ParentPtr pointing to the node with the key 9. If we were calling FindNode with the intention of subsequently inserting a node with the key 7, we would now know two things:

1. Since NodePtr = NIL, we know that there is no node with the key 7 in the tree.
2. Since ParentPtr points to the last node visited before we fell out of the tree, we know that the new node, with a key value of 7, will be attached to Node(ParentPtr).

Figure 9-4
Tracing the Find-
Node Operation

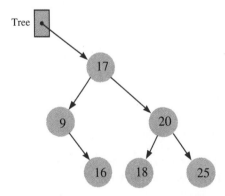

This information will be very helpful when we are developing the InsertElement operation.

The RetrieveElement Operation

The RetrieveElement operation described in our ADT specification looks for a node that has a given key value and then returns a copy of its Info field, the part of the node that belongs to the user. The algorithm for the operation looks like this:

RetrieveElement

FindNode in Tree that contains KeyValue

ValueInTree ← (node was found in tree?)

IF ValueInTree
    THEN Copy Info field of node into Element

Since we already have Procedure FindNode, the RetrieveElement operation is trivial. The first part of the operation, to locate the node, is performed by FindNode. If the key value is in the tree, the NodePtr parameter will point to the node that contains it; otherwise NodePtr will be NIL. The rest of the algorithm can be coded without further explanation:

```
PROCEDURE RetrieveElement
   (Tree           : TreeType;
    KeyValue       : KeyType;
    VAR Element       : TreeElementType;
    VAR ValueInTree : Boolean);

   (* Searches the binary search tree for the element whose *)
   (* key is KeyValue, and returns a copy of the element.   *)
VAR
   NodePtr   : TreePtrType; (* pointer to node with KeyValue *)
   ParentPtr : TreePtrType; (* used for FindNode interface   *)
BEGIN (* RetrieveElement *)

   (* Find node in tree that contains KeyValue. *)
   FindNode (Tree, KeyValue, NodePtr, ParentPtr);
   ValueInTree := (NodePtr <> NIL);

   IF ValueInTree
     THEN Element := NodePtr^.Info
END;  (* RetrieveElement *)
```

In an effort to encapsulate the tree structure, we have designed the retrieve operation to return a *copy* of the node's Info field rather than letting the user access the node directly (by giving back a pointer to the node, for instance). With this design, the tree users don't need to deal with Right and Left pointers; they just deal with the Info field.

Because Element contains a copy of the data in the tree, modifying the values in Element after a call to RetrieveElement does not make changes to the data stored in the tree. To change the values in the tree, you must call ModifyElement.

The ModifyElement Operation

The ModifyElement tree operation inputs Tree, which points to the root node of a binary search tree, and ModElement, an element of TreeElementType. It causes the tree element with the same key as ModElement to be replaced with the new value. Since FindNode will give us a pointer to the correct tree node, the design for ModifyElement is simple:

ModifyElement

FindNode containing ModElement.Key
Copy ModElement into the Info field of the node in the tree.

We do not even have to check whether the pointer value returned from FindNode is NIL, since the preconditions of ModifyElement state that the node is known to be in the tree. Here is the procedure:

```
PROCEDURE ModifyElement
    (VAR Tree    : TreeType;
     ModElement : TreeElementType);

    (* ModElement replaces existing tree element with same key. *)

VAR
    NodePtr   : TreePtrType; (* pointer to node with KeyValue *)
    ParentPtr : TreePtrType; (* used for FindNode interface   *)

BEGIN (* ModifyElement *)

    (* Find the node with the same key as ModElement.Key. *)
    FindNode (Tree, ModElement.Key, NodePtr, ParentPtr);

    (* NodePtr points to the tree node with same key. *)
    NodePtr^.Info := ModElement

END;  (* ModifyElement *)
```

There is one interesting issue in the coding of this procedure. Since the binary search tree changes as a result of this operation, Tree is specified as an output of this operation. Thus we marked Tree as a VAR parameter. In fact, though, Tree cannot be modified by this procedure, even if we are modifying the root node. True, we may modify the Info field of this node, but since we are not changing the structure of the tree in any way, Tree—a *pointer*—is never modified by this operation.

So should Tree be a VAR parameter? We answer yes to this question for two reasons. First, it is strange to see an operation called "modify" that does not have any VAR parameters—it doesn't look as if anything is changed. The value in the tree is changed almost as a side effect of the operation. So even though Tree itself is not changed by the call, we mark it as a VAR parameter to indicate that data that it accesses will be modified by the procedure.

A second reason for marking Tree as a VAR parameter is because we do not know, from the heading, how the tree is implemented. If we decided to change the implementation to an array-based tree (similar to the array-based linked list in Chapter 7), changing the value of a field would require Tree to be a VAR parameter. We don't want to change the procedure heading, however, if we change the implementation. So we have made Tree a VAR parameter for a second reason. Both of these reasons are stylistic, not syntactic, and another programmer might choose otherwise.

The InsertElement Operation

To create and maintain the information stored in a binary search tree, we must have an operation that will insert new nodes into the tree. We will use the following insertion approach: A new node will always be inserted into its appropriate position in the tree as a *leaf*. Figure 9-5 shows a series of insertions into a binary tree.

The algorithm for the InsertElement operation has three tasks that must be performed:

InsertElement

Create a node to contain the new element.
Find the insertion place.
Change pointers to insert the new node into the tree.

We get space for the new node by calling the Pascal New procedure. Because the new node will be inserted as a leaf in the tree, we can set both of its pointer fields to NIL. Then the new data will be stored in the node's Info field.

Create a Node

New (NewNode)
Left(NewNode) ← NIL
Right(NewNode) ← NIL
Info(NewNode) ← Element

Now that the new node has been created, we can search for its insertion point. Let's see how Procedure FindNode can be used to perform this task for us. We call FindNode, asking it to find the node with the key Element.Key:

FindNode (Tree, Element.Key, NodePtr, ParentPtr)

Suppose we want to insert an element with the key value 13 to the binary search tree pictured in Figure 9-6. In Procedure FindNode, NodePtr is initialized to point to

Figure 9-5 *Insertions into a Binary Search Tree*

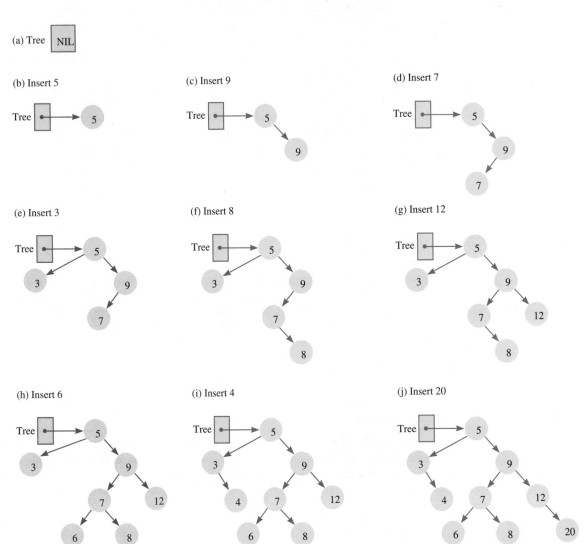

the root of the tree, and ParentPtr is initialized to NIL [Figure 9-6(a)]. The key of the root node (7) is smaller than KeyValue (13), so we move NodePtr to the right, dragging ParentPtr along behind it [Figure 9-6(b)]. Now Key(NodePtr), 15, is greater than KeyValue, so we move NodePtr to the left, with ParentPtr following [Figure 9-6(c)]. The key of Node(NodePtr), 10, is now smaller than KeyValue, so ParentPtr catches up, and NodePtr moves to the right [Figure 9-6(d)]. At this point, NodePtr is NIL, so we exit Procedure FindNode with the pointers as shown in Figure 9-6(d).

Of course, KeyValue wasn't *supposed* to be found in the tree, for we are just now inserting its node. The good news is that NodePtr has fallen out of the tree just at the

Figure 9-6
**Using Procedure
FindNode to Find
the Insertion Point**

(a)

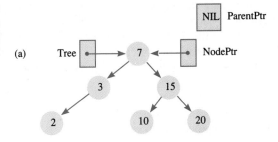

(b)

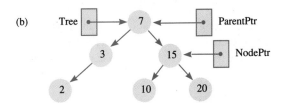

(c)

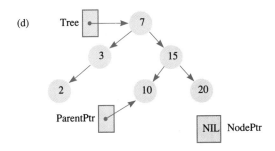

(d)

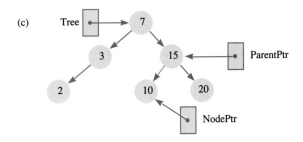

(d)

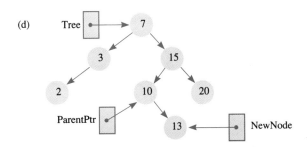

spot where the new node should be inserted. Since ParentPtr is trailing right behind NodePtr, we can simply attach the new node to Node(ParentPtr) [Figure 9-6(e)].

Now we're ready for the third task: to fix the pointers in Node(ParentPtr) to attach the new node. In the general case we compare the key of the new element to the key of Node(ParentPtr). Either the Left or the Right pointer field of Node(ParentPtr) must be set to NewNode:

Attach New Node

IF Key(ParentPtr) > Key(NewNode)
   THEN Left (ParentPtr) ← NewNode
   ELSE Right(ParentPtr) ← NewNode

In the case of inserting the first node into an empty tree, however, ParentPtr still equals NIL and references to Node(ParentPtr) are illegal. We need to make inserting the first node into the tree a special case. We can test for ParentPtr = NIL to determine whether the tree is empty; if so, we will change Tree to point to the new node.

Attach New Node (Revised)

IF ParentPtr = NIL
   THEN Tree ← NewNode
   ELSE (tree is not empty)
     IF Key(ParentPtr) > Key(NewNode)
       THEN Left(ParentPtr) ← NewNode
       ELSE Right(ParentPtr) ← NewNode

Taken together, the pieces of the insert design can be coded as procedure InsertElement, with the interface described in the Binary Search Tree ADT specification. Note that in this procedure, Tree *must* be a VAR parameter; if we are inserting into an empty tree, the value of Tree will be changed from NIL to NewNode.

```
PROCEDURE InsertElement
  (VAR Tree : TreeType;
   Element  : TreeElementType);

  (* Add Element to the binary search tree. Assumes that no *)
  (* element with the same key exists in the tree.          *)

VAR
  NewNode   : TreePtrType;  (* pointer to new node        *)
  NodePtr   : TreePtrType;  (* used for FindNode call      *)
  ParentPtr : TreePtrType;  (* points to new node's parent *)

BEGIN (* InsertElement *)

  (* Create a new node. *)
  New (NewNode);
  NewNode^.Left  := NIL;
  NewNode^.Right := NIL;
  NewNode^.Info  := Element;
```

```
(* Search for the insertion place. *)
FindNode (Tree, Element.Key, NodePtr, ParentPtr);

(* If this is first node in tree, set Tree to NewNode; *)
(* otherwise, link new node to Node(ParentPtr).        *)
IF ParentPtr = NIL
  THEN Tree := NewNode  (* first node in the tree *)
  ELSE (* Add to the existing tree. *)
    IF ParentPtr^.Info.Key > Element.Key
      THEN ParentPtr^.Left  := NewNode
      ELSE ParentPtr^.Right := NewNode

END; (* InsertElement *)
```

A Recursive InsertElement

We can also implement the InsertElement operation recursively. This algorithm does not use the FindNode operation; the looping part of the search for the insertion place is replaced by recursion. Before we go into the development of the algorithm, we want to reiterate that *every* node in a binary search tree is the root node of a binary search tree. In Figure 9-7(a), we want to insert a node with the key value 13 into the tree

Figure 9-7
The Recursive
InsertElement
Operation

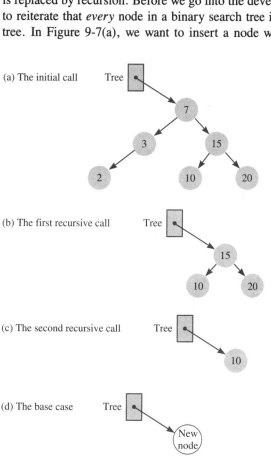

(a) The initial call   Tree

(b) The first recursive call   Tree

(c) The second recursive call   Tree

(d) The base case   Tree   New node

whose root is the node containing 7. Since 7 is less than 13, we know that the new node belongs in the root node's right subtree. We have now redefined a smaller version of our original problem: We want to insert a node with the key value 13 into the *tree whose root is Tree^.Right* [Figure 9-7(b)]. Of course, we have a procedure to insert elements into binary search tree: InsertElement. InsertElement is called recursively:

```
InsertElement (Tree^.Right, Element);
```

InsertElement begins its execution, looking for the place to insert Element in the tree whose root is the node with the key value 15. We compare the key of the root node to the key of Element (13); 13 < 15, so we know that the new Element belongs in the tree's left subtree. Again we have redefined a smaller version of the problem: We want to insert a node with the key value 13 into the tree *whose root is Tree^.Left* [Figure 9-7(c)]. We call InsertElement recursively to perform this task. Remember that in this (recursive) execution of InsertElement, Tree points to the node whose key is 15, not the original Tree root:

```
InsertElement (Tree^.Left, Element);
```

Again we recursively execute InsertElement. We compare the key of Element to the key of the (current) root node, then call InsertElement to insert the new Element into the correct subtree—the left subtree if Element.Key is less than the key of the root node; the right subtree if Element.Key is greater than the key of the root node.

Where does it all end? There must be a base case, in which space for the new element is allocated and the value of Element copied into it. This case occurs when Root = NIL, when the subtree we wish to insert into is empty. (Remember, we are going to add Element as a leaf node.) Figure 9-7(d) illustrates the base case. We can create the new node and link it to the correct field of its logical parent with the call:

```
New (Tree);
```

Wait a minute! How does this call to New link the new node to the existing tree? To understand this point, we must consider what *Tree* is in a recursive execution of the procedure. The last recursive call [Figure 9-8(a)] is InsertElement (Tree^.Right, Element). Since Tree is a VAR parameter, in the final recursive execution of InsertElement, Tree *is* the Right field of the node containing 10 (the logical parent of the new node). The call to New(Tree) puts the address of the new node into the Right field of the node containing 10, thus linking the new node into the tree structure [Figure 9-8(b)].

This point is critical to understanding how the recursive version of InsertElement works correctly: If Tree is a VAR parameter, the pointer that is being passed to InsertElement is not an external pointer like NodePtr in the FindNode procedure; it is the actual Left or Right field of a node in the tree. Tree is *not a copy* of a node's Left or Right child's address; it is actually a pointer field *in the tree*.

Figure 9-8
The Tree Parameter
Is a Pointer within
the Tree

(a) The last call to InsertElement

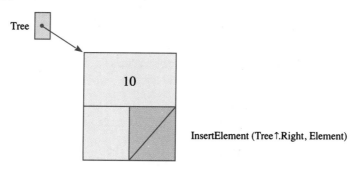

Tree

10

InsertElement (Tree↑.Right, Element)

(b) Within the last execution of InsertElement

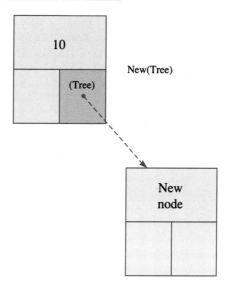

10

(Tree)

New(Tree)

New
node

The recursive procedure is summarized below:

InsertElement (Tree, Element)

Definition:	Insert Element into binary search Tree.
Size:	The number of elements in path from root to insertion place.
Base Case:	If Tree = NIL, then allocate new leaf Node(Tree) to contain Element.
General Cases:	(1) If Element.Key < Key(Tree), then InsertElement (Tree^.Left, Element) (2) If Element.Key > Key(Tree), then InsertElement (Tree^.Right, Element)

Here is the recursive version of the InsertElement procedure.

```
PROCEDURE InsertElement
  (VAR Tree   : TreeType;
   Element    : TreeElementType);
BEGIN (* InsertElement *)

  IF Tree = NIL
    THEN  (* Base Case: Allocate new leaf Node(Tree). *)
      BEGIN
        New (Tree);
        Tree^.Left  := NIL;
        Tree^.Right := NIL;
        Tree^.Info  := Element
      END (* IF Tree = NIL *)

    ELSE
      IF Element.Key < Tree^.Info.Key
        THEN (* General Case 1: Insert in left subtree. *)
          InsertElement (Tree^.Left, Element)
        ELSE (* General Case 2: Insert in right subtree. *)
          InsertElement (Tree^.Right, Element)
END;  (* InsertElement *)
```

Is this a "good" use of recursion? To make this decision, we must answer several questions:

Is the depth of recursion relatively shallow?

Yes. The depth of recursion is dependent on the height of the tree. If the tree is well balanced (relatively short and bushy, not tall and stringy), the depth of recursion will be closer to $O(\log_2 N)$ than to $O(N)$.

Is the recursive solution shorter or clearer than the nonrecursive version?

Yes. The recursive solution is certainly shorter than the combination of the nonrecursive procedure InsertElement *plus* its supporting procedure FindNode. Is it more clear? Once you accept that in every recursive execution of InsertElement, the Tree parameter is actually a pointer field within the tree, the recursive version becomes intuitively obvious.

Is the recursive version much less efficient than the nonrecursive version?

No. Both the recursive and nonrecursive versions of the InsertElement are $O(\log_2 N)$ operations, assuming a well-balanced tree. The only efficiency issue of concern is that of space. Element is an input parameter; our procedure passes a copy of it on each recursive call. If Element is a large record, these copies may cause an overflow of the run-time stack. (It would be better to make Element a VAR parameter if TreeElementType is large or the tree has great height.)

We give the recursive version of the procedure an 'A'; it is a good use of recursion.

Insertion Order and Tree Shape

Because nodes are always added as leaves, the order in which nodes are inserted determines the shape of the tree. Figure 9-9 illustrates how the same data, inserted in different orders, will produce very differently shaped trees. If the values are inserted in order (or in reverse order), the tree will be very skewed. A random mix of the elements will produce a shorter, "bushy" tree. Since the height of the tree determines the maximum number of comparisons in a binary search, the tree's shape is very important. Obviously, minimizing the height of the tree will maximize the efficiency of the search. There are algorithms to adjust a tree to make its shape more desirable; these schemes are subject matter for more advanced courses.

Figure 9-9
The Input Order
Determines the
Shape of the Tree

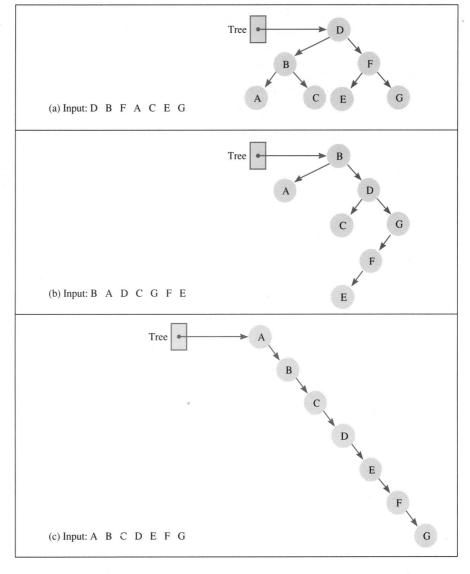

(a) Input: D B F A C E G

(b) Input: B A D C G F E

(c) Input: A B C D E F G

The DeleteElement Operation

The DeleteElement operation inputs the external pointer to a binary search tree (Tree) and a delete key (KeyValue), and finds and deletes the node containing that key from the tree. According to the specifications of the operation, the KeyValue is known to exist in the tree. These specifications suggest a two-part operation:

DeleteElement

FindNode in Tree that contains KeyValue.
DeleteNode from the tree.

Procedure FindNode will perform the first task. The second part of the operation—deleting this node from the tree—is more complicated. This task varies according to the position of the node in the tree. Obviously it is simpler to delete a leaf than to delete the root of the tree. In fact, we can break down the DeleteNode algorithm into three cases, depending on the number of children linked to the node we want to delete:

1. *Deleting a leaf (no children):* As shown in Figure 9-10, deleting a leaf is simply a matter of setting the appropriate link of its parent to NIL and then disposing of the unnecessary node.
2. *Deleting a node with only one child:* The simple solution for deleting a leaf will not suffice for deleting a node with children, because we don't want to lose all of its descendants from the tree. We want to make the pointer from the parent skip over the deleted node and point instead to the child of the node we intend to delete. We then dispose of the unwanted node (see Figure 9-11).

Figure 9-10   *Deleting a Leaf Node*

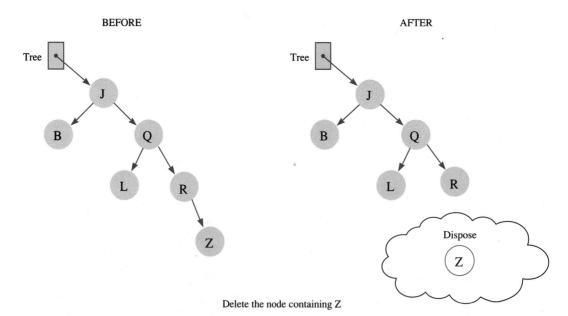

Delete the node containing Z

Figure 9-11   *Deleting a Node with One Child*

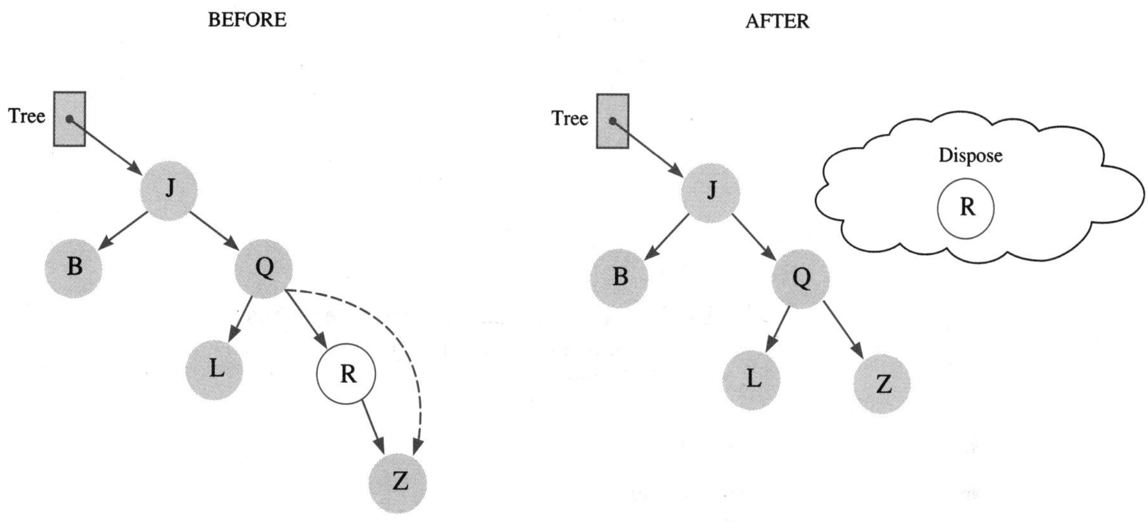

Delete the node containing R

3. *Deleting a node with two children.* This case is the most complicated because we cannot make the parent of the deleted node point to *both* of the deleted node's children. There are several ways to accomplish this deletion. The method we will use is to replace the Info part of the node we wish to delete with the Info part of its logical predecessor—the node whose key is closest in value to, but less than, the key of the node to be deleted. This replacement node will have either 0 or 1 child. We then delete the *replacement node* by changing one of its parent's pointers (see Figure 9-12).

Examples of all of these types of deletions are shown in Figure 9-13.

Developing the Delete Operation

It is clear that the delete task will involve changing pointers of the *parent* of the node to be deleted. Luckily, we thought of this ahead of time and implemented Procedure FindNode accordingly. We call FindNode to locate the node that contains KeyValue. Since the specifications state that KeyValue exists in the tree, on return from FindNode, NodePtr will be pointing to the node containing KeyValue, and ParentPtr will be pointing to its parent node [or will be NIL if Node(NodePtr) is the root of the tree].

Now for the fun part: deleting Node(NodePtr). In the interest of keeping our program modules to a reasonable (short) length, let's isolate the DeleteNode task by making it a nested procedure of the DeleteElement operation. What inputs and outputs does this procedure need? First, we need ParentPtr, so that we can change the appropriate pointer field in the parent node. We also need NodePtr, so that we will know which of Node(ParentPtr)'s children to delete—the left one or the right one. Finally, we need

Figure 9-12   Deleting a Node with Two Children

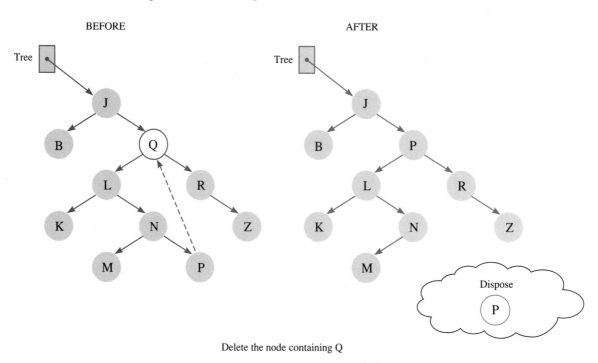

Delete the node containing Q

the root pointer of the tree; this pointer may be changed if we delete the root node of the tree. Here is Procedure DeleteElement, which calls Procedure DeleteNode:

```
PROCEDURE DeleteElement
  (VAR Tree : TreeType;
   KeyValue : KeyType);

  (* Deletes the element containing KeyValue from the binary *)
  (* search tree pointed to by Tree. Assumes that this key   *)
  (* value is known to exist in the tree.                    *)

VAR
  NodePtr   : TreePtrType; (* pointer to node to be deleted *)
  ParentPtr : TreePtrType; (* pointer to parent node        *)

BEGIN (* DeleteElement *)

  (* Find node containing KeyValue. *)
  FindNode (Tree, KeyValue, NodePtr, ParentPtr);

  (* Delete node pointed to by NodePtr. ParentPtr points *)
  (* to the parent node, or is NIL if deleting root node. *)
  DeleteNode (Tree, NodePtr, ParentPtr)

END;  (* DeleteElement *)
```

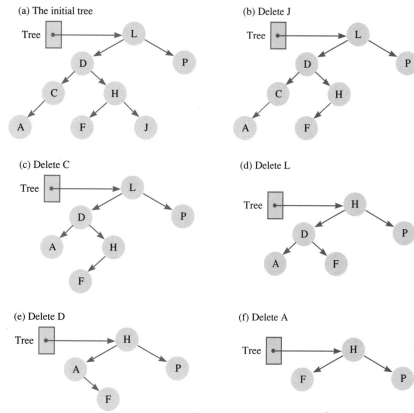

Figure 9-13
Deletions from a
Binary Search Tree

(a) The initial tree

(b) Delete J

(c) Delete C

(d) Delete L

(e) Delete D

(f) Delete A

Let's develop the algorithm for DeleteNode case by case. The first case involves deleting a leaf. Figure 9-14 shows the part of the tree we are working on.

Delete Leaf

IF (Right(NodePtr) = NIL) AND (Left(NodePtr) = NIL)
  THEN set appropriate field of Node(ParentPtr) to NIL

Which field of the parent node is the appropriate one: Left or Right? We check to see which of the parent node's pointer fields points to Node(NodePtr):

Set ParentPtr

IF Right(ParentPtr) = NodePtr
  THEN Right(ParentPtr) ← NIL
  ELSE Left(ParentPtr) ← NIL

If Node(Ptr) is not a leaf, we need to determine how many children it has:

IF (Right(NodePtr) <> NIL) AND (Left(NodePtr) <> NIL)
  THEN Delete node with two children

Figure 9-14
Deleting a Leaf

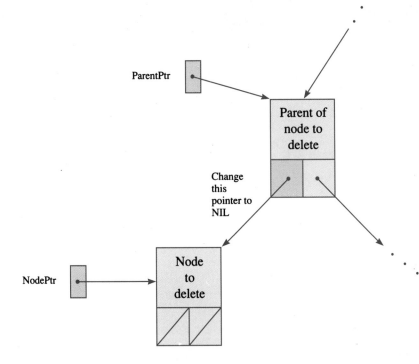

This is the most complicated case; we'll come back to it later.

ELSE Delete node with one child

Is it a right child or a left child? (See Figure 9-15.) Let's check first for a right child, then for a left. We know it can't have both.

Delete Node with One Child
IF Right(Ptr) <> NIL
  THEN
    Set the appropriate field of Node(ParentPtr) to Right(NodePtr)
  ELSE
    Set the approriate field of Node(ParentPtr) to Left(NodePtr)

Which is the "appropriate" field of Node(ParentPtr)? As in the case of deleting a leaf, we can examine the fields of Node(ParentPtr) to find which pointer field points to Node(NodePtr). (See the Set ParentPtr algorithm above.)

To delete a node with two children, we search the tree for the *immediate predecessor* of the node to be deleted. We are not talking about the parent node, but rather the node whose key value is closest to, but less than, the key value of the node to be deleted. *We will not actually delete Node(NodePtr).* Instead we will replace its *contents* with the Info field of its logical predecessor. Of course we don't want to have two copies of this node in the tree, so we will delete the node we copied from. Why is deleting this

Figure 9-15
Deleting a Node
with One Child

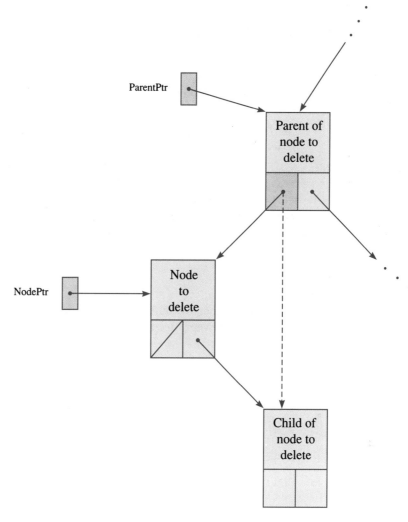

node easier than deleting the node with two children? As you will see, the replacement node has at most one child, so its deletion is a relatively simple matter.

Where is the replacement node? The largest key value in the tree that is less than Key(NodePtr) must be the *largest key in Node(NodePtr)'s left subtree.* Let's write a little "helper" procedure, FindAndRemoveMax, that will return a pointer to the largest node in a (sub)tree, after unlinking it from the tree.

The maximum value in a tree is in its *rightmost node.* A recursive procedure to find and unlink this node is very simple:

```
PROCEDURE FindAndRemoveMax
   (VAR Tree    : TreePtrType;
    VAR MaxPtr  : TreePtrType);
```

```
BEGIN (* FindAndRemoveMax *)

  IF Tree^.Right = NIL
    THEN (* Base Case: maximum found *)
      BEGIN
        MaxPtr := Tree;           (* return pointer to max node *)
        Tree   := Tree^.Left   (* unlink max node from tree  *)
      END (* Base Case *)

    ELSE (* General Case: find and remove from right subtree *)
      FindAndRemoveMax (Tree^.Right)

END; (* FindAndRemoveMax *)
```

As in the recursive InsertElement procedure, Tree is passed as a VAR parameter. Thus Tree is an actual pointer field in the tree, not an external pointer. Therefore, the modification to Tree in the Base Case:

```
Tree := Tree^.Left;
```

actually changes the tree.

Let's walk through the procedure, using the example in Figure 9-16. On the initial call to FindAndRemoveMax, Tree accesses the node containing M. Tree^.Right is not

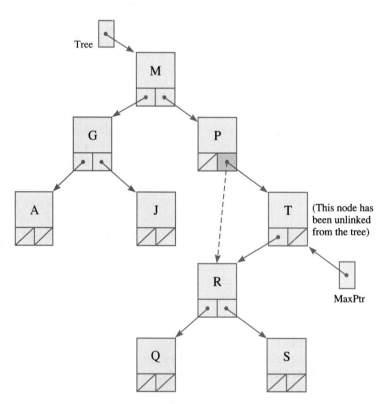

Figure 9-16
FindAnd-RemoveMax

NIL, so we call FindAndRemoveMax recursively to process the right subtree. In the first recursive execution, Tree is the Right field of the node containing M, which points to the node that contains P. Tree^.Right is not NIL, so we call FindAndRemoveMax recursively to process the right subtree. In the next recursive execution of FindAnd-RemoveMax, Tree is the Right field of the node containing P. Now Tree^.Right *is* NIL, so we take the base case. MaxPtr is set to Tree, and Tree (the Right field of the node containing P) is reset to Tree^.Left. Note that we set Tree to Tree^.Left, not to NIL. We know that the node containing the maximum key has no right child, but it may have a left subtree, as in this example.

What is the initial call to this procedure from DeleteNode? We want to find and remove the maximum value in Node(NodePtr)'s left subtree, and to return a pointer to the node with the maximum key in ReplacePtr:

```
FindAndRemoveMax (Tree^.Left, ReplacePtr);
```

Figure 9-17 shows two different situations: If the node to the left of Node(NodePtr) has no right child, then this node contains the replacement value [see Figure 9-17(a)]. Otherwise, the replacement value is found in the rightmost descendant in Node(NodePtr)'s left subtree [see Figure 9-17(b)]. Walk through FindandRemoveMax to see how the replacement node is successfully unlinked in each case.

Now we effect the "deletion" of the unwanted element by copying the Info part of the replacement node into the node to delete:

Info(NodePtr) ← Info(ReplacePtr)

Finally, we call Dispose to deallocate the unneeded space. If there is 0 or 1 child, we simply Dispose(NodePtr). In the case of deleting a node with two children, however, we want to dispose of Node(ReplacePtr).

The DeleteNode design has one remaining problem: If we try to delete the root node, we may run into difficulties. If the root node has two children, there is no problem, since we only copy information into it; we don't change its address. If the root node has no children or one child, however, we must change the value of Tree, the external pointer to the tree. In addition, the references to Left(ParentPtr) and Right(ParentPtr) will cause run-time errors, because ParentPtr = NIL. We can add a few more IF checks to the DeleteNode operation to check for this situation and handle it as a special case. We're ready to code. Procedure DeleteNode is shown below.

```
PROCEDURE DeleteNode
  (VAR Tree  : TreePtrType;  (* pointer to root of tree   *)
   NodePtr   : TreePtrType;  (* pointer to node to delete *)
   ParentPtr : TreePtrType); (* pointer to parent node    *)
  (* Deletes Node(NodePtr) from the binary search tree *)
  (* with root pointer Tree.                           *)
VAR
  ReplacePtr : TreePtrType; (* used in 2-child case *)
```

Figure 9-17 **Deleting a Node with Two Children**

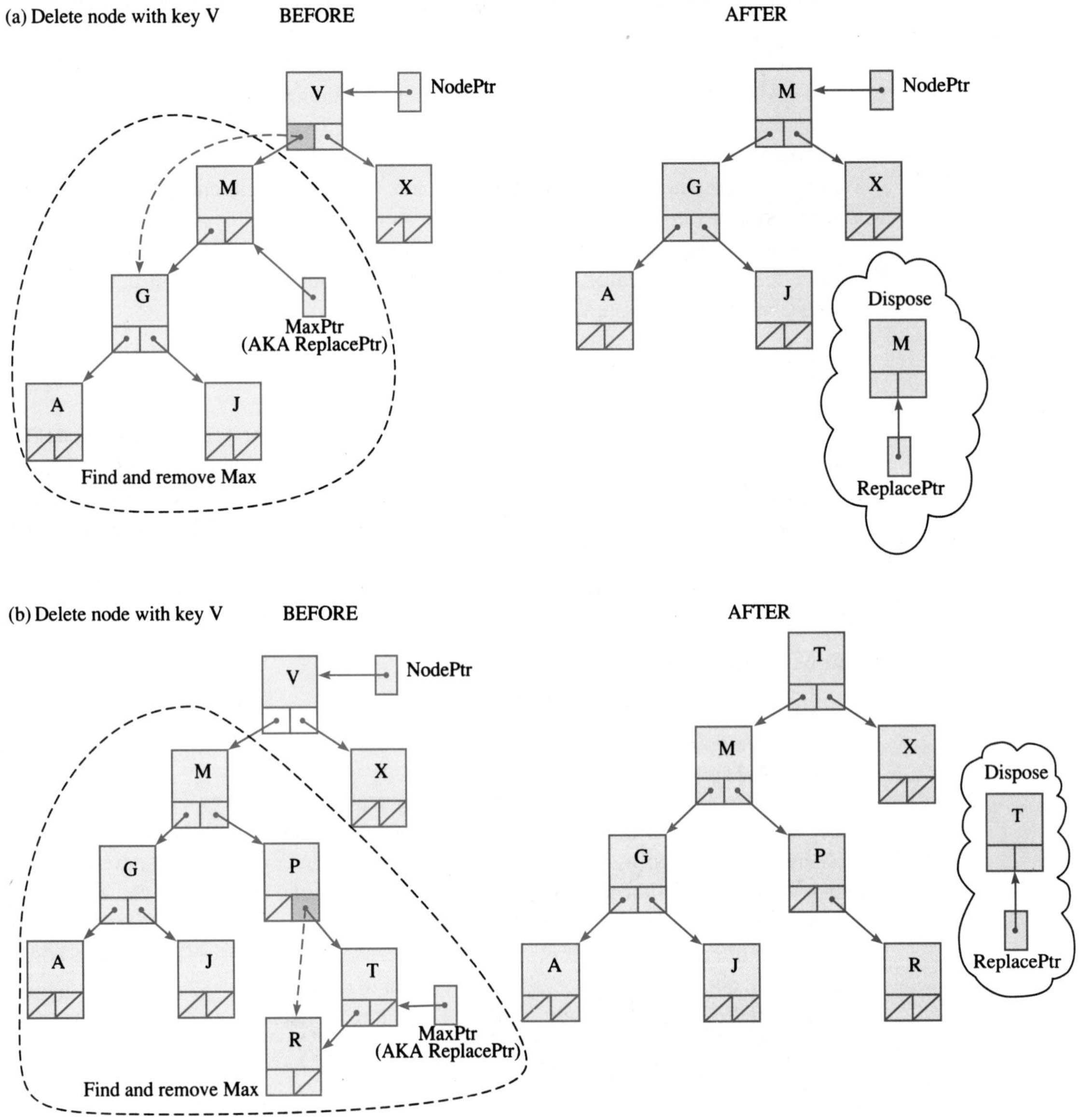

(a) Delete node with key V

(b) Delete node with key V

```
BEGIN (* DeleteNode *)
  (* Case of deleting a leaf: *)
  IF (NodePtr^.Right = NIL) AND (NodePtr^.Left = NIL)
    THEN
      IF ParentPtr = NIL
        THEN  (* Node(NodePtr) is the last node in tree. *)
          Tree := NIL
        ELSE (* Delete the leaf. *)
          IF ParentPtr^.Right = NodePtr
            THEN ParentPtr^.Right := NIL
            ELSE ParentPtr^.Left  := NIL
    ELSE
      (* Case of deleting node with two children: *)
      IF (NodePtr^.Right <> NIL) AND (NodePtr^.Left <> NIL)
        THEN
          BEGIN (* node has two children *)

            (* Find and remove the replacement value from *)
            (* Node(NodePtr)'s left subtree.              *)
            FindAndRemoveMax (NodePtr^.Left, ReplacePtr);

            (* Replace the delete element. *)
            NodePtr^.Info := ReplacePtr^.Info;

            (* Set NodePtr to ReplacePtr for Dispose call. *)
            NodePtr := ReplacePtr

          END  (* case node has two children *)

        ELSE (* Case node has one child: *)
          (* Reset one of the pointer fields of parent *)
          (* node according to whether the node being  *)
          (* deleted has a right or a left child.       *)
          IF NodePtr^.Right <> NIL
            THEN (* There is a right child. *)
              IF ParentPtr = NIL
                THEN Tree := NodePtr^.Right (* delete root *)
                ELSE (* delete nonroot node *)
                  IF ParentPtr^.Right = NodePtr
                    THEN ParentPtr^.Right := NodePtr^.Right
                    ELSE ParentPtr^.Left  := NodePtr^.Right
            ELSE (* there is a left child. *)
              IF ParentPtr = NIL
                THEN Tree := NodePtr^.Left (* delete root *)
                ELSE (* delete nonroot node *)
                  IF ParentPtr^.Right = NodePtr
                    THEN ParentPtr^.Right := NodePtr^.Left
                    ELSE ParentPtr^.Left  := NodePtr^.Left;
  (* Free the unneeded node. *)
  Dispose (NodePtr)
END; (* DeleteNode *)
```

A Simpler Delete Algorithm

We have coded this procedure directly from our design. It's the brute force approach to deleting a node, with heavy and confusing use of nested IF statements. The main reason for this situation is the need to determine which pointer field of Node(ParentPtr) must be modified. Consider the source of NodePtr and ParentPtr from Procedure DeleteElement. This procedure called FindNode to search the tree for a node with a particular key value. FindNode returned the pointers NodePtr and ParentPtr.

Figure 9-18 illustrates this approach with the KeyValue 'B'. The search ends when NodePtr is pointing to the node whose key is 'B' and ParentPtr is pointing to the parent node, whose key is 'J'. *Copies* of these two pointers are returned from FindNode, and are then sent to Procedure DeleteNode as value parameters. When DeleteNode wants to modify the appropriate field of the parent node, it has no information regarding the relative positions of Node(ParentPtr) and Node(NodePtr). Is the node to be deleted to the right or to the left? The need to test explicitly for this information results in a large number of IF statements.

It would be nice if, instead of an external pointer to Node(NodePtr), we could send the DeleteNode routine the actual pointer *from inside the tree* (see Figure 9-19). This approach worked well for the recursive procedures InsertElement and FindAndReplaceMax; now let's see if it will help us streamline the DeleteNode procedure.

DeleteNode no longer needs to have a pointer to the parent node at all, because the input parameter will actually *be* the correct pointer field from the parent node. By making this pointer a VAR parameter, the field in the parent node can be modified

Figure 9-18
Pointers NodePtr and ParentPtr Are External to the Tree

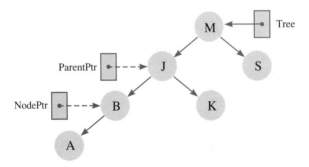

Figure 9-19
Pointer ParentPtr Is External to the Tree, but Parent-Ptr^.Left Is an Actual Pointer in the Tree

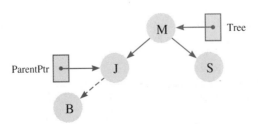

directly. As a matter of fact, in Procedure DeleteElement we even know the name of this pointer. If the node to be deleted is the root node, the pointer to be modified is Tree. If the node to be deleted is to the left of the parent node, then we want to modify ParentPtr^.Left; otherwise we want to modify ParentPtr^.Right.

To use this single-parameter version in Procedure Delete, we modify the Delete-Element procedure to replace the last line (the call to DeleteNode) with an IF statement.

```
PROCEDURE DeleteElement
  (VAR Tree : TreeType;
   KeyValue : KeyType);

  (* Deletes element containing KeyValue from the binary   *)
  (* search tree pointed to by Tree. Assumes that this key *)
  (* value is known to exist in the tree.                  *)

VAR
  NodePtr   : TreePtrType; (* pointer to node to be deleted *)
  ParentPtr : TreePtrType; (* pointer to parent node        *)
BEGIN (* DeleteElement *)

  (* Find node containing KeyValue. *)
  FindNode (Tree, KeyValue, NodePtr, ParentPtr);

  (* Delete node pointed to by NodePtr. ParentPtr points  *)
  (* to the parent node, or is NIL if deleting root node. *)
  IF NodePtr = Tree
    THEN (* Delete the root node. *)
      DeleteNode (Tree)
    ELSE
      IF ParentPtr^.Left = NodePtr
        THEN (* Delete the left child node. *)
          DeleteNode (ParentPtr^.Left)
        ELSE (* Delete the right child node. *)
          DeleteNode (ParentPtr^.Right)

END;  (* DeleteElement *)
```

Note that this change is made *within* the DeleteElement procedure, and that its function and interface remain the same as before. We haven't changed the specification of the DeleteElement procedure from the user's point of view. (DeleteNode is not logically visible to the user; it is internal to the tree ADT.)

Let's look at the changes in our algorithm case by case. Remember that NodePtr is an *actual pointer* in the tree from the parent node to the node to be deleted.

Delete Leaf Node

IF Node(NodePtr) is a leaf node
    THEN NodePtr ← NIL

That was easy. ELSE . . .

Delete Node with One Child

```
IF Node(NodePtr) has one child
   THEN
      IF Right(NodePtr) = NIL
         THEN NodePtr ← Left(NodePtr)
         ELSE NodePtr ← Right(NodePtr)
```

Actually the cases of no children and one child can be considered together. In either case, if Right(NodePtr) = NIL, we want to set NodePtr to Left(NodePtr). [When Node(NodePtr) is a leaf, Left(NodePtr) will be NIL, which is correct.] Otherwise, if Left(NodePtr) = NIL, we set NodePtr to Right(NodePtr). Let's start again.

Delete Node with Zero or One Child

```
IF Right(NodePtr) = NIL
   THEN NodePtr ← Left(NodePtr)
   ELSE (There is at least one child.)
      IF Left(NodePtr) = NIL
         THEN NodePtr ← Right(NodePtr)
```

ELSE we know that Node(NodePtr) has two children. As before, we will replace the Info part of this node with the Info part of the node from its left subtree with the largest key value.

Delete Node with Two Children

```
FindAndRemoveMax (NodePtr^.Left, TempPtr)
Info(NodePtr) ← Info(TempPtr)
```

The only task left to do is to dispose of the deleted node. In the case of the node with two children, we can now delete Node(TempPtr). But in the other two cases, we have "jumped over" the deleted node without saving its pointer. This problem is easily remedied by setting TempPtr to NodePtr at the beginning of the procedure. Now in all cases we'll finish with a call to Dispose (TempPtr).

The single-parameter version of DeleteNode is given below.

```
PROCEDURE DeleteNode
  (VAR NodePtr : TreePtrType);

   (* Deletes the node pointed to by NodePtr from the binary *)
   (* search tree. NodePtr is a real pointer from the parent *)
   (* node in the tree, not an external pointer.             *)

VAR
  TempPtr : TreePtrType;   (* node to delete *)

BEGIN   (* DeleteNode *)

   (* Save the original pointer for freeing the node. *)
   TempPtr := NodePtr;

   (* Case of no children or one child: *)
   IF NodePtr^.Right = NIL
     THEN NodePtr := NodePtr^.Left
```

```
        ELSE (* There is at least one child. *)
          IF NodePtr^.Left = NIL
            THEN (* There is one child. *)
              NodePtr := NodePtr^.Right

            ELSE (* There are two children. *)
              BEGIN
                (* Find and remove the replacement value from *)
                (* Node(NodePtr)'s left subtree.              *)
                FindAndRemoveMax (NodePtr^.Left, TempPtr);

                (* Replace the delete element. *)
                NodePtr^.Info := TempPtr^.Info

              END; (* There are two children. *)
      (* Free the unneeded node. *)
      Dispose (TempPtr)
  END;  (* DeleteNode *)
```

A Recursive DeleteElement

We can also implement the DeleteElement operation recursively, by replacing the search loop (in FindNode) with successive recursive calls to search smaller and smaller subtrees until the delete node is found. When the node to delete is found, we simply call the version of DeleteNode above.

```
PROCEDURE DeleteElement
  (VAR Tree : TreeType;
   KeyValue : KeyType);

  (* Deletes element containing KeyValue from the binary  *)
  (* search tree pointed to by Tree. Assumes that this key *)
  (* value is known to exist in the tree.                 *)

BEGIN (* DeleteElement *)

  IF KeyValue = Tree^.Info.Key
    THEN (* Base Case : delete this node *)
      DeleteNode (Tree)

    ELSE
      IF KeyValue < Tree^.Info.Key
        THEN (* General Case 1: delete from left subtree *)
          DeleteElement (Tree^.Left, KeyValue)
        ELSE (* General Case 2: delete from right subtree *)
          DeleteElement (Tree^.Right, KeyValue)
END;  (* DeleteElement *)
```

Since Tree is a VAR parameter, in each recursive execution Tree is a pointer field within the tree—the Left or Right field of some node. When the correct node has been found, DeleteElement passes this pointer to DeleteNode, which deletes the node according to the number of children. If the node has two children, DeleteNode calls Find-AndRemoveMax, another recursive procedure. This makes for an interesting situation: a recursive procedure called from within the execution of another recursive procedure. This sounds like an efficiency nightmare! Before you lapse into a reverie of recursive procedures spinning off each other *ad infinitum,* let's review the situation. The call to DeleteNode is in DeleteElement's base case, the nonrecursive path. Therefore DeleteNode, with its call to FindAndRemoveMax, will only be executed once. In terms of Big-O, the recursive DeleteElement procedure is no less efficient than the nonrecursive version.

Tree Traversals

To traverse a tree means to visit all its nodes—for example, to print all of the values in the tree or to delete all the elements in the tree. To traverse a linear linked list, we set a temporary pointer equal to the start of the list, and then follow the links from one node to the other until we reach a node whose pointer value is NIL. Similarly, to traverse a binary tree, we initialize our pointer to the root of the tree. But where do we go from there—to the left or to the right? Do we print the root or the leaves first?

Suppose we decide to print out the values in the tree in order, from the smallest to the largest. We first need to print the root's *left* subtree, all the values in the tree that are smaller than the value in the root node. Then we print the value in the root node. Finally we print the values in the root's *right* subtree, all the values that are larger than the value in the root node (see Figure 9-20).

Some considerations become immediately apparent. As we move our traversal pointer, Ptr, to the left, in order to begin traversing the left subtree, we lose our access to the nodes above it. We can't get back up. In fact, this problem is a general one as we move through the tree. When Ptr points to the node to the left of the root node (see Figure 9-21), we need to repeat the whole procedure: Print the nodes to the left, print Node(Ptr), then print the nodes to the right. We will move our pointer again to the left, not yet printing anything, but again we won't be able to get back to nodes we have passed. We need some way of keeping track of these nodes as we pass them. Later we will want to retrieve them, beginning with the node that was most recently saved and proceeding backward.

Figure 9-20
Printing All the
Nodes in Order

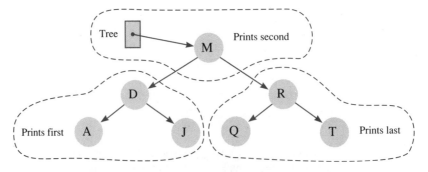

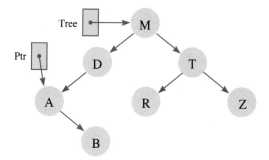

Figure 9-21
When You Have
Finished with the
Left Subtree, How
Can You Get Back
Up to Print the Root
and the Right
Subtree?

Luckily we know of a data structure that is ideal for this backtracking task: the *stack!* As we travel down the left branch as far as possible, we'll push onto a stack the pointer to each node we pass.

WHILE Ptr <> NIL DO
    Push Ptr onto the stack
    Move Ptr to the left

When Ptr is NIL, we know that the left subtree is empty, and we can climb back into the tree. How? By popping the stack of node pointers. We print the value in the node pointed to by Ptr. Then we want to traverse that node's *right* subtree by setting Ptr to Right(Ptr) and repeating the whole routine.

How do we know when we are finished? When we are traversing a linear linked list, we need only note when Ptr is equal to NIL. When we are traversing a binary tree, this condition is not sufficient; Ptr will be NIL after we pass *any* leaf node. Thus we also need to look at the status of the stack. When Ptr is NIL *and* the stack is empty, we are finished.

The following procedure implements this "in-order" tree traversal, using operations from the Stack ADT that was developed in Chapter 4. (Note that we do not have to know anything about the stack implementation. As users, this information is none of our business!) We will also use a procedure called PrintNode, which prints out the Info part of a single node.

```
PROCEDURE PrintInorder
  (Tree : TreeType);

  (* Prints out the elements in the binary tree pointed *)
  (* to by Tree, in order from smallest to largest.     *)

VAR
  PtrStack : StackType;
    (* stack of pointers used to keep track of nodes *)
    (* until the appropriate time to print them      *)

  Ptr      : TreePtrType; (* used to traverse the tree *)
BEGIN (* PrintInorder *)

  (* Start out with an empty stack. *)
  CreateStack (PtrStack);
```

```
(* Begin at the root of the tree. *)
Ptr := Tree;

REPEAT (* Process until the whole tree is finished. *)

  (* Go to the left as far as possible, pushing pointer   *)
  (* to each node as it is passed. Stop when Ptr falls out *)
  (* of the tree.                                          *)
  WHILE Ptr <> NIL DO
    BEGIN
      Push (PtrStack, Ptr); (* Push node ptr onto stack. *)
      Ptr:= Ptr^.Left       (* Keep moving to the left.  *)
    END; (* WHILE *)

  (* If there's anything left in the stack, pop, print, *)
  (* and move to the right.                             *)
  IF NOT EmptyStack (PtrStack)
    THEN
      BEGIN
        Pop (PtrStack, Ptr);   (* Climb back into tree.    *)
        PrintNode (Ptr^.Info); (* Print Info part of node. *)
        Ptr := Ptr^.Right      (* Move once to the right.  *)
      END  (* If stack is not empty *)

UNTIL (Ptr = NIL) AND (EmptyStack (PtrStack))

END; (* PrintInorder *)
```

Figure 9-22 traces through this procedure, using a tree with four nodes.

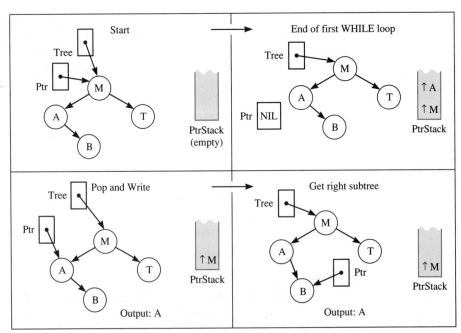

Figure 9-22
Printing InOrder

Figure 9-22
(Continued)

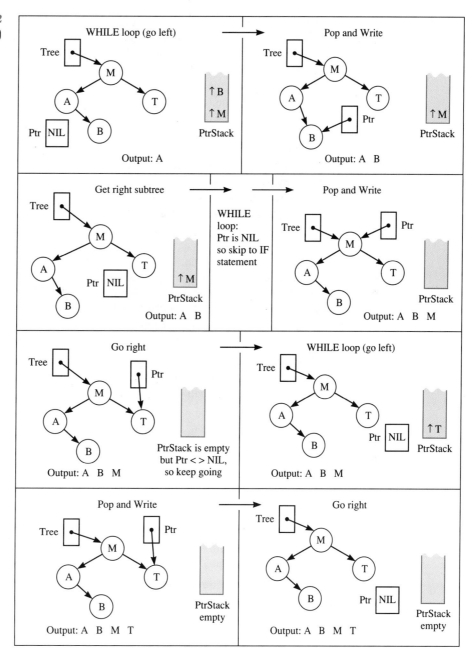

Recursive Tree Traversals

Procedure PrintInorder is not exactly intuitive, and only walking through an example like the one in Figure 9-22 makes it really clear how the tree is traversed. All the pointer stacking is kind of confusing. But Pascal provides us with another way of performing the stacking necessary to keep track of the nodes in the tree: *recursion*.

Let's describe this problem again, thinking recursively. We want to print the elements in the binary search tree rooted at Tree in order; that is, first we print the left subtree in order, then we print the root, and finally we print the right subtree in order. Tree^.Left points to the root of the left subtree. Since the left subtree is also a binary search tree, we can call procedure PrintInorder to print it, using Tree^.Left as the root parameter. When PrintInorder finishes printing out the left subtree, we print out the value in the root node, using Procedure PrintNode. Then, we call procedure PrintInorder to print the right subtree with Tree^.Right as the root parameter.

Of course each of these two calls to Procedure PrintInorder uses the same approach to print the subtree: print the left subtree with a call to PrintInorder, print the root, then print the right subtree with another call to PrintInorder.

What happens if the input parameter is NIL on one of the recursive calls? This situation means that the input parameter is the root of an empty tree. (This is the case whenever we pass a leaf node.) In this case, we just want to exit the procedure—clearly there's no point to printing an empty subtree.

We can write a very short recursive procedure to do the inorder traversal, and let Pascal take care of the stack, hidden from our view. To describe the problem, let's use the technique we developed in Chapter 8.

■ Procedure PrintInorder

Definition:	Print out all the elements in the binary search tree in order from smallest to largest.
Size:	The nodes in the tree whose root is Tree.
Base Case:	IF Tree = NIL, do nothing.
General Case:	Traverse the left subtree in order. Then print Info(Tree). Then traverse the right subtree in order.

This description can be coded into a recursive procedure PrintInorder:

```
PROCEDURE PrintInorder
  (Tree : TreeType);

  (* Prints out the elements in a binary search tree in *)
  (* order from smallest to largest. This procedure is  *)
  (* a recursive solution.                              *)

BEGIN  (* PrintInorder *)

  (* Base Case: If Tree is NIL, do nothing. *)
  IF Tree <> NIL
    THEN

      BEGIN (* General Case *)

        (* Traverse left subtree to print smaller values. *)
        PrintInorder (Tree^.Left);
```

```
         (* Print the information in this node. *)
         PrintNode(Tree^.Info);

         (* Traverse right subtree to print larger values. *)
         PrintInorder(Tree^.Right)

    END (* General Case *)
END; (* PrintInorder *)
```

To print out the whole tree, we initially call this procedure with the statement PrintInorder (Tree). The initialization of Tree to the root of the tree is accomplished through the original calling argument.

Is this a good use of recursion? We think you can answer this question yourself.

Other Tree Traversal Orders

In our tree package specification, we referred to two other traversal orders that the tree user might want to use: preorder and postorder. The traversal we have already discussed is called "in-order" because each node is visited *in between* its left and right subtrees. A preorder traversal visits each node *before* its left and right subtrees, and a postorder traversal visits each node *after* its left and right subtrees.

A *preorder traversal* of a binary tree

- visits the root
- traverses the left subtree in preorder
- traverses the right subtree in preorder

Given the tree in Figure 9-23, a preorder traversal would print

P F B H G S R Y T W Z

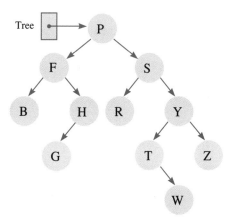

Figure 9-23
Three Tree
Traversals

In order:	B	F	G	H	P	R	S	T	W	Y	Z
Preorder:	P	F	B	H	G	S	R	Y	T	W	Z
Postorder:	B	G	H	F	R	W	T	Z	Y	S	P

The preorder print procedure can be written recursively simply by changing the order of the statements in the in-order print routine:

```
PROCEDURE PrintPreorder
    (Tree : TreeType);

    (* Print out the elements in a binary search tree in *)
    (* preorder. This procedure is a recursive solution. *)

BEGIN (* PrintPreorder *)

    (* Base Case: IF Tree is NIL, do nothing. *)
    IF Tree <> NIL
        THEN (* General Case *)
            BEGIN

                (* Print the information in this node. *)
                PrintNode(Tree^.Info);

                (* Traverse the left subtree in preorder. *)
                PrintPreorder (Tree^.Left);

                (* Traverse the right subtree in preorder. *)
                PrintPreorder (Tree^.Right)

            END   (* General Case *)
END; (* PrintPreorder *)
```

A *postorder traversal* of a binary tree

- traverses the left subtree in postorder
- traverses the right subtree in postorder
- visits the root

A postorder traversal of the tree in Figure 9-23 would print

    B G H F R W T Z Y S P

A procedure to print out the elements in a binary tree in postorder is given below. Like Procedure PrintPreorder, it rearranges the order of the three statements in the general case to change the order of the printing.

```
PROCEDURE PrintPostorder
    (Tree : TreeType);

    (* Prints out the elements in a binary search tree in *)
    (* postorder. This procedure is a recursive solution. *)

BEGIN (* PrintPostorder *)

    (* Base Case: If Tree is NIL, do nothing. *)
    IF Tree <> NIL
        THEN (* General Case *)
            BEGIN

                (* Traverse the left subtree in postorder. *)
                PrintPostorder (Tree^.Left);
```

```
    (* Traverse the right subtree in postorder. *)
    PrintPostorder (Tree^.Right);

    (* Print the information in this node. *)
    PrintNode (Tree^.Info)

  END (* General Case *)
END; (* PrintPostorder *)
```

When might one want to use a postorder traversal of a binary tree? Consider the following situation. We want to traverse the tree and delete all the nodes that meet some criteria. In this case we could use any of the traversal orders with the same final results. We know that deleting a leaf node is simpler than deleting a node with children, however. If we start the traversal at the bottom of the tree (where the leaves are) using a postorder search, we will increase the likelihood of deleting leaves.

The PrintTree operation in the binary search tree ADT specification takes a tree root and a value of an enumerated type designating which traversal is desired, and calls the appropriate traversal routine. (The traversal procedures listed above are internal to the binary search tree ADT.) Below is the code to support this procedure:

```
TraversalType = (Preorder, Inorder, Postorder);

PROCEDURE PrintTree
  (Tree           : TreeType;
   TraversalOrder : TraversalType);

  (* Print all the elements in the tree, in the order *)
  (* specified by TraversalOrder.                     *)

BEGIN (* PrintTree *)

  (* Call print procedure according to TraversalOrder. *)
  CASE TraversalOrder OF
    Preorder  : PrintPreorder  (Tree);
    Inorder   : PrintInorder   (Tree);
    Postorder : PrintPostorder (Tree)
  END (* CASE *)

END;  (* PrintTree *)
```

The DestroyTree Operation

The DestroyTree operation inputs the pointer to a binary search tree and destroys all the nodes, leaving the tree empty. To delete all the elements we will have to traverse the tree. Instead of printing each element, as we did in the previous section, we will remove the node from the tree. Which traversal order would be best? While any of the traversal orders would result in the procedure performing correctly, one traversal order is more efficient than the others. Knowing that the DeleteNode operation does less work to delete a leaf node than a node with children, we want to delete leaves first. If you delete the nodes in postorder, each node is a leaf by the time of its turn to be deleted.

The code for the DestroyTree operation is nearly the same as the PrintPostorder procedure we coded above, with a call to Dispose replacing the call to PrintNode.

```
PROCEDURE DestroyTree
  (VAR Tree : TreeType);

  (* Removes all the elements from the binary search tree *)
  (* rooted at Tree, leaving the tree empty.             *)

BEGIN (* DestroyTree *)

  (* Base Case: If Tree is NIL, do nothing. *)
  IF Tree <> NIL
    THEN (* General Case *)
      BEGIN

        (* Traverse the left subtree in postorder. *)
        DestroyTree (Tree^.Left);

        (* Traverse the right subtree in postorder. *)
        DestroyTree (Tree^.Right);

        (* Delete this leaf node from the tree. *)
        Dispose (Tree)

      END (* General Case *)
END; (* DestroyTree *)
```

Comparing Binary Search Trees to Linear Lists

A binary search tree is an appropriate structure for many of the same applications discussed previously in conjunction with other ordered list structures. The special advantage of using such a tree is that it facilitates *searching*, while conferring the benefits of linking the elements. It provides the best features of both the sequential and linked lists: Like a sequential list, it can be searched quickly, using a binary search. Like a linked list, it allows insertions and deletions without having to move data. Thus it is particularly suitable for applications in which search time must be minimized or in which the nodes will not necessarily be processed in sequential order.

As usual, there is a trade-off. The binary search tree, with its extra pointer in each node, will take up more memory space than a singly linked list. In addition, the algorithms for manipulating the tree are somewhat more complicated. If all of the list's uses involve sequential rather than random processing of the elements, the tree may not be as good a choice.

Suppose we have 1000 customer records in a list. If the main activity in the application is to send out updated monthly statements to the customers and if the order in which the statements are printed is the same as the order in which the records appear on the list, a linked list would be suitable. But suppose we decide to keep a terminal available to give out account information to the customers whenever they ask. If the data are kept in a linked list, the first customer on the list can be given information almost instantly, but the last customer will have to wait while the other 999 records are examined. When direct access to the records is a requirement, a binary search tree is a more appropriate structure.

Big-O and Execution Time Comparisons

To illustrate the difference between the operations that manipulate a linked list and a binary search tree, we ran a timed test. Before we tell you how the tests came out, let's describe the operations in terms of their Big-O approximations. Then we can see how well we would expect the operations to perform.

The FindNode operation, as we would expect in a structure dedicated to searching, is the most interesting operation to analyze. In the best case—if the order that the elements were inserted results in a short and bushy tree—we can find any node in the tree with at most $\log_2 N + 1$ comparisons. We would expect to be able to locate a random element in such a tree much faster than finding an element in an ordered linear list. In the worst case—if the elements were inserted in order from smallest to largest or vice versa—the tree won't really be a tree at all; it will be a linear list, linked through either the Left or Right pointer field. (This is called a "degenerate" tree.) In this case, the tree operations should perform much the same as the operations on a linked list.

The InsertElement, ModifyElement, and RetrieveElement operations are basically FindNode [$O(\log_2 N)$] plus tasks that are $O(1)$—for instance, creating a node, resetting pointers, or copying data. Thus these operations are all described as $O(\log_2 N)$. The DeleteElement operation consists of FindNode plus DeleteNode. In the worst case (deleting a node with two children), DeleteNode must find the replacement value, an $O(\log_2 N)$ operation. (Actually, the two tasks together add up to $\log_2 N$ comparisons, since if the delete node is higher in the tree, fewer comparisons are needed to find it, and more comparisons may be needed to find its replacement node.) Otherwise, if the deleted node has 0 or 1 child, DeleteNode is an $O(1)$ operation. So DeleteElement too may be described as $O(\log_2 N)$.

The PrintTree and DestroyTree operations require the tree to be traversed, processing each element once. Thus these are $O(N)$ operations. The orders of magnitude for the tree and list operations are compared in the first table on page 576.

Now let's see how our test came out. For each structure (linear list and binary search tree), we inserted elements with the Integer keys 1 through 1000, printed them in order, and then deleted them one by one. We ran each test three times. In the first test, we inserted the elements in random order, hoping to produce a short, bushy tree. We then deleted the elements one by one, in the same order in which they were inserted. As you can see in the second table on page 576, the results were as expected: Both the tree insertions and deletions were faster than the comparable linear list operations.

In the second test, we inserted elements with the keys 1 through 1000 in order, and then deleted them one by one in the same order. In this case, the tree produced was essentially a linear list, and the tree operations were no better than the list operations.

In the third test, we inserted elements with the keys 1 through 1000 in reverse order, and then deleted them one by one in the same order. In this case, the list insertions

Big-O Comparison of Tree and List Operations

	Binary Search Tree	Linked List
Create operation	O(1)	O(1)
Destroy operation	O(N)	O(N)
Print operation	O(N)	O(N)
Find node operation		
if elements were inserted		
randomly	**O(log$_2$N)**	**O(N)**
in order	O(N)	O(N)
Insert operation		
FindNode plus	O(1)	O(1)
Total	**O(log$_2$N)***	**O(N)**
Retrieve operation		
FindNode plus	O(1)	O(1)
Total	**O(log$_2$N)***	**O(N)**
ModifyElement		
FindNode plus	O(1)	O(1)
Total	**O(log$_2$N)***	**O(N)**
DeleteElement		
FindNode plus	**O(log$_2$N)**	**O(1)**
Total	**O(log$_2$N)***	**O(N)**

*Assuming random insertion of tree elements

Timed Comparisons of Tree and List Operations

	Binary Search Tree	Linked List
Test 1:		
(1000 elements in random order)		
Insert	0.11	1.48
Print	5.17	5.17
Delete	0.38	1.48
Test 2:		
(1000 elements in order)		
Insert	3.57	2.86
Print	5.21	5.27
Delete	0.06	0.05
Test 3:		
(1000 elements in reverse order)		
Insert	3.57	0.06
Print	5.21	5.28
Delete	0.05	2.85

All times are in seconds. Tests were run on an IBM-compatible computer (Intel 386 25-MHz) using a test driver, tree code, and list code compiled under Turbo Pascal 5.5.

were essentially O(1) operations, as we were always inserting at the front of the list. Again, the tree was a linear structure, this time leaning in the opposite direction. Since tree insertions are always made to leaf nodes, however, the insertions were much slower—we were always inserting the "last" node—O(N) operations. The deletions worked in reverse: The first (root with one child) element was always deleted from the tree [an O(1) operation], but the last node was always deleted from the list [an O(N) operation]. The timing results are as we would expect.

This exercise illustrates an important point about binary search trees: The order in which the elements were inserted is critical in determining the efficiency of the tree operations. This order will determine the shape of the tree—short and bushy (good) or tall and stringy (bad). The shorter the tree (fewer levels to search), the faster we can access *random* elements. The speed of a tree *traversal* is unaffected by the shape. A short bushy tree, a tall stringy tree, or a linked list will all take about the same time to traverse. However, there are space implications; the overhead from the recursive calls to traverse a tall, stringy tree may cause overflow of the run-time stack.

Summary

In this chapter we have seen how the binary tree may be used to structure ordered information to reduce the search time for any particular element. For applications where direct access to the elements in an ordered structure is needed, the binary search tree is a very useful data type. If the tree is balanced, we can access any node in the tree with an $O(\log_2 N)$ operation. The binary search tree combines the advantages of quick random-access (like a binary search on a sequential list) with the flexibility of a linked structure.

We also saw that the tree operations could be implemented very elegantly and concisely using recursion. This makes sense, since a binary tree is itself a "recursive" structure: Any node in the tree is the root of another binary tree. Each time we moved down a level in the tree, taking either the right or left path from a node, we cut the size of the (current) tree in half, a clear case of the smaller-caller. We saw cases of recursion that replaced iteration (InsertElement and DeleteElement), as well as recursion that replaced the use of a stack (tree traversals).

In the application section at the end of this chapter, we will add a cross-reference generator to Program ListAndCount. As we process the program, line by line, we need a place to store the program's identifiers. Since we want to be able to access random identifiers in the cross-reference quickly, and we also want to be able to print the structure in order, a binary search tree is an ideal structure to contain the cross-reference data.

Application

Software Development Tools 2: Cross Reference

Abstract Data Types
- Binary search trees
- FIFO queues
- Strings

Software Techniques
- Top-down design
- Program modification

In Chapter 1 we designed and implemented a tool to help us in the software development process—a program that produces a numbered listing of the source code of a Pascal program and counts its executable and comment lines. Now we want to add another feature to this program: a **cross reference** generator. A cross reference is like an index into the program; it tells us all the lines in which each of the program's identifiers is used. Figure 9-24 shows a sample program and its cross reference.

It is clear from this example that we do not need to include every word and symbol of the program in the cross reference. The cross reference generator only needs to keep track of *identifiers:* the names of constants, types, variables, procedures, and functions. It does not need to include reserved words (PROCEDURE, VAR, BEGIN, IF, and so on), symbols and punctuation marks (such as ' + ', '*', and ';'), or words used within comments.

Figure 9-24   Sample Program and its Cross Reference

```
 1. PROGRAM TestCrossRef (Input, Output);

 2. CONST
 3.    Ten = 10;

 4. VAR
 5.    Value : Integer; (* global variable *)

 6. FUNCTION Increment
 7.    (Number : Integer) : Integer;

       (* Return the value of Number + 1. *)

 8. BEGIN (* Increment *)
 9.    Increment := Number + 1;
10. END;  (* Increment *)

    (****************************************)

11. BEGIN (* TestCrossRef *)
12.    Readln (Value);
13.    IF Increment (Value) < Ten
14.       THEN Writeln (Value)
15.       ELSE Writeln (Ten);
16. END.  (* TestCross Ref *)
```

```
Cross Reference

Increment:      6   9   13

Number:         7   9

Readln:         12

Ten:            3   13   15

TestCrossRef:   1

Value:          5   12   13   14

Writeln:        14   15
```

The specifications of the cross reference generator are listed in Figure 9-25. The inputs to the program include those for Program ListAndCount: the file name (from the keyboard) and ProgramFile, which contains the source code to process. The cross reference generator requires a third input. ReservedFile is a Text file that contains all the reserved words that should not be included in the cross reference. The outputs of

---

Specification: Cross Reference Generator

Function:

The Cross Reference Generator function is to be added to Program ListAndCount to create and print a cross reference listing of all the identifiers used in the program.

Input: (in addition to the inputs for Program ListAndCount)

File RESERVED.TXT is a text file that contains all of the reserved words that should not be entered into the cross reference. The reserved words are strings of uppercase letters, listed one per line in alphabetical order.

Output: (in addition to Outputs 1 and 2 of ListAndCount)

3. The Cross Reference report will consist of an alphabetical listing of all the identifiers used in the program. Each identifier name is followed by a list of the line numbers in which the identifier was declared or used. These line numbers should match the numbers in the Program Listing (Output 1).

Processing Requirements:

1. The recognition of identifiers must be case insensitive. (For instance, 'GetWord', 'GETWORD', and 'getword' refer to the same identifier.)
2. In the Cross Reference report, each identifier name should be printed in upper- and/ or lowercase, in the same form as it was *first* encountered in the program.
3. The alphabetic ordering of the identifiers in the Cross Reference report must be case insensitive. (For instance, 'A' comes before 'b', even if ORD('b') < ORD('A').)
4. If an identifier is used more than once in a line (for example, "Count := Count + 1;"), you may list the line number more than once in the Cross Reference.

Assumptions:

1. The Pascal program in the ProgramFile is syntactically correct.
2. The program's source lines contain only printable characters, including blanks. There are no more than 80 characters per line of source code.
3. Identifiers begin with a letter (upper- or lowercase), and contain only letters and numbers.
4. Only (*   *) comment delimiters are supported. A comment must terminate with '*)' on the same line in which it began; it cannot span across more than one line. No executable source code may follow a comment on a line.
5. You do not need to include special processing to ignore literal strings within quote marks. (This will be left as a programming assignment.)

---

the program are the numbered source listing and the line count reports, as in Program ListAndCount, as well as a formatted listing of the cross reference data.

To simplify this problem we have included a number of restrictive assumptions. For instance, we assume that no "executable" source code follows a comment within a line, and that every comment ends in the line in which it began.

The Design

How does the cross reference generator fit into the structure of Program List-AndCount? Let's review the design from Chapter 1. The top level of this design is shown below, with the modifications necessary for the cross reference generator printed in italics.

ListAndCount   /   *Level 0*

GetFiles—*including Reserved File*
Process Program File—*including generation of cross reference*
PrintCountData
PrintCrossRef
TerminateProcessing

The main modification to ListAndCount will be in the ProcessProgramFile module. As we process ProgramFile line by line, listing and counting, we must perform an additional task—to extract all the identifiers from each executable line and to add their line references to the cross reference. After the whole ProgramFile is processed, we will print out the cross reference data, following the line count report.

What is this "cross reference data"? At this phase of our design, we decide that a data structure, CrossReference, will contain the names of all the identifiers used in ProgramFile, as well as a set of line references for each. We do not need any more details at this level. Now let's return to the program design.

In the ProcessProgramFile module, whose design is listed on page 38, we must add a task to the CASE statement's processing of an executable line.

ExecLine : (*In the CASE statement*)
    Increment ExecCount.
    Print executable line to ReportFile, preceded by ExecCount.
    ProcessLine

The ProcessLine module goes through TextLine, extracting all the "words." It rejects any words that are included in ReservedFile, since we only want to include identifiers in the cross reference. If this is the first time an identifier is encountered, it will be added to the cross reference, along with its line number; otherwise the existing cross reference entry for this identifier is updated to add the current line number. Here is the specification of this module:

ProcessLine (TextLine, LineNumber, CrossReference, ReservedWords)   /
Level 2

   Function: Extracts all identifiers from TextLine and updates Cross-Reference to include references for this LineNumber.

Input:	TextLine (StringType)
	LineNumber (Integer)
	CrossReference (CrossRefType)
	ReservedWords (ReservedListType)
Preconditions:	All inputs are defined.
Output:	CrossReference
Postconditions:	A reference to LineNumber exists in the CrossReference entry of each identifier used in TextLine.

The algorithm for this module follows:

ProcessLine

CurPos ← start of line

WHILE more words in TextLine DO
  GetWord from TextLine (updates CurPos)

  IF a Word is found
    THEN

       CapWord ← upper-case equivalent of Word

      IF CapWord is not in ReservedWords
        THEN
          RetrieveElement - retrieve CapWord's entry in
            CrossReference, if it exists

         IF CapWord's entry found in CrossReference
          THEN
            Add LineNumber to line references for this entry
            ModifyElement
         ELSE (CapWord not yet in CrossReference)
            Build an entry for CapWord
            Add LineNumber to line references for this entry
            InsertElement

    In the loop body, we must first extract the next "word" from TextLine. The GetWord module searches TextLine for a string of characters that might be an identifier, beginning at the "current" position (CurPos). It returns Word (a string) and resets CurPos to jump over the Word in TextLine. The specification of this module follows.

GetWord (TextLine, CurPos, Word)   /   *Level 3*

Function:	Extracts Word from TextLine, beginning at CurPos.
Input:	TextLine (StringType)
	CurPos (Integer)
Preconditions:	1 <= CurPos <= Length (TextLine)
Output:	CurPos
	Word (StringType)

> *Postconditions:*   Word = string starting with a letter and terminating with first non-alphanumeric character. If no word found in TextLine, starting at CurPos, Word is empty string. CurPos = position of first character following Word string in TextLine. If no word found, CurPos = Length (TextLine) + 1.

The design for this module is:

GetWord   /   *Level 3*

EmptyString (Word)
SkipLeadChars
BuildWord

EmptyString is one of the String ADT operations defined in Chapter 3. Skip-LeadChars and BuildWord need further decomposition. Their designs use the CharAt, Length, and Append operations from the String ADT.

Since a Pascal identifier must begin with a letter, SkipLeadChars resets CurPos to skip past all the non-alphabetic characters—operators, numbers, parentheses, brackets, and so on. The program's assumptions state that executable code will not follow a comment within a line, so we can stop processing this line (by setting CurPos past the end of TextLine) if we encounter the beginning of a comment. We use the Identify-CommentStart module from Program ListAndCount to determine if a comment is beginning.

SkipLeadChars   /   *Level 4*

WHILE CurPos < = Length (TextLine) AND
    CharAt (TextLine, CurPos) is not a letter DO
  IdentifyCommentStart (TextLine, CurPos, InComment)
  IF InComment
    THEN CurPos ← Length (TextLine) + 1
    ELSE CurPos ← CurPos + 1

When we exit this loop, CurPos either indicates the first alphabetic character or it exceeds Length (TextLine), indicating that there are no more words in TextLine.

BuildWord appends characters to Word until a non-alphanumeric character (or the end of TextLine) is encountered. (The specifications state that only letters and numbers are permitted in identifiers.)

BuildWord   /   *Level 4*

More ← True
WHILE CurPos < = Length (TextLine) AND More DO
  IF CharAt (TextLine, CurPos) is a letter or a number
    THEN Append (Word, CharAt (TextLine, CurPos))
    ELSE More ← False
  CurPos ← CurPos + 1

If a word was found, on exit from this loop CurPos indicates the position in TextLine that follows the word. Thus it is set correctly for the call to GetWord in the next iteration of the loop body in ProcessLine.

Should GetWord convert all the letters in the Word to the same case? We don't want to mistake 'GetWord' and 'Getword' for two different identifiers, though the string Compare operation would consider them to be two different strings. On the other hand, we want to preserve the readability of mixed-case identifiers in our cross reference report. We decide to have our cake and eat it too. GetWord returns Word as it was written in TextLine, and ProcessLine creates a second, all-upper-case version of Word (CapWord) to use as this entry's key in the CrossReference.

Next ProcessLine checks whether CapWord is a reserved word. The specifications say that a Text file of reserved words (strings of upper-case letters) is one of the inputs to the program. It would be inefficient to search this file every time we want to check a word. Instead, as part of our initialization processing in GetFiles, we will build some kind of data structure to contain these strings. In fact, we can consider ReservedWords to be a little ADT, for which two operations are specified:

GetReservedWords (ReservedWords)

Function:	Read the reserved words from ReservedFile and store in ReservedWords.
Input:	From ReservedFile (Text): reserved words (StringType)
Preconditions:	ReservedFile exists and is not open.
Output:	ReservedWords (ReservedListType)
Postconditions:	ReservedWords contains all the reserved words that should not be added to the cross reference. ReservedFile is unchanged.

WordIsReserved (ReservedWords, Word) Returns Boolean

Function:	Determines if Word is included in ReservedWords.
Input:	ReservedWords (ReservedListType) Word (StringType)
Preconditions:	ReservedWords has been initialized by GetReservedWords.
Output:	WordIsReserved (Boolean)
Postconditions:	WordIsReserved = (Word is included in ReservedWords)

We'll come back to the design of ReservedWords later; for now let's continue with the design of ProcessLine.

ReservedWords is one of the inputs to ProcessLine. To check whether CapWord is a reserved word, we invoke Function WordIsReserved:

```
IF NOT WordIsReserved (ReservedWords, CapWord)
    THEN (update the cross reference)
```

To update the cross reference data and to complete the design of ProcessLine, we must stop and add a level of detail to the data design.

Designing CrossReference

We have said that CrossReference is a structure that contains the names and line references of all the identifiers in the program. What is the overall structure of CrossReference? When we print out the CrossReference data at the end of the program, we must access the elements in alphabetical order; thus CrossReference must be a structure that supports the sequential processing of its elements. However, as we build the CrossReference within ProcessProgramFile, we need to access its elements in whatever order they are encountered. Thus CrossReference should be a structure that can be searched quickly. This description suggests that either a sequential list (which can be searched with a binary search) or a binary search tree would be an appropriate data representation for CrossReference.

Since the number of identifiers can vary widely, depending on the size of the program, we cannot predict how many entries will be in the CrossReference. In addition, a sequential list requires data movement to insert new elements; a linked structure would not require such data movement. For these reasons, we decide to implement CrossReference as a binary search tree.

Each element in the tree contains the cross reference data for one identifier—its name and a set of line references. The upper-case version of the identifier name, a string, is the key field. We will also store the original version of the identifier name, to use in printing the cross reference data. What is the set of line references? Line references are added as they are encountered in the line-by-line processing of the program. Later, when we print the contents of the CrossReference, we will access the line references for each identifier in the same order in which they were added. Logically the line references can be considered a FIFO queue. The declarations for Tree-ElementType are shown below:

```
TYPE
  TreeElementType = RECORD
    Key       : StringType;    (* upper-case ID name   *)
    ID        : StringType;    (* original identifier  *)
    LineQueue : QueueType      (* line references      *)
  END;    (* TreeElementType *)
```

The key field is declared as StringType (a record). This has implications for the tree operations, for we cannot compare two strings with the comparison operators $=$, $>$, and $<$. The key comparisons in the tree procedures FindNode and InsertElement must be edited to use the Compare operation defined for the String ADT in Chapter 3.

In earlier chapters, we have implemented the FIFO Queue ADT as an array, as a linear linked list, and as a circular linked list. Which of these should be used for implementing the LineQueue? While we could choose any of these representations, we have selected a linked queue implementation because the number of line references may vary greatly from one identifier to another. For instance, the program name will have one reference in the program, while a variable name like Index may have many.

We can now complete the design of the ProcessLine module. The references to RetrieveElement, ModifyElement, and InsertElement in its design will be implemented as calls to the operations in the Binary Search Tree ADT. When we "build an entry for Word," we set its Key field to CapWord and its ID field to Word, and then call CreateQueue to initialize the LineQueue to the empty state. To "Add LineNumber to the line references" simply requires a call to Enqueue the LineNumber.

Changes to the GetFiles Module

The GetFiles module in ListAndCount opens the ProgramFile and ReportFile. We will give this module an additional task—to create ReservedWords from the data in ReservedFile. This adds another output to the specification of GetFiles:

▪ **GetFiles (ProgramFile, Reportfile, ReservedWords)** / *Level 1*

Function:	Gets name of program file from the user. Opens the program file for reading and the report file for writing.
Input:	From the user: File name of program file
Preconditions:	ProgramFile exists.
Output:	ProgramFile (Text) ReportFile (Text) ReservedWords (ReservedListType)
Postconditions:	ProgramFile is open for reading. ReportFile is open for writing. ReservedWords contains all the reserved words that should not be added to the cross reference.

The only change to the algorithm for this module is to add a call to the ReservedWords ADT operation, GetReservedWords, which was specified earlier.

Printing the Cross Reference Data

The final modification to Program ListAndCount is to add a procedure to print the cross reference data. This procedure will be called at the end of the program, immediately after the call to PrintCountData. The PrintCrossRef module is specified as follows.

▪ **PrintCrossRef (ReportFile, CrossReference)** / *Level 1*

Function:	Prints the identifiers and their line references to the ReportFile.
Input:	ReportFile (Text) CrossReference (CrossRefType)
Preconditions:	ReportFile is open for writing.
Output:	ReportFile, CrossReference
Postconditions:	ReportFile is open and contains cross reference data. Line queues in CrossReference are empty.

The algorithm for this module is:

PrintCrossRef

Print title to ReportFile
PrintTree (ReportFile, CrossReference, InOrder)

We have made a minor change to PrintTree. Since we want the cross reference output to be written to ReportFile, not to the screen, we must specify a file name on the calls to Writeln. Therefore we have added the file name as the first parameter (ToFile) of PrintTree. This change must trickle down to the PrintInorder and PrintNode procedures as well. The PrintNode procedure in the chapter text only prints the key field; we must modify this procedure to print out the cross reference data for one identifier. Note in the design below that the ID field, not the Key field (the upper-case version of the identifier), is printed as the identifier name.

PrintNode (ToFile, Element)

PrintString (ToFile, Element.ID)
Writeln (ToFile)

WHILE NOT EmptyQueue (Element.LineQueue) DO
    Dequeue (Element.LineQueue, LineNumber)
    Write (ToFile, LineNumber)

Writeln (ToFile)

There is an interesting side effect of printing the CrossReference: As we Dequeue the line numbers from each line queue, the line queues are destroyed. This side effect is noted in the specifications of PrintCrossRef.

The ReservedWords ADT

GetReservedWords reads the contents of the RESERVED.TXT file, and constructs a structure containing the words that are to be disregarded in creating the cross reference. The reserved words are strings of upper-case letters, stored in the file in alphabetical order, one word per line. (In our test copy of the file, we have included all the reserved words from Appendix A at the end of this book, as well as the standard constants (True, False, and Maxint), types (Integer, Boolean, Real, Char, and Text), and files (Input and Output) from Appendix B.

Since the number of reserved words is small and predictable (less than 50), we do not need to be concerned about the efficiency of searching the ReservedWords structure. Therefore, in the program listing that follows, ReservedWords has been implemented as a simple sequential list of strings, stored in an array. The WordIsReserved function performs a sequential search [$O(N)$] on this list.

You may want to add other words to this file; for instance, you may not want to include the standard functions and procedures (such as EOF, New, and Writeln) in the cross reference. (These are listed in Appendix B.) If the number of words in the file grows large, you may want to consider improving the efficiency of the search in the WordIsReserved function. One way to do this is to use a binary search; a second alternative is to reimplement the ReservedWords structure as a binary search tree. These modifications to the program are left as a programming exercise.

The Program

The modified Program ListAndCount is listed below. To save space, we have abbreviated the program listing by inserting comments in place of the source code of procedures and functions that are unchanged from the version of the program in Chapter 1, as well as the operations from the String, FIFO Queue, and Binary Search Tree ADT's.

File CROSSREF.PAS on the program disk contains the complete source listing.

```
PROGRAM ListAndCount
  (Input, Output, ProgramFile, ReportFile, ReservedFile);

  (* Program specification goes here. *)

CONST

  (* Comment delimiters *)
  LeftPar  = '(';
  Star     = '*';

  (* Maximum characters in StringType variables *)
  MaxString   = 80;  (* maximum number of chars per string *)
  MaxReserved = 50;  (* maximum number of reserved words   *)

TYPE
  LineType = (BlankLine, CommentLine, ExecLine);

  (*************** String Declarations *******************)
  (* Include string declarations from Chapter 3 here.    *)
  (*****************************************************)

  (***************** Reserved Words Types ***************)
  WordListType  = ARRAY [1 .. MaxReserved] OF StringType;
  WordRangeType = 0 .. MaxReserved;

  ReservedListType = RECORD
    Words    : WordListType;
    NumWords : WordRangeType
  END; (* ReservedListType *)

  (**************** Cross Reference Types ****************)
  QueueElementType = Integer;     (* queue of line numbers  *)
  (* Include QueueType declarations from Chapter 5 here.    *)
  (*****************************************************)

  (************* Binary Search Tree Types *****************)
  KeyType = StringType;

  TreeElementType = RECORD
    Key       : StringType;  (* key = cap ID    *)
    Id        : StringType;  (* identifier name *)
    LineQueue : QueueType    (* line references *)
  END; (* TreeElementType *)

  (*****************************************************)
  (* Include TreeType declarations from Chapter 9 here.   *)
  (*****************************************************)

  CrossRefType = TreeType;

VAR

  (* Files *)
  ProgramFile : Text; (* text of Pascal program to process *)
  ReportFile  : Text; (* report output of this program     *)
```

```
(* Count information *)
CommentCount : Integer;    (* count of comment-only lines   *)
ExecCount    : Integer;    (* count of executable lines     *)

(* Cross reference data *)
ReservedWords : ReservedListType; (* words to ignore        *)
CrossReference : CrossRefType;    (* ids used in program    *)
(***************************************************************)
(*                  String Operations                       *)
(***************************************************************)
(* Include source code for the String ADT operations Length, *)
(* CharAt, EmptyString, Append, ReadLine, PrintString, and   *)
(* Compare from Chapter 3. Include FindNonBlank from the      *)
(* original ListAndCount in Chapter 1.                        *)
(***************************************************************)

PROCEDURE UpCase
  (VAR Strng : StringType);

  (* Convert Strng to all upper-case equivalent. *)

VAR
  Index : Integer;

BEGIN (* UpCase *)

  FOR Index := 1 TO Strng.Length DO
    IF Strng.Chars[Index] IN ['a' .. 'z']
      THEN Strng.Chars[Index] :=
        CHR (ORD (Strng.Chars[Index])
          - (ORD ('a') - ORD ('A')))

END; (* UpCase *)
(***************************************************************)
(*                   Tree Operations                        *)
(***************************************************************)
(* Include source code for Binary Search Tree ADT operations *)
(* CreateTree, FindNode, RetrieveElement, ModifyElement,     *)
(* InsertElement, and PrintTree from Chapter 9. NOTE: Key     *)
(* field comparisons in FindNode and InsertElement must be    *)
(* modified to use string Compare operation in place of <.    *)
(* Use the version of PrintNode shown below:                  *)
(***************************************************************)

PROCEDURE PrintNode
  (VAR ToFile : Text;
   Element    : TreeElementType);

VAR
  LineNumber : QueueElementType;
```

```
BEGIN (* PrintNode *)

  PrintString (ToFile, Element.Id);
  Writeln (ToFile, ':');
  Write   (ToFile,'  ');

  WHILE NOT EmptyQueue (Element.LineQueue) DO
    BEGIN
      Dequeue (Element.LineQueue, LineNumber);
      Write   (ToFile, LineNumber, '  ')
    END; (* WHILE *)

  Writeln (ToFile);
  Writeln (ToFile)

END;  (* PrintNode *)

(*************************************************************)
(*                  ReservedWords Operations                *)
(*************************************************************)

PROCEDURE GetReservedWords
  (VAR ReservedWords : ReservedListType);

  (* Read the reserved words from text file, and create the *)
  (* list of ReservedWords.                                 *)

CONST
  FileName = 'RESERVED.TXT';

VAR
  ReservedFile : Text;
  Error        : Boolean;

BEGIN (* GetReservedWords *)

  (* Open ReservedFile for reading. *)
  Assign (ReservedFile, FileName); (* Turbo Pascal Code *)
  Reset  (ReservedFile);

  WITH ReservedWords DO
    BEGIN

      (* Set up for loop. *)
      NumWords := 0;

      (* Read ReservedFile, and store reserved words in      *)
      (* the ReservedWords list. File contains one reserved *)
      (* word per line.                                      *)
      WHILE NOT EOF (ReservedFile) DO
        BEGIN

          NumWords := NumWords + 1;

          (* Read next reserved word from file. *)
          ReadLine (ReservedFile, Words[NumWords], Error)

        END (* WHILE *)
```

```
    END  (* WITH *)
END;   (* GetReservedWords *)

(*************************************************************)

FUNCTION WordIsReserved
  (VAR ReservedWords : ReservedListType;
   Word              : StringType)  : Boolean;

  (* Determine if Word is in ReservedWords.          *)
  (* ReservedWords is passed as a VAR parameter because *)
  (* of its size and is not modified in this function.  *)

VAR
  Comparison : Relation;
  Index      : Integer;
BEGIN  (* WordIsReserved *)

  (* Search the ReservedWords list. *)
  Comparison := Less;
  Index := 1;

  WHILE (Comparison <> Equal) AND
        (Index <= ReservedWords.NumWords) DO
    BEGIN
      Comparison := Compare (Word, ReservedWords.Words[Index]);
      Index := Index + 1
    END; (* WHILE *)

  WordIsReserved := (Comparison = Equal)

END;   (* WordIsReserved *)

(*************************************************************)
(*                Application Operations                  *)
(*************************************************************)

PROCEDURE GetFiles
  (VAR ProgramFile   : Text;
   VAR ReportFile    : Text;
   VAR ReservedWords : ReservedListType);

  (* Get name of program file from the user. Open the   *)
  (* program file (reset) and the report file (rewrite). *)
  (* Read file containing reserved words and return the  *)
  (* ReservedWords list.                               *)

  (* NOTE: This procedure contains Turbo Pascal code.   *)

CONST
  ReportName = 'COUNTOUT';

VAR
  FileName : String[20];   (**** Turbo Pascal type ****)
```

```
BEGIN (* GetFiles *)

  Writeln ('What file would you like to list and count?');
  Readln (FileName);

  (****** Turbo Pascal code *******)
  Assign (ProgramFile, FileName);
  Reset  (ProgramFile);

  Assign (ReportFile,  ReportName);
  Rewrite (ReportFile);

  GetReservedWords (ReservedWords)

END;  (* GetFiles *)
```

```
(*************************************************************)
(* Include Functions Min and LineStatus and Procedures      *)
(* PrintCountData and IdentifyCommentStart from the         *)
(* original Program ListAndCount in Chapter 1.              *)
(*************************************************************)
```

```
PROCEDURE PrintCrossRef
  (VAR ReportFile  : Text;
   CrossReference  : CrossRefType);

BEGIN (* PrintCrossRef *)

  (* Print cross reference heading. *)
  Writeln (ReportFile);
  Writeln (ReportFile);
  Writeln (ReportFile,
    '*****************************************************');
  Writeln (ReportFile,
    '                    Cross Reference');
  Writeln (ReportFile);

  (* Print cross reference in alphabetical order. *)
  PrintTree (ReportFile, CrossReference, InOrder)

END;  (* PrintCrossRef *) .

(**************************************************************)

PROCEDURE GetWord
  (TextLine      : StringType;
   VAR CurPos    : Integer;
   VAR Word      : StringType);

  (* Extract Word from TextLine, beginning at CurPos. CurPos *)
  (* is reset to jump over the word, if it exists.           *)

VAR
  InComment : Boolean;
  More      : Boolean;
```

```
BEGIN (* GetWord *)

  EmptyString (Word);

  More := True;

  (* Skip leading characters that don't belong     *)
  (* in an identifier (nonalphabetic characters). *)
  WHILE (CurPos <= Length (TextLine)) AND More DO
    IF NOT (CharAt (TextLine, CurPos) IN
            ['a' .. 'z', 'A' .. 'Z'])
      THEN
        BEGIN

          (* If a comment is starting here, reset CurPos *)
          (* to jump past the end of TextLine; otherwise *)
          (* increment CurPos.                           *)
          IdentifyCommentStart (TextLine, CurPos, InComment);
          IF InComment
            THEN CurPos := Length (TextLine) + 1
            ELSE CurPos := CurPos + 1
        END (* if not alphabetic *)
      ELSE More := False;

  More := True;

  (* Append all legal identifier characters. *)
  WHILE (CurPos <= Length (TextLine)) AND More DO
    BEGIN
      (* If character is letter or number, append it; *)
      (* otherwise, stop looking for characters.      *)
      IF CharAt (TextLine, CurPos)
         IN ['a' .. 'z', 'A' .. 'Z', '0' .. '9']
        THEN Append (Word, CharAt(TextLine, CurPos))
        ELSE More := False;

      CurPos := CurPos + 1

    END (* WHILE *)

END;  (* GetWord *)

(****************************************************************)

PROCEDURE ProcessLine
   (TextLine           : StringType;
    LineNumber         : Integer;
    VAR CrossReference : CrossRefType;
    VAR ReservedWords  : ReservedListType);

  (* Extract all identifiers from this line and add to *)
  (* CrossReference. ReservedWords list is passed as a *)
  (* VAR parameter because of its size, but is not     *)
  (* modified by this procedure.                       *)
```

```
VAR
  Finished : Boolean;              (* finished this line?      *)
  CurPos   : Integer;              (* current string position *)
  Word     : StringType;           (* current Word in line     *)
  CapWord  : StringType;           (* uppercase Word           *)
  Element  : TreeElementType;      (* tree element for Word    *)
  Found    : Boolean;              (* Word in CrossReference   *)

BEGIN (* ProcessLine *)

  (* Set up to process the line. *)
  Finished := False;
  CurPos   := 1;

  WHILE NOT Finished DO
    BEGIN

      (* Get next "word" from the line. *)
      GetWord (TextLine, CurPos, Word);

      IF Length (Word) = 0
        THEN Finished := True
        ELSE
          BEGIN

            (* Convert Word to uppercase for exact match. *)
            CapWord := Word;
            UpCase (CapWord);

            (* If CapWord is not in ReservedWords list, then  *)
            (* add LineNumber to its entry in CrossReference. *)
            IF NOT WordIsReserved (ReservedWords, CapWord)
              THEN
                BEGIN
                  RetrieveElement
                    (CrossReference, CapWord, Element, Found);

                  IF Found
                    THEN
                      BEGIN  (* update Element *)
                        Enqueue (Element.LineQueue, LineNumber);
                        ModifyElement (CrossReference, Element)
                      END (* IF Found *)

                    ELSE
                      BEGIN (* add Element to CrossReference *)
                        Element.Key := CapWord;
                        Element.Id  := Word;
                        CreateQueue (Element.LineQueue);
                        Enqueue (Element.LineQueue, LineNumber);
                        InsertElement (CrossReference, Element)
                      END (* add Word to CrossReference *)
```

```
                        END (* IF not a reserved word *)
                   END (* If Word not empty *)
            END   (* WHILE *)
   END;  (* ProcessLine *)

   (***************************************************************)

   PROCEDURE ProcessProgramFile
      (VAR ProgramFile    : Text;
       VAR ReportFile     : Text;
       VAR ExecCount      : Integer;
       VAR CommentCount   : Integer;
       VAR CrossReference : CrossRefType);

      (* Process the Pascal program in ProgramFile, creating a *)
      (* numbered program listing in ReportFile.               *)

   VAR
      TextLine : StringType;   (* line being processed   *)
      Error    : Boolean;      (* returned from ReadLine *)

   BEGIN (* ProcessProgramFile *)

      (* Initialize for processing. *)
      ExecCount     := 0;
      CommentCount := 0;
      CreateTree (CrossReference);

      WHILE NOT EOF (ProgramFile) DO
        BEGIN

          (* Get the next line from the program file. *)
          ReadLine (ProgramFile, TextLine, Error);

          (* Echoprint TextLine to the screen. *)
          PrintString (Output, TextLine);
          Writeln (Output);

          (* Process according to whether this line is blank, *)
          (* comment-only, or contains "executable" code.     *)
          CASE LineStatus (TextLine) OF

            BlankLine   :
              BEGIN
                (* Print the line to the report file. *)
                Writeln (ReportFile)
              END; (* BlankLine *)

            CommentLine :
              BEGIN
                CommentCount := CommentCount + 1;

                (* Print the line to the report file. *)
                Write (ReportFile, '        ');
                PrintString (ReportFile, TextLine);
                Writeln (ReportFile)

              END; (* CommentLine *)
```

```
          ExecLine   :
            BEGIN
              ExecCount := ExecCount + 1;

                (* Print the line to the report file. *)
                Write (ReportFile, ExecCount:4, '.  ');
                PrintString (ReportFile, TextLine);
                Writeln (ReportFile);

                (* Update cross reference. *)
                ProcessLine (TextLine, ExecCount,
                  CrossReference, ReservedWords)

          END (* ExecLine *)
      END  (* CASE *)
    END (* WHILE NOT EOF *)
END;  (* ProcessProgramFile *)

(**************************************************************)

PROCEDURE TerminateProcessing
  (VAR ProgramFile : Text;
   VAR ReportFile  : Text);

  (* Close ProgramFile and ReportFile.              *)
  (* NOTE: This procedure contains Turbo Pascal code. *)

BEGIN (* TerminateProcessing *)

  (* Close the files. *)
  Close (ReportFile);
  Close (ProgramFile)

END;  (* TerminateProcessing *)

(**************************************************************)

BEGIN (* ListAndCount *)

  (* Get Program file name from user; open Program (Reset) *)
  (* and Report (Rewrite) files for processing. Read file  *)
  (* of reserved words and return ReservedWords list.      *)
  GetFiles
    (ProgramFile,
     ReportFile,
     ReservedWords);

  (* Process the Pascal program in ProgramFile, creating a  *)
  (* numbered program listing in ReportFile.                *)
  ProcessProgramFile
    (ProgramFile,
     ReportFile,
     ExecCount,        (* returned *)
     CommentCount,     (* returned *)
     CrossReference);  (* returned *)
```

```
(* Print the count information to the ReportFile. *)
PrintCountData
  (ReportFile,
   ExecCount,
   CommentCount);

(* Print the CrossReference to the ReportFile. *)
PrintCrossRef
  (ReportFile,
   CrossReference);

(* Close the files. *)
TerminateProcessing
  (ProgramFile,
   ReportFile)

END.   (* ListAndCount *)
```

▪ *Exercises**

1. (a) What does the level of a binary search tree mean in relation to the searching efficiency?
   (b) What is the maximum number of levels that a binary search tree with 100 nodes can have?
   (c) What is the minimum number of levels that a binary search tree with 100 nodes can have?

2. What is the maximum total number of nodes in a tree that has N levels? (Remember that the root is Level 0.)
   (a) $N^2 - 1$ (c) $2^{N+1} - 1$
   (b) 2^N (d) 2^{N+1}

3. What is the maximum number of nodes in the Nth level of a binary tree?
   (a) N^2 (c) 2^{N+1}
   (b) 2^N (d) $2^N - 1$

4. How many ancestors does a node in the Nth level of a binary search tree have?

5. (a) How many different *binary trees* can be made from three nodes that contain the key values 1, 2, and 3?
   (b) How many different *binary search trees* can be made from three nodes that contain the key values 1, 2, and 3?

6. Draw all the possible binary trees that have four leaves and all the nonleaf nodes have two children.

Answer the questions in Exercises 7–9 independently, using the tree at the top of the next page.

7. (a) What are the ancestors of node P?
   (b) What are the descendants of node K?
   (c) What is the maximum possible number of nodes in the tree at the level of node W?
   (d) What is the maximum possible number of nodes in the tree at the level of node N?
   (e) Insert node O. How many nodes would be in the tree if it were completely full down to and including the level of node O?

*Questions with italicized numbers are answered in the back of the book.

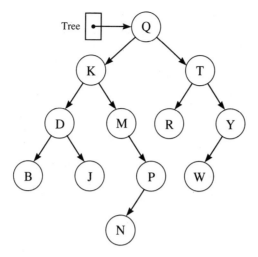

8. Show what the tree would look like after each of the following changes. (Use the original tree to answer each part.)
   (a) Add node C.
   (b) Add node Z.
   (c) Add node X.
   (d) Delete node M.
   (e) Delete node Q.
   (f) Delete node R.

9. Show what would be printed by each of the following.
   (a) an inorder traversal of the tree
   (b) a postorder traversal of the tree
   (c) a preorder traversal of the tree

10. Draw the binary search tree whose elements are inserted in the following order:
    50 72 96 94 107 26 12 11 9 2 10 25 51 16 17 95

Exercises 11–15 use the following tree.

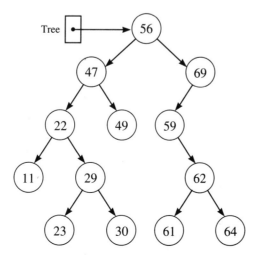

11. (a) What is the height of the tree?
    (b) What nodes are on level 3?
    (c) Which levels have the maximum number of nodes that they could contain?
    (d) What is the maximum height of a binary search tree containing these nodes? Draw such a tree.
    (e) What is the minimum height of a binary search tree containing these nodes? Draw such a tree.

12. (a) Trace the path that would be followed in searching for a node containing 61.
    (b) Trace the path that would be followed in searching for a node containing 28.

13. Show what would be printed by each of the following.
    (a) an inorder traversal of the tree
    (b) a postorder traversal of the tree
    (c) a preorder traversal of the tree

14. Show how the tree would look after the deletion of 29, 59, and 47.

15. Show how the (original) tree would look after the insertion of nodes containing 63, 77, 76, 48, 9, and 10 (in that order).

16. True or False.
    (a) Invoking the delete procedure in this chapter might create a tree with more levels than the original tree had.
    (b) A preorder print traversal will print the exact reverse of what a postorder traversal will print.
    (c) An inorder traversal will always print the elements of a tree in the same order, regardless of the order in which the elements were inserted.
    (d) A preorder traversal will always print the elements of a tree in the same order, regardless of the order in which the elements were inserted.

17. If you wanted to traverse a tree, writing all the elements to a file, and later (the next time you ran the program) rebuild the trees by reading and inserting, would an inorder traversal be appropriate? Why or why not?

18. (a) One hundred integer elements are chosen at random and inserted into an ordered linked list and a binary search tree. Describe the efficiency of searching for an element in each structure, in terms of Big-O.
    (b) One hundred integer elements are inserted in order, from smallest to largest, into an ordered linked list and a binary search tree. Describe the efficiency of searching for an element in each structure, in terms of Big-O.

19. The Info field of the nodes in a binary search tree contains short character strings.
    (a) Show how such a tree would look after the following words were inserted (in the order indicated):

    monkey canary donkey deer zebra yak walrus vulture penguin quail

    (b) Show how the tree would look if the same words were inserted in this order:

    quail walrus donkey deer monkey vulture yak penguin zebra canary

    (c) Show how the tree would look if the same words were inserted in this order:

    zebra yak walrus vulture quail penguin monkey donkey deer canary

20. Modify the DeleteNode procedure from the chapter so that it uses the immediate *successor* (rather than the predecessor) of the value to be deleted in the case of deleting a node with two children.

21. (a) Use the Three-Question method to verify the recursive version of InsertElement.
(b) Use the Three-Question method to verify the recursive version of DeleteElement.

22. Write a nonrecursive version of FindAndRemoveMax.

23. Procedure ChangeKey modifies the key value of an element in a binary search tree. It assumes that there is a node in the tree whose key is OldKey, and changes the key of this node to NewKey.
(a) Write the specifications of ChangeKey.
(b) Write ChangeKey as an application operation that does not know how the tree is implemented.

24. Write a nonrecursive procedure Ancestors that prints the ancestors of a given node whose Info field contains a value Num. Num only occurs once in the tree. Do not print Num. You may assume that the tree is not empty. Use the following procedure heading:

```
PROCEDURE Ancestors
  (Tree : TreeType;
   Num  : Integer);
```

25. (a) Write a recursive version of Procedure Ancestors described in Exercise 24.
(b) Write a call to Procedure Ancestors to print the ancestors of the node containing the value 27.

26. Write a recursive version of Procedure Ancestors (see Exercise 24) that prints out the ancestors in reverse order (first the parent, then the grandparent, and so on).

27. The Binary Search Tree ADT is extended to include Boolean function IsBST, which determines if a binary tree is a binary search tree.
(a) Write the specifications of IsBST.
(b) Write a recursive implementation of this function.

28. The Binary Search Tree ADT is extended to include functions that input a pointer to a binary search tree, and return the number of nodes that meet certain requirements.
(a) Write a recursive function NodeCount, which returns the number of nodes in the tree.
(b) Write a recursive function LeafCount, which returns the number of leaf nodes in the tree.
(c) Write a recursive function SingleParentCount, which returns the number of nodes in the tree that have only one child.
(d) Write a recursive function BigValueCount, which returns the number of nodes in the tree whose key value is greater than Value (an input parameter to the function).

29. The Binary Search Tree ADT is extended to include Procedure CopyTree, which inputs a pointer to the root node of a binary search tree, and outputs a pointer to the root node of a duplicate tree.
(a) Write the specifications of CopyTree.
(b) Write Procedure CopyTree.

30. The Binary Search Tree ADT is extended to include a Boolean function SimilarTrees, which inputs pointers to two binary trees, and determines if the shapes of the trees are the same. (The nodes do not have to contain the same values, but each node must have the same number of children.)
    (a) Write the specifications of SimilarTrees.
    (b) Write function SimilarTrees.

31. Procedure Mirror inputs a pointer to the root node of a binary search tree, and creates a mirror image of the tree.
    (a) Write the specifications of Mirror.
    (b) Write Procedure Mirror.
    (c) Can the binary tree returned from this procedure be used for binary searching? If so, how?

Use the following declarations for Exercises 32 and 33.

```
TYPE
  ListType = RECORD
    Elements    : ARRAY [1 .. MaxElements] OF Integer;
    NumElements : 0 .. MaxElements
  END; (* ListType *)

  TreeElementType = Integer;
  (* use the other tree declarations from this chapter *)
```

32. Write a procedure, MakeTree, that will create a binary search tree from the elements in a sorted list of integers. You cannot traverse the list inserting the elements in order, since that would produce a tree that would have N levels. You must create a tree with at most $\log_2 N + 1$ levels.

33. Write a Boolean function, MatchingElements, that determines if a binary search tree and a sequential list contain the same values.

Use the following declarations for TreeElementType in Exercises 34 and 35.

```
TYPE
  AppraisalType = (Superior, Good, Fair, Warning, PinkSlip);

  TreeElementType = RECORD
    EmployeeID : Integer; (* key *)
    Salary     : Real;
    Appraisal  : AppraisalType
  END; (* TreeElementType *)
```

34. Write a procedure RaiseTime, which inputs a pointer to the root node of a binary search tree of employee records, and modifies the salary of every employee according to their last appraisal rating:

Superior	raise current salary by 10%
Good	raise current salary by 5%
Fair	raise current salary by 3%
Warning	no change
PinkSlip	set salary to 0

35. Write a procedure PrintByAppraisal that inputs a pointer to the root node of a binary search tree, and prints out the EmployeeID's of every record with each Appraisal rating. (First all the EmployeeID's of the Superior employees should be printed (in order), then the Employee ID's of the Good employees, and so on. Each set of EmployeeID's should be preceded by a label describing the Appraisal rating.

Use the following declarations for TreeElementType in Exercises 36–38.

```
TYPE

    StringType = PACKED ARRAY [1..20] OF Char;

    SexType   = (Male, Female);
    ClassType = (Freshman, Sophomore, Junior, Senior, Grad);

    TreeElementType = RECORD
      LastName  : StringType;
      FirstName : StringType;
      IDNum     : Integer;
      Sex       : SexType;
      Class     : ClassType;
      GPA       : Real
    END; (* TreeElementType *)
```

36. The binary search tree is ordered by GPA from smallest to largest. A women's organization wants to select some graduating female students to receive awards. Write a procedure PrintSeniorWomen to print the name, GPA, and IDNum of each of the women in the senior class, ordered from highest to lowest GPA.

37. The binary search tree is ordered by GPA from smallest to largest. The dean wants to specially honor all of the students with a GPA of 4.0. Write a procedure PrintGenius that takes a pointer to the binary search tree and prints the name of each student with a GPA of 4.0. The names can be printed in any order. (*Hint:* You don't need to traverse the whole tree.)

38. The binary search tree of student records is ordered by IDNum. Write a procedure that takes an IDNum and either prints out all of the corresponding student information (if the specified student is found) or prints "No student found with" and then the IDNum. You can call Procedure RetrieveElement from the Binary Search Tree ADT to get the student information, using the IDNum key.

Use these declarations for Problems 39 and 40:

```
CONST
  Null = 0;

TYPE
  NodeType = RECORD
    Info       : Char;
    Left, Right : 0 .. MaxNodes
  END; (* NodeType *)

  NodeSpace = ARRAY [1 .. MaxNodes] OF NodeType;

VAR
  Nodes : NodeSpace;
```

39. You decide to store the nodes of a binary search tree in an array of records, rather than using dynamic storage allocation. Given the declarations above, show how the array would look after these elements had been inserted:

    Q L W F M R N S

    Free space is linked through the Left field. Be sure to fill in all the spaces. If you do not know the contents of a space, use '?'.

Nodes	.Info	.Left	.Right
[1]	Q		
[2]	L		
[3]	W		
[4]	F		
[5]	M		
[6]	R		
[7]	N		
[8]	S		
[9]			
⋮			

    Tree ☐

    Free ☐

40. Show the contents of the array in Exercise 22 after 'B' has been inserted and 'R' deleted.

Nodes	.Info	.Left	.Right
[1]			
[2]			
[3]			
[4]			
[5]			
[6]			
[7]			
[8]			
[9]			
⋮			

Tree ☐

Free ☐

Exercises 41–44 refer to the Cross Reference application at the end of this chapter.

41. Two possibilities are mentioned in the text for improving the efficiency of searching ReservedWords. How does the order of the data in the input file relate to this issue?

42. Why is the LineQueue of each CrossReference element destroyed as a side effect of printing the CrossReference? If we wanted to do something else with the cross reference data after

printing, this side effect would cause problems. Suggest ways that the LineQueues could be preserved.

43. The following statement contains a literal string:

```
Writeln ('The value of Number = ', Number);
```

How does the cross reference generator in the text deal with such literal strings? How could the program be modified to deal with them "correctly"? Modify the design of the module where the changes belong.

44. The following statement contains two references to an identifier in the same line:

```
Index := Index + 1;
```

(a) How does the cross reference generator in the text deal with such duplicate references?
(b) Modify the design of the program to allow duplicates to be put into the LineQueue, but not to be printed in the Cross Reference report.
(c) Modify the design of the module so that only one reference to a line is put in the line queue. If you need to use any additional Queue operations, specify them.

Trees Plus

GOALS

- To be able to show how a binary tree can be represented in an array, with implicit positional links between the elements.
- To be able to define the following terms:
  - full binary tree
  - complete binary tree
  - heap
- To be able to describe the shape and order properties of a heap, and to implement a heap in a nonlinked tree representation in an array.
- To be able to describe a priority queue at the logical level and to implement a priority queue as a heap.
- To be able to compare the implementation of a priority queue using a heap, linked list, and binary search tree.
- To be able to define the following terms related to graphs:
  - directed graph
  - undirected graph
  - vertex
  - edge
  - path
  - complete graph
  - weighted graph
  - adjacency matrix
  - adjacency list
- To be able to implement a graph using an adjacency matrix to represent the edges.
- To be able to explain the difference between a depth-first and a breadth-first search and to implement these searching strategies using stacks and queues for auxiliary storage.
- To be able to implement a shortest-paths operation, using a priority queue to access the edge with the minimum weight.

So far we have examined several basic data structures in depth, discussing their uses and operations, as well as one or more implementations of each. As we have constructed these programmer-defined data structures out of the built-in types provided by our high-level language, we have noted variations that adapt them to the needs of different applications. In Chapter 9 we looked at how a tree structure, the binary search tree, facilitates searching data stored in a linked structure. In this chapter we will see how other branching structures are used to model a variety of applications.

A Nonlinked Representation of Binary Trees

Our discussion of the implementation of binary trees has so far been limited to a scheme in which the pointers from parent to children are *explicit* in the data structure. A field was declared in each node for the pointer to the left child and the pointer to the right child.

A binary tree can be stored in an array in such a way that the relationships in the tree are not physically represented by link fields, but are *implicit* in the algorithms that manipulate the tree stored in the array. The code is, of course, much less self-documenting, but we save memory space because there are no pointers.

Let's take a binary tree and store it in an array in such a way that the parent–child relationships are not lost. We will store the tree in the array level by level, left to right. This mapping is illustrated in Figure 10-1. The number of nodes in the tree is NumElements. The tree elements are stored with the root in Tree[1] and the last node in Tree[NumElements].

Figure 10-1
A Binary Tree and
Its Array
Representation

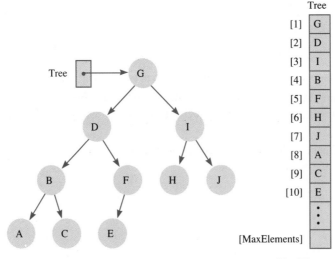

NumElements = 10

To be able to implement the algorithms that manipulate the tree, we must be able to find the left and right child of a node in the tree. Comparing the tree and the array in Figure 10-1, we see that

Tree[1]'s children are in Tree[2] and Tree[3].
Tree[2]'s children are in Tree[4] and Tree[5].
Tree[3]'s children are in Tree[6] and Tree[7].

Do you see the pattern? For any node Tree[Index], its left child is in Tree[Index * 2] and its right child is in Tree[Index * 2 + 1] (provided that these child nodes exist). Notice that the nodes in the array from Tree[NumElements DIV 2 + 1] to Tree[NumElements] are leaf nodes.

Not only can we easily calculate the location of a node's children, we can also determine the location of its *parent* node. This is not an easy task in a binary tree linked together with pointers from parent to child nodes, but it is very simple in our implicit link implementation:

Tree[Index]'s parent is in Tree[Index DIV 2].

Because Pascal's integer division operator truncates the remainder, Index DIV 2 is the correct parent index for either a left or right child. Thus this implementation of a binary tree is linked in both directions: from parent to child, and from child to parent. We will take advantage of this fact later in this chapter.

This tree representation works well for any binary tree that is full or complete. A **full binary tree** is a binary tree in which all of the leaves are on the same level and every nonleaf node has two children. The basic shape of a full binary tree is triangular:

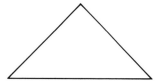

A **complete binary tree** is a binary tree that is either full or full through the next-to-last level, with the leaves on the last level as far to the left as possible. The shape of a complete binary tree is either triangular (if the tree is full) or something like the following:

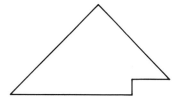

Figure 10-2
Examples of Binary
Trees

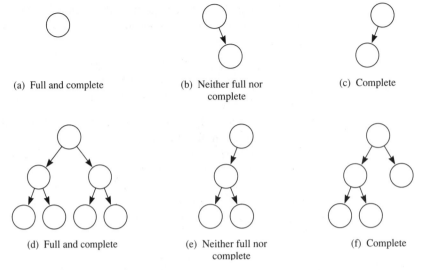

(a) Full and complete   (b) Neither full nor   (c) Complete
                                   complete

(d) Full and complete   (e) Neither full nor   (f) Complete
                                   complete

Figure 10-2, above, shows some examples of binary trees.

The array-based representation is simple to implement for trees that are full or complete, since the elements occupy contiguous array slots. If a tree is not full or complete, however, we must account for the gaps where nodes are missing. To use the array representation, we must store a dummy value in those positions in the array in order to maintain the proper parent–child relationship. The choice of a dummy value depends on what information is stored in the tree. For instance, if the elements in the tree are positive integers, a negative value can be stored in the dummy nodes.

Figure 10-3 illustrates a tree that is not complete and its corresponding array. NumElements indicates how many contiguous array slots are in use. Some of these slots do not contain actual tree elements, however; they contain dummy values. The algorithms to manipulate the tree must reflect this situation. For example, to determine whether the node in Tree[Index] has a left child, you must check whether Index * 2 <= NumElements, and then compare the value in Tree[Index * 2] to the dummy value.

We have seen how an array can be used to represent a binary tree. We can also reverse this process, creating a binary tree from the elements in an array. In fact, we can regard *any* one-dimensional array as representing a tree structure, but the data values that happen to be stored in it may not match this structure in a meaningful way.

Heaps

A **heap** is a binary tree that satisfies two properties, one concerning its shape and the other concerning the order of its elements. The **shape property** is simple: A heap must be a complete binary tree. The **order property** says that, for every node in the heap, the value stored in that node is greater than or equal to the value in each of its children.

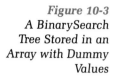

Figure 10-3
A BinarySearch
Tree Stored in an
Array with Dummy
Values

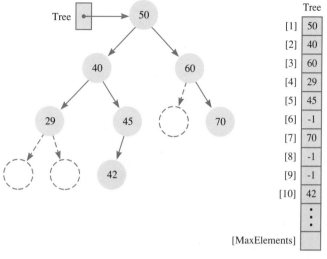

NumElements = 10

Heap A complete binary tree, each of whose elements contains a value that is greater than or equal to the value of each of its children.

Figure 10-4 shows two heaps that contain the values 'A' through 'J'. Notice that the placement of the values differs in the two trees, but the shape is the same: a complete binary tree of ten elements. Note also that the two heaps have the same root node. A group of values can be stored in a binary tree in many ways and still satisfy the order property of heaps. Because of the shape property, we know that the shape of all the heaps with a given number of elements will be the same. We also know, because of the order property, that the root node will always contain the largest value in the heap. This fact gives us a hint as to what this data structure might be good for. The special feature of heaps is that we always know where the maximum value is: It is in the root node.

NOTE: When we refer to a "heap" in this section, we are referring to the structure defined above. This might also be called a "maximum heap," since the root node contains the maximum value in the structure. It is also possible to create a "minimum heap," each of whose elements contains a value that is *less* than or equal to the value of each of its children.

Let's say that we want to remove the element with the largest value from a heap. The largest element is in the root node, so we can easily remove it, as illustrated in Figure 10-5(a). But this leaves a hole in the root position. Because the heap's tree must be complete, we decide to fill the hole with the bottom rightmost element from the heap; now the structure satisfies the shape property [Figure 10-5(b)]. However, the replacement value came from the bottom of the tree, where the smaller values are; the tree no longer satisfies the order property of heaps.

Figure 10-4
Two Heaps Contain-
ing the Letters A–J

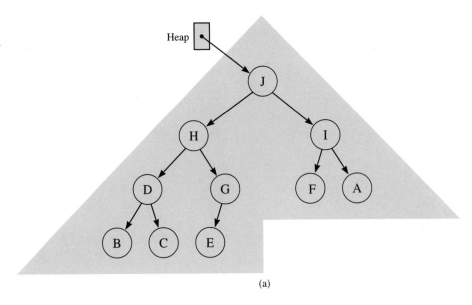

(a)

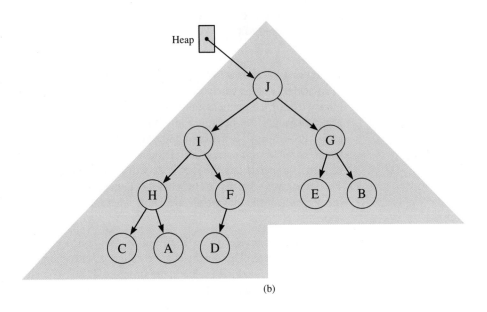

(b)

Figure 10-4
Two Heaps Contain-
ing the Letters A–J

This situation suggests one of the basic heap operations: Given a complete binary tree whose elements satisfy the heap order property *except in the root position*, repair the structure so that it will again be a heap. This operation involves moving the element down from the root position until it ends up in a position where the order property is satisfied [see Figure 10-5(c)]. The ReheapDown operation has the following specification:

Figure 10-5
The ReheapDown Operation

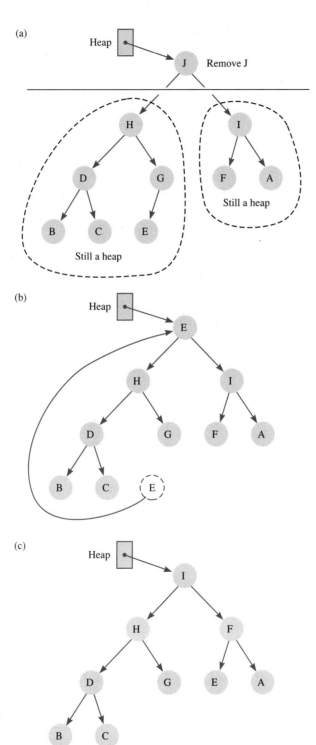

(a)

(b)

(c)

ReheapDown (Heap, Root, Bottom)

Function:	Restores the order property of heaps to the (sub) tree beginning at Root.
Input:	Heap, Root, Bottom
Preconditions:	The order property of heaps is violated only by the root node of the (sub) tree.
Output:	Heap (changed)
Postconditions:	The order property applies to all elements of the heap.

We have tried to make this operation fairly general, by telling it where to find the root and the bottom rightmost element of the heap and passing it the set of elements. Letting Root be a parameter, instead of just assuming that we start at the root of the whole heap, generalizes this routine, allowing us to perform the reheap operation on any subtree, as well as on the original heap. (This will be helpful in Chapter 11, when we develop the HeapSort algorithm.)

Now let's say that we want to add an element to the heap—where do we put it? The shape property tells us that the tree must be complete, so we put the new element in the next bottom rightmost place in the tree, as illustrated in Figure 10-6(a). Now the shape property is satisfied, but the order property may be violated. This situation illustrates the need for another basic heap operation: Given a complete binary tree containing N elements, whose first $N - 1$ elements satisfy the order property of heaps, repair the structure so that it will again be a heap. To fix this structure, we need to float the Nth element up in the tree until it is in its correct place [see Figure 10-6(b)]. Let's call this operation ReheapUp and give it the following specification:

ReheapUp (Heap, Root, Bottom)

Function:	Restores the order property to the heap.
Input:	Heap, Root, Bottom
Preconditions:	The order property is satisfied from the root of the heap through the next-to-last node; Bottom rightmost node may violate the order property.
Output:	Heap
Postconditions:	The order property applies to all the elements of the heap from Root through Bottom.

Heap Implementations

Although we have graphically depicted heaps as binary trees with nodes and links, it would be very impractical to implement the heap operations using the usual linked tree representation. The shape property of heaps tells us that the binary tree is complete, so we know that it will never have any holes in it. Thus we could easily store the tree in an array with implicit links, as discussed earlier in this chapter. Figure 10-7 shows how the values in a heap would be stored in this array representation. If a heap with

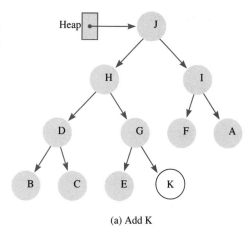

(a) Add K

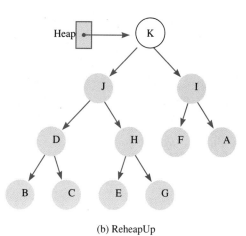

(b) ReheapUp

Figure 10-6
The ReheapUp
Operation

Figure 10-7
Heap Values in an
Array
Representation

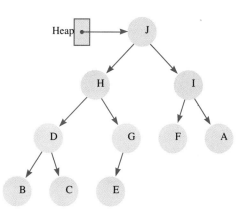

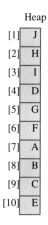

N elements is implemented this way, the shape property says that the heap elements will be stored in N consecutive slots in the array, with the root element in the first slot and the last leaf node in the Nth slot. The order property says that, for every nonleaf node Heap[Index],

Heap[Index] $>=$ Heap[Index * 2]

and, if there is a right child,

Heap[Index] $>=$ HeapElements[Index * 2 + 1].

We will use the following declarations to support this heap implementation:

```
CONST
  MaxElements = 100;
TYPE
  ElementType = Char: (* Whatever is stored in the heap *)

  ArrayType = ARRAY [1 .. MaxElements] OF ElementType;
VAR
  Heap : ArrayType;
```

We've specified two utility operations to fix heaps that are "broken" at one end or the other. Now let's look at these operations in more detail.

When the ReheapDown operation is first called, there are two possibilities. If the value of the root node (Heap[1]) is greater than or equal to the values of its children, the order property is still intact and we don't have to do anything. Otherwise we know that the maximum value of the tree is in either the root node's left child (Heap[2]) or the right child (Heap[3]). One of these values must be swapped with the smaller value in the root. Now the subtree rooted at the node that was swapped is a heap—except (possibly) for *its* root node. We apply the same process again, asking whether the value in this node is greater than or equal to the values in its children. We test smaller and smaller subtrees of the original heap, moving our original root node down until

1. the root of the current subtree is a leaf node; or
2. the value in the root of the current subtree is greater than or equal to the values of both its children.

The algorithm for this procedure is given below and illustrated with an example in Figure 10-8. At the start, Root is the index of the node that (possibly) violates the heap order property.

ReheapDown (Heap, Root, Bottom)

IF Heap[Root] is not a leaf
   THEN
      MaxChild ← index of child with larger value

     IF Heap[Root] < Heap[MaxChild]
       THEN (General Case)
         Swap them
         ReheapDown (Heap, MaxChild, Bottom)

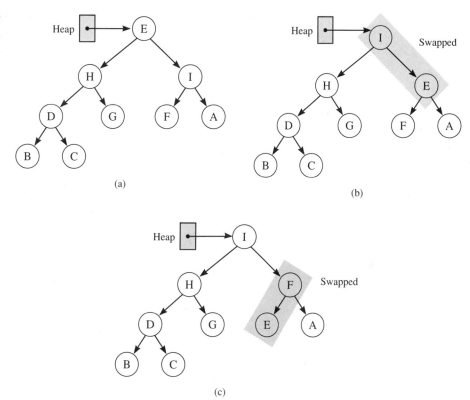

Figure 10-8
The ReheapDown
Operation

ELSE (Base Case)
    Do nothing—Order property intact

ELSE (Base Case)
    Do nothing—Heap[Root] is a leaf

This is a recursive algorithm. In the general case, we swap the values in the root node with its largest child, and then repeat the process. On the recursive call, we specify MaxChild as the root of the heap; this shrinks the size of the tree still to be processed, satisfying the smaller-caller question. There are two base cases: (1) if Heap[Root] is a leaf, and (2) if the heap order property is already intact. In either of these cases, we do nothing.

To determine MaxChild, we first check to see whether the current root node has only a single child. If so, it will be a left child (because the tree is complete), and we set MaxChild to its index. Otherwise we compare the values of the two child nodes and set MaxChild to the index of the node that has the larger value.

The whole procedure is shown below. It uses a utility procedure, Swap, which swaps the values of its two parameters. (Since this procedure is trivial, we do not show its implementation here.)

```
PROCEDURE ReheapDown
    (VAR Heap    : ArrayType;
    Root, Bottom : Integer);
```

```
(* Restores the heap order property to the subtree starting *)
(* at Root. On invocation of ReheapDown, the order property *)
(* is violated (if at all) only by root node.               *)
VAR
  MaxChild   : Integer; (* index of child with larger value *)
  RightChild : Integer; (* index of the right child node    *)
  LeftChild  : Integer; (* index of the left child node     *)
BEGIN (* ReheapDown *)

  LeftChild  := Root * 2;
  RightChild := Root * 2 + 1;

  (* Check for Base Case 1: Heap[Root] is a leaf *)
  IF LeftChild <= Bottom
    THEN
      BEGIN  (* Heap[Root] is not a leaf *)

        (* MaxChild := index of child with larger value *)
        IF LeftChild = Bottom
          THEN (* There is only one child node. *)
            MaxChild := LeftChild
          ELSE (* Pick the greater of the two children. *)
            IF Heap[LeftChild] > Heap[RightChild]
              THEN MaxChild := LeftChild
              ELSE MaxChild := RightChild;

        (* Check for Base Case 2: order property intact *)
        IF Heap[Root] < Heap[MaxChild]
          THEN
            BEGIN (* General Case: swap and reheap *)
              Swap (Heap[Root], Heap[MaxChild]);
              ReheapDown (Heap, MaxChild, Bottom)
            END (* IF Heap[Root] < Heap[MaxChild] *)

      END (* IF Heap[Root] is not a leaf *)
END;   (* ReheapDown *)
```

The converse operation, ReheapUp, takes a leaf node that violates the order property of heaps and moves it up until its correct position is found. We compare the value of the bottom node with the value of its parent node. If the parent's value is smaller, the order property is violated, so the two nodes are swapped. Then we examine the parent, repeating the process until

1. the current node is the root of the heap; or
2. the value in the current node is less than or equal to the value of its parent node.

The algorithm for this procedure is given below and illustrated in Figure 10-9.

ReheapUp (Heap, Root, Bottom)

IF Heap[Bottom] is not the Root node
  THEN
    Parent ← index of parent of Heap[Bottom]

Figure 10-9
The ReheapUp
Operation

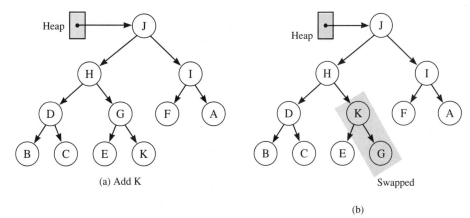

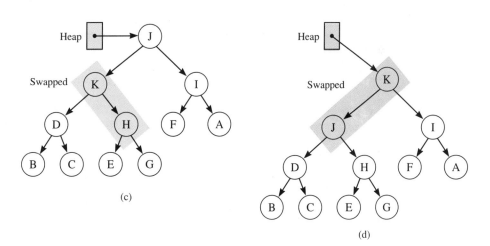

```
IF Heap[Parent] < Heap[Bottom]
   THEN (General Case)
      Swap them
      ReheapUp (Heap, Root, Parent)

   ELSE (Base Case)
      Do nothing—Order property intact

ELSE (Base Case)
   Do nothing—Heap[Bottom] is the root
```

This is also a recursive algorithm. In the general case, we swap the (current) "bottom" node with its parent and reinvoke the procedure. On the recursive call, we specify Parent as the bottom node; this shrinks the size of the tree still to be processed, so the smaller-caller question can be answered affirmatively. There are two base cases: (1) if we have reached the root node, or (2) if the heap order property is satisfied. In either of these cases, we exit the procedure without doing anything.

How do we find the parent node? This is not an easy task in a binary tree linked together with pointers from parent to child nodes, but, as we saw earlier, it is very simple in our implicit link implementation:

```
Parent := Bottom DIV 2;
```

We can now code the whole procedure:

```
PROCEDURE ReheapUp
  (VAR Heap      : ArrayType;
   Root, Bottom : Integer);

  (* Restores the order property to the heap. Assumes that *)
  (* at invocation the order property is violated only at  *)
  (* the bottom leaf node position.                        *)

VAR
  Parent : Integer; (* index of the parent node *)

BEGIN (* ReheapUp *)
  (* Check for Base Case 1: Heap[Bottom] is the root *)
  IF Bottom > Root
    THEN
      BEGIN  (* Heap[Bottom] is not the root *)
        Parent := Bottom DIV 2;

      (* Check for Base Case 2: order property intact *)
        IF Heap[Parent] < Heap[Bottom]
          THEN
            BEGIN (* General case: swap and reheap *)
              Swap (Heap[Parent], Heap[Bottom]);
              ReheapUp (Heap, Root, Parent)
            END (* IF Heap[Parent] < Heap[Bottom] *)

      END (* IF Heap[Bottom] is not root *)
END;  (* ReheapUp *)
```

⊟   The source code for the declarations and operations on a heap is in file HEAP.PAS on the program disk.

Heap Applications

In discussing FIFO queue applications in Chapter 5, we said that the operating system of a multiuser computer system may use job queues to save users' requests in the order in which they are made. Another way such requests may be handled is according to how important the job request is. That is, the head of the company might get higher priority than the lowly junior programmer. Or an interactive program might get higher priority than a "batch job" to print out a report that isn't needed until the next day. To handle these requests efficiently, the operating system may use a structure called a *priority queue*. Because a heap gives us fast access to the largest (or highest-priority) element in the structure, it is a good way to implement a priority queue. We will look at this structure in detail in the next section.

Heaps are also useful in sorting. It's easy to imagine how heaps relate to sorting an array if you consider a simple sorting technique that makes repeated searches through the array to locate the next-largest value and move it into its correct place. With heaps, we always know where to find the largest value. We'll look more at how heaps can be used in sorting in Chapter 11.

Priority Queues

The Logical Level

A priority queue is an abstract data type with an interesting accessing function: Only the *highest-priority* element can be accessed. "Highest priority" can mean different things, depending on the application. Consider, for example, a small company with one secretary. When the other employees leave work on the secretary's desk, which jobs get done first? The jobs are processed in order of the employee's importance in the company; the secretary completes the president's work before starting the vice-president's, and does the marketing director's work before staff programmer's. That is, the *priority* of each job relates to the level of the employee who initiated it.

In a telephone answering system, calls are answered in the order that they are received. That is, the highest-priority call is the one that has been waiting the longest. Thus a FIFO queue can be considered a priority queue whose highest-priority element is the one that has been queued the longest time.

In this section, we'll describe a priority queue whose highest-priority element is the one with the largest value.

The operations defined for the Priority Queue ADT include procedures to create and destroy a priority queue, as well as functions to test for an empty or full priority queue. These operations are very similar to those specified for the FIFO queue discussed in Chapter 5. The PriorityEnq operation adds a given element to the priority queue. The PriorityDeq operation removes the highest-priority element from the priority queue and returns it to the user. The specification for this abstract data type follows:

Priority Queue ADT Specification

Structure   The Priority Queue is arranged to support access to the highest-priority element.

(The CreatePQueue, DestroyPQueue, FullPQueue, and EmptyPQueue operations are analogous to the FIFO queue operations.)

PriorityEnq (PQueue, NewElement)

Function:	Adds NewElement to the priority queue.
Input:	PQueue (PriorityQueueType)
	NewElement (ElementType)

Preconditions:	PQueue is not full.
Output:	PQueue
Postconditions:	PQueue is a priority queue that contains the original elements of PQueue + NewElement.

PriorityDeq: (PQueue, PriorityElement)

Function:	Removes the highest-priority element from the priority queue and returns its value in PriorityElement.
Input:	PQueue (PriorityQueueType)
Preconditions:	PQueue is not empty.
Output:	PQueue (changed) PriorityElement (ElementType)
Postconditions:	PQueue is a priority queue that contains all the original elements in PQueue, except for its highest-priority element. PriorityElement = highest-priority element from original PQueue

Implementation of Priority Queues

There are many ways to implement a priority queue. In any implementation, we want to be able to access the largest element quickly and easily. For instance, we can keep the elements in a linked list ordered from largest to smallest element, or in a binary search tree. We'll discuss these implementations more at the end of this section.

An excellent way to implement a priority queue is by using a heap. Suppose that the number of elements in a priority queue is NumElements. Using the heap implementation described earlier, the elements are stored in the first NumElements array slots. Because of the order property, we know that the largest element is in the root—that is, in the first array slot.

Let's look first at the PriorityDeq operation. The root element is returned to the caller. After we remove the root, we are left with two subtrees, each of which satisfies the heap property (review Figure 10-5 on page 611). Of course, we cannot leave a hole in the root position, for that violates the shape property. Since we have removed an element, there are now NumElements − 1 elements left in the priority queue, stored in array slots 2 through NumElements. If we fill the hole in the root position with the bottom element, array slots 1 through NumElements − 1 contain the heap elements. The heap shape property is now intact, but the order property may be violated. The resulting structure is not a heap, but it is almost a heap—all of the nodes *except the root node* satisfy the order property. This is an easy problem to correct, for we have a heap operation to do exactly this task: ReheapDown. The algorithm for PriorityDeq is given below.

PriorityDeq

PriorityElement ← root element from PQueue

Move last leaf element into the root position
Decrement NumElements

ReheapDown

The PriorityEnq operation involves adding an element in its "appropriate" place in the heap. Where is this place? If the new element is larger than the current root element, we know that the new element belongs in the root. But that's not the typical case; we want a more general solution. To start, we can put the new element at the bottom of the heap, in the next available leaf position (review Figure 10-6 on page 613). Now the array contains elements in the first NumElements + 1 slots, preserving the heap shape property. The resulting structure is probably not a heap, but it's *almost* a heap—the order property is violated in the last leaf position. This problem is easy to solve, using the ReheapUp operation. The algorithm for PriorityEnq is given below.

PriorityEnq

Increment NumElements
Put NewElement in next available leaf position
ReheapUp

The declarations for the priority queue stored in a heap are as follows:

```
CONST
   MaxElements = 100;      (* maximum possible of elements *)
TYPE
   ArrayType = ARRAY [1 .. MaxElements] OF ElementType;

   PriorityQueueType = RECORD
     NumElements : Integer;      (* number of elements *)
     Elements    : ArrayType     (* heap of elements   *)
   END;  (* PriorityQueueType *)
```

Using these declarations, we can now write procedures to implement the priority queue operations we discussed above. (We leave the specification and implementation of CreatePQueue, DestroyPQueue, FullPQueue, and EmptyPQueue as exercises. They should be similar to their equivalent FIFO queue operations in Chapter 5.)

```
PROCEDURE PriorityDeq
   (VAR PQueue          : PriorityQueueType;
    VAR PriorityElement : ElementType);

   (* Removes the highest-priority element from the queue *)
   (* and returns its value in PriorityElement. Assumes    *)
   (* that the priority queue is not empty.                *)
BEGIN  (* PriorityDeq *)

   WITH PQueue DO
     BEGIN

       (* PriorityElement is in the root node of the heap. *)
       PriorityElement := Elements[1];

       (* Move the last leaf element into the root position. *)
       Elements[1] := Elements[NumElements];
       NumElements := NumElements - 1;
```

```
                    (* At this point the heap order property applies    *)
                    (* from Elements[2] .. Elements[NumElements]; it     *)
                    (* is violated only by the root node. Fix it.        *)
                    ReheapDown (Elements, 1, NumElements)

          END (* WITH *)
    END;    (* PriorityDeq *)

    (**************************************************************)

    PROCEDURE PriorityEnq
      (VAR PQueue : PriorityQueueType;
       NewElement : ElementType);

      (* Add NewElement to the priority queue. Assumes that *)
      (* the priority queue is not full.                    *)

    BEGIN (* PriorityEnq *)

      WITH PQueue DO
        BEGIN

          (* Put NewElement into the next free slot in the array. *)
          NumElements := NumElements + 1;
          Elements[NumElements] := NewElement;

          (* At this point the heap order property applies to *)
          (* Elements[1] .. Elements[NumElements - 1]; it is  *)
          (* violated only by the last leaf node. Fix it.     *)
          ReheapUp (Elements, 1, NumElements)

        END (* WITH *)
    END;    (* PriorityEnq *)
```

The source code for the declarations and operations on a priority queue is in file PQUEUE.PAS on the program disk.

Heaps vs. Other Representations of Priority Queues

How efficient is the heap implementation of a priority queue? The create, full, and empty operations are trivial, so we will only examine the operations to add and remove elements. PriorityEnq puts the new element into the next free leaf node in the tree. This array position can be accessed directly, so this part of the operation is O(1). ReheapUp is then invoked to correct the order. This operation moves the new element up the tree, level by level; since a complete tree is of minimum height, there are at most $\log_2 N$ levels above the new element (N = NumElements). So PriorityEnq is an $O(\log_2 N)$ operation. PriorityDeq removes the element in the root node, and replaces it with the bottom rightmost leaf node. Since both of these elements in the array can be accessed directly, this part of the operation is O(1). Then ReheapDown is invoked to correct the order. This operation moves the root element down in the tree, level by level. There are at most $\log_2 N$ levels below the root, so PriorityDeq is also an $O(\log_2 N)$ operation.

How does this implementation compare to the others we mentioned earlier in this section? If we implement the priority queue with a linked list, ordered from largest to smallest element, PriorityDeq merely removes the first node from the list—an O(1) operation. PriorityEnq, however, must search up to all the elements in the list to find the appropriate insertion place; thus it is an O(N) operation.

If the priority queue is implemented using a binary search tree, the efficiency of the operations depends on the shape of the tree. When the tree is balanced, both PriorityEnq and PriorityDeq are $O(\log_2 N)$ operations. In the worst case, if the tree degenerates to a linked list, ordered from smallest to largest element, both PriorityEnq and PriorityDeq are O(N). The following table summarizes the efficiency of the different implementations.

Comparison of Priority Queue Implementations

	Priority Queue Operation	
	PriorityEnq	*PriorityDeq*
Heap	$O(\log_2 N)$	$O(\log_2 N)$
Linked List	O(N)	O(1)
Binary Search Tree		
Balanced	$O(\log_2 N)$	$O(\log_2 N)$
Badly skewed	O(N)	O(N)

Overall, the binary search tree looks good, if it is balanced. However, a binary search tree can become skewed, which reduces the efficiency of the operations. The heap, on the other hand, is always a tree of minimum height. The heap is not a good structure for accessing *any* randomly selected element, but that is not one of the operations defined for priority queues. The accessing function of a priority queue specifies that only the largest (or highest-priority) element can be accessed. The linked list is excellent for this operation (assuming the list is ordered from largest to smallest), but we may have to search the whole list to find the place to add a new element. For the operations specified for priority queues, therefore, the heap is an excellent choice.

Graphs

The Logical Level

Binary trees provide a very useful way of representing relationships in which a hierarchy exists. That is, a node is pointed to by at most one other node (its parent), and each node points to at most two other nodes (its children). If we remove the restriction that each node can have at most two children, we have a nonbinary tree, as pictured on page 624.

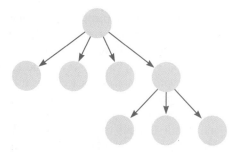

If we also remove the restriction that each node may only have one parent node, we have a data structure called a **graph**. A graph is made up of a set of nodes called **vertices** and a set of lines called **edges** (or **arcs**) that connect the nodes.

The set of edges describes relationships between the vertices. For instance, if the vertices are the names of cities, the edges that link the vertices could represent roads between pairs of cities. Since the road that runs between Houston and Austin also runs between Austin and Houston, the edges in this graph have no direction. This is called an **undirected graph**. However, if the edges that link the vertices represent flights from one city to another, the direction of each edge *is* important. The existence of a flight (edge) from Houston to Austin does not assure the existence of a flight from Austin to Houston. A graph whose edges are directed from one vertex to another is called a **directed graph**, or **digraph**.

There is a great deal of formal mathematics associated with graphs. In fact, there is an area of mathematics called "graph theory." In other computing courses, you will probably analyze graphs and prove theorems about them. This section introduces the graph as an abstract data type, teaches some basic terminology, discusses how a graph might be implemented, and describes how algorithms that manipulate graphs make use of stacks, queues, and priority queues.

Formally, a graph is defined as follows:

$$G = (V, E)$$

where

    V(G) is a finite, nonempty set of vertices
    E(G) is a set of edges (pairs of vertices)

The set of vertices is specified by listing them in set notation, within { } brackets. (This is mathematical notation; not Pascal syntax.) The following set defines the four vertices of the graph pictured in Figure 10-10(a):

    V(Graph1) = {A, B, C, D}

The set of edges is specified by listing a sequence of edges. Each edge is denoted by writing the names of the two vertices it connects in parentheses, with a comma between them. For instance, the vertices in Graph1 in Figure 10-10(a) are connected by the four edges described below:

    E(Graph1) = {(A,B), (A,D), (B,C), (B,D)}

Figure 10-10
Some Examples of
Graphs

(a) Graph1 is an undirected graph.

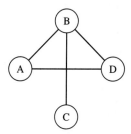

V(Graph1) = { A, B, C, D }
E(Graph1) = { (A, B), (A, D), (B, C), (B, D) }

(b) Graph2 is a directed graph.

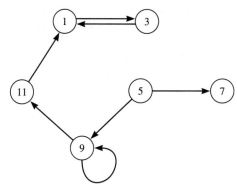

V(Graph2) = { 1, 3, 5, 7, 9, 11 }
E(Graph2) = { (1, 3), (3, 1), (5, 7), (5, 9), (9, 11), (9, 9), (11, 1) }

(c) Graph3 is a directed graph.

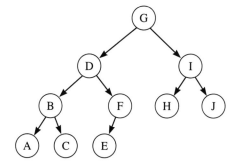

V(Graph3) = { A, B, C, D, E, F, G, H, I, J }
E(Graph3) = { (G, D), (G, I), (D, B), (D, F), (I, H), (I, J), (B, A), (B, C), (F, E) }

Since Graph1 is an undirected graph, the order of the vertices in each edge is unimportant. The set of edges in Graph1 can also be described as follows:

E(Graph1) = {(B,A), (D,A), (C,B), (D,B)}

If the graph is a digraph, the direction of the edge is indicated by which vertex is listed first. For instance, in Figure 10-10(b), the edge (5,7) represents a link from vertex 5 to vertex 7. However, there is no corresponding edge (7, 5) in Graph2. Note that in pictures of digraphs, the arrows indicate the direction of the relationship.

If two vertices in a graph are connected by an edge, they are said to be **adjacent**. In Graph1 [Figure 10-10(a)], vertices A and B are adjacent, but vertices A and C are not. If the vertices are connected by a directed edge, then the first vertex is said to be *adjacent to* the second, and the second vertex is said to be *adjacent from* the first. For example, in Graph2 [in Figure 10-10(b)], vertex 5 is adjacent to vertices 7 and 9, while vertex 1 is adjacent from vertices 3 and 11.

The picture of Graph3 in Figure 10-10(c) may look familiar; it is the tree we looked at earlier in connection with nonlinked representation of a binary tree. A tree is a special case of a directed graph, in which each vertex may only be adjacent from one other vertex (its parent node) and one vertex (the root) is not adjacent from any other vertex.

A **path** from one vertex to another consists of a sequence of vertices that connect them. For a path to exist, there must be an uninterrupted sequence of edges from the first vertex, through any number of vertices, to the second vertex. For example, in Graph2, there is a path from vertex 5 to vertex 3, but not from vertex 3 to vertex 5. Note that in a tree, such as Graph3 [Figure 10-10(c)], there is a unique path from the root to every other node in the tree.

A **complete* graph** is one in which every vertex is adjacent to every other vertex. Figure 10-11 shows two complete graphs. If there are N vertices, there will be N * (N − 1) edges in a complete directed graph and N * (N − 1)/2 edges in a complete undirected graph.

A **weighted graph** is a graph in which each edge carries a value. Weighted graphs can be used to represent applications in which the *value* of the connection between the vertices is important, not just the *existence* of a connection. For instance, in the weighted graph pictured in Figure 10-12, the vertices represent cities and the edges indicate the AirBusters Airlines flights that connect the cities. The weights attached to the edges represent the air distances between pairs of cities.

To see whether we can get from Denver to Washington, we look for a path between them. If the total travel distance is determined by the sum of the distances between each pair of cities along the way, we can calculate the travel distance by adding the weights attached to the edges that constitute the path between them. Note that there may be multiple paths between two vertices. Later in this chapter, we will talk about a way to find the shortest path between two vertices.

We have described a graph at the logical level as a set of vertices and a set of edges that connect some or all of the vertices one to another. What kind of operations are defined on a graph? In this chapter we will specify and implement a small set of useful graph operations. Many other operations on graphs can be defined; we have chosen

---

*Note that the term "complete" means different things when applied to trees and to graphs.

Figure 10-11
Two Complete
Graphs

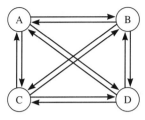

(a) Complete directed graph.

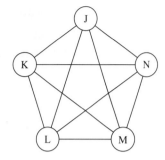

(b) Complete undirected graph.

Figure 10-12
A Weighted Graph

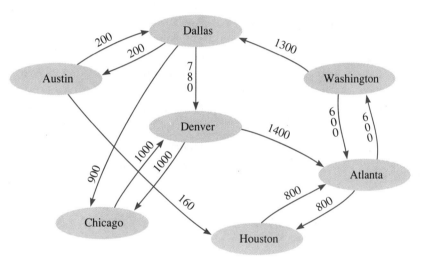

operations that will be useful in the graph applications described later in the chapter. Here is the specification of a weighted graph:

Graph ADT Specification

> ***Structure***   The graph consists of a set of vertices and a set of weighted edges that connect some or all of the vertices one to another.

Operations:

CreateGraph (Graph)

Function:	Create empty graph.
Input:	None
Preconditions:	None
Output:	Graph (GraphType)

Postconditions: V(Graph) = empty
E(Graph) = empty

AddVertex (Graph, Vertex)

Function: Add Vertex to the graph.

Input: Graph (GraphType)
Vertex (VertexType)

Preconditions: Graph has been created and is not full.

Output: Graph

Postconditions: Vertex is a vertex in V(Graph).

AddEdge (Graph, FromVertex, ToVertex, Weight)

Function: Add an edge with specified Weight in Graph from From-Vertex to ToVertex.

Input: Graph (GraphType)
FromVertex, ToVertex (VertexType)
Weight (EdgeValueType)

Preconditions: Graph has been created. FromVertex and ToVertex exist in V(Graph).

Output: Graph

Postconditions: (FromVertex, ToVertex) is an edge in E(Graph) with specified Weight.

Weight (Graph, FromVertex, ToVertex) Returns EdgeValueType

Function: Determines the weight of the edge from FromVertex to ToVertex.

Input: Graph (GraphType)
FromVertex, ToVertex (VertexType)

Preconditions: Graph has been created. FromVertex and ToVertex exist in V(Graph).

Output: Weight (EdgeValueType)

Postconditions: Weight = weight of edge from FromVertex to ToVertex. If an edge does not exist, a null-edge value is returned.

GetAdjacentList (Graph, Vertex, AdjList)

Function: Creates a list of the vertices that are adjacent from Vertex.

Input: Graph (GraphType)
Vertex (VertexType)

Preconditions: Graph has been created. Vertex exists in V(Graph).

Output: AdjList (VertexListType)

Postconditions: AdjList contains the names of all the vertices that are adjacent from Vertex.

Implementing Graphs

A simple way to represent the edges in a graph is by using an **adjacency matrix**, a two-dimensional array of edge values. We will use the following declarations to implement a weighted graph:

```
CONST
  MaxVertices = 10;      (* maximum vertices in the graph  *)
  NullEdge    = 0;       (* edge value when no edge exists *)
TYPE
  StringType      = PACKED ARRAY [1 .. 10] OF Char;
  VertexType      = StringType;        (* vertex information *)
  EdgeValueType   = Integer;           (* weight of edge     *)

  VertexListType = RECORD
    NumVertices  : 0 .. MaxVertices;
    VertexList   : ARRAY [1 .. MaxVertices] OF VertexType
  END; (* VertexListType *)

  MatrixType      = ARRAY [1 .. MaxVertices, 1 .. MaxVertices]
                    OF EdgeValueType;

  GraphType       = RECORD
    Vertices    : VertexListType;
    Edges       : MatrixType
  END; (* GraphType *)

VAR
  Graph : GraphType;
```

The Vertices array contains whatever information about a vertex is needed; for instance, if the graph vertices represent cities, VertexType might be a string indicating the city name. The two-dimensional array Edges is the adjacency matrix. It indicates which vertices are connected by edges. Since this is a weighted graph, we have declared EdgeValueType to be Integer. If this were not a weighted graph, EdgeValueType would be Boolean, and each matrix position would be True if an edge exists between the pair of vertices, and False if no edge exists.

At any time, within Graph

- Vertices.NumVertices is the number of vertices in the graph.
- The vertex data is contained in Vertices.VertexList[1] .. Vertices.Vertex—List[Vertices.NumVertices].
- The edge data is in a square subarray, Edges[1, 1] .. Edges[Vertices.NumVertices, Vertices.NumVertices].

For example, if Graph has seven vertices, the first seven slots of Graph.Vertices.VertexList contain vertex information (such as the names of the seven cities served by the airline), and the first seven rows and seven columns of Graph.Edges describe the connections between the vertices.

Figure 10-13 depicts the implementation of the graph of AirBusters flights between seven cities. (A drawing of this graph is found in Figure 10-12.) The names of the cities are the vertices in the graph, and are contained in Graph.Vertices. The weight of each edge in the Edges adjacency matrix represents the air distance between two cities that are connected by a flight. For example, the value in Graph.Edges[2,4] tells us that there is a direct flight between Austin and Dallas, and that the air distance is 200 miles. The NullEdge value (0) in Graph.Edges[2,7] tells us that the airline has no direct flights between Austin and Washington.

Now let's look at how the graph operations specified earlier would be implemented using these declarations. The CreateGraph operation sets Graph to its empty state. By setting the NumVertices field to zero, we indicate that there are no vertices in Graph.Vertices and that the part of Graph.Edges that is in use is a 0 × 0 subarray; that is, there are no edges.

```
PROCEDURE CreateGraph
  (VAR Graph : GraphType);

  (* Create empty graph. *)

BEGIN (* CreateGraph *)
  Graph.Vertices.NumVertices := 0
END;  (* CreateGraph *)
```

Figure 10-13 *Graph of Flight Connections Between Cities*

Graph

.Vertices
  .NumVertices 7
  .VertexList

	.VertexList		.Edges	[1]	[2]	[3]	[4]	[5]	[6]	[7]	[8]	[9]	[10]
[1]	'Atlanta '		[1]	0	0	0	0	0	800	600	•	•	•
[2]	'Austin '		[2]	0	0	0	200	0	160	0	•	•	•
[3]	'Chicago '		[3]	0	0	0	0	1000	0	0	•	•	•
[4]	'Dallas '		[4]	0	200	900	0	780	0	0	•	•	•
[5]	'Denver '		[5]	1400	0	1000	0	0	0	0	•	•	•
[6]	'Houston '		[6]	800	0	0	0	0	0	0	•	•	•
[7]	'Washington'		[7]	600	0	0	1300	0	0	0	•	•	•
[8]			[8]	•	•	•	•	•	•	•	•	•	•
[9]			[9]	•	•	•	•	•	•	•	•	•	•
[10]			[10]	•	•	•	•	•	•	•	•	•	•
				[1]	[2]	[3]	[4]	[5]	[6]	[7]	[8]	[9]	[10]

(Array positions marked with '•' are undefined)

The AddVertex operation puts Vertex in the next free space in the Vertices array. Since the new vertex has no edges defined yet, we also initialize the appropriate row and column in the Edges matrix to contain NullEdge values.

```
PROCEDURE AddVertex
  (VAR Graph : GraphType;
   Vertex    : VertexType);

  (* Add Vertex to Graph. *)

VAR
  Index : Integer;

BEGIN  (* AddVertex *)

  WITH Graph.Vertices DO
    BEGIN

      (* Put Vertex in Vertices array. *)
      NumVertices := NumVertices + 1;
      VertexList [NumVertices] := Vertex;

      (* Initialize Edges to False. *)
      FOR Index := 1 TO NumVertices DO
        BEGIN
          Graph.Edges[NumVertices, Index] := NullEdge;
          Graph.Edges[Index, NumVertices] := NullEdge
        END  (* FOR *)

    END  (* WITH *)
END;   (* AddVertex *)
```

To add an edge to the graph, we must first locate the FromVertex and ToVertex that define the edge. These inputs to the AddEdge procedure are VertexType (in our example, the names of the cities); to index the correct matrix slot, we need the *index* in the Vertices array that corresponds to each vertex. Once we know the indexes, it is a simple matter to set the weight of the edge. Here is the algorithm:

AddEdge

FromIndex ← index of FromVertex in Graph.Vertices
ToIndex   ← index of ToVertex in Graph.Vertices
Graph.Edges[FromIndex, ToIndex] ← Weight

To find the index of the vertices, let's write a little search function that inputs the name of a vertex and outputs its location (index) in the VertexList array. Since the preconditions of the AddEdge operation state that FromVertex and ToVertex are known to be defined in the graph, the search function is very simple:

```
FUNCTION VertexIndex
  (VAR Graph : GraphType;
   Vertex    : VertexType) : Integer;
```

```
(* Returns index of Vertex in Graph.Vertices.VertexList. *)
(* Assumes that Vertex is in the array. Graph is passed  *)
(* as a VAR parameter because of its size, but is not    *)
(* changed by this function.                             *)
VAR
  Index : Integer;
BEGIN (* VertexIndex *)

  Index := 1;

  WITH Graph.Vertices DO
    (* Loop Invariant: Vertex is not in VertexList[1] *)
    (* .. VertexList[Index - 1].                      *)
    WHILE VertexList[Index] <> Vertex DO
      Index := Index + 1;

  VertexIndex := Index

END;  (* VertexIndex *)
```

This function is internal to the Graph ADT; it is only for the use of the other graph operations. Using the VertexIndex function, coding Procedure AddEdge is simple:

```
PROCEDURE AddEdge
  (VAR Graph  : GraphType;
   FromVertex : VertexType;
   ToVertex   : VertexType;
   Weight     : EdgeValueType);

  (* Add an edge in Graph between FromVertex and ToVertex. *)
  (* Assumes FromVertex and ToVertex exist in V(Graph).    *)
BEGIN (* AddEdge *)
  (* Set the slot in Edges matrix to the Weight. *)
  Graph.Edges[VertexIndex (Graph, FromVertex),
           VertexIndex (Graph, ToVertex)] := Weight

END;  (* AddEdge *)
```

Note that, if the graph is undirected, we make two calls to AddEdge—one for each direction.

The Weight operation returns the weight of the edge from FromVertex to ToVertex. To implement this function, we first find the indexes of the two vertices; then we set Weight to the value of the appropriate slot in the Edges matrix. We can use the VertexIndex function to convert the Vertex name to its index.

```
FUNCTION Weight
  (VAR Graph  : GraphType;
   FromVertex : VertexType;
   ToVertex   : VertexType) : EdgeValueType;
```

```
(* Determines value of edge from FromVertex to ToVertex. *)
(* Graph is passed as a VAR parameter because of its     *)
(* size, but is not changed by this function.            *)
BEGIN (* Weight *)

  (* Get Weight from Graph.Edges. *)
  Weight := Graph.Edges[VertexIndex (Graph, FromVertex),
                        VertexIndex (Graph, ToVertex) ]

END;  (* Weight *)
```

The last graph operation that we specified is GetAdjacentList. This procedure inputs a graph and the name of a vertex, and outputs a list of vertices that are adjacent from the designated vertex. That is, it returns a list of all the vertices that you can get to from this vertex. Using an adjacency matrix to represent the edges, it is a simple matter to determine which nodes are adjacent to Vertex. We merely loop through the appropriate row in Edges; whenever a non-NullEdge value is found, we add another vertex to the list.

```
PROCEDURE GetAdjacentList
   (VAR Graph    : GraphType;
    Vertex       : VertexType;
    VAR AdjList  : VertexListType);

  (* Create a list of vertices that are adjacent from Vertex. *)
  (* Graph is passed as a VAR parameter because of its        *)
  (* size, but is not changed by this function.               *)
VAR
  FromIndex : Integer;
  ToIndex   : Integer;
BEGIN (* GetAdjacentList *)

  (* Find index associated with Vertex in Graph. *)
  FromIndex := VertexIndex (Graph, Vertex);

  WITH AdjList DO
    BEGIN

      NumVertices := 0;

      (* Put all adjacent vertices into AdjList. *)
      FOR ToIndex := 1 TO Graph.Vertices.NumVertices DO
        IF Graph.Edges[FromIndex, ToIndex] <> NullEdge
          THEN
            BEGIN
              NumVertices := NumVertices + 1;
              VertexList[NumVertices] :=
                Graph.Vertices.VertexList[ToIndex]
            END (* IF *)

    END (* WITH *)
END;  (* GetAdjacentList *)
```

A call to GetAdjacentList (Graph, Vertex, AdjList), when Vertex = Dallas, searches the fourth row of Edges, looking for nonzero values. It returns AdjList containing three vertices: Austin, Chicago, and Denver. Note that, since this example is a directed graph, GetAdjacentList does not put Washington in AdjList; Dallas is adjacent *from* Washington, but there are no direct flights from Dallas *to* Washington.

The source code for the graph declarations and operations is in file GRAPH.PAS on the program disk.

Graph Traversals

In Chapter 9, we discussed the postorder tree traversal, which goes to the deepest level of the tree and works up. This strategy of going down a branch to its deepest point and moving up is called a *depth-first* strategy. Another systematic way to visit each vertex in a tree is to visit each vertex on level 0 (the root), then each vertex on level 1, then each vertex on level 2, and so on. Visiting each vertex by level in this way is called a *breadth-first* strategy. With graphs, both depth-first and breadth-first strategies are useful. We will outline both algorithms within the context of the airline example.

Depth-First Searching   One question we can answer with the graph in Figure 10-14 is "Can I get from city X to city Y on my favorite airline?" This is equivalent to asking "Does a path exist in the graph from vertex X to vertex Y?" Using a depth-first strategy, let's develop an operation that finds a path from StartVertex to EndVertex.

We need a systematic way to keep track of the cities as we investigate them. With a depth-first search, we will examine the first vertex that is adjacent from StartVertex; if this is EndVertex, the search is over. Otherwise, we will examine all the vertices that are adjacent from this vertex. Meanwhile, we need to store the other vertices that are adjacent from StartVertex. If a path does not exist from the first vertex, we will come back and try the second, third, and so on. Because we want to travel as far as we can down one path, backtracking if the EndVertex is not found, a stack would be a good structure for storing the vertices. Here is the algorithm we will use:

DepthFirstSearch

Found ← False
CreateStack (Stack)
Push (Stack, StartVertex)

REPEAT

  Pop (Stack, Vertex)

  IF Vertex = EndVertex
    THEN
      Print final vertex
      Found ← True

    ELSE (not yet found)
      Print this Vertex

GetAdjacentList—get list of adjacent vertices

Push all the adjacent vertices onto Stack

UNTIL EmptyStack (Stack) OR Found

IF NOT Found
  THEN Print 'Path does not exist'

Let's apply this algorithm to the sample airline route graph in Figure 10-13. We want to fly from Austin to Washington. The places we can reach directly from Austin are Dallas and Houston; we push both these vertices onto the stack [Figure 10-14(a)]. Then we pop the top vertex from the stack—Houston. Houston is not our destination, so we resume our search from there. There is only one flight out of Houston, to Atlanta; we push Atlanta onto the stack [Figure 10-14(b)]. Again we pop the top vertex from the stack. Atlanta is not our destination, so we continue searching from there. Atlanta has flights to two cities: Houston and Washington [Figure 10-14(c)].

But we just came from Houston! We don't want to fly back to cities that we have already visited; this could cause an infinite loop. We have to take care of cycling in this algorithm just as we did in the maze problem in Chapter 8. There we marked a square as having been visited by putting a little stone in the square. Here we must mark a city as having been visited so that it will not be investigated a second time. Let's assume that we have marked the cities that have already been tried, and continue our example. Houston has already been visited, so we ignore it. The second adjacent vertex, Washington, is our destination, so the search is complete. The path from Austin to Washington, using a depth-first search, is illustrated in Figure 10-15.

This search is called a depth-first search because we go to the deepest branch, examining all the paths beginning at Houston before we come back to search from Dallas. (The maze problem also used a depth-first search.) When you have to backtrack, you take the branch closest to where you dead-ended. That is, you go as far as you can down one path before you take alternative choices at earlier branches.

Before we look at the source code of the DepthFirstSeach operation, let's talk a little more about "marking" vertices on the Graph. Before we begin the search, all the vertices must be marked as not yet visited. As we visit each vertex during the search, we want to mark it as visited. Before we process each vertex we can ask, "Have we

Figure 10-14
Using a Stack to Store the Routes

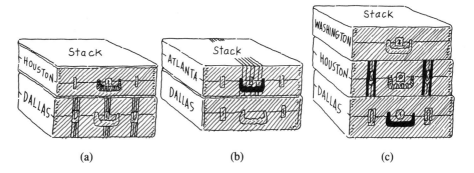

(a)   (b)   (c)

Figure 10-15
The Depth-First
Search

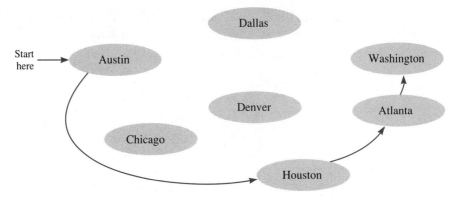

visited this vertex before?" If so, we will ignore this vertex and go on. To support this vertex-marking feature, we will add three operations to the Graph ADT. These operations are specified below:

■ **InitMarks (Graph)**

Function:	Initialize marks for all vertices to False.
Input:	Graph (GraphType)
Preconditions:	None
Output:	Graph
Postconditions:	All marks are set to not visited.

MarkVertex (Graph, Vertex)

Function:	Mark the specified Vertex to visited.
Input:	Graph (GraphType)
	Vertex (VertexType)
Preconditions:	Vertex exists in V(Graph).
Output:	Graph
Postconditions:	Vertex is marked as visited.

VertexMarked (Graph, Vertex) Returns Boolean

Function:	Determines if Vertex has been visited.
Input:	Graph (GraphType)
	Vertex (VertexType)
Preconditions:	Vertex exists in V(Graph).
Output:	VertexMarked (Boolean)
Postconditions:	VertexMarked = (Vertex has been visited).

We will use these graph operations, as specified above, in the graph search procedures. To support these operations, GraphType may be modified, but for now, as graph *users*, we will not deal with this issue. The implementation of the "mark" operations is left as an exercise.

Procedure DepthFirstSearch inputs a graph, a starting vertex, and a target vertex. It uses the depth-first strategy to find a path from the starting vertex to the ending vertex, printing out the names of all the vertices in the path. Note that there is nothing in the procedure listed below that depends on the implementation of the graph. The procedure is implemented as a graph application; it uses the Graph ADT (including the mark operations), without knowing how the graph is represented. The procedure also uses the Stack ADT specified in Chapter 4.

```
PROCEDURE DepthFirstSearch
   (VAR Graph    : GraphType;
    StartVertex : VertexType;
    EndVertex   : VertexType);

(* Search Graph for path from StartVertex to EndVertex, *)
(* using a depth-first search strategy.                 *)

VAR
   Stack   : StackType;
     (* stores vertices for later LIFO retrieval *)

   AdjList : VertexListType; (* list of adjacent vertices *)
   Index   : Integer;        (* index into AdjList        *)
   Vertex  : VertexType;     (* Vertex from stack         *)
   Found   : Boolean;        (* EndVertex found?          *)

BEGIN (* DepthFirstSearch *)

   (* Initialize for search. *)
   Found := False;
   InitMarks (Graph);
   CreateStack (Stack);
   Push (Stack, StartVertex);

   (* Search until EndVertex found, or until there are no *)
   (* more vertices to examine.                           *)
   REPEAT

     (* Get the last vertex seen from the stack. *)
     Pop (Stack, Vertex);

     IF Vertex = EndVertex (* destination is found *)
       THEN
         BEGIN
           Writeln (Vertex); (* print out final vertex *)
           Found := True
         END (* IF Vertex = EndVertex *)
```

```
      ELSE (* destination not yet found *)
        BEGIN

          (* If vertex has not been visited, visit it. *)
          IF NOT VertexMarked (Graph, Vertex)
            THEN
              BEGIN

                (* Mark the vertex as "visited." *)
                MarkVertex (Graph, Vertex);

                (* Print out this vertex. *)
                Writeln (Vertex);

                (* Get list of all vertices that are *)
                (* adjacent to this vertex.          *)
                GetAdjacentList (Graph, Vertex, AdjList);

                (* Push all adjacent vertices that *)
                (* have not yet been visited.      *)
                FOR Index := 1 TO AdjList.NumVertices DO
                  IF NOT VertexMarked (Graph,
                          AdjList.VertexList[Index]
                      THEN
                        Push (Stack, AdjList.VertexList[Index])

              END (* IF not visited *)
          END (* IF not found *)

    UNTIL EmptyStack(Stack) OR Found;

    IF NOT Found
      THEN Writeln ('Path not found')

END;   (* DepthFirstSearch *)
```

Breadth-First Search   A breadth-first search looks at all possible paths at the same depth before it goes to a deeper level. In our flight example, a breadth-first search would check all possible one-stop connections before checking any two-stop connections. For most travelers, this would be the preferred approach in this context. How do we change a depth-first search into a breadth-first search? A stack keeps track of things or events in the order opposite that of their occurrence. To keep track of things in the order in which they happened, we use a FIFO queue instead of a stack.

To modify the search to use a breadth-first strategy, we change all the calls to stack operations to the analogous FIFO queue operations. Searching for a path from Austin to Washington, we first Enqueue all the cities that can be reached directly from Austin: Dallas and Houston [Figure 10-16(a)]. Then we Dequeue the front queue element. Dallas is not the destination we seek, so we Enqueue all the adjacent cities that have not yet been visited: Chicago and Denver [Figure 10-16(b)]. (Austin has been visited already, so it is not Enqueue'd.) Again we Dequeue the front element from the queue. This element is the other "one-stop" city, Houston. Houston is not the desired destination, so we continue the search. There is only one flight out of Houston, and it is to Atlanta. Because we haven't visited Atlanta before, it is Enqueue'd [Figure 10-16(c)].

Figure 10-16
Using a Queue to
Store the Routes

Now we know that we cannot reach Washington with one stop, so we start examining the two-stop connections. We Dequeue Chicago; this is not our destination, so we put its adjacent city, Denver, into the queue [Figure 10-16(d)]. Now this is an interesting situation: Denver is in the queue twice. Should we mark a city as having been visited when we put it in the queue or after it has been Dequeue'd, when we are examining its outgoing flights? If we mark it only after it is Dequeue'd, there may be multiple copies of the same vertex in the queue. (This is why we check to see if a city is marked after it is Dequeue'd.)

An alternative approach is to mark the city as having been visited before it is put into the queue. Which is better? It depends on the processing. You may want to know whether there are alternative routes, in which case you would want to put a city into the queue more than once.

Back to our example. We have put Denver into the queue in one step and removed its previous entry at the next step. Denver is not our destination, so we put its adjacent cities into the queue. This processing continues until Washington has been put into the queue (from Atlanta), and is finally Dequeue'd. Now Vertex = EndVertex, and the search is complete. This search is illustrated in Figure 10-17.

The source code for the BreadthFirstSearch procedure is identical to DepthFirst-Search, except for the replacement of the stack with a FIFO queue.

```
PROCEDURE BreadthFirstSearch
   (VAR Graph   : GraphType;
    StartVertex : VertexType;
    EndVertex   : VertexType);

   (* Search Graph for path from StartVertex to EndVertex, *)
   (* using a breadth-first search strategy.               *)
```

Figure 10-17 The Breadth-First Search

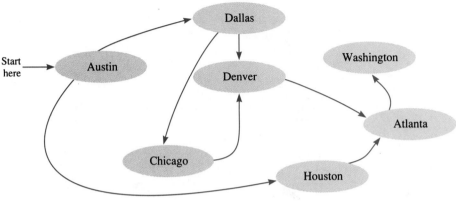

```
VAR
  Queue  : QueueType;
    (* stores vertices for later FIFO retrieval *)

  AdjList : VertexListType; (* list of adjacent vertices *)
  Index   : Integer;        (* index into AdjList       *)
  Vertex  : VertexType;     (* Vertex from queue        *)
  Found   : Boolean;        (* EndVertex found?         *)
BEGIN (* BreadthFirstSearch *)

  (* Initialize for search. *)
  Found := False;
  InitMarks (Graph);
  CreateQueue (Queue);
  Enqueue (Queue, StartVertex);

  (* Search until EndVertex found, or until there are no *)
  (* more vertices to examine.                           *)
  REPEAT

    (* Get a Vertex from the queue. *)
    Dequeue (Queue, Vertex);

    IF Vertex = EndVertex (* destination is found *)
      THEN
        BEGIN
          Writeln (Vertex); (* print out final vertex *)
          Found := True
        END (* IF Vertex = EndVertex *)
```

```
      ELSE (* destination not yet found *)
        BEGIN

          (* If vertex has not been visited, visit it. *)
          IF NOT VertexMarked (Graph, Vertex)
            THEN
              BEGIN

                (* Mark the vertex as "visited." *)
                MarkVertex (Graph, Vertex);

                (* Print out this vertex. *)
                Writeln (Vertex);

                (* Get list of all vertices that are *)
                (* adjacent to this vertex.          *)
                GetAdjacentList (Graph, Vertex, AdjList);

                (* Enqueue all the adjacent vertices. *)
                FOR Index := 1 TO AdjList.NumVertices DO
                  IF NOT VertexMarked
                    (Graph, AdjList.VertexList[Index])
                    THEN
                      Enqueue (Queue, AdjList.VertexList[Index]);

              END (* IF not visited *)
        END (* IF not found *)

  UNTIL EmptyQueue (Queue) OR Found;

  IF NOT Found
    THEN Writeln ('Path not found')

END; (* BreadthFirstSearch *)
```

The Single-Source Shortest Paths Problem   We know from the two search operations above that there may be multiple paths from one vertex to another. Suppose that we want to find the *shortest path* from Austin to each of the other cities that AirBusters serves. By "shortest path" we mean the path whose edge values (weights), added together, have the smallest sum. Consider the following two paths from Austin to Washington:

Austin		Austin	
}	160 miles	}	200 miles
Houston		Dallas	
}	800 miles	}	780 miles
Atlanta		Denver	
}	600 miles	}	1400 miles
Washington		Atlanta	
		}	600 miles
		Washington	

| Total miles | 1560 | Total miles | 2980 |

Clearly the first path is preferable, unless you want to collect frequent-flyer miles.

Let's develop an operation that will print out the shortest path from a designated starting vertex to every other vertex in the graph. As in the other graph traversals, we need an auxiliary structure for storing vertices that we will process later. In the depth-first search, we retrieved the vertex that was most recently put into the structure. In the breadth-first search, we retrieved the vertex that had been in the structure the longest time. What kind of access will help us retrieve the vertex in the shortest path? We want to retrieve the vertex that is *closest* to the current vertex—that is, the vertex connected with the minimum weight.

If we consider the edge with the minimum weight to be the *highest-priority* element in the structure, then we know of a perfect structure—the priority queue. We'll develop the algorithm using a priority queue whose elements are edge descriptions, containing the following information:

<FromVertex, ToVertex, Distance>

where FromVertex and ToVertex are vertices in the graph, and Distance is the weight of the edge between them. Each call to PriorityDeq removes and returns the highest-priority element, the element with the *smallest* weight value. (Note that we have redefined "highest priority" in this application; we'll discuss the ramifications for the priority queue implementation later.) Here is the algorithm for the ShortestPaths operation:

ShortestPaths
InitMarks (Graph)
CreatePQueue (PQ)
PriorityEnq (PQ, <StartVertex, StartVertex, 0>)

REPEAT
  PriorityDeq (PQ, ShortEdge)

  IF ToVertex of ShortEdge is not marked
    THEN
      MarkVertex (Graph, ToVertex)
      Print FromVertex, ToVertex, Distance
      FromVertex ← ToVertex
      MinDist ← Distance

      GetAdjacentList—get list of vertices adjacent to FromVertex

      PriorityEnq all unmarked adjacent vertices, with Distance = MinDist + weight
        of edge that connects it to FromVertex
UNTIL EmptyPQueue (PQ)

In coding this algorithm, we have used the following declaration for the priority queue's ElementType:

```
TYPE
  ElementType  = RECORD
    Distance   : Integer; (* key field *)
    FromVertex : VertexType;
    ToVertex   : VertexType
  END; (* ElementType *)
```

The priority queue itself can be implemented with a *minimum heap*, as described earlier in this chapter. That is, for every element in the heap, Node.Distance is less than or equal to the Distance field of each of its children. The implementation of this structure is left as an exercise.

Here is the ShortestPaths procedure:

```
PROCEDURE ShortestPaths
  (VAR Graph : GraphType;
   StartVertex : VertexType);

(* Determine the shortest paths from StartVertex to *)
(* every other vertex in Graph.                     *)

VAR
  PQ         : PriorityQueueType;
    (* stores edge info for later priority retrieval *)

  ShortEdge : ElementType;     (* edge with minimum weight  *)
  MinDist   : Integer;         (* minimum distance from PQ  *)
  AdjList   : VertexListType;  (* list of adjacent vertices *)
  Index     : Integer;         (* index into AdjList        *)

BEGIN (* ShortestPaths *)
  (* Initialize for processing. *)
  InitMarks (Graph);
  CreatePQueue (PQ);
  ShortEdge.FromVertex := StartVertex;
  ShortEdge.ToVertex   := StartVertex;
  ShortEdge.Distance   := 0;
  PriorityEnq (PQ, ShortEdge);
  Writeln ('  Shortest Path from ', StartVertex);
  Writeln ('Last Vertex   Destination   Distance');
  Writeln ('----------------------------------------');

  (* Process until done. *)
  REPEAT

    (* Retrieve the edge with the minimum weight. *)
    PriorityDeq (PQ, ShortEdge);

    WITH ShortEdge DO
      BEGIN
        IF NOT VertexMarked (Graph, ToVertex)
          THEN
            BEGIN

              (* Mark the vertex as "visited." *)
              MarkVertex (Graph, ToVertex);
```

```
                        (* Print the edge information. *)
                        Writeln (FromVertex, '   ', ToVertex,
                           '   ', Distance);

                        FromVertex := ToVertex;
                        MinDist    := Distance;

                        (* Get list of vertices adjacent to FromVertex. *)
                        GetAdjacentList (Graph, FromVertex, AdjList);

                        (* Add edge info for all unmarked adjacent *)
                        (* vertices to the priority queue.          *)
                        FOR Index := 1 TO AdjList.NumVertices DO
                          IF NOT VertexMarked
                               (Graph, AdjList.VertexList[Index])
                             THEN
                               BEGIN
                                 ToVertex := AdjList.VertexList[Index];
                                 Distance := MinDist +
                                   Weight (Graph, FromVertex, ToVertex);
                                 PriorityEnq (PQ, ShortEdge)
                               END (* IF NOT VertexMarked *)
                     END (* IF NOT VertexMarked *)
              END (* WITH ShortEdge *)

       UNTIL EmptyPQueue (PQ)
    END;  (* ShortestPaths *)
```

The output from this algorithm is a table of edges (FromVertex, ToVertex), showing the total distance from StartVertex to each of the other vertices in the graph, as well as the last vertex visited before the destination. If Graph contains the information shown in Figure 10-13, the procedure call

```
Shortest Paths (Graph, 'Washington');
```

prints out the following table:

```
  Shortest path from Washington

Last Vertex     Destination    Distance
───────────────────────────────────────
Washington      Washington     0
Washington      Atlanta        600
Washington      Dallas         1300
Atlanta         Houston        1400
Dallas          Austin         1500
Dallas          Denver         2080
Dallas          Chicago        2200
```

The shortest-path distance from Washington to each destination is shown in the two columns to the right. The left-hand column shows which vertex immediately preceded the destination in the traversal. Let's figure out the shortest path from Washington to

Chicago. We see from the left-hand column that the next-to-last vertex in the path is Dallas. Now we look up Dallas in the Destination (middle) column: The vertex before Dallas is Washington. The whole path is Washington–Dallas–Chicago. (We might want to consider another airline for a more direct trip.)

The source code for these graph applications (the DepthFirst, BreadthFirst, and ShortestPath procedures) is in file GRAPHAPP.PAS on the program disk.

Other Graph Implementations

The advantage to representing the edges in a graph with an adjacency matrix is its simplicity. Given the indexes of two vertices, determining the existence (or the weight) of an edge between them is an $O(1)$ operation. The problem with adjacency matrices is that their use of *space* is $O(N^2)$, where N is the *maximum* number of vertices in the graph. If the maximum number of vertices is large, adjacency matrices may waste a lot of space. In the past, we have tried to save space by allocating it as we need it at run time, using linked structures. We can use a similar approach to implementing graphs. **Adjacency lists** are linked lists, one per vertex, that contain the names (or indexes) of the vertices to which each vertex is connected. There are several ways to implement adjacency lists. Figure 10-18 shows two different adjacency list representations of the graph in Figure 10-12. Implementing the graph operations for an adjacency list implementation is left as a programming assignment.

Figure 10-18
Adjacency List
Representations
of Graphs

(a)

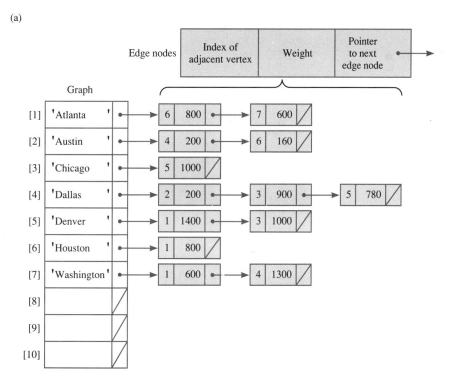

Figure 10-18
(Continued)

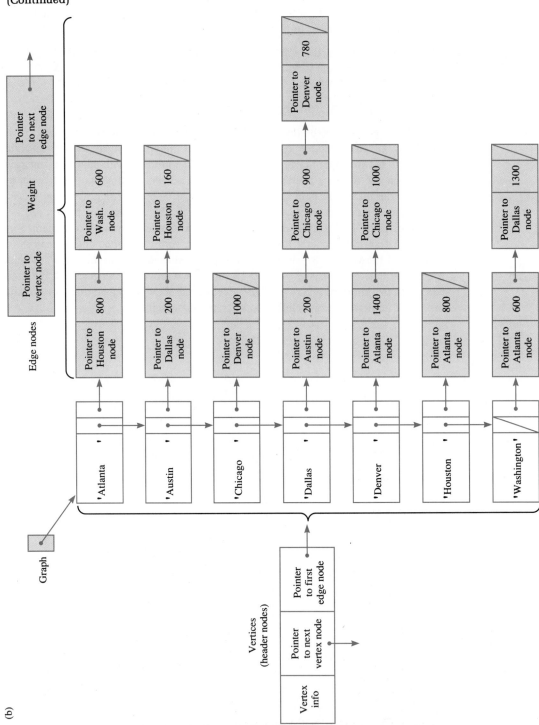

(b)

Summary

In this chapter we have discussed several branching structures: heaps, priority queues, and graphs. Branching structures are very versatile and are a good way to model many real-world objects and situations. Because there are many different types of applications for these data structures, there are all kinds of variations and generalizations of trees and graphs. These topics are introduced here in order to show the wide variety of applications for which programmers must create appropriate data structures. They are generally covered in detail in more advanced computer science courses.

■ *Exercises**

1. Tell whether the following trees are complete, full, heaps, or none of the above.

(a)

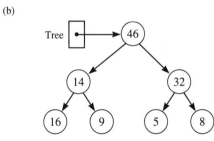

(b)

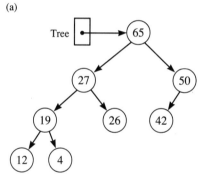

(c)

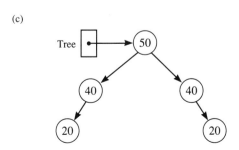

(d)

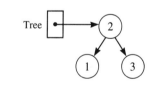

(e)

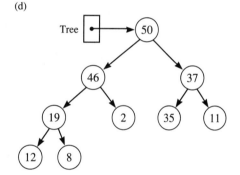

(f)

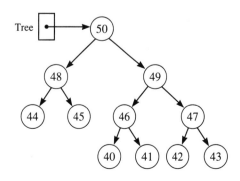

*Questions with italicized numbers are answered in the back of the book.

2. The elements in a binary tree are to be stored in an array, as described in the chapter. Each element is a nonnegative real number.
   (a) What value can you use as the dummy value, if the binary tree is not complete?
   (b) Show the contents of the array, given the tree illustrated below:

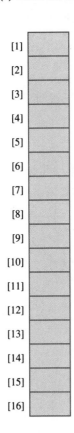

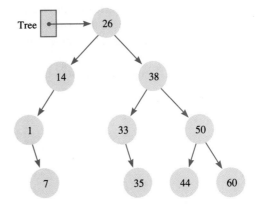

3. The elements in a complete binary tree are to be stored in an array, as described in the chapter. Each element is a nonnegative real number.
   (a) Show the contents of the array, given the tree illustrated below:
   (b) Is this tree a heap?

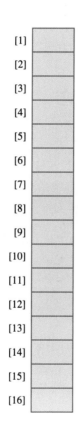

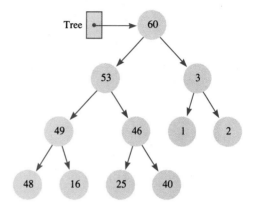

4. (a) Given the array pictured below, draw the binary tree that can be created from its elements. (The elements are arranged in the array as discussed in the chapter.)

NumElements = 9

[1]	1
[2]	55
[3]	59
[4]	44
[5]	33
[6]	58
[7]	57
[8]	22
[9]	11
[10]	99

(b) Is this tree a heap? If not, what procedure call(s) can be used to make the tree into a heap?

5. Draw a tree that satisfies both the binary search property and the order property of heaps.

6. A binary tree is stored in an array called Tree, which is indexed from 1 to 100, as described in the chapter. The tree contains 85 elements. Mark each of the following statements as True or False, and correct any false statements.
   (a) Tree[43] is a leaf node.
   (b) Tree[42] has only one child.
   (c) The right child of Tree[13] is Tree[26].
   (d) The subtree rooted at Tree[8] is a full binary tree with four levels.
   (e) The tree has seven levels that are full, and one additional level that contains some elements.

7. A *minimum heap* has the following order property: The value of each element is *less* than or equal to the value of each of its children. What changes to the heap operations are needed to make the heap satisfy this property?

8. (a) Write a nonrecursive version of ReheapDown.
   (b) Write a nonrecursive version of ReheapUp.
   (c) Describe the nonrecursive versions of these operations in terms of Big-O.

9. A priority queue containing characters is implemented as a heap stored in an array. The precondition states that this priority queue cannot contain duplicate elements. There are 10 elements currently in the priority queue. What values might be stored in array positions 8–10 so that the properties of a heap will be satisfied?

Heap

[1]	Z
[2]	F
[3]	J
[4]	E
[5]	B
[6]	G
[7]	H
[8]	?
[9]	?
[10]	?

10. A priority queue is implemented as a heap:

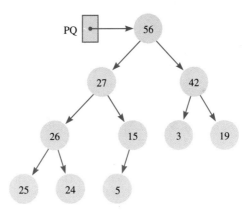

(a) Show how the heap above would look after this series of operations:

PriorityEnq (PQ, 28);
PriorityEnq (PQ, 2);
PriorityEnq (PQ, 40);
PriorityDeq (PQ, X);
PriorityDeq (PQ, Y);
PriorityDeq (PQ, Z)

(b) What would the values of X, Y, and Z be after the series of operations in part (a)?

11. The PriorityEnq and PriorityDeq operations are to be modified to check for overflow/underflow before performing the operation. PriorityEnq will return a Boolean value, Overflow, to indicate whether the queue was full on entrance to the procedure. PriorityDeq will

return a Boolean value, Underflow, in addition to PriorityElement, to indicate whether the queue was empty on entrance to the procedure.

(a) Show the modified specifications for the PriorityEnq operation.

(b) Show the modified specifications for the PriorityDeq operation.

(c) Code the modified PriorityEnq procedure.

(d) Code the modified PriorityDeq procedure.

12. A priority queue is implemented as a linked list, ordered from largest to smallest element.

    (a) Write the declarations needed for this implementation.

    (b) Write the PriorityEnq operation (from the chapter specification), using this implementation.

    (c) Write the PriorityDeq operation (from the chapter specification), using this implementation.

    (d) Compare the PriorityEnq and PriorityDeq operations to those for the heap implementation, in terms of Big-O.

13. A priority queue is implemented as a binary search tree.

    (a) Write the declarations needed for this implementation.

    (b) Write the PriorityEnq operation (from the chapter specification), using this implementation.

    (c) Write the PriorityDeq operation (from the chapter specification), using this implementation.

    (d) Compare the PriorityEnq and Priority Deq operations to those for the heap implementation, in terms of Big-O. Under what conditions would this implementation be better or worse than the heap implementation?

14. (a) Write the specifications for the CreatePQueue, DestroyPQueue, FullPQueue, and EmptyPQueue operations.

    (b) Write the operations specified in part (a), using the heap implementation discussed in this chapter.

15. A stack is implemented using a priority queue. Each element is time-stamped as it is put into the stack. (The time stamp is a number between 0 and MaxInt. Each time an element is pushed onto the stack, it is assigned the next larger number.)

    (a) What is the the highest-priority element?

    (b) Write the Push and Pop algorithms, using the specifications in Chapter 4.

    (c) Compare these Push and Pop operations to the ones implemented in Chapter 4, in terms of Big-O.

16. A FIFO queue is implemented using a priority queue. Each element is time-stamped as it is put into the queue. (The time stamp is a number between 0 and MaxInt. Each time an element is Enqueue'd, it is assigned the next larger number.)

    (a) What is the the highest-priority element?

    (b) Write the Enqueue and Dequeue operations, using the specifications in Chapter 5.

    (c) Compare these Enqueue and Dequeue operations to the ones implemented in Chapter 5, in terms of Big-O.

17. A priority queue of strings is implemented using a heap. The heap contains the following elements:

NumElements = 10

[1]	'introspective'
[2]	'intelligent '
[3]	'intellectual'
[4]	'intimate'
[5]	'intensive'
[6]	'interesting'
[7]	'internal '
[8]	'into '
[9]	'in'
[10]	'intro '

(a) What feature of these strings is used to determine their priority in the priority queue?

(b) Show how this priority queue would be affected by calling PriorityEnq to add the string 'interviewing'.

18. The highest-priority element in a priority queue is the one with the smallest Real-type value. How do the priority queue algorithms need to be modified?

Use the following description of an *undirected graph* in Exercises 19–22:

```
EmployeeGraph        = (V, E)
V(EmployeeGraph)     = {Susan, Darlene, Mike, Fred, John, Sander, Lance, Jean, Brent,
                         Fran}
E(EmployeeGraph)     = {(Susan, Darlene), (Fred, Brent), (Sander, Susan), (Lance, Fran),
                         (Sander, Fran), (Fran, John), (Lance, Jean), (Jean, Susan), (Mike,
                         Darlene), (Brent, Lance), (Susan, John)}
```

19. Draw a picture of EmployeeGraph.

20. Draw EmployeeGraph, implemented as an adjacency matrix. Store the vertex values in alphabetical order.

21. Using the adjacency matrix for EmployeeGraph from Exercise 20, describe the path from Susan to Lance
    (a) using a breadth-first strategy,
    (b) using a depth-first strategy.

22. Which one of the following phrases best describes the relationship represented by the edges between the vertices in EmployeeGraph?
    (a) "works for"
    (b) "is the supervisor of"
    (c) "is senior to"
    (d) "works with"

Use the following specification of a *directed graph* in Exercises 23–26:

ZooGraph = (V, E)

V(ZooGraph) = {dog, cat, animal, vertebrate, oyster, shellfish, invertebrate, crab, poodle, monkey, banana, dalmation, dachshund}

E(ZooGraph) = {(vertebrate, animal), (invertebrate, animal), (dog, vertebrate), (cat, vertebrate), (monkey, vertebrate), (shellfish, invertebrate), (crab, shellfish), (oyster, shellfish), (poodle, dog), (dalmation, dog), (dachshund, dog)}

23. Draw a picture of ZooGraph.

24. Draw the adjacency matrix for ZooGraph. Store the vertices in alphabetical order.

25. To tell if one element in ZooGraph has relation X to another element, you look for a path between them. Show whether the following statements are true, using the picture or adjacency matrix.
    (a) dalmation X dog
    (b) dalmation X vertebrate
    (c) dalmation X poodle
    (d) banana X invertebrate
    (e) oyster X invertebrate
    (f) monkey X invertebrate

26. Which of the following phrases best describes relation X in the previous question?
    (a) "has a"
    (b) "is an example of"
    (c) "is a generalization of"
    (d) "eats"

Use the following graph for Exercises 27–29.

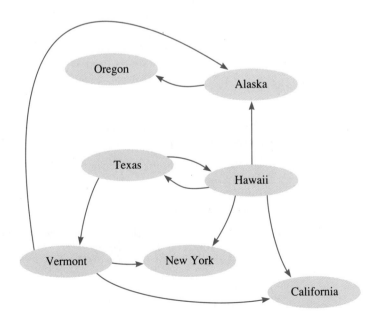

27. Describe the graph pictured above, using the formal graph notation.

    V(StateGraph) =
    E(StateGraph) =

28. (a) Is there a path from Oregon to any other state in the graph?
    (b) Is there a path from Hawaii to every other state in the graph?
    (c) From which state(s) in the graph is there a path to Hawaii?

29. Show the adjacency matrix that would describe the edges in this graph. Store the vertices in alphabetical order.

30. The Graph ADT in this chapter is to be extended to include the following Boolean functions: FullGraph (determines if a graph's set of vertices is "full"), EmptyGraph (determines if a graph has no vertices), EdgeExists (determines two vertices are connected by an edge).
    (a) Write the specifications of these functions.
    (b) Using the adjacency matrix implementation developed in the chapter, implement the three functions.

31. The Graph ADT in this chapter is to be extended to include a DeleteEdge operation, which deletes the edge between two specified vertices.
    (a) Write the specification of this operation.
    (b) Using the adjacency matrix implementation developed in the chapter and the specification from part (a), implement the procedure.

32. The Graph ADT in this chapter is to be extended to include a DeleteVertex operation, which deletes a vertex from the graph.
    (a) Write the specification of this operation.
    (b) Deleting a vertex is more complicated than deleting an edge from the graph. Discuss why.

33. Implement the graph "mark" operations specified in the chapter. The marks are to be stored in Visited, an array of Boolean values, that is added as a field in GraphType.

34. (a) Modify the DepthFirstSearch operation to check each adjacent vertex before pushing it onto the stack, to make sure that it is not the destination vertex. Mark the adjacent vertex as "visited" before adding it to the stack.
    (b) Trace the execution of this procedure in searching for a path from Dallas to Washington. Show the contents of the stack after each iteration of the loop body. What elements are on the stack when Washington is found?

35. The DepthFirstSearch operation can be implemented without a stack by using recursion.
    (a) Name the base case(s). Name the general case(s).
    (b) Write the algorithm for a recursive depth-first search.
    (c) Code the recursive procedure.

36. (a) Modify the BreadthFirstSearch operation to mark each adjacent vertex as "visited" before adding it to the queue.
    (b) Trace the execution of the modified procedure in searching for a path from Denver to Washington. Show the contents of the queue after each iteration of the loop body. What elements are on the queue when Washington is found?

Use the following graph for Exercises 37–39. The vertices are single-character values. The graph is undirected.

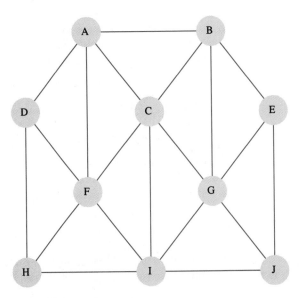

The graph is to be implemented as an adjacency matrix indexed by the characters 'A' through 'Z', using the following declarations:

```
TYPE
   AlphaType = 'A' .. 'Z';

   GraphType = ARRAY [AlphaType, AlphaType] OF Boolean;

VAR
   AlphaGraph : GraphType;
```

37. Show the contents of AlphaGraph, given the graph pictured above. (You only need to show the subarray that is in use.)

   NOTE: The edge (D,F) is represented by AlphaGraph['D', 'F'] and AlphaGraph['F', 'D'].

38. Reimplement the graph operations specified in the chapter to use the declarations above.

39. Implement a graph operation to delete a vertex from the graph. The edges to all adjacent vertices must also be deleted.

Sorting Algorithms

GOALS

- To be able to design and implement the following sorting algorithms:
    straight selection sort
    bubble sort (two versions)
    merge sort
    quick sort
    heap sort
- To be able to compare the efficiency of the sorting algorithms, in terms of Big-O and of space requirements.
- To be able to discuss other efficiency considerations: sorting small numbers of elements, programmer time, sorting arrays of large data elements.
- To be able to sort on several keys.

At many points in this book, we have gone to great trouble to keep lists of elements in sorted order: student records sorted by ID number, integers sorted from smallest to largest, words sorted alphabetically. The goal of keeping sorted lists, of course, is to facilitate searching: Given an appropriate data structure, a particular list element can be found faster if the list is sorted.

Putting an unordered list of data items into order—**sorting**—is a very common and useful operation. Whole books have been written about various sorting algorithms, as well as algorithms for searching an ordered list to find a particular element. The goal is to come up with better, *more efficient*, sorts. Because sorting a large number of elements can be extremely time consuming, a good sorting algorithm is very desirable. This is one area in which programmers are sometimes encouraged to sacrifice clarity in favor of speed of execution.

How do we describe efficiency? We will pick an operation central to most sorting algorithms: the operation that compares two values to see which is smaller. In our study of sorting algorithms, we will relate the number of comparisons to the number of elements in the list (N) as a rough measure of the efficiency of each algorithm.

In this chapter we will develop a number of sorting algorithms that will sort the *sequential list* from Chapter 6. To focus our attention on the sorting algorithms, we will simplify ListElementType to be a scalar type. This means that we will be sorting a list of scalar values, not a list of records ordered according to a Key field. To modify the resulting procedures to sort a list of records, you must add ".Key" (or whatever the key field name is) in statements that compare list elements.

```
CONST
  MaxElements = 100;   (* maximum number of elements in list *)

TYPE
  ListElementType = Integer;  (* simplified for discussion! *)

  IndexType = 0 .. MaxElements;
  ArrayType = ARRAY [1 .. MaxElements] OF ListElementType;

  ListType = RECORD
    Length : IndexType;
    Info   : ArrayType
  END; (* ListType *)
VAR
  List : ListType;
```

From the perspective of the sort user (who may not care *how* the elements are sorted), Procedure SortList has the following specification:

▶ SortList (List)

Function:	Sort List.Info[1] .. List.Info[List.Length] from smallest to largest element.
Input:	List (ListType)

Preconditions:	Info contains at least List.Length values, and 1 <= List.Length <= MaxElements. Array elements can be compared using <.
Output:	List
Postconditions:	List.Info[1] .. List.Info[List.Length] are sorted in order of increasing value.

Procedure SortList is very simple to write:

```
PROCEDURE SortList
  (VAR List : ListType);

  (* Sort list elements in increasing order. *)
BEGIN (* SortList *)
  (*********************************************************)
  (* Call one of the sorting procedures in this chapter. *)
  (*********************************************************)
END;   (* SortList *)
```

The code for all of the sorts developed in this chapter is contained in file SORTS.PAS on the program disk.

Straight Selection Sort

If you were handed a list of names and asked to put them in alphabetical order, you might use this general approach:

1. Find the name that comes first in the alphabet, and write it on a second sheet of paper.
2. Cross the name out on the original list.
3. Continue this cycle until all the names on the original list have been crossed out and written onto the second list, at which point the second list is sorted.

This algorithm is simple to translate into a computer program, but it has one drawback: It requires space in memory to store two complete lists. Although we have not talked about memory space considerations, this duplication is clearly wasteful. A slight adjustment to this manual approach does away with the need to duplicate space, however. As you cross a name off the original list, a free space opens up. Instead of writing the minimum value on a second list, you can exchange it with the value currently in its correct place in the original list. Let's look at an example—sorting the five-element list shown in Figure 11-1(a).

1. The smallest value in Info is in location [4]. Therefore we swap the contents of Info[1] and Info[4]. Now the smallest value is in its correct position in the array [Figure 11-1(b)].

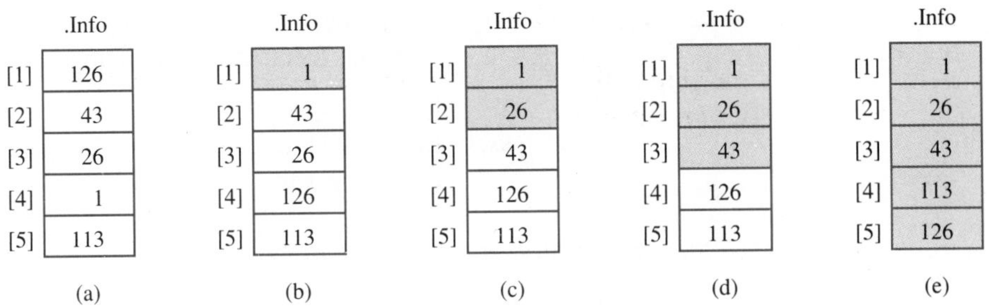

Figure 11-1

Example of Straight Selection Sort. (The sorted elements are shaded.)

	.Info		.Info		.Info		.Info		.Info
[1]	126	[1]	1	[1]	1	[1]	1	[1]	1
[2]	43	[2]	43	[2]	26	[2]	26	[2]	26
[3]	26	[3]	26	[3]	43	[3]	43	[3]	43
[4]	1	[4]	126	[4]	126	[4]	126	[4]	113
[5]	113	[5]	113	[5]	113	[5]	113	[5]	126
	(a)		(b)		(c)		(d)		(e)

2. The smallest value in the unordered part of the array (Info[2] .. Info[5]) is in location [3], so we swap Info[2] and Info[3]. Now the first two positions in the array are sorted [Figure 11-1(c)].
3. The smallest value in the unsorted part of the array (Info[3] .. Info[5]) is in Info[3], its correct position, so we do nothing [Figure 11-1(d)].
4. The smallest value in the unsorted part of the array (Info[4] .. Info[5]) is in position [5], so we swap Info[4] and Info[5]. The only element left is Info[5], which must be the largest value in the array. We now have a sorted array, as shown in Figure 11-1(e).

Let's see how this approach can be described in terms of a programming algorithm:

Selection Sort

Current ← index of first element in the list

WHILE more elements in unsorted part of list DO
    Find the index of the smallest unsorted element.
    Swap the Current element and the smallest unsorted element.
    Shrink the unsorted part of the list by incrementing Current.

We use a variable, Current, to mark the beginning of the unsorted part of the list. We start out by setting Current to the index of the first list position. That means that the unsorted part of the list goes from index Current to List.Length.

The main sort processing is a loop. In each iteration of the loop body, the smallest value in the unsorted part of the list is swapped with the value in the Current location. After the swap, Current is in the sorted part of the list, so we shrink the size of the unsorted part by incrementing Current. The loop body is now complete.

Back at the top of the loop body, the unsorted part of the list goes from the (now incremented) Current index to the end of the list. We know that every value in the unsorted part is greater than (or equal to, if duplicates are permitted) any value in the sorted part of the list. This observation suggests the loop invariant:

Loop Invariant: The values in Info[1] .. Info[Current − 1] are sorted, and are less than or equal to the values in Info[Current] .. Info[Length].

How do we know when "there are more elements in the unsorted part"? As long as Current < = Length, the unsorted part of the list (Info[Current] .. Info[Length]) contains values. In each iteration of the loop body, Current is incremented, shrinking the unsorted part of the list. When Current = Length, the "unsorted" part (Info[Length] .. Info[Length]) contains only one element, and we know from the loop invariant that this value is greater than (or equal to) any value in the sorted part. So the value in Info[Length] is in its correct place, and we are done. The limitation on the size of Current adds another piece to the loop invariant: 1 < = Current < = Length. The condition for the WHILE loop is *WHILE Current < Length*. A "snapshot" picture of the selection sort algorithm is illustrated in Figure 11-2.

Now all we have to do is to locate the smallest value in the unsorted part of the list. Let's write a function to do this task. Function Mindex inputs the array of list elements and the first and last indexes of the unsorted part, and returns the index of the smallest value in this part of the list.

Mindex (Info, StartIndex, EndIndex)

Min ← StartIndex

FOR Index : = StartIndex + 1 TO EndIndex DO
    IF Info[Index] < Info[Min]
        THEN Min ← Index

Mindex ← Min

Trace this algorithm on the data in Figure 11-1(a). Did you come up with Mindex = 4?

Back to the SelectionSort algorithm: Now that we know where the smallest unsorted element is, we swap it with the element at index Current. Since swapping data values between two array locations is common to many sorting algorithms, let's write a little procedure, Swap, to accomplish this task.

Figure 11-2
The Straight Selection Sort

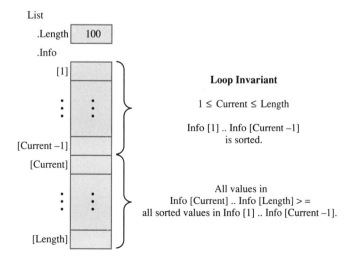

Loop Invariant

1 ≤ Current ≤ Length

Info [1] .. Info [Current −1]
is sorted.

All values in
Info [Current] .. Info [Length] > =
all sorted values in Info [1] .. Info [Current −1].

```
PROCEDURE Swap
  (VAR Element1, Element2 : ListElementType);

  (* Swap the values of Element1 and Element2. *)

VAR
  Temp : ListElementType;

BEGIN (* Swap *)
  Temp := Element1;
  Element1 := Element2;
  Element2 := Temp
END;  (* Swap *)
```

Now we are ready to code Procedure SelectionSort:

```
PROCEDURE SelectionSort
  (VAR List : ListType);

  (* Sort List elements in order of increasing value. *)

VAR
  Current  : IndexType;
  Smallest : IndexType;

  (*************** Nested Function Mindex **************)

  FUNCTION Mindex
    (Info       : ArrayType;
     StartIndex : IndexType;
     EndIndex   : IndexType)  : IndexType;

    (* Mindex = index of smallest element in the subarray *)
    (* Info[ StartIndex] .. Info[EndIndex].              *)

  VAR
    Min   : IndexType; (* index of smallest element so far *)
    Index : IndexType; (* loop control variable            *)

  BEGIN (* Mindex *)
    Min := StartIndex;

    (* Loop Invariant: Info[Min] is the smallest element *)
    (* in Info[StartIndex] .. Info[Index - 1] AND        *)
    (* StartIndex <= Index <= EndIndex + 1.              *)
    FOR Index := StartIndex + 1 TO EndIndex DO
      IF Info[Index] < Info[Min]
        THEN Min := Index;

      Mindex := Min

  END;  (* Mindex *)

  (**********************************************************)
```

```
BEGIN (* SelectionSort *)
  WITH List DO
    BEGIN

      Current := 1;    (* index of first unsorted element *)

      (* Loop Invariant: 1 <= Current <= Length AND the     *)
      (* values in Info[1] .. Info[Current - 1] are sorted *)
      (* and are less than or equal to the unsorted values *)
      (* in Info[Current] .. Info[Length].                 *)
      WHILE Current < Length DO
        BEGIN

          (* Find the smallest element in the unsorted part. *)
          Smallest := Mindex (Info, Current, Length);

          (* Swap the Current element and the smallest    *)
          (* element in the unsorted part of the array.   *)
          Swap (Info[Current], Info[Smallest]);

          (* Shrink the unsorted part of the array. *)
          Current := Current + 1

        END (* WHILE *)
    END (* WITH *)
END;  (* SelectionSort *)
```

Now let's try measuring the amount of "work" required by this algorithm. We will describe the number of comparisons as a function of the number of elements in the list. To be concise, in this discussion we will refer to List.Length as N.

The comparison operation is in the Mindex function. We know from the loop condition, *WHILE Current < Length DO,* that Mindex is called N − 1 times. Within the function, the number of comparisons varies, depending on the values of StartIndex and EndIndex:

```
FOR Index := StartIndex + 1 TO EndIndex DO
  IF Info[Index] < Info[Min]
    THEN Min := Index;
```

In the first call to Mindex, StartIndex is 1 and EndIndex is Length, so there are N − 1 comparisons; in the next call there are N − 2 comparisons, and so on, until in the last call, there is only one comparison. The total number of comparisons is

$$(N - 1) + (N - 2) + (N - 3) + \cdots + 1 = N(N - 1)/2$$

To accomplish our goal of sorting a list of N elements, the straight selection sort requires $N(N - 1)/2$ comparisons. Note that the particular arrangement of values in the list does not affect the amount of work done at all. Even if the array is in sorted order *before* the call to SelectionSort, the procedure will still make $N(N - 1)/2$ comparisons. The following table shows the number of comparisons required for lists of various sizes. Note that doubling the list size roughly quadruples the number of comparisons.

Number of Comparisons Required to Sort Arrays of Different Sizes Using SelectionSort

Number of Elements	Number of Comparisons
10	45
20	190
100	4,950
1,000	499,500
10,000	49,995,000

How do we describe this algorithm in terms of Big-O? If we express $N(N - 1)/2$ as $\frac{1}{2}N^2 - \frac{1}{2}N$, it is easy to see. In Big-O notation we only consider the term $\frac{1}{2}N^2$, because it increases fastest relative to N. (Remember the elephants and goldfish?) Further, we ignore the constant, $\frac{1}{2}$, making these algorithms $O(N^2)$. This means that, for large values of N, the computation time will be *approximately proportional to N^2*. Looking back at the previous table, we see that multiplying the number of elements by 10 increases the number of comparisons by more than a factor of 100. That is, the number of comparisons is multiplied by approximately the square of the increase in the number of elements. Looking at this chart makes us appreciate why sorting algorithms are the subject of so much attention: Using SelectionSort to sort a list of 1000 elements requires almost a half million comparisons!

The identifying feature of a selection sort is that, on each pass through the loop, one element is put in its proper place. In the straight selection sort, each iteration finds the smallest unsorted element and puts it in its correct place. If we had made the nested function find the *largest* value, instead of the smallest, the algorithm would have sorted in descending order. We could also have made the loop go down from Length to 1, putting the elements in the bottom of the array first. All these are variations on the straight selection sort. The variations do not change the basic way that the minimum (or maximum) element is found.

Bubble Sort

The **bubble sort** is a selection sort that uses a different scheme for finding the minimum (or maximum) value. Each iteration puts the smallest unsorted element in its correct place, but it also makes changes in the location of the other elements in the list. The first iteration will put the smallest element in the list in the first array position. Starting with the last list element we compare successive pairs of elements, swapping whenever the bottom element of the pair is smaller than the one above it. In this way the smallest element "bubbles" up to the top of the array. The next iteration puts the smallest element in the unsorted part of the list into the second array position, using the same technique. As we walk through sorting the five-element list in Figure 11-3(a), note that in addition

Figure 11-3
Example of Bubble
Sort

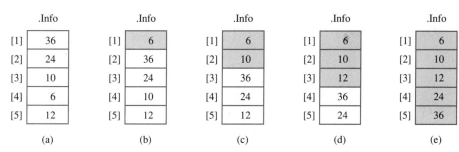

to putting one element in its proper place, each iteration causes some intermediate changes in the array.

The first iteration puts 6 in Info[1] [Figure 11-3(b)]. Unlike the straight selection sort, which would make only the single swap between 6 and 36, the bubble sort causes two additional intermediate swaps. It first compares the values in Info[5] and Info[4]. Because 12 >= 6, no swap occurs. Then Info[4] and Info[3] are compared; 6 < 10, so the two are swapped. The new value in Info[3], which is 6, is compared to Info[2]; 6 < 24, so they are swapped. Finally, the new value in Info[2] (6 again) is compared to Info[1]; 6 < 36, so a swap occurs. Now the smallest value (6) is in the top position in the array. The second iteration will put the next smallest value (10) in the second position, causing one additional swap [Figure 11-3(c)], and so on.

The basic algorithm for the bubble sort is

Bubble Sort

Current ← index of first element in the array

WHILE more elements in unsorted part of list DO
    "Bubble up" the smallest element in the unsorted part of the list, causing intermediate
        swaps as needed.
    Shrink the unsorted part of the list by incrementing Current.

The structure of the loop is much like that of the SelectionSort. The unsorted part of the list is the area from Info[Current] to Info[Length]. Current begins at 1, and we loop until Current reaches Length, with Current incremented in each iteration. On entrance to each iteration of the loop body, the first Current − 1 values are already sorted, and all the elements in the unsorted part of the list are greater than or equal to the sorted elements.

The inside of the loop body is different, however. Each iteration of the WHILE loop "bubbles up" the smallest values in the unsorted part of the list to the Current position. The algorithm for the bubbling task is

BubbleUp (Info, StartIndex, EndIndex)

FOR Index := EndIndex DOWNTO StartIndex + 1 DO
    IF Info[Index] < Info[Index − 1]
        THEN Swap Info[Index] with Info[Index − 1])

A snapshot of this algorithm is shown in Figure 11-4. Using the Swap procedure coded earlier, the code for Procedure BubbleSort is listed on page 666.

Figure 11-4
Algorithm for the
Bubble Sort

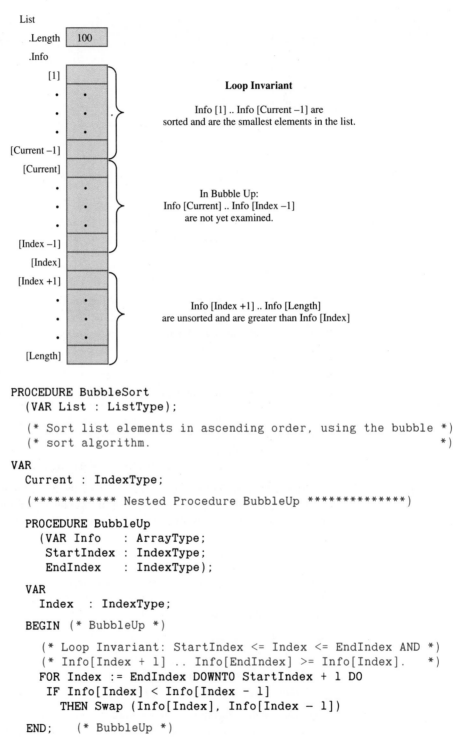

PROCEDURE BubbleSort
  (VAR List : ListType);

  (* Sort list elements in ascending order, using the bubble *)
  (* sort algorithm.   *)

VAR
  Current : IndexType;

  (*********** Nested Procedure BubbleUp **************)

  PROCEDURE BubbleUp
    (VAR Info   : ArrayType;
     StartIndex : IndexType;
     EndIndex   : IndexType);

  VAR
    Index : IndexType;

  BEGIN (* BubbleUp *)

    (* Loop Invariant: StartIndex <= Index <= EndIndex AND *)
    (* Info[Index + 1] .. Info[EndIndex] >= Info[Index].   *)
    FOR Index := EndIndex DOWNTO StartIndex + 1 DO
    IF Info[Index] < Info[Index - 1]
      THEN Swap (Info[Index], Info[Index - 1])

  END;   (* BubbleUp *)

```
    (*******************************************************)
BEGIN  (* BubbleSort *)
  WITH List DO
    BEGIN

      Current := 1;   (* index of first unsorted element *)

      (* Loop Invariant: 1 <= Current <= Length AND     *)
      (* the values in Info[1] .. Info[Current - 1] are  *)
      (* sorted and are less than or equal to the values *)
      (* in Info[Current] .. Info[Length].               *)
      WHILE Current < Length DO
        BEGIN
          (* Bubble up the smallest element from the unsorted *)
          (* part of the list, with intermediate swaps.       *)
          BubbleUp (Info, Current, Length);

          (* Shrink the unsorted part of the list. *)
          Current := Current + 1

      END (* WHILE *)
    END (* WITH *)
END; (* BubbleSort *)
```

To analyze the work required by BubbleSort is easy. It is the same as for the straight selection sort algorithm. The comparisons are in BubbleUp, which is called $N - 1$ times. There are $N - 1$ comparisons the first time, $N - 2$ comparisons the second time, and so on. Therefore BubbleSort and SelectionSort require the same amount of work, in terms of the number of comparison. BubbleSort does more than just make comparisons, though; while SelectionSort has only one data swap per iteration, BubbleSort may do many additional data swaps.

What is the purpose of these intermediate data swaps? By reversing out-of-order pairs of data as they are noticed, the procedure might get the list in order before $N - 1$ calls to BubbleUp. However, this version of the bubble sort makes no provision for stopping when the list is completely sorted. Even if the list is already in sorted order when BubbleSort is called, this procedure continues to call BubbleUp (which changes nothing) $N - 1$ times.

We could quit before the maximum number of iterations if BubbleUp returns a Boolean flag, Sorted, to tell us when the list is sorted. Within BubbleUp, we set Sorted to True; then in the loop, if any swaps are made, we reset Sorted to False. If no elements have been swapped, we know that the list is already in order. Now the bubble sort only needs to make *one* extra call to BubbleUp when the list is in order. This version of the bubble sort is shown below:

```
PROCEDURE ShortBubble
  (VAR List : ListType);

  (* Sorts List elements in ascending order, using bubble *)
  (* sort algorithm; stops when elements are in order.     *)
```

```
VAR
  Current : IndexType;
  Sorted  : Boolean;

(*********** Nested Procedure BubbleUp **************)

PROCEDURE BubbleUp
  (VAR Info   : ArrayType;
   StartIndex : IndexType;
   EndIndex   : IndexType;
   VAR Sorted : Boolean);

VAR
  Index  : IndexType;

BEGIN (* BubbleUp *)

  Sorted := True;     (* start out optimistic *)

  (* Loop Invariant: StartIndex <= Index <= EndIndex AND *)
  (* Info[Index + 1] .. Info[EndIndex] >= Info[Index].   *)
  FOR Index := EndIndex DOWNTO StartIndex + 1 DO
    IF Info[Index] < Info[Index - 1]
      THEN
        BEGIN
          Swap (Info[Index], Info[Index - 1]);
          Sorted := False
        END (* IF *)

  END;   (* BubbleUp *)

(******************************************************)

BEGIN  (* ShortBubble *)

  WITH List DO
    BEGIN

      Current := 1;   (* index of first unsorted element *)
      Sorted  := False;

      (* Loop Invariant: 1 <= Current <= Length AND       *)
      (* the values in Info[1] .. Info[Current - 1] are    *)
      (* sorted and are less than or equal to the values   *)
      (* in Info[Current] .. Info[Length].                 *)
      WHILE (Current < Length) AND NOT Sorted DO
        BEGIN
          (* Bubble up the smallest element from unsorted *)
          (* part of the list, with intermediate swaps.   *)
          BubbleUp (Info, Current, Length, Sorted);

          (* Shrink the unsorted part of the list. *)
          Current := Current + 1

        END (* WHILE *)
    END (* WITH *)
END; (* ShortBubble *)
```

The analysis of ShortBubble is more difficult. Clearly, if the list is already sorted, one call to BubbleUp will tell us so. In this best case scenario, ShortBubble is O(N); only N − 1 comparisons are required for the sort. What if the original list was actually sorted in *descending* order before the call to ShortBubble? This is the worst possible case: ShortBubble requires as many comparisons as BubbleSort and SelectionSort, not to mention the "overhead"—all the extra swaps and setting and resetting the Sorted flag. Can we calculate an average case? In the first call to BubbleUp, when Current is 1, there are Length − 1 comparisons; on the second call, when Current is 2, there are Length − 2 comparisons. The number of comparisons in any call to BubbleUp is Length − Current. If we let N indicate Length and K indicate the number of calls to BubbleUp executed before ShortBubble finishes its work, the total number of comparisons required is

$$(N - 1) \quad + \quad (N - 2) \quad + \quad (N - 3) \quad + \quad \cdots \quad + \quad (N - K)$$
$$\text{1st call} \qquad\qquad \text{2nd call} \qquad\qquad \text{3rd call} \qquad\qquad\qquad\qquad \text{K'th call}$$

A little algebra* changes this to

$$(2KN - K^2 - K)/2$$

In Big-O notation, the term that is increasing the fastest relative to N is 2KN. We know that K is between 1 and N − 1. On the average, over all possible input orders, K is proportional to N. Therefore 2KN is proportional to N^2; that is, the ShortBubble algorithm is also $O(N^2)$. Because the straight selection sort and both bubble sorts are all on the order of N^2, they are all too time-consuming for sorting large lists. Thus there is a need for sorting methods that work better when N is large.

O(N log₂ N) Sorts

Considering how fast N^2 grows as the size of the list gets larger, can't we do better? We note that N^2 is a lot larger than $(\frac{1}{2}N)^2 + (\frac{1}{2}N)^2$. If we could cut the list into two pieces, sort each segment, and then merge the two back together, we should end up sorting the entire list with a lot less work. An example of this approach is shown in Figure 11-5.

The idea of "divide and conquer" has been applied to the sorting problem in different ways, resulting in a number of algorithms that can do the job much more efficiently than $O(N^2)$. We will look at three of these sorting algorithms here—MergeSort, QuickSort, and HeapSort. As you might guess, the efficiency of these algorithms is achieved at the expense of the simplicity seen in the straight selection and bubble sorts.

---

*For those of you who want to see the algebra:

$$(N - 1) + (N - 2) + \cdots (N - K)$$
$$= \quad KN - (\text{sum of 1 through K})$$
$$= \quad KN - (\tfrac{1}{2} K(K + 1)) \quad [\text{as we saw in Chapter 1}]$$
$$= \quad KN - (\tfrac{1}{2} K^2 + \tfrac{1}{2} K)$$
$$= \quad (2KN - K^2 - K) /2$$

*Figure 11-5
Rationale for
Divide-and-Con-
quer Sorts*

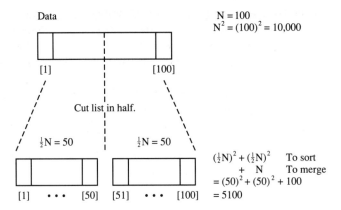

Merge Sort

The merge sort algorithm is taken directly from the idea in the previous section:

MergeSort

Cut the list in half
Sort the left half
Sort the right half
Merge the two sorted halves into one sorted list

Merging the two halves together is an O(N) task: We merely go through the sorted halves, comparing successive pairs of values (one in each half) and putting the smaller value into the next slot in the final solution. Even if the sorting algorithm used for each half is $O(N^2)$, we should see some improvement over sorting the whole list at once.

Actually, because MergeSort is itself a sorting algorithm, we might as well use it to sort the two halves. That's right—we can make MergeSort a *recursive* procedure and let it call itself to sort each of the two sublists:

MergeSort—Recursive

Cut the list in half
MergeSort the left half
MergeSort the right half
Merge the two sorted halves into one sorted list

This is the general case, of course. What is the base case, the case that does not involve any recursive calls to MergeSort? If the "half" to be sorted doesn't have more than one element, we can consider it already sorted and just return.

As usual with recursive procedures, we will need to pass some extra information on the parameter list. In the other sorts that we have discussed, we have defined the "unsorted part of the list" using a local variable, Current, and the list Length field. Each iteration processed the unsorted part of the list, the elements between index Current and index Length. However, for a recursive sort routine, we must explicitly define the unsorted part of the list on each recursive call. Therefore, we add both the first and last indexes of the sublist to be MergeSort'ed to the parameter list. Each call to MergeSort will process the unsorted part of the list—from index First to index Last. Since the Length field of List is not used within procedure MergeSort, we will just input the array part of List. The initial call to MergeSort (in Procedure SortList) is *MergeSort (List.Info, 1, List.Length)*.

Let's summarize MergeSort in the format we used in Chapter 8.

Procedure MergeSort (Info, First, Last)

Definition:	Sort the list elements in ascending order.
Size:	Info[First] .. Info[Last]
Base Case:	IF less than 2 elements to compare in Info[First] .. Info[Last], do nothing.
General Case:	Cut the array in half.
	MergeSort the left half.
	MergeSort the right half.
	Merge the sorted halves into one sorted list.

Cutting the array in half is simply a matter of finding the midpoint between the first and last indexes:

Middle ← (First + Last) DIV 2

Then, in the smaller-caller tradition, we can make the recursive calls to MergeSort:

MergeSort (Info, First, Middle)
MergeSort (Info, Middle + 1, Last)

So far this is pretty simple. Now we only have to merge the two halves and we're done.

Merging the Sorted Halves

Obviously all the serious work is in the merge step. Let's first look at the general algorithm for merging two sorted lists, and then we can look at the specific problem of our subarrays.

To merge two sorted lists, we compare successive pairs of elements, one from each list, moving the smaller of each pair to the "final" list. We can stop when the shorter list runs out of elements, and then move all the remaining elements (if any) from the other list to the final list. Figure 11-6 illustrates the general algorithm.

We use a similar approach in our specific problem, in which the two "lists" to be merged are actually subarrays of the original array (Figure 11-7). Just as in the previous example we merged List1 and List2 into a third list, we will need to merge our two subarrays into some auxiliary data structure. We will only need this data structure, another array, temporarily. After the merge step, we can copy the now-sorted elements back into the original array. The whole process is shown in Figure 11-8.

Let's specify a subprocedure, Merge, to do this task:

Figure 11-6
Strategy for Merging Two Sorted Lists

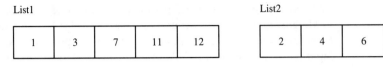

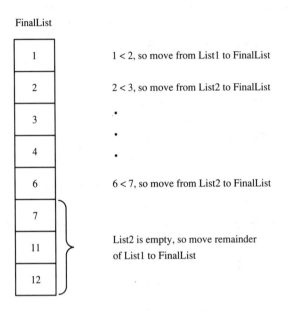

Figure 11-7
Two Subarrays

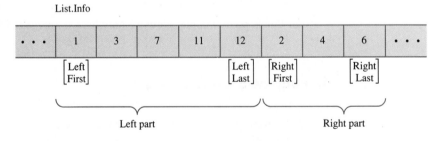

▪	**Merge (Info, LeftFirst, LeftLast, RightFirst, RightLast)**	
	Function:	Merge two sorted subarrays into a single sorted piece of the array.
	Input:	Info (ArrayType) LeftFirst, LeftLast, RightFirst, RightLast
	Preconditions:	Info[LeftFirst] .. Info[LeftLast] is sorted; Info[RightFirst] .. Info[RightLast] is sorted.
	Output:	Info (changed)
	Postconditions:	Info[LeftFirst] .. Info[RightLast] is sorted.

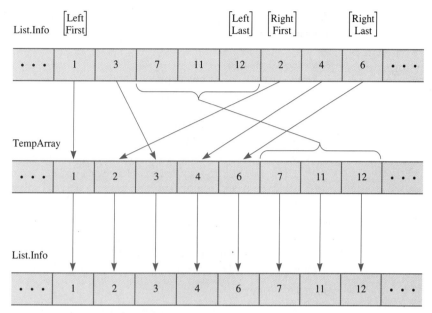

Figure 11-8
Merging Sorted
Halves

Here is the algorithm for Merge:

Merge (Uses a local array, TempArray)

Index ← LeftFirst

WHILE more elements in left half AND more elements in right half DO
  IF Info[LeftFirst] < Info[RightFirst]
    THEN
      TempArray[Index] ← Info[LeftFirst]
      Increment LeftFirst
    ELSE
      TempArray[Index] ← Info[RightFirst]
      Increment RightFirst
  Increment Index

Copy any remaining elements from left half to TempArray
  (or)
Copy any remaining elements from right half to TempArray

Copy the sorted elements from TempArray back into Info

In the coding of Procedure Merge, we use LeftFirst and RightFirst to indicate the "current" position in the left and right halves, respectively. Since these are not VAR parameters, copies of these parameters are passed to Procedure Merge. These copies are changed in the procedures, but the changed values are not passed out of Merge. Note that both of the "copy any remaining elements . . ." loops are included. During the execution of this procedure, one of these loops will never execute. Can you explain why?

```
PROCEDURE Merge
   (VAR Info    : ArrayType;
    LeftFirst   : Integer;
    LeftLast    : Integer;
    RightFirst  : Integer;
    RightLast   : Integer);

   (* Merge the two sorted subarrays, Info [LeftFirst] ..      *)
   (* Info[LeftLast] and Info[RightFirst] .. Info[RightLast] *)
   (* into a single sorted subarray, Info[LeftFirst] ..       *)
   (* Info[RightLast].                                         *)

VAR
   TempArray : ArrayType;     (* auxiliary array        *)
   Index     : IndexType;     (* index into TempArray   *)
   SaveFirst : IndexType;     (* saves left first index *)
BEGIN (* Merge *)

   (* Initialize indexes before the loop. *)
   Index     := LeftFirst;
   SaveFirst := LeftFirst;

   (* Process while more elements are in both subarrays. *)
   WHILE (LeftFirst <= LeftLast) AND
         (RightFirst <= RightLast) DO
     BEGIN
       IF Info[LeftFirst] < Info[RightFirst]
         THEN
           BEGIN  (* copy from left half into TempArray *)
             TempArray[Index] := Info[LeftFirst];
             LeftFirst := LeftFirst + 1
           END (* Left element is smaller *)
         ELSE
           BEGIN (* copy from right half into TempArray *)
             TempArray[Index] := Info[RightFirst];
             RightFirst := RightFirst + 1
           END; (* Right element is smaller or equal. *)

       Index := Index + 1
     END; (* WHILE more elements in loop *)

   (* Copy any remaining elements from left half. *)
   WHILE LeftFirst <= LeftLast DO
     BEGIN
       TempArray[Index] := Info[LeftFirst];
       LeftFirst    := LeftFirst + 1;
       Index := Index + 1
     END; (* While more elements in left half *)
```

```
    (* Copy any remaining elements from right half. *)
    WHILE RightFirst <= RightLast DO
      BEGIN
        TempArray[Index] := Info[RightFirst];
        RightFirst := RightFirst + 1;
        Index := Index + 1
      END;  (* While more elements in right half *)

    (* Copy the sorted elements from TempArray back into Info. *)
    FOR Index := SaveFirst TO RightLast DO
      Info[Index] := TempArray[Index]
  END;  (* Merge *)
```

The MergeSort Procedure

As we said, most of the work is in the merge task. The actual MergeSort procedure is short and simple:

```
PROCEDURE MergeSort
  (VAR Info : ArrayType;
   First    : Integer;
   Last     : Integer);

  (* Sort Info[First]..Info[Last] in increasing order. *)

VAR
  Middle : Integer;          (* middle index in range to sort *)

BEGIN (* MergeSort *)

  (* Base Case: Check for empty list or single element. *)
  IF First < Last
    THEN
      BEGIN (* General Case *)

        (* Cut the array into two halves. *)
        Middle := (First + Last) DIV 2;

        (* Sort the left subarray. *)
        MergeSort (Info, First, Middle);

        (* Sort the right subarray. *)
        MergeSort (Info, Middle + 1, Last);

        (* Merge the two sorted halves together. *)
        Merge
          (Info,          (* array to sort            *)
           First,         (* first index in left half  *)
           Middle,        (* last index in left half   *)
           Middle + 1,    (* first index in right half *)
           Last)          (* last index in right half  *)

      END (* General Case *)
END;     (* MergeSort *)
```

Analyzing MergeSort

We already pointed out that sorting two half-lists is less work than sorting one whole list. How much less work is it? The bulk of the work occurs in the merge processing. In the Merge procedure we make comparisons on each element in the subarrays; this is an O(N) operation. We also copy all the elements in the subarray back from TempArray into the original list, which is also O(N). This makes a total of 2N, but we drop constants. So the Merge procedure is O(N).

Now, how many times is the Merge procedure called? It is called in Procedure MergeSort after the array has been divided in half and each of those halves has been sorted (using MergeSort, of course). In each of the recursive calls, one for the left half and one for the right, the array is divided in half again, making four pieces. Each of these pieces is similarly subdivided. At each level the number of pieces doubles (see Figure 11-9). We can keep dividing the array in half $\log_2 N$ times. (This is just like the analysis of the binary search algorithm in Chapter 2.)

Each time the array is divided, we perform the O(N) Merge procedure to put it back together again. This gives us a product of $N \times \log_2 N$. Thus the whole algorithm is O($N \log_2 N$). Figure 11-10 illustrates that, for large values of N, O($N \log_2 N$) is a big improvement over O(N^2).

The disadvantage of MergeSort is that it requires an auxiliary array that is as large as the original array to be sorted. If the array is large and space is a critical factor, this sort may not be an appropriate choice. Next we'll discuss two sorts that move elements around in the original array and do not need an auxiliary array.

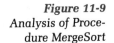

Figure 11-9
Analysis of Proce-
dure MergeSort

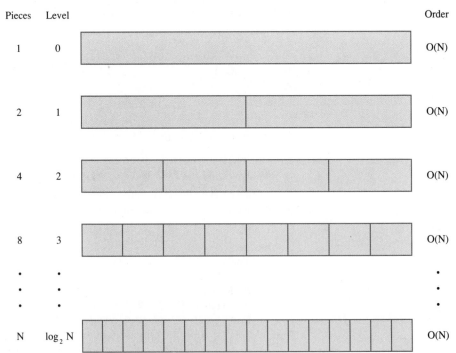

Pieces	Level		Order
1	0		O(N)
2	1		O(N)
4	2		O(N)
8	3		O(N)
.	.		.
.	.		.
.	.		.
N	$\log_2 N$		O(N)

Figure 11-10
Comparing N² and
N log₂ N

N	$\log_2 N$	N^2	$N\log_2 N$
32	5	1,024	160
64	6	4,096	384
128	7	16,384	896
256	8	65,536	2,048
512	9	262,144	4,608
1024	10	1,048,576	10,240
2048	11	4,194,304	22,528
4096	12	16,777,216	49,152

Quick Sort

The quick sort is another sorting algorithm based on the fact that it is faster and easier to sort two small lists than one larger one. The name comes from the fact that, in general, quick sort can sort a list of data elements significantly faster than any of the common simple sorts. The basic strategy of QuickSort, like that of MergeSort, is to divide and conquer.

If you were given a large stack of final exams to sort by name, you might use the following approach: Pick a splitting value, say L, and divide the stack of tests into two piles, A–L and M–Z. (Note that the two piles will not necessarily contain the same number of tests.) Then take the first pile and subdivide it into two piles, A–F and G–L. The A–F pile can be further broken down into A–C and D–F. This division process goes on until the piles are small enough to be easily sorted. The same process is applied to the M–Z pile.

Eventually all the small sorted piles can be stacked one on top of the other to produce an ordered set of tests. (See Figure 11-11.)

This strategy is based on recursion—on each attempt to sort the stack of tests the stack is divided and then the same approach is used to sort each of the smaller stacks (a smaller case). This process goes on until the small stacks do not need to be further divided (the base case). Like Procedure MergeSort, the parameter list of the QuickSort procedure will reflect the part of the list that is currently being processed: We will pass List.Info (the array) and the First and Last indexes that define the part of the array to be processed on this call. The initial call to QuickSort in Procedure SortList is *QuickSort (List.Info, 1, List.Length)*.

▪ **Procedure QuickSort (Info, First, Last)**

Definition:	Sort the elements in array Info.
Size:	Info[First] .. Info[Last]
Base Case:	IF less than 2 elements to compare in Info[First] .. Info[Last], do nothing.
General Case:	Split the array according to splitting value. QuickSort the elements <= splitting value. QuickSort the elements > splitting value.

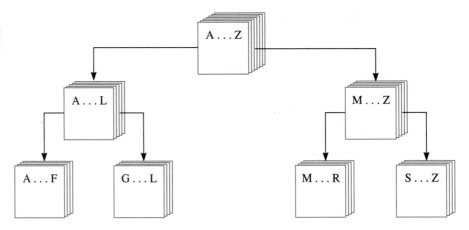

Figure 11-11
Ordering a List
Using QuickSort

QuickSort

IF there is more than one element in Info[First] .. Info[Last]
  THEN
    Select SplitVal

    Split the array so that:
      Info[First] .. Info[SplitPoint − 1] <= SplitVal
      Info[SplitPoint] = SplitVal
      Info[SplitPoint + 1] .. Info[Last] > SplitVal.

    QuickSort the left half.
    QuickSort the right half.

How do we select SplitVal? One simple solution is to use the value in Info[First] as the splitting value.

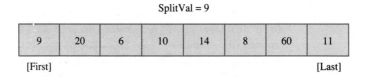

After the call to Split, all the elements less than or equal to SplitVal will be on the left side of the array and all those greater than SplitVal will be on the right side of the array:

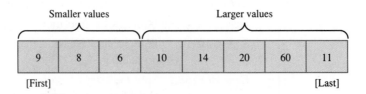

The two "halves" meet at SplitPoint, the index of the last element that is less than or equal to SplitVal. Note that we don't know the value of SplitPoint until the splitting process is complete. We can then swap SplitVal with the value at SplitPoint:

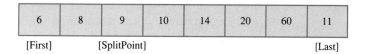

| 6 | 8 | 9 | 10 | 14 | 20 | 60 | 11 |

[First] [SplitPoint] [Last]

Our recursive calls to QuickSort will use this index (SplitPoint) to reduce the size of the problem in the general case.

QuickSort (Info, First, SplitPoint − 1) sorts the left "half" of the array. QuickSort (Info, SplitPoint + 1, Last) sorts the right "half" of the array. (The "halves" are not necessarily the same size.) SplitVal is already in its correct position in Info[SplitPoint].

What is the base case? When the segment being examined has less than two elements, we do not need to go on. So "there is more than one element in Info[First] .. Info[Last]" can be translated into "IF First < Last". We can now code Procedure QuickSort.

```
PROCEDURE QuickSort
  (VAR Info : ArrayType;
   First    : Integer;
   Last     : Integer);

VAR
  SplitPoint : IndexType;

BEGIN  (* QuickSort *)

  IF First < Last  (* General Case *)
    THEN
      BEGIN

        (* Procedure Split chooses the splitting value and *)
        (* rearranges the array so that:                   *)
        (* Info[First] .. Info[SplitPoint - 1] <= SplitVal *)
        (* Info[SplitPoint] = SplitVal                     *)
        (* Info[SplitPoint + 1] .. Info[Last] > SplitVal.  *)
        Split (Info, First, Last, SplitPoint);

        (* Sort the left "half." *)
        QuickSort (Info, First, SplitPoint - 1);

        (* Sort the right "half." *)
        QuickSort (Info, SplitPoint + 1, Last)

      END    (* IF First < Last *)

  (* ELSE Base Case: Do nothing. *)
END;  (* QuickSort *)
```

Let's verify QuickSort according to the Three Question Method.

1. *Is there a nonrecursive base case?* Yes. When First $>=$ Last (there is at most one element in the segment), QuickSort does nothing.
2. *Does each recursive call involve a smaller case of the problem?* Yes. Split divides the segment into two not necessarily equal pieces, and each of these smaller pieces is then QuickSorted. Note that even if SplitVal is the largest or smallest value in the segment, the two pieces will still be smaller than the original one: If SplitVal is smaller than all the other values in the segment, then QuickSort (Info, First, SplitPoint $-$ 1) will terminate immediately, because First $>$ SplitPoint $-$ 1. QuickSort (Info, SplitPoint $+$ 1, Last) will quick sort a segment one element smaller than the original.
3. *Assuming that the recursive calls succeed, does the whole procedure work?* Yes. We assume that QuickSort (Info, First, SplitPoint $-$ 1) actually sorts the first SplitPoint $-$ 1 elements, whose values are less than or equal to SplitVal. Info[SplitPoint], containing SplitVal, is in its correct place. We also assume that QuickSort (Info, SplitPoint $+$ 1, Last) has correctly sorted the rest of the list, whose values are all greater than SplitVal. So we know that the whole list is sorted.

In good top-down fashion, we have shown that our algorithm will work if Procedure Split works. Now we must develop our splitting algorithm. We must find a way to get all of the elements equal to or less than SplitVal on one side of SplitVal and the elements greater than SplitVal on the other side.

We do this by moving the indexes, First and Last, toward the middle of the array, looking for elements that are on the wrong side of the split point (Figure 11-12). As in Procedure Merge, since First and Last are not VAR parameters, we can change their values without affecting the calling procedure. We save the original value of First in a local variable, SaveFirst.

We start out by moving First to the right, toward the middle, comparing Info[First] to SplitVal. If Info[First] $<=$ SplitVal, we keep incrementing First; otherwise we leave First where it is and begin moving Last toward the middle. [See Figure 11-12(b).]

Now Info[Last] is compared to SplitVal. If it is greater than SplitVal, we continue decrementing Last; otherwise we leave Last in place. [See Figure 11-12(c).] At this point it is clear that Info[Last] and Info[First] are each on the wrong side of the array. Note that the elements to the left of Info[First] and to the right of Info[Last] are not necessarily sorted; they are just on the correct side *with respect to SplitVal*. To put Info[First] and Info[Last] into their correct sides, we merely swap them, then increment First and decrement Last. [See Figure 11-12(d).]

Now we repeat the whole cycle, incrementing First until we encounter a value that is greater than SplitVal, then decrementing Last until we encounter a value that is less than or equal to SplitVal. [See Figure 11-12(e).]

When does the process stop? When First and Last meet each other, no further swaps are necessary. They meet at the SplitPoint. This is the location where SplitVal belongs, so we swap Info[SaveFirst], which contains SplitVal, with the element at Info[SplitPoint] [Figure 11-12(f)]. The index SplitPoint is returned from the procedure, to be used by QuickSort to set up the next recursive call.

Figure 11-12
Procedure Split

(a) Initialization

SplitVal = Info [First] = 9

9	20	6	10	14	8	60	11

[First]   [Last]

(b) Increment First until Info [First] > SplitVal.

9	20	6	10	14	8	60	11

[SaveFirst] [First]   [Last]

(c) Decrement Last until Info [Last] < = SplitVal.

9	20	6	10	14	8	60	11

[SaveFirst] [First]   [Last]

(d) Swap Data [First] and Data [Last]; move First and Last toward each other.

9	8	6	10	14	20	60	11

[SaveFirst]   [First]   [Last]

(e) Increment First until Info [First] > SplitVal, or First > Last.
    Decrement Last until Info [Last] < = SplitVal, or First > Last.

9	8	6	10	14	20	60	11

[SaveFirst]   [Last] [First]

(f) First > Last so no swap occurs within the loop.
    Swap Info [SaveFirst] and Info [Last].

6	8	9	10	14	20	60	11

[SaveFirst]   [Last]
                         (SplitPoint)

```
PROCEDURE Split
  (VAR Info       : ArrayType;
   First          : Integer;
   Last           : Integer;
   VAR SplitPoint : IndexType);

  (* Choose SplitVal and rearrange Info so that:        *)
  (* Info[First]..Info[SplitPoint - 1] <= SplitVal and   *)
  (* Info[SplitPoint] = SplitVal and                     *)
  (* Info[SplitPoint + 1] .. Info[Last] > SplitVal.      *)

VAR
  SplitVal  : ListElementType; (* value on which to split *)
  SaveFirst : IndexType; (* original value of First       *)

BEGIN (* Split *)

  (* SplitVal is chosen from the First array slot. *)
  SplitVal := Info[First];

  (* Set up for split loop. *)
  SaveFirst := First;
  First := First + 1;

  (* Loop invariant: elements to the left of First are *)
  (* less than or equal to SplitVal; elements to the   *)
  (* right of Last are greater than SplitVal.          *)
  REPEAT

    (* Increment First until element > SplitVal. *)
    WHILE (First < Last) AND (Info[First] <= SplitVal) DO
      First := First + 1;

    (* Check end condition. *)
    IF (First = Last) AND (Info[First] <= SplitVal)
      THEN First := First + 1;

    (* Decrement Last until element <= SplitVal. *)
    WHILE (First <= Last) AND (Info[Last] > SplitVal) DO
      Last := Last - 1;

    (* If First and Last are on the wrong side of the *)
    (* split point, then swap them; update First and  *)
    (* Last to set up to continue splitting.          *)
    IF First < Last
      THEN
        BEGIN
          Swap (Info[First], Info[Last]);
          First := First + 1;
          Last := Last - 1
        END (* IF *)

  UNTIL First > Last;

  (* Set SplitPoint to place where the halves meet. *)
  SplitPoint := Last;
```

```
(* Swap SplitVal with element at SplitPoint. *)
Swap (Info[SaveFirst], Info[SplitPoint])
END; (* Split *)
```

Note that we could not use the expression "While (First <= Last) AND (Info[First] <= SplitVal)" because it would cause an array index to be out of bounds in the case where Last = MaxElements and SplitVal is the largest value in the array.

What happens if our splitting value is the largest or the smallest value in the segment? The algorithm will still work correctly, but because of the lopsided splits it will not be quick.

Is this situation likely to occur? That depends on how we choose our splitting value and on the original order of the data in the array. If we use Info[First] as the splitting value and the array is already sorted, then *every* split will be lopsided. One side will contain one element, while the other side will contain all but one of the elements. Thus our QuickSort will not be a quick sort. This splitting algorithm favors an array in random order.

It is not unusual, however, to want to sort an array that is already in nearly sorted order. If this is the case, a better splitting value would be the middle value,

Info[(First + Last) DIV 2]

This value could be swapped with Info[First] at the beginning of the procedure.

There are many possible splitting algorithms. One that is a slight variation of the one we have just developed is given below. It uses the value in the middle of the array as the splitting value without moving it to the first slot. As a result the value in Info[SplitPoint] may or may not be in its permanent place.

```
PROCEDURE Split2
   (VAR Info    : ArrayType;
    First       : Integer;
    Last        : Integer;
    VAR SplitPt1 : Integer;
    VAR SplitPt2 : Integer);

   (* Chooses a splitting value and arranges Info so that   *)
   (* Info[First] .. Info[SplitPt2] <= SplitVal and          *)
   (* Info[SplitPt1 + 1] .. Info[Last] > SplitVal.           *)
VAR
   SplitVal : ListElementType;

BEGIN (* Split2 *)

   (* Let SplitVal be the middle value. *)
   SplitVal := Info[(First + Last) DIV 2];

   (* Loop invariant: elements to the left of First are *)
   (* less than or equal to SplitVal; elements to the    *)
   (* right of Last are greater than SplitVal.           *)
   REPEAT
```

```
        (* Increment First until element > SplitVal. *)
        WHILE Info[First] < SplitVal DO
          First := First + 1;

        (* Decrement Last until element < SplitVal.  *)
        WHILE Info[Last] > SplitVal DO
          Last := Last - 1;

        (* If First and Last are on the wrong side of the split *)
        (* point, swap the elements and update First and Last.  *)
        IF First <= Last
          THEN
            BEGIN
              Swap (Info[First], Info[Last]);
              First := First + 1;
              Last := Last - 1
            END (* IF *)

      UNTIL First > Last;

      SplitPt1 := First;
      SplitPt2 := Last

  END;   (* Split2 *)
```

If this algorithm is used, Procedure QuickSort will have to be adjusted slightly.

```
PROCEDURE QuickSort2
  (VAR Info : ArrayType;
   First     : Integer;
   Last      : Integer);

  (* Sorts Info from index First to index Last. *)

VAR
  SplitPt1, SplitPt2 : Integer;

BEGIN  (* QuickSort2 *)

  IF First < Last
    THEN
      BEGIN
        Split2 (Info, First, Last, SplitPt1, SplitPt2);
        IF SplitPt1 < Last
          THEN QuickSort2 (Info, SplitPt1, Last);
        IF First < SplitPt2
          THEN QuickSort (Info, First, SplitPt2)
      END  (* IF *)

END; (* QuickSort2 *)
```

Notice that QuickSort2 only makes the recursive call if there is more than one element in a segment. This makes the code more efficient.

Analyzing QuickSort

The analysis of QuickSort is very similar to that of MergeSort. On the first call, every element in the list is compared to the dividing value, so the work done is O(N). The array is divided into two parts (not necessarily halves), which are then examined.

Each of these pieces is then divided in two, and so on. If each piece is split approximately in half, there will be $O(\log_2 N)$ splits. At each split, we make O(N) comparisons. So QuickSort is also an $O(N\log_2 N)$ algorithm, which is quicker than the $O(N^2)$ sorts we discussed at the beginning of this chapter.

But QuickSort isn't *always* quicker. Note that there will be $\log_2 N$ splits *if* each split divides the segment of the array approximately in half. As we've seen, QuickSort is sensitive to the order of the data.

What will happen if the array is already sorted when our first version of QuickSort is called? The splits will be very lopsided, and the subsequent recursive calls to QuickSort will sort into a segment of one element and a segment containing all the rest of the array. This situation will produce a sort that is not at all quick. In fact, there will be $N - 1$ splits; in this case QuickSort will be $O(N^2)$.

Such a situation is very unlikely to occur by chance. By way of analogy, consider the odds of shuffling a deck of cards and coming up with an ordered deck. On the other hand, in some applications you may know that the original array is likely to be sorted or nearly sorted. In such cases you would want to use either a different splitting algorithm or a different sort.

Heap Sort

In each iteration of the selection sort, we searched the array for the next smallest element and put it in its correct place in the array. Another way to write a selection sort is to find the maximum value in the array and swap it with the last array element, then find the next-to-largest element and put it in its place, and so on. Most of the work in this sorting algorithm comes from searching the remaining part of the array in each iteration, looking for the maximum value.

In Chapter 10 we discussed the *heap*, a data structure with a very special feature—we always know where to find its greatest element. Because of the order property of heaps, the maximum value of a heap is in the root node. We can take advantage of this situation by using a heap to help us sort. The general approach of HeapSort is as follows:

1. Take the root (maximum) element off the heap, and put it in its place.
2. Reheap the remaining elements. (This puts the next-largest element back in the root position.)
3. Repeat until there are no more elements.

The first part of this algorithm sounds a lot like the straight selection sort. What makes the HeapSort fast is the second step: finding the next-largest element. Because the shape property of heaps guarantees a binary tree of minimum height, we make only $O(\log_2 N)$ comparisons in each iteration, as compared with $O(N)$ comparisons in each iteration of the selection sort.

Building a Heap

By now you are probably protesting that we are dealing with an unsorted array of elements, not a heap. Where will the original heap come from? Before we go on, we'll have to convert the unsorted array, Info, into a heap.

Let's take a look at how the heap relates to our array of unsorted elements. In Chapter 10 we saw how heaps can be represented in an array with implicit links. Because of the shape property, we know that the heap elements will take up consecutive positions in the array. In fact, the unsorted array of data elements already satisfies the shape property of heaps. Figure 11-13 shows an unsorted array and its equivalent tree.

Figure 11-13
An Unsorted Array
and Its Tree

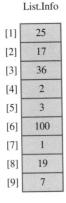

List.Info

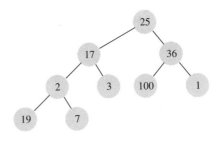

We also need to make the unsorted array elements satisfy the order property of heaps. First let's see if there's any part of the tree that already satisfies the order property. All of the leaf nodes (subtrees with only a single node) are heaps. In Figure 11-14(a) the subtrees whose roots contain the values 19, 7, 3, 100, and 1 are heaps because they are root nodes.

Now let's look at the first *nonleaf* node, the one containing the value 2 [Figure 11-14(b)]. The subtree rooted at this node is not a heap, but it is *almost* a heap. It is the root of a complete binary tree whose subtrees are heaps. We know how to fix this problem. In Chapter 10 we developed a heap utility procedure, ReheapDown, that can be used to correct this exact situation. Given a tree whose elements satisfy the order property of heaps except (perhaps) at the root node, ReheapDown rearranges the nodes, leaving the (sub)tree as a heap.

We apply this procedure to all the subtrees on this level, then we move up a level in the tree and continue reheaping until we reach the root node. After ReheapDown has been called for the root node, the whole tree should satisfy the order property of heaps. This heap-building process is illustrated in Figure 11-14; the changing contents of the array are shown in Figure 11-15.

Figure 11-14
The Heap-Building
Process

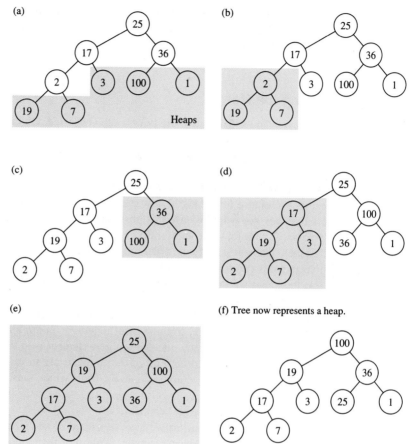

(f) Tree now represents a heap.

Figure 11-15
Changing Contents
of the Array

	[1]	[2]	[3]	[4]	[5]	[6]	[7]	[8]	[9]
Original Info	25	17	36	2	3	100	1	19	7
After ReheapDown Index = 4	25	17	36	19	3	100	1	2	7
After Index = 3	25	17	100	19	3	36	1	2	7
After Index = 2	25	19	100	17	3	36	1	2	7
After Index = 1	100	19	36	17	3	25	1	2	7

Tree is a heap.

The algorithm for this process is summarized below:

BuildHeap

FOR Index := first nonleaf node DOWNTO root node DO
    ReheapDown (Info, Index, Length)

We know where the root node is stored in our array representation of heaps—it's in Info[1]. Where is the first nonleaf node? Because half the nodes of a complete binary tree are leaves (prove this yourself), the first nonleaf node may be found at Info[Length DIV 2].

Sorting the Heap

Now that we are satisfied that we can turn the unsorted array of elements into a heap, let's take another look at the sorting algorithm.

We can easily access the largest element from the original heap—it's in the root node. In our array representation of heaps, that is Info[1]. This value belongs in the last-used array position Info[Length], so we can just swap the values in these two positions. Because Info[Length] now contains the largest value in the array (its correct sorted value), we want to leave this position alone. Now we are dealing with a set of elements, from Info[1] through Info[Length − 1], that is almost a heap. We know that all of these elements satisfy the order property of heaps, except (perhaps) the root node. To correct this condition, we call our heap utility, ReheapDown.

At this point we know that the next-largest element in the array is in the root node of the heap. To put this element in its correct position, we swap it with the element in Info[Length − 1]. Now the two largest elements are in their final correct positions, and the elements in Info[1] through Info[Length − 2] are almost a heap. So we call ReheapDown again, and now the third-largest element is in the root of the heap.

This process is repeated until all of the elements are in their correct positions; that is, until the heap contains only a single element, which must be the smallest item in the array, in Info[1]. This is its correct position, so the array is now completely sorted from the smallest to the largest element.

The HeapSort algorithm, as we have described it, sounds like a recursive process. Each time we swap and reheap a smaller portion of the total array. The repetition can just as clearly be coded using a simple FOR loop, however, and the iterative solution is generally more efficient. The node sorting algorithm is

SortNodes

FOR Index := last node DOWNTO next-to-root node DO
    Swap root node element with Info [Index]
    ReheapDown (Info, 1, Index − 1)

Procedure HeapSort first builds the heap and then sorts the nodes, using the algorithms just discussed.

```
PROCEDURE HeapSort
  (VAR List : ListType);

  (* Sort the elements in List in ascending order, using *)
  (* the HeapSort algorithm.                             *)
```

```
VAR
  Index : IndexType;

BEGIN (* HeapSort *)

  WITH List DO
    BEGIN

      (* Build the original heap from the unsorted elements. *)
      FOR Index := (Length DIV 2) DOWNTO 1 DO
        ReheapDown (Info, Index, Length);

      (* Sort the elements in the heap by swapping the root *)
      (* (current largest) value with the last unsorted    *)
      (* value, then reheaping remaining part of the list.  *)
      (* Loop invariant: Info[1] .. Info[Index] represents  *)
      (* a heap AND Info[Index + 1] .. Info[Length] are     *)
      (* sorted in ascending order.                         *)
      FOR Index := Length DOWNTO 2 DO
        BEGIN
          Swap (Info[1], Info[Index]);
          ReheapDown (Info, 1, Index - 1)
        END  (* FOR loop *)
    END (* WITH *)
END;   (* HeapSort *)
```

Figure 11-16 shows how each iteration of the sorting loop (the second FOR loop) would change the heap created in Figure 11-15. Each line represents the array after one operation. The sorted elements are shaded.

We entered the HeapSort routine with a simple array of unsorted values and returned to the caller with an array of the same values sorted in ascending order. Where did the heap go? The heap in HeapSort is just a temporary structure, internal to the sorting algorithm. It is created at the beginning of the procedure, to aid in the sorting process, and then is methodically diminished element by element as the sorted part of the array grows. At the end of the procedure, the sorted part fills the array and the heap has completely disappeared. When we used heaps to implement priority queues in Chapter 10, the heap structure stayed around for the duration of the use of the queue. The heap in HeapSort, in contrast, is not a retained data structure. It only exists for a while inside the HeapSort procedure.

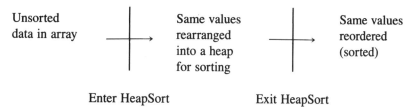

Analyzing HeapSort

The code for procedure HeapSort is very short—only a few lines of new code plus the utility procedure ReheapDown, which we can reuse from Chapter 10. These few lines

Figure 11-16

Effect of HeapSort on the Array

	[1]	[2]	[3]	[4]	[5]	[6]	[7]	[8]	[9]
List.Info	100	19	36	17	3	25	1	2	7
Swap	7	19	36	17	3	25	1	2	100
ReheapDown	36	19	25	17	3	7	1	2	100
Swap	2	19	25	17	3	7	1	36	100
ReheapDown	25	19	7	17	3	2	1	36	100
Swap	1	19	7	17	3	2	25	36	100
ReheapDown	19	17	7	1	3	2	25	36	100
Swap	2	17	7	1	3	19	25	36	100
ReheapDown	17	3	7	1	2	19	25	36	100
Swap	2	3	7	1	17	19	25	36	100
ReheapDown	7	3	2	1	17	19	25	36	100
Swap	1	3	2	7	17	19	25	36	100
ReheapDown	3	1	2	7	17	19	25	36	100
Swap	2	1	3	7	17	19	25	36	100
ReheapDown	2	1	3	7	17	19	25	36	100
Swap	1	2	3	7	17	19	25	36	100
ReheapDown	1	2	3	7	17	19	25	36	100
Exit from sorting loop	1	2	3	7	17	19	25	36	100

of code, however, do quite a bit: All of the elements in the original array are rearranged to satisfy the order property of heaps, moving the largest element up to the top of the array, only to put it immediately into its place at the bottom. It's hard to believe from a small example such as the one in Figure 11-16 that HeapSort is really very efficient.

For small arrays, HeapSort is not very efficient because of all the "overhead." For large arrays, however, HeapSort is very efficient. Let's consider the sorting loop. We loop through N − 1 times, swapping elements and reheaping. Swapping two elements takes a small, constant amount of time [O(1)]. The other activity, Reheaping, is more complex. A complete binary tree with N nodes has $O(\log_2(N + 1))$ levels. In the worst cases, then, if the root element had to be bumped down to a leaf position, the ReheapDown procedure would take $O(\log_2 N)$ swaps. So the swap plus ReheapDown is $O(\log_2 N)$. Multiplying this activity by the N − 1 iterations [O(N)] shows that the sorting loop is $O(N\log_2 N)$.

Combining the original heap build, which is O(N), and the sorting loop, we can see that HeapSort requires $O(N\log_2 N)$ data swaps or comparisons. Note that, unlike QuickSort, HeapSort's efficiency is not affected by the initial order of the elements.

Other Efficiency Considerations

When N Is Small

As we have stressed throughout this chapter, our analysis of efficiency has been based on the number of comparisons made by a sorting algorithm. This number gives us a rough estimate of the computation time involved. The other activities that accompany the comparison (swapping, keeping track of Boolean flags, and so forth) contribute to the "constant of proportionality" of the algorithm.

In comparing Big-O evaluations, we ignored constants and smaller-order terms, for we wanted to know how the algorithm would perform for large values of N. In general, an $O(N^2)$ sort requires few extra activities in addition to the comparisons, so its constant of proportionality is fairly small. On the other hand, an $O(Nlog_2N)$ sort may be more complex, with more overhead and thus a larger constant of proportionality. This situation may cause anomalies in the relative performances of the algorithms when the value of N is small. In this case N^2 is not much greater than $Nlog_2N$, and the constants may dominate instead, causing an $O(N^2)$ sort to run faster than an $O(Nlog_2N)$ sort.

Eliminating Calls to Procedures and Functions

We mentioned at the beginning of this chapter that it may be desirable, for efficiency considerations, to streamline the code as much as possible, even at the expense of readability. For instance, we have consistently written

```
Swap (X,Y)
```

instead of the in-line expansion:

```
Temp := X;
X := Y;
Y := Temp
```

Similarly, in SelectionSort, we coded the operation to find the minimum element as a nested function, Mindex, and in BubbleSort, we coded a nested procedure BubbleUp. Coding such operations as procedures and functions made the code simpler to write and to understand, avoiding a more complicated nested loop structure.

Though the procedure and function calls are clearer, in the actual coding it may be better to use the in-line expansion. Procedure and function calls require extra overhead that you may prefer to avoid in a sort, where these routines are called within a loop.

The recursive sorting procedures, MergeSort and QuickSort, have a similar situation: They require the extra overhead involved in executing the recursive calls. You may want to avoid this overhead by coding nonrecursive versions of these procedures, as we did for HeapSort.

Programmer Time

If the recursive calls are less efficient, why would anyone ever decide to use a recursive version of a sort? The decision involves a choice between types of efficiency. Up until now, we have only been concerned with minimizing computer time. While computers are becoming faster and cheaper, however, it is not at all clear that computer *programmers* are following that trend. Therefore in some situations programmer time may be an important consideration in choosing a sort algorithm and its implementation. In this respect, the recursive version of QuickSort is more desirable than its nonrecursive counterpart, which requires the programmer to simulate the recursion explicitly.

Space Considerations

Another efficiency consideration is the amount of memory space required. In general, memory space is not a very important factor in choosing a sorting algorithm. We only looked at one sort, MergeSort, in which space would be a serious consideration. The usual time versus space trade-off applies to sorts—more space often means less time, and vice versa.

Because processing time is the factor that applies most often to sorting algorithms, we have considered it in detail here. Of course, as in any application, the programmer must determine goals and requirements before selecting an algorithm and starting to code.

More About Sorting in General

Keys

In our descriptions of the various sorts, we showed examples of sorting arrays of integers. In reality one is more likely to be sorting arrays of records that contain several fields of information, ordering the records according to a **key** field. Each record must contain some unique identifying key, such as an IDNumber field. In addition, a record may contain secondary keys, which may or may not be unique. For instance, a student record may contain the following fields:

StudentNumber   *Primary unique key*
Name
Address   }   *Secondary keys*
Major

If the data elements are only single integers, it doesn't matter whether the original order of duplicate values is kept. As you will see, however, preserving the original order of records with identical key values may be desirable. If a sort preserves this order, it is said to be **stable**. (Of the sorts we discussed in this chapter, HeapSort is the only one that is inherently unstable. Equal values can work their way up different paths in the heap, without consideration of their original order.)

Suppose that List is a list of personnel records with the following record declarations:

```
TYPE
   StringType  = PACKED ARRAY [1 .. 20] OF Char;

   AddressType = RECORD
      Street,
      City,
      State     : StringType;
      Zip       : Integer
   END;    (* AddressType *)

   PersonType = RECORD
      IDNum    : Integer;
      Name     : StringType;
      Address  : AddressType;
      Dept     : Integer;
      Salary   : Real
   END;    (* PersonType *)

   ListElementType = PersonType;
```

The list may normally be ordered by the unique key IDNum. For some purposes we might want to see a listing in order by name. In this case the sort key would be the Name field. To sort by city, we would use the Address.City field as a sort key. To sort by zip code, we would sort on the Address.Zip key.

If the sort is stable, we can get a listing by zip code, with the names in alphabetical order within each zip code, by sorting twice: the first time by name and the second time by zip code. A stable sort preserves the order of the records when there is a match on the key. The second sort, by zip code, will produce many such matches, but the alphabetical order imposed by the first sort will be preserved.

To get a listing by city, with the zip codes in order within each city and the names alphabetically ordered within each zip code, we would sort three times, on the following keys:

```
Name
Address.Zip
Address.City
```

The file would first be put into alphabetical order by name. The output from the first sort would be input to a sort on zip code. The output from this sort would be input to a sort on city name. If the sorting algorithms used were stable, the final sort would give us what we were looking for.

Sorting Pointers

Sorting large records using some kind of exchange sort may require a lot of computer time just to move sections of memory from one place to another every time we make a swap. This move time can be reduced by setting up an array of pointers to the records and then sorting the pointers instead of the actual records. This scheme is illustrated in Figure 11-17.

Figure 11-17
Sorting Arrays with
Pointers

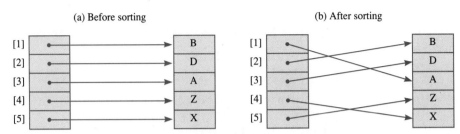

Note that after the sort the records are still in the same physical arrangement, but they may be accessed in order through the sorted array of pointers.

This scheme may be extended to allow us to keep a large array of data sorted on more than one key. For instance, with the declarations

```
TYPE
    EmployeeType = RECORD
        IDNum   : Integer;
        Name    : StringType;
        Salary  : Integer
    END;  (* EmployeeType *)

    ListElementType = EmployeeType;
```

the data in Figure 11-18 is physically stored according to the primary key, IDNum. The arrays NameOrd and SalOrd contain pointers (indexes) to the records in the large array, EmployeeData. In this way we can keep the array ordered with respect to the secondary keys, Name and Salary, as well.

Figure 11-18
Data Sorted on
More Than One Key

EmployeeData

[1]	15 JONES 20000
[2]	20 SMITH 40000
[3]	34 ABLE 29246
[4]	100 BAKER 20000
[5]	144 OWENS 6000

NameOrd

[1]	3
[2]	4
[3]	1
[4]	5
[5]	2

SalOrd

[1]	5
[2]	1
[3]	4
[4]	3
[5]	2

Summary

We have not attempted in this chapter to give every known sorting algorithm. We have presented a few of the popular sorts, of which many variations exist. It should be clear from this discussion that no single sort is best for all applications. The simpler, generally $O(N^2)$ sorts work as well, and sometimes better, for fairly small values of N. Because they are simple, these sorts require relatively little programmer time to write and maintain. As you add features to improve sorts, you also add to the complexity of the algorithms, increasing both the work required by the routines and the programmer time needed to maintain them.

Another consideration in choosing a sort algorithm is the order of the original data. If the data are already ordered (or almost ordered), ShortBubble will be $O(N)$, whereas some versions of a QuickSort will be $O(N^2)$.

As always, the first step in choosing an algorithm is to determine the goals of the particular application. This step will usually narrow down the options considerably. After that, knowledge of the strong and weak points of the various algorithms will assist you in making a choice.

The following table summarizes the comparison among the sorts discussed in this chapter, in terms of Big-O. So that you can see that there really is a difference between an $O(N^2)$ sort and an $O(N\log_2 N)$ sort, we ran a timed test. With a list of 1000 elements, we executed each of the sorts in this chapter, first on an array of mixed-up numbers, and then on an array of the numbers 1 through 1000 in order. Each sort was called by a test driver that read the system clock before and after the call to the sorting routine, and calculated the elapsed time in seconds. The results of the test, summarized in the first table on page 696, are just as you would expect.

Big-O Comparison of Sorting Algorithms

	Order of Magnitude		
Sort	*Best case*	*Average*	*Worst case*
SelectionSort	$O(N^2)$	$O(N^2)$	$O(N^2)$
BubbleSort	$O(N^2)$	$O(N^2)$	$O(N^2)$
ShortBubble	$O(N)$ data already sorted	$O(N^2)$	$O(N^2)$
MergeSort	$O(N \log_2 N)$	$O(N \log_2 N)$	$O(N \log_2 N)$
QuickSort	$O(N \log_2 N)$	$O(N \log_2 N)$	$O(N^2)$ depends on order/split
HeapSort	$O(N \log_2 N)$	$O(N \log_2 N)$	$O(N \log_2 N)$

Timed Comparison* of Sorting Procedures

Sort	Mixed-up	In-Order
SelectionSort	1.59	1.59
BubbleSort	3.52	1.59
ShortBubble	3.62	0.00
MergeSort	0.11	0.06
QuickSort	0.06	1.21
QuickSort2	0.05	0.44
HeapSort	0.16	0.17

*Time in seconds for sorting 1000 integers. Sorts and test driver were compiled under Turbo Pascal 5.5, and run on an IBM-compatible 386 (25MHz) computer.

Finally, so that you will appreciate the value of programmer time, the next table compares the size of the sorting procedures as coded in this chapter, measured in executable lines of code.

Source Line Count Comparison of Sorting Procedures

Sort	Lines of Code
Swap	9
SelectionSort	31
BubbleSort	26
ShortBubble	34
MergeSort	65
QuickSort	44
QuickSort2	43
HeapSort	42

■ *Exercises**

1. Show the contents of the array

43	7	10	23	18	4	19	5	66	14
[1]	[2]	[3]	[4]	[5]	[6]	[7]	[8]	[9]	[10]

after the fourth iteration of
(a) BubbleSort
(b) SelectionSort

*Questions with italicized numbers are answered in the back of the book.

2. (a) Show how the values in the array in Exercise 1 would have to be rearranged to satisfy the heap property.
   (b) Show how the heap would look with four values in place, after reheaping.

3. Show how the values in the array in Exercise 1 would be arranged immediately before the execution of Procedure Merge in the original (nonrecursive) call to MergeSort.

4. Given the array

26	24	3	17	25	24	13	60	47	1
[1]	[2]	[3]	[4]	[5]	[6]	[7]	[8]	[9]	[10]

tell which sorting algorithm would produce the following results after four iterations:

(a)

1	3	13	17	26	24	24	25	47	60
[1]	[2]	[3]	[4]	[5]	[6]	[7]	[8]	[9]	[10]

(b)

1	3	13	17	25	24	24	60	47	26
[1]	[2]	[3]	[4]	[5]	[6]	[7]	[8]	[9]	[10]

5. How many comparisons would be needed to sort an array containing 100 elements using ShortBubble
   (a) in the worst case?
   (b) in the best case?

6. A sorting procedure is called to sort a list of 100 integers that have been read from a file. If all 100 values are zero, what would the execution requirements (in terms of Big-O) be if the sort used was
   (a) QuickSort, with the first element used as the split value?
   (b) ShortBubble?
   (c) SelectionSort?
   (d) HeapSort?
   (e) MergeSort?

7. How many comparisons would be needed to sort an array containing 100 elements using SelectionSort if the original array values were already sorted?
   (a) 10,000
   (b) 9,900
   (c) 4,950
   (d) 99
   (e) None of the above

8. A merge sort is used to sort an array of 1000 test scores in descending order. Which of the following statements is true?
   (a) The sort will be fastest if the original test scores are ordered from smallest to largest.
   (b) The sort will be fastest if the original test scores are in completely random order.
   (c) The sort will be fastest if the original test scores are ordered from largest to smallest.
   (d) The sort will be the same, no matter what the order of the original elements.

9. A list is ordered from smallest to largest when a sort is called. Which sort would take the longest time to execute and which would take the shortest time?
   (a) HeapSort
   (b) ShortBubble
   (c) QuickSort (with the first element as the split value)
   (d) SelectionSort

10. (a) In what case(s), if any, is the bubble sort O(N)?
    (b) In what case(s), if any, is the selection sort O($\log_2 N$)?
    (c) In what case(s), if any, is QuickSort O(N^2)?

11. A very large array of elements is to be sorted. The program is to be run on a personal computer with limited memory. Which sort would be a better choice: HeapSort or MergeSort? Why?

12. Use the Three-Question Method to verify the MergeSort procedure.

13. True or False? Correct the False statements.
    (a) MergeSort requires more space to execute than HeapSort.
    (b) QuickSort (first version) is better for nearly sorted data than HeapSort.
    (c) The efficiency of HeapSort is not affected by the order of the elements on entrance to the procedure.

14. Which is true about QuickSort?
    (a) A recursive version executes faster than a nonrecursive version.
    (b) A recursive version has fewer lines of code than a nonrecursive version.
    (c) A nonrecursive version takes more space on the run-time stack than a recursive version.
    (d) It can only be programmed as a recursive procedure.

15. What is meant by the statement that programmer time is an efficiency consideration? Give an example of a situation in which programmer time is used to justify the choice of an algorithm, possibly at the expense of other efficiency considerations.

16. Identify one or more correct answers: Sorting an array of pointers to list elements, rather than sorting the elements themselves, is a good idea when
    (a) the number of elements is very large.
    (b) the individual elements are large in size.
    (c) the sort is recursive.
    (d) there are multiple keys on which to sort the elements.

17. The following statement is found in a stable sort:

```
IF Data[I].Key < Data[J].Key
  THEN Swap (Data[I], Data[J]);
```

Tell whether each of the following modifications will also result in a stable sort:
```
(a) IF Data[I].Key < Data[J].Key
      THEN Swap (Data[J], Data[I]);
```

(b) IF Data[I].Key <= Data[J].Key
        THEN Swap (Data[I], Data[J]);
(c) IF Data[I].Key <= Data[J].Key
        THEN Swap (Data[J], Data[I]);
(d) IF Data[I].Key < Data[J].Key
        THEN Swap (Data[I].Key, Data[J].Key);

18. Give arguments for and against using procedures (such as Swap) to encapsulate frequently used code in a sorting procedure.

19. Write a version of the bubble sort algorithm that sorts a list of integers in descending order. Write the procedure so that it is very efficient for lists whose elements are "almost" sorted from largest to smallest.

20. The *insertion sort* uses the following algorithm: Each successive element in the array to be sorted is put into its proper place relative to the other (already sorted) elements.

InsertSort

FOR Index : = 2 TO List.Length DO
    Put List.Info[Index] in its proper place, relative
    to List.Info[1] .. List.Info[Index − 1].

(a) Write procedure InsertSort.
(b) Describe this algorithm in terms of Big-O.
(c) How does the order of the original data affect the order of the algorithm, in terms of Big-O?

21. In the *shaker sort* version of the bubble sort, the smallest element bubbles to the top during the first iteration, but during the second iteration the largest element bubbles to the bottom. The sort alternates bubbling up and bubbling down until the list is sorted.
(a) Modify BubbleSort to create ShakerSort.
(b) Describe this algorithm in terms of Big-O.

22. (a) Write a version of SelectionSort that does not make any procedure calls.
(b) Name an advantage and disadvantage to using this version of SelectSort.

23. Write a recursive version of SelectionSort.

24. Write a procedure SortLinked that sorts the elements in an unordered linked list. (Use the declarations of a linear singly linked list from Chapter 6.)

25. QuickSort works best for large randomly ordered lists, but when the sublists become small, it might be more efficient to call another sort. Modify QuickSort to make the recursive calls only when the number of elements to be sorted on that call is greater than a constant called Limit; otherwise, it calls SelectionSort.

Use the following declarations for Exercises 26–29.

```
TYPE
    SuitType = (Club, Diamond, Heart, Spade);
    NumberType = (Two, Three, Four, Five, Six, Seven,
        Eight, Nine, Ten, Jack, Queen, King, Ace);
```

```
CardType = RECORD
  Suit : SuitType;
  Number : NumberType
END;  (* CardType *)

DeckType = ARRAY [1 .. 52] OF CardType;

RelationType = (Smaller, Equal, Greater);

SortFieldType = (SuitField, NumField);
```

26. Write a function, CompareCards, that inputs two cards of CardType and a SortField, and returns a value of RelationType, after comparing the two cards using the specified field.

27. Write a procedure, SortCards, that inputs an unsorted deck of cards (DeckType) and a SortField (SortFieldType), and outputs the deck of cards, sorted according to the specified field. (Use function CompareCards to compare two cards.) Your sort must be *stable*.

28. Write a procedure, SortDeck, that sorts a deck of cards. The cards should be sorted by suit, and within each suit, by number. You may use procedure SortCards.

29. Why does the sorting algorithm in SortCards need to be stable?

Use the following declarations for Exercises 30–32.

```
CONST
  MaxStudents = 1000;

TYPE
  StringType  = PACKED ARRAY [1 .. 20] OF Char;
  ClassType   = (Freshman, Sophomore, Junior, Senior);
  IndexType   = 1 .. MaxStudents;

  NameType    = RECORD
    LastName  : StringType;
    FirstName : StringType;
    MidInitial: Char
  END;   (* NameType *)

  StudentType   = RECORD
    StudentName : NameType;
    StudentID   : Integer;
    GPA         : Real;
    HoursEarned : Integer;
    Class       : ClassType;
    ZipCode     : Integer
  END;   (* StudentType *)

  RecArrayType = ARRAY[IndexType] OF StudentType;

  StudentList  = RECORD
    NumStudents: Integer;
    Students   : RecArrayType
  END;   (* StudentList *)
```

The array of student records is sorted according to the StudentID field as the primary key. For some types of processing, we need to order the student data according to a secondary key, StudentName. To save space, we decide to keep an array of index pointers ordered on the name field.

30. Values of NameType cannot be compared directly, because this type is a record. Write a function CompareNames that can be used to perform the comparison. It should take two "names" (records of NameType) and return one of the following values: LessThan, EqualTo, GreaterThan.

31. Write a procedure to create the list of pointers sorted on the StudentName field of the records. Use Function CompareNames to do the comparison.

32. Write a procedure to print out the names and IDs of all the students, ordered alphabetically by name, in this format:

ID   LastName, FirstName

33. Sooey County is about to have its annual Big Pig Contest. Because the sheriff's son, Wilbur, is majoring in computer science, the county hires him to computerize the Big Pig judging. Each pig's name (string) and weight (integer) is to be read in from the keyboard. The county expects 500 entries this year.

The output needed is a listing of the ten heaviest pigs, ordered from biggest to smallest. Because Wilbur has just learned some sorting methods in school, he feels up to the task of writing this "pork-gram." He writes a program to read in all the entries into an array of records, then uses a selection sort to put the whole array in order according to the PigWeight field. He then prints the 10 largest values from the array.

Can you think of a more efficient way to write this program? If so, write the algorithm.

34. State University needs a listing of the overall SAT percentiles of the 14,226 students it has accepted in the past year. The data is in a text file, with one line per student. That line contains the student's ID number, SAT overall percentile, math score, English score, and high school grade point average. (There is at least one blank between each two fields.) The output needed is a listing of all the percentile scores, one per line, ordered from highest to lowest. Duplicates should be printed. Write an O(N) procedure to produce the listing.

Searching

C H A P T E R

12

GOALS

- To be able to demonstrate the steps in the algorithms and to implement the following search algorithms:
  - sequential search of unordered list
  - sequential search of ordered list
  - binary search
- To be able to define the following terms:
  - hashing
  - rehashing
  - collisions
  - linear probing
  - clustering
- To be able to design and implement an appropriate hashing function for an application.
- To be able to design and implement a collision-resolution algorithm for a hash table.
- To be able to discuss the efficiency considerations for the searching and hashing algorithms, in terms of Big-O.

As we discussed in Chapter 3, for each particular structure used to hold data, the functions that allow access to elements in the structure must be defined. In some cases access is limited to the elements in specific positions in the structure, such as the top element in a stack or the front element in a queue. Often, when data is stored in a list or a table, we want to be able to access any element in the structure.

Sometimes the retrieval of a specified element can be performed directly. For instance, the fifth element of the list stored *sequentially* in an array called List is found in List[5]. Often, however, you want to access an element according to some key value. For instance, if a list contains student records, you may want to find the record of the student named Suzy Brown (the key field is StudentName) or the record of the student whose ID number is 203557 (the key field is IDNum). In cases like these, some kind of *searching technique* is needed to allow retrieval of the desired record. We will describe several algorithms for searching a list for the element with a specified key value. The list is ordered sequentially in an array, as described in Chapter 6. The declarations of this list type are repeated here:

```
CONST
   MaxElements = 100;   (* maximum number of elements in list *)
TYPE
   KeyType = Integer;      (* or any type that can be compared *)
                          (* using <, >, <=, >=, <>, and =     *)
   ListElementType = RECORD           (* the user's data type *)
      Key    : KeyType;      (* field on which list is ordered *)
      .
      .                   (* other fields in user's data as needed *)
      .
   END; (* ListElementType *)
   IndexType = 0 .. MaxElements;
   ArrayType = ARRAY [1 .. MaxElements] OF ListElementType;

   ListType = RECORD
      Length : IndexType;   (* number of elements in list *)
      Info   : ArrayType    (* array of list elements     *)
   END; (* ListType *)
```

For each of the search techniques we discuss, we will write a procedure that inputs a list and a key value to search for, and outputs the location of the element with the desired key and a Boolean flag Found, indicating whether the key was in the list. Since the search procedures return an index into the array, they are not seen by the user of the List ADT. These procedures, like the FindElement procedure in Chapter 6, are used by operations like RetrieveElement and ModifyElement to find the element to process.

Sequential Searching

We cannot discuss efficient ways to find an element in a list without considering how the elements were inserted into the list. Therefore, our discussion of search algorithms will be related to the issue of the List's InsertElement operation. Suppose that we want to insert elements as quickly as possible, and we are not as concerned how long it will take to find them. We could use the following insertion algorithm:

InsertElement

Increment List.Length
Put element in List.Info[List.Length]

This is an O(1) insertion algorithm. The resulting list is ordered according the time of insertion, not according to key value.

To search this list for the element with a given key, we would use a simple *sequential search*. Beginning with the first element in the list, we search for the desired element by examining each subsequent record's key until either the search is successful or the list is exhausted:

Sequential Search (unordered data)

Access the first element in the list
Found ← False

WHILE more elements in list AND NOT Found DO
   IF key of this element = KeyVal
      THEN Found ← True
      ELSE Access next element in list

Using the parameter Location to traverse this list, we can code this algorithm as the following procedure:

```
PROCEDURE SequentialSearch
  (VAR List     : ListType;
   KeyVal       : KeyType;
   VAR Location : Integer;
   VAR Found    : Boolean);

  (* Locate the record whose Key field contains the value  *)
  (* KeyVal and, if Found, return the index of the element  *)
  (* in Location; otherwise Found is False and Location is  *)
  (* undefined.                                             *)

  (* NOTE: The List is passed as a VAR parameter for space  *)
  (* considerations, and is not modified by this procedure. *)
```

```
BEGIN   (* SequentialSearch *)
  WITH List DO
    BEGIN

      (* Initialize for search. *)
      Location := 1;
      Found    := False;

      (* Search until the element is found or the array is *)
      (* exhausted. If the element is found, Location will *)
      (* indicate its index in the Info array.             *)
      (* Loop Invariant: 1 <= Location <= Length + 1 AND    *)
      (* KeyVal is not in Info[1] .. Info[Location - 1].    *)
      WHILE NOT Found AND (Location <= Length) DO
        IF Info[Location].Key = KeyVal
          THEN Found := True
          ELSE Location := Location + 1
    END (* WITH *)
END; (* SequentialSearch *)
```

Based on the number of comparisons, it should be obvious that this search is O(N), where N represents the number of elements. In the worst case, in which we are looking for the last element in the list or for a nonexistent element, we will have to make N key comparisons. On the average, assuming that there is an equal probability of searching for any item in the list, we will make N/2 comparisons for a successful search; that is, on the average we will have to search half of the list.

High-Probability Ordering

The assumption of equal probability for every element in the list is not always valid. Sometimes certain list elements are in much greater demand than others. This observation suggests a way to improve the search: Put the most-often-desired elements at the beginning of the list. Using this scheme, you are more likely to make a hit in the first few tries, and rarely will you have to search the whole table.

If the elements in the list are not static or if you cannot predict their relative demand, you need some scheme to keep the most frequently used elements at the front of the list. One way to accomplish this goal is to move each element accessed to the front of the list. Of course, there is no guarantee that this element will later be frequently used. If the element is not retrieved again, however, it will drift toward the end of the list as other elements are moved to the front. This scheme is easy to implement for linked lists, requiring only a couple of pointer changes, but it is less desirable for lists kept sequentially in arrays, because of the need to move all the other elements down to make room at the front.

A second approach, which causes elements to move toward the front of the list gradually, is appropriate for either linked or sequential list representations. As each element is accessed, it is swapped with the element that precedes it. Over many list retrievals, the most frequently desired elements will tend to be grouped at the front of the list. To implement this approach, we only need to add the following statement at the end of the SequentialSearch procedure:

```
(* If found, move this element up in the list. *)
IF Found AND (Location > 1)
  THEN Swap (Info[Location], Info[Location - 1])
```

In the original version of SequentialSearch, we passed List as a VAR parameter for space reasons—we did not want to make a copy of a potentially large structure. In this version, however, List becomes a real VAR parameter, as it is actually changed by the search operation. This change should be documented; it is an unexpected side effect of searching the list.

Keeping the most active elements at the front of the list will not affect the worst case; if the search value is the last element or is not in the list, the search will still take N comparisons. This is still an O(N) search. The *average* performance on successful searches should be better, however. Both of these algorithms depend on the assumption that some elements in the list are used much more often than others. If this assumption is not applicable, a different ordering strategy is needed to improve the efficiency of the search technique.

Key Ordering

If a list is ordered according to the key value, we can write more efficient search routines. To support a key-ordered list, we must either insert the elements in order, as the InsertElement procedure does in Chapter 6, or we must sort the list before searching it, as we discussed in Chapter 11. (Note that inserting the elements in order is an $O(N^2)$ process; as each insertion is O(N). If we insert each element in the next free slot, and then sort the list with a "good" sort, the process is $O(N\log_2 N)$.)

If the list is sorted, a sequential search no longer needs to search the whole list to discover that a element does not exist. It only needs to search until it has passed the element's logical place in the list—that is, until an element with a larger key value is encountered. The sequential and linked versions of the FindElement procedure in Chapter 6 implement this search technique. A simple version is shown below:

```
PROCEDURE SequentialSearch2
    (VAR List      : ListType;
     KeyVal        : KeyType;
     VAR Location  : Integer;
     VAR Found     : Boolean);

  (* Locate the record whose Key field contains the value  *)
  (* KeyVal and, if Found, return the index of the element *)
  (* in Location; otherwise Found is False and Location is *)
  (* undefined. The list is ordered according to Key field.*)
  (* NOTE: List is passed as a VAR parameter for space     *)
  (* considerations, and is not modified by this procedure.*)
```

```
VAR
  MoreToSearch : Boolean;
BEGIN (* SequentialSearch2 *)

  WITH List DO
    BEGIN
      (* Initialize for search. *)
      Location := 1;                (* start of list *)
      MoreToSearch := True;         (* not done yet  *)

      (* Loop Invariant: 1 <= Location <= Length + 1 AND *)
      (* KeyVal is not in Info[1] .. Info[Location - 1]. *)
      WHILE MoreToSearch AND (Location <= Length) DO
        IF Info[Location].Key < KeyVal
          THEN Location := Location + 1
          ELSE MoreToSearch := False;

      (* Set Found output parameter. *)
      IF Location > Length
        THEN Found := False
        ELSE Found := (Info[Location].Key = KeyVal)
    END (* WITH *)
END; (* SequentialSearch2 *)
```

The advantage of sequentially searching an ordered list is the ability to stop searching before the list is exhausted if the element does not exist. Again, the search is O(N)—the worst case, searching for the largest element, still requires N comparisons. The average number of comparisons for an unsuccessful search is now N/2, however, instead of a guaranteed N.

The advantage of sequential searching is its simplicity. The disadvantage is its performance: In the worst case you will have to make N comparisons. If the list is sorted and stored in an array, however, you can improve the search time to a worst case of $O(\log_2 N)$ by using a binary search. However, efficiency is improved at the expense of simplicity.

Binary Searching

We know of a way to improve searching from O(N) to $O(\log_2 N)$: If the data elements are ordered and stored sequentially in an array, we can use a *binary* search. The binary search algorithm improves the search efficiency by limiting the search to the area where the element might be. The binary search algorithm takes a divide-and-conquer approach: It continually pares down the area to be searched until either the element is found or the search area is gone (the element is not in the list). We developed the BinarySearch procedure in Chapter 2, and converted it to a recursive procedure in Chapter 8.

The binary search, however, is not guaranteed to be faster for searching very small lists. Notice that even though the binary search generally requires fewer comparisons, each comparison involves more computation. When N is very small, this extra work (the constants and smaller terms that we ignore in determining the Big-O approximation) may dominate. Although fewer comparisons are required, each involves more processing. For instance, in one assembly language program, the sequential search required five time units per comparison, whereas the binary search took 35. For a list size of 16 elements, therefore, the worst-case sequential search would require 5 * 16 = 80 time units. The worst-case binary search would only require four comparisons, but at 35 time units each, the comparisons would take 140 time units. In cases where the number of elements in the list is small, a sequential search is certainly adequate and sometimes faster than a binary search.

As the number of elements increases, however, the disparity between the sequential search and the binary search grows very quickly. Look back at Figure 2-8 to compare the rates of growth for the two algorithms.

How is this disparity reflected in actual executions of the sequential and binary search procedures? The table below shows the results of timed tests that compared the performance of SequentialSearch2 and the BinarySearch (iterative version) from Chapter 2. Various sizes of arrays (as listed in the first column of the table) were loaded with integer values, and the search procedures were called to search for every value in the list. For instance, in the first test, an array of 1000 slots was loaded with the values 1 to 1000. The sequential search procedure was invoked repeatedly to search for list elements:

```
FOR Value := 1 TO List.Length DO
  SequentialSearch2 (List, Value, Location, Found);
```

The elapsed time was calculated; then the process was repeated for the binary search. The results columns show two sets of values for each search procedure: the total elapsed time for the set of searches and the average time per call. As you can see in the table, the average time to process each call to SequentialSearch2 doubles as the number of elements doubles; this result is what we would expect to see from an O(N) search. The average time to complete each call to the BinarySearch procedure rises much more slowly in comparison, consistent with what we would expect from an $O(\log_2 N)$ search.

Comparing the Sequential and Binary Search Procedures

Number of Elements in List	Sequential Search		Binary Search	
	Elapsed seconds	msec per call	Elapsed seconds	msec per call
1000	2.30	2.300	0.11	0.110
2000	9.17	4.585	0.11	0.055
4000	36.75	9.188	0.27	0.068
8000	146.81	18.351	0.66	0.082

Note that the binary search discussed here is appropriate only for lists stored in a sequential array representation. After all, how can you efficiently find the midpoint of a linked list? However, you already know of a structure that allows you to perform a binary search on a linked data representation, the binary search tree. The operations used to search a binary tree are discussed in Chapter 9.

Hashing

So far, we have succeeded in paring down our O(N) search to O(log$_2$N) by keeping the list ordered sequentially with respect to the value of the key field—that is, the key in the first element is less than (or equal to) the key in the second element, which is less than the key in the third, and so on. Can we do better than that? Is it possible to design a search of O(1)—that is, one that takes the same search time to find any element in the list?

In theory, that is not an impossible dream. In Program AdManager (Chapter 6 and 7 application sections), we designed a CommandTable that supported O(1) access of random elements. The user's input was a single character that represented a command: 'A' to AcceptAd, 'B' to BillAdvertisers, etc. The program needed to convert this single-letter form of the command to a value of the enumerated type CommandType. We implemented the CommandTable with the following declarations:

```
TYPE
  CommandTableType = ARRAY ['A'..'Z'] OF CommandType;
```

and stored the appropriate CommandType value in the array slot whose index matched the command's single-letter "key"—in CommandTable['A'] we stored AcceptAd, in CommandTable['B'] we stored BillAdvertisers, and so on. To retrieve the correct CommandType value, given the single-letter key ComLetter, we perform an O(1) search operation: The value that we want is in CommandTable[ComLetter].

This scheme worked well for the CommandTable, where we had complete control over the values in the list. Can we use a similar approach to help us implement an O(1) "search" when the elements are inserted dynamically? To answer this question, let's look at an example, a list of employees of a fairly small company. Each of the 100 employees has an ID number in the range 1 to 100, and we want to access the employee records by the key IDNum. If we store the elements in an array that is indexed from 1 to 100, we can directly access any employee's record through the array index. There is a one-to-one correspondence between the element keys and the array index; in effect the array index functions as the key field of each element.

In practice, however, this perfect relationship between the key value and the address of an element is not easy to establish or maintain. Consider a similar small company that uses its employees' five-digit ID number as the primary key field. Now the range of key values is from 00000 to 99999. Obviously it is impractical to set up an array of 100,000 elements, of which only 100 will be needed, just to make sure that each employee's element will be in a perfectly unique and predictable location.

What if we keep the array size down to the size that we actually need (an array of 100 elements) and just use the last two digits of the key field to identify each employee? For instance, the element of employee 53374 will be in EmployeeList[74], and the element of employee 81235 will be in EmployeeList[35]. Note that the elements will not be ordered according to the *value* of the key field as they were in our earlier discussion; the position of Employee 81235's record precedes that of Employee 53374 in the array, even though the value of its key is larger. Instead, the elements are ordered with respect to some *function* of the key value.

This function is called a **hash function**, and the search technique we are using is called **hashing**. In the case of the employee list above, the hash function is Key MOD 100. The key (IdNum) is divided by 100, and the remainder is used as an index into the array of employee elements, as illustrated in Figure 12-1. This function assumes that the array is indexed from 0 to 99 (MaxElements = 100). The Pascal function to perform the conversion of IdNum values to indexes is very simple:

```
FUNCTION Hash
  (IdNum : Integer) : IndexType;

  (* Turns unique 5-digit IdNumbers into 2-digit index *)
  (* values for an array that is indexed from 0 to 99. *)
BEGIN (* Hash *)
  Hash := IdNum MOD 100
END;  (* Hash *)
```

This hash function has two uses. As we have seen, it is used as a method of accessing the element. The output of the hash function tells us where to look for a particular element. On page 712 is a simple version of Procedure RetrieveElement, which assumes that the element is in the list.

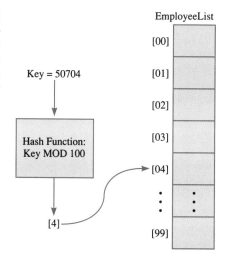

Figure 12-1
Using a Hash Function to Determine the Location of the Element in an Array

```
PROCEDURE RetrieveElement
  (VAR List      : ListType;
   KeyVal        : KeyType;
   VAR Element   : ListElementType);

  (* Find element in List with KeyVal, return copy in Element. *)
  (* Assumes that the element is in the list.                  *)
VAR
  Location : IndexType;

BEGIN (* RetrieveElement *)

  (* Use the hash function to find the element with KeyVal. *)
  Location := Hash (KeyVal);

  (* Access the element through the hashed key. *)
  Element := List.Info[Location]

END;   (* RetrieveElement *)
```

There is a second use of the hash function: It determines where in the array to *store* the element. If the employee list elements were inserted into the list using the InsertElement operation from Chapter 6—into sequential array slots with their relative order determined by the Key field—we could not use the hash function to retrieve them. We would have to create a version of the InsertElement operation that puts each new element into the correct slot *according to the hash function*. Here is a simple version of Insert-Element, which assumes that the array slot at the index returned from the hash function is not in use:

```
PROCEDURE InsertElement
  (VAR List    : ListType;
   NewElement : ListElementType);

  (* Insert NewElement in List, in slot indicated by Hash. *)
  (* Assumes that this slot is free.                       *)
VAR
  Location : IndexType;

BEGIN (* InsertElement *)

  (* Find the insertion location, using the hash function. *)
  Location := Hash (NewElement.Key);

  (* Insert the new element into this array slot. *)
  List.Info[Location] := NewElement;

  List.Length := List.Length + 1

END;   (* InsertElement *)
```

Figure 12-2(a) shows an array whose elements—records for the employees with the Key values (unique ID numbers) 12704, 31300, 49001, 52202, and 65606—were added using the InsertElement procedure above. Note that Procedure InsertElement does not fill the array positions sequentially. Since we have not yet inserted any elements whose

Figure 12-2
Comparing Hashed
and Sequential
Lists of Identical
Elements

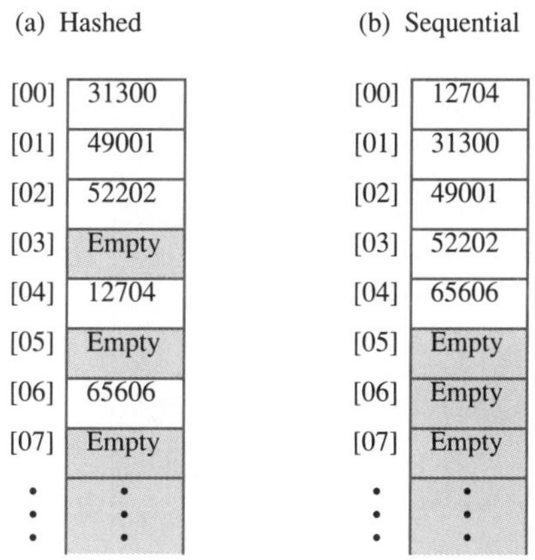

(a) Hashed

[00]	31300
[01]	49001
[02]	52202
[03]	Empty
[04]	12704
[05]	Empty
[06]	65606
[07]	Empty

(b) Sequential

[00]	12704
[01]	31300
[02]	49001
[03]	52202
[04]	65606
[05]	Empty
[06]	Empty
[07]	Empty

keys produce the hash values 3 and 5, the array slots [3] and [5] are logically "empty." This is different from the approach we used in Chapter 6 to create a sequential list. In Figure 12-2(b), the same employee records have been inserted into a sequential list using the InsertElement operation from Chapter 6. Note that, unless the hash function was used to determine where to insert an element, the hash function is *useless* for finding the element.

Collisions

By now you are probably objecting to this scheme on the grounds that it does not guarantee unique addresses. IdNum 01234 and IdNum 91234 both "hash" to the same address: List.Info[34]. The problem of avoiding these **collisions** is the biggest challenge in designing a good hash function. A good hash function *minimizes collisions* by spreading the elements uniformly throughout the array. We say "minimizes collisions," for it is extremely difficult to avoid them completely.

Assuming that there will be some collisions, where do you store the elements that produce them? We will briefly describe several popular collision-handling algorithms in the next sections. Note that the scheme that is used to find the place to store an element determines the method subsequently used to retrieve it.

Linear Probing

A simple approach to resolving collisions is to store the colliding element in the next available space. This technique is known as **linear probing**. In the situation in Figure 12-3, we want to add the employee element with the key IdNum 77003. The hash function returns the Location (index) [03]. But there is already an element stored in this array slot, the record for Employee 50003. We increment Location to [04] and examine the next array slot. EmployeeList[4] is also in use, so we increment the index again. This time we find a slot that is free, so we store the new element in EmployeeList[5].

What happens if the key hashes to the last index in the array and that space is in use? We can consider the array as a circular structure and continue looking for an empty slot at the beginning of the array.

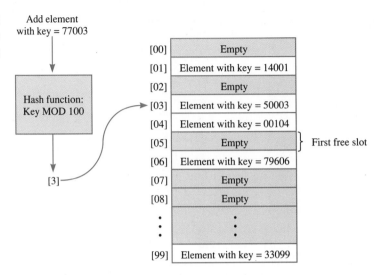

Figure 12-3
Handling Collisions with Linear Probing

How do we know whether an array slot is "free"? We can initialize all of the array slots to contain a special EmptyKey value in the CreateList operation. This value is selected much as we select values for header or trailer nodes in a list—it must be syntactically legal, but semantically illegal. For instance, if all employees have positive integer IdNum keys, we can use −1 as the key value of an "empty" slot. Now it is easy to tell if the slot is free.

Here is a version of InsertElement that uses linear probing to find a place to store a new element. It assumes that there is room in the array for another element; that is, a check has been made for FullList before this procedure was called. (We have retained the Length field of ListType. Even if it does not tell us where the "end" of the list is, it is still useful in determining if the list is full.)

```
PROCEDURE InsertElement
  (VAR List    : ListType;
   NewElement : ListElementType);

  (* Insert NewElement into the list, using Function Hash  *)
  (* to determine the insertion location. If the index     *)
  (* supplied by the hash function indicates a slot that   *)
  (* is not free, linear probing is used to find           *)
  (* the next free slot. Assumes that list is not full.    *)

VAR
  Location  : IndexType;  (* returned from Hash function  *)

BEGIN (* InsertElement *)

  WITH List DO
    BEGIN

      (* Find insertion place, using Hash function. *)
      Location := Hash (NewElement.Key);
```

```
    (* Search for a place to insert NewValue. *)
    WHILE Info[Location].Key <> EmptyKey DO
      Location := (Location + 1) MOD MaxElements;

    (* Insert the new element into this array slot. *)
    Info[Location] := NewElement;
    Length := Length + 1

  END (* WITH *)
END;  (* InsertElement *)
```

To search for an element using this collision-handling technique, we perform the hash function on the key, then compare the desired key to the actual key in the element at the designated location. If the keys do not match, we use linear probing, beginning at the next slot in the array. Following is a version of the RetrieveElement operation that uses this approach. If the element is not found in the list, the output parameter Found is False, and Element is undefined:

```
PROCEDURE RetrieveElement
  (VAR List      : ListType;
   KeyVal        : KeyType;
   VAR Element   : ListElementType;
   VAR Found     : Boolean);

  (* Find element in List with KeyVal, return copy in Element. *)
  (* Uses linear probing to resolve collisions                 *)
VAR
  Location : IndexType;
  StartLoc : IndexType;
  MoreToSearch : Boolean;

BEGIN (* RetrieveElement *)

  WITH List DO
    BEGIN

      (* Find likely Location using Hash function. *)
      StartLoc := Hash (KeyVal);

      (* Initialize for search. *)
      Location := StartLoc;
      MoreToSearch := True;

      (* Search for element with KeyVal. Stop searching when *)
      (* KeyVal or a free slot found, or when all slots in   *)
      (* the array have been searched.                       *)
      REPEAT
        IF (Info[Location].Key = KeyVal) OR
           (Info[Location].Key = EmptyKey)
          THEN MoreToSearch := False
          ELSE Location := (Location + 1) MOD MaxElements
      UNTIL (Location = StartLoc) OR NOT MoreToSearch;
```

```
                    (* Set output parameters. *)
                    Found    := (Info[Location].Key = KeyVal);
                    Element := Info[Location]
              END (* WITH *)
        END;  (* RetrieveElement *)
```

We have discussed the insertion and retrieval of elements in a hash table, but we have not yet mentioned how to delete an element from the table. If we did not need to concern ourselves with collisions, the deletion algorithm would be simple:

DeleteElement

Location ← Hash (DeleteVal)
Info[Location].Key ← EmptyKey

Collisions, however, complicate the matter. We can find the element using the same search approach as we used for RetrieveElement. But when we locate the element in the hash table, we cannot merely set its key value to EmptyKey. A review of the RetrieveElement procedure above shows the problem: In the REPEAT loop, the detection of an EmptyKey value sets MoreToSearch to False. Setting the key value of a deleted record to EmptyKey may cause us to terminate a subsequent search prematurely.

Let's look at an example. In Figure 12-4, suppose we delete the element with the key 77003 by setting the key field of array slot [05] to EmptyKey. A subsequent search for the element with the key 42504 would begin at the hash address [04]. The record in this slot is not the one we are looking for, so we increment the hash address to [5]. This slot, which formerly was occupied by the record that we deleted, now contains EmptyKey, so we terminate the search. We haven't really finished searching, however—the record that we are looking for is in the next slot.

One solution to this problem is to create another special key value, DeleteKey, to use in place of EmptyKey in slots that were occupied by deleted records. We would

Figure 12-4
A Hash Table with Linear Probing

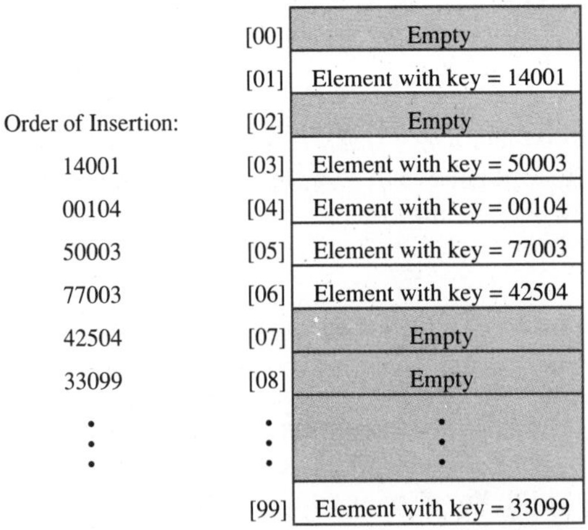

Order of Insertion:

14001
00104
50003
77003
42504
33099

[00]	Empty
[01]	Element with key = 14001
[02]	Empty
[03]	Element with key = 50003
[04]	Element with key = 00104
[05]	Element with key = 77003
[06]	Element with key = 42504
[07]	Empty
[08]	Empty
⋮	⋮
[99]	Element with key = 33099

need to modify both the insertion and retrieval operations to process slots with this key value correctly.

This solution corrects the search problem, but generates another: After many deletions, the search "path" to a record may travel through many array slots that contain DeleteKey. This may cause the efficiency of retrieving an element to deteriorate. These problems illustrate that hash tables, in the forms that we have studied thus far, are not the most effective data structure for implementing tables whose elements may be deleted.

Clustering

One problem with linear probing is that it results in a situation called **clustering**. A good hash function results in a uniform distribution of indexes throughout the array's index range. Initially, therefore, records are inserted throughout the array, each slot equally likely to be filled. Over time, however, after a number of collisions have been resolved, the distribution of records in the array becomes less and less uniform. The records tend to cluster together, as multiple keys begin to compete for a single address.

Consider the hash table in Figure 12-4. Only a record whose key produces the hash address 8 would be inserted into array slot [08]. However, any records with keys that produce the hash addresses 3, 4, 5, 6, or 7 would be inserted into array slot [07]. That is, array slot [07] is five times as likely as array slot [08] to be filled. Clustering results in inconsistent efficiency of insertion and retrieval operations.

Rehashing

The technique of linear probing discussed above is an example of collision resolution by **rehashing**: If the hash function produces a collision, the hash address is used as the input to a *rehash function* to compute a new address. In the previous section, we added 1 to the hash address to create a new hash address; that is, we used the rehash function:

(HashAddress + 1) MOD 100.

For rehashing with linear probing, you can use any function

(HashAddress + *constant*) MOD *array-size*

as long as *constant* and *array-size* are relatively prime—that is, if the largest number that divides both of them evenly is 1. For instance, given the 100-slot array in Figure 12-5, we might use the constant 3 in the rehash function:

(HashAddress + 3) MOD 100.

(Though 100 is not a prime number, 3 and 100 are relatively prime; they have no common factor larger than 1.)

Suppose that we want to add a record with the key 14001 to the hash table in Figure 12-5. The original hash function (Key MOD 100) returns the hash address [01], but this array slot is in use; it contains the record with the key 44001. To determine the next array slot to try, we apply the rehash function using the results of the first hash

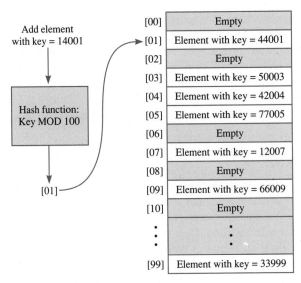

Figure 12-5
Handling Collisions
with Rehashing

function as input: $(1 + 3)$ MOD $100 = 4$. The array slot at index [04] is also in use, so we reapply the rehash function until we get an available slot. Each time, we use the address computed from the previous rehash as input to the rehash function. The second rehash gives us $(4 + 3)$ MOD $100 = 07$; this slot is in use. The third rehash gives us $(7 + 3)$ MOD $100 = 10$; the array slot at index [10] is free, so NewElement is inserted there.

To understand why the constant and the number of array slots must be relatively prime, consider the rehash function

(HashAddress + 2) MOD 100.

We want to add the record with the key 14001 to the hash table pictured in Figure 12-5. The original hash function, Key MOD 100, returns the hash address [01]. This array slot is already occupied. We resolve the collision by applying the rehash function above, examining successive odd-numbered indexes until a free slot is found. What happens if *all* of the slots with odd-numbered indexes are already in use? The search would fail—even though there are free slots with even-numbered indexes. This rehash function does not cover the index range of the array. However, if the constant and the number of array slots are relatively prime (like 3 and 100), the function will produce successive rehashes that will eventually cover every index in the array.

Rehash functions that use linear probing do not eliminate clustering (although the clusters are not always visually apparent in a figure). For example, in Figure 12-5, any record with a key value that produces the hash address 1, 4, 7, or 10 would be inserted in the slot at index [10].

In linear probing, we add a constant (usually 1) in each successive application of the rehash function. Another approach, called **quadratic probing**, makes the result of rehashing dependent on how many times the rehash function has been applied. In the *I'th* rehash, the function is

(HashAddress + I^2) MOD *array-size*.

The first rehash adds 1 to the HashAddress, the second rehash adds 4, the third rehash adds 9, and so on. Quadratic probing reduces clustering, but it does not necessarily examine every slot in the array. For example, if *array-size* is a power of 2 (512 or 1024, for example), relatively few array slots will be examined.

A third approach uses a pseudorandom number generator to determine the increment to HashAddress in each application of the rehash function. **Random probing** is excellent for eliminating clustering, but it tends to be slower than the other techniques we have discussed.

Buckets and Chaining

Another alternative for handling collisions is to *allow* multiple element keys to hash to the same location. One solution is to let each computed hash address contain slots for multiple elements, rather than just a single element. Each of these multi-element locations is called a **bucket**. Figure 12-6 shows a hash table with buckets that can contain three elements each. Using this approach, we can allow collisions to produce duplicate entries at the same hash address, up to a point. When the bucket becomes full, we must again deal with handling collisions.

Another solution, which avoids this problem, is to use the hash address not as the actual location of the element, but as the index into an array of pointers. Each pointer accesses a **chain** of elements that share the same hash address. Figure 12-7 illustrates this solution to the problem of collisions. Rather than rehashing, we simply allow both elements to share hash address [03]. The entry in the array at this location contains a pointer to a linked list that includes both elements.

To search for a given element, you first apply the hash function to the key and then search the chain for the element. Searching is not eliminated, but it is limited to elements that actually share a hash address. Using the first hash-and-search technique discussed,

Figure 12-6   *Handling Collisions by Hashing with Buckets*

[00]	Empty	Empty	Empty
[01]	Element with key = 14001	Element with key = 72101	Empty
[02]	Empty	Empty	Empty
[03]	Element with key = 50003	Add new element here	Empty
[04]	Element with key = 00104	Element with key = 30504	Element with key =56004
[05]	Empty	Empty	Empty
⋮	⋮	⋮	⋮
[99]	Element with key = 56399	Element with key = 32199	Empty

Add element with key = 77003

Hash function: Key MOD 100

[3]

Figure 12-7

Handling Collisions by Hashing with Chaining

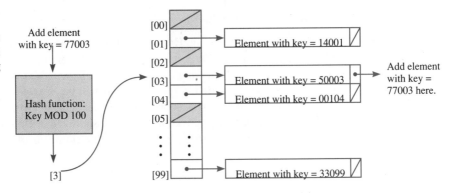

you may have to search through many additional elements if the slots following the hash address are filled with elements from collisions on other addresses.

Figure 12-8 illustrates a comparison of the chaining and hash-and-search schemes. The elements were added in the following order:

45300
20006
50002
40000
25001
13000
65905
30001
95000

Figure 12-8(a) represents the linear probing approach to collision handling; Figure 12-8(b) shows the result of chaining the colliding elements. Let's search for the element with the key 30001.

Using linear probing, we apply the hash function to get the index [1]. Because List.Info[1] does not contain the element with the key 30001, we search sequentially until we find the element in List.Info[7].

Using the chaining approach, we apply the hash function to get the index [1]. List.Info[1] directs us to a chain of elements whose keys hash to 1. We search this linked list until we find the element with the desired key.

Another advantage of chaining is that it simplifies the deletion of records from the hash table. We apply the hash function to obtain the index of the array slot that contains the pointer to the appropriate chain. The node can then be deleted from this chain, using the linked-list deletion algorithm from Chapter 6.

Choosing a Good Hash Function

One way to minimize collisions is to use a data structure that has more space than is actually needed for the number of elements, in order to increase the range of the hash

Figure 12-8   Comparison of Linear Probing and Chaining Schemes

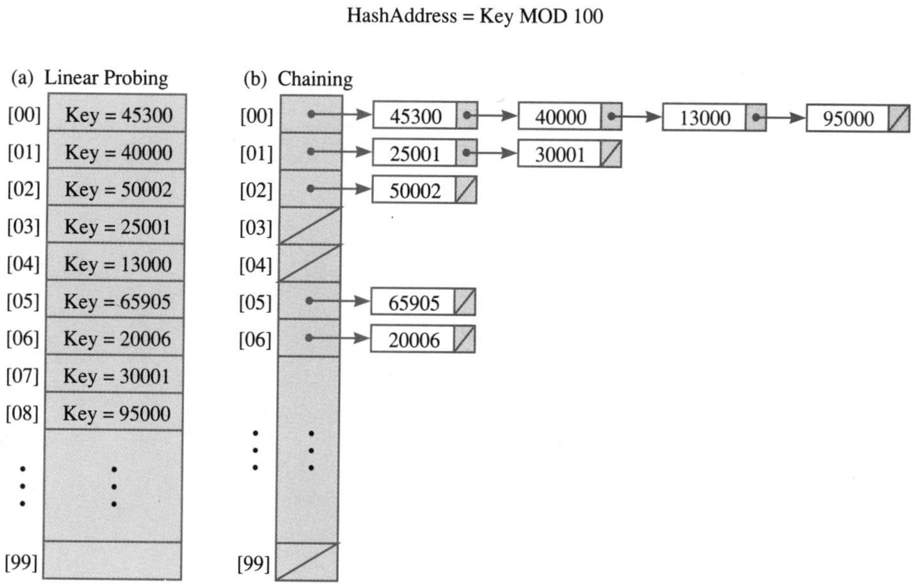

HashAddress = Key MOD 100

(a) Linear Probing

[00]	Key = 45300
[01]	Key = 40000
[02]	Key = 50002
[03]	Key = 25001
[04]	Key = 13000
[05]	Key = 65905
[06]	Key = 20006
[07]	Key = 30001
[08]	Key = 95000
⋮	
[99]	

(b) Chaining

[00]	→ 45300 → 40000 → 13000 → 95000
[01]	→ 25001 → 30001
[02]	→ 50002
[03]	
[04]	
[05]	→ 65905
[06]	→ 20006
⋮	
[99]	

function. In practice it is desirable to have the array size somewhat larger than the number of elements requires to reduce the number of collisions.

Selecting the table size involves a space vs. time trade-off. The larger the range of hash addresses, the less likely it is that two keys will hash to the same location. However, allocating an array that contains a large number of empty spaces wastes space.

More important, you can design your hash function to minimize collisions. The goal is to distribute the elements as uniformly as possible throughout the array. Therefore you want your hash function to produce unique addresses as often as possible. Once you admit collisions, you must introduce some sort of searching, either through array or chain searching or through rehashing. The access to each element is no longer direct, and the search is no longer $O(1)$. In fact, if the collisions cause very disproportionate chains, the worst case may be almost $O(N)$!

To avoid such a situation, you need to know something about the distribution of keys. Imagine a company whose employee elements are ordered according to a company ID six digits long. There are 500 employees, and we decide to use a chained approach to handling collisions. We set up 100 chains (expecting an average of five elements per chain) and use the hash function

IdNum MOD 100

That is, we use the last two digits of the six-digit IdNum as our index. The planned hash scheme is shown in Figure 12-9(a).Figure 12-9(b) shows what happened when the hash scheme was implemented. How could the distribution of the elements have

Figure 12-9
Hash Scheme to
Handle Employee
Elements

(a) The plan

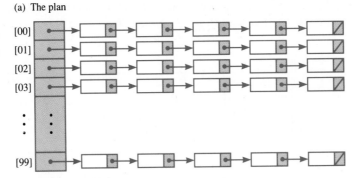

Average 5 records/chain
5 records × 100 chains = 500 employees
Expected search —O(5)

(b) The reality

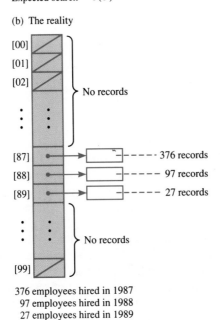

376 employees hired in 1987
 97 employees hired in 1988
 27 employees hired in 1989
─────────────────────
500 employees
Actual search O(N)

come out so skewed? It turns out that the company's IdNum is a concatenation of three
fields:

X X X	X	X X
3 digits, unique number (000–999)	1 digit, dept. number (0–9)	2 digits, year hired (e.g., 89)

The hash scheme depended solely on the year hired to produce unique addresses. Because the company was founded in 1987, all the elements were crowded very disproportionately into a small subset of the hash addresses. A search for an employee element, in this case, will be O(N). Although this is an exaggerated example, it illustrates the need to understand as completely as possible the domain and predicted values of keys in a hash scheme.

Division Method

The most common hash functions use the division method (MOD) to compute hash addresses. This is the type of function used in the preceding examples. The general function is

Key MOD TableSize

(or Key MOD TableSize + 1 to index the table beginning at 1, rather than at 0). We have already mentioned the idea of making the table somewhat larger than the number of elements requires, in order to increase the range of hash addresses. In addition, it has been found that better results are produced with the division method when the table size is prime.

The advantage of the division hash function is simplicity. Sometimes, however, it is necessary to use a more complicated (or even exotic) hash function to get a good distribution of hash addresses.

Other Hash Methods

How can we use hashing if the key field is a string instead of an integer? One approach is to use the ordinal values (ORD) of the string's characters to create a number that can be used as an index. For instance, here is a simple hash function that converts a key of StringType (defined in Chapter 3) to an index:

```
FUNCTION Hash
   (Key : StringType) : IndexType;

   (* Converts StringType Key to an array index by dividing *)
   (* the sum of the ordinal values of the characters by    *)
   (* MaxElements. The remainder is the new index.          *)
   (* Uses string operations Length (returns length of the  *)
   (* string) and CharAt (returns Ith character in string). *)
VAR
   StrIndex : Integer;
   Sum      : Integer;

BEGIN (* Hash *)

   Sum := 0;

   (* Add up the ORD's of all the characters. *)
   FOR StrIndex := 1 TO Length(Key) DO
      Sum := Sum + ORD (CharAt(Key, StrIndex));
```

```
(* Hash = remainder of division of Sum by MaxElements. *)
Hash := Sum MOD MaxElements
```

END;   (* Hash *)

A hash method called **folding** involves breaking the key into several pieces and concatenating or exclusive-OR'ing some of them to form the hash address. Another method is to square the key and then use some of the digits (or bits) of the key as a hash address. There are a number of other techniques, all of which are intended to make the hash address as unique and random (within the allowed range) as possible.

So that you will be familiar with the idea of folding, we will give an example here. This example cannot be implemented in standard Pascal. Turbo Pascal (and many other Pascal compilers), however, provides the XOR operation for integers. We leave the implementation of this algorithm for the adventurous student with a cooperative compiler. Suppose we want to devise a hash function that will result in an index between 0 and 255, and the internal representation of the Integer-type key is a bit string of 32 bits. We know that it takes 8 bits to represent the 256 index values ($2^8 = 256$). A folding algorithm to create a hash function might

1. break the key into four bit strings of 8 bits each,
2. exclusive-OR the first and last bit strings,
3. exclusive-OR the two middle bit strings, and
4. exclusive-OR the results of steps 2 and 3 to produce the 8-bit index into the array.

We will illustrate this scheme using the key 618403. The binary representation of this key is

00000000000010010110111110100011.

We break this bit string into four 8-bit strings:

```
00000000    (leftmost 8 bits)
00001001    (next 8 bits)
01101111    (next 8 bits)
10100011    (rightmost 8 bits)
```

The next step is to exclusive-OR the first and last bit strings. (The exclusive OR of two bits is 0 if the two bits are the same, and 1 if they are different. To exclusive-OR, (denoted as XOR) bit strings, we apply this rule to successive pairs of bits.)

```
          00000000
(XOR)     10100011
          10100011
```

Then we exclusive-OR the middle 2-bit strings:

```
          00001001
(XOR)     01101111
          01100110
```

Finally we exclusive-OR the results of the preceding two steps:

```
        10100011
(XOR)   01100110
        11000101
```

This binary number is equivalent to the decimal number 197. So the key 618403 hashes into the index 197.

The relationship between the key and the index is not intuitively obvious, but the indexes produced are likely to be uniformly distributed through the range of possible values.

When using an exotic hash function, you should keep two considerations in mind. First, the efficiency of calculating the function should be considered. Even if a hash function always produces unique addresses, it is not a good hash function if it takes longer to calculate the address than to search half the list. Second, programmer time should be considered. An extremely exotic function that somehow produces unique addresses for all of the known key values may fail if the domain of possible key values changes in a later modification. The programmer who has to modify the program may then waste a lot of time trying to find another hash function that is just as clever.

Summary

Searching, like sorting, is a topic that is closely tied to the goal of efficiency. We speak of a sequential search as an $O(N)$ search, because it may require up to N comparisons to locate an element. (N refers to the number of elements in the list.) Binary searches are considered to be $O(\log_2 N)$ and are appropriate for arrays only if they are sorted. A binary search tree may be used to support binary searches on a linked structure. The goal of hashing is to produce a search that approaches $O(1)$. Because of collisions of hash addresses, some searching or rehashing is usually necessary. A good hash function minimizes collisions and distributes the elements randomly throughout the table.

To solve a problem, programmers usually would rather create a new procedure than review someone else's solution. Why then have we devoted the past two chapters to a discussion of well-known sorting and searching algorithms? First, it is important to be familiar with several of the basic sorting and searching techniques. These are tools that you will use over and over again in a programming environment, and you will need to know which ones are appropriate solutions to different problems. Second, a review of sorting and searching techniques has given us another opportunity to examine a measuring tool—the Big-O approximation—that helps us determine how much work is required by a particular algorithm. Both building and measuring tools are needed to construct sound program solutions.

■ *Exercises**

For Exercises 1–4 use the following data file:

14 27 95 12 26 5 33 15 9 99

1. DataList is an array of 10 integer positions. Show what DataList would look like if it were loaded sequentially with the integers from the file (the first number in the first slot, the second in the second slot, and so on).

DataList

[1]	[2]	[3]	[4]	[5]	[6]	[7]	[8]	[9]	[10]

2. OrderedList is an array of 10 integer positions. Show what OrderedList would look like if it were loaded with the integers from the file and then the elements were sorted from smallest to largest.

OrderedList

[1]	[2]	[3]	[4]	[5]	[6]	[7]	[8]	[9]	[10]

3. Tree is a binary search tree of integer elements. Show what Tree would look like if the integers from the file were inserted into the tree in the order in which they were read into the file.

4. Fill in the following table, showing the number of comparisons needed either to find the value or to determine that the value is not in the list.

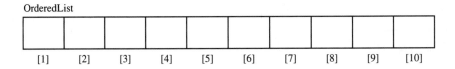

Number of comparisons

Value	Search DataList sequentially	Search OrderedList sequentially	Binary-search OrderedList	Search Tree
15				
17				
14				
5				
99				
100				
0				

*Questions with italicized numbers are answered in the back of the book.

For Exercises 5–9 use the following values:

66 47 87 90 126 140 145 153 177 285 393 395 467 566 620 735

5. Store the values in a hash table with 20 positions, using the division method of hashing and the linear probing method of resolving collisions.

6. Store the values in a hash table with 20 positions, using rehashing as the method of collision resolution. Use Key MOD TableSize as the hash function, and (Key + 3) MOD TableSize as the rehash function.

7. Store the values in a hash table with 10 buckets, each containing three values. If a bucket is full, use the next (sequential) bucket that contains a free slot.

8. Store the values in a hash table that uses the hash function Key MOD 10 to determine which of 10 chains to put the value into.

9. Fill in the following table, showing the number of comparisons needed to find each value using the hashing representations given in Exercises 5–8.

Number of comparisons

Value	Problem 5	Problem 6	Problem 7	Problem 8
66				
467				
566				
735				
285				
87				

10. If you know the index of an element stored in an array of N unordered elements, which of the following best describes the order of the algorithm to retrieve the element?
    (a) $O(1)$
    (b) $O(N)$
    (c) $O(\log_2 N)$
    (d) $O(N^2)$
    (e) $O(0.5\ N)$

11. The element being searched for is *not* in an array of 100 elements. What is the *average* number of comparisons needed in a sequential search to determine that the element is not there
    (a) if the elements are completely unordered?
    (b) if the elements are ordered from smallest to largest?
    (c) if the elements are ordered from largest to smallest?

12. The element being searched for is *not* in an array of 100 elements. What is the *maximum* number of comparisons needed in a sequential search to determine that the element is not there
    (a) if the elements are completely unordered?
    (b) if the elements are ordered from smallest to largest?
    (c) if the elements are ordered from largest to smallest?

13. The element being searched for *is* in an array of 100 elements. What is the *average* number of comparisons needed in a sequential search to determine the position of the element
    (a) if the elements are completely unordered?
    (b) if the elements are ordered from smallest to largest?
    (c) if the elements are ordered from largest to smallest?

14. Choose the answer that correctly completes the following sentence: The elements in an array may be ordered by highest probability of being requested in order to reduce
    (a) the average number of comparisons needed to find an element in the list.
    (b) the maximum number of comparisons needed to detect that an element is not in the list.
    (c) the average number of comparisons needed to detect that an element is not in the list.
    (d) the maximum number of comparisons needed to find an element that is in the list.

15. Identify each of the following statements as True or False. Correct any false statements.
    (a) A binary search of an ordered set of elements in an array is always faster than a sequential search of the elements.
    (b) A binary search is an $O(N\log_2 N)$ algorithm.
    (c) A binary search of elements in an array requires that the elements be sorted from smallest to largest.
    (d) A high-probability ordering scheme would be a poor choice for arranging an array of elements that are equally likely to be requested.
    (e) When a hash function is used to determine the placement of elements in an array, the order in which the elements are added will not affect the resulting array.
    (f) When hashing is used, increasing the size of the array will always reduce the number of collisions.
    (g) If we use buckets in a hashing scheme, we will not have to worry about collision resolution.
    (h) If we use chaining in a hashing scheme, we will not have to worry about collision resolution.
    (i) The procedures in this chapter are used only for external searching.
    (j) The goal of a successful hashing scheme is an $O(1)$ search.

16. Choose the answer that correctly completes the following sentence: The number of comparisons required to find an element in a hash table with N buckets, of which M are full,
    (a) is always 1.
    (b) is usually only slightly less than N.
    (c) may be large if M is only slightly less than N.
    (d) is approximately $\log_2 M$.
    (e) is approximately $\log_2 N$.

17. A list is ordered in such a way that the elements most often accessed are closest to the top. The list is then searched sequentially to find the desired element. When it is found, it is moved toward the top of the list by swapping it with its immediate predecessor. Over time, the most frequently requested records migrate to the top of the list.
    (a) Show how the specifications of FindElement (from Chapter 6) would be modified by this list representation.
    (b) Assuming the list is implemented sequentially, using the declarations in Chapter 6, reimplement the FindElement procedure.

18. A linked list is ordered in such a way that the elements most recently accessed are closest to the top. The list is searched sequentially to find the desired element. When it is found, it is moved to the beginning of the list.

(a) Show how the specifications of FindElement (from Chapter 6) would be modified by this list representation.

(b) Assuming the list is implemented using the declarations of a linear linked list in Chapter 6, reimplement the FindElement procedure.

(c) Would this approach be good for a sequential list? Why or why not?

19. How might you order the elements in the ReservedWords list (from the Chapter 9 application section) to use the idea of high-probability ordering?

20. A record has a key field of type StringType (PACKED ARRAY[1 .. 20] OF Char). A list of such records is stored in an array, using the following hash function: Each character in the string is turned into its integer equivalent (using the standard function ORD) and then the integers are added up to make one number, which is MOD'ed by TableSize. The result is used as the index in the array.

Write Function CharHash, which takes the key string and returns the resulting index. (You may assume that all the characters in the packed array are legitimate; the "string" is padded with blanks to fill the packed array.)

21. Indicate whether each of the following changes would or would not be a good revision to Function CharHash from Exercise 20.

(a) Instead of adding up the integer versions of all the characters, only add up the consonants.

(b) Only add up the integer versions of the odd-indexed elements in the packed array.

(c) Only add up the integer versions of the vowels.

(d) Only use the integer version of the first letter in the string.

(e) Only use the integer versions of the first five characters in the packed array.

(f) Only use the integer versions of the last five characters in the packed array.

(g) Instead of adding up the integer versions of all the letters, multiply them.

22. It was shown in the chapter that the folding method hashed the key 618403 to the index 197.

(a) What is another key between 32768 and 65536 that hashes to this index?

(b) What is another key between 16384 and 65536 that hashes to this index?

23. The *insertion sort* uses the following algorithm:

InsertSort

FOR Index := 2 TO List.Length DO
    Put List.Info[Index] in its proper place, relative to List.Info[1] .. List.Info[Index - 1].

In each iteration of the loop body, the elements in List.Info[1] .. List.Info[Index - 1] are sorted with respect to each other. The next element in the list, List.Info[Index], is then put into its correct place by moving all the larger elements in the "sorted" are down to make room for it.

One way to find the proper place for List.Info[Index] is to use a binary search function that inputs the list, the key of the element, and the indexes that define the area of the array to search. The function returns the index of the correct place to insert the element.

```
FUNCTION BinSearch
  (VAR List : ListType;
   Key      : KeyType;
   Start    : IndexType;
   Finish   : IndexType) : IndexType;
```

(a) Write Function BinSearch.

(b) Write Procedure InsertSort, using BinSearch to find the correct insertion place for each successive element.

Use the following hash table for Exercises 24–26. Seven elements have been inserted, using a hash function to determine the insertion place. The linear probing method of collision resolution has been used.

[0]	51
[1]	34
[2]	
[3]	20
[4]	3
[5]	4
[6]	38
[7]	7
[8]	
[9]	
[10]	
[11]	28
[12]	11
[13]	

24. What is the hash function?

25. For each element in the hash table, show the result of the hash function and the number of places that had to be searched to find the insertion place.

26. Which of the following are possible insertion orders that would have produced the table above? (There may be more than one correct answer.)
    (a) 51 34 20 3 38 4 7 28 11
    (b) 51 20 34 3 4 38 28 11 7
    (c) 28 11 7 51 34 20 3 4 38
    (d) 7 28 11 51 34 3 4 38 20

27. A hash table contains 1000 slots, indexed from 1 to 1000. The elements stored in the table have keys that range in value from 1 to 99999. Which, if any, of the following hash functions would work correctly? (There may be more than one correct answer.)
    (a) Key MOD 1000
    (b) (Key − 1) MOD 1000
    (c) ((Key + 1) MOD 999)
    (d) (Key MOD 1000) + 1

28. A hash table contains 1000 slots, indexed from 0 to 999. The elements in the table have keys that range from 1 to 100000. The original hash function is Key MOD 1000. Which, if any, of the following collision resolution schemes would work correctly? (There may be more than one correct answer.)

    (a) Rehashing, with function = (Key + 1) MOD 1000.

    (b) Rehashing, with function = (Key + 2) MOD 1000.

    (c) Rehashing, with function = Key MOD 999.

    (d) Rehashing, with function = (Key + 3) MOD 1000.

29. A hash table is used to store approximately 350 employee records of EmployeeType, whose key field is called IdNum. The key field may range in value from 1000 to 9999. The hash table contains five buckets per hash address. The original hash function is Key MOD 100.

    (a) Write the declarations for the hash table.

    (b) Write Procedure CreateTable, which initializes all the slots in the hash table to empty.

    (c) Write Procedure InsertElement, which inserts an employee record into the first free slot in the appropriate bucket. (If the bucket is full, search the following buckets until a free slot is available.)

    (d) Write Procedure RetrieveElement, which returns a copy of the employee record with a designated key.

30. A hash table is used to store employee records of EmployeeType, whose key field is called IdNum. The key field may range in value from 1000 to 9999. The original hash function is Key MOD 100. There is a chain of records for each hash address.

    (a) Write the declarations for the hash table.

    (b) Write Procedure CreateTable, which initializes all the slots in the hash table to empty.

    (c) Write Procedure InsertElement, which inserts an employee record into the appropriate chain.

    (d) Write Procedure RetrieveElement, which returns a copy of the employee record with a designated key.

    (e) Write Procedure DeleteElement, which deletes the employee record from its chain.

Appendixes

Appendix A   Reserved Words

The following are reserved words in Standard Pascal:

AND	END	MOD	REPEAT
ARRAY	FILE	NIL	SET
BEGIN	FOR	NOT	THEN
CASE	FORWARD	OF	TO
CONST	FUNCTION	OR	TYPE
DIV	GOTO	PACKED	UNTIL
DO	IF	PROCEDURE	VAR
DOWNTO	IN	PROGRAM	WHILE
ELSE	LABEL	RECORD	WITH

The following are reserved words in Turbo Pascal:

ABSOLUTE	INLINE	SHL	UNIT
EXTERNAL	INTERFACE	SHR	USES
IMPLEMENTATION	INTERRUPT	STRING	XOR

Check the reference manual of your compiler for other reserved words.

Appendix B   Standard Identifiers

Standard Constants

False   True   MaxInt

Standard Types

Integer   Boolean   Real   Char   Text

Standard Files

Input   Output

Standard Functions

Function	Parameter Type	Result Type	Returns
ABS(X)	Integer or Real	Same as parameter	Absolute value of X
ARCTAN(X)	Integer or Real	Real	Arctangent of X in radians
CHR(X)	Integer	Char	Character whose ordinal number is X
COS(X)	Integer or Real	Real	Cosine of X (X is in radians)
EOF(F)	File	Boolean	End-of-file test of F
EOLN(F)	File	Boolean	End-of-line test of F
EXP(X)	Real or Integer	Real	e to the X power
LN(X)	Real or Integer	Real	Natural logarithm of x
ODD(X)	Integer	Boolean	Odd test of X
ORD(X)	Ordinal (scalar except Real)	Integer	Ordinal number of X
PRED(X)	Ordinal (scalar except Real)	Same as parameter	Unique predecessor of X (except when X is the first value)
ROUND(X)	Real	Integer	X rounded
SIN(X)	Real or Integer	Real	Sine of X (X is in radians)
SQR(X)	Real or Integer	Same as parameter	Square of X
SQRT(X)	Real or Integer	Real	Square root of X
SUCC(X)	Ordinal (scalar except Real)	Same as parameter	Unique successor of X (except when X is the last value)
TRUNC(X)	Real	Integer	X truncated

Standard Procedures

Procedure Name	Description
Dispose (P)	Destroys the dynamic variable referenced by pointer P, returning its space to the available space list.
Get (F)	Advances the current position of file F to the next component and assigns the value of the component to F↑.
New (P)	Creates a variable of the type referenced by pointer P, and stores a pointer to the new variable in P.
Pack (U, I, P)	Copies the elements of unpacked array U, beginning at subscript position I, into packed array P, beginning at the first subscript position of P.
Page (F)	Advances the printer to the top of a new page before printing the next line of text file F.
Put (F)	Appends the value of the buffer variable F↑ to the file F.
Read (F, variable list)	Reads data values from the file F and assigns these values to the variable(s) in the variable list in order until the list is satisfied. (If F is not specified, default is Input.)

Readln (F, variable list)	Same as Read, then advances the file pointer past the end-of-line.
Reset (F)	Resets file F to its beginning for reading.
Rewrite (F)	Resets file F to its beginning for writing; old contents of F are lost.
Unpack (P, U, I)	Copies the elements of packed array P, beginning at the first subscript position, into unpacked array U, beginning at subscript position I.
Write (F,parameter list)	Writes the data to file F, in the order specified in the parameter list. (If F is not specified, default is Output).
Writeln (F,parameter list)	Same as Write, then generates an end-of-file marker.

(Some compilers provide additional types, files, functions and/or procedures. Check the reference manual for your compiler to see what is available.)

Appendix C   Pascal Operators and Symbols

+			plus or set union
−			minus or set difference
*			times or set intersection
/			real divide
DIV			integer divide
MOD			remainder from integer divide (modulus)
<			is less than
< =			is less than or equal to
=			is equal to
<>			is not equal to
> =			is greater than or equal to
>			is greater than
AND			Boolean conjunction
OR			Boolean inclusive disjunction
NOT			Boolean negation
IN			test set membership
: =			becomes, is assigned
,			separates items in a list
;			separates statements
:			separates variable name and type; separates case label and statement; separates statement label and statement
'			delimits character and string literals
.			decimal point, record selector, and program terminator
..			subrange specifier
↑	^	@	file and pointer variable indicator
(			starts parameter list or nested expression
)			ends parameter list or nested expression
[	(.		starts subscript list or set expression
]	.)		ends subscript list or set expression
(*	{		starts a comment
*)	}		ends a comment

Appendix D   Precedence of Operators

NOTE:

1. Parentheses can be used to change the order of precedence.
2. When operators of equal precedence are used, they are executed in left to right order.

NOT	*Highest precedence*
* / DIV MOD AND	
+ − OR	
< <= => = > <> IN	*Lowest precedence*

Appendix E   Syntax Diagrams

PROGRAM

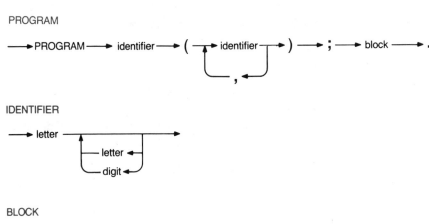

IDENTIFIER

BLOCK

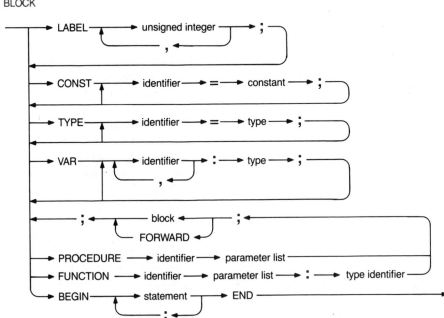

CONSTANT

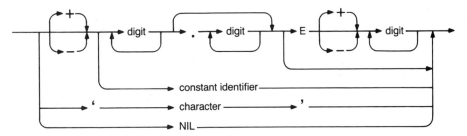

TYPE

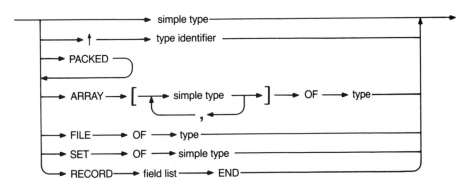

SIMPLE TYPE

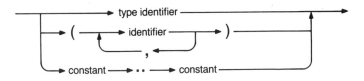

FIELD LIST

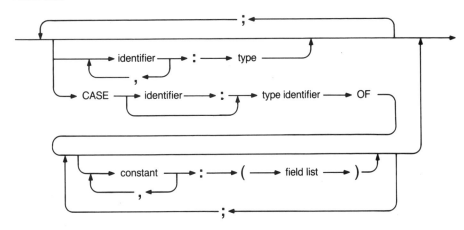

PARAMETER LIST

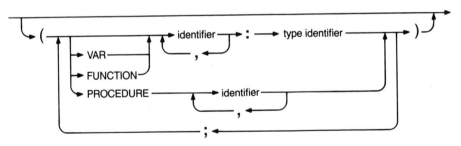

STATEMENT

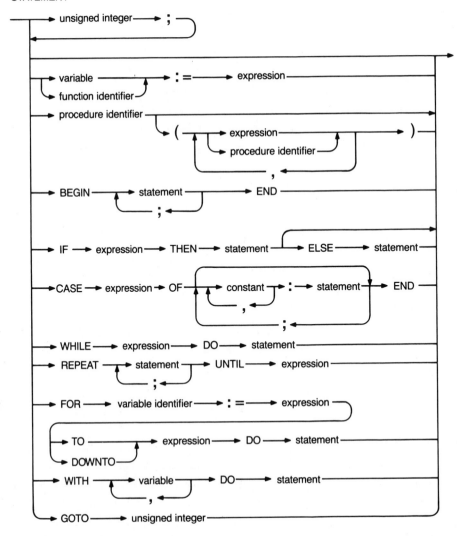

VARIABLE

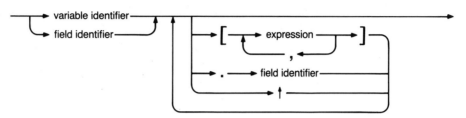

EXPRESSION

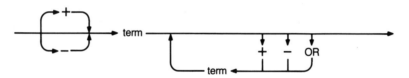

SIMPLE EXPRESSION

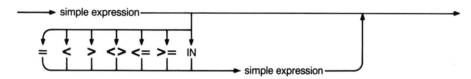

TERM

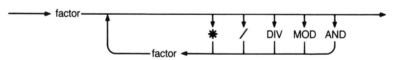

FACTOR

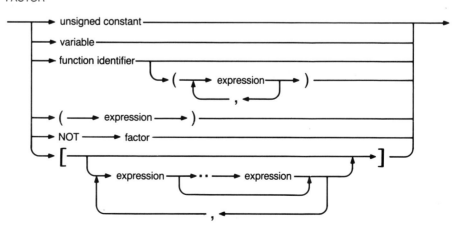

Appendix F   Character Sets

The following charts show the ordering of the most common character sets: ASCII (American Standard Code for Information Interchange), EBCDIC (Extended Binary Coded Decimal Interchange Code) and CDC Scientific. Only printable characters are shown. The ordinal number for each character is shown in decimal. The blank character is denoted by a "□".

Left Digit(s)	Right Digit	ASCII									
		0	1	2	3	4	5	6	7	8	9
3				□	!	"	#	$	%	&	'
4		(	)	*	+	,	−	.	/	0	1
5		2	3	4	5	6	7	8	9	:	;
6		<	=	>	?	@	A	B	C	D	E
7		F	G	H	I	J	K	L	M	N	O
8		P	Q	R	S	T	U	V	W	X	Y
9		Z	[	\	]	∧	—	`	a	b	c
10		d	e	f	g	h	i	j	k	l	m
11		n	o	p	q	r	s	t	u	v	w
12		x	y	z	{	|	}	~			

Codes 00–31 and 127 are nonprintable control characters.

Left Digit(s)	Right Digit	EBCDIC									
		0	1	2	3	4	5	6	7	8	9
6						□					
7						¢	.	<	(	+	|
8		&									
9		!	$	*	)	;	¬	−	/		
10								∧	,	%	—
11		>	?								
12				:	#	@	'	=	"		a
13		b	c	d	e	f	g	h	i		
14							j	k	l	m	n
15		o	p	q	r						
16				s	t	u	v	w	x	y	z
17									\	{	}
18		[	]								
19						A	B	C	D	E	F	G
20		H	I								J
21		K	L	M	N	O	P	Q	R		
22								S	T	U	V
23		W	X	Y	Z						
24		0	1	2	3	4	5	6	7	8	9

Codes 00–63 and 250–255 are nonprintable control characters.

Left Digit(s)	Right Digit	CDC									
		0	1	2	3	4	5	6	7	8	9
0		:	A	B	C	D	E	F	G	H	I
1		J	K	L	M	N	O	P	Q	R	S
2		T	U	V	W	X	Y	Z	0	1	2
3		3	4	5	6	7	8	9	+	−	*
4		/	(	)	$	=	□	,	.	≡	[
5		]	%	≠	↦	∨	∧	↑	↓	<	>
6		≤	≥	¬	;						

Appendix G   Verification Methods

Debugging gets rid of known bugs in programs. Good testing helps you to find more bugs. Unless the test data checks every possible combination of branches with every possible input, however, testing cannot really prove conclusively that the program is correct. In a large program, the number of possible combinations of branches makes this approach unfeasible.

For this reason, one of the theoretical areas of computer science research involves *program verification*. The goal of this research is to establish a method of proving programs correct that is analogous to the method of proving theorems in geometry. One such technique for doing this is shown below.

The Verification Technique

The essence of the verification technique is to say, "If the input satisfies some condition P, and S (a program segment) is executed, then if S terminates, the output condition Q is satisfied." Formally we say:

{P}   S   {Q}

This notation comes from propositional calculus, which is not a prerequisite for this course, so we will define our notation intuitively as we go along.

{P} and {Q} are statements about the state of the machine (the computer). They are called *assertions*. Formally, {P} S {Q} is interpreted as "If P is true and S is executed, then (assuming S terminates) Q is true." P is called the *precondition* for S, and Q is called the *postcondition* of S.

To verify a program, you have to verify each statement and use the rule for sequences to collect the statements into larger and larger proved units. The rule for sequences is as follows:

({P} S1 {R}) AND ({R} S2 {Q}) → {P} S1;S2 {Q}

The final step in verifying a program is to show

{P}   S   {Q}
 ↑   ↑   ↑
Initial state   Program   Final state

In addition to this rule for sequences, there are rules for assignment statements, selection statements, and iteration statements.

Assignment Statement

The general rule for assignment statements is as follows:

$$\{Q_e^v\} \; v = e \; \{Q\}$$

This rule states that the precondition is the postcondition with every occurrence of v replaced with e. That is, given the postcondition and the assignment statement, we can prove what the precondition must be. Let's apply this rule to the following:

$$\{?\} \; x := x - 1 \; \{x = 4\}$$

Substituting $x - 1$ for x in $\{x = 4\}$ we get

$$x - 1 = 4$$
$$x = 5$$

Therefore $\{x - 5\}$ is the precondition.

It seems backward to work from the postcondition to the precondition. Indeed there is a general rule that works from the precondition, but it is much more complex.

The following table illustrates this rule:

$\{Q_e^v\}$	S	$\{Q\}$
$\{J = 6\}$	$J := J + 1$	$\{J = 7\}$
$\{K = 3\}$	$L := K + 3$	$\{K = 3 \text{ AND } L = 6\}$
$\{Data[I] = J\}$	$J := J + 1$	$\{Data[I] = J - 1\}$

Selection (IF statements)

Given a Boolean expression E, the rule for selection or branching is as follows:

$$\{P \text{ AND } E\} \; S1 \; \{Q\}, \; \{P \text{ AND NOT } E\} \; S2 \; \{Q\} \rightarrow \{P\} \text{ IF E THEN S1 ELSE S2 } \{Q\}$$

This rule says that we want $\{Q\}$ to be true eventually. Now if E is true initially, S1 will be executed with $\{P \text{ AND } E\}$ as the initial condition. If E is not true, S2 will be executed with $\{P \text{ AND NOT } E\}$ as the initial condition.

This can be pictured as follows:

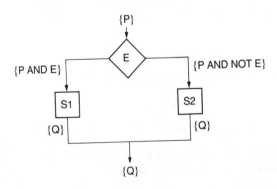

Note that if there is no ELSE clause, S2 is the identity function; that is, everything keeps its previous identity.

The following example to set Max to the maximum of X and Y demonstrates how the verification of the selection statement works.

{P}	{true}	(* no preconditions exist *)
	IF X > Y	
	THEN	{X > Y} {X = maximum (X, Y)}
{S1}	Max := X	{Max = maximum (X, Y)} is True
	ELSE	{X <= Y} {Y = maximum (X, Y)}
{S2}	Max := Y	{Max = maximum (X, Y)} is True
{Q}	{Max = maximum (X, Y)}	

In the THEN branch we know that X is greater than Y, and thus maximum (X, Y) equals X. In the ELSE branch we know that X is not greater than Y, and thus maximum (X, Y) equals Y.

The next example shows a case where the verification fails. Again, the segment of code is supposed to set Max to the maximum of X and Y.

{P}	{true}	(* no preconditions exist *)
	IF X > Y	
{S1}	THEN	{X > Y} {X = maximum (X, Y)}
	Max := X	{Max = maximum (X, Y)} is True
	(* no ELSE *)	{X <= Y} {Max = Max}
{S2}	(* identity *)	{Max = maximum (X, Y)} is undefined
{Q}	{Max = maximum(X,Y)} is False.	

In the THEN branch we know that X is greater than Y, and thus maximum (X, Y) equals X. In the ELSE branch, we know that X is not greater than Y. However, because there is no action, maximum is unchanged and it may be left containing an incorrect or undefined value.

Iteration (WHILE statements)

The rule for loops is

$$\{P \text{ AND } E\} \ S \ \{P\} \rightarrow \{P\} \text{ WHILE } E \text{ DO } S \ \{P \text{ AND NOT } E\}$$

Let's rewrite this rule adding an additional assertion, {I}. The backward C means *implies*.

$$\{P\} \supset \{I\}, \ \{I \text{ AND } E\}, \ \{I \text{ AND NOT } E\} \supset \{Q\}$$

{I} is called the **invariant** of the loop. {I} must be true before the loop is entered, and the loop must maintain the truth of {I} at the end of each iteration. When condition E becomes FALSE, the loop is terminated, and {I} is still true. We talked about using loop invariants to help us design correct loops in Chapter 2. Now let's look at how we can use loop invariants to prove the correctness of loops.

In order to make use of the important principles here, let's rewrite this as a chart showing where certain things must be shown to be true.

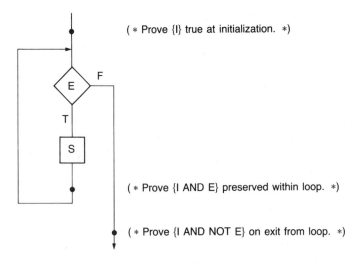

(* Prove {I} true at initialization. *)

(* Prove {I AND E} preserved within loop. *)

(* Prove {I AND NOT E} on exit from loop. *)

Just what is this loop invariant {I} that we are trying to prove? It is a statement about the relationships of the variables involved in the loop. It expresses the semantics of the loop, as opposed to the mechanics. The expression E, which controls the loop repetition, is used to tell when the semantics of the loop would be violated if another repetition were performed. Let's tie all this together by looking at an example: summing the N integer values in an array, Data.

```
Sum := 0;
Index := 1;

WHILE Index <= N DO
  BEGIN
    Sum := Sum + Data[Index];
    Index := Index + 1
  END (* WHILE *)
```

To prove this section of code, we must do the following:

1. Define the loop invariant (actually, as we said in Chapter 2, this should be done before the code is written).
2. Show that the loop invariant is true before entering the loop.
3. Show that the invariant is preserved within the loop.
4. Show that the loop halts and that the invariant {I} and the terminating condition {E} imply {Q}.

The loop invariant is "Sum contains the sum of all the elements in the array up to (but not including) Data[Index], as long as Index is less than or equal to one more than the number of elements in Data." We can write this more precisely as follows:

Loop Invariant: $1 <= \text{Index} <= N + 1$ AND Sum contains the sum of the elements in Data[1] . . Data[Index − 1].

A picture of the relationships in the loop is shown on the following page.

Data

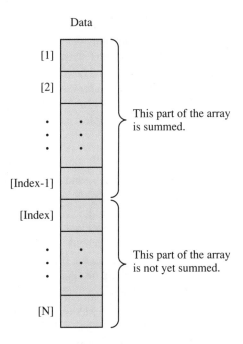

[1]

[2]

.
.
.

[Index-1]

This part of the array
is summed.

[Index]

.
.
.

This part of the array
is not yet summed.

[N]

To verify this loop, we must prove the invariant is true at the initialization point and
at the exit from the loop. We must then show that the code of the loop maintains the
invariant within the loop.

Initialization   The loop invariant says that at the end of any iteration, the area
of the array from Data[1] . . Data[Index $-$ 1] is already summed. Substituting the
initial value 1 for Index in the loop invariant, we get "Sum contains the sum of all the
elements in the array from Data[1] . . Data[0]." This range of array elements is empty,
so Sum, as expected, is 0.

Termination   When we reach this point, we know that the condition of the WHILE
loop (Index $<=$ N) is not true. Since our loop invariant says that Index $<=$ N + 1
and we know that Index $>$ N, Index must now be N + 1.

Substituting N + 1 for Index in the loop invariant, we get "Sum contains the sum
of all the elements in the array from Data[1] . . Data[(N + 1) $-$ 1]"—that is, Sum
contains the sum of the whole array.

How do we know that we actually reach this point? That is, how do we know that
the section of code actually terminates? We don't. We have proved partial correctness.
If this section of code terminates, the results are correct. To prove termination, we
have to add a precondition that N, the number of elements, is greater than or equal to
1. Index begins at 1 and is incremented by 1 each time. N is not changed within the
loop. Therefore Index will eventually be greater than N, and the loop will terminate.

Preservation   We know from the loop invariant that Sum contains the sum of the
elements from Data[1] . . Data[Index $-$ 1]. The first statement in the loop adds the

value in Data[Index] to Sum. So now Sum contains the values from Data[1] . . Data[Index]. The next statement increments Index. Applying the rule for assignment statements, we replace Index with Index − 1 in the previous statement. Now Sum contains the sum of the values from Data[1] . . Data[Index − 1], which is our loop invariant.

This seems like an awful lot of work to show something that is obvious anyway: The code *is* correct. It may be obvious in this small example, but the technique can be used to verify much more complicated examples.

The Case Against GOTO

We have discussed the verification of the assignment statement and the three basic program structures: the sequence, the branch, and the loop. Those of you who have previous programming experience in FORTRAN or BASIC, or who like to read the fine print in the Pascal manual, may be familiar with another kind of statement that determines program control: the **GOTO** statement. The GOTO statement means just what is says: *go to* the line in the program indicated by the label following GOTO. It is an unconditional branch to another place in the program.

How can program segments that include GOTO statements be verified? A GOTO statement within one of the basic program structures—sequence, selection, or loop—can take control away so that the structure does not terminate normally. A GOTO inside a WHILE loop, for instance, may make the loop terminate while the condition is still true. The following example sets Place to the location of Val in an array called List:

```
LABEL
  10;
CONST
  Max = 100;
VAR
  List  : ARRAY [1 .. Max] OF ValueType;
  Val   : ValueType;
  Place : Integer;
    .

    .

    .
  Place := 1;
  WHILE Place <= Max DO
    IF List[Place] = Val
      THEN GOTO 10
      ELSE Place := Place + 1
    .

    .

    .
10: Writeln ('Place = ', Place)
```

The invariant of this LOOP is "1 <= Place <= Max + 1 AND Val is not contained in the array from List[1] .. List[Place − 1]." The terminating condition on the loop control is Place <= Max. But if Val is found in the array, the terminating condition will still be true at the exit of the loop. Note that the code is functionally correct; it works. However, it is very difficult to verify programs that include GOTO statements.

The difficulty of verification is not the only problem with the GOTO statement. The use of GOTO leads to unstructured programs with multiple entries into and exits from control structures. This is sometimes called *spaghetti code* because trying to read it can be like trying to untangle a bowl of spaghetti. Programs with GOTO statements are harder to read, understand, modify, and debug.

Glossary

abstract data type   The logical picture of a data type plus the specifications of the operations required to create and manipulate objects of this data type.

abstract data type specification   A specification that describes the logical organization and the operations that encapsulate an abstract data type.

ACM   Association for Computing Machinery, a professional society of computer scientists, programmers, and others interested in computers and data processing.

activation record   A record used at run-time to store information about a procedure or function call, including the parameter, local variables, register values, and return address.

actual parameter   A variable or expression contained in a procedure or function call and passed to that procedure or function.

actual parameter list   The list of actual parameters contained in a procedure or function call.

Ada   High-level programming language commissioned by the Department of Defense (DoD); created to provide a single language in which to implement the many large and complex DoD programming projects.

address   A label (name, number, or symbol) designating a location in memory.

adjacency list   Linked lists, one for each node in a graph, that contain the names of the nodes to which each node is connected.

adjacency matrix   For a graph with N nodes, an N × N table that shows the existence (or weights) of all edges in the graph.

adjacent nodes   Two nodes in a graph that are connected by an edge.

adjacent vertices   Vertices in a graph that are connected by an edge.

ADT   *See* abstract data type.

algorithm   A logical sequence of discrete steps that describe a complete solution to a given problem in a finite amount of time.

allocate   To set aside space in memory. *See* dynamic and static allocation.

alphanumeric   A general term for human-readable alphabetic letters, numeric digits, and special characters that are machine processable.

ancestor   A node in a tree that is the parent of another node or the parent of another ancestor of that node.

anonymous type   A type defined in the VAR section of a program, so called because it does not have an identifier (a name) associated with it.

ANSI   American National Standards Institute, an organization that promotes voluntary standards in the United States.

arc   The connection between two vertices in a graph.

argument   *See* parameter.

arithmetic logic unit (ALU)   The computer component that performs arithmetic operations (addition, subtraction, multiplication, division) and logical operations (comparison of two values).

arithmetic operator   A symbol used in a numeric expression whose operation results in a numeric value.

array   A structured data type composed of a fixed number of components of the same type, with each component directly accessed by the index.

ASCII   American Standard Code for Information Interchange, a widely used encoding scheme for a character set composed of printable and control characters.

assembler   A program that translates an assembly language program into machine code.

assembly language   A language, similar to machine code, that uses mnemonics to represent operations and identifiers to represent addresses.

assignment operator   The Pascal symbol ": = " used in an assignment statement.

assignment statement   A statement that uses the assignment operator to assign a value to a variable or function.

atomic data type   A data type that allows only a single value to be associated with an identifier of that type.

automatic range-checking   The automatic detection of the assignment of an out-of-range value to a variable.

auxiliary storage device   A device that stores data in

coded form, external to the computer's memory.

base   The number of digits used in a number system (e.g., decimal uses 10, binary uses 2).

base address   The starting location in memory of a variable.

base case   The case for which the solution can be stated nonrecursively.

base type   The set of allowable values that a variable may take.

batch processing   A technique for executing programs and data without intermediate user interaction with the computer.

Big–O   *See* order of magnitude.

binary   Expressed in terms of combinations of the numbers 1 and 0 only.

binary expression tree   Binary tree in which each nonleaf node contains a binary operator and each leaf node contains one of the operands of its parent node.

binary file   A file that is created within one program to be read by another program or by the same program at a later date; such a file is written in the internal representation of a machine.

binary operator   An operator requiring two operands. *See* arithmetic operator, logical operator, relational operator.

binary search   A search algorithm for sorted lists that involves dividing the list in half and determining, by value comparison, whether the item would be in the upper or lower half; the process is performed repeatedly until either the item is found or it is determined that the item is not on the list.

binary search tree   A binary tree in which the key value in any node is greater than the key value in its left child and any of its children (left subtree) and less than the key value in its right child and any of its children (right subtree).

binary tree   A data structure with a unique starting node (the root), in which each node is capable of having two child nodes and in which a unique path exists from the root to every other node.

binding   The association of a memory address with a variable name.

binding time   The point in the compile/execution cycle when variable names are associated with addresses in memory.

bit   A binary digit (1 or 0) used to represent information in a computer. Several bits make up a byte. *See* byte, word.

black box testing   Testing a program or module based on covering the possible input values, treating the code as a "black box."

block   A program unit consisting of an optional declarations part and a compound statement; program and procedure/function declarations consist of a heading and a block. Pascal is known as a block-structured language.

Boolean   Data type consisting of only two values: True and False.

Boolean expression   An assertion that can be evaluated as being either True or False, the only values of the Boolean data type.

Boolean operator   *See* logical operator.

branch   *See* selection.

breadth-first search   Searching strategy of visiting nodes one level at a time.

buckets   Collection of records associated with a particular hash address.

buffer   An intermediate data storage area usually used to balance the different operating speeds of computer components (e.g., slow I/O and the faster CPU).

buffer variable   *See* file buffer variable.

bug   An error in a program that prevents compilation or execution or causes incorrect results.

byte   A sequence of bits (often 8) used to encode a character within a computer. See word.

call   A transfer of control from one portion of a program to a named subroutine (procedure or function).

cancellation error   A loss in accuracy during addition or subtraction of numbers of widely differing sizes, due to limits of precision. *See* representational error.

cardinality   The number of values contained in an ordinal type.

case label list   A list of values of the same type as the case selector, appearing in the body of the CASE statement.

case selector   The ordinal expression or variable whose value determines which case label list is selected (cannot be Real).

case statement   A selection control structure that provides for multi-way selection of different courses of action; a generalization of the IF statement equivalent to nested IF-THEN-ELSE statements.

cathode ray tube (CRT) screen   An electronic tube with a screen upon which visual information may be displayed (used in computer video terminals and television sets).

central processing unit (CPU)   The "brain" of a

computer, which interprets and executes instructions; the combination of the control unit and the arithmetic logic unit.

Char Data type consisting of one alphanumeric character (letter, digit, or special symbol).

character set The set of machine-representable characters encoded according to a specific coding system. *See* collating sequence.

character string A string of alphanumeric characters. *See* string.

circular linked list Linked list in which every node has a successor; the "last" element is succeeded by the "first" element.

clear box testing Testing a program or module based on covering all of the branches or paths in the code; also called "white box" testing.

clustering The tendency of records to become unevenly distributed in a hash table, with many records clustering around a single address.

code All or part of a program. To write all or part of a program in a programming language. *See* programming language.

code coverage *See* clear box testing.

code inspection Meeting of a technical team to perform a formal reading of the source code of a computer program, with the goal of identifying errors.

code walkthrough Meeting of a technical team to perform a manual simulation of the source code of a computer program with sets of sample test data, with the goal of finding errors.

coding Translating an algorithm into a programming language; also, the process of assigning bit patterns to pieces of information.

collating sequence The ordering of a computer's character set.

collision Condition resulting when two or more keys produce the same hash address.

column-major order An array organization where the elements are stored in memory column by column.

comment A note in a program intended for human understanding but ignored by the compiler.

comparison operator *See* relational operator.

compile To translate a program in a high-level language into machine language, using a compiler.

compile time The phase of program translation (as opposed to the phase of program execution known as run-time).

compiler A program that translates a high-level language program (source code) into machine code (object code).

compiler listing A copy of a program into which have been inserted messages from the compiler (indicating errors in the program that prevent its translation into machine language if appropriate).

compiler options Selectable options chosen through command lines or program comment lines directing the compiler to perform compilation in certain ways.

complete binary tree Binary tree that is either full or full through the next-to-last level, with the leaves on the last level as far left as possible.

complete graph Graph in which every vertex is connected to every other vertex.

component A logical part or element of a data structure.

component type *See* base type.

compound statement A group of statements between the Pascal reserved words BEGIN and END that are treated as a single statement.

computer A programmable electronic device that can store, retrieve, and process data.

computer program A sequence of instructions outlining the steps to be performed by a computer.

computer programming The process of planning a sequence of instructions for a computer to perform.

condition A Boolean expression used to determine the action of a selection or looping control structure.

conditional *See* selection.

constant A location in memory, referenced by a program constant name (identifier), where a data value is stored (this value cannot be changed).

control abstraction The separation of the logical properties of a control structure from its implementation.

control structure A construct that determines the flow of control in part of a program and is usually represented by a statement, with the basic types being the sequence, selection, and loop.

control unit The computer component that controls the actions of the other components in order to execute instructions (A program) in sequence.

crash The cessation of a computer's operations as a result of the failure of one of its components.

cross reference An index of the identifiers used in a program indicating the lines on which each was used.

data Information that has been put into a form usable by a computer—that is, a form suitable for analysis or decision making.

data abstraction The separation of the logical properties of the organization of a program's data from its implementation, ignoring inessential details.

data encapsulation   Separation of the representation of data from the applications that use the data at a logical level.

data structure   A collection of data elements whose organization is characterized by accessing functions that are used to store and retrieve individual data elements.

data type   *See* type.

debugging   The task of removing errors, or "bugs," from a computer program.

declaration   A statement that associates an identifier with a process or object so that the user can refer to that process or object by name.

declaration section   The part(s) of a Pascal program where identifiers to be used in a procedure or program are specified.

default value   An assumed value used by a system or compiler when no specific choice is given by the program or the user.

depth-first search   Searching strategy of going down a branch to its deepest point before examining other nodes on the same level.

descendant   A node in a tree that is the child of another node, or the child of another descendant of that node.

design inspection   Meeting of a technical team to perform a formal reading of the design of a computer program, with the goal of identifying errors.

design walkthrough   Meeting of a technical team to perform a manual simulation of the design of a computer program with sets of sample test data, with the goal of finding errors.

deskchecking   A verification technique whereby the programmer writes down essential data then walks through the program marking any changes in the data to see if the results are as expected.

digraph   *See* directed graph.

direct access   *See* random access.

directed graph   Graph in which each edge is directed from one vertex to one (may be the same) vertex; sometimes called digraph.

disk   A secondary mass storage medium providing a large amount of permanent storage; a rotating magnetic disk used to store and retrieve magnetically encoded data through a read-write head that is in close proximity to the surface of the disk.

documentation   Written descriptions, specifications, design, code, and comments (internal and external to a program) which make a program readable, understandable, and more easily modified; also, a user's manual for a program. *See* self-documenting code.

dope vector   A table of information that is used by the compiler to keep track of the characteristics of an array.

doubly linked list   Linked list in which each node is linked to both its successor and its predecessor.

down   A descriptive term applied to a computer when it is not in a usable condition.

dynamic allocation   Creation of storage space in memory for a variable during run-time (as opposed to static allocation during compile-time). *See* referenced variable.

dynamic data structure   A data structure that may expand and contract during run-time.

dynamic storage   *See* dynamic allocation.

dynamic variable   A variable created during execution of a program and hence not declared in the declaration section of a program.

echo printing   Printing the data values input to a program so that it can be verified that they are correct.

edge   Connection between two nodes in a graph; sometimes called arc.

editor   An interactive program that allows the user to create and alter test files such as data, programs, manuscripts, etc.

empty set   The set with no members at all.

empty statement   An allowable Pascal syntax, implying no action, that is created when two statement separators (such as a semi-colon and END) are used consecutively. Sometimes needed when no action is required after a case label list.

end-of-file (EOF) marker   The mechanism for indicating the end of a file.

end-of-line (EOLN) marker   The mechanism for indicating the end of a line. (Pascal returns a blank when this marker is read.)

enumerated type   *See* user-defined type.

error checking   Explicit checking for invalid and error conditions in a program.

executing   The action of a computer performing as instructed by a given program.

execution time   *See* run time.

exponential notation   *See* scientific notation.

expression   A sequence of identifiers and/or constants, separated by compatible operators, that is evaluated at run-time.

external documentation   Program specification, design, and development history that are external to the body of executable code.

external file   A permanently stored file separate from the executing program.

external pointer (to a list)   A named pointer variable that references the first node in a linked list.

field identifier   The name of a component in a record.

field selector   The expression used to access components of a Pascal record variable, consisting of the record variable name and the field identifier separated by a period.

fieldwidth   The total number of columns (character positions) allotted to an output value in a Write or Writeln statement.

FIFO queue   A data structure in which elements are added to the rear and removed from the front of the list; a "first-in, first-out" (FIFO) structure.

file   A data structure consisting of a sequence of components that are all of the same type; a collection of related data, usually stored on disk or tape, and referenced by a single name.

file buffer   *See* file buffer variable.

file buffer variable   A variable of the same type as the components of the file with which it is associated, and used as a "window" through which we can read or write file components.

file data type   A collection of components, all of the same data type, accessed sequentially, one component at a time.

flag   A Boolean variable that is set in one part of the program and tested in another to control the logical flow of a program.

floating point number   The value stored in a type Real variable, so called because part of the memory location is assumed to hold the exponent and the balance of the location contains the number itself, with the decimal point floating as necessary among the significant digits.

flow of control   The order in which statements are executed in a program. *See* control structure.

folding   A hash method that breaks the key into several pieces and concatenates or exclusive-OR's some of them to form the hash address.

FOR statement   A looping control structure similar to a WHILE loop but with predefined initial and final values for the loop control variable, as well as automatic incrementing (or decrementing) of the loop control variable.

formal parameter   A variable, declared and used in a procedure or function declaration, that is replaced by an actual parameter when the procedure or function is called.

formal parameter list   The list of formal parameters contained in a procedure or function heading.

formatting   The planned positioning of statements or declarations and blanks on a line of a program; the arranging of program output so that it is neatly spaced and aligned.

free format   An allowable formatting of program statements characterized by no rules governing the indentation or number of syntax elements that may appear on a line of code.

full binary tree   Binary tree in which all the leaves are on the same level and every nonleaf node has two children.

function   A subroutine that returns a value when called. *See* subroutine, parameter.

functional domain   The set of valid input data for a program or subprogram.

function call   An expression in the main program requiring the computer to execute a function subprogram.

function result   The value computed by the function subprogram and then returned to the main program; often called just the result.

general case   In a recursive definition, the case for which the solution is expressed in terms of a smaller version of itself; recursive case.

global identifier   An identifier declared in the outermost block (main program); an identifier that is not local to a block but whose scope includes that block.

GOTO   Unconditional branch to a statement in a program; almost never seen in structured programs.

graph   Data structure that consists of a set of nodes and a set of edges that relate the nodes to each other.

hardware   The physical components of a computer.

hash function   Function used to manipulate the key of a record in a list to produce a unique location.

hashing   Technique used for ordering and accessing elements in a list in a relatively constant amount of time by manipulating the key to produce a (hopefully) unique location.

header node   Dummy node at the beginning of a list; used to simplify list processing and/or to contain information about the list.

heap   A complete binary tree, each of whose elements contains a value that is greater than or equal to the value of each of its children.

hierarchical records   Records in which at least one of the fields is itself a record.

high-level language   A programming language that is

closer to natural language than assembly language and whose statements each translate into more than one machine language instruction.

homogeneous   A descriptive term applied to structures in which all components are of the same data type (such as an array).

identifiers   Names that are associated with processes and objects and used to refer to those processes and objects. Pascal identifiers are made up of letters and numbers but must begin with a letter.

implementing   Coding and testing an algorithm.

index   An ordinal value identifying a particular component of a data structure such as an array.

infinite loop   A loop whose terminating condition would never be reached; the loop would (theoretically) execute indefinitely and the program would never terminate.

infinite recursion   The situation in which a subprogram calls itself over and over without end.

infix notation   Notation for expressions in which the binary operator is placed between its operands.

information hiding   Principle of making details of a function or data structure inaccessible to other parts of the program.

initialize   To assign an initial value to a variable.

inorder traversal   Traversal of a binary tree in which each node is visited between its left and right subtrees.

input   Any external data used by a program, from whatever source, such as a keyboard or disk file.

input/output (I/O)   Media and devices used to achieve human/machine communication.

input prompts   Messages printed by an interactive program, explaining what data is to be entered.

insertion sort   A sorting algorithm in which values are placed one at a time into their proper position within a list that was originally empty.

integer number   A positive or negative whole number made up of a sign and digits (when the sign is omitted, a positive sign is assumed).

integration testing   Testing which is performed to integrate program modules that have already been independently unit tested.

interactive processing   Use of an interactive program; user interaction with a program usually by prompts, data entry, and commands made through a terminal.

interactive programming   Use of an interactive system to create and compile programs through the use of an editor, compiler, debugger, and other tools.

interactive system   Direct communication between the user and the computer; a terminal/computer connection allowing direct entry of programs and data and providing immediate feedback to the user.

interface   A shared boundary where independent systems meet and act on or communicate with each other.

internal documentation   Features within the executable code that make a program easy to read and understand; includes comments, prettyprinting, and self-documenting code.

interpreter   A program that translates each statement of a (usually) high-level language source program into a sequence of machine code instructions which are executed before the next statement of the source program is translated.

invoke   *See* call.

ISO   International Organization for Standardization, an organization that promotes voluntary standards.

iteration   An individual pass through, or repetition of, the body of a loop.

key   Field in a record whose value is used to determine the logical (and/or physical) order of the records in a list or file.

key-ordered list   A list in which the elements are ordered according to the value of a key field of each element.

label   A name used in a computer program to identify an instruction, statement, data value, record, or file; an integer in the range 1 to 9999 declared in a Pascal label declaration and used to mark a particular statement, usually as the destination of an unconditional jump (GOTO).

language independence   A feature of abstract data types and algorithms that allows them to be implemented in almost any general-purpose programming language.

leaf   Node in a tree that has no children.

leaf node   Node in a tree that has no children.

left child   Node to the left of a given node in a binary tree; sometimes called left son.

left subtree   All the nodes to the left of a given node in a binary tree.

linear probing   Resolving a hash collision by sequentially searching a hash table beginning at the hash address.

linked list   List in which the order of the elements is determined by an explicit link field in each element rather than sequential order in memory.

listing   *See* source listing.

literal   A symbol that defines itself; a constant value such as a literal string or number.

local identifier An identifier declared in the block where it is used. *See* name precedence.

local variable Variable declared within a procedure subprogram and accessible only within the block in which it was declared; the value of this variable is destroyed when the procedure returns control to the calling program.

logical operator A symbol used in a Boolean expression whose operation results in a Boolean value of True or False.

loop A control structure that allows a statement(s) to be executed more than once (until a termination condition is reached).

loop control variable A variable (usually ordinal) used to control the number of times the body of a loop is executed.

loop invariant An assertion of what conditions must be true on entry into an iteration of a loop body and on exit from the loop.

machine language The language used directly by the computer and composed of binary coded instructions.

main storage Also main memory. *See* memory.

mainframe A large computing system designed for high-volume processing or for use by many people at once.

maintenance The modification of a program, after it has been completed, in order to meet changing requirements or to take care of any errors that show up.

memory The ordered sequence of storage cells (locations, words, places) in a computer that are accessed by address and used to temporarily hold the instructions and variables of an executing program. *See* secondary storage.

memory unit The internal data storage of a computer. *See* memory.

metric-based testing Testing in which goals are based on certain measurable factors.

modular decomposition *See* top-down design.

modular design A design methodology that breaks the program down into independent logical units or modules.

module An independent unit that is part of a whole; a logical part of a design or program, such as a procedure.

multi-dimensional array An array of one or more arrays.

name precedence The priority of a local identifier over a more global identifier, where the identifiers have the same name. *See* scope.

nested logic A control structure contained within another control structure.

NIL A constant in Pascal that can be assigned to a pointer type variable, indicating that the pointer points to nothing.

NIL pointer A pointer that points to nothing.

node Element in a list or tree.

object code The machine code produced by a compiler or assembler from a source program. Also called object program.

object-oriented programming (OOP) A programming methodology that uses the properties of encapsulation, inheritance, and polymorphism to build and manipulate data types.

operating system The set of programs that manage computer resources.

operator A symbol that indicates an operation to be performed.

operator precedence *See* precedence rules.

order of magnitude Ways of expressing relationships between large numbers by using formal approximation. Used in computing to express amount of work done.

ordinal type A set of distinct values that are ordered such that each value (except the first) has a unique predecessor and each value (except the last) has a unique successor; any scalar type except REAL.

output Data produced by a program and sent to an external file or device.

overflow A condition where the results of a calculation are too large to represent on a given machine. *See* precision.

packed array An array which occupies as little memory space as possible by having as many array components as possible packed into each memory word.

packed option A Pascal feature allowing more efficient storage of records and arrays.

palindrome String that reads the same backward or forward (e.g., RADAR).

parameter An expression passed in a procedure or function call. *See* actual parameter, formal parameter.

parameter list *See* actual parameter list, formal parameter list.

path Sequence of vertices that connects two nodes in a graph. Also, a combination of branches that might be traveled when a program is executed.

path testing A testing technique whereby the programmer tries to execute all possible paths in a program or subprogram.

peripheral device   An input, output, or auxiliary storage device of a computer.

pointer   A simple data type, consisting of an unbounded set of values, which addresses or otherwise indicates the location of a variable of a given type.

pointer type variable   A variable that contains an address in memory.

portability   The ability of software written for one computer to run successfully on different machines.

postconditions   Assertions that state what results are to be expected at the exit of an operation or procedure, assuming that the preconditions are true.

postfix notation   Notation for expressions in which the binary operator follows its operands.

postorder traversal   Traversal of a binary tree in which each node is visited after its left and right subtrees.

powerset   *See* universal set.

precedence rules   The order in which operations are performed in an expression.

precision   The maximum number of significant digits.

preconditions   Assertions that must be true on entry into an operation or procedure for the postconditions to be guaranteed.

prefix notation   Notation for expressions in which the binary operator precedes its operands.

preorder traversal   Traversal of a binary tree in which each node is visited before its right and left subtrees.

prettyprinting   Program formatting to make a program more readable.

priority queue   A data structure in which only the highest priority (e.g., largest value of some field representing priority) element can be accessed.

procedure   A subroutine that is executed when called. *See* subroutine, parameter.

procedure call   *See* call.

programming   The planning, scheduling, or performing of a task or an event. *See* computer programming.

programming language   A set of rules, symbols, and special words used to construct a program.

programming language implementation   The representation of a programming language on a particular computer system; a specific compiler and associated run-time support subroutines.

program verification   The process of determining the degree to which a software product fulfills its specifications.

pseudo-code   A mixture of English and Pascal-like control structures used to specify a design.

quadratic probing   Resolving a collision by applying a rehash function of the form (HashAddress + I2) MOD ArraySize, where I is the number of times that the rehash function has been applied.

queue   *See* FIFO queue, priority queue.

queuing system   System made up of servers and queue(s) of objects to be served.

random access   The process of retrieving or storing elements in a data structure where the time required for such access is independent of the order of the elements.

random probing   Resolving a collision by reaching random locations in a hash table for the hash target.

range   The interval within which values must fall, specified in terms of the largest and smallest allowable values.

range-checking   The automatic detection of an out-of-range value being assigned to a variable.

real number   A number that has a whole and a fractional part and no imaginary part.

record   A structured data type with a fixed number of components (not necessarily of the same type) that are accessed by name (not subscript).

recursion   The ability of a procedure or function to call itself.

recursive algorithm   A solution that is expressed in terms of (a) smaller instances of itself and (b) a base case.

recursive call   A subprogram call in which the subprogram being called is the same as the one making the call.

recursive definition   A definition in which something is defined in terms of smaller versions of itself.

referenced variable   A variable accessed not by name but through a pointer variable; a dynamic variable; a variable created by the procedure NEW in Pascal.

refinement   In top-down design, the expansion of a module specification to form a new module that solves a major step in the computer solution of a problem.

regression testing   Re-execution of program tests after modifications have been made in order to ensure that the program still works correctly.

rehashing   Resolving a collision by computing a new hash address using a hash function.

relational operator   A symbol that forms an expression with two values of compatible types, and whose operation comparing these values results in a Boolean value of True or False.

repeat statement   A looping control structure similar to a WHILE loop, except that there will always be at least one execution of the loop since the loop condition is tested after the body of the loop.

representational error An arithmetic error that occurs when the precision of the result of an arithmetic operation is greater than the precision of a given machine.

requirements Statement of what is to be provided by a computer system or software product.

reserved word An identifier that has a specific meaning in a programming language and may not be used for any other purpose in a program.

return The point at which execution of a subprogram is completed and execution resumes with the statement immediately following the call.

right child Node to the right of a given node in a binary tree; sometimes called right son.

right-justified Placed as far to the right as possible.

right subtree All the nodes to the right of a given node in a binary tree.

robustness The ability of a program to recover following an error and to continue operating within its environment.

root node The external pointer to a tree data structure; the top or base node of a tree.

round off To truncate (or make zero) one or more least significant digits of a number, and to increase the remaining least significant digit by one if the truncated value is more than half of the number base. Pascal provides a function to round off a real value to the nearest integer.

row-major order An array organization where the elements are stored in memory row by row.

run-time The phase of program execution during which program instructions are performed.

run-time error Software error that occurs during the execution of the program.

run-time stack A data structure that keeps track of activation records during the execution of a program.

scalar data type A set of distinct values (constants) that are ordered.

scientific notation A method of representing a number as an expression consisting of a number between 1 and 10 multiplied by the appropriate power of 10. Also called floating point notation.

scope The range or area within a program in which an identifier is known.

searching The locating of a particular element in a data structure.

secondary storage Backup storage for the main storage (memory) of a computer, usually permanent in nature (such as tape or disk).

seed Global variable that initializes a random number generator.

selection A control structure that selects one of possibly several options or paths in the flow of control, based upon the value of some expression.

self-documenting code Source code that uses meaningful identifier names, as well as effective use of clarifying comments.

semantics The set of rules which give the meaning of a statement.

sentinel A special data value used to mark the end of a data file.

sequential access The process of retrieving or storing elements in a fixed order in a data structure where the time required for such access is dependent on the order of the elements.

sequential search A search technique in which elements are examined sequentially until the target element is found.

set A structured data type composed of an unordered collection of distinct elements (members) chosen from the values of the base type.

siblings Nodes in a tree that have the same parent node; sometimes called brothers.

side effects A change, within a procedure or function, to a variable that is external to, but not passed to, the procedure or function.

significant digits Those digits that begin with the first non-zero digit on the left and end with the last non-zero digit on the right (or a zero digit that is exact).

simple type A scalar type; a type that is not structured; any of the Pascal types Integer, Real, Boolean, Char or any user-defined (ordinal) type.

simulation A problem solution that has been arrived at through the application of an algorithm designed to model the behavior of physical systems, materials, or processes.

software Computer programs; the set of all programs available to a computer.

software engineering Disciplined approach to the design, production, and maintenance of computer programs that are developed on time and within cost estimates, using tools that help manage the size and complexity of the resulting software products.

software specifications Detailed description of the function, inputs, processing, outputs, and special requirements of a software product, which provides the information needed to design and implement the program.

sorted (value-ordered) list A list in which the elements are ordered according to their value or the value of a key field of each element.

sorting Arrangement of elements in a list according to the increasing (or decreasing) values of some key field of each element.

source code Also called source program; a program in its original form, in the language in which it was written, prior to any compilation or translation.

source listing A printout of a source program processed by a compiler and showing compiler messages, including any syntax errors in the program.

specifications The formal definition of a problem to be solved, describing its inputs and outputs and pre- and post-conditions.

stack A data structure in which elements are entered and removed from only one end; a "last in, first out" (LIFO) structure.

stack overflow The condition resulting from trying to push an element onto a full stack.

stack underflow The condition resulting from trying to pop an empty stack.

statement An instruction in a programming language.

statement separator A symbol used to tell the compiler where one instruction ends and another begins in a program, such as the semi-colon in Pascal.

static allocation Creation of storage space in memory for a variable at compile-time (cannot be changed at run-time).

static data structure A data structure fixed in size at compile-time. *See* static allocation.

step-wise refinement A design method in which an algorithm is specified at an abstract level and additional levels of detail are added in successive iterations throughout the design process. *See* top-down design.

storage *See* memory.

string A collection of characters interpreted as a single data item; a packed character array.

structured design A design methodology incorporating a high degree of modularity, and employing generic control structures having only one entry and one exit. *See* top-down design.

structured programming The use of structured design and the coding of a program that parallels the structure of the design. *See* top-down programming.

structured type A type composed of more than one element, which at its lowest level is a simple type; any of the Pascal types ARRAY, RECORD, SET, and FILE.

stub Dummy procedure or function that is used in top-down testing to stand in for a lower-level subprogram.

subprogram *See* subroutine.

subrange type A data type composed of a specified range of any standard or user-defined ordinal type.

subroutine A collection of statements in a program, but not part of the main program, that is treated as a named entity, performs a specific task, and is capable of being called (invoked) from more than one point in the program; a function or procedure in Pascal.

subscript *See* index.

subscripted variable *See* array.

subset The set A is a subset of the set B if each element of A is an element of B.

symbol table Table, defined by the compiler, that maps variables to memory locations.

syntax The formal rules governing the construction of valid statements in a language.

syntax diagram A pictorial definition of the syntax rules of a programming language.

syntax error Invalid construction of statements in a programming language, which is detected during the compilation of the program.

system software The set of programs that improves the efficiency and convenience of using a computer, such as the operating system, editor, and compiler.

tag field Field in a variant record that determines which set of variant fields will be included in a particular instance of the record.

tail recursion Condition when a subprogram contains a single recursive invocation that is the last statement in the subprogram.

tape A secondary mass storage medium providing a large amount of permanent storage; a thin plastic strip having a magnetic surface used to store and retrieve magnetically encoded data through a read/write head that is in close proximity to the surface of the tape.

test driver Program that sets up the testing environment by declaring and assigning initial values to variables, then calls the subprogram to be tested.

test plan A document showing the test cases planned for a program or module, their purposes, inputs, expected outputs, and criteria for success.

text file A file of characters that is also divided into lines.

time sharing A method of operation in which a computer is shared by several users simultaneously.

top-down design A design methodology that works from an abstract functional description of a problem (top) to a detailed solution (bottom); a hierarchical approach to problem solving that divides a problem into functional sub-problems represented by modules, which are easier to solve and which may themselves be further broken down into modules. The design consisting of a hierarchy of separate modules (solutions), with lower level modules containing greater detail than higher level modules. *See* structured design.

top-down programming Programming that incorporates top-down design, and, through the use of procedures, functions, and control structures, maintains in the program the modularity and structure of the design.

top-down testing A technique for testing the modules (procedures and functions) of a program, as they are written, by calling them with actual parameters and providing stub (dummy) modules for those modules not yet written but referenced in the program.

trace To follow the logical flow of a program and determine the value of variables after each instruction. Also known as code walk-through and playing computer.

trailer node Dummy node at the end of a list used to simplify list operations.

translator A program that translates from one programming language to another (usually machine code). *See* assembler, compiler, interpreter.

tree A data structure composed of a root node having offspring that are also nodes that can have offspring, and so on.

tree diagram A hierarchical chart showing the relationships of modules in a top-down design.

truncation The decrease in precision of a number by the loss or removal of one or more least significant digits.

type A formal description of the set of values that a variable of a given type may take or to which a datum of that type must belong.

type definition A definition of a data type in Pascal in the type declaration of a block, with the type identifier on the left of the equal sign (" = ") and the definition on the right.

unary operator An operator requiring only one operand such as the logical operator NOT.

underflow A condition that occurs when the results of a calculation are too small to represent in a given machine.

undirected graph A graph in which the edges have no direction.

unit testing Testing which is performed to verify that a single "unit" (procedure, module, or package) of a program meets its specifications.

universal set The set consisting of all values of the base type.

user-defined (enumerated) type The ordered set of distinct values (constants) defined as a data type in a program. *See* ordinal type.

value parameter A formal parameter that is a local variable of a procedure or function, but whose value is initialized to the value of an actual parameter in a call to the procedure or function.

variable A location in memory, referenced by a program variable name (identifier), where a data value can be stored (this value can be changed during program execution).

variable declaration The creation of a variable in Pascal in the variable declaration section of a block with the variable identifier on the left of the colon (":") and the type definition or identifier on the right.

variable parameter A formal parameter that is replaced by an actual parameter in a call to procedure or function.

variant record Record type which may contain different collections of fields, according to the value of a tag field.

verification The process of determining the degree to which a software product fulfills its specifications.

vertex (pl. vertices) A node in a graph.

weighted graph Graph in which each edge carries a value.

white box testing *See* clear box testing.

window *See* file buffer variable.

word A group of bits, one or more bytes in length, treated as a unit or location in memory, and capable of being addressed.

word size The number of bits comprising a word or location in memory.

Answers to Selected Exercises

Chapter 1

1. Software engineering is a disciplined approach to the creation and maintenance of computer programs throughout their whole life cycle.

4. Some software tools used in developing computer programs are text editors, compilers, assemblers, operating systems, and debugging programs.

7. Software specifications tell exactly *what* a program will do, but *not* how it will do it.

9. Ways to make your programs readable and easily understood include modular programming; use of comments, self-documenting code, prettyprinting, and constants; and avoidance of "tricky" code.

12. The first step in developing any software program is to *think*.

13. When requirements in a programming assignment are ambiguous, you should ask the instructor to clarify them. If that is not possible (for instance, if it is 2:30 Sunday morning), you should make your best guess as to what is required and explicitly document your interpretation in the program's Assumptions section.

15. (a) *Examples of O(1) algorithms:* printing a character to the screen, incrementing a variable, adding two numbers together.

    (b) *Examples of O(N) algorithms:* initializing all of the elements in a one-dimensional array to zero, incrementing all the elements in a one-dimensional array, multiplying two numbers by performing successive addition operations, raising a number to a power by performing successive multiplication operations.

    (c) *Examples of $O(N^2)$ algorithms:* initializing all of the elements in a two-dimensional array to zero, printing out all the elements in a two-dimensional array, searching for the smallest element in an unsorted two-dimensional array.

18. Algorithm 3 [$O(\log_2 N)$] should execute the fastest; Algorithm 2 [$O(N)$] should execute the slowest.

20. If a program needs to be finished quickly, sometimes the programmer's time is a more important efficiency consideration than how fast the resulting program will run on a computer.

23. *Details* should never be found in the top level of a top-down design.

25. "Implementation" refers to the actual solving of the problem in a way that can be executed on a computer. Implementation answers the *how* questions.

27. Examples of data abstraction include "list of student information," "file of employee records," "bank account database," "grocery list."

29. "External documentation" is program documentation that exists outside of the program's source code. Some examples are user manuals, specification documents, the program's top-down design, and historical records of the program's development.

30. Examples of internal documentation include comments, variable names, procedure names, and constants.

32.
```
CONST
   Pi = 3.1417;

VAR
   Height      : Real;
   Radius      : Real;
   CylinderArea : Real;

   .

   .

   .

   CylinderArea := Height * Pi * SQR (Radius);
```

34. The *main program* is analogous to the main module of the top–down design.

36. *This Week*

Monday	THINK.
Tuesday	Write detailed description. Get answers to questions about requirements.
Wednesday	Write top-down design level 0.
Thursday– Sunday	Write detailed levels of top-down design.

Next Week

Monday	Begin coding from detailed design.
Tuesday	Complete coding (program compiles without error).
Wednesday–Friday	Test program. (Finish before 2:00 P.M. Friday.)
Weekend	Attend sister's wedding.

Two Weeks from Now

Monday	Double-check that all documentation is ready to be turned in with program.
Tuesday	Turn in program.

38. The functions Length and CharAt were created to encapsulate StringType, so that implementation details were not accessible to the string user. Software engineering principles: information hiding, data encapsulation.

41. ProcessProgramFile: O(N)
    LineStatus: O(1)

Chapter 2

1. (a) False; software verification begins at the start of the software lifecycle.
   (b) False; testing is just one part of the program verification effort.
   (c) False; testing does not "prove" program correctness.
   (d) True.
   (e) False; syntax errors are usually detected by the compiler.

4. A syntax error is an error in the use of the programming language, and will most likely be found at compile time, if it has not been detected by visual inspection of

the program. A logical error is an error in how the program works, and will most likely be detected at run time, by causing the program to crash or to produce wrong results.

7. Some examples of run-time errors occurring as the result of a programmer making too many assumptions include: attempting to divide without checking the value of the denominator (to avoid dividing by 0), attempting to use data read from user inputs without checking its value, attempting to use the value in a data structure without checking to see if the structure is empty.

9. *Designing for correctness* involves using program design strategies in an attempt to ensure that the program will be correct. The types of assertions described in this chapter that can contribute to the correctness of a design are preconditions/postconditions and loop invariants.

12. (a) A loop invariant is an assertion of the conditions that must be true on entry into an iteration of the loop body, and that are true on exit from the loop.

    (b) Loop Invariant: 1 < = Index < = ElementCount + 1 AND TargetValue does not exist in DataList[1] . . DataList[Index − 1].

15. We must always check that the loop will terminate.

18. The purpose of conducting design and code inspections is to identify errors in programs as early as possible, before the actual execution of the program during testing.

22. (a) There would be an infinite loop, with nothing printed.

    (b) Remove the semicolon after DO.

25. A single programmer could use the inspection process as a way to do a structured "desk check" of his or her program and would especially benefit from inspection checklists of errors to look for.

28. *Unit testing* is the testing of a single unit of the program (for instance, a procedure or function). *Integration testing* is the testing of groups of already tested units to make sure that they interact correctly and that the whole program works according to its specifications.

31. *Data coverage* refers to testing the possible inputs or classes of inputs that may occur in the execution of the program. *Code coverage* refers to testing the structure of the program's solution by driving the execution into the various paths or branches of the program. Neither strategy is necessarily better than the other. The best type of testing to use depends on the testing strategy and requirements.

34. *Branches* and *paths* refer to code segments (and combinations of segments) that should be executed in various test cases. It is possible to attempt 100% branch coverage of a program; this means that every branch in the program will be executed in some test case. It is not possible to attempt 100% path coverage of anything but the most trivial programs because of the explosion of test cases that would have to be generated. Metric-based testing refers to the idea of measuring the amount or percent of the program tested, using some unit of measure (e.g., statements or branches).

37. A *test driver* is needed for testing lower-level program modules independently of the source of their call. This type of testing is very effective for testing utility routines without having to deal with the parts of the program that input the values used for parameters. It is especially useful when several programmers are working

on different parts of a program and need to test their sections independently before integrating the program.

Chapter 3

1. *Data abstraction* refers to the logical picture of data—what the data represents rather than how it is represented.

4. (a) Objects of type Text are files of character data. The operations defined for variables of type Text are the procedures Reset, Rewrite, Read, Readln, Write, and Writeln, and the functions EOF and EOLN. (Some versions of Pascal provide other file operations.)

   (b) The implementation of Text-type file variables is inaccessible to the file user. The physical file can only be modified through calls to the file operations. Thus type Text is encapsulated by its operations.

6. Two components of a data structure are a logical arrangement of data elements and a set of operations to access the elements.

9. The structured data types that are built in to Pascal are: arrays, records, variant records, sets, and files. Some versions of Pascal have other built-in data types (for instance, strings).

12. The accessing function of a Pascal one-dimensional array is direct access through the element's index.

15. The accessing function of a two-dimensional array is

   ArrayName [*FirstDimension*, *SecondDimension*]

   where *ArrayName* is the name of a two-dimensional array variable, *FirstDimension* is the desired index in the first array dimension, and *SecondDimension* is the desired index in the second array dimension. An example of a two dimensional array is a chess board.

17. (a) TYPE
```
      WeatherListType = ARRAY [MonthType] OF WeatherRecType;
   VAR
      YearlyWeather : WeatherListType;
```
   (b) `YearlyWeather[July].ActualRain := 1.05;`
   (c) 238

20. *Field*

Field	Length	Offset
FirstName	10	0
LastName	10	10
ID	1	20
GPA	2	21
CurrentHours	1	23
TotalHours	1	24

24. (a) The following is one suggestion (by someone who doesn't know anything about meteorology). The answer must include a variant record.

```
TYPE
  String20 = PACKED ARRAY[1 .. 20] OF Char;

DateType = RECORD
  Day    : 1 .. 31;
  Month  : 1 .. 12;
  Year   : 1900 .. 2100
END;  (* DateType *)

TempType       =  -100 .. 150;
HumType        =  0 .. 100;
DirectionType  = (N, NE, E, SE, S, SW, W, NW);
WeatherType    =
  (Snow, Thunderstorm, Hurricane, Drought, Windstorm);

WeatherRecord  = RECORD
  (* fixed part *)
  Date          : DateType;
  HighTemp      : TempType; (* degrees Fahrenheit *)
  LowTemp       : TempType; (* degrees Fahrenheit *)
  RainFall      : Real;     (* inches            *)
  Humidity      : HumType;  (* percent           *)

  (* variant part *)
  CASE Weather  :  WeatherType OF
    Snow        :  (Inches  : Real);
    Thunderstorm :  ();
    Hurricane   :  (HurricaneWind : Integer;
                    HurricaneName : String20);
    Drought     :  ();
    Windstorm   :  (WindSpeed      : Integer;
                    WindDirection : DirectionType)

END;  (* WeatherRecord *)
```

(b)

Date	Date	Date	Date
HighTemp	HighTemp	HighTemp	HighTemp
LowTemp	LowTemp	LowTemp	LowTemp
RainFall	RainFall	RainFall	RainFall
Humidity	Humidity	Humidity	Humidity
Weather = Snow	Weather = Thunderstorm or Drought	Weather = Hurricane	Weather = Windstorm
Inches	(Unused)	HurricaneWind	WindSpeed
(Unused)		HurricaneName	WindDirection
			(Unused)

27. Pascal supports data abstraction through the use of data type declarations, but does not enforce data encapsulation for programmer-defined types. There is nothing to prevent the user of the data type from accessing or updating the data directly without going through the specified operations.

31. (a)
```
CONST
   Max = 3;
   EmptySpace = '.';

TYPE
   RangeType = 1 .. Max;
   MarkType  = Char; (* 'X', '0', or EmptySpace *)
   BoardType = ARRAY [RangeType, RangeType] OF MarkType;
```

(b)
```
PROCEDURE Initialize
   (VAR Board : BoardType);

   (* Initialize Tic Tac Toe board to empty spaces. *)

VAR
  Row, Col : RangeType;

BEGIN (* Initialize *)
  FOR Row := 1 TO Max DO
    FOR Col := 1 TO Max DO
      Board[Row, Col] := EmptySpace
END;  (* Initialize *)

PROCEDURE Mark
 (VAR Board : BoardType;
  Row, Col  : RangeType;
  Value     : MarkType);

   (* Set designated space to Value. Assumes that *)
   (* the space is EmptySpace.                    *)

BEGIN (* Mark *)
  Board[Row,Col] := Value
END;  (* Mark *)

PROCEDURE Display
   (Board : BoardType);

   (* Display the Tic Tac Toe board. *)

VAR
  Row, Col : RangeType;

BEGIN (* Display *)
  FOR Row := 1 TO Max DO
    BEGIN  (* print the row *)
      FOR Col := 1 TO Max DO
        Write (Board[Row, Col]);
      Writeln
    END (* FOR Row *)
END;  (* Display *)
```

32. (a) The specification:

> **ReadFixedString (Data, Number, String)**
>
> | | |
> |---|---|
> | *Function:* | Reads Number of characters from Data file and returns them in String. |
> | *Input:* | Data (Text)
Number (Integer) |
> | *Preconditions:* | EOF will not be encountered; EOLN will be treated as a blank.
0 < Number < = MaxString. |
> | *Output:* | String (StringType) |
> | *Postconditions:* | String = string made up of Number of characters beginning at the current position on Data file. |

(b) The algorithm:

ReadFixed String

FOR Pos : = 1 TO Number DO
   Read next character and place in string.

Set string length.

(c)
```
PROCEDURE ReadFixedString
   (VAR Data   : Text;
    Number     : Integer;
    VAR String : StringType);

   (* See the previous specification. *)

VAR
  Pos : IndexType;

BEGIN  (* ReadFixedString *)

  (* Read characters and place in string. *)
  FOR Pos := 1 TO Number DO
    Read (Data, String.Chars[Pos]);

  (* Set string length. *)
  String.Length := Number

END; (* ReadFixedString *)
```

36. (a) $O(1)$.
   (b) Assumes StringType = PACKED ARRAY[1 . . MaxString] OF Char, with string characters left-justified, and the rest of the array padded with blanks.

```
FUNCTION Length
  (String : StringType) : StringRangeType;

  (* Returns the length characteristic of String. *)

VAR
  Pos : StringRangeType;

BEGIN (* Length *)

  Pos := MaxString;
```

```
(* Search for rightmost nonblank character.  *)
(* Loop Invariant: The array contains blanks *)
(* in String[Pos + 1] .. String[MaxString].  *)
WHILE (Pos > 1) AND (String[Pos] = ' ') DO
  Pos := Pos - 1;

IF String[Pos] = ' '
  THEN Length := 0
  ELSE Length := Pos

END; (* Length *)
```

This Length function is O(N).

Chapter 4

1. A stack is an ordered group of homogeneous elements; elements are added to and removed from only the top of the stack.

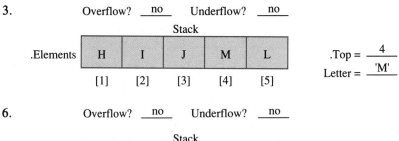

3.

Overflow? __no__   Underflow? __no__

Stack

.Elements | H | I | J | M | L | .Top = __4__

[1] [2] [3] [4] [5]   Letter = __'M'__

6.

Overflow? __no__   Underflow? __no__

Stack

.Elements | A | B | X | Y | Z | .Top = __4__

[1] [2] [3] [4] [5]   Letter = __'Z'__

8. (c)

9. (a) Pop (Stack, X − 1) would cause a syntax error at compile time, because the second parameter is a VAR parameter and X − 1 is an expression.

12. (a) As a stack-user:

```
FUNCTION StackTop
  (Stack : StackType) : StackElementType;

VAR
  Temp : StackElementType;

BEGIN (* StackTop *)
  Pop (Stack, Temp);
  Push (Stack, Temp);
  StackTop := Temp
END;  (* StackTop *)
```

(b) As a stack ADT operation:

```
FUNCTION StackTop
  (Stack : StackType) : StackElementType;

BEGIN (* StackTop *)
  StackTop := Stack.Elements[Stack.Top]
END;  (* StackTop *)
```

(c) If StackElementType were a record type, you would need to make this operation a procedure, since functions return scalar types.

14. CreateStack initializes the stack to its empty state, regardless of its previous state; it has no preconditions. The preconditions of the DestroyStack operation require the stack to have been created. This precondition is not important for the array-based stack, but is necessary for the linked version. If the stack had not been created, the pointer may contain garbage, and a call to DestroyStack would try to Dispose of node(s) whose addresses are meaningless.

16. (a) This implementation violates the idea of an array as a homogeneous collection of data. Though the elements are the same type (Integer) as the index of the top element, they are different, in terms of their purpose in the program. The use of the array is syntactically correct, but might be considered to be semantically incorrect.

    (b) This implementation choice would make no change in the stack specifications. The procedures and functions would need to be modified slightly from the array-based implementation in the chapter, changing references to "Stack.Top" to "Stack[0]" and references to "Stack.Elements" to "Stack".

17. The last node does not point to another node. Rather, its Next field contains a NIL value to indicate that this is the end of the stack.

19. (a) pointer
    (b) record
    (c) array
    (d) integer
    (e) pointer
    (f) record
    (g) integer

23. CreateStack (TempStack)

```
WHILE NOT EmptyStack (Pez) DO
  Pop (Pez, Candy)
  IF Candy = Yellow
    THEN Eat it
    ELSE Push (TempStack, Candy)

WHILE NOT EmptyStack (TempStack) DO
  Pop (TempStack, Candy)
  Push (Pez, Candy)
```

25.

Number of Elements	Static Array-Based	Dynamic Linked Stack
0	1202	4
10	1202	164
50	1202	804
100	1202	1604

27.
```
FUNCTION FullStack
    (Stack : StackType) : Boolean;

BEGIN (* FullStack *)
  FullStack := (MaxAvail < SizeOf(StackElementType))
END;  (* FullStack *)
```

28. If every expression was fully parenthesized, including parentheses around the outermost operands, we could modify the ProcessToken module to skip the call to PerformOperation in the case of an EndExpression token.

32. (a) True
    (b) False
    (c) False
    (d) True

33. (a) 25
    (b) 15
    (c) 23

36. (a) A 2 + B 4 + * 1 −
    (b) Z X 1 + 2 * 5 − Y / −
    (c) C 2 * 1 + A B + /

Chapter 5

1. A FIFO queue is an ordered group of homogeneous elements that satisfy the following property: New elements are added at the rear, and old elements are removed from the front.

4.   Overflow? __yes__   Underflow? __no__

Queue.Elements

V	W	X	Y	Z
[1]	[2]	[3]	[4]	[5]

Queue.Front = __5__
Queue.Rear = __4__

6.   Overflow? __no__   Underflow? __no__

Queue.Elements

V	W	X	Y	L
[1]	[2]	[3]	[4]	[5]

Queue.Front = __1__
Queue.Rear = __5__

8.   Overflow? __no__   Underflow? __no__

Queue.Elements

V	W	X	Y	Z
[1]	[2]	[3]	[4]	[5]

Queue.Front = __1__

Queue.Rear = __3__

QueueValue = __'V'__

10. (a) no
    (b) yes
    (c) no
    (d) no
    (e) yes
    (f) yes
    (g) no
    (h) yes
    (i) no

13. FUNCTION QueueCount
       (Queue : QueueType) : Integer;

    (* Return the number of elements in Queue. *)

    BEGIN (* QueueCount *)
      QueueCount := Queue.Count
    END; (* QueueCount *)

16. PROCEDURE Enqueue
       (VAR Queue   : QueueType;
        NewElement : QueueElementType);

    BEGIN (* Enqueue *)

      (* Get new rear position. *)
      Queue.Rear := (Queue.Rear MOD MaxQueue) + 1;

      (* Add new element to the rear of the queue. *)
      Queue.Elements[Queue.Rear] := NewElement;

      Queue.Count := Queue.Count + 1

    END; (* Enqueue *)

    PROCEDURE Dequeue
       (VAR Queue   : QueueType;
        VAR DeqElement : QueueElementType);

    BEGIN   (* Dequeue *)

      (* Get the front element. *)
      DeqElement := Queue.Elements[Queue.Front];

      (* Update the count and queue front indicator. *)
      Queue.Count := Queue.Count - 1;
      Queue.Front := (Queue.Front MOD MaxQueue) + 1

    END; (* Dequeue *)

19. FUNCTION EmptyQueue
    (Queue : QueueType) : Boolean;

```
BEGIN (* EmptyQueue *)
  EmptyQueue := (Queue.Front = NIL)
  (* alternately: EmptyQueue := (Queue.Count = 0) *)
END; (* EmptyQueue *)
```

```
(* Assuming that there is a MaxQueue size specified, *)
(* you could use the following function; otherwise,  *)
(* the FullQueue stub in the chapter text is used.   *)
FUNCTION FullQueue
  (Queue : QueueType) : Boolean;
```

```
BEGIN (* FullQueue *)
  FullQueue := (Queue.Count = MaxQueue)
END; (* FullQueue *)
```

22. (a) The space for the queue elements is allocated dynamically. (The space for all possible elements is allocated at the same time.)

    (b) The space for the variable Queue is the size of a pointer.

    (c) The create, destroy, and empty queue operations:

```
PROCEDURE CreateQueue
  (VAR Queue : QueueType);

BEGIN (* CreateQueue *)
  New (Queue);
  Queue^.Front := MaxQueue;
  Queue^.Rear  := MaxQueue
END;  (* CreateQueue *)
```

```
PROCEDURE DestroyQueue
  (VAR Queue : QueueType);

BEGIN (* DestroyQueue *)
  Dispose (Queue);
  Queue := NIL
END;  (* DestroyQueue *)
```

```
FUNCTION EmptyQueue
  (Queue : QueueType) : Boolean;

BEGIN  (* EmptyQueue *)
  EmptyQueue := (Queue^.Rear = Queue^.Front)
END;  (* EmptyQueue *)
```

    (d) FullQueue is a meaningful operation; it indicates whether there is space available in the array.

```
FUNCTION FullQueue
  (Queue : QueueType) : Boolean;
```

```
BEGIN (* FullQueue *)
  FullQueue := ((Queue^.Rear MOD MaxQueue) + 1 =
                   Queue^.Front)
END;  (* FullQueue *)
```

(e) You should modify the source code for the array-based implementation. The only change to the code is to replace references to "Queue" with "Queue^".

24. (a)

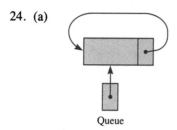

Queue

(b) Create, destroy, and empty queue operations:

```
PROCEDURE CreateQueue
  (VAR Queue : QueueType);

BEGIN (* CreateQueue *)
  Queue := NIL
END;  (* CreateQueue *)

PROCEDURE DestroyQueue
  (VAR Queue : QueueType);

VAR
  Ptr : QueuePtrType;

BEGIN (* DestroyQueue *)

  IF Queue <> NIL
    THEN  (* Queue is not empty *)
      BEGIN
        (* Mark the rear of the queue with NIL flag. *)
        Ptr := Queue;
        Queue := Queue^.Next;
        Ptr^.Next := NIL;

        (* Dispose of all the nodes in the Queue. *)
        WHILE Queue <> NIL DO
          BEGIN
            Ptr := Queue;
            Queue := Queue^.Next;
            Dispose (Ptr)
          END (* WHILE *)
      END (* IF *)
END;  (* DestroyQueue *)
```

```
FUNCTION EmptyQueue
    (Queue : QueueType) : Boolean;

BEGIN  (* EmptyQueue *)
  EmptyQueue := (Queue = NIL)
END;  (* EmptyQueue *)
```

(c)   Enqueue and Dequeue operations:

```
PROCEDURE Enqueue
    (VAR Queue      : QueueType;
     NewElement     : QueueElementType);

VAR
  NewNode : QueuePtrType;

BEGIN (* Enqueue *)

  (* Create a node for the new element. *)
  New (NewNode);
  NewNode^.Info := NewElement;

  (* Insert new node at rear of Queue. *)
  IF Queue = NIL (* queue is empty *)
    THEN NewNode^.Next := NewNode
    ELSE
      BEGIN (* insert into existing queue *)
        NewNode^.Next := Queue^.Next;
        Queue^.Next := NewNode
      END; (* ELSE *)

  (* Update external pointer to rear of Queue. *)
  Queue := NewNode

END;  (* Enqueue *)

PROCEDURE Dequeue
    (VAR Queue       : QueueType;
     VAR DeqElement : QueueElementType);
VAR
  TempPtr : QueuePtrType;

BEGIN (* Dequeue *)

  TempPtr := Queue^.Next;
  DeqElement := TempPtr^.Info;

  (* Check whether last node is being removed. *)
  IF Queue = TempPtr
    THEN Queue := NIL  (* last node *)
    ELSE Queue^.Next := TempPtr^.Next;

  Dispose (TempPtr)

END;  (* Dequeue *)
```

27. (a)   record
    (b)   pointer
    (c)   record

(d) integer

(e) record

(f) pointer

28. ```
PROCEDURE AddJob
    (ID   : Integer;
     Token : TokenType);
    (* Adds Token to appropriate queue for user's priority *)
    (* level, determined by ID number. Jobs used globally. *)

BEGIN (* AddJob *)
   Enqueue (Jobs[ID DIV 100], Token)
END; (* AddJob *)
```

31. ```
FUNCTION FullQueue
    (Queue : QueueType) : Boolean;

BEGIN (* FullQueue *)
   FullQueue := (MaxAvail < SizeOf(QueueElementType))
END;   (* FullQueue *)
```

33. The following are sample answers to this question:

(a) 1. A phone answering system with multiple operators (the servers) and a single waiting queue for incoming calls (the objects being served).

2. A bank with multiple tellers (the servers) and a single waiting line for customers (the objects being served).

(b) 1. A grocery store with multiple cashiers (the servers), each with a line of customers waiting to check out (the objects being served).

2. A student registration system, with desks (the servers) containing student registration packets. Each desk serves a particular portion of the alphabet (for instance, students whose last names begin with A–C, D–F, and so on); there is a separate line of students (the objects being served) waiting at each desk.

35. (a) Replace the Queue ADT declarations and operations with the array-based implementation and recompile.

(b) ```
PROCEDURE UpdateQueue
    (VAR Queue : QueueType);

    (* Increment all queue elements by 1. *)

VAR
   Index : Integer;

BEGIN (* UpdateQueue *)

   IF Queue.Front <> Queue.Rear
      THEN (* Queue not empty *)
         BEGIN
            Index := Queue.Front;

            REPEAT
               Index := (Index MOD MaxQueue) + 1;
               Queue.Elements[Index] :=
                  Queue.Elements[Index] + 1
            UNTIL Index = Queue.Rear
         END (* IF *)
END;   (* UpdateQueue *)
```
```

    (c) Add checks for queue overflow.

38. (a) The input and output procedures were implemented as stubs to allow us to focus on the simulation processing.

    (b)
```
FUNCTION ReadyToStop : Boolean;
    (* Stub for Function ReadyToStop *)

BEGIN (* ReadyToStop *)
  ReadyToStop := True
END;  (* ReadyToStop *)
```

Chapter 6

1. (a) In a sequential list, the successor of each element is implicit from the element's physical position in the list; elements are placed in sequential slots within the structure. In a linked representation, the order of the elements is determined by explicit links between them.

    (b) Sequential lists are better solutions for problems in which random access to the elements is needed and in which the number of elements is known and stable. A sequential list might be employed, for example, for a list of student information for a class of 40 students, each with a student number from 1 to 40. Such a list might be used in meeting with individual students to discuss their progress and in generating report cards.

    (c) Linked lists are better solutions for problems in which you cannot predict the number of elements or in which the number of elements varies widely. Linked lists are more appropriate for accessing elements one after another than for accessing elements randomly. A linked list might be employed, for example, for a list of employee records that is used for creating phone lists and for producing paychecks.

4. (a) 30

    (b) 90

    (c) 45

7. (a) `List := A^.Next;`

    (b) `B := B^.Next;`

    (c) `List := NIL;`

    (d) `A^.Next^.Info.Key := 46;`

8. 7 7

11. (c) Syntactically incorrect, because of the forward reference to DataType in the record declaration.

13. (d) Syntactically incorrect, because the anonymous type ^DataNode cannot be used in a procedure heading.

16.
```
FUNCTION FullList
    (List : ListType) : Boolean;

BEGIN (* FullList *)
  FullList := (MaxAvail < SizeOf(ListElementType))
END;  (* FullList *)
```

18. (a)   The specification:

InsertElement (List, NewElement, ElementExists)

Function:	Adds NewElement to List if an element with this key is not already in the list.
Input:	List (ListType) NewElement (ListElementType)
Preconditions:	List is not full.
Output:	List ElementExists (Boolean)
Postconditions:	ElementExists = (element with key of NewElement is already in list). IF ElementExists, List is unchanged; otherwise List = original list plus NewElement.

(b)   The sequential-list implementation:

```
PROCEDURE InsertElement
  (VAR List          : ListType;
   NewElement        : ListElementType;
   VAR ElementExists : Boolean);

VAR
  Location : IndexType;   (* for FindElement interface  *)
  PredLoc  : IndexType;   (* index of preceding element *)
  Index    : IndexType;   (* used for moving data       *)
BEGIN (* InsertElement *)

  (* Find the insertion place. *)
  FindElement (List, NewElement.Key, Location, PredLoc);

  (* Set ElementExists based on Location info. *)
  ElementExists := (Location <> 0);

  (* If element is not already in the list, add it. *)
  IF NOT ElementExists
    THEN
      BEGIN

        (* Create space for new element. *)
        FOR Index := List.Length DOWNTO PredLoc + 1 DO
          List.Info[Index + 1] := List.Info[Index];

        (* Put new element in list. *)
        List.Info[PredLoc + 1] := NewElement;
        List.Length := List.Length + 1
      END (* IF NOT ElementExists *)

END; (* InsertElement *)
```

(c)   The linked-list implementation:

```
PROCEDURE InsertElement
  (VAR List          : ListType;
   NewElement        : ListElementType;
   VAR ElementExists : Boolean);

(* Add NewElement to List, leaving key value-ordered *)
(* structure of List intact.                         *)

VAR
  NewNode   : PointerType; (* pointer to the new node *)
  Location  : PointerType; (* ptr to element          *)
  PredLoc   : PointerType; (* ptr to preceding node   *)

BEGIN (* InsertElement *)

  (* Find the insert location. *)
  FindElement (List, NewElement.Key, Location, PredLoc);

  (* Set ElementExists, based on value of Location. *)
  ElementExists := (Location <> NIL);

  (* If the element is not already in the List, add it. *)
  IF NOT ElementExists
    THEN
      BEGIN

        (* Allocate a new node; put NewElement into it. *)
        New (NewNode);
        NewNode^.Info := NewElement;

        (* Insert the new node into the list. *)
        IF PredLoc = NIL
          THEN (* inserting first element *)
            BEGIN
              NewNode^.Next := List;
              List := NewNode
            END (* inserting first element *)

          ELSE (* inserting in the middle or at the end *)
            BEGIN
              NewNode^.Next := PredLoc^.Next;
              PredLoc^.Next := NewNode
            END (* inserting in middle or at end *)
      END (* IF NOT ElementExists *)
END; (* InsertElement *)
```

21. (a)   The sequential-list implementation:

```
PROCEDURE SplitList
   (VAR MainList : ListType;
    SplitValue   : KeyType;
    VAR List1    : ListType;
    VAR List2    : ListType);
```

```
(* Splits the nodes in MainList into two lists: Listl   *)
(* will contain all the nodes with values less than     *)
(* SplitValue, and List2 will contain all the nodes     *)
(* with key values greater than or equal to SplitValue. *)
(* MainList is left empty.                               *)
VAR
  Location, PredLoc : IndexType;

BEGIN (* SplitList *)

  (* Find the split place. *)
  FindElement (List, SplitValue, Location, PredLoc);

  (* Split the lists at the split place. *)
  IF PredLoc = NIL
    THEN (* main list is empty or splits before lst element *)
      BEGIN
        Listl.Length := 0;

        FOR Location := 1 TO MainList.Length DO
          List2.Info[Location] := MainList.Info[Location];

        List2.Length := MainList.Length
      END (* IF *)

    ELSE (* main list splits in middle or end *)
      BEGIN
        (* Move MainList elements from index 1 to *)
        (* PredLoc into Listl.                    *)
        FOR Location := 1 TO PredLoc DO
          Listl.Info[Location] := MainList.Info[Location];
        Listl.Length := PredLoc;

        (* Move MainList elements from index PredLoc + 1 *)
        (* .. MainList.Length (if any) into List2.       *)
        FOR Location := PredLoc + 1 TO MainList.Length DO
          List2.Info[PredLoc - Location] :=
            MainList.Info[Location];
        List2.Length := MainList - PredLoc

      END; (* ELSE *)
  MainList.Length := 0

END; (* SplitList *)
```

(b)   The linked-list implementation:

```
PROCEDURE SplitList
  (VAR MainList : ListType;
   SplitValue   : KeyType;
   VAR Listl    : ListType;
   VAR List2    : ListType);
```

```
(* Splits the nodes in MainList into two lists: List1   *)
(* will contain all the nodes with values less than      *)
(* SplitValue, and List2 will contain all the nodes      *)
(* with key values greater than or equal to SplitValue. *)
(* MainList is left empty.                               *)
VAR
  Location, PredLoc : PointerType;
BEGIN (* SplitList *)

  (* Find the split place. *)
  FindElement (List, SplitValue, Location, PredLoc);

  (* Split the lists at the split place. *)
  IF PredLoc = NIL
    THEN (* main list is empty or splits before 1st element *)

      BEGIN
        List1 := NIL;
        List2 := MainList
      END (* IF *)

    ELSE  (* main list splits in middle or end *)
      BEGIN
        List1 := MainList;
        List2 := PredLoc^.Next;
        PredLoc^.Next := NIL
      END; (* ELSE *)

  MainList := NIL

END;  (* SplitList *)
```

(c) Both implementations are O(N).

(d) The sequential-list implementation requires three lists, each large enough to contain the maximum number of list elements. The linked-list implementation, which moves nodes from one list to another, does not require any space in addition to that used by the elements that are actually in the lists (the user's data + a pointer field).

24. (a) The specifications:

ReversePrint (List)

Function:	Print out the elements in List in reverse order.
Input:	List (ListType)
Preconditions:	List has been created.
Output:	To standard output: all the elements in the List, in reverse order.
Postconditions:	The elements in List have been printed in reverse order. List is unchanged.

(b) The sequential-list implementation:

```
PROCEDURE ReversePrint
  (List : ListType);

VAR
  Index : Integer;

  (* Code for nested procedure PrintElement goes here *)

BEGIN (* ReversePrint *)

  (* Loop invariant: Elements from List.Info[Index + 1] *)
  (* .. List.Info[List.Length] have been printed in     *)
  (* reverse order.                                      *)
  FOR Index := List.Length DOWNTO 1 DO
    PrintElement (List.Info[Index])

END;  (* ReversePrint *)
```

(c) A stack could be used as a supporting data structure. The linked-list implementation:

```
PROCEDURE ReversePrint
  (List : ListType);

VAR
  Stack : StackType;    (* stack of pointers *)  .
  Ptr   : PointerType;

  (* Code for nested procedure PrintElement goes here *)

BEGIN (* ReversePrint *)

  CreateStack (Stack);
  Ptr := List;

  (* Push pointers to all the list nodes onto Stack. *)
  WHILE Ptr <> NIL DO
    BEGIN
      Push (Stack, Ptr);
      Ptr := Ptr^.Next
    END; (* WHILE *)

  (* Pop and print until stack is empty. *)
  WHILE NOT EmptyStack (Stack) DO
    BEGIN
      Pop (Stack, Ptr);
      PrintElement (Ptr^.Info)
    END (* WHILE *)

END;  (* ReversePrint *)
```

(d) *Code Length:* The sequential-list version of ReversePrint is substantially more concise (8 source lines vs. 19 for the linked-list version, which also needs the supporting stack routines).

Space Requirements: The sequential-list version only requires an Index in addition to the list itself, while the linked-list version also uses a stack of pointers.

Big-O Comparison: The sequential-list version accesses each element once; it is a O(N) operation. The linked-list version must access each node once to put a pointer to it on the stack (O(N)), and then accesses each node again as its pointer is popped from the stack and the node's value is printed (also O(N)). The total is O(N) + O(N) = O(N). In terms of execution time, the sequential-list version is quicker, but in terms of Big-O, the two procedures are O(N).

27. ```
CONST
   MaxStudents = 100;

TYPE
   StringType = PACKED ARRAY [1 .. 20] OF Char;

   StudentDataType = RECORD
      IdNum   : Integer;   (* key field *)
      FirstName : StringType;
      LastName : StringType;
      GPA   : Real
   END; (* StudentDataType *)

   IndexType = 0 .. MaxStudents;

   ListType = RECORD
      Length : IndexType;
      Info   : ARRAY [1 .. MaxStudents] OF StudentDataType
   END; (* ListType *)

VAR
   StudentList : ListType;
```

28. List

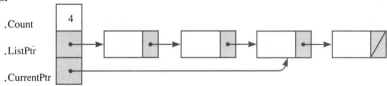

.Count

.ListPtr

.CurrentPtr

31. ```
CONST
   MaxCompanies = 100;
TYPE
   CreditRatingType = (Poor, Fair, Good, Excellent);

   ListElementType = RECORD
      AccountNumber : Integer;
      CompanyName   : StringType;
      BalanceDue    : Real;
      CreditRating  : CreditRatingType
   END; (* ListElementType *)
```

```
            IndexType = 0 .. MaxCompanies;

            ListType  = RECORD
               Count   : IndexType;      (* number of elements in list *)
               Info    : ARRAY [1 .. MaxCompanies] OF ListElementType;
               Current : IndexType       (* index of current element  *)
            END;  (* ListType *)
 33. PROCEDURE PrintWinners
        (VAR List      : ListType);

        (* Print all companies with Excellent CreditRating. *)
        (* Assumes List is not empty.                       *)

     VAR
        EndOfList : Boolean;
        Element   : ListElementType;

     BEGIN (* PrintWinners *)

        (* Start at beginning of List. *)
        ResetList (List);

        REPEAT

           (* Get copy of the next element from List. *)
           GetCurrentElement (List, Element, EndOfList);

           IF Element.CreditRating = Excellent
              THEN PrintLine (Element.CompanyName)

        UNTIL EndOfList (* no more elements follow  *)

     END;   (* PrintWinners *)
 34. FUNCTION MakeReal
        (IntNumber : IntType) : Real;

        (* Converts IntNumber (an integer number stored in a *)
        (* linked list) into a real number. IntNumber is the *)
        (* pointer to a linked list, each node of which has  *)
        (* a digit in the Info field and a pointer to the    *)
        (* next node in the Next field.                      *)

     VAR
        RealNumber : Real;    (* calculated real number *)

     BEGIN (* MakeReal *)

        RealNumber := 0.0;

        WHILE IntNumber <> NIL DO
           BEGIN
              RealNumber := 10.0 * RealNumber + IntNumber^.Info;
              IntNumber  := IntNumber^.Next
           END; (* WHILE *)

        MakeReal := RealNumber

     END; (* MakeReal *)
```

37. ListType was modified in order a allow sequential positional access to its elements. The version of ListType in the chapter text only provides access by key value.

38. (a) The array-based queue simplified the storage of the queue in a file between executions of the program. Since the size of the queue is known at compile time, the queue can be included as a field in a record-type binary file component.

(b) The ad queues could be stored in another file between executions of the program. The ad queues in the AdList would need to be reconstructed as part of the initial program processing. During the ReadListFromFile processing, the ad data would be read in and new nodes allocated as needed to reconstruct the queues.

Chapter 7

1. CreateList, EmptyList, FullList, RetrieveElement, and ModifyElement are the same as the equivalent linear-list operations. DestroyList is modified as shown below:

```
PROCEDURE DestroyList
  (VAR List : ListType);

VAR
  Ptr : PointerType;

BEGIN (* DestroyList *)
  IF List <> NIL
    THEN (* destroy nonempty list *)
      BEGIN

        (* Mark "end" of list with NIL. *)
        Ptr := List^.Next;
        List^.Next := NIL;
        List := Ptr;

        (* Delete and dispose every node in the list. *)
        WHILE List <> NIL DO
          BEGIN
            List := List^.Next;
            Dispose (Ptr);
            Ptr := List
          END (* WHILE *)

      END (* IF list not empty *)
END; (* DestroyList *)
```

3. ```
PROCEDURE PrintReverse
  (List : ListType);

VAR
  Stack : StackType;   (* stack of pointers *)
  Ptr   : PointerType;
```
```

```
                      (* Code for nested procedure PrintElement goes here *)
            BEGIN (* PrintReverse *)

              CreateStack (Stack);
              Ptr := List;

              (* Push pointers to all the list nodes onto Stack. *)
              WHILE Ptr <> NIL DO
                BEGIN
                  Push (Stack, Ptr);
                  Ptr := Ptr^.Next
                END; (* WHILE *)

              (* Pop and print until stack is empty. *)
              WHILE NOT EmptyStack (Stack) DO
                BEGIN
                  Pop (Stack, Ptr);
                  PrintElement (Ptr^.Info)
                END (* WHILE *)

            END;  (* PrintReverse *)
```

4. Assuming that the four-digit employee ID is implemented as type Integer, the minimum value for the header could be any negative number, and the maximum value for the trailer could be any number greater than 9999.

8. (a) `C^.Next^.Info`
   (b) `B^.Back^.Info`
   (c) `A^.Next^.Next`
   (d) `C^.Back^.Next`
   (e) `B^.Back^.Back^`
   (f) `C^.Back^.Back`
   (g) `A^.Back`

9. (a) a pointer
   (b) a record
   (c) a character string
   (d) an integer
   (e) a pointer
   (f) a character

11.
```
PROCEDURE DeleteElement
    (VAR List  : ListType;
     DeleteVal : ElementType);

    (* List points to a doubly linked list, without *)
    (* headers or trailers. Assumes DeleteVal is    *)
    (* in the list.                                 *)

VAR
  Location, PredLoc : PointerType;

BEGIN (* DeleteElement *)
```

```
        (* Find location of DeleteVal in List. *)
        FindElement (List, DeleteVal, Location, PredLoc);

        (* Remove the node from the list and dispose of it. *)
        IF Location = List
          THEN (* Delete first node. *)
            List := List^.Next

          ELSE (* Delete middle or end node. *)
            Location^.Back^.Next := Location^.Next;

        (* If this is not the last node, correct Back ptr. *)
        IF Location^.Next <> NIL
          THEN
            Location^.Next^.Back := Location^.Back;

        Dispose (Location)

    END;  (* DeleteElement *)
```

13. The code segments will work the same if Ptr is not NIL on entry to the loop. If Ptr is NIL (i.e., the list is empty), the REPEAT loop will cause a run-time error. Therefore, the WHILE loop needs no preconditions, but the REPEAT loop needs the precondition Ptr <> NIL.

14.
```
PROCEDURE InsertLast
    (VAR List : ListType;
     Val      : ListElementType);

VAR
  NewNode : PointerType;

BEGIN (* InsertLast *)

  (* Create node for new element. *)
  New (NewNode);
  NewNode^.Info := Val;

  (* Link new node to the existing list. *)
  IF List = NIL
    THEN (* add first node to empty list *)
      NewNode^.Next := NewNode
    ELSE (* add last node to existing list *)
      BEGIN
        NewNode^.Next := List^.Next;
        List^.Next    := NewNode
      END; (* IF *)

  (* Make List point to the last list element. *)
  List := NewNode

END;  (* InsertLast *)
```

17. (a) The elements in the list are 6, 11, 32, 67, 68, and 95.
    (b) The array positions in the free space list are 3, 2, 5, and 1.

(c) After deletion of 68:

List

Nodes	.Info	.Next
[1]	12	0
[2]	19	5
[3]	8	2
[4]	6	10
[5]	14	1
[6]	32	7
[7]	67	8
[8]	95	0
[9]	68	3
[10]	11	6

Start 4

Free 9

(d) After insertion of 17:

List

Nodes	.Info	.Next
[1]	12	0
[2]	19	5
[3]	17	6
[4]	6	10
[5]	14	1
[6]	32	7
[7]	67	9
[8]	95	0
[9]	68	8
[10]	11	3

Start 4

Free 2

18. (a) After initialization:

List

Nodes	.Info	.Next	.Back
[1]		2	
[2]		3	
[3]		4	
[4]		5	
[5]		6	
[6]		7	
[7]		8	
[8]		9	
[9]		10	
[10]		0	

Start 0

Free 1

(b)   After insertion of 17, 4, 25:

List

Nodes	.Info	.Next	.Back		Start	2
[1]	17	3	2		Free	4
[2]	4	1	0			
[3]	25	0	1			
[4]		5				
[5]		6				
[6]		7				
[7]		8				
[8]		9				
[9]		10				
[10]		0				

(c)   After deletion of 17:

List

Nodes	.Info	.Next	.Back		Start	2
[1]	17	4	2		Free	1
[2]	4	3	0			
[3]	25	0	2			
[4]		5				
[5]		6				
[6]		7				
[7]		8				
[8]		9				
[9]		10				
[10]		0				

23. The **Interface** section contains all of the declarations (constants, types, and variables) and subprogram interfaces that are exported from the unit. The **Implementation** section contains all of the declarations and subprogram implementations that are entirely encapsulated by the unit.

24. The initialization section of a Turbo Pascal unit is used to specify actions that must take place before the unit is used.

26. The call to GetAdRates must be removed from the unit's Initialization section. The heading of GetAdRates must be included in the Interface section of the unit, so that the call to the procedure from the main program will compile successfully.

27. In GetPayment (the input operation that is called by ProcessPayment), the call to Readln expects an integer value to be input. If the user types in nonnumeric data, the program will crash. This operation could be made more robust by inputting the number as character data and converting it to an integer.

Chapter 8

1. (a) The *base case* is a nonrecursive exit from the recursive routine.
   (b) The *general (or recursive) case* is a path that includes a recursive call to the routine, to solve a smaller version of the original problem.
   (c) The *run-time stack* is a structure that keeps track of the activation records at run time, in order to preserve the values of parameters, return addresses, registers, and so on.
   (d) *Binding time* refers to the point in the compile/execution cycle when variable names are associated with addresses in memory.
   (e) *Tail recursion* occurs when the recursive call is the last statement executed in a recursive procedure or function.

4. Answering yes to Question 1 provides us with a base case which works correctly. In answering Question 3, we make an assumption that the function will work for some arbitrary case; we can then show that applying the function to the next value results in the correct answer in the general case.

5. A stack.

7. The base cases and general case are commented in the function.

```
FUNCTION Puzzle
    (Base, Limit : NonNegative) : Integer;

BEGIN (* Puzzle *)
    IF Base > Limit
        THEN Puzzle := -1          (* Base Case 1  *)
        ELSE
            IF Base = Limit
                THEN Puzzle := 1      (* Base Case 2  *)
                ELSE                  (* General Case *)
                    Puzzle := Base * Puzzle (Base + 1, Limit)
    END; (* Puzzle *)
```

8. (a) −1
   (b) 120
   (c) 1

12. (a) This answer is incorrect; it resets the value of SumSquares to 0 inside the recursive function. The assignment of SumSquares to 0 should occur in the base case (when List = NIL). Half credit is awarded for getting the general case correct, though.
    (b) This answer will correctly calculate the sum of the squares, but it gets no credit because the assignment was to write a *recursive* function. This is an iterative (looping) solution.
    (c) Correct recursive solution. Full credit is awarded.
    (d) This solution is functionally equivalent to (c); it just avoids the last recursive can (to an empty list) by setting SumSquares to the square of the last list element in the base case. This answer runs into problems if the list is empty, for List^.Next is accessed in the IF condition. However, the specification said that we can assume that the list is not empty, so full credit is awarded.

(e)   This solution is incorrect; the general case will not correctly calculate the sum of the squares. Quarter credit is given, though, for using the correct control structure (IF) for a recursive solution and for getting the base case correct.

13. (a)   Recursive solution:

```
FUNCTION Fib
  (N : Integer) : Integer;

BEGIN (* Fib *)
  IF N <= 1
    THEN (* Base Case *)
      Fib := N
    ELSE (* General Case *)
      Fib := Fib (N - 2) + Fib (N - 1)
END;   (* Fib *)
```

(b)   The recursive solution is inefficient because some of the intermediate values are calculated more than once.

(c)   Iterative solution:

```
FUNCTION Fib
  (N : Integer) : Integer;

VAR
  Lo, Hi, Count, Temp : Integer;

BEGIN (* Fib *)
  IF N <= 1
    THEN Fib := 1
    ELSE
      BEGIN (* N > 1 *)
        Lo := 0;
        Hi := 1;
        FOR Count := 2 TO N DO
          BEGIN
            Temp := Lo;
            Lo := Hi;
            Hi := Temp + Lo
          END; (* FOR *)
        Fib := Temp
      END (* ELSE *)
END;   (* Fib *)
```

17. (a)   It is difficult to establish that the recursive calls satisfy Question 2, that they are moving towards the base case.

(b)   Ulam (7) makes 16 recursive calls.
Ulam (8) makes 3 recursive calls.
Ulam (15) makes 17 recursive calls.

18. Dynamic storage allocation provides a separate workspace for each invocation of a procedure or function, which is a requirement for recursion.

19. Binding time refers to the point in the compile/execute cycle when variable names are associated with addresses in memory. For recursion to be possible, variables must be bound to addresses at run time, not at compile time.

22. (a) False. Recursive solutions are often less efficient in terms of computing time.
    (b) True—assuming that the recursive solution is not much less efficient.
    (c) False. Recursive solutions generally require more space in the run-time stack.
    (d) True. (Don't you want a good grade in this course?)

23. The base cases occur when the current position has already been tried or is the exit or a trap, or when we are already free from the maze. The general case occurs in every other case.

Chapter 9

2. (c) $2^{N+1} - 1$.
4. A node in the Nth level (where the root level = 0) has N ancestors.
5. (a) 30 (5 different shapes with 6 different combinations of values for each)
   (b) 5 (5 different shapes with one legal combination of values for each)

8.

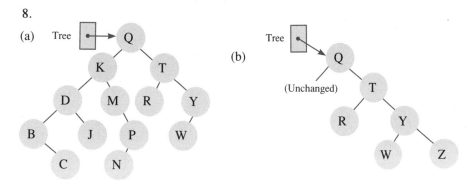

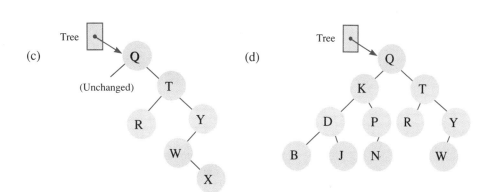

(e)   (f)

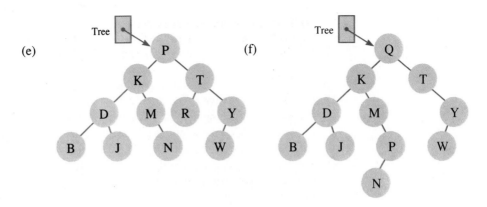

10.

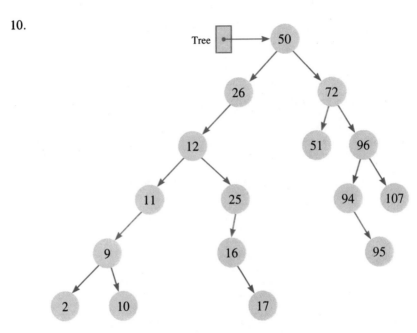

12. (a) The path to search for 61 would go through the nodes containing 56, 69, 59, 62, and 61.
    (b) The path to search for 28 would go through the nodes containing 56, 47, 22, 29, and 23, before determining that 28 is not in the tree.
16. (a) False
    (b) False
    (c) True
    (d) False
17. No; an inorder traversal would leave the elements in a sorted order, so that when you went to rebuild the tree, you would have a stalk instead of a tree.
20. Replace call to FindAndRemoveMax with the following procedure call:
    FindAndRemoveMin (NodePtr^.Right, TempPtr);

```
    PROCEDURE FindAndRemoveMin
      (VAR Tree   : TreePtrType;
       VAR MinPtr : TreePtrType);

  BEGIN (* FindAndRemoveMin *)

    IF Tree^.Left = NIL
      THEN (* Base Case: minimum found *)
        BEGIN
          (* Return pointer to minimum node and unlink *)
          (* the node from the tree.                   *)
          MinPtr := Tree;
          Tree   := Tree^.Right
        END (* Base Case *)

      ELSE (* General Case *)
        FindAndRemoveMin (Tree^.Left, MinPtr)

  END;  (* FindAndRemoveMin *)
```

22.
```
    PROCEDURE FindAndRemoveMax
      (VAR Tree   : TreePtrType;
       VAR MaxPtr : TreePtrType);

    (* Find and remove node with largest value from Tree. *)
    (* Assumes that Tree is not NIL.                       *)

  VAR
    ParentPtr : TreePtrType;

  BEGIN (* FindAndRemoveMax *)

    ParentPtr := NIL;
    MaxPtr := Tree;

    (* Find the node with the maximum value. *)
    WHILE MaxPtr^.Right <> NIL DO
      BEGIN
        ParentPtr := MaxPtr;
        MaxPtr := MaxPtr^.Right
      END; (* WHILE *)

    (* Unlink the maximum value node from the tree. *)
    IF ParentPtr = NIL
      THEN Tree := MaxPtr^.Left
      ELSE ParentPtr^.Right := MaxPtr^.Left

  END;  (* FindAndRemoveMax *)
```

26.
```
    PROCEDURE Ancestor
      (Tree : TreeType;
       Num  : Integer);
```

```
BEGIN (* Ancestor *)

  IF Tree^.Info <> Num
    THEN   (* General Case *)
      BEGIN (* this is an ancestor *)

        (* Print the rest of the ancestors. *)
        IF Tree^.Info < Num
          THEN Ancestor (Tree^.Right, Num)
          ELSE Ancestor (Tree^.Left, Num);

        (* Print the key value of the ancestor node. *)
        Writeln (Tree^.Info)

      END (* IF *)
    (* ELSE Base Case: Node containing Num is found, *)
    (* so stop processing.                           *)

END;  (* Ancestor *)
```

29. (a)   The specification:

> **CopyTree (Tree, DupeTree)**
>
> | | |
> |---|---|
> | *Function:* | Creates a copy of Tree. |
> | *Input:* | Tree (TreeType) |
> | *Preconditions:* | Tree accesses a binary search tree (which may be empty). |
> | *Output:* | DupeTree (TreeType) |
> | *Postconditions:* | DupeTree accesses a binary search tree that is identical to Tree. Original Tree is unchanged. |

(b)   The procedure:

```
PROCEDURE CopyTree
  (Tree        : TreeType;
   VAR DupeTree : TreeType);

BEGIN (* CopyTree *)

  IF Tree = NIL
    THEN (* Base Case *)
      DupeTree := NIL

    ELSE (* General Case *)
      BEGIN
        (* Create this node. *)
        New (DupeTree);
        DupeTree^.Info := Tree^.Info;

        (* Create copy of left subtree. *)
        CopyTree (Tree^.Left, DupeTree^.Left);

        (* Create copy of right subtree. *)
        CopyTree (Tree^.Right, DupeTree^.Right)
```

```
      END (* General Case *)
END;  (* CopyTree *)
```

31. (a)   The specification:

▎ **Mirror (Tree, MirrorTree)**

Function:	Creates a mirror-image copy of Tree.
Input:	Tree (TreeType)
Preconditions:	Tree accesses a binary search tree (which may be empty).
Output:	MirrorTree (TreeType)
Postconditions:	MirrorTree accesses a binary search tree that is a mirror image of Tree. Original Tree is unchanged.

(b)   The procedure:

```
PROCEDURE Mirror
  (Tree          : TreeType;
   VAR MirrorTree : TreeType);

BEGIN (* Mirror *)

  IF Tree = NIL
    THEN (* Base Case *)
      MirrorTree := NIL

    ELSE (* General Case *)
      BEGIN
        (* Create this node. *)
        New (MirrorTree);
        MirrorTree^.Info := Tree^.Info;

        (* Create mirror image of left subtree. *)
        Mirror (Tree^.Left, MirrorTree^.Right);

        (* Create mirror image of right subtree. *)
        Mirror (Tree^.Right, MirrorTree^.Left)
      END (* General Case *)

END;  (* Mirror *)
```

(c)   This tree can be used for binary searching, if the search conditions are reversed:

   IF Key(NodePtr) > KeyValue
   THEN NodePtr ← Right(NodePtr)
   ELSE NodePtr ← Left(NodePtr)

34.
```
PROCEDURE RaiseTime
   (VAR Tree : TreeType);

   (* Note: The traversal order is not important. *)
```

```
    VAR
      Raise : Real;

  BEGIN  (* RaiseTime *)

    IF Tree <> NIL
      THEN   (* General Case *)
        BEGIN

          (* Determine salary increase by appraisal. *)
          CASE Tree^.Info.Appraisal OF
            Superior : Raise := 1.10;
            Good     : Raise := 1.05;
            Fair     : Raise := 1.03;
            Warning  : Raise := 1.00;
            PinkSlip : Raise := 0.00
          END;  (* CASE *)

          (* Calculate new salary for this record. *)
          Tree^.Info.Salary := Raise * Tree^.Info.Salary;

          (* Process the left subtree. *)
          RaiseTime (Tree^.Left);

          (* Process the right subtree. *)
          RaiseTime (Tree^.Right)

        END  (* IF Tree <> NIL *)

      (* ELSE Base Case: Do nothing. *)

  END;   (* RaiseTime *)



37.  PROCEDURE PrintGenius
        (TreeRoot : TreeType);

      (* Prints a list of all of the students in the Tree *)
      (* who have a GPA of 4.0. The tree is ordered by     *)
      (* GPA from smallest to largest.                     *)
      (* This procedure assumes duplicates are handled by  *)
      (* inserting them in the right subtree of the node    *)
      (* with a duplicate key. Since 4.0 is the highest     *)
      (* value key in the tree, we search for the first     *)
      (* instance of this value, and then print the Info    *)
      (* parts of all of the nodes to its right.            *)

    VAR
      Ptr         : TreePtrType;
      GeniusFound : Boolean;

  BEGIN  (* PrintGenius *)

    (* Look through right subtree to find a 4.0 key. *)
    Ptr := TreeRoot;
    GeniusFound := False;
```

```
WHILE (Ptr <> NIL) AND NOT GeniusFound DO
  IF Ptr^.Info.GPA = 4.0
    THEN GeniusFound := True
    ELSE Ptr := Ptr^.Right;

(* If 4.0 key was found, print Info part of that node *)
(* and all of its right subtree descendants.         *)
WHILE Ptr <> NIL DO
  BEGIN
    Writeln (Ptr^.Info.LastName, ', ',
             Ptr^.Info.FirstName);
    Ptr := Ptr^.Right
  END (* WHILE more *)

END;   (* PrintGenius *)
```

39.

Nodes	.Info	.Left	.Right
[1]	Q	2	3
[2]	L	4	5
[3]	W	6	0
[4]	F	0	0
[5]	M	0	7
[6]	R	0	8
[7]	N	0	0
[8]	S	0	0
[9]	?	10	?
[10]	?	11	?

Tree [1]

Free [9]

40.

Nodes	.Info	.Left	.Right
[1]	Q	2	3
[2]	L	4	5
[3]	W	8	0
[4]	F	9	0
[5]	M	0	7
[6]	R	10	8
[7]	N	0	0
[8]	S	0	0
[9]	B	0	0
[10]	?	11	?

Tree [1]

Free [6]

41. Because the input file contains reserved words in alphabetical order, simply reading the words from the file and inserting them into a binary search tree would result in a skewed tree, with O(N) searching. This is no more efficient than the sequential list implementation in the chapter. A binary search of the sequential list, however, would provide $O(\log_2 N)$ searching.

Chapter 10

1. (a) none of the above
   (b) full (and complete)
   (c) none of the above
   (d) heap (and complete)
   (e) full (and complete)
   (f) none of the above
4. (a) Note that NumElements = 9; thus 99 is not in the tree.

Num = 9

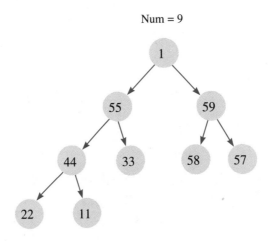

   (b) ReheapDown (Heap, 1, 9)
7. The algorithms for the minimum heap operations follow:

ReheapDown (Heap, Root, Bottom)

IF Heap[Root] is not a leaf
    THEN
        MinChild ← index of child with smaller value

        IF Heap[Root] > Heap[MinChild]
           THEN
               Swap them
               ReheapDown (Heap, MinChild, Bottom)

ReheapUp (Heap, Root, Bottom)

IF Heap[Bottom] is not the Root node
    THEN
        Parent ← index of parent of Heap[Bottom]

        IF Heap[Parent] > Heap[Bottom]
           THEN
               Swap them.
               ReheapUp (Heap, Root, Parent)

10. (a)

After PriorityEnq (PQ, 28)

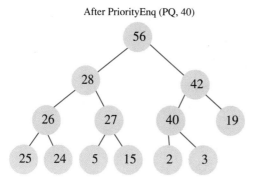

After PriorityEnq (PQ, 2)

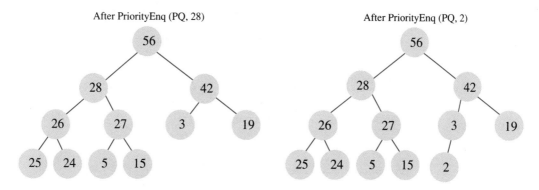

After PriorityEnq (PQ, 40)

After PriorityDeq (PQ, X)

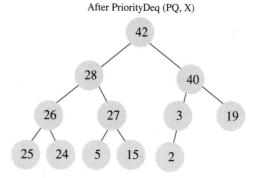

After PriorityDeq (PQ, Y)

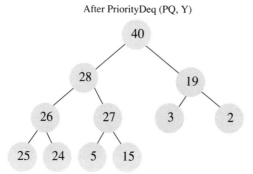

After PriorityDeq (PQ, Z)

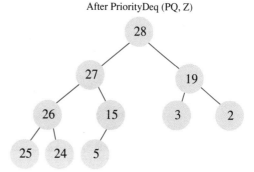

(b)   X = 56, Y = 42, Z = 40.

14. (a) The specifications:

CreatePQueue (PQueue)

Function:	Create empty priority queue.
Input:	None
Preconditions:	None
Output:	PQueue (PriorityQueueType)
Postconditions:	PQueue is empty.

DestroyPQueue (PQueue)

Function:	Destroy a priority queue.
Input:	PQueue (PriorityQueueType)
Preconditions:	PQueue has been created.
Output:	PQueue
Postconditions:	PQueue is empty.

FullPQueue (PQueue) returns Boolean

Function:	Determines if a priority queue is full.
Input:	PQueue (PriorityQueueType)
Preconditions:	PQueue has been created.
Output:	FullPQueue (Boolean)
Postconditions:	FullPQueue = (PQueue is full)

EmptyPQueue (PQueue) returns Boolean

Function:	Determines if a priority queue is empty.
Input:	PQueue (PriorityQueueType)
Preconditions:	PQueue has been created.
Output:	EmptyPQueue (Boolean)
Postconditions:	EmptyPQueue = (PQueue is empty)

(b) The implementations:

```
PROCEDURE CreatePQueue
  (VAR PQueue : PriorityQueueType);

BEGIN (* CreatePQueue *)
  PQueue.NumElements := 0
END;  (* CreatePQueue *)

PROCEDURE DestroyPQueue
  (VAR PQueue : PriorityQueueType);

BEGIN (* DestroyPQueue *)
  PQueue.NumElements := 0
END;  (* DestroyPQueue *)
```

```
FUNCTION FullPQueue
  (PQueue : PriorityQueueType) : Boolean;

BEGIN (* FullPQueue *)
  FullPQueue := (PQueue.NumElements = MaxElements)
END;  (* FullPQueue *)

FUNCTION EmptyPQueue
  (PQueue : PriorityQueueType) : Boolean;

BEGIN (* EmptyPQueue *)
  EmptyPQueue := (PQueue.NumElements = 0)
END;  (* EmptyPQueue *)
```

15. (a) The highest priority element is the one with the largest time stamp. (This assumes that time stamps never reach MaxInt.)

(b) The Push operation:
Assign the new element the next largest time stamp.
Put the new element into the stack (position is unimportant).

The Pop operation:
Find the element with the largest time stamp.
Assign this element to PoppedElement.
Remove this element from the stack.

(c) The Push operation, like those in Chapter 1, is O(1). The Pop operation is O(N), as compared with the O(1) operations developed in Chapter 1.

17. (a) The string length attribute is used to determine their priority (longer length = higher priority).

(b)   NumElements = 10

[1]	'introspective'
[2]	'interviewing'
[3]	'intellectual'
[4]	'intimate'
[5]	'intelligent'
[6]	'interesting'
[7]	'internal'
[8]	'into'
[9]	'in'
[10]	'intro'
[11]	'intensive'

18. If the priority queue is ordered to access the smallest, rather than the largest, element, the algorithms for the priority queue operations will remain the same. We will need to make minor changes to the Reheap operations (to change < to > and vice versa).

22. (d) "Works with" is the best description of the relationship represented by the edges between the vertices in EmployeeGraph, because it is an undirected graph. The other relationships listed have an order implicit in them.

23.

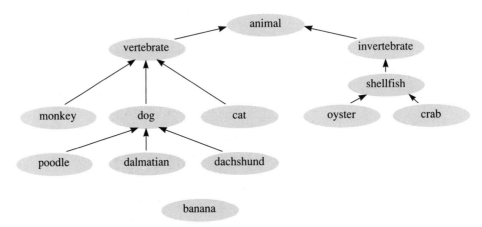

25. (a) yes
    (b) yes
    (c) no
    (d) no
    (e) yes
    (f) no
26. (b) For instance, dalmation *is an example of* dog.
28. (a) no
    (b) yes
    (c) Texas
32. (a) The specification:

■ **DeleteVertex (Graph, Vertex)**

Function:	Delete a Vertex from Graph.
Input:	Graph (GraphType)
Preconditions:	Graph has been created and contains the specified Vertex.
Output:	Graph
Postconditions:	Vertex is not a vertex in V(Graph).

(b) Deleting a vertex is more complicated than deleting an edge because, in addition to removing the vertex from V(Graph), we must also remove the edges to all its adjacent vertices from E(Graph).

35. **(a)** **Base Cases:** (1) IF EndVertex previously found, stop; Found = True. (2) IF StartVertex = EndVertex found, print StartVertex and stop; Found = True. (3) IF no more untried vertices adjacent to StartVertex, stop; Found = False. **General Case:** IF EndVertex is not yet found, DepthFirstSearch all the untried adjacent vertices.

(b) Algorithm:

DepthFirstSearch

IF Not Found
    THEN
         IF StartVertex = EndVertex
            THEN (Base Case)
                Print StartVertex
                Found ← True
            ELSE
                IF StartVertex is not yet tried
                    THEN
                        Mark StartVertex as tried
                        Print StartVertex
                        Get list of adjacent vertices
                        DepthFirstSearch all untried adjacent vertices

(c) The procedure:

```
PROCEDURE DepthFirstSearch
   (VAR Graph    : GraphType;
    StartVertex : VertexType;
    EndVertex   : VertexType);

VAR
   Found : Boolean;

(*************** Nested recursive procedure **********)
PROCEDURE Search
   (VAR Graph    : GraphType;
    StartVertex : VertexType;
    EndVertex   : VertexType;
    VAR Found    : Boolean);

VAR
   AdjList : VertexListType; (* adjacent vertices  *)
   Index   : Integer;        (* index into AdjList *)

BEGIN (* Search *)
   IF NOT Found (* Base Case 1 *)
      THEN
```

```
                    IF StartVertex = EndVertex (* Base Case 2 *)
                      THEN
                        BEGIN
                          Writeln (StartVertex);
                          Found := True
                        END (* IF StartVertex = EndVertex *)

                      ELSE (* destination not yet found *)
                        BEGIN
                          (* If vertex has not been visited, visit it. *)
                          IF NOT VertexMarked (Graph, StartVertex)
                            THEN
                              BEGIN

                                (* Mark the vertex as "visited." *)
                                MarkVertex (Graph, StartVertex);

                                (* Print out this vertex. *)
                                Writeln (StartVertex);

                                (* Get list of vertices that are *)
                                (* adjacent to this vertex.      *)
                                GetAdjacentList
                                  (Graph, StartVertex, AdjList);

                                (* Search all adjacent vertices     *)
                                (* that have not yet been visited. *)
                                FOR Index := 1 TO AdjList.NumVertices DO
                                  IF NOT VertexMarked (Graph,
                                    AdjList.VertexList[Index])
                                      THEN (* General Case *)
                                        (* Make the recursive call. *)
                                        Search
                                          (Graph,
                                           AdjList.VertexList[Index],
                                           EndVertex,
                                           Found)

                              END (* IF not visited *)
                        END (* IF not found *)
END; (* Search *)
(*************** End of nested procedure ***************)

BEGIN (* DepthFirstSearch *)

  InitMarks (Graph);
  Found := False;

  Search (Graph, StartVertex, EndVertex, Found);

  IF NOT Found
    THEN Writeln ('Path not found')

END;  (* DepthFirstSearch *)
```

37. In the adjacency matrix below, if AlphaGraph[V1, V2] = True (T), there is an edge between vertex V1 and vertex V2; if AlphaGraph[V1, V2] is False (F), there is no edge between them.

	[A]	[B]	[C]	[D]	[E]	[F]	[G]	[H]	[I]	[J]
[A]	F	T	T	T	F	T	F	F	F	F
[B]	T	F	T	F	T	F	T	F	F	F
[C]	T	T	F	F	F	T	T	F	T	F
[D]	T	F	F	F	F	T	F	T	F	F
[E]	F	T	F	F	F	F	T	F	F	T
[F]	T	F	T	T	F	F	F	T	T	F
[G]	F	T	T	F	T	F	F	F	T	T
[H]	F	F	F	T	F	T	F	F	T	F
[I]	F	F	T	F	F	T	T	T	F	T
[J]	F	F	F	F	T	F	T	F	T	F

Chapter 11

2. (a)

66	43	19	23	18	4	10	5	7	14
[1]	[2]	[3]	[4]	[5]	[6]	[7]	[8]	[9]	[10]

(b)

18	14	10	5	7	4	19	23	43	66
[1]	[2]	[3]	[4]	[5]	[6]	[7]	[8]	[9]	[10]

4. (a) bubble sort
   (b) selection sort
6. (a) $O(N^2)$
   (b) $O(N)$
   (c) $O(N^2)$
   (d) $O(N\log_2 N)$
   (e) $O(N\log_2 N)$
9. QuickSort (c) would take the longest; ShortBubble (b) would be the fastest.
11. HeapSort would be a better choice than MergeSort, because MergeSort needs a copy of the array for its processing whereas HeapSort sorts within the original array.
14. Only (b) is true.

16. Both (b) and (d) are true.
18. *For:* Making Swap a procedure will make the code easier to read and understand. *Against:* It would be more efficient, in terms of execution time, to code the swap algorithm "in line" instead of requiring a procedure call, which takes extra time to execute.
22. (a) The procedure:

```
PROCEDURE SelectionSort
  (VAR List : ListType);

  (* Sorts List elements in order of increasing value. *)

VAR
  Current : IndexType;      (* current index to process *)
  Mindex  : IndexType;     (* index of smallest element *)
  Temp    : ListElementType;          (* used for swap *)

BEGIN (* SelectionSort *)

  WITH List DO
    BEGIN

      Current := 1;   (* index of first unsorted element *)

      (* Loop Invariant: 1 <= Current <= Length AND       *)
      (* the values in Info[1] .. Info[Current - 1] are *)
      (* sorted and are <= to the unsorted values in     *)
      (* Info[Current] .. Info[Length].                  *)
      FOR Current := 1 TO Length - 1 DO
        BEGIN
          (* Find smallest element in the unsorted part. *)
          Mindex := Current;

          (* Loop Invariant: Info[Mindex] is smallest    *)
          (* element in Info[Current] .. Info[Index-1]. *)
          FOR Index := Current + 1 TO Length DO
            IF Info[Index] < Info[Mindex]
              THEN Mindex := Index;

          (* Swap the Current element and the smallest   *)
          (* element in the unsorted part of the array.  *)
          Temp := Info[Current];
          Info[Current] := Info[Mindex];
          Info[Mindex] := Temp

        END (* FOR *)
    END (* WITH *)
END;  (* SelectionSort *)
```

(b) *Advantage:* Because there are no procedure or function calls, the sort should execute more quickly.
Disadvantage: The code is not as readable.

26. FUNCTION CompareCards
```
      (Cardl, Card2 : CardType;
       SortField    : SortFieldType) : RelationType;

      (* Compare Cardl and Card2 using the specified field. *)

  BEGIN (* CompareCards *)

    CASE SortField OF
      SuitField :
        IF Cardl.Suit = Card2.Suit
          THEN CompareCards := Equal
          ELSE
            IF Cardl.Suit < Card2.Suit
              THEN CompareCards := Smaller
              ELSE CompareCards := Greater;

      NumField  :
        IF Cardl.Number = Card2.Number
          THEN CompareCards := Equal
          ELSE
            IF Cardl.Number < Card2.Number
              THEN CompareCards := Smaller
              ELSE CompareCards := Greater
    END (* CASE *)

  END; (* CompareCards *)
```

30. FUNCTION CompareNames
```
      (Namel, Name2 : NameType) : RelationType;

      (* Compare Namel and Name2. *)

  BEGIN (* CompareNames *)

    (* Compare the LastNames. *)
    IF Namel.LastName < Name2.LastName
      THEN CompareNames := LessThan
      ELSE
        IF Namel.LastName > Name2.LastName
          THEN CompareNames := GreaterThan

        ELSE
          (* LastNames are the same; compare FirstNames. *)
          IF Namel.FirstName < Name2.FirstName
            THEN CompareNames := LessThan
            ELSE
              IF Namel.FirstName > Name2.FirstName
                THEN CompareNames := GreaterThan
```

```
                        ELSE
                          (* FirstNames are the same; *)
                          (* compare MidInitials.     *)
                          IF Name1.MidInitial < Name2.MidInitial
                            THEN CompareNames := LessThan
                            ELSE
                              IF Name1.MidInitial > Name2.MidInitial
                                THEN CompareNames := GreaterThan
                                ELSE CompareNames := EqualTo

            END;  (* CompareNames *)
```

33. Wilbur could use a modification of the selection sort: Each iteration would put the next largest element in place (rather than the next smallest, as shown in this chapter). He wouldn't have to sort the whole array, because he needs only the top 10. Therefore the outer loop would run from 1 to 10 rather than from 1 to NumPigs.

Chapter 12

1.

14	27	95	12	26	5	33	15	9	99
[1]	[2]	[3]	[4]	[5]	[6]	[7]	[8]	[9]	[10]

3.

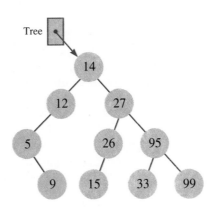

5.

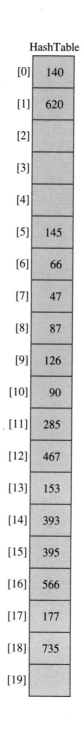

7.

HashTable

[0]	90	140	620
[1]			
[2]			
[3]	153	393	
[4]			
[5]	145	285	395
[6]	66	126	566
[7]	47	87	177
[8]	467	735	
[9]			

9.

Number of Comparisons

Value	Problem 5	Problem 6	Problem 7	Problem 8
66	1	1	1	1
467	6	6	4	4
566	11	3	3	3
735	4	2	11	4
285	7	2	2	2
87	2	2	2	2

11. (a) 100
    (b) 50
    (c) 50
13. (a) 50
    (b) 50
    (c) 50
15. (a) False; a binary search of an ordered set of elements in an array is usually faster than a sequential search of the elements, but it will not be faster if the number of elements is very small.

(b) False; a binary search is an $O(\log_2 N)$ algorithm.

(c) False; a binary search of elements in an array requires only that the elements be sorted; they may be ordered from smallest to largest or vice versa. (Of course, the algorithm will be determined by the ordering scheme.)

(d) True.

(e) False; this statement would be true only if we could guarantee that there would be no collisions. If there are collisions, the order in which elements are added determines their place in the array.

(f) False; increasing the size of the array will reduce the number of collisions only if the hash function will distribute the elements throughout the larger array.

(g) False; we will still need to resolve collisions when the buckets are full.

(h) True.

(i) False; the procedures in this chapter are used only for internal searching.

(j) True.

19. Arrange the most commonly used reserved words toward the beginning of the list. For instance, reserved words like IF, THEN, ELSE, BEGIN, and END are commonly used. On the other hand, PROGRAM is only used once per program; FORWARD and GOTO are rarely used at all. These less common reserved words would be placed at the end of the list.

21. (a) This change would not be any better than the original hash function but would probably work well.

(b) This change would be okay.

(c) This would not be a good modification, because the likelihood of collisions is increased.

(d) This would not be a good modification, because the likelihood of collisions is increased.

(e) This change would be okay, because the variety of characters would probably give a good hash address.

(f) This change would not be good, because the hash address would be calculated from the blank padding for strings that are shorter than the maximum length.

(g) This change would not be good, because the product of the integer version of all the letters in the string would likely be greater than MaxInt.

24. Key MOD 17

27. (d) only

Programming Assignments

In this section, we have included a number of programming assignments, keyed by chapter. Some of the programs are to be written "from scratch," to give students the opportunity to design, code, and test a whole program from written specifications. Other programming assignments are designed to give students experience in modifying an existing program. For instance, for each chapter that contains an application section, there are suggested modifications to the original program. We hope that, by having the opportunity to modify an existing program, students will gain important experience in program reading and "maintenance."

There are many additional programming assignments included in the *Instructor's Guide*. All of the assignments printed here and those in the *Instructor's Guide* are included as ASCII files on the disk provided with the *Instructor's Guide* for easy editing.

A collection of programming assignments, each much altered over time, is part of the folklore of every department. In the assignments that follow we have tried to attribute ones we didn't write ourselves to their original authors. If you recognize one of your own and we didn't credit you, forgive us; the oversight was unintentional.

Chapter 1

1. Your assignment is to modify Program ListAndCount, found in file COUNT.PAS on the program disk, from the application section to:
   (1) accept { } comments;
   (2) accept comments that span a line;
   (3) (optional Turbo Pascal modification) error-proof the GetFiles operation.

Accepting { } Comments

According to the definition of Pascal, the { } comment delimiters are interchangeable with the (* *) delimiters. That is, the following is a legitimate comment:

```
(* This is a comment. }
```

However, some implementations of Pascal (such as Turbo Pascal) require comments to terminate with the same type of comment delimiter that began it. The advantage to this restriction is that it allows us to nest comments. We can use one type of comment delimiter in our code. Then we can use the other type of comment delimiter to "comment out" sections of code—comments and all.

Your modification to Program ListAndCount will take this second approach: It will assume that a comment that begins with (* will terminate with *), even if a } delimiter is encountered. Similarly, a comment that begins with { must terminate with }, even if the *) delimiter is encountered. The program must keep track of which comment delimeter is expected.

Accepting Comments that Span a Line

The specification of ListAndCount allowed the assumption that a comment terminates on the line in which it begins. The modification to the program removes this assumption. Your program must be able to correctly identify the following types of lines:

```
X := 1; (* assign 1 to X *)                    Executable
Y := 2; (* assign 2                            Executable
        to Y *)                                Comment
Z := X + Y; (* assign X + Y to Z and           Executable
print Z *) Writeln (Z);                        Executable
```

Note that in the last example line, your program must recognize that the line began with the comment that started on the previous line, but contained executable code following the comment. (We do not claim that this is good programming style, only that it is permissible.)

You may assume that an executable line will not begin with more than one comment. That is, the following line is *not* permitted:

```
(* Two *)  (* Comments *) Writeln ('Hi');
```

In the line-by-line processing of the source program, ListAndCount must keep track of whether it is inside an unfinished comment when it begins a new line. Because of the earlier modification, it must also keep track of what kind of comment it is in.

Error-proofing the GetFiles Operation

(This is an optional Turbo Pascal modification.) The specifications of Program ListAndCount allow the assumption that the user will correctly type in the name of a file that exists and contains Pascal source code. If the file does not exist, the program will crash on the call to Reset. The reason why the failed call to Reset causes the program to crash has to do with Pascal's dedicated approach to error checking. The compiler automatically checks the result of all I/O operations; if there is a failure, the program terminates (crashes).

Turbo Pascal, however, provides a *compiler directive* to tell the compiler to turn the automatic I/O checking off ($I−) and on ($I+). Following the $I− compiler directive, the system no longer performs error checking on calls to I/O operations like Reset, until a $I+ compiler directive reenables the automatic I/O error checking. While automatic error checking is disabled, it is the programmer's responsibility to check the result of I/O operations. However, the Reset procedure does not return a parameter that tells whether an error occurred; Turbo Pascal has a nonstandard predefined function called IOResult. If IOResult is 0, the operation was successful; otherwise something went wrong. (The *Reference Manual* explains the meaning of all the error values.) The way that a "conditional" Reset is performed in Turbo Pascal is as follows:

```
(*$I-*)        (* Disable automatic I/O error checking. *)
Reset (ProgramFile);   (* Try to open the ProgramFile *)
(*$I+*)        (* Enable automatic I/O error checking.  *)


IF IOResult = 0          (* Check the result of Reset. *)
  THEN (* the call to Reset succeeded *)
  ELSE (* the call to Reset failed    *)
```

If the call to Reset failed, your modified GetFiles procedure should print a message and prompt the user for another file name. This process should continue until the user supplies the name of a file that does exist. Alternately, you could allow the user to type a special character ('*', for instance) to indicate that he wants to quit without going on. Note that this requires a change to the specifications of ListAndCount.

Turn In:

1. Modified specifications of ListAndCount.
2. Top-down design for the parts of the original program that had to be modified.
3. Program listing. (Use your program as input to itself, and turn in the numbered and counted listing.)
4. Test program listing. Write a short program that contains examples of the kinds of source lines that ListAndCount has been modified to handle. Run this program through ListAndCount and turn in a listing of the output.

2. You are the manager of a team of ten programmers who have just completed a seminar in structured programming and top-down design. To prove to your boss that these techniques pay off, you decide to run the following contest: You number the programmers 1 through 10, based on their performance in the seminar (1 is poorest, 10 is best) and monitor their work. As each does his or her part of your project, you keep track of the number of lines of debugged code turned in by each programmer. (You get this information from Program ListAndCount.) You record this number as a programmer turns in a debugged module. The winner of the contest is the first person to reach 1000 lines of debugged code. (You hope this will be programmer #9 or #10.) As further proof of the value of these new techniques, you want to determine how many poor programmers it takes to surpass the winner's figure; that is, find the smallest k such that programmers 1 through k have turned in more lines than the winner.

Input

The input consists of a sequence of pairs of integers. The first integer in each pair is the programmer's number (an integer from 1 to 10), and the second is the number of lines of code turned in. The pairs occur in the same order as that in which the modules were turned in.

Processing/Output

Read in pairs of integers until someone's total goes over 1000. Print out (echoprint) each pair as you read it. Ignore any input after someone's total exceeds 1000. Then print out a table listing the ten programmers and their totals, with the winner flagged as shown in the example below. Finally, find the smallest k such that the sum of the totals for programmers $1 - k$ exceeds the winner's total. Print k in a an explanatory sentence.

Sample Input:

```
10        230
 8        206
 7        111
 3        159
 9        336
 1         51
10        250
 4        101
 9        341
 2        105
 8        256
10        320
 3        150
 5        215
 7        222
 9        400        #9 goes over 1000.
```

Sample Output:

```
PROGRAMMER PROGRESS
Programmer  Lines of Code
10              230 ⎫
    .                ⎪
    .                ⎬  Echoprint the first 16 pairs.
    .                ⎪
 9              400 ⎭

       FINAL TOTALS
Programmer  Lines of Code
 1               51
 2              105
 3              309
 4              101
 5              215
 6                0
 7              333
 8              462
 9             1077     *** THE WINNER ***
10              800
```

It took programmers 1 through 7 to produce more than the winner.

Turn In:

1. Your top-down design.
2. A program listing produced by running your program through ListAndCount.
3. Run your program twice with different input data. Turn in a listing of the program output for each test.

Chapter 2

1. You will design, code, and test a *sequential search* procedure; then you will compare this procedure to the binary search that was developed in the Application section of this chapter.

The Sequential Search

Given an array, List, that contains NumElements values (sorted from smallest to largest) and a Value to search for, the sequential search uses the following approach: Compare Value to successive List elements, starting with the first element, and searching until (1) Value has been found, (2) we have passed Value's place in the sorted list without finding it, or (3) there are no more elements in the array to examine. You must develop the algorithm using a loop invariant.

When you have finished coding the SequentialSearch procedure, test it, using the test driver from the Application section. (Simply replace the call to BinarySearch with a call to SequentialSearch.) The binary search procedure and test driver are in files BINSRCH.PAS and TESTSRCH.PAS on the program disk.

Comparing the Search Procedures

To compare the two searching procedures, you should modify each procedure to count the number of comparisons made before Value is found. Using the test driver, search for values in various positions in the array, and for values that are not in the array, using each search procedure. Following each call to a search procedure, the search Value, location, and the comparison count should be printed. These results should be printed in table format, with the following column headings:

```
                              Comparison Count

Value   Location      BinarySearch    SequentialSearch
```

Test Data   For more interesting results, you should increase the array size to 100, and fill the array. Remember that the values must be ordered from smallest to largest. Leave some gaps in the values, in order to search for medium-sized values that are not in the array. Because of the large array size, you should modify PrintList to print the elements vertically, not horizontally. You only need to print the list once, before you begin to search for values. Modify the test driver to print all data to a file, in addition to the screen. At the end of your experiment, make a hard copy of the file to turn in.

Conclusions Compare the SequentialSearch and BinarySearch procedures in terms of lines of code and number of comparisons. Were the results of your experiment consistent with the discussion in the Application section?

Turn In:

1. The design of procedure SequentialSearch. (It must contain a loop invariant.)
2. Listing of procedure SequentialSearch.
3. Output from your comparison test runs.
4. Your conclusions, in paragraph form.

2. Your assignment is to design, code, and test a sorting procedure that uses the *insertion sort algorithm*. The procedure will sort the integer elements in a list that has the following declarations:

```
CONST
  MaxElements = 100;   (* maximum number of elements in list *)
TYPE
  IndexType = 0 .. MaxElements;

  ListType = RECORD
    Length : IndexType;
    Info   : ARRAY [1 .. MaxElements] OF Integer
  END; (* ListType *)
```

The procedure has the following specifications:

SortList (List)

Function:	Sort the elements in List.Info[1] . . List.Info[List.Length] from *largest to smallest* value.
Input:	List (ListType)
Preconditions:	List.Info contains at least List.Length values, and 1 <= List.Length <= MaxElements.
Output:	List
Postconditions:	List.Info[1] . . List.Info[List.Length] are sorted in order of decreasing size.

The Insertion Sort Algorithm

The basic approach of the insertion sort is as follows: Each successive element in the list is inserted into its proper place relative to the other (already sorted) elements. We begin with the first element. There is only one element in the part of the list being examined, so it must be in its correct place. Now we put the second element in the list into its correct place, so that List.Info[1] is larger than List.Info[2]. (Note that they are not necessarily in their *final* positions in the sorted list; they are simply in their correct positions with respect to each other.) Then the value in the third array slot is put into its proper place, with respect to List.Info[1] . . List.Info[3].

This process continues until all the list elements have been sorted. The changing values of the arrays below illustrate the algorithm.

List.Length = 5

.Info	.Info	.Info	.Info	.Info
20	33	33	33	45
33	20	25	25	33
25	25	20	22	25
22	22	22	20	22
45	45	45	45	20

The sorting algorithm involves repeated examination of the elements in a list, which suggests the use of looping constructs. You should develop the design for procedure InsertionSort using loop invariants, then code the procedure. The code for the procedure must include Writeln's that output debugging data to a file called DEBUG.

Testing the InsertionSort

Your next step is to create a test plan, showing the various test cases, along with inputs and expected outputs. Your grade will be determined, in part, by the design of your test cases.

To test the procedure, you should write a *batch* test driver. Your test driver should open the debug file, set up the array with values as specified in the test plan, and then call the InsertionSort procedure. The values in the array should be printed before and after sorting. The number of times that you will need to set up array data and call InsertionSort will depend on the test cases in your test plan. Make sure that the output of each test case clearly identifies it by test number. Write a stub for procedure InsertionSort to use in testing the test driver.

When your test driver is debugged, you will comment out the InsertionSort stub, and replace it with the actual InsertionSort procedure. Record the results of your tests on the test plan. When you have completed testing, comment out the debugging Writeln's.

Turn In:

1. The design of procedure InsertionSort. (It must include loop invariants for any loops.)
2. The test plan, with results recorded.
3. Listing of the test driver and InsertionSort. The stub for InsertionSort and the debugging Writeln's should be in the listing, commented out.
4. Hard copy of the DEBUG file produced by your test.

Chapter 3

1. Your assignment is to extend and test the String ADT that was developed in the Application Section of this chapter. You will add the following four operations to the String ADT:

ReadString (FileToRead, EndSet, String, Error)

Function:	Read a string of characters, terminating with a character from EndSet, from FileToRead, and return it in String.
Input:	FileToRead (Text file) EndSet (SET OF Char)
Preconditions:	FileToRead is open for reading, with file read cursor at first character of current line; EndSet is defined; EOF will not be encountered.
Output:	FileToRead — file read cursor updated String (StringType) Error (Boolean)
Postconditions:	Error = (number of characters in the current line > MaxString) String = up to MaxString characters, from the current cursor position in FileToRead up to, but not including, the first occurrence of a character in EndSet. File cursor is at character following occurrence of character in EndSet.

Delete (String, StartPos, NumChars, Error)

Function:	Delete NumChars characters from String, beginning with the character in the StartPos position.
Input:	String (StringType) StartPos (IndexType) NumChars (IndexType)
Preconditions:	String is not undefined. 1 <= StartPos <= Length (String) 1 <= Num <= Length (String)
Output:	String Error (Boolean)
Postconditions:	Error = (StartPos + NumChars − 1 > Length(String)). IF NOT Error, String = original String with NumChars characters deleted, beginning at position StartPos. Any characters in String that follow the deleted characters are move up to fill the gap. If Error, String is unchanged.

Insert (String, InString, Pos, Error)

Function:	Insert InString into String at the position specified by Pos, moving the following characters in String to make room for the new characters.
Input:	String (StringType) InString (StringType) Pos (IndexType)
Preconditions:	String and InString are not undefined. 1 <= Pos <= Length (String) + 1
Output:	String Error (Boolean)
Postconditions:	Error = (Length (String) + Length (InString) > MaxString). IF NOT Error, String = original String with InString inserted, beginning at position Pos. Any characters in String that follow the inserted characters are moved to make room for InString. If Error, String is unchanged.

Search (String, Pattern, Found, Pos)

Function:	Search for first occurrence of Pattern in String. If it is found, Pos indicates its starting position in String.
Input:	String (StringType) Pattern (StringType)
Preconditions:	String and Pattern are not undefined.
Output:	Found (Boolean) Pos (IndexType)
Postconditions:	Found = (Pattern was found in String) IF Found, Pos = position of first Pattern character within String; otherwise Pos is undefined.

As part of the String ADT, the operations specified above should be implemented to manipulate the strings directly, without the use of other string operations. For instance, Delete and Insert should be implemented from scratch; they should not call Substring and Concat as described in the Application section.

Testing the String Operations

You must create a test plan to test each of the operations specified above. Your grade will depend in part on the completeness of your test design. Write a batch test driver to execute the test cases. Make sure that your output is labelled to identify the various test cases. The output should be written to a file, and printed following the test. Record the results of all tests on the test driver.

Turn In:

1. The design of the new String procedures.
2. The test plan, with results recorded.
3. Listing of the test driver and the new string procedures.
4. Hard copy of the output file produced by your test.

Chapter 4

1. This problem requires you to write a program to convert an infix expression to postfix format. The evaluation of an infix expression such as A + B * C requires knowledge of which of the two operations, + or *, should be performed first. In general, A + B * C is to be interpreted as A + (B * C) unless otherwise specified. We say that multiplication takes *precedence* over addition. Suppose that we would now like to convert A + B * C to postfix. Applying the rules of precedence, we begin by converting the first portion of the expression that is evaluated, namely the multiplication operation. Doing this conversion in stages, we obtain

A + B * C	*Given infix form*
A + B C *	*Convert the multiplication*
A B C * +	*Convert the addition*

(The part of the expression that has been converted is underlined.)

The major rules to remember during the conversion process are that the operations with highest precedence are converted first and that after a portion of an expression has been converted to postfix it is to be treated as a single operand. Let us now consider the same example with the precedence of operators reversed by the deliberate insertion of parentheses:

(A + B) * C	*Given infix form*
A B + * C	*Convert the addition*
A B + C *	*Convert the multiplication*

Note that in the conversion from "A B + * C" to "A B + C *", "A B +" was treated as a single operand. The rules for converting from infix to postfix are simple, provided that you know the order of precedence.

We consider four binary operations: addition, subtraction, multiplication, and division. These operations are denoted by the usual operators, + , − , *, and /, respectively. There are two levels of operator precedence. Both * and / have higher precedence than + and − . Furthermore, when unparenthesized operators of the same precedence are scanned, the order is assumed to be left to right. Parentheses may be used in infix expressions to override the default precedence.

As we discussed in this chapter, the postfix form requires no parentheses. The order of the operators in the postfix expressions determines the actual order of operations in evaluating the expression, making the use of parentheses unnecessary.

Input

The input file contains a collection of *error-free* infix arithmetic expressions, one expression per line. Expressions are terminated by semicolons, and the final expression is followed by a period. An arbitrary number of blanks and end-of-lines may occur between any two symbols in an expression. A symbol may be an operand (a single upper-case letter), an operator ($+$, $-$, $*$, or $/$), a left parenthesis, or a right parenthesis.

Sample Input:

```
A + B - C ;
A + B * C ;
( A + B ) / ( C - D ) ;
( ( A + B ) * ( C - D ) + E ) / ( F + G ) .
```

Output

Your output should consist of each input expression, followed by its corresponding postfix expression. All output (including the original infix expressions) must be clearly formatted (or reformatted) and also clearly labeled.

Sample Output

```
Infix:    A + B - C ;
Postfix:  A B + C -

Infix:    A + B * C ;
Postfix:  A B C * +

Infix:    ( A + B ) / ( C - D ) ;
Postfix:  A B + C D - /

Infix:    ( ( A + B ) * ( C - D ) + E ) / ( F + G ) .
Postfix:  A B + C D  -  * E + F G + /
```

Discussion

In converting infix expressions to postfix notation, the following fact should be taken into consideration: In infix form the order of applying operators is governed by the possible appearance of parentheses and the operator precedence relations; however, in postfix form the order is simply the "natural" order—i.e., the order of appearance from left to right.

Accordingly, subexpressions within innermost parentheses must first be converted to postfix, so that they can then be treated as single operands. In this fashion, parentheses can be successively eliminated until the entire expression has been converted. The *last* pair of parentheses to be opened within a group of nested parentheses encloses the *first* subexpression within that group to be transformed. This last-in, first-out behavior should immediately suggest the use of a stack. Your program may utilize any of the operations in the Stack ADT.

In addition, you must devise a Boolean function that takes two operators and tells you which has higher precedence. This will be helpful because in Rule 3 below you need to compare the next input symbol to the top stack element. Question: What precedence do you assign to ' (' ? You need to answer this question since ' (' may be the value of the top element in the stack.

You should formulate the conversion algorithm using the following six rules:

Rule 1:   Scan the input string (infix notation) from left to right. One pass is sufficient.

Rule 2:   If the next symbol scanned is an operand, it may be immediately appended to the postfix string.

Rule 3:   If the next symbol is an operator,
      (a) Pop and append to the postfix string every operator on the stack that
            (i)   is above the most recently scanned left parenthesis, and
            (i)   has precedence higher than or equal to that of the new operator symbol.
      (b) Then push the new operator symbol onto the stack.

Rule 4:   When an opening (left) parenthesis is seen, it must be pushed onto the stack.

Rule 5:   When a closing (right) parenthesis is seen, all operators down to the most recently scanned left parenthesis must be popped and appended to the postfix string. Furthermore, this pair of parentheses must be discarded.

Rule 6:   When the infix string is completely scanned, the stack may still contain some operators. (No parentheses at this point. Why?) All these remaining operators should be popped and appended to the postfix string.

Data Structure

You may use either stack implementation from the chapter. Outside of the Stack ADT operations, your program may not assume knowledge of the stack implementation. If you need to extend the Stack ADT with other operations, you should specify and implement them.

Examples

Here are two examples to help you understand how the algorithm works. Each line on the following page demonstrates the state of the postfix string and the stack when the corresponding next infix symbol is scanned. The rightmost symbol of the stack is the top symbol. The rule number corresponding to each line demonstrates which of the six rules was used to reach the current state from that of the previous line.

Example 1: Input expression is A + B * C / D − E.

Next symbol	Postfix string	Stack	Rule
A	A		2
+	A	+	3
B	A B	+	2
*	A B	+ *	3
C	A B C	+ *	2
/	A B C *	+ /	3
D	A B C * D	+ /	2
−	A B C * D / +	−	3
E	A B C * D / + E	−	2
	A B C * D / + E −		6

Example 2: Input expression is (A + B * (C − D)) / E.

Next symbol	Postfix string	Stack	Rule
(		(	4
A	A	(	2
+	A	(+	3
B	A B	(+	2
*	A B	(+ *	3
(	A B	(+ * (	4
C	A B C	(+ * (	2
−	A B C	(+ * (−	3
D	A B C D	(+ * (−	2
)	A B C D −	(+ *	5
)	A B C D − * +		5
/	A B C D − * +	/	3
E	A B C D − * + E	/	2
	A B C D − * + E /		6

Turn In:

1. Program listing.
2. Output of test run of the program.

Chapter 5

1. Your assignment is to modify Program Simulation from file SIM.PAS on the program disk to:
   (1) use time-stamping to determine waiting time;
   (2) allow varying transaction times; and
   (3) keep track of the amount of time that the tellers are free, expressed as a percentage of clock time.

Time Stamping

In the Application section, the jobs waiting in line to be processed were described as a queue of "wait timers." We kept track of how long a job was in the wait queue by incrementing its wait time every clock cycle. Updating the wait queue this way is an O(N) operation. A more efficient way to keep track of how long a job has been waiting is to treat the wait queue as a queue of *time stamps*. When a job arrives, the current clock value is Enqueue'd. When that job is later Dequeue'd, its wait time is calculated by subtracting its time stamp from the current clock value.

Varying Transaction Times

As we mentioned at the end of the Application section, in real-life situations there may not be a single "typical" transaction time. For instance, we described a pediatric clinic where there are three typical types of patients: 20% come in for innoculations (2 minutes), 50% come in sick (6 minutes), and 30% come in for annual checkups (10 minutes). Your modification will allow the user to specify up to 5 different transaction times, along with the probability of each. (They must add up to 100%.) During the execution of the simulation, a call to the random number generator will determine how long a particular job will take.

Free Tellers

Your modification will determine the amount of time that tellers are not busy, expressed as a percentage of clock time. (Note that, if there are 3 tellers and the simulation runs for 1000 "minutes," the free time is expressed as a percentage of 3000, not 1000.) You do not need to report free time on a teller-by-teller basis; only the totals are required.

NOTE: Modifications 2 and 3 will require changes to the table output in file REPORT.SIM.

Turn In:

1. Listing of the modified Simulation program.
2. Hard copy of REPORT.SIM (output from executing the Simulation).

2. The local medical clinic has decided to automate its scheduling services. You have been assigned to design the initial version of the schedules. The basic functions that the clinic has in mind are doctor check-in and check-out and patient check-in and check-out.

A doctor checks in by telling the scheduler his or her name, an examination room number, and a medical specialty code. Each doctor has a favorite room. The scheduler checks to see whether the room is free. If so, it assigns this doctor to the room; if not, it rejects the request with a message, and the doctor can try again to check in. When a doctor checks out, the examination room is freed.

A patient checking in gives a name, age, specialist code, and emergency indication. The scheduler will try to match up the patient with a doctor according to a set of rules that will be described below. If there is a match, the patient is seen by the assigned doctor. If this doctor is currently seeing a patient, the new patient is queued to see the doctor according to the emergency indicator. Usually there is no emergency, and the patient is put at the end of the doctor's waiting list; if there is an emergency, however, the patient is put at the front of the waiting list ahead of any other patients.

The rules for assigning doctors to patients are as follows:

1. Any patient under age 16 is assigned to see a pediatrician.
2. Patients age 16 and older are assigned a doctor according to the specialty requested. If there is no doctor in the clinic with the requested specialty, the patient is assigned to a general practitioner (GP). If there is no GP, the patient can be assigned to any doctor.
3. If there is more than one doctor of the requested specialty, the patient is assigned to the doctor with the shortest waiting list.

When a patient checks out, the doctor he or she was assigned to is available to see the next patient if there is anyone in the waiting list.

Input

Since this will be an interactive system, your program should prompt the users to input the correct information. The initial prompt is

'Type D for Doctor or P for Patient: '

The next prompt is

'Type I for checkin or O for checkout: '

According to the request, your program should prompt the user for any other needed information, as indicated in the following table:

Action	Additional information
Doctor check-in	Doctor's name
	Room number
	Specialty code
Doctor check-out	Doctor's name
Patient check-in	Patient's name
	Age
	Specialty (code requested)
	Emergency flag
Patient check-out	Patient's name
	Room number

You may define the format for the input processed by your program.

Output

The output for each request is in the form of messages to the user, according to the request, as indicated in the table on the following page:

Action	Message
Doctor check-in	Confirmation that room is available *or* Error message if room is in use
Doctor check-out	Goodbye message
Patient check-in	Message telling patient which room to go to and which doctor has been assigned. If no doctor available, apologetic message.
Patient check-out	Goodbye message. At a later time we may add billing information at this point.

In addition to printing the messages on the screen, you should also write the requests and messages to a transaction file (TRANSACT.OUT), to be turned in with your program listing.

Details and Assumptions

1. There are 100 examination rooms at the clinic, each with a waiting room attached.
2. Specialty codes are as follows:

PED	Pediatrics
GEN	General practice
INT	Internal medicine
CAR	Cardiology
SUR	Surgeon
OBS	Obstetrics
PSY	Psychiatry
NEU	Neurology
ORT	Orthopedics
DER	Dermatology
OPT	Opthomology
ENT	Ear, Nose, and Throat

3. You may assume that no patient leaves without checking out. (That is, every doctor becomes free eventually.)
4. No one leaves before he or she sees the assigned doctor. (That is, no one has to be taken out of the waiting queue.) The clinic is open 24 hours a day, 7 days a week.
5. If a doctor checks out while there is still a waiting list of patients assigned to him or her, the patients must be reassigned to other doctors.

Data Structures

The basic data structure is a list of examination rooms with waiting lists attached to each. Since the number of rooms is fixed, you may use an array of records to represent it. It is the waiting list attached to each examination room that is of interest to us. We have seen that patients are seen in the order in which they are added to the list (a simple queue), with one exception: Emergency patients are added at the front of the queue. What we have here is a special data structure, kind of a *deque,* in which additions may be made to either end, but deletions are always made at the front of the list.

Use the kind of data design process described in Chapter 5 to figure out how to best represent this structure. However you decide to implement it, you should encapsulate the details by creating utility routines to make the necessary additions and deletions to the waiting lists. (Consider, for instance, that you may have to find the shortest waiting list for a given specialty code, so the number of elements in the list is important.)

Turn In:

1. Listing of the program
2. Hard copy of TRANSACT.OUT file.

Chapter 6

1. Your assignment is to modify Program AdManager found in file ADMGR.PAS on the program disk, to include the following additional commands:
   (1) ListAdvertisers ('L'): List the names of all the advertisers on the screen.
   (2) *Save* ('S'): Save all the data without quitting the program.
   (3) *Dummy* ('D'): Generate a list of ads to use for "dummying" the magazine.

Creating the Dummy Listing

The ads in the dummy listing must be ordered from largest to smallest size; within a size group, the ads may be listed in any order. If color is specified, it must be marked, as shown in the sample output below:

```
              Full Page Ads

LIONEL                              FULL COLOR
MATTEL                              RED

              Half Page Ads

TRAIN STOP
LGB EXPRESS                         BLUE
DENVER STATION                      RED

                 Quarter Page Ads

CALIFORNIA HOBBY CO.
CALIFORNIA HOBBY CO.     (a second quarter page ad)
RIVERDALE RAIL
  .
  .
  .
```

And so on. Write the dummy listing to a Text file called DUMMY, to be printed later.

To prepare the dummy listing, you will need to design a temporary data structure to contain the listing information until it is printed. Use good data design practices: specify the structure as an ADT, and then implement it. If the structure uses dynamically allocated space, this space should be freed when the Dummy operation is complete.

While creating this data structure, you must not change the AdList in any way. In particular, note that in examining the ad queues, you must not destroy them. If you Dequeue an ad, you must Enqueue it again. (Don't forget to mark the end of the queue.)

Initializing AdFile

In the Application section, we discussed the problem that occurs the first time you run the AdManager program: Since the AdFile has never been created, the call to Reset will fail. The solution to this problem is to create an empty AdFile before the first execution of AdManager. Before you can test your program, you should create this file by running the DUMFILE.PAS program on the program disk.

Testing

Test your modifications to AdManager by adding the following advertisers and ads:

```
LIONEL:
  Full page, Full color
MATTEL:
  Full page, Red
TRAIN STOP:
  Half page, Blue
  Half page, No color
  Quarter page, Red
LGB EXPRESS:
  Quarter page, No color
  Quarter page, Red
  Half page, Blue
DENVER STATION:
  Half page, Red
CALIFORNIA HOBBY CO.:
  Quarter page, No color
  Quarter page, No color
RIVERDALE RAIL:
  Eighth page, No color
  Quarter page, No color
  Eighth page, No color
GARDEN RAIL VIDEOS:
  Half page, Full color
KIT 'N' CABOOSE:
  Eighth page, No color
DYNARAIL:
  Quarter page, Blue
  Quarter page, No color
```

```
MODEL WAREHOUSE:
  Half page, Green
AMERICAN ENGINE CO.:
  Quarter page, No color
```

Turn In:

1. Listing of the modified Program AdManager.
2. Hard copy of file DUMMY, created by the execution of AdManager using the data above.

2. Your assignment is to extend the List ADT by adding the following operations:

Name	Type	Purpose
ValueInList	Function	Determine whether there is an element with the specified Key value in List.
MergeLists	Procedure	Merge the elements in List1 and List2 into a single list, NewList.
SplitList	Procedure	Split the elements in MainList into two lists, List1 and List2, according to the key value of each element. All elements with keys less than SplitValue will be put into List1; all elements with keys greater than or equal to SplitValue will be put into List2.
GetElement	Procedure	Return a copy of the element in the *Nth* position in the List.
ReversePrint	Procedure	Print out the List elements in reverse key order (from largest to smallest key).

The first part of your assignment is to write the specifications of each operation, in the following format:

Operation (parameter list)

> *Function:*   _____
>
> *Inputs:*   _____
>
> *Preconditions:* _____
>
> *Outputs:*   _____
>
> *Postconditions:* _____

Once you have specified the operations, you should implement them using the *linked* list representation developed in the chapter.

Testing the Operations

Write a test plan describing the test cases needed for each operation. Your grade will be determined in part by the completeness of your test plan.

Create a batch test driver that will execute these test cases. Write the test output to a file, as well as to the screen. Be sure to identify each test case with labels in your output. Print "before" and "after" values to show the results of each operation.

Your test driver may use any of the operations in the List ADT from this chapter.

Turn In:

1. The written specifications for the new operations.
2. Program listing of the test driver, including the operations to be tested.
3. Copy of the test plan, with the results of the test cases recorded.

3. Your assignment is to track the corporate careers of some up-and-coming executives who are busily changing jobs, being promoted and demoted, and, of course, getting paid.

In this (admittedly unrealistic) version of the corporate world, people either belong to a company or are unemployed. The list of people the program must deal with is not fixed; initially there are none, and new people may be introduced by the JOIN command (see below).

Executives within a company are ordered according to a seniority system and are numbered from 1 to N (the number of people in the company) to indicate their rank: 1 is the lowest rank and N is the highest. A new employee always enters at the bottom of the ladder and hence will *always* start with a rank of 1. When a new person joins a company, the rank of everyone in the company is increased by one, and when an employee quits, the rank of employees above him or her in that company is decreased by one. Promotions can also occur and affect the ranks in the obvious way.

Naturally, salaries are based on rank. An employee's salary is Rank * $1000. Unemployed people draw $50 in unemployment compensation.

Input

1. From file COMPANY: The company names are listed one per line. There will be at most 20 companies. Company names are at most 10 characters and do not contain embedded blanks.
2. From the keyboard: Commands, as listed below. <Person> and <Company> names are at most 10 characters and do not contain embedded blanks.

JOIN <person> <company>

   <Person> joins the specified <company>. This may be the first reference to this person, or he or she may be unemployed. The person will not currently belong to another company. Remember that when a person joins a company he or she always starts at the bottom.

QUIT <person>

   <Person> quits his or her job and becomes unemployed. You may assume that the person is currently employed.

CHANGE <person> <company>

   <Person> quits his or her job and joins the specified new <company>. You may assume that the person is currently employed.

PROMOTE <person>

> <Person> is moved up one step in the current company, ahead of his or her immediate superior. If the person has highest rank within the company, no change occurs.

DEMOTE <person>

> <Person> is moved one step down in the current company, below his or her immediate subordinate. If the person has lowest rank within the company, no change occurs.

PAYDAY

> Each person is paid his or her salary as specified above. (You must keep track of the amount each person has earned from the start of the program.)

EMPLOYEES <company>

> The current list of employees should be printed for the specified <company>. The employees must be printed in order of rank; either top to bottom or bottom to top is appropriate.

UNEMPLOY

> The list of unemployed people should be printed.

DUMP

> Print the employees in each company, as specified under the EMPLOYEES command above, then print the unemployeed people. Label the output appropriately.

END

> Stop accepting commands.

Note that the CHANGE, PROMOTE, and DEMOTE commands do not tell you the person's current employer; you will have to search the data structure to find the person.

Output (to screen and file EMPLOY.OUT)

1. Echoprint all commands, and print out a message that indicates what action has been taken. (For the EMPLOYEES and UNEMPLOY commands, print out the information specified in the Input section above.)
2. After all the commands have been processed, print out one list consisting of all the people who have been mentioned in any command and the total amount of money they have accumulated. The list should be sorted by decreasing order of total salary accumulated.

Data Structures

The list of employees for each company should be implemented as a linked list. You may modify and use any of the List ADT operations from the chapter. You

may not use knowledge of the list implementation outside of List ADT operations.
If necessary, you may specify and implement additional operations for the List ADT.

Testing

You may want to test your program on the following sample data:

File COMPANY:

```
Borland
Microsoft
IBM
Digital
Compaq
NEC
XEROX
```

Commands from keyboard:

```
JOIN David XEROX
JOIN Mario XEROX
JOIN John Digital
JOIN Fred Digital
JOIN Phil IBM
CHANGE Fred NEC
JOIN Miriam Digital
JOIN Sharon Microsoft
JOIN Harvey Digital
CHANGE Miriam Borland
PAYDAY
EMPLOYEES Digital
JOIN Marge Borland
JOIN Lesley Microsoft
JOIN Sam Digital
JOIN George NEC
JOIN Bob Borland
JOIN Susan IBM
JOIN Joshua Digital
JOIN Max NEC
PAYDAY
EMPLOYEES IBM
EMPLOYEES Digital
EMPLOYEES NEC
JOIN Tim IBM
DEMOTE Harvey
PROMOTE Max
DEMOTE Marge
CHANGE Marge IBM
QUIT John
PAYDAY
QUIT Mario
```

```
QUIT David
PROMOTE Marge
PROMOTE Marge
PAYDAY
UNEMPLOY
EMPLOYEES IBM
EMPLOYEES XEROX
JOIN John Compaq
JOIN Ralph Compaq
QUIT Phil
JOIN Phil Compaq
DUMP
CHANGE Marge Compaq
CHANGE Miriam Compaq
CHANGE Fred Compaq
CHANGE Susan Compaq
QUIT Tim
PAYDAY
EMPLOYEES Compaq
JOIN Mario XEROX
JOIN David XEROX
EMPLOYEES XEROX
JOIN Tim Compaq
PROMOTE Tim
PROMOTE Fred
DEMOTE Miriam
JOIN Laszlo Digital
PROMOTE Laszlo
CHANGE Joshua Compaq
PAYDAY
PROMOTE Sharon
DEMOTE Lesley
PROMOTE Bob
DEMOTE Bob
DEMOTE John
PAYDAY
DUMP
END
```

Turn In:

1. Source program listing.
2. Hard copy of file EMPLOY.OUT, containing the output of the test execution.

(This programming assignment was developed from an idea by Jim Bitner.)

Chapter 7

1. Your assignment is to modify Program AdManager, found in file ADMGR2.PAS on the program disk, to add the following commands:
   (1) PrintRates ('R'): Print out the ad size and color rates.

(2) UpdateRates ('U'): Update the ad size and color rates.

You will need to decide which interfaces to add to the AdRates Unit. Document your decision by writing specifications for the operations. (Do not forget to save updated rates to the ADPRICES file.)

Any user inputs must be handled from separate user interface operations. Do not make calls to Read or Readln from your "application" procedures. The style of the prompts for user inputs should be consistent with the program's existing user interface.

Turn In:

1. The specifications of any new modules added to AdManager.
2. Listing of the modified Program AdManager.

2. (Turbo Pascal) Your assignment is modify Program AdManager, found in file ADMGR2.PAS, by reimplementing the CommandTable ADT as a Turbo Pascal Unit.

Turn In:

1. Listing of COMTABLE.PAS.
2. Listing of Program AdManager. Use a highlighting marker to indicate program additions or modifications that result from this assignment.

3. Write the up-and-coming executives program (Chapter 6, #3), using doubly linked lists for each company's employee list. (This may simplify the PROMOTE and DEMOTE processing.)

Chapter 8

1. *(Turbo Pascal)* Modify Program ListAndCount (file COUNT.PAS) to accept *Include* compiler directives, using recursion to keep track of levels of included file nesting.

Including Files

One way to make a long program more readable is to break it up into a number of separate files and then to "include" them in your main program file using Turbo Pascal's Include compiler directive. This compiler directive was discussed at the end of Chapter 5. To review, the syntax for the Include compiler directive is

```
(*$I filename *)
```

The directive simply means "include all the code from the specified text file at this point."

Modifying ListAndCount

If Program ListAndCount were to come across such a compiler directive, it would be treated as a simple comment line. Your assignment is to modify ListAndCount to print included files, at the point at which they are included. After the included file is printed, you should resume printing the file from which it was included, at the line following the compiler directive. To make the assignment more interesting, included files may themselves include other files. Thus, after each included file is printed, you must backtrack to resume printing the file from which it was included.

To modify Program ListAndCount to handle included files as described above, you should make the ProcessProgramFile procedure *recursive*. That is, within the WHILE loop, if an Include compiler directive is encountered, the new file is opened and ProcessProgramFile is called recursively. Make sure that the program line numbering continues throughout the program; it should not start numbering each included file at line 1.

Testing the Modification

To test the modification of ListAndCount, you must create a test program that contains included files. The program does not need to do anything useful, as long as it contains Include compiler directives. There should be some nested Include files. The name of each included file should be identified in comments at the beginning and end of the file, as illustrated by the following example:

```
(************* Beginning of File TEST1.PAS *************)


(* This included file contains variable declarations.*)
VAR
   Number : Integer;
   Letter : Char;


(**************** End of File TEST1.PAS ****************)
```

Turn In:

1. Listing of modified Program ListAndCount.
2. Hard copy of file COUNTOUT, containing the output of your test run.

2. In this assignment you will write and compare two procedures that count the number of paths possible to move in a 2-dimensional *square* grid from row 1, column 1 to row N, column N. Steps are restricted to going up or to the right, but not diagonally. The illustration below shows 3 of many paths, if N = 10:

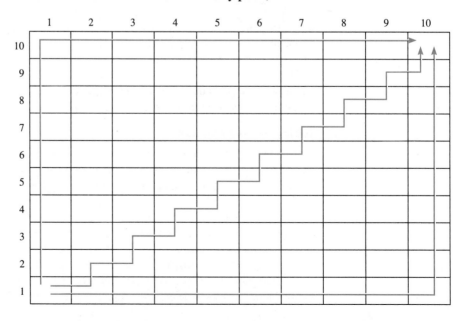

The functions that you will write have the following specification:

NumPaths (Row, Col, N) returns Integer

Function:	Returns the number of paths possible to move in a 2-dimensional square grid from starting Row/Col to row N/column N.
Input:	Row (Integer) — starting row Col (Integer) — starting column N (Integer) — maximum row/column
Preconditions:	1 <= Row <= N 1 <= Col <= N
Output:	NumPaths (Integer)
Postconditions:	NumPaths = number of paths possible to move from starting row and column to terminal position at row N/column N.

Both versions of NumPaths will be recursive functions.

Version 1

The first version (call it NumPaths1) uses the "brute force" approach:

IF Row = N OR Col = N
   THEN NumPaths ← 1
   ELSE NumPaths ← sum of NumPaths starting at next row/same column and
               NumPaths starting at same row/next column.

After you have coded the function, walk through the execution of NumPaths (4) by hand. Why is this algorithm inefficient? (Save the walkthrough and the answer to the question to turn in with your program listings.)

Version 2

The efficiency of this operation can be improved by keeping intermediate values of NumPaths in a two-dimensional array of Integer values. This keeps the function from having to recalculate values that it has already done. Design and code a version of NumPaths (call it NumPaths2) that uses this approach. Be careful about where and how the array is declared and initialized! (You may want to make the recursive part a nested function inside of NumPaths2.)

Testing the Implementations

Write a test driver to test these functions. The driver should prompt the tester to input the value of N, then call each version of NumPaths to calculate the number of paths. The result of each call should be printed. The initial (nonrecursive) calls are:

```
PathCount := NumPaths1 (1, 1, N);
```

and

```
PathCount := NumPaths2 (1, 1, N);
```

The test driver should continue prompting the tester to supply values of N until 0 is input.

Run the program, using values of 1, 2, 3, . . ., and so on, for N. Both versions should get the same results. At what point does the answer get too large for type Integer? (You may want to change the result type of the functions to Real.)

Comparing the Implementations

To compare the two versions of NumPaths, add a statement to each function to increment a variable called CallCount. CallCount will be used to see how many times the function is called. This variable should be declared as a global variable in the test driver. Before each invocation of a NumPaths function, initialize CallCount to 0. After each call, print out CallCount. Record the results of CallCount for each function for N values of 1 to 10. Answer the following questions:

(1) How do the two versions of NumPaths compare in terms of execution-time efficiency?
(2) How do the two versions of NumPaths compare in terms of space efficiency?

Turn In:

1. Walkthrough of NumPaths1 (1, 1, 4). Why is it inefficient?
2. Program listing of test driver, including the two versions of NumPaths.
3. The answers to questions (1) and (2) in the previous section.
4. Fill in the following chart with values calculated by your program:

N	Number of paths	CallCount	
		NumPaths1	NumPaths2
1			
2			
3			
4			
5			
6			
7			
8			
9			
10			

3. Your assignment is to (1) write a function that computes an approximation to a definite integral that is within a given tolerance of the exact answer, (2) write a sorting procedure that will help monitor the behavior of the integration function, and (3) test your function on several prescribed integrals.

Method

The integration function implements an adaptive algorithm based on the trapezoid rule of integration and its associated error estimate. The trapezoid rule for integration is

$$\int_a^b f(x)dx = (f(a) + f(b)) * (b - a)/2$$

If the interval [a, b] is divided into two equal subintervals, another estimate of the integral can be obtained by applying the trapezoid rule to each half interval and adding the two results. This new result is normally more accurate, and an estimate of the error in the better result is given by

Error = (T(a, b) − (T(a, c) + T(c, b))) / 3.0

where c = (a + b)/2 and T(x, y) is the result of applying the trapezoid rule to f on the interval [x, y].

The integral is to be computed to within a given degree of accuracy by a divide-and conquer strategy. With the above formulas, the integral can be approximated and the error in the approximation can be estimated. If the absolute value of the error is small enough, the calculation terminates. Otherwise, the integral is computed on each half interval separately with an error tolerance that is half the original one.

All the real numbers at which the function is evaluated are to be stored in an array. After the integration routine terminates, these values should be sorted and printed out. (Use any sorting method to sort the array of values in increasing order). This will help monitor the behavior of the integration algorithm by showing where the function f was evaluated. The evaluations should be concentrated where the function is badly behaved (that is, poorly approximated by straight-line pieces).

Specification

The integration function should be

FUNCTION Q (f, A, B, Eps, MaxFun, Err)

f	is the name of the function to be integrated.
A	is the left endpoint of the interval.
B	is the right endpoint of the interval.
Eps	is the maximum allowed absolute value of the error.
MaxFun	is the maximum number of function evaluations to be used.
Err	is a Boolean error flag: Err is true if more than MaxFun function values would be needed to satisfy the error test.
Q	is returned as the estimate of the integral.

Implementation Details

1. The name of the function f, which is to be integrated, should be passed by the main program as a parameter to the integration function Q. One execution of the main program should call the integration function for each of the functions whose integrals are to be estimated. It is not acceptable to include the code of a function to be integrated inside the integration function Q.
2. To prevent the possibility of infinite recursion, the integration function should terminate if the function f is called MaxFun times. In this case, the best available approximation to the integral should be returned and an error flag should be set.

3. The primary cost of using an integration routine is in the cost of evaluating the function f. Write your code so that it never evaluates the function twice at the same point.
4. The divide-and-conquer approach should be implemented by a recursive function. This recursive function is not called directly, but is called by the nonrecursive driver function Q, described above.
5. The straightforward way to compute the midpoint of an interval is not the best. To ensure that the computed midpoint of an interval [a, b] is not outside the interval, the formula a + (b − a)/2 should be used.
6. The main program should do the following, once for each function in the test data:
   (a) Call Q with the appropriate arguments.
   (b) Print the estimate of the interval.
   (c) Print an error message if Err is true.
   (d) Sort the array of real numbers at which the function f was evaluated.
   (e) Print the sorted values.

Testing the Function

Test your integration function by computing the following integrals:

f	A	B	Eps	MaxFun
1	0.0	1.0	10^{-3}	5
x	−1.0	3.0	10^{-5}	3
x	−1.0	3.0	10^{-5}	2
e^{-x*x}	0.0	5.0	10^{-3}	1000
$(\frac{1}{3} - x)^{1/3}$	0.0	1.0	10^{-2}	10
$(\frac{1}{3} - x)^{1/3}$	0.0	1.0	10^{-3}	1000
$\dfrac{4}{(1 + x^2)}$	0.0	1.0	10^{-3}	1000

NOTE: Standard Pascal does not require that an exponential function be provided. If your version of Pascal does not include an exponential function, you should enter the code for an exponential function as a procedure in the main program. Also, most exponential functions will not allow you to raise a negative number to a real number power. This problem occurs with the fifth and sixth functions above. However, you can take the absolute value of the base, raise it to a power, and then append the correct sign.

(This programming assignment was written by Alan Cline and David Scott.)

Chapter 9

1. Your assignment is to modify Program ListAndCount (with cross reference generator), found in file CROSSREF.PAS on the program disk to make the following changes:

   (1) Ignore reserve words in RESERVED.TXT if there is a '*' in the first column.
   (2) Do not update the cross reference for multiple references to an identifier in the same line. (You may want modify the Queue ADT to add a "peek" operation, which returns the value of the rear element without changing the queue.)
   (3) Ignore text between quotes. For instance, in the following statement, 'Hello' should not be considered an identifier:

   ```
   Writeln ('Hello');
   ```

   (4) Implement the reserved list to support $O(log_2N)$ searching.
   (5) Allow executable code after a comment.
   (6) Prompt the user to ask if a cross reference is wanted; only build the cross reference if the user requests it.
   (7) In the cross reference listing, format the line numbers ten per line, separated by a blank.

   ### Testing the Program Modifications

   Record the test cases necessary for testing these program modifications on a test plan. Create a Pascal program to use as input data; be sure to mark the test case numbers in comments in the program. Run the modified program using the test input.

   ### Turn In:

   1. Listing of modified Program ListAndCount.
   2. Test plan, with results recorded.
   3. Output from file COUNTOUT, showing the results of your test.

2. Your assignment is to extend the Binary Search Tree ADT by adding the following operations:

Name	Type	Purpose
IsBST	Function	Determine if a binary tree is a binary search tree.
SimilarTrees	Function	Determine if two binary trees have the same shape. (The nodes do not have to contain the same values, but they must have the same number of children.)
NodeCount	Function	Determine the number of nodes in a binary search tree.
LeafCount	Function	Determine the number of leaf nodes in a binary search tree.
CopyTree	Procedure	Create a copy of a binary search tree.
Mirror	Procedure	Creates a mirror image of a binary search tree.
Ancestor	Procedure	Prints the ancestors of the tree node with the specified KeyValue.

The first part of your assignment is to write the specifications of each operation, in the following format:

Operation (parameter list)

Function: _____

Inputs: _____

Preconditions: _____

Outputs: _____

Postconditions: _____

Once you have specified the operations, you should implement them. Use recursion wherever possible.

Testing the Operations

Write a test plan describing the test cases needed for each operation. Your grade will be determined in part by the completeness of your test plan.

Create a batch test driver that will execute these test cases. Write the test output to a file, as well as to the screen. Be sure to identify each test case with labels in your output. Print "before" and "after" values to show the results of each operation.

Your test driver may use any of the operations in the Binary Search Tree ADT from this chapter. Once an operation is tested, you may use it to test other operations. For instance, after testing procedure Mirror, you may use the mirror-image tree for testing IsBST. (Is it a binary search tree?)

Turn In:

1. The written specifications for the new operations.
2. Program listing of the test driver, including the operations to be tested.
3. Copy of the test plan, with the results of the test cases recorded.

3. There is a real program developed by a computer company that reads in written reports, issues warnings on bad style, and partially corrects the style. Your assignment is to create a simplified version of this program. It will examine a report for the use of annoying words, caution the author on the tendencies to use such words, and then correct the report. After the corrected report is printed, the program user may issue commands to add or delete entries from the collection of annoying words.

Input

1. From file BADWORDS: The list of annoying words, in the following format:

   <annoying word> <synonym>,<synonym>, . . . ,<synonym>.

   The first word on each line is an annoying word, followed by a blank space and a maximum of five synonyms, separated by commas. The last synonym is followed by a period. Each word is a maximum of 15 characters. Sample line:

   grungy dirty,soiled,grimy,encrusted.

   The entries are not arranged in any particular order.

2. From file TEXTFILE: A paragraph of text over several lines, in which the words are separated from one another by blanks, commas, periods, or quotes. There need not be a blank before the word at the beginning of the line.
3. From the user (keyboard): Any number of the following commands in any order, one per line.

ADD <annoying word> <synonym>, .. ,<synonym>.
    Add <annoying word> and its synonyms to the collection of annoying words.

DELETE <annoying word>
    Delete <annoying word> and its synonyms from the collection of annoying words.

QUIT
    Stop processing user commands.

Output

1. Alphabetical listing of the collection of annoying words and their synonyms (to file NEWFILE).
2. Echoprinted original text from TEXTFILE (to screen and file NEWFILE).
3. The corrected text after the substitutions of synonyms for annoying words (to the screen and NEWFILE).
4. List of slight tendencies to use annoying words. Print a heading ('Slight Tendencies to use Annoying Words'), followed by any annoying word that occurred 1 to 4 times in the input text. The list of words should be printed one word per line, alphabetized, to the screen and NEWFILE.
5. A list of extreme tendencies to use annoying words. Print a heading ('Extreme Overuse of Annoying Words'), followed by a list of annoying words that occurred 5 or more times in the input text. The list of words should be printed one word per line, alphabetized to the screen and NEWFILE.
6. Issue prompts for commands to screen. Echo print commands issued by program user to NEWFILE.
7. After QUIT command, reprint the text from TEXTFILE, using the current collection of annoying words and synonyms to correct the text (to screen and NEWFILE).

Processing

The program begins by reading in the collection of annoying words from file BAD-WORDS. The annoying words should be stored in a binary search tree (BadTree). The list of synonyms associated with each annoying word should also be stored. To make things more interesting, note that when the program finds an annoying word in the text, it must replace it by a more acceptable synonym. It is nearly as annoying to have the same synonym replace every occurrence of the annoying word. The list of synonyms for each annoying word should be stored in a circular list, so that the program cycles through the synonyms for each occurrence of a particular annoying word (see example). After the BadTree has been built, print out the annoying words alphabetically, with their synonyms, to NEWFILE.

The program then processes the TEXTFILE, by reading the text and replacing any annoying words with the next synonym associated with it. The modified text is printed to both the screen and NEWFILE.

After the user sees which words the program has, the author may use the DELETE and ADD commands to modify the collection of annoying words and their synonyms. After all modifications have been made, the user issues the QUIT command. The program then reprocesses the TEXTFILE, by reading the text and replacing any words that are currently considered to be annoying with their synonyms. The final text and the lists of slight and extreme tendencies are printed to the screen and NEWFILE.

Sample Input

File BADWORDS:

```
grungy dirty,soiled,grimy,encrusted.
awesome amazing,incredible.
teeny small,tiny.
```

File TEXTFILE:

```
The apartment was so grungy it was totally awesome. The
sofa was grungy, the floor was grungy, the fridge was
grungy, and even the grass outside was grungy. When I
think that could have been where I would live this year,
all I could say was, "Totally awesome."
```

Commands:

```
ADD fridge refrigerator.
DELETE awesome
QUIT
```

Sample Output (File NEWFILE)

```
Annoying words and synonyms:

awesome    amazing,incredible
grungy     dirty,soiled,grimy,encrusted
teeny      small,tiny
```

```
Text from TEXTFILE:
```

```
The apartment was so grungy it was totally awesome. The
sofa was grungy, the floor was grungy, the fridge was
grungy, and even the grass outside was grungy. When I
think that could have been where I would live this year,
all I could say was, "Totally awesome."
```

Corrected Text:

The apartment was so dirty it was totally amazing. The
sofa was soiled, the floor was grimy, the fridge was
encrusted, and even the grass outside was dirty. When I
think that could have been where I would live this year,
all I could say was "Totally incredible."

Slight Tendencies to Use Annoying Words:
awesome

Extreme Overuse of Annoying Words:
grungy

ADD fridge refrigerator
DELETE awesome

Final text:

The apartment was so dirty it was totally awesome. The
sofa was soiled, the floor was grimy, the refrigerator was
encrusted, and even the grass outside was dirty. When I
think that could have been where I would live this year,
all I could say was, "Totally awesome."

Slight Tendencies to Use Annoying Words:
fridge

Extreme Overuse of Annoying Words:
grungy

Turn In:

1. Program Listing
2. Hard copy of file NEWFILE.

(This programming assignment was developed from an idea by Gael Buckley.)

Chapter 10

1. Your assignment is to write and compare two implementations of a priority queue
   whose highest priority element is the one with the *smallest key* value. The elements
   have the following declarations:

```
TYPE
  StringType  = PACKED ARRAY [1 .. 10] OF Char;

  ElementType = RECORD
    Key       : Integer;
    Name      : StringType;
  END; (* ElementType *)
```

The Priority Queue Implementations

The first implementation will use a minimum heap. You will need to modify the heap operations to keep the minimum, rather than maximum, element in the root. You must also make comparisons based on the Key field, rather than the whole element.

The second implementation will use a linear linked list, whose elements are ordered by key value.

Testing the Implementations

After the operations for each implementation are written, test them with a batch test driver that performs the following operations:

PriorityEnq the following elements:

Key	Name
43	Robert
5	Miriam
8	Joshua
36	Susan
11	David
1	Leah

Priority Deq
PriorityDeq

PriorityEnq the following elements:

Key	Name
2	Abigail
9	Adriane
10	Dori

PriorityDeq all the rest of the elements

After each PriorityDeq operation, print the Key and Name of the element returned. Print all output to both the screen and a file called PQUEUE.OUT.

(Turbo Pascal) If you are using Turbo Pascal, you should put the code for each implementation in a separate file. Your test driver should Include (using the $I compiler directive) the correct file to be tested.

Comparing the Implementations

To compare the operations, you must modify the PriorityEnq and PriorityDeq operations to count how many elements are accessed (compared or swapped, in the case of reheaping) during its execution. Run the test cases described in the previous section, recording the number of elements accessed by each operation.

Turn In:

1. Source listing of each priority queue implementation.
2. Source listing of the test driver.
3. Report comparing the number of elements accessed in executing each operation.

2. Reimplement the Graph ADT using an *adjacency list* representation. Figure 10-19 suggests two ways that the graph could be implemented. You should implement the originally specified Graph operations and the Mark operations.

Testing the Graph Operations

Test the graph operations with a test driver that builds the graph depicted in Figure 10-13, and performs the following depth-first *and* breadth first searches:

Houston to Denver
Washington to Chicago
Austin to Washington

All output should be directed to both the screen and file GRAPH.OUT.

Turn In:

1. Source listing of test driver, including the graph declarations and operations.
2. Hard copy of file GRAPH.OUT, containing the output from the test driver.

Chapter 11

1. The object of this programming assignment is twofold. First, you are to compare the relative performance of different sorting algorithms on the same data set. Second, you are to compare the relative performance of the same algorithm on two different data sets.

   Five sorting algorithms are to be tested:
   1. SelectionSort
   2. BubbleSort
   3. MergeSort
   4. Quicksort
   5. HeapSort
   You may use either version of BubbleSort and QuickSort. You must modify each sort to include a counter in each sort to keep track of the number of comparisons made. The sorting procedures are in file SORTS.PAS on the program disk.

Input

Two files of integers to be sorted. There are a maximum of 10 integers in the first data set and a maximum of 100 integers in the second data set.

Output

The following output should be repeated for each sort:
1. The name of the sort
2. Echoprint of the input
3. The sorted file
4. The number of comparisons required

Finally, for each data file, your program should print a summary table that lists the type of sort and number of comparisons.

Turn In:

1. Program listing.
2. Program output listed above.

Chapter 12

1. The object of this assignment is twofold. First, you are to compare the relative performance of different searching algorithms on the same data set. Second, you are to compare the performance of the same algorithm on data sets of different sizes.

   Your program will compare the following three search strategies:
   1. Linear search in an unordered list
   2. Linear search in an ordered list
   3. Binary search
   You will need to write each search procedure with a counter that keeps track of how many comparisons are made.

   Input

   Create a data set of 100 integers. Do ten searches with each algorithm. Be sure the searches include values not in the list as well as those in the list.

   Create a second data set made up of three different sets of data to be searched. The first set of data should have 6 values, the second 50, and the third 150. Run each routine with five searches within each of the three data sets.

   Output

   The following should be printed for each data set:
   1. Echoprint the input data.
   2. Print, for each search value:
      (a) the value being searched for
      (b) the algorithm name, the success of the search, and the number of comparisons made.

   Turn In:

   1. Program listing.
   2. Program output listed above.

2. Create a data set with 100 integer values. Use the division method of hashing to store the data values into hash tables with table sizes of 7, 51, and 151. Use the linear probing method of collision resolution. Print out the tables after the data values have been stored. Search for 10 different values in each of the three hash tables, counting the number of comparisons necessary. Print out the number of comparisons necessary in each case, in tabular form.

   Turn In:

   1. Program listing.
   2. Program output listed above.

Index

Syntax Element	Example
Program Body	`BEGIN  (* Reference *)`
Comment	`  (* These code segments are examples of proper syntax *)`
	`  (* and style only. This isn't a working program.     *)`
Assignment	
integer +,*	`    Number := (Number + 1) * 100;`
MOD, −, DIV	`    Number := Number MOD 10 - Number DIV 100;`
real *, −, /, +	`    Overtime := Overtime * 15.0 - Overtime / 20.0 = 0.5;`
boolean, =, >, <	`    Flag := (Number = 1) OR (Number > 4) OR (Number < 0);`
NOT, AND, OR	`    Flag := NOT EOF AND NOT EOLN OR Flag;`
Input/Output	
Read DataFile	`    Read (DataFile, Overtime, Regular);`
Readln Input	`    Readln (InChar, Number);`
Write DataFile	`    Write (DataFile, 'Overtime = ', Overtime:8:2);`
Writeln Output	`    Writeln (Individual.Name:30, ' ':5, Number:1);`
IF-THEN-ELSE	
condition	`    IF (Number <> 0) AND (0.001 >= Abs(Overtime))`
true branch	`      THEN`
	`        BEGIN`
	`          Writeln('Regular work week.');`
	`          Individual.Pay := 400.0`
	`        END   (* IF *)`
false branch	`      ELSE`
	`        Writeln('Special work week. ');`
IF-THEN	
condition	`    IF Flag`
true branch	`      THEN Number := 0;`
WHILE Loop	`    Number := 1;`
test	`    WHILE Number <= 20 DO`
	`      BEGIN`
	`        Read (Individual.Name[Number]);`
	`        Number := Number + 1`
	`      END;   (* WHILE *)`
REPEAT Loop	`    REPEAT`
	`      Writeln ('Enter Y or N. ');`
	`      Readln (InChar)`
test	`    UNTIL InChar IN ['Y', 'N', 'y', 'n'];`
FOR Loop	`    FOR Number := 1 TO 10 DO`
	`      Writeln (Number:10, Sqr(Number) : 10);`
CASE	
selector	`    CASE InChar OF`
label list	`      'P', 'N' : BEGIN`
	`                    Table[PtTime]  := Table[PtTime] + 1;`
	`                    Table[NonUnit] := Table[NonUnit] + 1`
	`                  END; (* P or N *)`
	`      'U'     : Table[Unit]  := Table[Unit] + 1;`
	`      'S'     : Table[Super] := Table[Super] + 1`
	`    END;  (* Case *)`
WITH	`    WITH Individual DO`
	`      Writeln (Name, ' ':5, Pay:8:2)`
End of Program	`END.  (* Reference *)`